Threats, Countermeasures, and Advances in Applied Information Security

Manish Gupta
State University of New York at Buffalo, USA

John Walp
M&T Bank Corporation, USA

Raj Sharman
State University of New York at Buffalo, USA

A volume in the Advances in Information
Security, Privacy, and Ethics (AISPE) Book
Series

Managing Director:	Lindsay Johnston
Senior Editorial Director:	Heather Probst
Book Production Manager:	Sean Woznicki
Development Manager:	Joel Gamon
Development Editor:	Myla Merkel
Acquisitions Editor:	Erika Gallagher
Typesetter:	Lisandro Gonzalez
Cover Design:	Nick Newcomer

Published in the United States of America by
Information Science Reference (an imprint of IGI Global)
701 E. Chocolate Avenue
Hershey PA 17033
Tel: 717-533-8845
Fax: 717-533-8661
E-mail: cust@igi-global.com
Web site: http://www.igi-global.com

Library of Congress Cataloging-in-Publication Data

Threats, countermeasures and advances in applied information security / Manish Gupta, John Walp, and Ra Sharman, editors.
    p. cm.
  Includes bibliographical references and index.
  Summary: "This book addresses the fact that managing information security program while effectively managing risks has never been so critical, discussing issues such as emerging threats and countermeasures for effective management of information security in organizations"--Provided by publisher.
  ISBN 978-1-4666-0978-5 (hardcover) -- ISBN 978-1-4666-0979-2 (ebook) -- ISBN 978-1-4666-0980-8 (print & perpetual access) 1. Information technology--Security measures. 2. Information technology--Management. 3. Management information systems. 4. Business enterprises--Computer networks--Security measures. 5. Risk management. I. Gupta, Manish, 1978- II. Walp, John, 1967- III. Sharman, Ra, 1956-
  HD30.2.T4953 2012
  658.4'78--dc23
                            2011049598

This book is published in the IGI Global book series Advances in Information Security, Privacy, and Ethics (AISPE) Book Series (ISSN: 1948-9730; eISSN: 1948-9749)

British Cataloguing in Publication Data
A Cataloguing in Publication record for this book is available from the British Library.

All work contributed to this book is new, previously-unpublished material. The views expressed in this book are those of the authors, but not necessarily of the publisher.

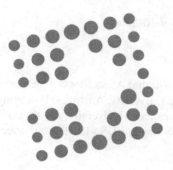

Advances in Information Security, Privacy, and Ethics (AISPE) Book Series

ISSN: 1948-9730
EISSN: 1948-9749

MISSION

In the digital age, when everything from municipal power grids to individual mobile telephone locations is all available in electronic form, the implications and protection of this data has never been more important and controversial. As digital technologies become more pervasive in everyday life and the Internet is utilized in ever increasing ways by both private and public entities, the need for more research on securing, regulating, and understanding these areas is growing.

The **Advances in Information Security, Privacy, & Ethics (AISPE) Book Series** is the source for this research, as the series provides only the most cutting-edge research on how information is utilized in the digital age.

COVERAGE

- Access Control
- Device Fingerprinting
- Global Privacy Concerns
- Information Security Standards
- Network Security Services
- Privacy-Enhancing Technologies
- Risk Management
- Security Information Management
- Technoethics
- Tracking Cookies

IGI Global is currently accepting manuscripts for publication within this series. To submit a proposal for a volume in this series, please contact our Acquisition Editors at Acquisitions@igi-global.com or visit: http://www.igi-global.com/publish/.

Titles in this Series

For a list of additional titles in this series, please visit: www.igi-global.com

Theory and Practice of Cryptography Solutions for Secure Information Systems
Atilla Elçi (Aksaray University, Turkey) Josef Pieprzyk (Macquarie University, Australia) Alexander G. Chefranov (Eastern Mediterranean University, North Cyprus) Mehmet A. Orgun (Macquarie University, Australia) Huaxiong Wang (Nanyang Technological University, Singapore) and Rajan Shankaran (Macquarie University, Australia)
Information Science Reference • copyright 2013 • 351pp • H/C (ISBN: 9781466640306) • US $195.00 (our price)

IT Security Governance Innovations Theory and Research
Daniel Mellado (Spanish Tax Agency, Spain) Luis Enrique Sánchez (University of Castilla-La Mancha, Spain) Eduardo Fernández-Medina (University of Castilla – La Mancha, Spain) and Mario Piattini (University of Castilla - La Mancha, Spain)
Information Science Reference • copyright 2013 • 390pp • H/C (ISBN: 9781466620834) • US $195.00 (our price)

Threats, Countermeasures, and Advances in Applied Information Security
Manish Gupta (State University of New York at Buffalo, USA) John Walp (M&T Bank Corporation, USA) and Raj Sharman (State University of New York, USA)
Information Science Reference • copyright 2012 • 319pp • H/C (ISBN: 9781466609785) • US $195.00 (our price)

Investigating Cyber Law and Cyber Ethics Issues, Impacts and Practices
Alfreda Dudley (Towson University, USA) James Braman (Towson University, USA) and Giovanni Vincenti (Towson University, USA)
Information Science Reference • copyright 2012 • 342pp • H/C (ISBN: 9781613501320) • US $195.00 (our price)

Information Assurance and Security Ethics in Complex Systems Interdisciplinary Perspectives
Melissa Jane Dark (Purdue University, USA)
Information Science Reference • copyright 2011 • 306pp • H/C (ISBN: 9781616922450) • US $180.00 (our price)

Chaos Synchronization and Cryptography for Secure Communications Applications for Encryption
Santo Banerjee (Politecnico di Torino, Italy)
Information Science Reference • copyright 2011 • 596pp • H/C (ISBN: 9781615207374) • US $180.00 (our price)

Technoethics and the Evolving Knowledge Society Ethical Issues in Technological Design, Research, Development, and Innovation
Rocci Luppicini (University of Ottawa, Canada)
Information Science Reference • copyright 2010 • 322pp • H/C (ISBN: 9781605669526) • US $180.00 (our price)

www.igi-global.com

701 E. Chocolate Ave., Hershey, PA 17033
Order online at www.igi-global.com or call 717-533-8845 x100
To place a standing order for titles released in this series, contact: cust@igi-global.com
Mon-Fri 8:00 am - 5:00 pm (est) or fax 24 hours a day 717-533-8661

Table of Contents

Detailed Table of Contents

    Chris Strasburg, The Ames Laboratory, US Department of Energy, USA
    Johnny S. Wong, Iowa State University, USA

The arms race between cyber attackers and defenders has evolved to the point where an effective counter-measure strategy requires the use of an automated, distributed, and coordinated response. A key difficulty in achieving this goal lies in providing reliable measures by which to select appropriate responses to a wide variety of potential intrusions in a diverse population of network environments. In this chapter, the authors provide an analysis of the current state of automated intrusion response metrics from a pragmatic perspective. This analysis includes a review of the current state of the art as well as descriptions of the steps required to implement current work in production environments. The authors also discuss the research gaps that must be filled to improve security professionals' ability to implement an automated intrusion response capability.

    Hai Thanh Nguyen, Gjøvik University College, Norway
    Katrin Franke, Gjøvik University College, Norway
    Slobodan Petrović, Gjøvik University College, Norway

Intrusion Detection Systems (IDSs) have become an important security tool for managing risk and an indispensable part of overall security architecture. An IDS is considered as a pattern recognition system, in which feature extraction is an important pre-processing step. The feature extraction process consists of feature construction and feature selection . The quality of the feature construction and feature selection algorithms is one of the most important factors that affects the effectiveness of an IDS. Achieving reduction of the number of relevant traffic features without negative effect on classification accuracy is a goal that largely improves the overall effectiveness of the IDS. Most of the feature construction as well as feature selection works in intrusion detection practice is still carried through manually by utilizing domain knowledge. For automatic feature construction and feature selection, the filter, wrapper, and embedded methods from machine learning are frequently applied. This chapter provides an overview of various existing feature construction and feature selection methods for intrusion detection systems. A comparison between those feature selection methods is performed in the experimental part.

Giuseppe Cattaneo, Università di Salerno, Italy
Pompeo Faruolo, Università di Salerno, Italy
Ivan Visconti, Università di Salerno, Italy

The established legal value of digital signatures and the growing availability of identity-based digital services are progressively extending the use of smart cards to all citizens, opening new challenging scenarios. Among them, motivated by concrete applications, secure and practical delegation of digital signatures and decryptions is becoming more and more critical. Unfortunately, all secure delegation systems proposed so far include various drawbacks with respect to some of the main functional requirements of any practical system. With the purpose of proposing a truly practical solution for signature and decryption delegation, in this chapter the authors put forth the notion of a "Proxy Smart Card System," a distributed system that allows a smart card owner to delegate part of its computations to remote users. They first stress the problematic aspects concerning the use of known proxy-cryptography schemes in synergy with current standard technologies, which in turn motivates the need of proxy smart card systems. Then they formalize the security and functional requirements of a proxy smart card system, identifying the involved parties, the adversary model, and the usability properties. Finally, the authors present the design and analysis of a proxy smart card system, which implements the required functionalities outperforming the current state of the art.

Mohammad Mahfuzur Rahman, Applied Research Centre for Business and Information
Technology (ARCBIT), UK
Karim Mohammed Rezaul, Centre for Applied Internet Research (CAIR), Glyndŵr University, UK

The expansion of electronic commerce (E-commerce) has become an increasing reality due to Internet's rapid growth during the last few years. E-commerce is growing at an exceptional rate with more organizations offering their goods and services online every day. Importantly, this growth is being matched by the number of people gaining access to the Internet in a variety of ways. E-commerce offers opportunities as well as threats. Information is crucial for any organization, especially in the e-market. The lack of an effective and trusted payment system that can be used in combination with online shopping has been limiting factor in the growth of Internet sales. Consumers are hesitant to provide personal information, including credit card details, over the Internet because of high perception of risk and concerns with privacy. Establishment of Information Security System can minimize the threats and risks. Technology can play an important role in intensifying trust in the information society and securing consumer rights. E-commerce will not be successful without protecting the consumers' rights, especially in the area of information security. The research highlights the relevant theories of information security within the e-commerce sectors, including identifying and investigating the problems.

Ella Kolkowska, Örebro University School of Business, Sweden
Karin Hedström, Örebro University School of Business, Sweden
Fredrik Karlsson, Örebro University School of Business, Sweden

One of the problems highlighted within the area of information security is that international standards are implemented in organisations without adopting them to special organisational settings. In this chapter the authors analyse information security goals found in hospital settings. They found that the CIA-triad fails to cover organisational specific information security goals in hospital settings. They found also that information security goals held by information security managers and business managers are not the same, implying that both these groups should be involved in designing of information security goals, in order to find information security goals relevant for the organisation. Finally, the authors found goal maps used in this study for analysis of empirical data, to be a useful tool for analysis and communication of information security goals in an organisation.

Authentication is probably one of the main security processes that almost everybody has at one point used. Currently, the most widespread authentication mechanism is based on textual passwords, a well-established approach that, with the growth of users and services, has increasing and serious drawbacks. With the rise of high quality displays and more ergonomic human computer interaction mechanisms such as mice, touch-pads and touch-screens, graphical passwords are credited as a valuable replacement to old-fashioned passwords. In contrast to alphanumerical passwords, graphical authentication mechanisms promise greater memorability and usability. In this chapter, an overview of the state-of-art of this topic is presented, introducing some of the main schemes proposed in current literature. The issues and concerns related to security and usability, which still challenge the researchers in this area, are also discussed.

Security evaluation is a complex problem. As more and more software systems become available, more diversity and alternatives can be found to accomplish the same tasks. However, there is still a lack of a standard approach that can be used to choose among the available alternatives or evaluate their configuration security. In this chapter, the authors present a methodology to devise security appraisals, which is based on the collection of widespread security knowledge for a specific domain. They demonstrate their methodology by devising two specific appraisals for the domain of transactional systems. The first one can be used to evaluate and assess the configuration of an already deployed database installation, while the target of the second one is to compare the capability of specific database brands concerning security aspects. The authors also present a real demonstration of both appraisals in real scenarios.

Regulatory compliance in areas such as privacy has become a major challenge for organizations. In large organizations there can be hundreds or thousands of projects that involve personal information. Ensuring that all those projects properly take privacy considerations into account is a complex challenge for accountable privacy management. Accountable privacy management requires that an organization makes sure that all relevant projects are in compliance and that there is evidence and assurance that this actually is the case. To date, there has been no suitable automated, scalable support for accountable privacy management; it is such a tool that the authors describe in this chapter. Specifically, they describe a privacy risk assessment and compliance tool which they are developing and rolling out within a large, global company – called HP Privacy Advisor (HP PA) – and its generalisation and extension. The authors also bring out those security, privacy, risk, and trust-related aspects they have been researching related to this work in particular.

Chapter 9

Marek R. Ogiela, AGH University of Science and Technology, Poland
Urszula Ogiela, AGH University of Science and Technology, Poland

Secure information splitting is used in many tasks of the intelligent sharing of secrets and key data in business organisations. The significance of information splitting depends on its nature, while the significance of information sharing may depend on its importance and the meaning it has for the organisation or institution concerned. This chapter presents models for multi-level information splitting and information management with the use of the linguistic approach and formal grammars. Such methods constitute a secure enhancement of traditional secret splitting algorithms and introduce an additional stage at which information is coded using the appropriately defined regular or context-free grammar. The many possible applications of such methods include their use for the intelligent management of important or confidential information in government institutions or businesses. Algorithms of multi-level information splitting allow information that is not available to all employees of a given organisation or its environment to be securely split or shared.

Chapter 10

Kasra Amirtahmasebi, Chalmers University of Technology, Sweden
Seyed Reza Jalalinia, Chalmers University of Technology, Sweden

Due to the huge growth in the need for using Web applications worldwide, there have been huge efforts from programmers to develop and implement new Web applications to be used by companies. Since a number of these applications lack proper security considerations, malicious users will be able to gain unauthorized access to confidential information of organizations. A concept called SQL Injection Attack (SQLIA) is a prevalent method used by attackers to extract the confidential information from organizations' databases. They work by injecting malicious SQL codes through the web application, and they cause unexpected behavior from the database. There are a number of SQL Injection detection/prevention techniques that must be used in order to prevent unauthorized access to databases.

Chapter 11

Siddhartha Baruah, Gauhati University, India
Anjana Kakoty Mahanta, Gauhati University, India
Kanak Ch Sarma, Gauhati University, India

Though embedded applications were originally built on standalone devices, nowadays these devices require a growing integration with other systems through their interconnection with TCP/IP networks. Web Services, which provide a service oriented distributed architecture for the interconnection of systems through TCP/IP networks, have been widely adopted for the integration of business applications, but this sort of integration is still not widely provided by embedded applications. The present work aims to demonstrate the feasibility of using Web Services for the integration of embedded applications running on heterogeneous architectures. This is achieved through the provision of a support for the development and deployment of web services for embedded applications. Basic objective of the system developed is to monitor and control Humidity and Temperature through Internet using interactive computer front end. The feasibility of this approach in terms of security and authentications of its Internet users is demonstrated by developing an mail server along with application deployed. Mail server keeps track of authorised users' with login password and email ID in a database table. This information is used to identify authorised users who are allowed to make changes in control parameters of the stated embedded application.

Chapter 12

Zhongwen Li, Chengdu University, China

Zhibin Xu, Xiamen University, China

Chen Liang, Xiamen University, China

P2P networks have characteristics of decentralization, autonomy, and dynamicity. The security problems caused by these characteristics have seriously affected further development of P2P networks. The authors did research on CL-PKC key management schemes. (1) They propose a certificateless-based key distribution scheme with multiple trusted centers that fits the characteristics of P2P networks, and analyzed its security. (2) They also propose an improved interactive key agreement protocol across multiple domains, and then compare it with some existing key agreement protocol from aspects of security and computational efficiency. (3) The authors have implemented the proposed key management schemes, then verified their correctness and tested their computational efficiency. Combined with master key share management and key management of nodes, this system constructed a complete certificateless-based key management model, which is an exploration to solve security problems in P2P networks.

Chapter 13

David S. Allison, The University of Western Ontario, Canada

Hany F. EL Yamany, Suez Canal University, Egypt

Miriam A. M. Capretz, The University of Western Ontario, Canada

Privacy for Service-Oriented Architecture (SOA) is required to gain the trust of those who would use the technology. Through the use of an independent Privacy Service (PS), the privacy policies of a service consumer and provider can be compared to create an agreed upon privacy contract. In this chapter, the authors further define a metamodel for privacy policy creation and comparison. A trust element is developed as an additional criterion for a privacy policy. The authors define the PS, outline what operations it must perform to accomplish its goals, and present how the PS operates in different scenarios. They believe the PS, combined with the enhanced metamodel, provides a strong solution for providing privacy in an SOA environment.

Chapter 14

Alessandra Bagnato, TXT e-solutions, Italy

Fabio Raiteri, TXT e-solutions, Italy

Christian Jung, ISQ Fraunhofer Institute for Experimental Software Engineering IESE, Germany

Frank Elberzhager, ISQ Fraunhofer Institute for Experimental Software Engineering IESE, Germany

Security inspections are increasingly important for bringing security-relevant aspects into software systems, particularly during the early stages of development. Nowadays, such inspections often do not focus specifically on security. With regard to security, the well-known and approved benefits of inspections are not exploited to their full potential. This book chapter focuses on the Security Goal Indicator Tree application for eliminating existing shortcomings, the training that led to their creation in an industrial project environment, their usage, and their reuse by a team in industry. SGITs are a new approach for modeling and checking security-relevant aspects throughout the entire software development lifecycle. This book chapter describes the modeling of such security goal based trees as part of requirements engineering using the GOAT tool dedicated plug-in and the retrieval of these models during the various phases of the software development lifecycle in a project by means of Software Vulnerability Repository Services (SHIELDS, Software Vulnerability Repository Services) created in the European project SHIELDS (SHIELDS, SHIELDS - Detecting known security vulnerabilities from within design and development tools).

Today, Peer-to-Peer SIP based communication systems have attracted much attention from both academia and industry. The decentralized nature of P2P might provide the distributed peer-to-peer communication system without help of the traditional SIP server. However, the decentralization features come to the cost of the reduced manageability and create new concerns. Until now, the main focus of research was on the availability of the network and systems, while few attempts were put on protecting privacy. In this chapter, the authors investigate P2PSIP security issues and introduce two enhancement solutions: central based security and distributed trust security, both of which have their own advantages and disadvantages. After that, they study appropriate combination of these two approaches to get optimized protection. Their design is independent of the DHT (Distributed Hash Table) overlay technology. The authors take the Chord overlay as the example, and then analyze the system in several aspects: security & privacy, number-of the hops, message flows, et cetera.

The role of human behaviour in enterprise security is one of the little studied aspects. The author proposes a reinforcement model of collaborative security employing basic concepts from game theory, socio-psychology, and probabilistic model-checking. The proposed model aims towards solving the problem of inducing positive network effect to enable user centric monitoring of security violations, in particular, against violations related to "semantic manipulation" of context dependent logical resources. Preventing such violations using existing security enforcement mechanisms is neither feasible nor cost effective. The author defines a payoff mechanism to formalize the model by stipulating appropriate payoffs as reward, punishment, and community price according to reporting of genuine or false violations, non-reporting of the detected violations, and proactive reporting of vulnerabilities and threats by the users. Correctness properties of the model are defined in terms of probabilistic robustness property and constraints for economic feasibility of the payoffs. For estimating the payoff parameters, system and user behaviours are further modelled in terms of probabilistic finite state machines (PFSM) and likelihood of the success of the model is specified using probabilistic computation tree logic (PCTL). PRISM model checker based automated quantitative analysis elicits the process of the estimation of various parameters in the model using PFSMs and PCTL formulas.

Chapter 17

Nabil Ajam, Institut Télécom, Télécom Bretagne, France
Nora Cuppens-Boulahia, Institut Télécom, Télécom Bretagne, France
Fréderic Cuppens, Institut Télécom, Télécom Bretagne, France

In this chapter, the authors propose the expression and the modelling of the most important principles of privacy. They deduce the relevant privacy requirements that should be integrated in existing security policy models, such as RBAC models. They suggest the application of a unique model for both access control and privacy requirements. Thus, an access control model is to be enriched with new access constraints and parameters, namely the privacy contexts, which should implement the consent and the notification concepts. For this purpose, the authors introduce the Privacy-aware Organisation role Based Access Control (PrivOrBAC) model.

Chapter 18

Komminist Weldemariam, Fondazione Bruno Kessler, Italy
Adolfo Villafiorita, Fondazione Bruno Kessler, Italy

In this chapter, first the authors discuss the current trends in the usage of formal techniques in the development of e-voting system. They then present their experiences on their usage to specify and verify the behaviors of one of currently deployed e-voting systems using formal techniques and verification against a subset of critical security properties that the system should meet. The authors also specified attacks that have been shown to successfully compromise the system. The attack information is used to extend the original specification of the system and derive what we called the extended model. This work is a step towards fostering open specification and the (partial) verification of a voting machine. The specification and verification was intended as a learning process where they would use formal techniques to improve the current development of e-voting systems.

Chapter 19

Aditya Raj, Netaji Subhas Institute of Technology, India
Tushar Pahwa, Netaji Subhas Institute of Technology, India
Ashish Jain, Netaji Subhas Institute of Technology, India

CAPTCHAs are employed on websites to differentiate between human users and bot programs that indulge in spamming and other fraudulent activities. With the advent and advancement of sophisticated computer programs to break CAPTCHAs, it has become imperative to continuously evolve the CAPTCHA schemes in order to keep the Internet network and website free of congestion and spam-bots. In light of these developments concerning information security, in this chapter, the authors introduce the novel concept of Scrambled CAPTCHA, which is a combination of OCR-based and Picture CAPTCHAs and exploits an inherent characteristic of human vision and perception. They also introduce Hindi CAPTCHA, developed in Hindi language (Devanagari script). This CAPTCHA will typically address spamming on Indian websites. It also contributes to the digitalization of books written in this script. The authors also discuss the features and security aspects of these schemes in detail, which, to the best their knowledge, had not been implemented earlier.

Embedded systems are extensively used in the field of pervasive computing. These systems are used to such an extent that embedded systems are now controlled and monitored from remote locations by using Web services. Internet authorities are able to assign every device a unique Internet protocol address with the introduction of IPv6 on the Web. Peer-to-peer communication between Internet-enabled devices helped Web services to make performance improvement. On the worse side, it created new attacks on the components used in the embedded systems. The chapter discusses the details of security issues on a Web-enabled embedded system used in greenhouse environment. The devices used in greenhouse environment are monitored and controlled by different software components used in the entire system. Various vulnerabilities are introduced during entire development process of the greenhouse environment. The problem is to search the real threats, then define security policies and implement them during development process. The chapter discusses most of the vulnerabilities of a generalized greenhouse project and tries to find out possible security techniques to deal with the vulnerabilities. Instead of showing the design to build a greenhouse embedded system, it shows to introduce security policies at various levels of life-cycle, be it before development, during development, or after development.

Security of wireless sensor networks (WSN) relates in many aspects to security of distributed systems. On the first sight WSNs form a large distributed ad-hoc system with lot of tiny devices that sense some phenomena and communicate wirelessly. Due to some limitations, among which the energy consumption problem is the most important one, security issues could demand different solutions than those used in the area of ordinary distributed systems. In this chapter, the authors briefly introduce the hardware and software approach to WSN design first, and then they define the main security aspects in such systems. Then some security mechanisms are presented, and their connection to possible countermeasures of the identified risks is described.

Network security is in a daily evolving domain. Every day, new attacks, viruses, and intrusion techniques are released. Hence, network devices, enterprise servers, or personal computers are potential targets of these attacks. Current security solutions like firewalls, intrusion detection systems (IDS), and virtual private networks (VPN) are centralized solutions, which rely mostly on the analysis of inbound network connections. This approach notably forgets the effects of a rogue station, whose communications cannot be easily controlled unless the administrators establish a global authentication policy using methods like 802.1x to control all network communications among each device. To the best of the authors' knowledge, a distributed and easily manageable solution for the global security of an enterprise network does not exist. In this chapter, they present a new approach to deploy a distributed security solution where communication between each device can be control in a collaborative manner. Indeed, each device has its own security rules, which can be shared and improved through exchanges with others devices. With this new approach, called grid of security, a community of devices ensures that a device is trustworthy and that communications between devices progress in respect of the control of the system policies. To support this approach, the authors present a new communication model that helps structuring the distribution of security services among the devices. This can secure both ad-hoc, local-area or enterprise networks in a decentralized manner, preventing the risk of a security breach in the case of a failure.

Fine-grained malware analysis requires various powerful analysis tools. Chief among them is a debugger that enables runtime binary analysis at the instruction level. One of the important services provided by a debugger is the ability to stop execution of code at arbitrary points during runtime, using breakpoints. Software breakpoints change the code being analyzed so that it can be interrupted during runtime. Most, if not all malware are very sensitive to code modification with self-modifying and/or self-checking capabilities, rendering the use of software breakpoints limited in their scope. Hardware breakpoints on the other hand, use a subset of the CPU registers and exception mechanisms to provide breakpoints that do not entail code modification. However, hardware breakpoints support limited breakpoint ability (typically only 2-4 locations) and are susceptible to various anti-debugging techniques employed by malware. This chapter describes a novel breakpoint technique (called stealth breakpoints) that provides unlimited number of breakpoints which are robust to detection and countering mechanisms. Further, stealth breakpoints retain all the features (code, data and I/O breakpoint abilities) of existing hardware and software breakpoint schemes and enables easy integration with existing debuggers.

One cannot develop effective economic models for information security and privacy without having a good understanding of the motivations, disincentives, and other influencing factors affecting the behavior of criminals, victims, defenders, product and service providers, lawmakers, law enforcement, and other interested parties. Predicting stakeholders' actions and reactions will be more effective if one has a realistic representation of how each of the various parties will respond to internal motivators and external stimuli. In this chapter, reactions of involved parties are assumed to be based on "personal utility functions." However, it is not sufficient merely to develop static utility functions, since the net value of security and privacy changes dynamically. External events, such as the announcement of a new threat, also have a significant effect on both subjective and objective net value. Knowing how such value functions vary over time helps determine the overall dynamic impact of security and privacy measures on the behavior of various participants and ultimately on the economic model that describes these behaviors. Also in this chapter, the authors enumerate the many factors that affect all the various parties and examine how these factors affect the responses of all those involved due to the economic impact of particular exploits and situations as they affect different groups.

Preface

Organizations are increasingly relying on information in electronic form to conduct business. While this evolution of an electronic-based society from a paper-based one has been advantageous to both enterprises and individuals alike, the amount of personal information has also grown exponentially. With rapid growth in the number of information systems and related processes, managing information security program, while effectively managing risks, has never been so critical. A recent survey of 600 IT and security executives (Baker, Waterman, & Ivanov, 2010) finds that there is a widespread lack of confidence in their organization's ability to defend against a cyberattack. "About 40% of those surveyed expected a major incident -- an attack resulting in major consequences -- within a year, and 80% said they expected a major incident within 5 years" (p. 13). On average, respondents estimated that 24 hours of down time from a major attack would cost their own organization U.S. $6.3 million and more than 60% say that the frequency and intensity of cyberattacks have increased in the past year. Given the rise of threats and technologies to launch and hide these attacks, the situation is clearly getting worse for organizations. Effective information security management and governance is the most important action organizations can take to thwart and manage these risks.

In today's rapidly changing and evolving environment, IT and security executives have to make difficult calculations and decisions about security with limited information. They need to make decisions that are based on analyzing opportunities, risks and security. In such an environment, information security management and governance issues are at the forefront of any discussions for security organization's information assets, which includes considerations for managing risks, data and costs. Organizations, worldwide, have adopted practical and applied approaches for mitigating risks and managing information security program. The book contains 24 Chapters on the most relevant and important issues and advances in applied information security management. The Chapters are authored by leading researchers and practitioners in the field of information security from across the globe. The Chapters represent emerging threats and countermeasures for effective management of information security at organizations.

With an increase in sophistication of technology, speed of propagation and relative ease of launching and coordinating a cyber-attack, an effective preventive and detective response should include automated and distributed mechanism. There are a variety of tools of available for cyber-attackers to change the attack pattern and signature, which only makes defense against them ever so challenging. To keep up with dynamic evolution of attack types, the detection methods should be constantly kept updated. In Chapter 1, titled *A Pragmatic Approach to Intrusion Response Metrics* by Chris Strasburg of The Ames Laboratory, US Department of Energy, USA and Johnny S. Wong of Department of Computer Science, Iowa State University, USA authors discuss their analyses of present-day automated intrusion response metrics; and how they can be used from a more practical standpoint. Authors review existing intrusion detection approaches and practical challenges faced by organizations in implementing and making the best use of them. They present practical solutions and recommendations for implementing intrusion response metrics, and identify research areas that need more focus for development of automated practical and effective response systems.

Intrusion Detection Systems (IDSs) are an important and critical part of any effective information security architecture and program. IDSs have evolved significantly over the last decade in response to efficiently thwart fast evolving threats and risks. At a basic level, IDS acts like a pattern recognition system, where patterns of attacks and malicious codes are used to detect threats. One of the most important steps, that plays a critical role in determining the overall effectiveness of intrusion detection, during pattern recognition is a process known as feature extraction. Use of domain knowledge in manual as well as automatic feature extraction is very pervasive. Hai Thanh Nguyen, Katrin Franke, and Slobodan Petrović of Gjøvik University College, Gjøvik, Norway provide an overview of various existing feature construction and feature selection methods for intrusion detection systems in Chapter 2. Using experiments, the Chapter 2 *(Feature Extraction Methods for Intrusion Detection Systems)* also presents a comparison between different feature selection methods. The experiments use public benchmarking data sets for demonstrating practical applications of feature extraction methods.

With increasing approval and regulation of digital signatures across globe, digital signatures are seen as faster and convenient way of legally signing and ratifying documents. In traditional paper based signatures, authority to sign documents on someone's behalf can be delegated. With rise in use of digital signatures, architectures and methods of similar delegation techniques for others to be able to legally and securely sign digital documents have been proposed. In Chapter 3, authors assert several shortcomings of these proposed methods from a practical implementation and adoption standpoint. Highlighting these shortcomings and stressing advantages of delegation through use of smart cards, in Chapter 3 *(A Distributed and Secure Architecture for Signature and Decryption Delegation through Remote Smart Cards* authors - Giuseppe Cattaneo, Pompeo Faruolo, and Ivan Visconti of Dipartimento di Informatica – Università di Salerno, Italy - put forth the notion of a "Proxy Smart Card System," a distributed system that allows a smart card owner to delegate part of its computations to remote users. Authors then formalize the security and functional requirements of a proxy smart card system, identifying the involved parties, the adversary model and the usability properties. The Chapter also demonstrates practical implementation of such a smart card based proxy system that includes all the functional requirements for secure delegation, while outperforming existing suggested methods.

Increase in dominance of ecommerce channels in delivering products and services could not be overemphasized. With such a rise in adoption rates, the challenges in securing these channels have never been more critical. In Chapter 4, titled *Information Security Management: Awareness of Threats in E-Commerce,* authors, Mohammad Mahfuzur Rahman of Applied Research Centre for Business and Information Technology (ARCBIT), London, UK and Karim Mohammed Rezaul of Glyndŵr University, Wrexham, *UK* present, identify, and investigate information security problems in the e-commerce sector within purview of extant theories of information security.

Information security standards and frameworks are increasingly adopted by companies of all sizes and forms. However, implementing a deployment scheme should be done within context of organizational specifics to ensure smoother adoption and effective enforcement. In this Chapter the authors analyse information security goals found in hospital settings. In Chapter 5 *(Analyzing Information Security Goals),* authors Ella Kolkowska, Karin Hedström and Fredrik Karlsson, of Örebro University School of Business, Sweden demonstrate that the CIA-triad fails to cover organisational specific information security goals in hospital settings. Authors present goal maps, which they used in their study for analysis of empirical data, as a useful tool for analysis and communication of information security goals in an organisation.

Authentication is one of the most basic as well as most important security processes that encompass protection of information from unauthorized use. With recent innovation in technology – both software and hardware – several innovative alternatives to simple text-based passwords have been suggested, which have shown to have higher security and usability. One such concept is graphical passwords. In Chapter 6 *(Graphical Passwords)*, Luigi Catuogno of Università degli Studi di Salerno, Italy and Clemente Galdi of Università degli Studi di Napoli "Federico II," Italy provide an overview of this state-of-art concept for stronger authentication using motivation and corroboration from extant literature.

Most of the vulnerabilities and threats in IT artifact arise from misconfigured software. Evaluating and testing security strength of any specific system is one of most crucial proactive countermeasures in ensuring security of any software system. In Chapter 7 *(Assessing the Security of Software Configurations)*, authors - Afonso Araújo Neto and Marco Vieira of University of Coimbra, Portugal - present a methodology to devise security appraisals, which is derived from available security knowledge about specific domains. Authors demonstrate their methodology by designing a couple of security appraisals for transactional systems. The authors also provide a real demonstration of both security appraisals using real scenarios.

Privacy issues in an organizational setting have fast emerged as one of the most challenging aspects of enterprise information security program. Recent instructions and mandates from government, in the form of regulations, have further burdened companies with finding effective ways to comply with those regulations and guidelines without compromising security and convenience. Authors of Chapter 8, Siani Pearson and Tomas Sander from Cloud and Security Research Lab, HP Labs, USA, in their work - *A Decision Support System for Privacy Compliance* – present a privacy risk assessment and compliance tool which they are developing and implementing in a large, global company – called HP Privacy Advisor (HP PA). Authors introduce concept of accountable privacy management in an organization that has several parallel projects while suggesting a compliance tool that also manages enterprise security, privacy, risk and trust-related aspects.

Information sharing and collaboration play a significant role in success of business processes and operations in an organizational environment. Cross-departmental and cross-functional teams have increasingly being leveraged for efficient deployment of products and services by businesses. At the same time securing the information that is being shared and collectively worked upon by has become equally critical. Data segregation and secure information splitting has been used in organizations to share confidential data. Chapter 9 *(Information Security Management Based on Linguistic Sharing Techniques)* by Marek R. Ogiela and Urszula Ogiela of AGH University of Science and Technology, Kraków, Poland presents models for multi-level information splitting and information management with the use of the linguistic approach and formal grammars. The proposed techniques and methods introduce major enhancements over traditional algorithms.

SQL injection attacks are one the most common ways by which confidential data is stolen by hackers. This is also one of the oldest techniques used to extract information from databases compromising the access and privilege requirements. Stronger input validation and detection techniques have been traditionally used to thwart SQL injection attacks. In Chapter 10, *SQL Injection Attacks Countermeasures*, authors - Kasra Amirtahmasebi and Seyed Reza Jalalinia *Chalmers* University of Technology, Sweden - present seven of the stronger countermeasures that cover a wide range of SQL injection attacks.

Each day, people's lives become more dependent on embedded systems and on digital information technology that is embedded in their environment. Embedded applications can be managed remotely using public network such as Internet. Web Services have been extensively used in traditional software systems for providing a wide variety of services including integration of applications, remote assistance and collaboration amongst others. Similar applications of web services for embedded systems haven't seen an emergence yet. In Chapter 11 *(Security and Authentication Issues of an Embedded System Designed and Implemented for Interactive Internet Users)*, authors - Siddhartha Baruah, Anjana Kakoty Mahanta and Kanak Ch Sarma *of Gauhati University, India* - present discussions to demonstrate the feasibility of using Web Services for the integration of embedded applications running on heterogeneous architectures. Authors present a model with an objective to demonstrate web services can be used to monitor and control humidity and temperature through Internet using interactive computer front end.

P2P networks are fast emerging as dependable forms of communications and for provding a large array of services, both for personal as well as commercial applications. P2P network's characteristics of decentralization, autonomy and dynamicity pose several unique security challenges, which can potentially hamper adoption and development of such networks. In Chapter 12 titled *Distributed Key Management Scheme Based on CL-PKC in P2P Networks,* authors - Zhongwen Li, Zhibin Xu, and Chen Liang of Xiamen University, Xiamen, Fujian, China - propose a certificate-less key distribution scheme with multiple trusted centers that fits the characteristics of P2P networks, and analyzed its security.

In Chapter 13 (*A Privacy Service for Comparison of Privacy and Trust Policies within SOA),* authors David S. Allison and Miriam A. M. Capretz of The University of Western Ontario, Canada, and Hany F. El Yamany of Suez Canal University, Egypt define a metamodel for privacy policy creation and comparison. The meta-model contains six elements using an independent privacy service (PS) and trust element, the privacy policies of a service consumer and provider are compared with an agreed upon privacy contract. The proposed enhanced metamodel provides a strong solution for providing privacy in an SOA environment.

Security of software and application development and implementation is one of the most common challenges facing companies. There are several approaches of evaluating security aspects of different stages in software development life cycle including fuzzing testing method, penetration testing and code walkthrough. One relatively new and novel inspection method known as Security Goal Indicator Trees is increasingly gaining relevance and importance. Alessandra Bagnato and Fabio Raiteri of Txt e-solutions Corporate Research Division, Italy, and Christian Jung and Frank Elberzhager of ISQ Fraunhofer Institute for Experimental Software Engineering, Germany, in Chapter 14 *(Creating and Applying Security Goal Indicator Trees in an Industrial Environment)* focus on the Security Goal Indicator Tree application for eliminating existing shortcomings. The Chapter describes the modeling of such security goal based trees as part of requirements engineering using a dedicated plug-in called toll called –GOAT.

Due to their relative convenience and cost savings, applications such as Skype and other mobile applications have seen tremendous growth in adoption in recent years. This has also brought unique and new security challenges for Peer-to-Peer SIP based communication systems that are underlying technologies for novel applications such as Skype. The decentralized nature of P2P makes security management and enforcement rather difficult. In Chapter 15 (*Security Enhancement of Peer-to-Peer Session Initiation),* Xianghan Zheng of Fuzhou University, P.R. China and Vladimir A. Oleshchuk of University of Agder, Norway investigate P2PSIP security issues and propose two enhancement solutions: central based security and distributed trust security. They discuss advantages and disadvantages of each of the proposed approaches. They also propose a combination of the two approaches in an attempt to find a better and more optimized protection.

In Chapter 16 *(Towards a Framework for Collaborative Enterprise Security)*, Janardan Misra, an *Independent Researcher* presents a principled approach to one of the many little-studied human and social aspects of enterprise security management. The chapter proposes a reinforcement model of collaborative security employing basic concepts from game theory, socio-psychology, and probabilistic model-checking. The proposed model aims to solve the problem of inducing positive network effect to enable user centric monitoring of security violations. The chapter presents a formal framework for devising policies to enable collaborative monitoring against policy violations without requiring employees and stakeholders of the company to own more roles for security policy monitoring and enforcement. The framework is based on 1) organic unity of biological systems under attacks and 2) socio- psychological studies on security and human motivation. The chapter proposes a reward-punishment based reinforcement model for enabling collaborative monitoring of policy violations by extrinsically inducing positive network effect in the system.

In Chapter 17 (*Privacy-Aware Organisation-Based Access Control Model (PrivOrBAC)*) authors - Nabil Ajam, Nora Cuppens-Boulahia and Fréderic Cuppens of Institut Télécom, Télécom Bretagne, France - identify the relevant privacy requirements that should be integrated in existing security policy models, such as RBAC models. The Chapter proposes Privacy-aware Organisation role Based Access Control (PrivOrBAC) model to identify and incorporate new access constraints and parameters, namely the privacy contexts, which should implement the consent and the notification concepts.

In Chapter 18, titled *Can Formal Methods Really Help: Analyzing the Security of Electronic Voting Systems?*, Komminist Weldemariam and Adolfo Villafiorita of Fondazione Bruno Kessler, Trento, Italy, discuss effective use of formal methods in e-voting systems development process. The Chapter also provides an overview of current trends in the usage of formal techniques in the development of e-voting system. Using their experience, authors specify and verify the behaviors of one of currently deployed e-voting systems using formal techniques and verification against a subset of critical security properties that the system should meet. Using specified attacks that have been shown to successfully compromise the system, the Chapter extends the original specification of the system and derives an extended model.

CAPTCHAs (Completely Automated Public Turing test to tell Computers and Humans Apart) are computer generated challenge-response tests employed on websites to differentiate between human users and bot programs which indulge in spamming and other fraudulent activities. CAPTCHAs rely on visual representation and have been vitally effective against several well-known attacks such as spam and denial of service. With the advent and advancement of sophisticated computer programs to break CAPTCHAs, it has become imperative to continuously evolve the CAPTCHA schemes in order to keep the Internet network and website free of congestion and spam-bots. In light of these developments concerning information security, in Chapter 19 (*Countering Spam Robots: Scrambled CAPTCHA and Hindi CAPTCHA*), authors, Aditya Raj, Tushar Pahwa, and Ashish Jain of Netaji Subhas Institute of Technology, New Delhi, India, introduce the novel concept of Scrambled CAPTCHA which is a combination of OCR-based and Picture CAPTCHAs and exploits an inherent characteristic of human vision and perception. They present unique security offerings of their concept and its implications. The Chapter also introduces Hindi CAPTCHA, based on Hindi language (Devanagari script).

Use of embedded systems has increased exponentially in recent years. They are extensively used in most of the common consumer electronics to industrial applications including transportation and airplanes. These applications of embedded systems are controlled and monitored from remote locations, over the Internet, using web services. While proving huge benefits, it has given rise to new security concerns. Trailokya Oraon of Jorhat Engineering College, Assam, India, in Chapter 20, titled *Security*

Risk of Embedded Systems in a Greenhouse Environment discusses the details of security issues in web-enabled embedded systems used in greenhouse environment. The discussions in the Chapter not only helps understand security issues of an embedded system but also provides insights into securing green computing systems. The Chapter identifies the security shortcomings in the system while providing solutions to overcome those challenges. It also demonstrates that security policies should be designed and enforced at each stage of development cycle.

Importance of security of a wireless network system (WSN) cannot be over emphasized. The security threats in such networks are heightened due to dynamic and highly distributed nature of the underlying infrastructural dependency. In Chapter 21, *Security in Wireless Sensor Networks with Mobile Codes*, Frantisek Zboril Jr., Jan Horacek, Martin Drahansky, and Petr Hanacek of Brno University of Technology, Brno, Czech Republic introduce design aspects of WSN, from both the hardware and software perspective, to unravel different components and services that can potentially be targeted. The Chapter presents main security challenges in such systems, while presenting security mechanisms and possible countermeasures.

Companies use a wide variety of technologies and their artifacts to protect their infrastructure including network, servers and software systems. Some of such artifacts include firewalls, intrusion detection systems, anti-virus, data leak prevention, content encryption amongst others. It becomes challenging to globally manage security of these disparate systems that work towards the same objective of providing comprehensive security. To address this common challenge, in Chapter 22 titled *Grid of Security: A Decentralized Enforcement of the Network Security*, Olivier Flauzac, Florent Nolot, Cyril Rabat, and Luiz-Angelo Steffenel, *of* University of Reims Champagne-Ardenne, France, present a new approach to deploy a distributed security solution where communication between each device can be control in a collaborative manner. In this novel proposed approach, called *grid of security*, each security component runs under guidance from its own security rules, which can be shared and improved through exchanges with others devices. This approach ensures that through compliance of security policies; and exchange and communication with other devices the complete system is more trustworthy.

Malware comes in different shapes and forms. They have shown to compromise security of software systems, from personal computers to utility grids. To design and develop countermeasures for any malware software, we need to analyze them first. Malware analysis is a challenging multi-step process providing insight into malware structure and functionality, facilitating the development of an antidote. In Chapter 23 (*Effective Malware Analysis Using Stealth Breakpoints*), Dr. Amit Vasudevan of CyLab/Carnegie Mellon University, USA describes a novel breakpoint technique (called stealth breakpoints), for efficient malware analysis, which provides unlimited number of breakpoints which are robust to detection and countering mechanisms.

In Chapter 24, titled *Dynamic Cyber Security Economic Model: Incorporating Value Functions for All Involved Parties*, Dr. C. Warren Axelrod of Delta Risk LLC, USA assert that it is important to understand and factor in motivations and reactions of all parties involved (such as criminals, victims, defenders, product and service providers, lawmakers, law enforcement, amongst others) for development of a comprehensive economic model or information security. The Chapter attempts to provide initial formulations of such dynamic economic models for information security, while providing insights into potential application of the model to assess the impact of different control mechanisms. Using dynamic "personal utility functions," the Chapter suggests factors that affect all the various parties and examines how these factors affect the responses due to the economic impacts.

The book hosts high-quality research papers and practice articles on management and governance issues in the field of information security. The Chapters in the book provide insights into practical and applied solutions, frameworks, technologies and practices on technological and organizational factors of an organization. Often, managers are overwhelmed with solutions and technologies for information security while squandering a lot of resources on trying to understand what would work for them and what not. The book presents information security management solutions being researched on or deployed through book Chapters from leading researchers and practitioners in the field, culminating in Chapters of the highest quality. The book fills gap in the existing literature on the latest advances in practice and in research in the areas of information security management and governance by providing the audience one comprehensive source of latest trends, issues and research in the field. The Chapters are authored by researchers and professionals from more than 10 countries, which further lend the global outlook and approach to the covered topics. The book hosts topics both on theoretical (research) aspects of information security management by presenting solutions and issues in the area while supplementing them with real- world implications and implementations (practice) of the research. By keeping the focus of the Chapters to the practices and solutions that are practical and implementable, it adds huge value to the extant literature, while helping organization around the world understand and effectively improve their overall information security posture. To the editors' knowledge, which collectively represents more than 60 years of practical and academic experience in information security and related fields, none of the existing books present this area, which has provided the opportunity to submit this book for publication. The editors would like to mention that though this will have some industry case studies to demonstrate the applicability and process of applied information security practices, it does not focus entirely in case studies, so thematically, the proposed book is not a case study book.

REFERENCE

Baker, S., Waterman, S., & Ivanov, G. (2010). In the crossfire: Critical infrastructure in the age of cyber war. *A Mcafee 2010 global security survey report.* Retrieved from http://resources.mcafee.com/content/ NACIPReport

Chapter 1
A Pragmatic Approach to Intrusion Response Metrics

Chris Strasburg
The Ames Laboratory, US Department of Energy, USA

Johnny S. Wong
Iowa State University, USA

ABSTRACT

The arms race between cyber attackers and defenders has evolved to the point where an effective counter-measure strategy requires the use of an automated, distributed, and coordinated response. A key difficulty in achieving this goal lies in providing reliable measures by which to select appropriate responses to a wide variety of potential intrusions in a diverse population of network environments. In this chapter, the authors provide an analysis of the current state of automated intrusion response metrics from a pragmatic perspective. This analysis includes a review of the current state of the art as well as descriptions of the steps required to implement current work in production environments. The authors also discuss the research gaps that must be filled to improve security professionals' ability to implement an automated intrusion response capability.

INTRODUCTION

With the increased use of automation by attackers, the number of attacks and degree of damage which can be caused in a short amount of time have also increased. Small increments of time on a system can mean significant additional damage done by the attacker. In 2002, the Computer Emergency Response Team (CERT) noted:

Attack tool developers are using more advanced techniques. Attack tool signatures are more difficult to discover through analysis and more difficult to detect through signature-based systems such as antivirus software and intrusion detection systems. Three important characteristics are the anti-forensic nature, dynamic behavior, and modularity of the tools. (Householder, 2002, p. 1)

For instance, the CodeRed worm was known for its rapid rate of infection, infecting nearly 400,000 hosts in less than 24 hours (Zou, 2002).

DOI: 10.4018/978-1-4666-0978-5.ch001

One researcher, presenting a biological model for Internet worm propagation, concluded: "Because high-speed worms are no longer a theoretical threat, we need to automate worm defenses; there is no conceivable way for system administrators to respond to threats of this speed." (Misslinger, 2005, p. 8)

To address this shortcoming, the DARPA/ISO Autonomic Information Assurance program studied high-speed and broad scale attacks, and suggested that effective response must also be fast (e.g. automated), and strategically coordinated rather than local and reactive (Lewandowski, 2002). This need has prompted the security research community to explore a variety of approaches to automated intrusion response systems (IRS). Currently few of these approaches have been applied in practice, and in fact there is still a lack of agreement on an effective assessment framework, much less a recognition of the most promising research directions. We will discuss the challenges to assessing and utilizing intrusion response approaches, and suggest directions of research and development which may alleviate these issues.

Organization

Intrusion response systems can be categorized along several dimensions, including degree of automation, ability to adjust, time of response, cooperation, and selection mechanism (See Figure 1) (Stakhanova, 2007).

Figure 1. Intrusion response taxonomy (Stakhanova, 2007)

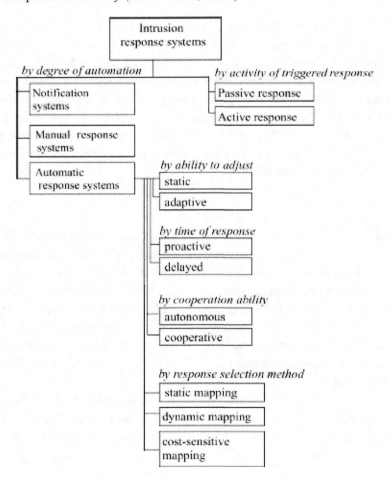

The class of dynamic and cost-sensitive response selection approaches also encompasses a range of complexity from heuristic response selection to attacker goal prediction. Heuristic selection identifies a guiding formula by which the optimal response can be estimated. A recent example is cost sensitive response selection, wherein an on-the-fly assessment of the potential impact of both the intrusion and each possible response is made, and the response with the best cost-benefit trade-off is chosen. These approaches usually center around an intuitive evaluation of system resources and the effect of intrusions and responses on them. In general, they sacrifice the predictive power of more complex approaches in favor of broader applicability and lower information gathering overhead for use.

At the other complexity extreme, goal prediction is based on a model of the attacker's behavior. By observing a set of alerts, a determination is made that an attacker is targeting a certain resource and has achieved some degree of progress toward that goal. In general, these approaches require detailed resource interaction maps as well as representations of attacks in terms of fundamental attack steps (Yu, 2007). Goal prediction places heavy emphasis on refining the ability to determine and anticipate attacker actions, responding to the higher-level activities which are occurring rather than individual events.

In this chapter we will focus on automated, adaptive, and dynamic intrusion response systems, including works of varying complexity, noting response time and alert correlation supported by each approach.

Practical Challenges

We identify three main challenges which impede the adoption of automated intrusion response systems in practice: information acquisition, accurate model generation, and confidence in response safety. There is another potential source of friction, the manual effort required to imple-ment responses, which is assumed to be a factor included in an organization's decision to pursue automated response.

Information Acquisition

An important consideration for organizations attempting to deploy a consistent automated response engine is the production of prerequisite information. Many approaches to intrusion response assessment assume the availability of detailed dependency graphs (Jahnke, 2007), fine-grained resource enumeration (Balepin, 2002), or exhaustive attack taxonomies (Lee, 2002). While this information is often producible on a small scale for use in experiments and demonstrations, real-world production environments have significant complexity differences precluding the manual generation of these inputs. In this chapter we evaluate the information requirements included in leading intrusion response approaches and discuss techniques for efficiently generating the required data.

Accurate Model Generation

Taking into account the trade-off between measurement granularity and computational complexity is another factor to be weighed in the application of security metrics. A direct relationship exists between the measurement granularity and the amount of information captured in the resultant value. This leads to a tendency for researchers to pursue fine-grained analysis of resources to produce the most promising experimental results at the cost of increased information requirements. We include performance and granularity in the information acquisition discussion to both estimate the balance in current work and to suggest future research directions to mitigate effects of more complex modeling.

Confidence in Response Safety

Many domains of application for intrusion response assessment are environment amalgamations, with different security requirements, controls, and management. Depending on the network and organizational structure, these application domains may be nested, disjoint, or partially overlapping. This prevents empirical studies from applying directly to production environments, leading administrators to a degree of skepticism when considering the safety of an automated response implementation.

The ability of a metric to produce consistent and comparable values across environments both within and between organizations is crucial to address this roadblock, as well as to enable information sharing and multi-organization collaboration. Our intention is to identify key research practices which provide a foundation for comparison both for academic and practical purposes.

Goals

Specific goals for this chapter include providing a starting point for researchers interested in intrusion response metrics, informing experienced members of the community about the continued open challenges impeding practical progress, and supplying a valuable reference for practitioners charged with improving automated intrusion response.

We discuss the practical application of metrics for intrusion response automation and provide a survey of the latest research developments in this area and their experimental results. In addition, consideration of each work includes an examination of the implementation requirements for use in production environments. Finally, a discussion of the open challenges provides direction for future research efforts.

RECENT APPROACHES

In 1977, Glaseman et al. presented an overview of the general problems facing those who seek to develop general metrics of security assessment and pointed to the assumption that administrators can provide all required data, and the lack of established foundation upon which to compare models of security. In addition, the need for more precision and granularity is identified as crucial for improved comparisons.

More recently, automated intrusion response has gained attention in the security research community, leading to a number of proposed approaches with various capabilities. This section is not intended to provide a comprehensive in-depth analysis of all intrusion response paradigms, but rather to focus on representative works utilizing various metrics for response selection.

Graph-Based Approaches

Graph-based modeling is a natural fit for describing relationships between resources, intrusions, and responses. Many approaches to dynamic response selection rely on graph structures to portray related resource types in a domain, resources in a system, and response and intrusion effects on resources (Toth, 2002; Balepin, 2002; Foo, 2005).

Several recent works (Jahnke, 2007; Kheir, 2010) developed approaches which utilize graphical dependency models to aid in assigning resource values. Dependency graphs model interrelationships between resources, and are useful to predict how an impact on one resource may spread to others.

Toth and Kruegel

The work by Toth and Kruegel (Toth, 2002) employed dependency trees, coupling resources with logical connectives and labeling edges with capability estimates to determine the overall effectiveness of the running system. This representa-

Figure 2. Graphs in IRS. A) High-level dependency graph; B) Excerpt of an attack graph; C) Low-level dependency graph of a VOIP system (Adapted from Toth, 2002; Foo, 2005; Jahnke, 2007)

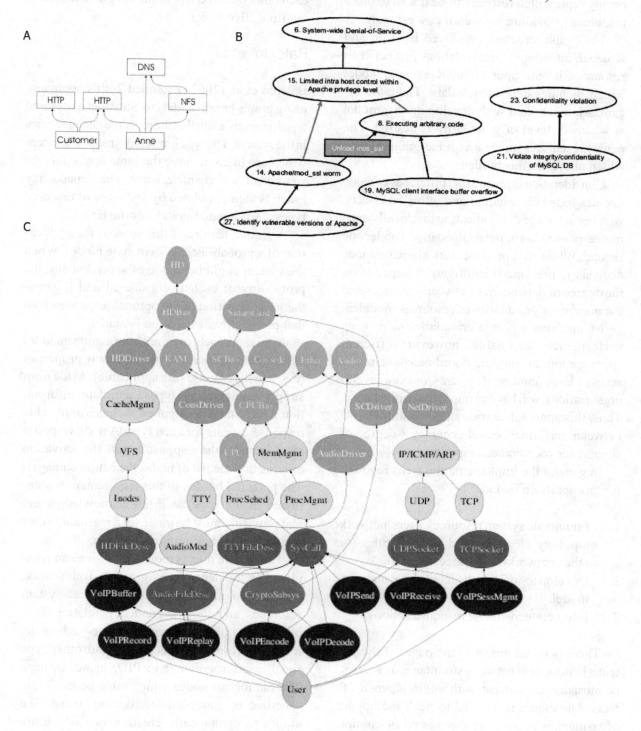

tion allows the impact of an attack (or response) on any represented resource to be traced to other resources, providing an overall cost estimate.

The graph structure employed by Toth and Kruegel, including logical relationships between resources, is built upon an input resource model which includes dependency data. Thus, the organization is tasked with developing this model at whatever level of granularity is desired. The paper presents resources at a course-grained level, which alleviates this burden.

Consideration is given to the efficiency of value updates based on response and intrusion effects, with performance data indicating that locally optimal responses can be determined in just under one second. While no formal theoretical performance analysis is presented, intuitively it depends on the degree of dependency between resources and the number or granularity of resources modeled.

Maintaining a coarse granularity helps keep performance reasonable, however sufficient specification to support coordinated response across a large number of systems, or even several organizations, will have an impact on performance. Thus, this approach carries an inherent trade-off between performance and accuracy / degree of support for coordinated response.

In general the implementation steps required for this approach include:

1. Enumerate system resources, users, network topology elements, and firewall rules (or other network-based access controls).
2. Develop a sufficiently detailed dependency model.
3. Enumerate available response actions.

There is no treatment in the paper of the potential interaction between simultaneous attacks, or intrusion concurrent with environmental effects. The model is updated to track the impact of sequential events, but there is no discussion addressing how to accurately represent this incremental degradation. For instance, concurrent intrusions and environmental effects may cancel each other out, overlap, or produce an additive or multiplicative effect.

Balepin, et al.

Balepin et al. (2002) extended Toth's approach, using graph-based models to construct a resource type hierarchy as well as the resource dependencies in the system. The type hierarchy groups resources which are likely to have the same applicable response set and characteristics. The dependency graph is then populated by instances of resource types, carrying additional information.

A unique feature of this work is the application of a probabilistic system state model. When the system could be in one of several states, the probability of each is considered and a game-theoretic selection of the optimal response given that probability distribution is made.

In this approach, required information includes defining the resource types and their properties (e.g. which responses are applicable). Aside from simply enumerating types, template information which must be supplied includes applicable response actions for each type. A node response entry includes the response action, the activation criteria, and the list of nodes the action damages. The potential burden of this requirement is mentioned in the paper with an acknowledgement that provision must be made for a reasonable user interface to add custom information.

The system map is more expressive and complex than the dependency graph in Toth's work. Information includes not only critical system resources and their dependency relationships, but also auxiliary information for each node, including resource value, type, and other type specific information (e.g. PID, name, owner). The number of nodes which must be explicitly specified is somewhat less onerous due to the ability to dynamically create nodes which are listed in an alert, but not present on the map. For example, given that "Web Server" is listed as a resource accompanied by a template for httpd host processes, each specific httpd process can be dynamically instantiated in the map from a suitable template.

A real-time probability estimate is also included, indicating the likelihood of each system state when multiple states are possible. However, to avoid requiring the predetermination of probabilities for all state-event combinations, the authors rely on historical data, and argue that the Laplace insufficiency criterion applies for cases where no historical data is available. This probability table is only employed in cases where an uncertain consequence of an event occurs, putting the system in one of several possible states. Thus the impact of mis-estimating these probabilities is very low.

The response selection mechanism itself involves choosing a response from each potentially affected node's response list, ensuring that all nodes are addressed. Responses are selected by their expected ability to restore that node to a safe state. Depending on the granularity of the system map, this may involve evaluating thousands of "compromised" nodes, e.g. in the case of an attacker creating thousands of hidden files, or creating many processes. While no explicit performance data is provided, the only execution costs which scale for a specific attack are the number of resources and the number of possible states (in the case of uncertainty).

Implementing such a system in practice requires the following steps:

1. Construct or obtain an appropriate type hierarchy for the system being protected.
2. Generate a list of responses for each node type.
3. Map each response to expected (damaging) changes in system state (e.g. nodes affected).
4. Specify static nodes in the map: all resources with non-zero cost, dependent resources, and service resources.
5. Assign cost values for each non-zero cost resource.
6. Represent any other dependencies between specified resources as edges in the system map.
7. Assign types to the objects which are mentioned in each intrusion alert generated by the IDS systems.
8. Map IDS alerts to expected changes in system state (e.g. nodes affected); estimate probabilities where several states may result.

Many of these tasks would be non-trivial for a modestly sized organization. Constructing a type hierarchy for each system type to be protected would be feasible for largely homogenous environments, and could be helped by publicly available data repositories of such hierarchies. The response list generation step will be more environment specific, but again a public repository may be helpful in bootstrapping this list. Popular IDS systems could include type information in their alert specifications, aiding with step 7 as well; care would need to be taken, however, to ensure that the types listed and those enumerated in the hierarchy were compatible.

Mapping responses to system state changes, however, would be more problematic. Even where the same system make, model, and operating system are employed throughout an organization, the impact of a response is also dependent on the use of the system in an environment. This extends to the specification of the system map and the cost values as well, much of which would need to be defined or heavily customized for each organization, if not for each system. Similarly, mapping IDS alerts to changes in system state would require at best an extensive manual review with customization prior to deployment. Considering that popular IDS systems such as Snort contain many thousands of alerts, this would be a considerable burden.

By updating the system map as events occur and addressing uncertainty, this model has the capability of dealing with coordinated attack and response. However, the version presented does not address the combinatorial complexity of considering sets of responses or response orderings in the system. Thus, this model essentially adopts a greedy approach, choosing locally optimal responses to global ones.

Foo, et al. (2005)

ADEPTS, initially targeted for e-commerce systems, is a system which models intruder goals and system dependencies, and also includes the ability to adapt future responses based on past behavior. Thus, if a response has failed several times in the past, it will be less likely to be selected in the future. In addition, a technique for determining when multiple alerts correspond to the same event is employed to address cases when simultaneous alerts are received. While originally web-oriented, the basic elements of ADEPTS could be applied to many types of systems.

ADEPTS incorporates two types of graphs. The SNet is an effect graph representing interactions between services in the system being protected. The I-DAG is a directed, acyclic graph which represents intrusions goals for the system. A response repository is an additional data source which must be instantiated, and several other pieces of information must be provided to support the survivability metric. Lastly, the organization must estimate the confidence of different intrusion alerts.

The I-DAG is created manually and captures final and intermediate goals which a particular intrusion is attempting to achieve. This structure requires an enumeration of the goals, and for each one the "cause service set" and "effect service set"; the pre-conditions and post-conditions for the goal to be achieved.

The S-Net must represent a superset of the services listed in the effect service sets of all nodes in the I-DAG. While not explicitly addressed, the S-Net appears to be manually constructed as well, with edges representing the ability of the source node to affect the destination node. Time estimates need to be applied to each edge giving the time required for the source to affect the destination, however, this data is obtained through statistical monitoring rather than manually.

Finally, the response repository stores all responses in the system. Each response is associated with an edge in the I-DAG which the response will disrupt, as well as edges in the S-Net which may be disrupted as side effects of the response. In addition, each response is tagged with a Disruptivity Index (DI), and an Effectiveness Index (EI), indicating how damaging the response is to normal users, and how effective previous deployments have been. With the exception of the EI, this information must be generated or obtained manually.

In addition to the system itself, the metric by which the system is measured, survivability, requires some information. This metric attempts to capture the ability of the system to serve its function, and begins with the enumeration of the abstract, high-level system goals. These goals are then functionally decomposed into weighted high level system transactions, where weights indicate the overall importance to the system owner. These transactions are compositions of service level transactions, which are specified as conjunctions or disjunctions of service interaction chains: causal orderings of two or more services. Each service interaction chain is also assigned a weight, which is the reduction in survivability if this chain is compromised. These parameters are additional models of the primary system functions which must be constructed by the administrator.

The authors conduct performance tests based on a test-bed implementation which show favorable results. The maximum latency is around 250ms, with the principle component being the number of alerts to consider and deploy. Due to the dynamic switching between low and high-level responses, their results reflect a peak delay when around 40% of the system is compromised.

The implementation of this system in practice requires the following steps:

1.   Specification of the I-DAG:
     a.   Enumerate all final and intermediate attack goals.
     b.   Develop the causal and effect sets of nodes.
2.   Specification of the S-Net for the system:
     a.   Enumerate significant services.
     b.   Define potential influences between all services.
     c.   Implement statistical monitoring to identify times to impact for influences between services.
3.   Associate available responses with I-DAG links and S-Net links.
4.   Develop survivability metric:
     a.   Enumerate high-level system goals.
     b.   Decompose goals into low-level contributing service chains.
5.   Associate confidence values with IDS alerts.

Unfortunately, in the ADEPTS case, most of these steps must be performed manually. It may be possible to re-use attack goal specifications and automate the specification of intermediate goals, but this will likely require per-system customization as capabilities and resources vary. Even confidence values for IDS alerts are highly environment specific and cannot easily be automated.

ADEPTS is geared toward coordinated response, with the ability to deploy combinations of responses to multiple simultaneous alerts. In addition, combining I-DAGs and S-Nets from multiple systems should require modifications at their boundaries of interaction only, assuming compatible concepts are included in models from both systems.

Kheir, et al.

Kheir et al. (2010) begins to address integrity and confidentiality by combining a formal model of trust with a heuristic approach for estimating the Return On Response Investment (RORI). While presented as a logical formalism, the concepts and relationships can easily be represented as a graphical model. Privileges are provided to users and services by other services. These privileges form the basis by which subjects are then trusted to perform certain actions. The authors employ Colored Petri Nets (CPNs) to model the propagation of privileges caused by intrusions and responses in the system.

A heuristic response selection metric is combined with logical semantics for privilege, trust, and dependency which can be represented via graph structures. The heuristic requires specification of several values including expected benefit of response, damage caused by response, operational cost of response, and cost of intrusion with and without response. This metric is very similar to that described in (Strasburg, 2009) with several of the parameters computed rather than assigned.

The logical semantics represents users, services, privileges, trust, and the relationships between them. This approach requires several pre-existing databases:

- Descriptions of equivalence classes (including required privileges), intrusion alerts, and responses.
- Descriptions of existing vulnerabilities (e.g. the publicly available National Vulnerability Database (NVD)).
- A static service dependency model, with similar information gathering requirements to those mentioned in the approaches above.

Only the first and third database sets must be manually specified. The equivalence classes define the levels of privilege in the system and each must be associated with the privileges they require and the service(s) which grant them. Intrusion alerts and responses must also be augmented with the privileges they revoke and the services they can affect. Intrusion alert descriptions may be automatically derived from the vulnerability database information.

As with other graph-based approaches, the correct construction of the system model is crucial to proper response selection. In this case, the system model includes not only the dependency graph, but also the precise definition of equivalence classes and privileges, and the relationships between them. Failure to model these correctly can result in mis-applied responses, failure to respond to an actual intrusion, or selection of the wrong response.

When an intrusion occurs, the CPN is used to simulate the effects on the system of:

1. The intrusion alone, to determine intrusion cost with no response.
2. Each candidate response alone, to determine response cost.
3. The intrusion plus each candidate response, to determine overall response benefit.

The first simulation must only be performed once, however the second and third must be performed for each candidate response. For a modest number of responses this should not be too onerous, but when considering responses with a large set of possible parameters, repeated simulations could introduce a large overhead. No explicit performance data was included in this work.

The implementation of this approach requires the following steps:

1. As with other graphical approaches, the system resources and dependencies must be modeled. Treated as a static input to the CPN, no automated approach to generating this model is suggested.
2. A vulnerability database must be selected and made available to the system.
3. A mapping between intrusion alerts and vulnerabilities must be obtained or constructed

(many IDS signatures include references, e.g. to the NVD).
4. The parameters required to support the RORI heuristic must be supplied, including:
   a. Operational Cost for all responses.
   b. Value estimates for all services / resources.
5. The logical framework must be developed, which includes:
   a. Assigning privileges to equivalence classes.
   b. Defining trust relationships (forming a privilege dependency model).

Given the listing above, this approach adds complexity to other dependency model approaches in the form of enumerating equivalence classes, privileges, and trust relationships. The granularity at which this model is developed will determine the additional hindrance this causes to organizations implementing this approach.

The use of CPNs allows the simultaneous propagation of privileges to be modeled, in theory permitting the evaluation of concurrent attacks and the selection of a globally optimal response. However, the problem of selecting a combination of response actions is not explicitly addressed in the paper.

Heuristic Approaches

Heuristic approaches use abstractions of resources, responses, and intrusions to enable fast response times and simple setup through closed-form equations which capture the potential costs and benefits of a response in any intrusion situation. While the real-world meaning of the heuristics themselves are often difficult to interpret, in practice they have been shown to produce competitive responses.

There is an unquestionable loss of precision in this abstraction, but it is important to remember that for the purposes of selecting a response, only the relative ranking of responses and intrusion matter. A response will not be selected if its cost exceeds the cost of the intrusion by 1 or by 1000. This principle is shared with the application of Naïve Bayesian models, e.g. in applications such as e-mail SPAM filtering. Naïve Bayes requires statistical independence between parameters to produce a valid probability. However, even in cases where this assumption is grossly violated, it has proven to be an effective classification engine.

Lee, et al. (2002)

In this work, the authors explored a cost-benefit approach to intrusion response. They enumerate major cost factors related to intrusion detection including the damage cost (DCost), response cost (RCost), and operational cost (OpCost). It is suggested that these measures be given relative values rather than attempting to supply absolute dollar costs, due to the difficulty in exhaustively reducing all pertinent cost factors to monetary units. These measures are then combined with an attack taxonomy, in which responses are statically assigned to enumerated intrusions and tagged with their associated costs. Thus, response selection amounts to a table lookup to determine if the response cost is worth preventing the intrusion.

The DCost in this work is a combination of criticality and lethality estimates proposed by Northcutt (Northcutt, 1999), using a fixed set of relative values based on target and attack type. The RCost also incorporates the criticality factor, combined with a base response cost derived from the complexity and delay in response. E.g., manual responses are generally more expensive than automated responses.

This approach extends into modeling the total costs associated with operating an intrusion detection system, however we will restrict our consideration to those issues which support intrusion response specifically to compare equitably with other approaches.

To complete the calculations required to determine a response deployment in this approach, the following pieces of information must be provided:

- A categorization of attacks including objective, technique, attack target, and estimated base damage and response costs.
- Assessment of the criticality of resources, and the lethality of various attacks against defined resources.
- Estimated complexity for each response.

Categorizing attacks according to objective, technique, and partly according to target, may be automated through the evaluation of existing signatures. For instance, a buffer overflow in a line of Cisco firewalls will clearly have an objective of remote admin access, a target type of firewall, and a known technique. However, in other cases, target, and possibly even objective will be environment specific, e.g. in the case where an attack on a web server may yield root or only local privileges on a system, and could target printers or a primary web server in an organization. Thus a significant amount of manual effort may be required for this step.

Given the simple ranking for attack and response costs (criticality, lethality, and complexity), the burden of specifying costs is very low. Estimating the complexity of each response will be organization and implementation dependent, however the number of different response types is generally fairly low, unless responses with different parameters are treated individually.

The abstraction and relative measures make this model less sensitive to small estimation errors, leaving the taxonomy of attacks and responses the most critical information piece. Given the partial automation, the crucial manual input is to ensure that all attack classes are covered and that response complexity is accounted for appropriately. Because RCost and DCost encompass so many implicit considerations (e.g. complexity, damage, per-incident direct costs, potential benefit, system administrator time) it is likely that the value assigned will not be accurate for all resources and attacks of a given type in an organization.

While no explicit performance data is provided, the authors report the implementation of a real-time system with the capability to evaluate an attack and deploy a response effectively on the fly. With the model being entirely specified in advance, there is no scaling with number of resources, responses, or attacks. Response deployment consists of looking up a response and determining if the cost is worth deploying.

Implementing this approach requires the following steps:

1. Select an intrusion detection system(s) to employ.
2. Determine the base damage cost, target, technique, and objective associated with each intrusion alert (note: some objectives may depend on the target).
3. Enumerate the responses which are available; define the base response cost for each.
4. Assign criticality values for all resource classes.
5. Assign lethality values for all attacks which affect each resource.

Due to the static mapping between attacks and responses, and the treatment of individual alerts as individual events to be responded to, multiple simultaneous attacks would trigger multiple responses, one for each attack. Thus, responses are locally selected and not coordinated globally.

Strasburg, et al. (2009)

The authors extended the heuristic components of prior approaches, adding parameters such as IDS confidence, operational cost for intrusions, and describing a measurement process which allows for adaptive and dynamic response selection rather than a static table-based scheme. The redefinition of the response assessment formula allows an intrusion response engine to learn from past performance, similar to the ADEPTS model, and decouples the response definitions from the intrusions, simplifying the addition of response measures. In addition, a methodology for assigning consistent and intuitive values is provided, giving an overview of the complexity of implementation.

To employ this approach, information required includes enumerating the responses and attacks which will be included in the response capability, enumerating resources which will be protected, assigning values for each resource, and rankings for each response and intrusion protection and impact value for each resource. In addition, each response needs the associated operational cost. Finally, an estimated confidence for each IDS needs to be supplied along with any static costs associated with an intrusion (e.g. mandatory reporting requirements, investigation costs). These information gathering requirements scale with the number of resources, responses, and attacks. Thus the required information may constitute a significant burden for an organization of more than modest size.

As with the Lee approach, the level of abstraction and the use of relative rankings reduces model sensitivity to minor variations in value. The use of more finely-grained parameters and dynamic values, while increasing the information gathering requirements, also improves the ability of the model to apply to a variety of environments.

Performance results indicate that, while latency does scale with the number of responses, resources, and simultaneous intrusions, even very large numbers (e.g. 1000+ for each category) still permit a response in real-time. The suggestion of the authors to keep resources abstract will mitigate scaling problems for larger environments, and as mentioned previously, the number of responses is generally small, unless parameter values are considered.

Implementing this approach requires the following steps:

1. Assign an overall value for the system in monetary terms (either in unit/time or straight units).

2. Assign overall system security priorities depending on the system type.

3. Enumerate resources of value and assign weights reflecting the potential to harm the overall security priorities.

4. Define the set of intrusions which are detectable, and determine which resources they may impact.

5. Estimate the confidence for each IDS and alert.

6. Define the set of available responses. For each response:

   a. Rank its ability to protect each resource, relative to other responses.

   b. Rank the degree of damage it causes for each resource, relative to other responses.

   c. Assign an operational cost relative to the overall value of the system. This is a static cost which is always incurred when the response is deployed, e.g. labor required, direct cost, or additional materials consumed such as disk space or bandwidth.

7. Determine the operational cost of an intrusion relative to the overall value of the system, such as mandatory reporting requirements.

One advantage of this approach is the ability to allow business decision makers to provide and change monetary values while allowing technical administrators to define system interaction properties independently. The bulk of the manual effort in this process is the assigning response and intrusion impacts for each resource. With a large number of resources this can quickly become overwhelming, requiring assignment of $(2 * N * M + N * L)$ values, where N is the number of resources, M is the number of responses, and L is the number of known intrusions. Since each response has a protection value and a damage value for each resource, there are twice as many assignments which must be made for a response, compared with an intrusion. Similarly to other approaches,

it may be possible to use existing vulnerability databases and signature information to automate the intrusion impacts to some degree, but the response rankings will be organization specific.

As in Lee et al. (2002), this heuristic does not address event correlation, and therefore will evaluate responses based on each individual alert. Thus, this approach also selects local responses rather than considering the global system state.

This system was implemented at Ames Laboratory (located at Iowa State University) as a proof-of-concept to assess the effort required to deploy an effective response selection engine in a real-world environment (see the architecture in Figure 3). A selection of intrusion alerts, resources, and responses were modeled and the system was tested on live network data. The implementation was reviewed by members of the operational cyber security team, who provided input on resource values, responses, and intrusion impacts.

The Automated Response System (ARS) reads parameters such as response impact, resource value, and system policy from XML input files which are generated using a GUI interface. While the selected responses were appropriate to the intrusion which was indicated by production alerts, assigning impact values to more than a handful of intrusions proved to be overwhelming. In addition, as new potential alerts were introduced daily into the IDS, maintaining appropriate impact values manually was infeasible. This exercise demonstrated that automated intrusion response was feasible, but also that even for a simplified set of heuristic metrics, work is required to facilitate consistent time-efficient assignment of values for resources, intrusion properties, and response impacts. We discuss this need further in Solutions and Recommendations.

Summary

As efforts to identify an effective cost-benefit representation for intrusion response continue, we move toward a more complete set of metrics

Figure 3. Ames Laboratory implementation architecture

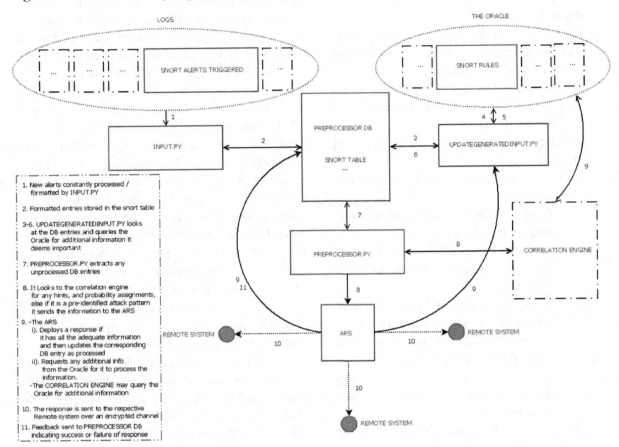

Table 1. Summary of metrics used in current approaches

Metric	Brief Description
Resource Priority / Cost / Value	An estimate of the relative importance of a resource in a system.
Effectiveness Index / Response Goodness	An estimate of how likely the response is to be effective in stopping an attack.
Disruptivity Index / Collateral Damage / Damage Cost / Response Cost / Intrusion Cost / Resource capability reduction.	An estimate of how severely an intrusion or response will impact a system.
Operational Cost	Costs associated with an intrusion or response which are not related to system damage (e.g. mandatory reporting, resource usage, system administrator time.
Compromised Confidence Index	A measure of the belief that a resource is compromised.
Response Index / Return on Response Investment (RORI) / Expected Response Benefit	The estimated positive effect of the response.

Table 2. Information requirements for each approach

Category \ First Author	Toth	Bale-pin	Foo	Jahn-ke	Kheir	Lee	Stras-burg
		Graph-based				Heuristic	
Enumerate high-level system goals in terms of chains of low-level transactions.			X				
Enumerate resources to be protected.	X	X	X	X	X	X	X
Organize resources into type-categories.		X				X	
Provide values for resources.		X					X
Define dependencies between resources.	X	X	X	X	X		
Define influence times between resources.			X				
Enumerate available responses.	X	X	X	X	X	X	X
Map responses to protected resources.		X		X			X
Rank response protection for resources.							X
Map responses to damaged resources.		X	X	X			X
Rank response damage for resources.			X				X
Map responses to intrusions which can be affected.						X	
Map responses to privileges revoked or conveyed.					X		
Define static costs associated with each response.					X	X	X
Enumerate detectable intrusions.						X	X
Define static costs associated with each intrusion.						X	X
Map intrusions to privileges revoked or conveyed.					X		
List attacker goals, causes, and effects.			X				
Define equivalence classes and required privileges.					X		
Estimate IDS alert confidence.		X					X

which must be incorporated to ensure that all related factors are accounted for. A listing of the commonly considered factors is given in Table 1.

In addition, the inclusion of response duration, and error-proneness have been suggested as additional metrics which may be included in the response selection formula. However, these measures have not been developed as quantified values.

Based on the overlapping response metrics used in many works, it is not surprising that many of the approaches have overlapping information requirements and implementation processes (see Table 2).

While these tables are not suitable for a formal information requirement analysis, it is clear that some information is required universally (e.g. some representation of the system resources, a description of available responses). In addition, graphical approaches all employ a form of dependency model, implying that dependency relationships are crucial during response selection and deployment.

The information requirements and implementation steps indicate a research trend toward increasingly complex architectures in order to improve the accuracy of approaches. However, this progress has not been matched by research targeting practical approaches to overcome the increased information gathering requirements and implementation complexity. Thus, while automated response research is improving response selection, at the same time, automated response is receding further from providing practical benefit.

SOLUTIONS AND RECOMMENDATIONS

When comparing the prerequisites required to support the metrics needed by each response selection approach, some patterns emerge which indicate fundamental elements required for an effective IRS. In this section we discuss the systemic challenges facing the practical application of automated intrusion response, and present solutions and recommendations for these key areas.

Generation of Input Data

Providing accurate input data (e.g. to describe system resources, responses, and intrusions) to apply a response selection metric is where the majority of effort is required for system administrators. Often the data requirements scale with the number of intrusions, number of responses, and number of resources to be included in the model.

In heuristic approaches, the resource model is a simple enumeration, while graph-based approaches include relationship information as well. The additional information provided by dependency graphs improves damage assessment accuracy, response accuracy, and correlation, while carrying a significant increase in the amount of information and setup required of a system administrator. In addition, system environments are dynamic by nature, and manually maintaining detailed system maps can quickly become overwhelming.

In addition to resources, specification of responses and intrusions is required, including which resources a response can protect, or which intrusions a response can address. While some early works employed a static mapping of responses to intrusions or resources (Lee, 2002; Toth, 2002), modeling resource effects as a layer of abstraction between intrusions and responses

is a more flexible approach. First, intrusions need not necessarily be exhaustively mapped to responses, a likely impossible task as new vulnerabilities are discovered daily. Second, as resources change, or resource values change, the response selection algorithm can adapt by selecting new responses more appropriate to the new environment. Categorizing intrusions based on characteristic behavior and expected impact on resources also permits automated response in the face of unknown attacks, as a response can be deployed to mitigate a certain type of damage rather than stop a specifically named attack.

Adequately modeling a response scenario in practice requires advances in dynamically generating and updating concrete, detailed, and scalable system maps, capable of expressing relationships between resources. Automating the construction of dependency graphs, categorization of intrusions, and estimation of response effects not only improves the practicality of complex models required for automated intrusion response, it also reduces the risk of manual errors causing system inconsistency.

Clearly some details must be supplied manually, such as security goals and overall system values. However, the pursuit of automatically identifying dependency relationships between systems, resources, and users in an automated and up-datable fashion is key to enabling the transfer of automated intrusion response from the laboratory to production networks.

Formal Knowledge Representation of Detection and Response

Another key development area is effective formal models of intrusion detection and response. Machine-consumable descriptions of attacks, responses, detection systems, and computational environments are pivotal to providing dynamic response selection and enabling automated response to unknown attacks.

This has been recognized and work has begun on developing formal knowledge representations, e.g. (Undercoffer, 2004; Morin, 2009). However, we do not know of any framework which unifies models of intrusion detection, attacks, system environments, and responses, and has been demonstrated in a live environment. Without such a framework, it is difficult to focus research efforts on the most promising directions, identify the most pressing problems, or develop a general basis of comparison for existing approaches.

Formal knowledge representation may also shed light on the problem of measuring confidentiality and integrity. Many existing works carry an implicit assumption that availability is the primary security objective in systems covered by an IRS. In practice, intuition dictates that additional, or more stringent, controls yield better confidentiality and integrity, but to our knowledge no theoretical foundation has been established which provides a direct basis of comparison, must less quantification, for the effectiveness of individual or a specific combination of controls.

Developing such a foundation will likely be an iterative process, and the works by (Jahnke, 2007; Kheir, 2010) are examples of attempting to formalize how confidentiality and integrity are compromised in the first place. With the goal of identifying a common formal basis for describing the security of a system, continued exploration of modeling confidentiality, integrity, and availability will clarify the invariant and transient properties that impact them.

Consistent Research Methods

While many of the existing approaches have merit, meaningful comparison and identification of useful directions for new research is hindered by the lack of some key discussion features.

First, a new approach needs to be evaluated on a comparable basis with an existing approach to argue for a real benefit. For instance, a new and more expressive metric should be able to capture the same inputs provided to some previous metric, and show a more accurate, intuitive, or consistent response. This process should include a description of mapping the existing inputs to inputs in the new metric, a description of how any new values are assigned, and a discussion of the resultant response selection.

A second important inclusion is a dictionary of which inputs are expected to be provided, and discussion of how inputs can be generated. While some existing approaches do explicitly address information gathering and setup, presenting a brief description of the steps involved will not only better inform potential implementers, but also inspire readers to future research in the automated assessment of those input values.

A third critical component is the presentation of intended application along with performance results. An IRS which is intended to provide fine-grained preemptive responses would be expected to have much different performance characteristics than an automated recovery system which assesses damage and restores resources. Such a discussion should also include the theoretical performance scaling in terms of environment characteristics or input complexity. This is another area in which measurable improvements can be presented in new approaches.

Finally, appendices or references to resources which present example input files are helpful to allow other researchers and practitioners to verify results, test new implementations, and gain a better understanding of the proposed approach. Consistently making such information available also encourages the community to gravitate toward a more standard description format where possible.

IMPLEMENTATION

Given the amount of manual information gathering and implementation complexity involved in deploying an automated response system, it is no surprise that most production environments at best have static responses mapped to specific intrusions. However, this does not mean it is impossible to develop an effective IRS. In fact, many commercial and open source intrusion response implementations are available, providing much of the intrusion and response related information as part of the product, e.g. SourceFire, (Network Awareness, 2010).

To utilize recent research directly, the implementation steps follow rather naturally from the information required for a response system. In addition to response selection, implementation of an automated response system also requires implementing responses to be deployed, securing communication between components of the detection and response systems, and ensuring that system administrators are provided ready access to information related to the IRS.

When considering automated intrusion response, the first question to ask is whether the benefit outweighs the cost. One of the biggest expected benefits is the ability to respond to intrusions even when those intrusions have not been specifically mapped to a response. Systems which provide this advantage are based on dependency graphs, and rely on a policy or anomaly based intrusion detection system.

The second question to ask is what types of environment information are already available. If a well-structured inventory of services, with estimates of value to the organization (or means to estimate value, e.g. sales through the web site per month), is available, developing a high-level dependency map may be feasible. If automated vulnerability scanning is already in place, approaches which also take advantage of attack graph information may also be more appealing. Considering the types of information readily producible at an organization can aid in selecting a response system which is implementable.

Given the evolving nature of cyber threats, sooner or later organizations will need automated response as much as firewalls and intrusion detection are needed today. Administrators and management must judge when the state of the art in automated response lowers the cost of implementation enough to make it worth pursuing.

FUTURE RESEARCH DIRECTIONS

It seems clear from the observations of researchers over the past 30 years that new directions need to be explored to develop a clear approach to automated intrusion response. The consistent issues mentioned in future work sections of publications and the lack of a demonstrably effective automated response system for general computing environments points to a few key problems. Based on the remaining obstacles to effective, comparable, and usable intrusion response systems, we have identified the following key research areas which need further work. To address the recommendations proposed above, we plan to pursue the following lines of research.

Automation

We plan to explore automated host and network based resource enumeration and dependency mapping. As a next step we will use resource interaction monitoring such as the use of system calls in a Linux system or network connections between services.

Formal Knowledge Representation

We are evaluating existing ontology and formal logic representation of intrusion detection and response with the goal of determining where additional abstract concepts can facilitate information sharing and automation. One specific concept we are exploring is the use of a signal, an observable effect of an intrusion or a response, as a component upon which intrusion signatures can be built and responses selected.

Knowledge-Based Metrics

With an ontology model in place, we will explore possible metrics by which to compare and judge existing and future approaches. Two metrics we will consider are the number of different attack classes covered by an automated response architecture and the types of intrusion detection system which are compatible with the response system. We will also develop approaches to include representations of resources and services to provide environment specific estimates of fitness, giving administrators an idea of which response system is likely to perform best for their organization.

CONCLUSION

Increased automation is a requirement to deal with the advancing threat posed by increasing sophisticated cyber attackers. While a significant body of work has been produced in the past fifteen years, a more focused approach to solving the problems related to intrusion response is needed. Rather than continued attempts to improve response selection techniques, we propose researchers focus on the following areas:

- Dynamic generation of resource dependency models.
- Formal knowledge representation of detection and response.
- Consistent research methods.

We believe that these areas are the key to laying a solid foundation upon which future researchers can make measured progress, developing approaches which practitioners can effectively implement.

REFERENCES

Balepin, I., Maltsev, S., Rowe, J., & Levitt, K. (2002). Using specification-based intrusion detection for automated response. In *Proceedings of 6th International Symposium on Recent Advances in Intrusion Detection*, (pp. 136–154). Springer.

Foo, B., Wu, Y., Mao, Y., Bagchi, S., & Spafford, E. (2005). ADEPTS: Adaptive intrusion response using attack graphs in an e-commerce environment. In *Proceedings of 35th IEEE/IFIP International Conference on Dependable Systems and Networks*. Retrieved from http://www.computer.org/portal/web/ csdl/doi/10.1109/DSN.2005.17

Glaseman, S., Turn, R., & Gaines, R. S. (1977). Problem areas in computer security assessment. In *Proceedings of the National Computer Conference* (pp. 13-16).

Householder, A., Houle, K., & Dougherty, J. (2002). Computer attack trends challenge internet security (Supplement to Computer Magazine). *Computer*, *35*(4), 5–7. doi:10.1109/MC.2002.1012422

Jahnke, M., Thul, C., & Martini, P. (2007). Graph based metrics for intrusion response measures in computer networks. In *Proceedings of the IEEE Conference on Local Computer Networks*, (pp. 1035–1042). doi:10.1109/LCN.2007.45

Kheir, N., Cuppens-Boulahia, N., Cuppens, F., & Debar, H. (2010). A service dependency model for cost-sensitive intrusion response. In *Proceedings of the 15th European Symposium on Research in Computer Security, Lecture Notes in Computer Science, 6345*, (pp. 626-642). doi:10.1007/978-3-642-15497-3_38.

Lee, W., Fan, W., Miller, M., Stolfo, S. J., & Zadok, E. (2002). Toward cost-sensitive modeling for intrusion detection and response. *Journal of Computer Security*, *10*, 5–22.

Lewandowski, S., Van Hook, D. J., O'Leary, G. C., Haines, J. W., & Rossey, L. M. (2002). SARA: Survivable autonomic response architecture. *DARPA Information Survivability Conference and Exposition, 1,* 0077. doi:10.1109/DISCEX.2001.932194

Misslinger, S. (2005). *Internet worm propagation*. Technical University of Munich. doi:10.1.1.94.7921.

Morin, B., Me, L., Debar, H., & Ducasse, M. (2009). A logic-based model to support alert correlation in intrusion detection. *Information Fusion, 10*(4), 285–299. doi:10.1016/j.inffus.2009.01.005

Network Awareness. (2010). Next-generation intrusion prevention system (NGIPS): Improved security and reduced administrative burden through contextual awareness. In *Sourcefire Cybersecurity*. Retrieved December 1, 2010, from http://www.sourcefire.com/content/ next-generation-intrusion-prevention-system-ngips

Northcutt, S., & Novak, J. (2000). *Network intrusion detection: An analysts handbook* (2nd ed.). New Riders Publishing.

Stakhanova, N., Basu, S., & Wong, J. (2007). A taxonomy of intrusion response systems. *International Journal of Information and Computer Security, 1*(1), 169–184. doi:10.1504/IJICS.2007.012248

Strasburg, C., Stakhanova, N., Basu, S., & Wong, J. S. (2009). A framework for cost sensitive assessment of intrusion response selection. In *Proceedings of 33rd Annual IEEE International Computer Software and Applications Conference,* (pp. 355-360).

Toth, T., & Kruegel, C. (2002). Evaluating the impact of automated intrusion response mechanisms. In *Proceedings of the 18th Annual Computer Security Applications Conference* (ACSAC), 2002

Undercoffer, J., Pinkston, J., Joshi, A., & Finin, T. (2004). A target-centric ontology for intrusion detection. In *Proceedings of the IJCAI-03 Workshop on Ontologies and Distributed Systems,* (pp. 47-58).

Yu, D., & Frincke, D. (2007). Improving the quality of alerts and predicting intruder's next goal with hidden colored Petri-Net. *Computer Networks: The International Journal of Computer and Telecommunications Networking, 51*(3), 632–654. doi:doi:10.1016/j.comnet.2006.05.008

Zou, C. C., Gong, W., & Towsley, D. (2002). Code red worm propagation modeling and analysis. In *Proceedings of the 9th ACM Conference on Computer and Communications Security,* (pp. 138–147). doi: 10.1145/586110.586130

ADDITIONAL READING

Alexander, K. (2010) *SANS: Intrusion detection FAQ: What is active response?* Retrieved from http://www.sans.org/security-resources/ idfaq/active.php

Bejtlich, R. (2004). *The Tao of network security monitoring: Beyond intrusion detection.* Addison-Wesley Professional.

Bishop, M. (2002). *Computer security: Art and science* (p. 1084). Addison-Wesley.

Cardenas, A. (2009). *A framework for the evaluation of intrusion detection systems.* Retrieved from http://www.isr.umd.edu/~baras/publications/papers/2006/CardenasBS_2006.pdf

Chandola, V., Banerjee, A., & Kumar, V. (2009). Anomaly detection: A survey. *ACM Computing Surveys, 41*(3). doi:10.1145/1541880.1541882

Cuppens, F., & Ortalo, R. (2000). LAMBDA: A language to model a database for detection of attacks. *Lecture Notes in Computer Science, 1907/2000,* 197–216. doi:10.1007/3-540-39945-3_13

Denning, D. E. (1987). An intrusion-detection model. *IEEE Transactions on Software Engineering, 13*(2), 222–232. doi:10.1109/TSE.1987.232894

Geib, C. (2002). *Plan recognition in intrusion detection systems.* Exposition II, 2001. DISCEX #39;01. Retrieved from http://ieeexplore.ieee.org/xpls/ abs_all.jsp?arnumber=932191

Glasgow, J., Macewen, G., & Panangaden, P. (1992). A logic for reasoning about security. *ACM Transactions on Computer Systems, 10*(3), 226–264. doi:10.1145/146937.146940

Gorodetski, V., & Kotenko, I. (2002). Lecture Notes in Computer Science: *Vol. 2516. Attacks against computer network: Formal grammar-based framework and simulation tool* (pp. 219–238).

Gu, G. (2009). *Measuring intrusion detection capability: An information theoretic approach.* Retrieved from http://members.home.nl/skoric/security/ ASIACCS06_revision1.pdf

Hawrylkiw, D. (2010). *SANS: Intrusion detection FAQ: Network intrusion and use of automated responses.* Retrieved from http://www.sans.org/security-resources/ idfaq/auto_res.php

Jansen, W. (2009). *Directions in security metrics research,* (p. 26). http://csrc.nist.gov/publications/drafts/ nistir-7564/Draft-NISTIR-7564.pdf.

Mankins, D., Krishnan, R., Boyd, C., Zao, J., & Frentz, M. (n.d.). *Mitigating distributed denial of service attacks with dynamic resource pricing.*

McHugh, J. (2001). Intrusion and intrusion detection. *International Journal of Information Security, 1*(1), 14–35. doi:doi:10.1007/s102070100001

Michel, C., & Me, L. (2001). *ADeLe: An Attack description language for knowledge-based intrusion detection* (pp. 353-368).

Porras, P. A., & Neumann, P. G. (1997). *EMERALD: Event monitoring enabling responses to anomalous live disturbances* (pp. 353-365).

Ranganathan, A., & Campbell, R. H. (2003). *An infrastructure for context-awareness based on first-order logic* (pp. 353–364). Personal and Ubiquitous Computing.

Rash, M., Orebaugh, A. D., Clark, G., Pinkard, B., & Babbin, J. (2005). *Intrusion prevention and active response: Deploying network and host IPS.* Syngress.

Raskin, V., Nirenburg, S., Hempelmann, C., & Triezenberg, K. (2002). *Ontology in information security: A useful theoretical foundation and methodological tool.*

Ryutov, T., Neuman, C., & Kim, D. (2009). *Dynamic authorization and intrusion response in distributed systems.* Retrieved from http://ieeexplore.ieee.org/stamp/ stamp.jsp?tp=&arnumber=1194872

Undercoffer, J., Pinkston, J., Joshi, A., & Finin, T. (2004). *A target-centric ontology for intrusion detection.* 18th International Joint Conference on Artificial Intelligence. Retrieved from http://citeseerx.ist.psu.edu/viewdoc/ download?doi=10.1.1.13.727&rep=rep1&type=pdf

Valdes, A., & Skinner, K. (2000). Adaptive, model-based monitoring for cyber attack detection. *Lecture Notes in Computer Science, 1907,* 80–92. doi:10.1007/3-540-39945-3_6

Vorobiev, A., & Bekmamedova, N. (2007). An ontological approach applied to information security and trust. *Information Systems,* 865–874.

Vorobiev, A., & Bekmamedova, N. (2010). An ontology-driven approach applied to information security. *Journal of Research and Practice in Information Technology, 42*(1), 61–76.

Wu, Y.-S. (2009). *Automated adaptive intrusion containment in systems of interacting services*. Retrieved from https://www.cerias.purdue.edu/ assets/ pdf/bibtex_archive/2005-87.pdf

KEY TERMS AND DEFINITIONS

Alert: A message generated by an IDS which indicates an attempted intrusion. An alert may contain information such as confidence, affected resources, and attack source.

ARS: An ARS (Automated Response System) is an IRS which does not require human intervention to deploy a response.

Attack Graph: An attack graph models the steps an attacker may take to elevate access to a system. Nodes represent the privileges an attacker has to a resource, and edges represent attack steps. Constructing these graphs may be partially automated through vulnerability scan analysis.

Dependency Graph: A dependency graph models the functional relationships between resources in a system. Nodes depict specific resources, and edges represent the dependency relation of one resource on another.

Intrusion: An intrusion is any attempt to subvert the confidentiality, integrity, or availability of data in a system.

IDS: An IDS (Intrusion Detection System) monitors a system and generates alerts when an intrusion is detected.

IRS: An IRS (Intrusion Response System) chooses and deploys a set of responses based on existing alerts and some model of the underlying system.

Measure: A quantification of an abstract quality such as IDS effectiveness or IRS performance.

Metric: A system of measurement or a unit of measure.

Response: A response is an action taken which prevents, stops, or mitigates the damage of an intrusion.

System: A system is any collection of resources managed by an organization. It may entail a single host, a company network, or a distributed web-based service.

Chapter 2
Feature Extraction Methods for Intrusion Detection Systems

Hai Thanh Nguyen
Gjøvik University College, Norway

Katrin Franke
Gjøvik University College, Norway

Slobodan Petrović
Gjøvik University College, Norway

ABSTRACT

Intrusion Detection Systems (IDSs) have become an important security tool for managing risk and an indispensable part of overall security architecture. An IDS is considered as a pattern recognition system, in which feature extraction is an important pre-processing step. The feature extraction process consists of feature construction and feature selection. The quality of the feature construction and feature selection algorithms is one of the most important factors that affects the effectiveness of an IDS. Achieving reduction of the number of relevant traffic features without negative effect on classification accuracy is a goal that largely improves the overall effectiveness of the IDS. Most of the feature construction as well as feature selection works in intrusion detection practice is still carried through manually by utilizing domain knowledge. For automatic feature construction and feature selection, the filter, wrapper, and embedded methods from machine learning are frequently applied. This chapter provides an overview of various existing feature construction and feature selection methods for intrusion detection systems. A comparison between those feature selection methods is performed in the experimental part.

INTRODUCTION

Intrusion Detection Systems (IDSs) have become an important security tool for managing risk and an indispensable part of overall security architecture (Northcutt, 1999). An Intrusion detection system

gathers and analyzes information from various sources within computers and networks to identify suspicious activities that attempt to illegally access, manipulate, and disable computer systems. The two main intrusion detection approaches are misuse detection and anomaly detection (Denning, 1986). Misuse detection systems, for instance,

DOI: 10.4018/978-1-4666-0978-5.ch002

Snort (Roesch, 1999), detect intrusions by looking at specific signatures of known attacks. This approach is similar to the way of detecting viruses in many antivirus applications. A set of patterns of known attacks is necessary be built in advance for further detections. It is easy to implement misuse detection systems. However, these systems are not effective against novel attacks that have no matched patterns yet. Anomaly detection systems, such as IDES (Lunt et al., 1992), can overcome the shortcoming of the misuse detection systems. An anomaly detector assumes that normal behaviors are different from abnormal behaviors. Therefore, abnormal activities can be detected by looking at normal activities only. In fact, in these system, a profile of normal behavior is set up and is utilized to flag any observed activities that deviate significantly from the established profile as anomalies or possible intrusions. Although anomaly detection systems have potentials of detecting novel attacks, it is not easy to define normal behaviors and these systems tend to generate more false positive alerts than the misuse detection systems.

An approach for building anomaly intrusion detection systems is to utilize machine learning and statistical techniques. By means of this approach, an intrusion detection system is considered as a statistical pattern recognition system. Figure 1 shows the model of a statistical pattern recognition

system that consists of two phases: training and classification. The test and training patterns as raw data are normalized, noise as well as unwanted data is removed by the preprocessing modules. In the training phase, the feature extraction/selection module looks for a representative feature set from the input patterns. Those features are then utilized for training a classifier. In the classification phase, the trained classifier is applied to assign the test patters to one of the pattern classes under consideration of the selected features from the training phase. In the following, we will focus on this approach for intrusion detection.

From Figure 1, it can be observed that feature extraction is an important part of a pattern recognition system. The feature extraction process consists of feature construction and feature selection. The quality of the feature construction and feature selection algorithms is one of the most important factors that influence the effectiveness of an IDS. Achieving reduction of the number of relevant traffic features without negative impact on classification accuracy is a goal that largely improves the overall effectiveness of the IDS. Most of the feature construction as well as feature selection works in intrusion detection practice is still carried out through manually utilizing domain knowledge. For automatic feature construction and feature selection, the filter, wrapper and em-

Figure 1. Model of a statistical pattern recognition (Jain et al., 2000)

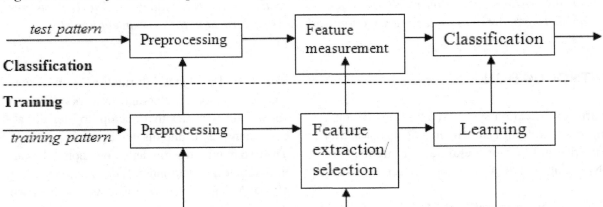

bedded methods from machine learning are frequently applied. This chapter provides an overview of various existing feature construction and feature selection methods for intrusion detection systems. A comparison between those feature selection methods is provided in the experimental part.

As this chapter aims to serve a wide audience from researchers to practitioners, we first introduce the basic concepts and describe the main feature extraction methods for intrusion detection; then present the practical applications of these methods to extract features from public benchmarking data sets for intrusion detection systems.

THEORETICAL BACKGROUND

Feature, which is a synonym for input variable or attribute, is any representative information that is extracted from the raw data set. A special pattern, which is directly selected from the data set, can be considered as a feature, for example, a representative substring of SQL injection code in a HTTP request. The distributions of characters or groups of characters are features. In some cases, the structures or semantics of data sets are considered as features. The relations between patterns or between features of the data are normally hidden, but are important for representing the data. Therefore, they are necessary be extracted from the data. The process of determining the most compact and informative features of a given data set is called Feature Extraction. By means of this process not only the efficiency of data storage is improved, but also the processing performance of intrusion detection systems is increased.

A feature extraction algorithm composes of two steps: feature construction and feature selection. Feature construction is one of the key steps in the data representation process for many tasks, such as classification or regression problems, largely conditioning the success of any subsequent statistic or modeling of a given raw data. This process refers to determining representative features from the original data. One can manually construct the features by looking at direct patterns in the data, for example, as we carry through when building signatures or rules for misuse intrusion detection systems. For automatic feature construction, several approaches, such as n-grams, association rule learning and frequency episode extraction, are usually applied. These methods will be introduced in more detail in the next sections.

At the feature construction stage, one should beware that any information could not be lost from the original data set. A common idea is to take into account all possible informative features. However, adding more features seems to come at a price: it increases the dimensionality of the data that is considered, thus increases the complexity of intrusion detection systems. Moreover, the irrelevant and redundant features are possibly contained in the set of features. How do we know when a feature is relevant or important? That is what feature selection is about and it is the main focus of this chapter. In general, feature selection can provide the following benefits (Guyon et al., 2006):

- General data reduction, i.e., to limit storage requirements and increase algorithm speed;
- Feature set reduction, i.e., to save resources in the next round of data collection or during utilization;
- Performance improvement, i.e., to gain predictive accuracy;
- Data understanding, i.e., to gain knowledge about the process that generated the data or simply visualize the data.

There are two ways of selecting features for intrusion detection systems: manual and automatic. Later on the automatic feature selection methods, which include filter, wrapper and embedded models from machine learning, will be emphasized.

Feature Construction

In this section, we present feature construction methods for intrusion detection systems that include association rule learning, frequency episode extraction and n-grams extraction.

Association Rule Learning

Association rule learning (Agrawal et al., 1993) is one of the most popular methods in data mining for discovering interesting relations between variables or features in large data sets. Such interesting relations are normally hidden in the raw data, and when they are extracted, they can be utilized for describing the data efficiently. For example, whenever one buys bread, she or he is likely to also buy butter and milk. Such information can be utilized as the basic for describing customers' behavior for making marketing activities. Another example in intrusion detection is that certain programs only get access to certain system files in specific directories, certain users (root, normal users or super users) have certain behavior or activities, such as normal users use mostly the utilities of the systems, whereas super users manage the systems, for instance, creating new users, new profiles or logging activities of other users, processes and so on. In this example, the interesting relations, which are associations between users and the used programs, are necessary be extracted and should be included in normal and suspicious usage profiles for further intrusion detection. For instance, if we have a profile of all users in a system, in which only super users have the right to modify a directory, then a normal user attempts to carry through the modification, his activity should be detected as suspicious, since in the profile of the system, there is no description of this activity for normal users.

The formal definition of association rule learning is given as follows: Let $I = \{i_1, i_2, ..., i_n\}$ be a set of n features called items of a system audit data. Let $D = \{r_1, r_2, ..., r_m\}$ be a set of records in this data set. Each record r_i contains a subset of features in I. A rule is defined as an implication of the form:

$X \Rightarrow Y$, where $X, Y \subseteq I$, and $X \cap Y = 0$.

When interpreting the above example in intrusion detection according to this definition, the followings are item sets:

$X = i_1 = programmer(users)$, and

$Y = i_2 = C\_compiler(used\_programs)$. The implication $X \Rightarrow Y$ is an association rule.

Before describing the main idea of association rules learning algorithms, two important concepts are introduced: the support $SUPP(X)$ of an item set X, and the confidence $CONF(X \Rightarrow Y)$ of a rule $X \Rightarrow Y$ as follows:

- The support of an item set X ($SUPP(X)$) is defined as the proportion of records in the data set that contain the item set X.

- The confidence $CONF(X \Rightarrow Y)$ of a rule ($X \Rightarrow Y$) is defined as follows:

$$CONF(X \Rightarrow Y) = \frac{SUPP(X \cup Y)}{SUPP(X)}$$

An association rule learning algorithm consists of two separate steps: Firstly, choosing a minimum threshold of the support values and looking for all possible frequent item sets in the data that have support values exceeding the chosen threshold. Secondly, these obtained frequent item sets are utilized to construct rules, which have confidence values exceeding the minimum threshold. There are several efficient algorithms for association rule learning, such as Apriori (Agrawal and Srikant, 1994) and Eclat (Zaki, 2000) algorithms.

Frequency Episode Extraction

Frequency episodes (Mannila et al., 1995 and Mannila & Toivonen, 1996) are normally utilized for representing a sequential audit data. In fact, frequent episodes are collections of events occurring frequently together. For example, in the sequence of Figure 2, the episode "E is followed by F" occurs several times:

Episodes, in general, are partially ordered sets of events. In intrusion detection, when discovering episodes in a system audit data, the goal is to look for relations between sequential patterns. Such relations will then be analyzed to understand the temporal as well as statistical nature of many attacks and normal users' behavior. From that, additional features will be extracted for detecting incoming traffic.

The formal definition of frequent episodes is given as follows: Let $I = \{i_1, i_2, ..., i_n\}$ be a set of n features called items of a system audit data. Let $D = P\{r_1, r_2, ..., r_m\}$ be a set of records in this data set. Each record r_i contains a subset of features in I. A frequent episode is defined as an expression of the form:

$X, Y \Rightarrow (Z, w)$, where $X, Y, Z \subseteq I$ and w is the width of considered time interval.

N-Grams Extraction

Many attacks that exploit vulnerabilities of protocols and services can be detected by analyzing header information from network packets or by monitoring the network traffic connection attempts and session behavior. For detecting attacks that tend to send bad payloads to vulnerable services or applications, such as viruses or malicious codes, consideration of the header information is not sufficient. The payload information of packets is necessary be analyzed. Some patterns of attacks can be selected from the payload by using domain knowledge in order to build a set of signatures. For automatic feature extraction, *n-grams* extraction method is usually applied (Wang et al., 2006 and Wang & Stolfo, 2004). An *n-gram* is a subsequence of *n* items from a given sequence. In the case of intrusion detection, if a payload is considered as a string, then an *n-gram* is a substring of *n* characters. With an assumption that payloads of normal traffic are different from payloads of attack traffic, the following is an automatic feature construction method based on *n-grams* extraction for intrusion detection: We consider *n-grams* ($n \geq 1$), thus the space S of all possible *n-grams* has the size of 2^{8n}, as considering 8 bits representation for each character:

$$S = \{n - grams_i \mid i = 1...2^{8n}\}$$

Given a payload p, a feature vector of p can be constructed as follows:

$$x_p = (x_1, x_2, ..., x_{2^{8n}}), \text{ where } x_i \text{ is the number of appearances of } n - gram_i \text{ in } p.$$

Feature Selection

In this section, we present automatic feature selection methods for intrusion detection systems

Figure 2. A sequence of events

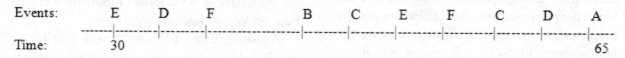

that include the filter model, the wrapper model and the embedded model from machine learning (Guyon et al., 2006 and Liu & Motoda, 2008).

The wrapper model assesses selected features by a learning algorithm's performance. In other words, in a wrapper model, one employs a learning algorithm and utilizes its performance to determine the quality of selected features. Therefore, the wrapper method requires a lot of time and computational resources to obtain the best feature subsets. However, these wrapper approaches are aimed at improving results of the specific classifiers they work with. In the following, one of the most popular machine learning algorithms, which are usually applied in wrapper models-Support Vector Machine (Vapnik, 1995), will be introduced.

The filter model considers statistical characteristics of a data set directly without involving any learning algorithm. Due to the computational efficiency, the filter method is usually utilized to select features from high-dimensional data sets, such as intrusion detection systems. The filter model encompasses two groups of methods: the feature ranking methods and the feature subset evaluating methods. The feature ranking methods assign weights to features individually based on their relevance to the target concept. The feature subset evaluating methods estimate feature subsets not only by their relevance, but also by the relations between features that make certain features redundant. It is well known that the redundant features can reduce the performance of a pattern recognition system (Guyon et al., 2006). Therefore, the feature subset evaluating methods are more suitable for selecting features for intrusion detection. A major challenge in the IDS feature selection process is to choose appropriate measures that can precisely determine the relevance and the relation between features of a given data set. Since the relevance and the relation are usually characterized in terms of correlation or mutual information (Guyon et al, 2006), in the following, two measures are considered: the correlation feature selection (CFS) measure (Hall, 1999) and the minimal-redundancy- maximal-relevance (mRMR) measure (Peng et al., 2005). It will be shown that these two measures can be fused and generalized into a generic feature selection (GeFS) measure for intrusion detection and also it will be presented how to obtain the best feature subsets by means of the GeFS measure.

In contrast to the filter and wrapper models, the embedded model of feature selection does not separate the learning from feature selection part. The embedded model integrates the selection of features in the model building. An example of such model is the decision tree induction algorithm (Duda, 2001), in which at each branching node, a feature has to be selected. Another example of the embedded model is SVM-based feature selection methods (Weston et al., 2001 and Guyon et al., 2002), in which the task of feature selection can be understood as looking for the feature subsets that lead to the largest possible generalization or equivalently to minimal risk. This SVM example will be shown in more detail in the next sections.

Wrapper Models for Feature Selection

Support Vector Machines

There are many machine learning algorithms that can be applied in the wrapper model for feature selection, such as Support Vector Machines, Neural Networks, Bayesian Networks and so on (Duda et al., 2001). In the following, one of the most popular algorithms, Support Vector Machine (SVM) (Vapnik, 1995), which is applied successfully in many application, is considered. SVM is a supervised learning technique, which can be utilized to both classification and regression problems. The main idea of the SVM is to construct a hyper-plane that tends to separate data points in the space. Below is the formal formulation of the Support Vector Machine algorithm.

A training data set D is given with m instances: $D = \{(a_i, c_i) \mid a_i \in R^n, c_i\{-1,1\}\}_{i=1}^m$, where

a_i is the instance that has n features and class label c_i; a_i can be represent as a data vector as follows: $a_i = (a_{i1}, a_{i2}, ..., a_{in})$, where a_{ij} is the value of the jth feature in instance a_i.

For the two-class classification problem, SVM learns the separating hyper-plane that maximizes the margin distance. The primal form of SVM is given below (Vapnik, 1995), where w is the weight vector and b is the bias:

$$\min_{w,b} \frac{1}{2} \|w\|_2^2 \qquad (1)$$

subject to the following constraints:

$$\left\{ c_i(wa_i - b) \geq 1, i = 1...m \right\}$$

In 1995, Cortes and Vapnik (Cortes and Vapnik, 1995) proposed a modified version of SVM that allows for mislabeled instances. They called this version of SVM Soft Margin, which has the following form:

$$\min_{w,b,\xi} \frac{1}{2} \|w\|_2^2 + C \sum_{i=1}^{m} \xi_i \qquad (2)$$

subject to the following constraints:

$$\begin{cases} c_i(wa_i - b) \geq 1 - \xi_i, \\ \xi_i \geq 0, i = 1...m, \\ \xi = (\xi_1, \xi_2, ..., \xi_m), \end{cases}$$

where ξ_i is a slack variable, which measures the degree of misclassification of instance a_i, $C > 0$ is the error penalty parameter.

The feature selection process is based on the evaluation of performances of the SVM algorithm. For a given feature subset, if the accuracy of the SVM is good, then the feature subset will be selected. In order to obtain the best feature subset, all 2^n possible feature subsets are necessary be tested. For more computational efficiency, heuristic search methods, such as backward search and forward search (Guyon et al., 2006), are usually applied.

Embedded Models for Feature Selection

SVM-Based Feature Selection

The SVM-based feature selection methods were studied in depth in previous works (Guyon et al., 2002 and Weston et al., 2001). As an example of the embedded models this section focuses on the feature selection method for linear SVMs (Vapnik, 1995) for two-class classification problems, such as for intrusion detection task. In particular, the utilization of L1-norm SVM for feature selection, which was first proposed by Bradley and Mangasarian in 1998 (Bradley and Mangasarian, 1998), is considered. Feature selection is an indirect consequence of the training process of SVMs. In fact, in the context of linear SVMs for binary classification tasks, the number of selected important features is the number of non-zero elements of the weight vectors after the training phase. Following the notations from the definition of the SVM method described above, the formal formulation of L1-norm SVM feature selection (Bradley and Mangasarian, 1998) is given below:

$$\min_{w,b,\xi} \|w\|_1 + C \sum_{i=1}^{m} \xi_i \qquad (3)$$

subject to the following constraints:

$$\begin{cases} c_i(wa_i - b) \geq 1 - \xi_i, \\ \xi_i \geq 0, i = 1...m, \\ \xi = (\xi_1, \xi_2, ..., \xi_m) \end{cases}$$

Define $w = p - q$ with $p, q \geq 0$. The problem (3) is then equivalent to the following linear programming problem (Bradley and Mangasarian, 1998):

$$\min_{p,q,b,\xi} e_n^T (p + q) + C \sum_{i=1}^{m} \xi_i$$

subject to the following constraints:

$$\begin{cases} c_i(pa_i - qa_i - b) \geq 1 - \xi_i, \\ \xi_i \geq 0, i = 1...m, \\ \xi = (\xi_1, \xi_2, ..., \xi_m), \\ p, q \geq 0, e_n^T = (1, 1, ..., 1) \in R^n \end{cases}$$

Bradley and Mangasarian (Bradley & Mangasarian, 1998 and Mangasarian, 2007) have shown in many applications that the utilization of L1-norm SVM leads to a feature selection method, whereas the utilization of the standard SVM (Vapnik, 1995) does not. However, it is realized that the Bradley and Mangasarian's method considers only one case of all n full-set features in the training phase. Since there probably exists irrelevant and redundant features (Guyon et al., 2006 and Liu & Motoda, 2008), it is necessary to test all 2^n possible combinations of features for training the SVM. In the following, a new general formulation of L1-norm SVM (GL1-SVM), which takes into account all 2^n possible feature subsets, is presented. Therefore, the traditional L1-norm SVM proposed by Bradley and Mangasarian is just only one case of the GL1-SVM introduced in this study. This is the reason why the method introduced in this study is called a general L1-norm SVM. The main idea of the GL1-SVM is that the weight vector and the data matrix are encoded by utilizing binary variables $x_j (j = 1...n)$ and additional non-negative variables $z = (z_1, ..., z_n, ..., z_{2n}) \geq 0$ as follows:

$$\begin{cases} p = (x_1 z_1, x_2 z_2, ..., x_n z_n), \\ q = (x_1 z_{n+1}, x_2 z_{n+2}, ..., x_n z_{2n}), \\ a_i = (a_{i1} x_1, a_{i2} x_2, ..., a_{in} x_n) \end{cases}$$

Following this encoding scheme, the GL1-SVM can be represented as a polynomial mixed 0-1 programming problem (PM01P), which can be solved to obtain the globally optimal solutions by applying the proposed methods described above in the section of filter models for feature selection.

$$\min_{x \in \{0,1\}^n} [\min_{z,b,\xi} (\sum_{j=1}^{n} x_j z_j + \sum_{j=1}^{n} x_j z_{n+j} + C \sum_{i=1}^{m} \xi_i)]$$

(4)

subject to the following constraints:

$$\begin{cases} \sum_{j=1}^{n} c_i a_{ij} x_j^2 z_j - \sum_{j=1}^{n} c_i a_{ij} x_j^2 z_{n+j} - c_i b \geq 1 - \xi_i, \\ x = (x_1, x_2, ..., x_n) \in \{0,1\}^n \\ \xi = (\xi_1, \xi_2, ..., \xi_m), \xi_i \geq 0, i = 1...m, \\ z = (z_1, ..., z_n, ..., z_{2n}), z_k \geq 0, k = 1...2n. \end{cases}$$

Proposition 7: Suppose that $S1, S2$ are minimal values of the objective functions from (3), (4), respectively. The following inequality is true:

$$S2 \leq S1$$

Proof: It is obvious, since the problem (3) is a case of the problem (4) when

$$x = (x_1, x_2, ..., x_n) = (1, 1, ..., 1). \;\square$$

Remark: As consequence of the Proposition 7, solving the problem (4) provides a smaller error penalty and enlarges the margin between two support vector hyper-planes, thus possibly provides better generalization capability of SVM than solving the traditional L1-norm SVM proposed by Bradley and Mangasarian (Bradley and Mangasarian, 1998).

Filter Models for Feature Selection

Correlation Feature Selection Measure

The Correlation Feature Selection (CFS) measure evaluates subsets of features on the basis of the following hypothesis: *"Good feature subsets contain features highly correlated with the classification, yet uncorrelated to each other"* (Hall, 1999). This hypothesis gives rise to two concepts. One is the feature-classification (r_{cf_i}) correlation and another is the feature-feature ($r_{f_i f_j}$) correlation. There exist broadly two measures of the correlation between two random variables: the classical linear correlation (Rodgers and Nicewander, 1988) and the correlation which is based on information theory (Shannon, 1948). The feature-classification correlation r_{cf_i} indicates how much a feature f_i is correlated to a target variable C, while the feature-feature correlation $r_{f_i f_j}$ is, as the very name says, the correlation between two features f_i and f_j. The following equation from (Ghiselli, 1964) applied in (Hall, 1999) provides the merit of a feature subset S consisting of k features:

$$Merit_S(k) = \frac{k\overline{r_{cf}}}{\sqrt{k + k(k-1)\overline{r_{ff}}}} \qquad (5)$$

Here, $\overline{r_{cf}}$ is the average feature-classification correlation, and $\overline{r_{ff}}$ is the average feature-feature correlation, as given below:

$$\overline{r_{cf}} = \frac{\sum_{i=1}^{k} r_{cf_i}}{k}, \quad \overline{r_{ff}} = 2\frac{\sum_{i,j=1,i\neq j}^{k} r_{f_i f_j}}{k(k-1)}$$

Therefore, equation (1) can be rewritten as follows:

$$Merit_S(k) = \frac{\sum_{i=1}^{k} r_{cf_i}}{\sqrt{k + 2(\sum_{i,j=1,i\neq j}^{k} r_{f_i f_j})}} \qquad (6)$$

In fact, the equation (5) is Pearson's correlation coefficient, where all variables have been standardized. It shows that the correlation between the feature subset S and the target variable C is a function of the number k of features in the subset S and the magnitude of the inter-correlations among them, together with the magnitude of the correlations between the features and the target variable C. From the equation (5), the following conclusions can be drawn: The higher the correlations between the features and the target variable C, the higher the correlation between the feature subset S and the target variable C; The lower the correlations between the features of the subset S, the more significant the correlation between the feature subset S and the target variable C.

The task of feature subset selection by means of the CFS measure: Suppose that there are n full set features. The subset S of k features, which has the maximum value of $Merit_S(k)$ over all 2^n possible feature subsets, is necessary be found:

$$\max_{S}\{Merit_S(k), 1 \leq k \leq n\}. \qquad (7)$$

Minimal-Redundancy-Maximal-Relevance Measure

In 2005, Peng et al. proposed a feature selection method, which is based on mutual information from information theory (Shannon, 1948). In this method, relevant and redundant features are considered simultaneously. In terms of mutual information, the relevance of a feature set S for the class C is defined by the mean value of all mutual information values between the individual feature f_i and the class C as follows:

$$D(S,C) = \frac{1}{|S|} \sum_{f_i \in S} I(f_i; C)$$

The redundancy of all features in the set S is the mean value R(S) of all mutual information values between the feature f_i and the feature f_j and is given below:

$$R(S) = \frac{1}{|S|^2} \sum_{f_i, f_j \in S} I(f_i; f_j)$$

The mRMR criterion is a combination of two measures given above and is defined as follows:

$$\max_S \phi_S(D, R) = \frac{1}{|S|} \sum_{f_i \in S} I(f_i; C) - \frac{1}{|S|^2} \sum_{f_i, f_j \in S} I(f_i; f_j) \tag{8}$$

The task of feature subset selection by means of the mRMR measure: Suppose that there are n full set features. The task of feature selection by means of this mRMR measure is to look for the subset S, which has the maximum value $\max_S \phi_S(D, R)$ of over all 2^n possible feature subsets:

For the tasks of feature subset selection by means of the CFS and the mRMR measures, the exhaustive search method can be applied to scan all possible feature subsets when the number n is small. But when this number becomes large, the heuristic and random search strategies, such as the best first search or genetic algorithm, are commonly chosen due to their computational efficiency. Consequently, the obtained results will always be approximate. It is desirable to obtain optimal subsets of features. In the sequel, the generalization of these two feature selection measures into a generic feature selection (GeFS)

measure and a new search method that ensures globally optimal feature subsets by means of GeFS will be introduced.

Generic Feature Selection Measure for Intrusion Detection

Definition 1: A generic feature selection measure applied in the filter model for intrusion detection is a function *GeFS(x)*, which has the following form (Nguyen et al., 2010b):

$$GeFS(x) = \frac{a_0 + \sum_{i=1}^{n} A_i(x)x_i}{b_0 + \sum_{i=1}^{n} B_i(x)x_i}, x \in \{0,1\}^n \tag{9}$$

In this definition, binary values of the variable x_i indicate the appearance $x_i = 1$ or the absence $x_i = 0$ of the feature f_i; a_0, b_0 are constants; $A_i(x)$, $B_i(x)$ are linear functions of variables x_1, x_2,..., x_n.

Definition 2: The feature selection problem is to look for $x \in \{0,1\}^n$ that maximizes the function *GeFS(x)* (Nguyen et al., 2010b)

$$\max_{x \in \{0,1\}^n} GeFS(x) = \frac{a_0 + \sum_{i=1}^{n} A_i(x)x_i}{b_0 + \sum_{i=1}^{n} B_i(x)x_i} \tag{10}$$

Proposition 1: The CFS measure and the mRMR measure are instances of the GeFS measure (Nguyen et al., 2010b).

Proof. The binary values of the variable x_i are utilized in order to indicate the appearance $x_i = 1$ or the absence $x_i = 0$ of the feature f_i in the globally optimal feature subset. The problems (7) and

(8) can be described as optimization problems (11) and (12), respectively as follows:

$$\max_{x \in \{0,1\}^n} \left[\frac{(\sum\limits_{i=1}^n r_{Cf_i} x_i)^2}{\sum\limits_{i=1}^n x_i + \sum\limits_{i \neq j} 2r_{f_i f_j} x_i x_j} \right] \qquad (11)$$

and

$$\max_{x \in \{0,1\}^n} \left[\frac{\sum\limits_{i=1}^n I(f_i; C) x_i}{\sum\limits_{i=1}^n x_i} - \frac{\sum\limits_{i,j=1}^n I(f_i; f_j) x_i x_j}{(\sum\limits_{i=1}^n x_i)^2} \right] \qquad (12)$$

It is obvious that the CFS measure and the mRMR measure are instances of the GeFS measure. $\square$

In the following, the optimization problems (11) and (12) are considered as polynomial mixed $0-1$ fractional programming (P01FP) problems and it is shown how to solve these problems.

Polynomial Mixed 0-1 Fractional Programming

A general polynomial mixed $0-1$ fractional programming (P01FP) problem (Chang, 2001) is represented as follows:

$$\min \sum_{i=1}^m \left(\frac{a_i + \sum\limits_{j=1}^n a_{ij} \prod\limits_{k \in J} x_k}{b_i + \sum\limits_{j=1}^n b_{ij} \prod\limits_{k \in J} x_k} \right) \qquad (13)$$

subject to the following constraints:

$$\begin{cases} b_i + \sum\limits_{j=1}^n b_{ij} \prod\limits_{k \in J} x_k > 0, i = 1, ..., m, \\ c_p + \sum\limits_{j=1}^n c_{pj} \prod\limits_{k \in J} x_k \leq 0, p = 1, ..., m, \\ x_k \in \{0,1\}, k \in J, \\ a_i, b_i, c_p, a_{ij}, b_{ij}, c_{pj} \in R. \end{cases}$$

By replacing the denominators in (13) by positive variables $y_i (i = 1...m)$, the P01FP then leads to the following equivalent polynomial mixed $0-1$ programming problem:

$$\min \sum_{i=1}^m \left(a_i y_i + \sum_{j=1}^n a_{ij} \prod_{k \in J} x_k y_i \right) \qquad (14)$$

subject to the following constraints:

$$\begin{cases} b_i y_i + \sum\limits_{j=1}^n b_{ij} \prod\limits_{k \in J} x_k y_i = 1, i = 1, ..., m, \\ c_p + \sum\limits_{j=1}^n c_{pj} \prod\limits_{k \in J} x_k \leq 0, p = 1, ..., m, \\ x_k \in \{0,1\}, k \in J, y_i > 0, \\ a_i, b_i, c_p, a_{ij}, b_{ij}, c_{pj} \in R. \end{cases} \qquad (15)$$

In order to solve this problem, Chang (Chang, 2001) proposed a linearization technique to transfer the terms $\prod\limits_{k \in J} x_k y_i$ into a set of mixed $0-1$ linear inequalities. Basing on this technique, the P01FP then becomes a mixed $0-1$ linear programming (M01LP) which can be solved by means of the branch-and-bound method to obtain the globally optimal solution.

Proposition 2: A polynomial mixed $0-1$ term $\prod\limits_{k \in J} x_k y_i$ from (14) can be represented by the following program (Chang, 2000):

$$\min z_i$$

subject to the following constraints:

$$\begin{cases} z_i \geq M(\sum_{k \in J} x_k - |J|) + y_i, \\ z_i \geq 0, \end{cases} \tag{16}$$

where M is a large positive value.

Proposition 3: A polynomial mixed $0-1$ term $\prod_{k \in J} x_k y_i$ from (15) can be represented by a continuous variable v_i, subject to the following linear inequalities (Chang, 2000):

$$\begin{cases} v_i \geq M(\sum_{k \in J} x_k - |J|) + y_i, \\ v_i \leq M(|J| - \sum_{k \in J} x_k) + y_i, \\ 0 \leq v_i \leq Mx_i, \end{cases} \tag{17}$$

where M is a large positive value.

In the following, the optimization problem of the GeFS measure (10) is formulated as a polynomial mixed $0-1$ fractional programming (P01FP) problem.

Proposition 4: The optimization problem of the GeFS measure (10) can be considered as a polynomial mixed $0-1$ fractional programming (P01FP) problem (Nguyen et al., 2010b).

Proof. The sign of *GeFS(x)* in (10) is changed to make a minimum problem. Therefore, (10) can be written as (13). □

Remark: By applying the Chang's method, this P01FP problem is transformed to the M01LP problem. The number of variables and constraints will depend on the square of n, where n is the number of features, because the number of terms $\prod_{k \in J} x_k y$, which are replaced by the new variables in forms $(\sum_{i \neq j} 2a_i a_j x_i x_j y)$ or $(\sum_{i \neq j} 2b_{ij} x_i x_j y)$,

is $n(n-1)/2$. The branch-and-bound algorithm then can be utilized to solve this M01LP problem. However, the efficiency of the method depends strongly on the number of variables and constraints. The larger the number of variables and constraints an M01LP has, the more computational complexity the branch-and-bound algorithm has.

In the next section, an improvement of the Chang's method is presented to obtain an M01LP with a linear number of variables and constraints in the number of full set variables. A new search strategy to obtain the relevant subsets of features by means the GeFS measure is also provided.

Optimization of the GeFS Measure

By introducing an additional positive variable, denoted by y, it is now considered that the following problem equivalent to (10):

$$\min_{x \in \{0,1\}^n} \{-GeFS(x)\} = -a_0 y - \sum_{i=1}^{n} A_i(x) x_i y \tag{18}$$

subject to the following constraints:

$$\begin{cases} y > 0, \\ x = (x_1, x_2, ..., x_n) \in \{0,1\}^n, \\ b_0 y + \sum_{i=1}^{n} B_i(x) x_i y = 1 \end{cases} \tag{19}$$

This problem is transformed into a mixed 0-1 linear programming problem as follows:

Proposition 5: A term $A_i(x) x_i y$ from (18) can be represented by the following program (Nguyen et al., 2010b):

$$\min z_i$$

subject to the following constraints:

$$\begin{cases} z_i \geq M(x_i - 1) + A_i(x)y, \\ z_i \geq 0, \end{cases} \qquad (20)$$

where M is a large positive value.

Proof:

a. If $x_i = 0$, then $z_i \geq M(0 - 1) + A_i(x)y \leq 0$ will cause $\min z_i$ to be zero, because $z_i \geq 0$ and M is a large positive value.

b. If $x_i = 1$, then $z_i \geq M(1 - 1) + A_i(x)y \geq 0$ will cause $\min z_i$ to be $A_i(x)y$, because $z_i \geq 0$.

Therefore, the above program on z_i reduces to:

$$\min z_i = \begin{cases} 0, & if\ x_i = 0 \\ A_i(x)y, & if\ x_i = 1 \end{cases}, \text{ which is the same}$$

as $A_i(x)x_i y = \min z_i$. □

Proposition 6: A term $B_i(x)x_i y$ from (19) can be represented by a continuous variable v_i, subject to the following linear inequality constraints (Nguyen et al., 2010b):

$$\begin{cases} v_i \geq M(x_i - 1) + B_i(x)y, \\ v_i \leq M(1 - x_i) + B_i(x)y \\ 0 \leq v_i \leq Mx_i, \end{cases} \qquad (21)$$

where M is a large positive value.

Proof:

a. If $x_i = 0$, then (15) becomes

$$\begin{cases} v_i \geq M(0 - 1) + B_i(x)y, \\ v_i \leq M(1 - 0) + B_i(x)y, \\ 0 \leq v_i \leq 0, \end{cases}$$

v_i is caused to be zero, as M is a large positive value.

b. If $x_i = 1$, then (15) becomes

$$\begin{cases} v_i \geq M(1 - 1) + B_i(x)y, \\ v_i \leq M(1 - 1) + B_i(x)y, \\ 0 \leq v_i \leq M, \end{cases}$$

v_i is caused to be $B_i(x)y$, as M is a large positive value.

Therefore, the constraints on v_i reduce to:

$$v_i = \begin{cases} 0, & if\ x_i = 0 \\ B_i(x)y, & if\ x_i = 1 \end{cases}$$

which is the same as $B_i(x)x_i y = v_i$. □

Each term $x_i y$ in (20), (21) is substituted by new variables t_i satisfying constraints from Proposition 2. Then the total number of variables for the M01LP problem will be *4n+1*, as they are x_i, y, t_i, z_i and $v_i (i = 1...n)$. Therefore, the number of constraints on these variables will also be a linear function of n. As mentioned above, in the Chang's method (Chang, 2001) the number of variables and constraints depends on the square of n, thus the new method introduced here actually improves Chang's method by reducing the complexity of branch and bound algorithm.

In the following, a new search strategy for obtaining the best subset of relevant features by means of the GeFS measure is presented:

The New Search Method for Relevant Feature Subsets by Means of the GeFS Measure

- **Step 1:** Analyzing the statistical properties of the given data set in order to choose an appropriate feature selection instance (CFS or mRMR) from the generic feature selection measure GeFS. The CFS is selected in the case if the data set has many features that linearly correlate to the class label and to each others. Otherwise, the mRMR measure is chosen.

- **Step 2:** Calculating all feature-feature and feature-classification correlations or mutual information corresponding to the statistical properties of the training data set.

  ○ Constructing the optimization problem (7) or (8) from the correlations or mutual information calculated above. In this step, domain knowledge can be utilized by assigning the value *1* to the variable x_i if the feature f_i should be in the final selected feature subset and the value *0* otherwise.

  ○ Transforming the optimization problem of GeFS to a mixed $0-1$ linear programming (M01LP) problem, which is to be solved by the branch-and-bound algorithm. A non-zero integer value of x_i from the globally optimal solution indicates the relevance of the feature f_i regarding to the GeFS measure.

METHOD APPLICATIONS

In this section, first, the 1998 DARPA data set (Lippmann et al., 1998 and Lippmann et al., 2000), which was generated by MIT Lincoln Laboratory for off-line intrusion detection evaluation, is described. Then it is shown how to construct the KDD CUP 1999 benchmarking data set (Lee, 1999) from the 1998 DARPA data set by utilizing feature construction methods that have been introduced in the previous sections. Various feature selection methods, which were applied to select features from the KDD CUP 1999 data set, will be described. Finally, a comparison of those feature selection algorithms for intrusion detection will be shown. The KDD CUP 1999 data set is considered, since it was a data set for evaluating IDSs and most the feature selection methods for intrusion detection were practiced on it.

The 1998 DARPA and the KDD CUP 1999 Data Sets

In 1998, MIT's Lincoln Laboratory launched a research project to evaluate the different intrusion detection systems, sponsored by the Air Force Research Laboratory (Lippmann et al., 1998). The goal of the project was mainly to create a benchmarking data set for intrusion detection by simulating background traffic and attack traffic. It took seven weeks to gather the training data and two weeks for the testing data were took place. The generated traffic was similar to that on a government sites containing hundreds of users. Custom software automata simulated hundreds of programmers, secretaries, managers and other types of users running common UNIX application programs. Many types of traffic were created by using a variety of network services. User automata sent and received emails, browsed websites, sent and received files using FTP or used Telnet to log into remote computers and performed works and so on. A more detail of the simulated network is described as follows. The inside of the Air Force base network contains three machines which were the most frequent victims of attacks (Linux2.0.27, SunOS 4.1.4 and Sun Solaris 2.5.1), and a gateway to hundreds of other inside emulated PCs and workstations. The outside of this network simulated the Internet. It contained a sniffer to capture traffic, a gateway to hundreds of emulated workstations on many other subnets and a second gateway to thousands of emulated web servers. Data collected for evaluating IDSs included network sniffing data from the outside sniffer, Sun Basic Security Module (BSM) audit data captured from the Solaris hosts and full disk dumps from the three UNIX victim machines.

For the normal traffic, a large amount of web, telnet and email traffic was generated between the inside PS's with workstations and the outside workstations with the websites. In addition, there are many user automata of various types (e.g. secretaries, managers and programmers) on outside workstations, who performed work using telnet and other services on the three inside victim machines, and the other inside workstations. The contents of network traffic, such as SMTP, HTTP and FTP file transfers, as they mentioned are either statistically similar to live traffic, or sampled from public-domain sources. For example, some email message contents were created using statistical bigrams frequencies to preserve word and two-word sequence statistics from a sampling of roughly 10,000 actual email messages to and from computer professionals filtered using a 40,000 word dictionary to remove names and other private information. Similar approaches were applied to produce content for FTP file transfer. The contents of the web servers were initially captured using a custom web automaton that was run on the real Internet. This automaton was programmed to visit thousands of websites popular with university and government personnel with a frequency that depends on the site's popularity and to visit a random number of links at each site before traversing to another sites.

For the attack traffic, there were more than 3,000 instances of 38 different simulated attacks against victim UNIX hosts. All the attacks can be categorized into 4 main groups: Denial of Service (DoS) attacks, Probe attacks, User to Root (U2R) attacks and Remote to Local (R2L) attacks. In more details, DoS attacks (e.g. smurt) load a legitimate network service, others (e.g. teardrop,

Ping of Death) create malformed packets, which are incorrectly handled by the victim machine, and others (e.g. apache2, back, syslogd) take advantage of software bugs in network daemon programs. The Probe attacks of Scan attacks are programs that can automatically scan a network of computers to gather information and search for known vulnerabilities. The U2R attacks attempt to obtain privileges normally reserved for the root or super users. In the case of R2L attacks, an attacker, who does not have an account on a victim machine. sends packets to that machine and gain local access. Some R2L attacks exploit buffer overflow in network server software (e.g. imap, named, sendmail), others exploit weak or misconfigured security policies (e.g. dictionary, ftp-write, guest) and one (xsnoop) is a trojan password capture program.

Feature Construction from the 1998 DARPA to the KDD CUP 1999 Data Sets

In 1999, Lee W. and Stolfo S. (Lee, 1999 and Lee & Stolfo, 2000) proposed a novel framework, MADAM ID, that applies data mining algorithms to extract frequent patterns from system audit data and construct predictive features from the patterns. Machine learning algorithms then were applied as intrusion detection systems to distinguish attacks from normal traffic in the audit records that are represented by feature vectors. They conducted the experiments on the 1998 DARPA data set as follows: the raw tcpdump data sets provided by the Lincoln Laboratory (Lippmann et al., 1998) were fist summarized into network connection records, in which a set of intrinsic features from domain knowledge was utilized. An example of network connection records and the list of intrinsic features are given in Table 1 and Table 2 as below:

The association rule learning algorithms were applied to search frequent associations or relations between intrinsic features. From those associations, Lee W. and Stolfo S. generated frequent

Table 1. An example of network connection records (Lee and Stolfo, 2000)

Timestamp	duration	Service	src_host	dst_host	src_bytes	dst_bytes	flag
1.1	0	http	spoofed_1	Victim	0	0	S0
1.1	0	http	spoofed_2	Victim	0	0	S0
10.2	2	ftp	A	B	200	300	SF
12.3	1	smtp	B	D	250	300	SF
13.4	60	telnet	A	D	200	12100	SF
...	...	...	...	...	...	...	...

Table 2. Intrinsic features of individual TCP connections (Lee and Stolfo, 2000)

ID	Feature Name	Description	Type
1	duration	length (number of seconds) of the connection	continuous
2	protocol_type	type of the protocol, e.g. tcp, udp, etc.	discrete
3	dervice	network service on the destination, e.g., http, telnet, etc.	discrete
4	src_bytes	number of data bytes from source to destination	continuous
5	dst_bytes	number of data bytes from destination to source	continuous
6	flag	normal or error status of the connection	discrete
7	land	1 if connection is from/to the same host/port; 0 otherwise	discrete
8	wrong_fragment	number of "wrong" fragments	continuous
9	urgent	number of urgent packets	continuous

episodes of sequential patterns of both the gathered normal and the attack traffic. They then compared the obtained patterns to look for the intrusion-only patterns that appear only in the intrusion data sets. Those intrusion patterns were utilized as guidelines for constructing additional features to build better classification models. In the Table 3, there is an example of frequent SYN flood patterns that they found in the audit data.

This SYN flood pattern guides to construct the following additional features: a count of con-

nections to the same *dst_host* in the past 2 seconds, and among these connections, the percentage of those that have the same *service*, and the percentage of those that have the "S0" *flag*.

Here the additional features automatically constructed by Lee's proposed method (Lee and Stolfo, 2000) are summarized as follows:

- The "same host" features that examine only the connections in the past 2 seconds that have the same destination host as the

Table 3. Example intrusion pattern (Lee and Stolfo, 2000)

Frequent Episode	Meaning
(flag=S0, service=http,dst_host=victim), (flag=S0, service=http,dst_host=victim) ⇒ (flag=S0, service=http,dst_host=victim) [0.93, 0.03, 2]	93% of the time, after two *http* connections with *S0* flag are made to host *victim*, within 2 seconds from the first of these two, the third similar connection is made, and this pattern occurs in 3% of the data.

current connection: the count of such connections, the percentage of connections that have the same service as the current one, the percentage of different services, the percentage of SYN errors, and the percentage of REJ (i.e., rejected connection) errors.

- The "same service" features that examine only the connections in the past 2 seconds that have the same service as the current connection: the count of such connections, the percentage of different destination hosts, the percentage of SYN errors, and the percentage of REJ errors.

They called these features "time-based" features for connection records. For several "slow" Probe attacks that scan the destination hosts or ports using more time than 2 seconds, there were not any intrusion-only patterns of these attacks within 2 seconds of connection. Therefore, Lee W. and Stolfo S. proposed to sort the connection records by the destination hosts and to consider 100 connections instead of the time window of 2 seconds. The automatic feature construction algorithms were applied again to obtain a mirror set of "host-based traffic" features as the "time-based traffic" features. All names of "time-based" and "host-based traffic" features are listed in the Table 4 and Table 5, respectively.

As many attacks, such as R2L and U2R attacks, are embedded in the payloads of the packets and involve only a single connection, the automatic feature construction algorithm, which is based on frequent sequential patterns of connection records, would fail to create any features of these attacks. Therefore, Lee W. and Stolfo S. proposed to look at the payloads of packets and combine it with domain knowledge to define suitable features for R2L and U2R attacks. These features are (Lee and Stolfo, 2000): number of failed logins, successfully logged in or not, whether logged in as root, whether a root shell is obtained, whether a *su* command is attempted and succeeded, number of access to access control files (e.g., "/etc/passwd", ".rhosts", etc.), number of compromised states on the destination host (e.g., file/path "not found" errors, and "Jump to" instructions, etc.), number of hot indicators, (e.g., access to system directories, creation and execution of programs, etc.), and number of outbound connections during a *ftp* session. These features are summarized in Table 6.

Table 4. Traffic features computed using a two-second time window (Lee and Stolfo, 2000)

ID	Feature Name	Description	Type
10	count	number of connections to the same host as the current connection in the past two seconds	Continuous
Note: The following features refer to these same-host connections.			
11	serror_rate	% of connections that have "SYN" errors	Continuous
12	rerror_rate	% of connections that have "REJ" errors	Continuous
13	same_srv_rate	% of connections to the same service	Continuous
14	diff_srv_rate	% of connections to different services	Continuous
15	srv_count	number of connections to the same service as the current connection in the past two seconds	Continuous
Note: The following features refer to these same-service connections.			
16	srv_serror_rate	% of connections that have "SYN" errors	Continuous
17	srv_rerror_rate	% of connections that have "REJ" errors	Continuous
18	srv_diff_host_rate	% of connections to different hosts	Continuous

Table 5. Traffic features computed using a window of 100 connections (Lee and Stolfo, 2000)

ID	Feature Name	Description	Type
19	dst_host_count	number of connections to the same host as the current connection in the past two seconds	Continuous
Note: The following features refer to these same-host connections.			
20	dst_host_serror_rate	% of connections that have "SYN" errors	Continuous
21	dst_host_rerror_rate	% of connections that have "REJ" errors	Continuous
22	dst_host_same_srv_rate	% of connections to the same service	Continuous
23	dst_host_diff_srv_rate	% of connections to different services	Continuous
24	dst_host_srv_count	number of connections to the same service as the current connection in the past two seconds	Continuous
Note: The following features refer to these same-service connections.			
25	dst_host_srv_serror_rate	% of connections that have "SYN" errors	Continuous
26	dst_host_srv_rerror_rate	% of connections that have "REJ" errors	Continuous
27	dst_host_srv_diff_host_rate	% of connections to different hosts	Continuous
28	dst_host_same_src_port_rate	% of connections to the same source port	Continuous

Feature Selection from the KDD CUP 1999 Data Set

In this section, we first describe the application of several existing feature selection methods, such as Markov Blanket, Support Vector Machine Wrapper and Classification and Regression Trees, on the KDD CUP 1999 data set. We then show the performance of the recently proposed generic feature selection (GeFS) measure for intrusion detection on this data set. Finally, a comparison between these feature selection methods is given.

Table 6. Content features within a connection suggested by domain knowledge (Lee and Stolfo, 2000)

ID	Feature Name	Description	Type
29	hot	number of "hot" indicators	Continuous
30	num_failed_logins	number of failed login attempts	Continuous
31	logged_in	1 if successfully logged in; 0 otherwise	Discrete
32	num_compromised	number of "compromised" conditions	Continuous
33	root_shell	1 if root shell is obtained; 0 otherwise	Discrete
34	su_attempted	1 if "su root" command attempted; 0 otherwise	Discrete
35	num_root	number of "root" accesses	Continuous
36	num_file_creations	number of file creation operations	Continuous
37	num_shells	number of shell prompts	Continuous
38	num_access_files	number of operations on access control files	Continuous
39	num_outbound_cmds	number of outbound commands in an ftp session	Continuous
40	is_hot_login	1 if the login belongs to the "hot" list; 0 otherwise	Discrete
41	is_guest_login	1 if the login is a "guest" login; 0 otherwise	Discrete

Markov Blanket

Markov blanket *MB(C)* of the output variable *C* is defined as the set of input variables such that all other variables are probabilistically independent of *C*. Knowledge of *MB(C)* is sufficient for perfectly estimating the distribution of the *C*. Therefore, Markov blanket can be applied for feature selection (Koller and Sahami, 1996). In 2005, Chebrolu et al. (Chebrolu et al., 2005) have proposed to apply Markov blanket for selecting important features for intrusion detection. In order to conduct the experiment, they constructed a Bayesian Network (BN) (Duda et al., 2001) from the original data set. A Bayesian network $B = (N, A, Q)$ is a Directed Acyclic Graph (DAG) (N, A) where each node $n \in N$ represents a domain variable (e.g. a data set attribute or variable), and each arc $a \in A$ between nodes represents a probabilistic dependency among the variables. A BN can be utilized to compute the conditional probability of one node, given values assigned to the other nodes. From the constructed BN, the Markov blanket of the class label *C* is the union of *C* 's parents, *C* 's children and eventually other parents of *C* 's children. For conducting the experiment, Chebrolu et al. (Chebrolu et al., 2005) randomly chose 11,982 instances from the overall (5 millions of instances) KDD CUP 1999 data set (Lee, 1999). 17 features were selected and the Bayesian Network (Duda et al, 2001) was applied for classifying the obtained data set after removing irrelevant features. The results are given in the Table 7.

Support Vector Machine Wrapper

Sung and Mukkamala (Sung and Mukkamala, 2003) have utilized the ranking methodology to select important features for intrusion detection: one input feature is deleted from the data at a time and the resultant data set is then utilized for training and testing the classifier Support Vector Machine (SVM) (Vapnik, 1995). Then the SVMs

Table 7. Performance of Bayesian Network using selected features (Chebrolu et al., 2005)

Classes	Number-of-selected-features	Accuracy
KDD99-normal	17	99.64%
KDD99-DoS	17	98.16%
KDD99-Probe	17	98.57%
KDD99-U2R	17	60.00%
KDD99-R2L	17	98.93%

performance was compared to that of the original SVM (based on all features) in terms of relevant performance criteria, such as overall accuracy of classification, training time and testing time. The deleted feature was ranked as "important", "secondary" or "insignificant" according to the following rules (Sung and Mukkamala, 2003):

- If accuracy decreases *and* training time increases *and* testing time decreases, *then* the feature is important.
- If accuracy decreases *and* training time increases *and* testing time increases, *then* the feature is important.
- If accuracy decreases *and* training time decreases *and* testing time increases, *then* the feature is important.
- If accuracy is not changed *and* training time increases *and* testing time increases, *then* the feature is important.
- If accuracy is not changed *and* training time decreases *and* testing time increases, *then* the feature is secondary.
- If accuracy is not changed *and* training time increases *and* testing time decreases, *then* the feature is secondary.
- If accuracy is not changed *and* training time decreases *and* testing time decreases, *then* the feature is insignificant.
- If accuracy increases *and* training time increases *and* testing time decreases, *then* the feature is secondary.

- If accuracy increases *and* training time decreases *and* testing time increases, *then* the feature is secondary.
- If accuracy increases *and* training time decreases *and* testing time decreases, *then* the feature is insignificant.

The experiment in (Sung and Mukkamala, 2003) was conducted on a part of KDD CUP'99 data set (Lee, 1999). This data set contains normal traffic and four main attack classes: Denial-of-Service (DoS) attacks, Probe attacks, User-to-Root (U2R) attacks and Remote-to-Local (R2L) attacks. Some important features were selected and the obtained data set after removing irrelevant features was classified by SVM. The results are given in Table 8.

Classification and Regression Trees

The Classification and Regression Trees (CART) (Breiman, 1984) is an approach of the decision tree learning techniques. This method is based on binary recursive partitioning. The process is binary because parent nodes are always split into exactly two child nodes and recursive because it is repeated by treating each child node as a parent. The key elements of CART methodology are a set of splitting rules in a tree; deciding when the tree is complete and assigning a class to each terminal node. Feature selection for intrusion detection is based on the contribution of the input variables to the construction of the decision tree from the original data set. The importance of features is determined by the role of each input variable either as a main splitter or as a surrogate. Surrogate splitters are considered as back-up rules that closely mimic the action of primary splitting rules. For example, in the given model, the algorithm splits data according to the variable *protocol type* and if a value for *protocol type* is not available then the algorithm might utilize the *service* feature as a good surrogate. Feature importance, for a particular feature is the sum across

Table 8. Performance of SVM using selected feature (Sung and Mukkamala, 2003)

Classes	Number-of-selected-features	Accuracy
KDD99-normal	25	99.59%
KDD99-DoS	19	99.22%
KDD99-Probe	7	99.38%
KDD99-U2R	8	99.87%
KDD99-R2L	6	99.78%

all nodes in the tree of the improvement scores that the predictor has when it acts as a primary or surrogate splitter. For example, for the node i, if the feature appears as the primary splitter then its importance could be given as $1.3 * 10^{-4}$. But if the feature appears as the nth surrogate instead of the primary variable, then the importance becomes $i_{IMPORTANCE} = (p^n) \times i_{IMPORTANCE}$, in which p is the *surrogate improvement weight* which is a user controlled parameter set between 0 and 1.

Chebrolu et al. (Chebrolu et al., 2005) have conducted the experiment on the data set, which contains randomly chosen 11,982 instances from the overall (5 millions of instances) KDD CUP 1999 data set (Lee, 1999). 12 features were selected and the CART (Breiman, 1984) was used for classifying the obtained data set after removing irrelevant features. The results are given in Table 9.

Generic Feature Selection Measure for Intrusion Detection

As the generic feature selection (GeFS) measure for intrusion detection has two instances: the correlation feature selection (CFS) measure and the minimal-redundancy-maximal-relevance (mRMR) measure, and following the new method proposed above for obtaining relevant feature subsets by means of the GeFS measure, it is necessary to choose an appropriate measure depending statistical properties of the KDD CUP 1999

Table 9. Performance of CART using selected features (Chebrolu et al., 2005)

Classes	Number-of-selected-features	Accuracy
KDD99-normal	12	100%
KDD99-DoS	12	85.34%
KDD99-Probe	12	97.71%
KDD99-U2R	12	64.00%
KDD99-R2L	12	95.56%

data set. In order to make the choice, the whole data set is visualized on two-dimension space to obtain a plot matrix, in which each element is the distribution of data points depending on the values of a feature and the class label or the values of two features. For example, Figure 3 shows the distribution of more than 32,000 data points of the KDD CUP 1999 data set according to values of "count" and "duration" features.

It can be observed that many features has no correlation with the class label, meanwhile they linearly correlate to each others. In fact, more than 65% of all feature-class correlation coefficients are very low (less than 0.01), meanwhile more than 35% of all feature-feature correlation coefficients are very high (more than 0.5). Therefore, the

CFS-based approach for selecting features from the KDD CUP 199 data set was opted. In the following, an experiment was conducted to validate the new CFS-based feature selection method as well as to compare it with the new mRMR-based approach and other heuristic algorithms.

Experimental Setting

For evaluating the performance of the new CFS-based feature selection approach for intrusion detection introduced in this study, the new mRMR-based approach and two available feature selection methods based on the CFS measure (Chen, 2006) were implemented. One is the best-first-CFS method, which employed the best first search strategy to obtain the locally optimal subset. The other employed the genetic algorithm for searching. Note that the best first search and genetic algorithm may not guarantee to obtain the globally optimal solution. However, this issue could be overcome with the new method. The exhaustive search method was not selected since it was not feasible for feature selection from data sets with a large number of features. Even for this experiment, no access to required computing resource was provided. Machine learning algorithms were applied for evaluating

Figure 3. Example distribution of data points from the KDD CUP 1999

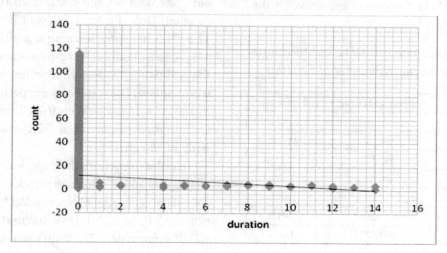

the classification accuracy on selected features, since there was no standard IDS.

The experiment was performed with 10% of the overall (5 millions) KDD CUP'99 IDS benchmarking labeled data. This data set contained normal traffic and four main attack classes: (i) Denial of Service (DoS) attacks, (ii) Probe attacks, (iii) User to Root (U2R) attacks, and (iv) Remote to Local (R2L) attacks. The number of instances for the four attack classes and normal class was relatively different, e.g. the relation of the number of U2R to the number of DoS was $1.3 * 10^{-4}$. Details of the number of class instances are given in Table 10.

In more details the performance of the newly proposed CFS-based feature selection method was testified as follows:

1. Feature selection is performed on the basis of the whole data set: (1a) Each attack class and the normal class are processed individually, so that a five-class problem can be formulated for feature extraction and classification with one single classifier. (1b) All attack classes are fused so that a two-class problem can be formulated, meaning the feature selection and classification for normal and abnormal traffic is performed. It might be well possible that the attack-recognition results are not satisfactory for all of the classes, since the number of class instances are unevenly dis-

tributed, in particular classes U2R and R2L are under-represented. The feature selection algorithm and the classifier, which is utilized for evaluation of the detection accuracy on selected features, might concentrate only on the most frequent class data and neglect the others. As a consequence, relevant characteristics of the less representative classes might be missed.

2. As the attack classes distributed differently, it is preferred to process these attack classes separately. With the specific application of IDS the four different two-class problems could also be formulated. Four classifiers were derived utilizing specific features for each classifier in order to detect (identify) a particular attack. The reason for this approach was that the most accurate classification was predicted if each of the four intrusion detectors (classifiers) was fine-tuned according to the significant features. This approach might also be very effective, since the four light-weight classifiers could be operated in parallel.

To understand the effect, as mentioned in 1), a small experiment was conducted. The aim was to show that the classifier highly neglected U2R attack instances. In order to carry through the experiment, all attack classes were mixed to obtain only one data set and considered the five-class (normal, DoS, Probe, U2R, and R2L) problem. The C4.5 machine learning algorithm was employed as a classifier. Five-folds cross-validation for evaluating the detection accuracy of the C4.5 were applied. The result of the experiment is given in Table 11. It can be seen from Table 11 that the C4.5 highly misclassified U2R attack instances with 34.6% error.

In order to perform the experiment 2), normal traffic was added into each attack class to obtain four data sets: KDD99-normal&DoS, KDD99-normal&Probe, KDD99-normal&U2R and KDD99-normal&R2L. With each data set, three

Table 10. The partition of KDD CUP'99 dataset utilized in experiment (Nguyen et al., 2010a)

Classes	Number-of-instances	Percentage
KDD99-normal	97,278	18.30%
KDD99-DoS	391,458	73.74%
KDD99-Probe	41,113	7.74%
KDD99-U2R	52	0.01%
KDD99-R2L	1,126	0.21%
Total	531,027	100%

feature-selection algorithms were run: the new CFS-based method proposed in this study, the best-first CFS-based, and the genetic algorithm CFS-based methods. The numbers of selected features and their identifications are given in Tables 12 and 13, respectively. Then the C4.5 and the BayesNet machine learning algorithm were applied on each original full set as well as each newly obtained data set that included only the selected features from feature selection algorithms. By applying 5-folds cross-validation evaluation on each data set, the classification accuracies are reported in Tables 14 and 15.

The new CFS-based method proposed in this study was compared with the new mRMR-based approach, the best first-CFS, and the genetic-algorithm-CFS methods regarding the number of selected features and regarding the classification accuracies of 5-folds cross-validation of the BayesNet and C4.5 learning algorithms. Weka tool (Witten et al., 1999) was employed to obtain the results. In order to solve the M01LP problem,

the TOMLAB tool (Kenneth et al., 2003) was utilized. All the obtained results are listed in Tables 12, 14, and 15.

Experimental Results

Table 12 shows the number of features selected by CFS-based approach and those selected by utilizing the mRMR-based method, the best-first and GA search strategies. The identification of selected features is given in Table 13 (for feature names, see Tables 2, 4, 5 and 6). Table 14 and Table 15 summarize the classification accuracies of the BayesNet and the C4.5, respectively, performed on four data sets (see above).

It can be observed from Table 12 that the CFS-based approach introduced in this study selects the smallest number of relevant features in comparison with the full and the feature sets selected by the mRMR-based method, the best-first and GA search strategies. In particular, in some cases, the new method introduced in this study extremely compresses the full set of features. For example, only one feature was selected out of 41 features of the KDD99-normal&U2R data set.

In the Table 14 and Table 15, it can be observed that with this study approach the average classification accuracies are slightly different from the ones obtained by utilizing the best-first search or the genetic algorithm. The absolute difference between them does not exceed 0.69%. In the case of the C4.5 classifier, the better performance was an evident. Even though the gain of classification accuracy is not very high compared to other meth-

Table 11. Unclassified instances (UI) by the C4.5 classifier (Nguyen et al., 2010a)

Classes	Number of UI	Percentage
Normal	65	0.07%
DoS	21	0.01%
Probe	39	0.10%
U2R	18	34.6%
R2L	39	3.46%

Table 12. Number of selected features (GA: genetic algorithm) (Nguyen et al., 2010a)

Data Set	Full-set	GeFS_CFS	GeFS_mRMR	Best-first	GA
KDD99-normal&Dos	41	3	22	6	11
KDD99-normal&Probe	41	6	14	7	17
KDD99-normal&U2R	41	1	5	4	8
KDD99-normal&R2L	41	2	6	5	8

Table 13. Identification of selected features by means of GeFS_CFS (Nguyen et al., 2010a)

Data Set	Identifications
KDD99-normal&Dos	4, 5, 31
KDD99-normal&Probe	4, 5, 13, 26, 27, 31
KDD99-normal&U2R	33
KDD99-normal&R2L	29, 41

ods, the overall gain of the feature selection classification procedure lies in significantly improved efficiency and in the obtained classification results due to the reduced number of relevant features.

Therefore, based on all these experiments it can be concluded that in general the new CFS-based method introduced in this study outperforms the mRMR-based approach, the best-first-CFS and genetic-algorithm-CFS methods by removing much more redundant features and still keeping the classification accuracies or even obtaining better performances.

A Comparison of Feature Selection Methods

In this section, we summarize the feature selection results described above to make a comparison between different methods. We use the general performance of intrusion detection systems as a measurement for this comparison. Since different intrusion detection systems used different feature selection methods and different classifiers with the aim of achieving the best classification results, we compared general performance of intrusion detection systems in terms of numbers of selected features and the classification accuracies of the machine learning algorithms giving the best classification results. The feature selection algorithms involved in this comparison are the SVM-wrapper, Markov Blanket, CART algorithms and the recently proposed generic feature selection (GeFS) method with 2 instances applicable in intrusion detection: the correlation-feature-selection (*GeFS_CFS*) and the minimal-

Table 14. Classification accuracies of C4.5 performed on KDD CUP'99 (Nguyen et al., 2010a)

Data Set	Full-set	GeFS_CFS	GeFS_mRMR	Best-first	GA
KDD99-normal&Dos	97.80	98.89	99.98	96.65	96.09
KDD99-normal&Probe	99.98	99.70	99.35	99.71	99.89
KDD99-normal&U2R	99.97	99.96	99.94	99.97	99.95
KDD99-normal&R2L	98.70	99.11	99.14	99.01	98.86
Average	**99.11**	**99.41**	**99.60**	**98.84**	**98.69**

Table 15. Classification accuracies of BayesNet performed on KDD CUP'99 (Nguyen et al., 2010a)

Data Set	Full-set	GeFS_CFS	GeFS_mRMR	Best-first	GA
KDD99-normal&Dos	99.99	98.87	99.36	99.09	99.72
KDD99-normal&Probe	98.96	97.63	98.65	97.65	99.19
KDD99-normal&U2R	99.85	99.95	99.94	99.97	99.93
KDD99-normal&R2L	99.33	98.81	99.17	98.95	99.28
Average	**99.53**	**98.82**	**99.28**	**98.91**	**99.52**

redundancy-maximal-relevance (*GeFS_mRMR*) measures.

Figure 4 shows the average number of selected features by various feature selection methods. Figure 5 summarizes the average classification accuracies of chosen machine learning algorithms as classifiers for intrusion detection process. It can be observed from Figure 4 that the proposed generic feature selection (GeFS) method selects the smallest number of relevant features. Figure 5 shows that with also the GeFS approach, the average classification accuracies are approximately the same or even better than those achieved by applying other methods.

DISCUSSIONS AND FUTURE DIRECTIONS

McHugh (McHugh, 2000) has criticized the 1998 DARPA dataset, arguing that several procedures utilized in the simulation for generating background traffic are questionable and described superficially. There was no statistical evidence proving the similarity between the synthesized data and the real data. McHugh suspected that

the 1998 DARPA dataset has statistically different characteristics from real traffic. Malhoney and Chan (Malhoney and Chan, 2003) has confirmed McHugh's criticisms by conducting experiments, in which the 1998 DARPA data set was compared with real traffic gathered from a network environment. It is shown that many features of the network traffic appeared to be relevant for detecting attacks in the 1998 DARPA, but less important in the real traffic. For example, there are only 9 of the possible 256 TTL values, which were found in the 1998 DARPA data set. In the real traffic, Malhoney and Chan (Malhoney and Chan, 2003) observed 177 different values.

Although the 1998 DARPA data set was highly innovative for its time and it was widely utilized by IDS community. Nowadays, the data set is out of date and does not contain many recent attacks. It would be necessary to generate a new benchmarking data set for IDSs and to test again the performance of the feature construction and the feature selection algorithms on the new data set.

Regarding future research directions on feature extraction for intrusion detection, the following list shows important questions that needs to be answered:

Figure 4. Number of selected features (on average)

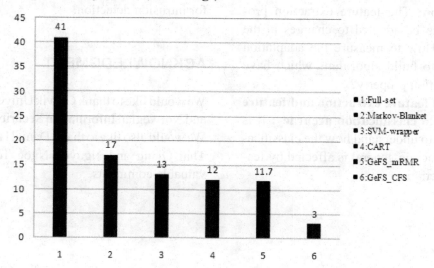

Figure 5. Classification accuracies (on average)

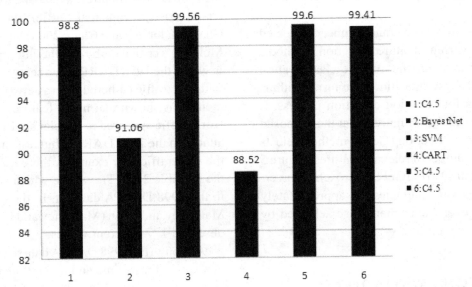

- **Stability:** How to build feature extraction methods that are stable with slight changes in the data sets? This issue is important in analyzing polymorphic attacks, such as virus or worms.
- **Imbalance:** The distributions of normal and attack traffic in data sets in general are different. How to build feature selection algorithms which considers most frequent traffic, without neglecting less frequent traffic?
- **Adaptation:** The feature extraction process has to be adapted to changes in the data set. How to measure the adaptation and how to build algorithms which have the adaptation property?
- **Impact of feature extraction and feature selection to classification accuracy:** It is important to understand how the classification accuracy in general is affected by feature extraction.

CONCLUSION

Feature extraction is an important part of an intrusion detection system. In the present chapter, we have described the theoretical background as well as the practical applications of various feature extraction methods for intrusion detection systems. A comparison of these methods performed on the public benchmarking data sets was also provided. Moreover, we have revealed several research directions on feature extraction for intrusion detection.

ACKNOWLEDGMENT

We would like to thank Gjøvik University College and Norwegian Information Security Laboratory. We would also like to thank Daniel Hartung, Dang Thai Giang and Nguyen Ngoc Toan for their valuable comments.

REFERENCES

Agrawal, R., Imielinski, T., & Swami, A. (1993). Mining association rules between sets of items in large databases. In P. Buneman & S. Jajodia (Eds.), *Proceedings of the 1993 ACM SIGMOD International Conference on Management of Data* (SIGMOD '93, Washington, DC, May 26-28), (pp. 207–216). New York, NY: ACM Press.

Agrawal, R., & Srikant, R. (1994). Fast algorithms for mining association rules in large databases. In J. B. Bocca, M. Jarke, & C. Zaniolo, (Eds.), *Proceedings of the 20th International Conference on Very Large Data Bases*, (p. 487). Santiago, Chile.

Bradley, P., & Mangasarian, O. L. (1998). Feature selection via concave minimization and support vector machines. In *Proceedings of the Fifteenth International Conference (ICML)*, (pp. 82-90).

Breiman, L., Friedman, J. H., Olshen, R. A., & Stone, C. J. (1984). *Classification and regression trees*. Belmont, CA: Wadsworth.

Chang, C.-T. (2000). An efficient linearization approach for mixed integer problems. *European Journal of Operational Research, 123*, 652–659. doi:10.1016/S0377-2217(99)00106-X

Chang, C.-T. (2001). On the polynomial mixed 0-1 fractional programming problems. *European Journal of Operational Research, 131*(1), 224–227. doi:10.1016/S0377-2217(00)00097-7

Chebrolu, S., Abraham, A., & Thomas, J. (2005). Feature deduction and ensemble design of intrusion detection systems. *Computers & Security, 4*, 295–307. doi:10.1016/j.cose.2004.09.008

Chen, Y., Li, Y., Cheng, X.-Q., & Guo, L. (2006). Survey and taxonomy of feature selection algorithms in intrusion detection system. In *Proceedings of Inscrypt 2006, LNCS 4318*, (pp. 153-167).

Cortes, C., & Vapnik, V. (1995). Support-vector networks. *Machine Learning, 20*(3). doi:10.1007/BF00994018

Denning, D. E. (1986). An intrusion detection model. In *Proceedings of the Seventh IEEE Symposium on Security and Privacy*, (pp. 119–131).

Duda, R. O., Hart, P. E., & Stork, D. G. (2001). *Pattern classification*. USA: Wiley-Interscience.

Ghiselli, E. E. (1964). *Theory of psychological measurement*. New York, NY: Mc GrawHill.

Guyon, I., Gunn, S., Nikravesh, M., & Zadeh, L. A. (2006). *Feature extraction: Foundations and applications. Series Studies in Fuzziness and Soft Computing, Physica-Verlag*. Springer.

Guyon, I., Weston, J., Barnhill, S., & Vapnik, V. (2002). Gene selection for cancer classification using support vector machines. *Machine Learning, 46*(1), 389–422. doi:10.1023/A:1012487302797

Hall, M. (1999). *Correlation based feature selection for machine learning*. Unpublished doctoral dissertation, University of Waikato, Department of Computer Science.

Jain, A. K., Duin, R. P. W., & Mao, J. (2000). Statistical pattern recognition: A review. *IEEE Transactions on Pattern Analysis and Machine Intelligence In Pattern Analysis and Machine Intelligence, 22*(1), 4–37. doi:10.1109/34.824819

Kenneth, H., Edvall, M. M., & Göran, A. O. (2003). TOMLAB-for large-scale robust optimization. In *Proceedings of the Nordic MATLAB Conference*.

Koller, D., & Sahami, M. (1996). Toward optimal feature selection. In *Proceedings of International Conference on Machine Learning*.

Lee, W. (1999). A data mining framework for building intrusion detection models. In *IEEE Symposium on Security and Privacy*, (pp. 120–132). Berkeley, California.

Lee, W., & Stolfo, S. (2000). A framework for constructing features and models for intrusion detection systems. *ACM Transactions on Information and System Security, 3*, 227–261. doi:10.1145/382912.382914

Lippmann, R. P., Fried, D., Graf, I., Haines, J., Kendall, K., & Mcclung, D. ... Zissman, M. (2000). Evaluating intrusion detection systems: The 1998 DARPA off-line intrusion detection evaluation. In *Proceedings of the on DARPA Information Survivability Conference and Exposition* (DISCEX'00, Hilton Head, South Carolina, Jan. 25-27), (pp. 12–26). Los Alamitos, CA: IEEE Computer Society Press.

Lippmann, R. P., Graf, I., Garfinkel, S. L., Gorton, A. S., Kendall, K. R., & McClung, D. J. ... Zissman, M. A. (1998). The 1998 DARPA/AFRL off-line intrusion detection evaluation. Presented to *the First Intl. Workshop on Recent Advances in Intrusion Detection (RAID-98)*, Lovain-la-Neuve, Belgium, 14–16 September.

Liu, H., & Motoda, H. (2008). *Computational methods of feature selection.* Boca Raton, FL: Chapman & Hall/CRC.

Lunt, T., Tamaru, A., Gilham, F., Jagannathan, R., Neumann, P., Javitz, H., ... Garvey, T. (1992). *A real-time intrusion detection expert system (IDES).* Final technical report.

Mahoney, M. V., & Chan, P. K. (2003). *An analysis of the 1999 DARPA/Lincoln laboratory evaluation data for network anomaly detection. Technical Report TR CS-2003-02.* Computer Science Department, Florida Institute of Technology.

Mangasarian, O. L. (2007). Exact 1-norm support vector machines via unconstrained convex differentiable minimization (special topic on machine learning and optimization). *Journal of Machine Learning Research, 7*(2), 1517–1530.

Mannila, H., & Toivonen, H. (1996). Discovering generalized episodes using minimal occurrences. In *Proceedings of the 2nd International Conference on Knowledge Discovery in Databases and Data Mining* (Portland, OR, Aug.).

Mannila, H., Toivonen, H., & Verkamo, A. I. (1995). Discovering frequent episodes in sequences. In *Proceedings of the First International Conference on Knowledge Discovery in Databases and Data Mining* (Montreal, Canada, Aug. 20-21).

McHugh, J. (2000). Testing intrusion detection systems: A critique of the 1998 and 1999 DARPA off-line intrusion detection system evaluation as performed by Lincoln Laboratory. *ACM Transactions on Information and System Security, 3*(4). doi:10.1145/382912.382923

Nguyen, H., Franke, K., & Petrovi'c, S. (2010a). Improving effectiveness of intrusion detection by correlation feature selection, In *Proceedings of the 2010 International Conference on Availability, Reliability and Security (ARES)*, Krakow, Poland, February 2010, (pp. 17-24).

Nguyen, H., Franke, K., & Petrovi'c, S. (2010b). Towards a generic feature-selection measure for intrusion detection. In *20th International Conference on Pattern Recognition*, Istanbul, Turkey, (pp. 1529-1532).

Northcutt, S. (1999). *Network intrusion detection: An analyst's handbook.* Sams.

Peng, H., Long, F., & Ding, C. (2005). Feature selection based on mutual information: Criteria of max-dependency, max-relevance, and min-redundancy. *IEEE Transactions on Pattern Analysis and Machine Intelligence, 27*(8), 1226–1238. doi:10.1109/TPAMI.2005.159

Quinlan, J. R. (1993). *C4.5: Programs for machine learning.* Morgan Kaufmann.

Rodgers, J. L., & Nicewander, W. A. (1988). Thirteen ways to look at the correlation coefficient. *The American Statistician, 42*(1), 59–66. doi:10.2307/2685263

Roesch, M. (1999). Snort - Lightweight intrusion detection for networks. In *Proceedings of the 13th USENIX Conference on System Administration,* (pp. 229-238).

Shannon, C. E. (1948). A mathematical theory of communication. *The Bell System Technical Journal, 27,* 379–423, 623–656.

Sung, A. H., & Mukkamala, S. (2003). Identifying important features for intrusion detection using support vectormachines and neural networks. In *Proceedings of the International Symposium on Applications and the Internet (SAINT),* (pp. 209–217). Los Alamitos, CA: IEEE Press.

Vapnik, V. (1995). *The nature of statistical learning theory.* Springer.

Wang, K., Parekh, J., & Stolfo, S. (2006). A content anomaly detector resistant to mimicry attack. In *Recent Adances in Intrusion Detection (RAID)* (pp. 226–248). Anagram. doi:10.1007/11856214_12

Wang, K., & Stolfo, S. (2004). Anomalous payload-based network intrusion detection. In *Recent Adances in Intrusion Detection* (pp. 203–222). RAID. doi:10.1007/978-3-540-30143-1_11

Weston, J., Mukherjee, S., Chapelle, O., Pontil, M., Poggio, T., & Vapnik, V. (2001). Feature selection for SVMs. *Advances in Neural Information Processing Systems,* 668–674.

Witten, I. H., Frank, E., Trigg, L., Hall, M., Holmes, G., & Cunningham, S. J. (1999). Weka: Practical machine learning tools and techniques with Java implementations. In *Proceedings of the ICONIP/ANZIIS/ANNES'99 Workshop on Emerging Knowledge Engineering and Connectionist-Based Information Systems* (pp. 192–196).

Zaki, M. J. (2000). Scalable algorithms for association mining. *IEEE Transactions on Knowledge and Data Engineering, 12*(3), 372–390. doi:10.1109/69.846291

ADDITIONAL READING

Cormen, T. H., Leiserson, C. E., Rivest, R. L., & Stein, C. (2001). *Introduction to algorithms,* 2nd ed. MIT Press & McGraw-Hill.

Crescenzo, G. D., Ghosh, A., & Talpade, R. (2005). Towards a theory of intrusion detection. In *Proceedings of the 10th European Symposium on Research in Computer Security (ESORICS'05),* (pp. 267-286). Springer.

Gu, G., Fogla, P., Dagon, D., Lee, W., & Skoric, B. (2006). Towards an information-theoretic framework for analyzing intrusion detection systems. In *Proceedings of the 11th European Symposium on Research in Computer Security (ESORICS'06),* (pp. 527-546). Springer.

Guyon, I., & Elisseeff, A. (2003). An introduction to variable and feature selection. *Journal of Machine Learning Research, 3,* 1157–1182.

Kohavi, R., & Sommerfield, D. (1995). Feature subset selection using the wrapper method: Overfitting and dynamic search space topology. In *Proceedings of First International Conference on Knowledge Discovery and Data Mining,* (pp. 192–197). Morgan Kaufmann.

Kononenko, I., & Kukar, M. (2007). *Machine learning and data mining: Introduction to principles and algorithms.* UK: Horwood Publishing Limited.

Mitchel, T. (1997). *Machine learning.* New York, NY: McGraw-Hill, Inc.

Nemhauser, G. L., & Wolsey, L. A. (1989). Integer programming. In *Handbooks in operations research and management science (Vol. 1)*. Amsterdam, The Netherlands: Elsevier/North Holland.

KEY TERMS AND DEFINITIONS

Feature Construction: The process of constructing representative features from the original data.

Feature Extraction: The process of extracting the most compact and informative features in a given data.

Feature Selection: The process of selecting the most relevant feature subset from a set of features.

Intrusion Detection System: A system (a device or a software application) that monitors network and/or system activities for detecting intrusions in the current networks or computers.

Pattern Recognition system: A system that assigns an output value (or label) to a given input value (or instance).

Risk Management: The identification, assessment, and prioritization of risks that are the effect of uncertainty on objectives, whether positive or negative.

Support Vector Machine: A supervised learning technique that is about to construct a hyper-plane, which tends to separate data points in the space.

Chapter 3
A Distributed and Secure Architecture for Signature and Decryption Delegation through Remote Smart Cards

Giuseppe Cattaneo
Università di Salerno, Italy

Pompeo Faruolo
Università di Salerno, Italy

Ivan Visconti
Università di Salerno, Italy

ABSTRACT

The established legal value of digital signatures and the growing availability of identity-based digital services are progressively extending the use of smart cards to all citizens, opening new challenging scenarios. Among them, motivated by concrete applications, secure and practical delegation of digital signatures and decryptions is becoming more and more critical. Unfortunately, all secure delegation systems proposed so far include various drawbacks with respect to some of the main functional requirements of any practical system. With the purpose of proposing a truly practical solution for signature and decryption delegation, in this chapter the authors put forth the notion of a "Proxy Smart Card System," a distributed system that allows a smart card owner to delegate part of its computations to remote users. They first stress the problematic aspects concerning the use of known proxy-cryptography schemes in synergy with current standard technologies, which in turn motivates the need of proxy smart card systems. Then they formalize the security and functional requirements of a proxy smart card system, identifying the involved parties, the adversary model, and the usability properties. Finally, the authors present the design and analysis of a proxy smart card system, which implements the required functionalities outperforming the current state of the art.

DOI: 10.4018/978-1-4666-0978-5.ch003

INTRODUCTION

Proxy cryptography is a widely developed research area that consists in providing cryptographic primitives that allow a user to safely delegate part of its tasks (typically decryptions and signatures of messages) to another user. Concrete applications of proxy cryptography are nowadays becoming more and more critical.

For instance digital signatures are now regulated and accepted by law in almost all countries and many entities playing crucial roles in both enterprises (e.g., CEOs) and public institutions (e.g., mayors, rectors), have to sign a large amount of documents per day. Moreover, it is often the case that documents have to be signed urgently, even when the signer is out of his office and unreachable. The possibility of delegating signing privileges should therefore be extended also to *digital* signatures.

Another major example is the increasing use of decryption features for e-mails, in order to keep private some relevant data. Again, one would like to delegate to someone else the capability of decrypting some of the emails (e.g., the ones with a specific subject) in order to reduce his own amount of work and not to stop his activities when he is disconnected from the Internet.

Unfortunately we observe a huge gap between features provided by proxy cryptography and their actual use in the real world. Indeed, it is well known that results produced by cryptographers need several years to be assessed and then used by practitioners. Moreover cryptography in standalone is not usable, it needs to be integrated in a system with security and privacy mechanisms that can make robust all the involved components. Proxy cryptography is affected by such delays, and indeed, while the literature already gives several provably secure schemes enjoying many features and reasonable efficiency, almost nothing of it is actually used in practice. This is in large part a consequence of the long distance between the requirements of proxy cryptography (e.g., system parameters, cryptographic operations) and the currently used technologies (e.g., PKIX (Housley *et al.*, 2002), Smart Cards). It is therefore urgent to provide mechanisms that allow delegation of signatures and decryptions using *current* standard technologies *only*.

Contribution

In this work we study the problematic aspects of using proxy cryptography along with current standard technologies to implement delegation of signatures and decryptions. Therefore, motivated by the worldwide spread of smart cards (SCs, for short), and their cryptographic operations (e.g., signatures and decryptions) for implementing various cryptographic services, we put forth the notion of a *Proxy Smart Card System* (PSCS, for short).

We investigate concrete real-world scenarios and according to them we formalize the security and functional requirements of a PSCS, identifying the involved parties, the adversary model and the critical usability properties. We finally present the design and analysis of a proxy smart card system (based on the use of a network security appliance) that outperforms the current state of the art. The development of our system required the combined use of several techniques and technologies in a novel way, which in some case could be also of independent interest.

Our solution is a "ready-to-use" framework that can be easily plugged in real-life scenarios. It does not resort to currently unused features of proxy cryptography and instead uses the synergy of existing crypto tools and security technologies to obtain a robust, easy to configure, scalable and cheap system to delegate, under some access control policies, signature and decryption privileges.

Organization of the Chapter

The chapter is organized as follows. In the next section we first briefly present the state of art of proxy signature and decryption, and then we stress their security and functional requirements. Then, we present the design and implementation of our PSCS. Successively, we analyze our PSCS with respect to the requirements discussed before. Finally, we list some concluding remarks.

PROXY SIGNATURES AND DECRYPTIONS

The concepts of proxy signatures and proxy decryptions were introduced respectively by Mambo & Okamoto (1997) and by Mambo *et al.* (1996). In such schemes a player called owner O, delegates to another player, called user U, the power to execute his own cryptographic tasks. In a proxy signature system, U can sign messages on O's behalf, while in a proxy decryption system he can decrypt ciphertexts encrypted under O's public key. In general, in such systems, O generates some *proxy secret keys* which Us can use to sign documents verifiable through O's public key and decrypt ciphertexts encrypted under O's public key.

In literature many generalizations and extensions have been proposed in the past. Among them we mention threshold proxy signatures (Shao *et al.*, 2007), blind proxy signatures (Kim & Chang, 2006; Liu *et al.*, 2007; Qin & Wu, 2008), nominative proxy signatures (Park & Lee, 2001), one-time proxy (Lu *et al.*, 2006), and proxy-anonymous signatures (Fan *et al.*, 2008) (Fuchsbauer & Pointcheval, 2008) (Hu *et al.*, 2007; Yumin, 2006; Zhou, 2008).

Originally, these building blocks were considered to be used in large enterprise scenarios, where a manager would like to delegate his signature capabilities, or could delegate his capabilities to decrypt some messages (e.g., e-mails) encrypted with his public key. Subsequently, the use of such schemes has been suggested in numerous other contexts as, mobile agent environment (Lee *et al.*, 2001a), grid computing (Foster *et al.*, 1998), distributed shared object systems (Leiwo *et al.*,

2000), global distribution networks (Bakker *et al.*, 2001), and mobile communications (Park & Lee, 2001).

SECURITY REQUIREMENTS

According to the relevant literature (Lee *et al.*, 2001b; Mambo *et al.*,1996), and the requirements of real-world applications, proxy signature and decryption schemes should enjoy the following (informal) properties.

Proxy Signature:

Verifiability: A verifier always accepts a proxy signature computed by a delegated honest user U.

Strong Unforgeability: It must be computationally hard for a player that is not a delegated honest U to compute a new proxy signature that is accepted by a verifier.

Strong Identifiability: From a proxy signature computed by a delegated user U, it must be possible to determine efficiently the identity of U.

Strong Undeniability: It must be computationally hard for a player that computed a proxy signature, to subsequently repudiate it.

Proxy Decryption:

Correctness: A delegated honest user U always correctly decrypts an encryption of a message under O's public key.

Indistinguishability: It is computationally hard for a player that is not O and neither a delegated honest user U to distinguish the plaintext encrypted in a ciphertext with respect to any other possible plaintext of the same length.

The above properties have been formally defined along with several variations and extensions in the related literature. Here, for the sake of focusing the chapter on the core of our contribution, we will consider the above informal security requirements only.

Functional Requirements

We notice that currently no proxy-signature/decryption scheme seems to be used in practice. Our investigations about the available schemes, the above security requirements and the available cryptographic tools, raised the following issues.

1. Proxy-cryptography schemes often use number-theoretic constructions and procedures that heavily deviate from the currently available standard technology. Their introduction in real-life scenarios would require too much effort for users to move to new/different systems.
2. Several schemes do not combine gracefully security and flexibility. Most of the proposed systems enjoy some properties and can not be easily adapted to bypass one of them.
3. Several schemes suffer of practical limitations (e.g., an efficient revocation mechanism, mechanisms to filter the type of document that can be signed or decrypted, tools for monitoring Us activities).

Summing up, the work done so far on proxy cryptography mainly focused on the design of powerful cryptographic primitives, but unfortunately it substantially ignored the concrete functional requirements of a practical and easy to use system. In order to be more concrete about such requirements, we studied different contexts where proxy signatures and decryptions are needed and we collected the *functional requirements* (beyond the usual security requirements) that we believe any practical proxy signature/decryption system should enjoy.

We summarize those requirements in the following categories.

Compatibility: schemes should use standard technologies only in order to be compatible with current software applications.
Flexibility: schemes should allow users to configure and select the appropriate features dynamically.
Efficiency: schemes should be reliable and satisfy some critical performance requirements.

Motivated by the above requirements, and the problematic use of proxy cryptography for satisfying them, we investigated the possibility of designing a system where all those security and functional requirements could be satisfied simultaneously. In the next section we show the design of our system that thus gives a positive answer to the challenging question of having a viable technology for digital signature and decryption delegation.

DESIGN OF A PROXY SMART CARD SYSTEM

Following the security and functional requirements identified in the previous section, we designed a PSCS, that is, a proxy smart cards system that can be used to safely delegate signing and decrypting capabilities of a personal smart card. In our system Os can allow authorized Us to remotely access their SCs in order to sign and decrypt messages using their private keys. Notice that smart cards are nowadays a standard technology deployed to all citizens by means of electronic ID cards. Moreover, the use of smart cards guarantees a high level of robustness of the system, because of the hardness of extracting private keys (i.e., the device is ideally considered tamper proof). Here we consider SCs as standard PKCS#11(RSA Laboratories, 2009) compliant smart cards, where critical operations are protected by a PIN (i.e., personal identification number).

A central role in our PSCS is the Proxy Server P, a hardware/software network security appliance equipped with smart card readers. The purpose of P is to allow Us to use the signing/decrypting capabilities of SC without compromising any critical information (e.g., private keys, PIN). O shares his SCs by plugging them into readers connected to P, while Us remotely interacts with P to use them according to the role-based access control (in short, RBAC (Ferraiolo & Kuhn, 1992)) configured by O. These interactions are implemented by PSCS through a *Remote PKCS#11*, that is, a library that exposes to Us standard PKCS#11 functionalities while computations are carried out on SCs plugged in P. Using this approach, Us can continue to use their standard applications also on O's SCs to compute proxy signatures or to decrypt messages.

Making SCs remotely available introduces the problem of filtering remote access to the SCs. This requires the assumption that P is a *tamper proof/ evident network security appliance* designed to provide the same services of a local smart card reader through the net.

Remote Smart Cards and Operating Modes

The remote smart cards that P exposes to Us do not necessarily correspond to the smart cards plugged in card readers. Indeed, in our system Os have the possibility to configure SCs in different operating modes giving to Us a virtual view of the SCs available. In detail, Os can define the *Remote Smart Card* (RSC) as *Single* (SRSC) or *Parallel* (PRSC). In the former case, a RSC corresponds exactly to a real SC while in the latter case several SCs, offering the same objects, will appear to Us as a single RSC. Any SC linked to a PRSC can execute a request.

Notice that an O can have several certificates (and thus several public keys) associated to his identity. Therefore PRSC is achievable by using a smart card for each certificate, so that each smart card stores a different private key. Indeed, a critical feature concerning the use of smart cards is

that the private key should never leave the smart card (and thus cloning procedures should not be performed).

Another important requirement is that the associated PIN should never be memorized in permanent storage, and we will deal with this later when we will discuss our PIN management system.

From the above discussion, we have that SCs with different keys can still be used for signatures delegation, while only one of them can be used for decrypting a message. The above mechanism makes signature delegation more efficient. Indeed, a PRSC allows one to parallelize the load of requests across its SCs.

Set up of the System

All Us and Os must enroll the system by registering their public keys. O plugs his SCs into the smart card readers connected to P. Through a remote administration web interface O sets the configuration of his RSCs and defines the related access policies for the delegated Us.

An authorized U for a given RSC, receives a special PIN that does not correspond to the real SC 's PIN, but instead is a *virtual PIN* that allows him to access that RSC. We discuss in the next section the problematic issues concerning PIN management, and the technical motivation of our non-trivial solution.

Os can revoke the delegated capabilities to each U in any moment by simply updating the access control policies. Such updates have immediate effects. Indeed a revoked U will not be able to invoke any further service on P. The past signatures will remain valid and can be invalidated through the publication of lists of revoked signatures (this can be done through mechanisms similar to those used for certificate revocation lists). The system allows Os to authorize the delegation only for a given time interval and/or on specific documents (e.g., decryption only of e-mails with a given subject). Moreover, O can decide if the proxy signatures will explicitly mention the performed delegation and in the affirmative case, whether it should contain a reference to U.

Proxy Signatures/Decryptions

First of all we remark that U can use his standard applications, which are PKCS#11 compatible, to sign or decrypt documents through O's SCs. These applications must only set the client side of *Remote* PKCS#11 as PKCS#11 layer. This module interacts with P in order to accomplish remotely the operation invoked by the application. Obviously, this task is done transparently to the application. The access to P is obtained by means of a strong authorization mechanism (i.e., TLS (Network Working Group, 2008) client authentication through digital certificates). Once the secure channel has been established, according to U privileges, it enumerates to the application all the RSCs available as PKCS#11 slots. When an RSC has been selected by U to sign or to decrypt documents, the client component of *Remote* PKCS#11 will sign the request with U's private key and will send it to the server component of the library. This signature is required in order to log the request on P, that thus can not be repudiated by U. If the PIN is correct and U has the required privileges, the operation is executed by the selected SC and the result is sent back to a local component of *Remote* PKCS#11 that will forward it to the application. More specifically, the system will dispatch the requests on a PRSC to the first available SC linked to that PRSC through a Round Robin scheme that therefore will balance the load of requests. Since signature/decryption computations are expensive, this mechanism radically improves system performance linearly scaling with the number of SCs configured for the PRSC.

The system allows obviously Os access (even remotely) to all the logs, in order to let them monitor completely the activity of their delegates.

Security Model

Given the critical use of smart cards in real world scenarios, a security model is required in order to show that a proposal is resilient to attacks mounted by malicious players. First of all, we follow the standard approach that assumes that an adversary has complete control over the communication channel. This includes the capability of reading and updating all messages that cross the network, of delaying the delivering of messages, and so on.

We assume that P is a trusted player. This means that when it is active it follows the prescribed procedures and his behavior cannot be compromised. This assumption is both 1) necessary, and 2) achievable in practice. Indeed, in case P is under the control of an adversary, since SCs are plugged into its readers, and remotely accessed through its software, the adversary would obtain the PINs of the SCs and thus could also ask them non-authorized services (e.g., signatures, decryptions). Notice that while it is known how to design protocols that are secure even in presence of such adversaries, the known solutions require that honest players (in this case SCs and honest Us) perform computations (e.g., running protocols for secure multi-party computation (Goldreich, Micali, & Wigderson, 1987)) that go much beyond the simple PKCS#11 interface that is currently available for accessing to standard smart cards. The need of obtaining a proxy system on top of standard technologies therefore requires that P behaves honestly.

The above assumption about P is also achievable in practice since the hardware infrastructure of P can be placed into a restricted access area (basically implementing a tamper evident mechanism) and moreover his software could be placed in EEROM (i.e., Electrically Erasable Read-Only Memory). Therefore the software is re-writable only when a special password is known. There must be instead a read-write (RW, for short) memory that will contain for instance log files and the RBAC policy files. We do not assume special requirements about such an RW memory, indeed its content remain valid and used by P as long as there is a valid message authentication code (MAC, for short) associated to them. Indeed, this memory could be maliciously corrupted and we require that the adversary must not be able to produce data along with a valid MAC. Moreover, erasing such data or trying to restore previous data will have no (substantial) effect since P is assumed to periodically send through S/MIME (Network Working Group, 1999) encrypted and signed backups of such data to the email addresses associated to Os.

We assume that *qualified* Us are honest while other Us can be corrupted. The distinction between such two categories depends on the RBAC policies configured for each smart card. Us that can access to services provided by some SCs are assumed to be honest for those SCs and potentially dishonest for the remaining services of those SCs and for the other SCs. Notice that since RBAC policies are dynamic, the set of qualified users is dynamic as well, and thus a user can be considered honest only temporarily (therefore one can not simply assume that the owner of a SC gives the PIN to qualified Us).

All honestly produced SCs are assumed to be incorruptible. Instead an adversary can produce some non-legitimate SCs that can be plugged into the readers of P and Us.

Pin Management

A major requirement for the design of a proxy smart-card system is the transparent use of remote smart cards as they were local. Indeed, clients would like to recycle their applications that access to local smart cards in order to also access to remote smart cards connected to the proxy smart-card system. Notice that access to a smart card is possible through a log on procedure where a personal identification number (PIN) has to be provided by the user and sent to the smart card. The need of recycling standard applications implies

that one can not simply assume that qualified users are identified by the system through passwords. In some countries laws mandatory require the use of PINs for accessing smart cards, therefore this restriction must be taken into account. Moreover, after a prescribed number of PIN log on failures a Personal Unblocking Key (PUK) is needed to restore access to the smart card.

The above problem could in general be solved by the following trivial solution: the PIN of the smart card is communicated to all users that have sufficient privileges to access the smart card. This solution however does not satisfy the flexibility requirement of a proxy smart-card system since user privileges are in general dynamic and thus removing a user from the system would require the generation of new PINs that then should be distributed to all qualified users. This is clearly unacceptable in systems with many users and dynamic assignment of privileges. We have therefore developed a more sophisticated system.

Virtual PINs

The failure of the trivial solution discussed above implies that the PIN on the client's side must be different from the real PIN that allows one to succeed in the log on procedure with the smart card. It is therefore fundamental to establish a virtual PIN system where users know some virtual PINs that can be translated into real PINs by the proxy smart-card system. In this direction one can consider the following simple but conceptually wrong solution. The RBAC policy is encoded through a table where each U has associated a mapping between virtual PIN and real PIN. Therefore, upon receiving a remote log on request with a given virtual PIN, P simply accesses the table and translates the virtual PIN to a real PIN to be used for the log on procedure with the smart card. This procedure would match the flexibility requirement of the system. However, it still includes a security drawback that we want to exclude from our architecture. Indeed, the above table should be stored somewhere in the permanent memory of P and would include the real PIN. Storing a real PIN on a permanent memory is conceptually wrong and in contrast with the common philosophy about the correct use of smart cards. Taking into account these issues, our solution is more sophisticated and requires the use of the virtual PIN as a key for the symmetric encryption of the real PIN. Therefore, when a new virtual PIN is generated and associated to a real PIN, P will be updated by adding a new entry in an access control table and it will contain an encryption of the real PIN computed by means of the virtual PIN as key. Notice that another trivial solution would consist in storing an encrypted table that associates virtual PINs to real PINs, and keeping in memory the decryption key. However, for the security of an encrypted real PIN, we require that the key must be in memory only for the limited time required for the decryption. Therefore using a virtual PIN as a decryption key seems to be the most compelling solution. We think that this technique can also have other applications. When U accesses remotely to a SC, he has to send the virtual PIN that then will be used by P to decrypt the corresponding entry in the RBAC table and to perform the log on procedure on the SC. Notice that using this approach we can still have flexibility and at the same time no key or PIN is stored unencrypted in the permanent memory of P.

Implementation Details

In this section we illustrate the main implementation details of our PSCS. First of all we implemented our PSCS using a Client/Server schema, between the PKCS#11 local component (on client side) and the PKCS#11 engine (on server side). The first one exposes a standard PKCS#11 interface to U's local application, but when applications invoke its functions, the module remotely calls the corresponding engine function on P. Invocations are encapsulated in a proprietary format and sent using the HTTP protocol through a secure channel (HTTPS) with mutual authentication based on the exchange of X.509 certificates (RSA Laboratories, 2009). The server engine forwards the requests to the plugged SCs and returns to the client the results. In the standard PKCS#11 interface some functions must be coded by the library while some others must be executed natively by SC. Some computations (e.g., AES symmetric encryptions, cryptographic hashing), are executed locally by the client module while others (e.g., signatures, decryptions) by SC on P through the engine component. We stress that this mechanism is transparent to Us and requires only the availability of U's authentication capabilities in the standard PKIX (RSA Laboratories, 2009) setting.

On the server side, to speed up the prototype realization we used a standard high level application server called Twisted (Fettig, 2006) coding all P modules using the language Python while the client component has been written using the language C.

As showed in Figure 1, the overall architecture of PSCS is set up by 4 modules: *Policy Manager*, *Log Service*, *RequestHandler* and the *CardHandler*. The functions implemented by the first two modules are straightforward: the first module implements the RBAC policies management while the second module provides high-level API to log all system activities along with the certification of the log file integrity.

The module *RequestHandler* listens to U's requests. Its main task consists in parsing the requests, verifying U's credentials according to the RBAC policies and, maintaining the sessions information for each Us. *RequestHandler* maps the requests trough a dictionary with the running configuration that is the list of the available objects, updating the structure each time a new SC is inserted or removed. For each physical card reader available to the PSCS there is an instance of the module *CardHandler*, which runs as a separate process, that handles the SC. It monitors SC's status changes (insertion, removal or failure), invokes on it a request at once and returns to the

Figure 1. PSCS architecture

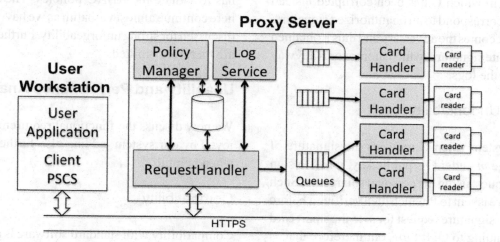

requester the corresponding result. Whenever during the processing phase an error is raised, the error message is forwarded to the client PKCS#11 module in order to let the application report the error message. The interactions between the RequestHandler and the various CardHandler is accomplished through a set of queues, one for each RSC. The RequestHandler puts on the target queue the verified requests. Each CardHandler picks up a request in front of a queue. From an SRSC queue only the CardHandler that handles the related SC can take the requests. From a PRSC queue any CardHandler that manages SCs linked to the PSCS can pick up requests. The CardHandler modules access this queue through a Round Robin schema.

ANALYSIS OF PSCS

We now show that the above system satisfies all the security and functional requirements discussed in previous sections.

Security Requirements

We start with the security requirements. We stress that in order to focus this work on the concrete use of a proxy smart card system, we will discuss informally only the security of our system.

Verifiability

In our system signatures are generated by using the private keys of Os stored in their SCs. Therefore the canonical verification procedure of the signature scheme can successfully assess the validity of the signature.

Strong Unforgeability

Assume that an adversary produces an unauthorized signature. Notice that since the signing keys are in the (ideal) tamper proof area of the smart card, such a signature must have been produced by the smart card after a successful log on procedure, which requires the use of a correct PIN. This case has negligible probability to happen since P follows the RBAC policies and therefore gives back a signature computed by SC only if U has the corresponding rights. Therefore it must be the case that the adversary impersonated U. This however can not happen as long as we U has not been corrupted and thus his smart card and computing resources have not been violated. The use of TLS and PKIX prevent further impersonations.

The case in which U has been corrupted instead does not correspond to an unauthorized signature, since U becomes the adversary and thus it obtained a legitimate signature, which moreover is anyway traced in the logs.

Strong Undeniability

In our system when U requests the signature of a message m under O's public key, it has to sign such a request using his personal smart card. Such a signature is sent to P, which then verifies it before sending a signature request for m to the smart card corresponding to O. It turns out therefore that as long as U' local computing system is not under attack, all his signature requests stored by P correspond to requests sent by U.

Strong Identifiability

The actual message that is signed by SC is a pair (m, id) where m is the message requested by U and id is the identity of U that has also been logged in P along with the signature request. Therefore each signed message uniquely and securely identifies U.

Correctness

The correctness of an decryption scheme is immediately translated in the correctness of the proxy system since SC will be able to decrypt a message upon receiving a request of P on behalf of a legitimate U.

Indistinguishability

The semantic security of the underlying decryption scheme ensures that an encrypted message does not disclose any information about the plaintext as long as the decryption key is not available to an adversary. However, the decryption key is stored in the (ideal) tamper proof area of the smart card, therefore in order to be able to decrypt a message without a legitimate authorization, an adversary

has to violate the RBAC policies. The analysis here continue almost verbatim as we have already discussed for strong unforgeability. Further details are therefore omitted.

Usability and Performance Analysis

We now discuss the functional requirements enjoyed by our system, adding also further details when helpful.

Compatibility

Compatibility with standard software is a critical requirement to obtain a usable system. Therefore P is accessed as a local device (SC reader) through a special PKCS#11 driver (library) which routes the application requests to the remote appliance through the local network connection. This is transparent to any application designed to operate through PKCS#11 functions. No change is necessary to applications when using the appliance services. This is necessary to preserve the certification process of the applications. Moreover, signatures produced by Us are verifiable with standard procedures since they are actually computed by SCs. Notice that in general, source codes of such applications are not publicly available, therefore we do not modify any component, including the user interface, (e.g., the PIN management) thus preserving laws compliances of applications. More in details, to enforce legal compliance, especially with respect to the PIN management, the appliance should exhibit the same behavior of a local SC blocking the card (service for the user) after 3 PIN log on failures.

Flexibility

Through the RBAC policies Os can allow access to their SCs in very different ways, such as, for a fixed time, only in the office time or according to the type of document to be signed/decrypted. The system allows O to configure the proxy signature

Table 1. Performance of the system

SC	Optimal Rate	Sign/Sec Rate	Sign/Sec Rate (per Card)	Efficiency
1	1,324	1,324	1,324	0,9995
2	1,398	2,796	1,400	0,9989
3	1,422	4,267	1,424	0,9989
4	1,202	4,806	1,210	0,9927
5	1,240	6,200	1,256	0,9874

service with or without adding the information about the identity of U. Moreover, adding a new SC makes automatically available the resource to all clients even if they are already connected to the appliance, and no reboot is required. On the other hand, since client applications are stateless, removing a card at run time is an issue that we considered. In any case before unmounting a card the corresponding queue is emptied out. Finally the network appliance is provided with an html-based management module, which enables the administrator to manage the available SCs, the various configurations, and to perform all the basic administrative tasks (e.g., upgrade, new module installation, power up, shutdown).

Efficiency

The system was designed to manage a high rate of requests. The main bottleneck is represented by SC operations that can be slow with respect to the request handling. In order to improve the system performance Os can use several SCs in the PRSC configuration so that several requests can be served in parallel. The system adopts a Round Robin scheme to dispatch the requests to the first available reader, providing the optimal concurrency degree with respect to the number of SC available. Then experimental analysis was conducted with the aim of verifying whether the system scales linearly in the number of smart cards. In our tests we measured the time required by the system to produce a large number of signatures in a given period of time. The tests were performed with one PRSC with an increasing number of SCs linked to it. Subsequently, to estimate the

efficiency of the system we compared the average rate of signatures per second produced by the system with the optimal one, i.e., those obtained by using the same number of smart cards in parallel with a standard application. The results of our experiments, reported in Table 1, show that the system overhead is minimal and thus confirms that it is able to scale linearly in the SCs linked to it. Indeed, the table shows in the last column that the efficiency of the system, (Optimal Rate / SignSecPerCard Rate), is very near one and it decrease slowly.

CONCLUSION

We have conducted several performance measurements with different use cases. In all of them, our system resulted sufficiently practical, flexible, efficient and secure as no other currently available proposal in the literature.

Our system is also easy to set up and we expect that our work will also give a chance for further extensions and improvements, thus generating follow up research on this topic.

ACKNOWLEDGMENT

This work has been supported in part by the joint project "SmartSEC," with Bit4ID S.r.l., financed by Italian Ministry of Economic Development in the framework P.O.N. 2000-2006 - Misura 2.1. A short version of this work appeared in Cattaneo *et al.* (2010).

REFERENCES

Bakker, A., van Steen, M., & Tanenbaum, A. S. (2001). A law-abiding peer-to-peer network for free-software distribution. *IEEE International Symposium on Network Computing and Applications* (pp. 60-67). IEEE Computer Society.

Cattaneo, C., Faruolo, P., Palazzo, V., & Visconti, I. (2010). Proxy smart card systems. *Proceedings of the 4th Workshop in Information Security Theory and Practice* (p. 213-220). Springer.

Fan, C., Zhou, S., & Li, F. (2008). Deniable proxy-anonymous signatures. *Proceedings of the 9th International Conference for Young Computer Scientists* (pp. 2131-2136). IEEE Computer Society.

Ferraiolo, D. F., & Kuhn, D. R. (1992). Role based access control. *National Computer Security Conference*, (pp. 554-563).

Fettig, A. (2006). *Twisted network programming essentials*. O'Reilly.

Foster, I. T., Kesselman, C., Tsudik, G., & Tuecke, S. (1998). A security architecture for computational grids. *ACM Conference on Computer and Communications Security*, (pp. 83-92).

Fuchsbauer, G., & Pointcheval, D. (2008). Anonymous proxy signatures. *Security and Cryptography for Networks, 6th International Conference, LNCS 5229* (p. 201-217). Springer.

Goldreich, O., Micali, S., & Wigderson, A. (1987). How to play any mental game or a completeness theorem for protocols with honest majority. *Nineteenth Annual ACM Symposium on Theory of Computing* (pp. 218-229). ACM.

Housley, R., Polk, W., Ford, W., & Solo, D. (2002). *Internet X509 public key infrastructure: Certificate and certificate revocation list (CRL) profile*. Retrieved from http://www.ietf.org/rfc/rfc3280.txt

Hu, C., & Li, D. (2007). A new type of proxy ring signature scheme with revocable anonymity. *Proceedings of the 8th ACIS International Conference on Software Engineering, Artificial Intelligence, Networking and Parallel/Distributed Computing* (pp. 866-868). IEEE Computer Society.

Hu, C., Liu, P., & Li, D. (2007). A new type of proxy ring signature scheme with revocable anonymity and no info leaked. *Multimedia Content Analysis and Mining, International Workshop, LNCS 4577*, (p. 262-266). Springer.

Kim, Y. S., & Chang, J. H. (2006). Provably secure proxy blind signature scheme. *Eigth IEEE International Symposium on Multimedia* (pp. 998-1003). IEEE Computer Society.

Laboratories, R. S. A. (2009). *PKCS #11: Cryptographic token interface standard*. Retrieved from http://www.rsa.com/rsalabs/ node.asp?id=2133

Lee, B., Kim, H., & Kim, K. (2001a). Secure mobile agent using strong non- designated proxy signature. *Information Security and Privacy, 6th Australasian Conference, LNCS 2119*, (p. 474).

Lee, B., Kim, H., & Kim, K. (2001b). Strong proxy signature and its applications. *Symposium on Cryptography and Information Security*, (pp. 603-608).

Leiwo, J., Hanle, C., Homburg, P., & Tanenbaum, A. (2000). Disallowing unauthorized state changes of distributed shared objects. *Information Security for Global Information Infrastructures, IFIP TC11 Fifteenth Annual Working Conference on Information Security, 175*, (pp. 381-390).

Liu, W., Tong, F., Luo, Y., & Zhang, F. (2007). A proxy blind signature scheme based on elliptic curve with proxy revocation. *Proceedings of the 8th ACIS International Conference on Software Engineering, Artificial Intelligence, Networking and Parallel/Distributed Computing* (pp. 99-104). IEEE Computer Society.

Lu, R., Cao, Z., & Dong, X. (2006). Efficient id-based one-time proxy signature and its application in e-cheque. *Cryptology and Network Security, LNCS, 4301,* 153–167. doi:10.1007/11935070_10

Mambo, M., & Okamoto, E. (1997). Proxy cryptosystem: Delegation of the power to decrypt ciphertexts. *IEICE Transaction Fundamentals. E (Norwalk, Conn.),* 80-A(1), 54–63.

Mambo, M., Usuda, K., & Okamoto, E. (1996). Proxy signatures for delegating signing operation. *ACM Conference on Computer and Communications Security* (p. 48-57). ACM.

Network Working Group. (1999). *S/MIME version 3 message specification.* Retrieved from http://tools.ietf.org/html/rfc2633

Network Working Group. (2008). *The transport layer security (TLS) protocol version 1.2.* Retrieved from http://tools.ietf.org/html/rfc5246

Park, H. U., & Lee, I. Y. (2001). A digital nominative proxy signature scheme for mobile communication. *Information and Communications Security, Third International Conference, LNCS 2229,* (pp. 451-455). Springer.

Qin, Y., & Wu, X. (2008). Cryptanalysis and improvement of two blind proxy signature schemes. *International Conference on Computer Science and Software Engineering* (pp. 762-765). IEEE Computer Society.

Shao, J., Cao, Z., & Lu, R. (2007). Improvement of Yang *et al.*'s threshold proxy signature scheme. *Journal of Systems and Software, 80*(2), 172–177. doi:10.1016/j.jss.2006.02.047

Yumin, Y. (2006). A threshold proxy signature scheme with nonrepudiation and anonymity. *Computer and Information Sciences, LNCS, 4263,* 1002–1010.

Zhou, X. (2008). Anonymous proxy authorization signature scheme with forward security. *International Conference on Computer Science and Software Engineering* (pp. 872-875). IEEE Computer Society.

KEY TERMS AND DEFINITIONS

Network Security Appliance: Domputing device placed in a safe are that exports to remote users various forms of access to local smart cards.

PIN: Personal Identification Number.

PIN Management: The suite of procedures that allow the network security appliance to associate virtual PINs to real PINs.

Proxy Decryption: A suite of algorithms that allow a user to securely delegate decryption privileges to another user.

Proxy Signature Scheme: A suite of algorithms that allow a user to securely delegate signature privileges to another user.

Smart Card: A PKCS#11 compliant device.

Twisted: A Python-based high-level application server.

Chapter 4
Information Security Management:
Awareness of Threats in E–Commerce

Mohammad Mahfuzur Rahman
Applied Research Centre for Business and Information Technology (ARCBIT), UK

Karim Mohammed Rezaul
Centre for Applied Internet Research (CAIR), Glyndŵr University, UK

ABSTRACT

The expansion of electronic commerce (E-commerce) has become an increasing reality due to Internet's rapid growth during the last few years. E-commerce is growing at an exceptional rate with more organizations offering their goods and services online every day. Importantly, this growth is being matched by the number of people gaining access to the Internet in a variety of ways. E-commerce offers opportunities as well as threats. Information is crucial for any organization, especially in the e-market. The lack of an effective and trusted payment system that can be used in combination with online shopping has been limiting factor in the growth of Internet sales. Consumers are hesitant to provide personal information, including credit card details, over the Internet because of high perception of risk and concerns with privacy. Establishment of Information Security System can minimize the threats and risks. Technology can play an important role in intensifying trust in the information society and securing consumer rights. E-commerce will not be successful without protecting the consumers' rights, especially in the area of information security. The research highlights the relevant theories of information security within the e-commerce sectors, including identifying and investigating the problems.

INTRODUCTION

E-Commerce plays a vital role in today's business, and that will continue growing in the future. E-Marketer predicts that worldwide e-commerce revenues are expected to total USD 2.7 trillion by 2004 (Reinsch, 2005). Information is a valuable asset in any organization particularly in the e-market. To effectively manage the threats and risks, the company should establish their Information Security System. There are several problems associated with information security, for example, phishing, slammer attack, stolen or ignorance by

DOI: 10.4018/978-1-4666-0978-5.ch004

the employee or organization itself and so on. To avoid or minimize these problems all organizations should practice the critical success factors (CSF) to implement an effective information security. In practice, most information systems need the active participation of staff throughout the organization.

E-shopping is now a popular method among all types of shopping; e-shopping covers everything from groceries to cars. As the number of e-shopper grows, the number of businesses that move into e-commerce also grows. Direct selling and buying are increasingly taking place on the Internet. One of the first to report sales in the millions of dollars directly from the Web was Dell Computer. Web research is becoming significant as the customers can book and check their Travel information through the Internet. Custom-orderable golf clubs and similar specialties are considered good prospects for the immediate future (Nelson, 2001). The expectation that e-commerce would quickly become a part of the consumer's everyday life has not been completely fulfilled in practice and one of the reasons for this failure is said to be the consumer trust, or rather the lack of it (Merrilees and Frye, 2003). So security is a very serious issue for e-commerce businesses.

Aims and Objectives

The aims and objectives of this research are:

- To discuss and analyze the relevant research about the theories of Information Security within the e-commerce sectors, including identifying and investigating the problems.
- Identifying the critical success factors (CSFs) for an effective information system and recommend the future of information security system.
- This study will also address the possible way to minimize or remove the risk of information security including why in-

formation security is important to the e-commerce.

- At the end, this study will provide a conclusion and recommendation for the future implementation of information security.

Research Questions

Research questions are:

1. What is the perception of the consumer about online shopping?
2. How information security threats effecting consumers' online shopping?
3. What are the problems faced by the consumers while shopping online?
4. Are the consumers aware of these threats?
5. What are the initiatives need to be taken to reduce the information security risks?

Limitations

The following limitations are placed on the proposed study:

1. The survey methods assume that the respondent will make an honest effort to understand and answer the questions truthfully.
2. One of the limitations of the study is relatively small amount of data. The number of samples used for the study is relatively small.
3. This survey might not represent all sectors of e-commerce.

LITERATURE REVIEW

E-Commerce

Conducting business on the Internet is known as E-Commerce, which includes buying and selling as well as customer service and dealing with other business organizations. It also includes purchasing goods and services online; as well as businesses communication with other businesses through the Internet. From the beginning of commerce, business has utilized technology. By the 1970s companies began to increasingly incorporate advanced information technology in their business models. From the 1980s onwards, advanced technology penetrated deep into the heart of business. These changes have introduced e-commerce (Papazoglou, 2003).

E-commerce is emerging at an incredible pace and indicating that it will continue to grow and many organizations will find themselves in a condition that either they have to go online or go out of business. With e-commerce, both small and large organization, have an equal opportunity to achieve success, because they have access to the same type of resources, like global and easy-to-use set of technologies and technology standards, no matter what type of computer system or platform the organizations are using (Henari and Mahboob, 2008). In online transactions, customers' reveal considerably more personal and financial information than in offline transactions (Miyazaki, 2001).

In the last few decades peoples were not much information sensitive and used to manage information negligently manually. As we are living in information age it is vital to protect information by giving highest priority.

Information Security

Information security is defined by the US National Security Telecommunications and Information Security Committee as the 'protection of information and the systems and hardware that use, store, and transmit that information' (Whitman and Mattord, 2003).

Martin (1995) reported that, without an uninterrupted flow for this vital resource, society would quickly run into difficulties, with business and industry, education, leisure, travel and communications, national and international affairs- all are vulnerable to disruption. In more advanced societies, this vulnerability is exalted by an in-creasing dependence on the enabling powers of information and communications technologies. The significance of information in the modern world can be measured by the three terms: The information society, the information economy and the information age.

One of the main issues of information security is lack of sufficient systems' security, reliability, standards, and communication protocols. Moreover, the software development tools are still evolving and changing rapidly (Schneider, 2004). Hackers can hack the system not only for the inadequate security system but also for the basic fundamental mistake made by the programmer while designing the system (Ben-Itzhak, 2004). "As developers strengthen security products in response, the attacks become more sophisticated, creating an ever-escalating and quickening cycle of attack and defense" (Bagchi and Udo, 2003).

Gauzente and Ranchhod (2001) depicted that customer service to the Internet also poses great challenges, including the emergence of serious privacy concerns and resulting negative consumer responses. This kind of threat to consumer privacy posed by the Internet requires urgent attention as it may undermine a firm's marketing performance in the long run.

Information is a precious asset in any organization whether it is printed or written on paper, stored electronically or by any means. To manage the threats and risks to any organization's information effectively the company needs to establish an Information Security Management System (ISMS).

Security Threats to E-Commerce

The rapid growth of Internet and number of online consumers has resulted in increased fears regarding the guarantees of privacy when using e-commerce (Desai, 2003). There are risks in transferring money electronically such as altering customers' account details. In Internet, the data can be accessed without physical access or presence. This facility not only assists the user but also gives advantage to the criminal (McCusker, 2006). Information infrastructures connected with public network are vulnerable to various attacks from both inside and outside the organization (Sharma, 2002 and Goan, 1999). The risk involved in e-commerce could be the compromise of customer confidentiality. Security issues are one of the biggest barriers to Internet sales growth (Worzala, *et al.*, 2001). Young as cited by Hopwood (2000) reported, "Competitors are the single greatest threat in computer crime". In addition to competitors, employee theft through e-commerce is an important issue. Disgruntled employees may wish to steal assets or sabotage the company as a means of revenge. Other employees may steal to satisfy a perceived need for cash (Hopwood, 2000). Purchasing on the Internet holds risks such as retailer might misuse customers' personal information (Grabner-Krauter and Kaluscha, 2003). According to McGuire (2000), there are nine basic threats to information security which are as follows:

1.   Data destruction,
2.   Interference,
3.   Modification/replacement,
4.   Misrepresentation/false use of data,
5.   Repudiation,
6.   Inadvertent misuse,
7.   Unauthorized altering/downloading,
8.   Unauthorized transaction, and
9.   Unauthorized disclosure.

Although companies are providing guarantees, still there exist two type of risk in the on-line: system-dependent risk where there is no control over the transmission of data and transaction-specific risk where data might be passed to the third parties or theft by employees (Hirshleifer, 1979). According to Van Slyke and Belanger (2003), "the level of trust that individuals and organizations are willing to place on online purchasing is one of the most important barriers to the use of the

Internet for conducting business today". However, Hagel and Armstrong reported, as cited by Durkan, *et al.* (2003), "the absence of personal contact to provide some sort of tangible measure of authenticity and reassurance, combined with the unfamiliarity of the online environment, can lead to consumer anxiety". Raja (2008) reported that transactions in electronic commerce can occur without any prior human contact or established interpersonal relationships and this lack of inter-personal trust creates a circumstance for a security threat. Fleischer (2007), Google's Privacy Chief, verifies that "Three quarters of the countries in the world have no privacy regimes at all". Some companies collect information about customers' through Internet without their consent (Desai, *et al.*, 2003).

Management of most organizations is reluctant to take any cohesive policies before the occurrence of an external threat (Smith, 1994). Web Merchants do not implement through privacy policies- often do not comply with minimum legal requirement (Gaauzente, 2004).

The internal security threat covers not only the misuse of confidential information or accidental use of information outside the organization by some employees, it also includes where and how the users are accessing systems and data which relates IT helpdesk utilization, password usages and security responsibility. The different features and use of e-commerce add security threats in it because of its mobile nature (Ghosh, 2001).

Although we are living in an information age but still some of the leading organization can not protect their customer's important personal information. It might be for the lack of security or just the ignorance. Symantec (2006) noted that in the latter half of 2005, 80% of the top 50 reported threats could be used for data theft. May be many organizations do not understand the value of the information. In the following paragraphs some of these will be discussed as examples.

Ulster Bank has lost at least 10 laptops through theft. The bank, which provides financial services to 1.8 million consumers and business customers in the UK and Ireland, between 8 to10 laptops had been stolen from one of its offices in Dublin containing thousands people's personal information (King, 2008).

The UK Financial Services Authority (FSA) said that it investigated 56 cases of data loss by financial services firms in 2007 and In December, it fined Norwich Union Life £1.26 million for identity theft. This accounted for just under a third of all financial crime cases dealt with by the team. In a study, Pennanen et al. (2007) found, "some informants suspected that their credit card number was accessible to some hostile third party when a transaction between the consumer and the e-service provider occurred".

In fact, data security was the most common type of financial crime incident dealt with during the year (FSA report, 2008) and it is highly likely that many data loss incidents go unreported". FSA said that these cases have revealed some serious weaknesses in firms' data security (Symantec, 2005).

A computer printout with 13,000 mortgage customer's account details was stolen from a member of staff in 2007 from the Halifax bank. Earlier of the last year, they also dumped customer account details in outside the bins (Shifrin, 2007).

One of the most popular and successful techniques employed by cyber thieves to steal a person's identity entails the use of deceptive e-mail phishing attacks (Emigh, as cited by Butler, 2007). According to the latest edition of the Symantec Internet Security Threat Report (2008), the number of blocked phishing attempts against targets in the financial services sector rose from a weekly average of 11.0 million attacks in January 2005 to a weekly average of 15.3 million in June 2005. Gartner, as cited by Butler (2007), a reputable research organization, reported that 10 million USA adults were victims of identity theft in 2005, causing almost $15 billion in losses.

Poor business practices create administrative threats in the form of password sniffing, data modification, spoofing, and repudiation (Ratnasingam,

2007). As a result most of the company is loosing trust to their customer and consequently earning bad will for their company. To avoid or minimize these problems all organizations should practice an effective information security management system within the organization.

Phishing is an activity, attempt by a third party to solicit confidential information from an individual, group, or organization often for the financial gain. Therefore, mainly financial services are mostly affected by this.

Critical Success Factors

According to Kesh, et al. (2002), one of the major critical success factors of e-commerce is security; without customers' confidence e-commerce will not work. Weakness in a single component can endanger security. E-marketplace security can be implemented by effective IT solutions, standard operating procedures and regulations (Ratnasingam, 2007).

To measure the safeguard of Internet privacy consumers look for both organizational and public policies. They consider these policies as a yardstick for reliability. Organizations that pay close attention to the regulatory aspects of web-based technologies would enjoy substantial marketing benefits in the long run. Consumers are more likely to turn to privacy-enhancing technologies to safeguard their online privacy (Wirtz, et al., 2007). Different technological security measures are not enough, company policies and employees' awareness is also needed to reduce security threats (Udo, 2001).

A Privacy Policy statement on web sites will also make consumers feel more comfortable about giving information online (Karakaya, 2001). Alder et al. (2006) and Kierkegaard (2005) emphasized the need of control that an employer should have over an employees' electronic communications and there are valid concerns regarding the impact of Internet monitoring on employees attitudes and behaviours.

Researchers have examined the requirements of information security which are: access control, privacy/confidentiality, authentication, non-repudiation, and availability, e.g., Daitel, et al., as cited by Kesh, et al. (2002). However, McGuire (2000) suggested that implementing the following sets of controls could help to prevent security threats:

1.   User ID/ Authentication controls,
2.   Authorization controls,
3.   Integrity Controls,
4.   Confidentiality controls,
5.   Accountability controls, and
6.   Availability controls.

Security mechanisms need to be updated regularly to fight against hackers (Bort, 2000). However, improvement of encryption mechanism and regular update of security system will prevent hackers from stealing information (Raja, 2008). Higher perceptions of privacy and security ensure the safeguards of personal information. Web site competency is also an important factor: a good reputation is regarded as a sign of a good and candid company with superior capabilities; willingness to customize is considered as an indication of company's benevolence and consideration of consumers (Chen and Barnes, 2007). And they also added, "higher degrees of online initial trust and familiarity with online purchasing stimulate higher degrees of consumers' purchase intentions; familiarity with online purchasing reduces consumers' perceived risks, brings positive attitudes in purchase intentions, and eases purchase decisions".

Karakaya and Charlton (2001) and Sanders, as cited by Desai et al. (2003), proposed for educating consumers by ad campaign about the benefits of information sharing and giving them tips about how to protect their privacy. Research conducted by Butler (2007), indicates that the education of online consumers, as well as the implementation and proper application of anti-phishing measures, can reduce the risk of consumers falling victim to phishing attacks. Gray et al. (1998) stated that "the current absence of global legislation and policies regarding e-commerce compounds consumers' dubious opinion of transacting on-line". However, data protection acts of the US are not as strong as the EU standard. Nowadays United States is trying to comply with EU standard.

Employees need to be trained to deal with the threats against information security. Risk managers must have sufficient knowledge of technology related risk (O'Rourke, 2003). Security technologies are not enough to control threats as studies showed that information security is socio-technological problem which requires through understanding the attitude and behavior towards using these security (Goodhue and Straub, 1991; Straub and Welke, 1998; Dhillon and Backhouse, 2001).

Companies need to combine security measures and regulatory directives to protect information (Tran, 2002). Internet specific regulation would be a useful development in the fight against financial fraud in cyberspace because government does not have enough regulation that specifically meets the needs of cyberspace (Fletcher, 2007). The lack of clear legal rules in international e-commerce have raised legitimate concerns about the adequacy of security and consumer protection measures. For instance, a recent study reflects a number of key concerns, including the need for effective redress mechanisms, confusion about self-regulatory controls, and lack of understanding of security technologies on the Internet. This makes it difficult for the consumer to evaluate the trustworthiness of Internet resources and services (Wilikens, 2001). International cooperation is a key factor of online protection of privacy and personal information (Aljifri et al., 2003). McCrohan (2003) said, "The involvement of senior managers in risk awareness and risk assessment initiatives, along with increased cooperation with the public sector, is required to achieve a realistic level of security". Hu and Dinev (2005) also emphasized on creating employee awareness.

METHODOLOGY

In order to investigate the research problem an appropriate methodological foundation is essential. Hence we characterize the research philosophy, methods, strategy and other relevant tactics, by which the research questions have been formulated, although researchers need to make a clear distinction between strategy and tactics. This section will describe the whole methodological works, aims and data collection methods, which have been done in order to achieve findings of this work.

Planning and Conducting Survey

This research is based on quantitative method. Two types of quantitative method have been studied here: experiments and survey. In order to collect the primary data, a questionnaire has been designed for survey. A letter has also been designed with explaining research topics and was sent by mail to the relevant informants. However, this strategy did not work well. In many cases, key researchers in this field did not receive the email on time, even some cases they were not available on that time and also some of the addresses collected were not up to date.

We had also planned for physical survey by short telephone interview which did work well. The authors had closed questions model and separated the numeric data to compare and contrast properly. The MS packages, namely Access and Excel, have been used for further data analysis.

Validity and Reliability

Validity is concerned with whether the information is really appropriate or not. Sometimes the interviewees may say what their executives or Board wanted them to follow. During collecting the primary data the researchers had arranged survey in order to take into account the issues of reliability. To reduce the rejection rate of survey, the authors took help from business experts, lecturers, other researchers and fellow colleagues. The authors also promised that they were not going to disclose any personal information without their (i.e. interviewees and others) permission.

Data Collection

In this research the authors collected both primary and secondary data.

Primary Data Collection

For collecting primary data the authors have designed a questionnaire for survey. Data for survey had been collected from a sizeable population by physical talking and group interview. For collecting the contemporary data, the authors had used closed questions' models.

The authors also arranged a survey of 624 people from various stakeholder groups such as students, service people and businessmen. For the ease of communication, the location chosen for the survey was Greater London as it was quite convenient to get all those people involved with online shopping.

Secondary Data Collection

According to experts, secondary data has significant advantages, because it has already been collected and analyzed, does not necessarily requires access to people who have supplied it, has historical value, and is useful for making assumptions and evaluating primary data (Thietart *et al.* 2001). Hence the purpose of using secondary data is to go deep in the research, analyze and to facilitate the primary data. The secondary data has been collected from the following sources:

- Internet Sites
- Books from different Libraries.
- Newspaper & magazine articles, news, reports

- Annual reports
- Conference & seminar report.
- National and international institutions such as university research report, Bank economic reviews.
- Government Statistics like Import/ export; production and sales statistics were collected from the governmental organizations.

Pilot Test

A pilot test is a preliminary test or study of the program or evaluation activities to try out procedures or systems in order to make any changes or adjustments. A pilot test was therefore used to identify clarity, difficulty levels, timing, and feasibility and to refine questionnaires in order to obtain some assessments of its validity and reliability. More than five respondents including teachers, students and people related with e-commerce were asked to make comments on the questionnaire and its design. After the criticism of different individuals, the authors reshape and redesign the questionnaire, which was finally used during interview and survey.

Ethical Consideration

Ethical concerns will emerge, as the researchers need to plan for research, seek access to organizations, individuals, to collect and analyse data for the project. In the context of research, ethics refers to the appropriateness of researcher's behaviour in relation to the rights of those who become the subject of his/her work, or are affected by it.

The data collection stage is associated with a range of ethical issues. The authors had to consider ethical issues throughout the period of research and to remain sensitive to the impact of this work on those whom they approached to help, those who co-operated, and those affected by the research work.

Respondents always had the option of refusing answering any question if they felt uncomfortable revealing certain information, or they may not be able to answer. However, in that case the authors had motivated interviewee to give an average answer.

During this research, communications occurred to a different level of people, organizations, institutions and even locations. Here the authors have carefully reviewed the ethical considerations such as privacy, dignity, confidentiality and self-determination as these are very important when conducting the research. Moreover, the following reasons are also important:

- Respect and protect interviewee's privacy.
- Motivate and encourage the honesty of responses from interviewee. It will also improve the standard of data provided by the respondents.
- Encouragement of participation in the research study in order to increase the number of samples.

The authors had also followed all the rules and regulations before using software, primary and secondary data collection as well as conducting interview and survey.

Hypothesis

This research investigates the following hypotheses:

Hypothesis 1: Consumers prefer online shopping provided that their personal information will be totally secured.

Hypothesis 2: Internal threats are the major factor behind Information security risk.

Hypothesis 3: Lack of awareness leads to information security risk.

Hypothesis 4: Regulation and Technology can help information security risk.

RESULTS AND ANALYSIS

This section presents the results of the questionnaire survey. Questionnaires were distributed

Figure 1. Age category of respondents

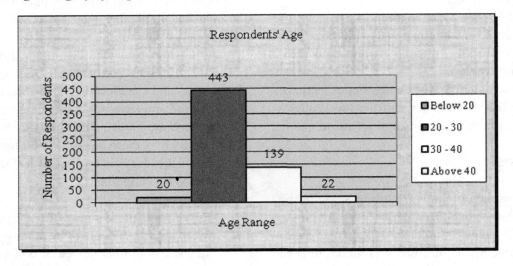

among the customer regardless they shop online or not. 624 questionnaires were filled up completely by the respondents. Each survey question is systematically analyzed with the percentage of response. The formulated hypotheses are tested in this section on the basis of the questionnaire survey.

Demographics

Respondents' Age

In Figure 1, 443 out of 624 respondents, that is 71% of the respondents belongs to age group of 20 to 30, 22% (139 out of 624) of the respondents belongs to age group between 30 to 40, 4% (22) respondents were above 40 and the rest 3% (20) were aged below 20.

Respondents' Occupation

In terms of occupation, 89% respondents (555 out of 624) were students, 6% (39) were in service and 5% (30) were in business (see Figure 2). Most of the respondents were students because of emphasising focus group.

General Information

Internet Availability

Figure 3 shows the availability of Internet at home. It shows most of the respondents (that is 89%) have Internet access at home and the rest 11% do not have Internet access at home.

It represents that most of the respondents can avoid transaction from public place. It might help them secure their personal information.

Online Shopping

Figure 4 intends to get the consumers opinion on purchasing online. It shows that 67% of the respondents shop online and 33% of the respondents do not shop online. The statistics represent the popularity of online shopping.

Shopping Preference

Figure 5 shows the shopping preference of the respondents. 49% of the respondents shop both online and direct shopping. 43% like going to shop directly and 8% prefer online shopping. This statistics shows that people are willing to shop online but due to concern of security and privacy they (43%) do not shop online.

Figure 2. Occupation of respondents

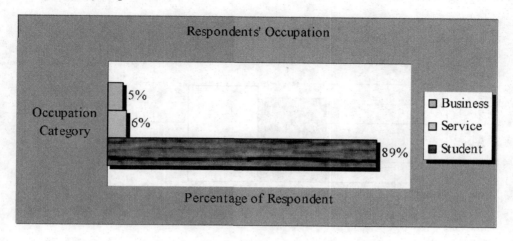

Figure 3. Internet availability at home

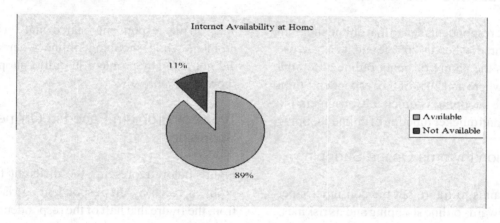

Figure 4. Online shopping

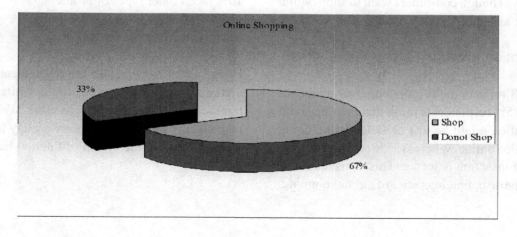

Figure 5. Shopping preference

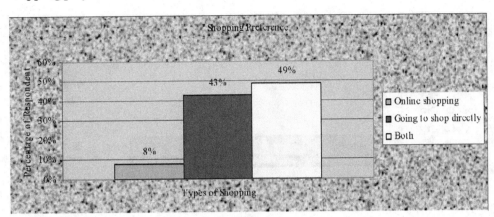

Consumers' Perception

Opinion about Online Shopping

29% of the respondents stated that online shopping is not secured, whereas 26% found it easy to use, 25% likes the nature of being online accessible from anywhere and 20% of the respondents think that online shopping is quicker. Consumers like the easier and quicker function of online shopping.

Perception towards Online Shopping

Figure 7 aims to figure out the consumer's perception towards online shopping and its riskiness. Most of the respondents (69%) found the online shopping risky and 31% think online shopping is not risky. Though consumers want to shop online they are afraid of its risky nature.

Perception towards Online Transaction

Figure 8 reflects the respondents fear about security. 75% respondents think that their personal information might be lost or stolen while doing transaction online. Whereas 25% consider that the online transaction is secure. This statistics signifies as the discouraging factor of online shopping.

Security Problem

Problem Faced in Online Shopping

30% of the respondents stated that they faced problem while shopping online whereas 70% did not face any problem in online shopping as shown in Figure 9.

Types of Problem Faced in Online Shopping

Figure below represents the different types of problem faced by the respondents. It is evident from the figure that half of the respondents (54%) faced identity theft problem, 19% were victim of hacking, 17% faced the Phishing problem and 10% faced other types of problem.

Victim of Internet Fraud

Figure 11 shows whether the respondents were victimized by any Internet fraud while doing transaction online. Result shows that 71% of the respondents were not victimized by any Internet fraud. 29% were the victim of Internet fraud.

Awareness

Online Transaction from Public Place

Figure 12 demonstrates that 57% respondents never make any transaction from any public place, 20% very rarely do the transaction, 18% sometimes and 5% always do the transaction from public place. It shows that respondents are aware of the fact that their personal information can be easily lost or stolen from public network because it is easy to access any public network.

Perception towards Spam Mail

More than half of the respondents (58%) consider spam mail as harmful, 12% think that it is not harmful and 30% were not sure about the harmfulness of spam mail. It is predictable from this statistics that nearly half (42%) of the respondents are not aware of this threat.

Use of Anti-Spam Software

52% of the respondents use anti-spam software whereas 48% do not use any anti-spam software. Use of anti-spam software helps reduce the chances being hacked. Here nearly half (48%) of the respondents do not use any anti-spam software. Results reveal that more than half of the respondents are vulnerable by getting hacked.

Phishing Awareness

More than half of the respondents (53%) were not aware of phishing whereas 47% know about phishing. So they are open to Phishing attack.

Use of Phishing Filter

Only 29% of the respondents use Phishing filter but 71% do not use the Phishing filter. This result shows that most of the respondents are open to a victim of data theft.

Hacking Awareness

Majority of the respondents (that is 79%) were aware of hacking, whereas only 21% were not aware of hacking.

Awareness of Identity Theft

Figure 18 shows that 73% of the respondents are aware of the identity theft but 27% do not have any idea in this regard.

Use of Antivirus Software

Majority of the respondents are aware of the virus attack which is reflecting by the Figure 19. It appears that 85% respondents use antivirus software and only 15% do not use that.

Security Threats

Most Vulnerable Threat to Data Theft

Respondents blame the organization for data theft. Employees are the most vulnerable to information security. 65% of the respondents think that internal threat is the most vulnerable to data theft and 35% consider external threats.

Customer Awareness towards Security Threat

Most of the respondents are not aware of different threats towards information security. Only 36% are aware of the threats but 64% are not aware of this.

Minimizing Security Threats

Customer Opinion about Minimizing Information Security Risk

Most of the respondents (75%) think that developing both employee and customer awareness can reduce information security risk. 19% suggested to develop customer awareness program whereas only 6% suggested to develop employee awareness program to minimize information security risk.

Use of Education and Training to Minimize Information Security Risk

Education and training are crucial tools to minimize information security risk. 90% of the respondents agreed to that whereas only 10% differ.

Effective Tools to Minimize Information Security Risk

Security policy by both government and the organization can help protect information. Advanced technology is also needed to establish security. 69% respondents state that both security policy and advanced technology are needed to minimize information security risk. 16% voted for only security policy and 15% suggested for advanced technology.

Evaluation of Hypotheses

Hypothesis 1: Consumers prefer online shopping provided that their personal information will be totally secured.

From the analyses, it is found that 67% of the respondents shop online while 33% does not shop online (Figure 4). 49% of the respondents prefer both online and direct shopping, while 43% prefer direct shopping and 8% prefer shopping online (Figure 5). 29% of the respondents found online shopping as not secured. 26% found online shopping easy, 25% likes online shopping and 20% found it quite convenient as it is quicker (Figure 6). But 69% of the respondents consider it as risky (Figure 7), 75% of the respondents had the experience of personal information stolen or theft (Figure 8). 29% of the respondents were victimized by Internet fraud (Figure 11).

So from the above analysis it is evident that the hypothesis 1 is valid.

Hypothesis 2: Internal threats are the major factor behind Information security risk.

Figure 6. Opinion about online shopping

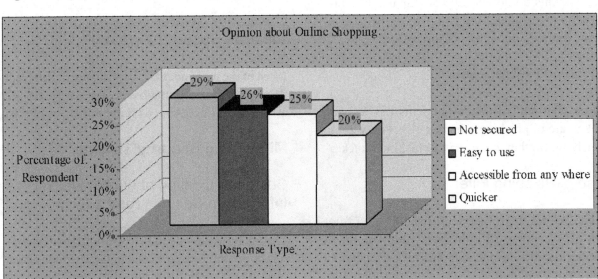

Figure 7. Perception towards online shopping

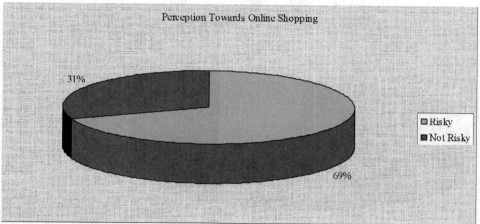

Figure 20 reflects the consumers' opinion about the risk factor and shows that 65% of the respondents state that internal threat is the most vulnerable towards information security and 35% voted for external threats which prove the hypothesis "Internal threats are the major factor behind Information security risk".

Hypothesis 3: Lack of awareness lead to information security risk.

Among the respondents, 43% (Figure 12) do transaction from public place, 30% (Figure 13) of them do not have any idea about spam mail and 52% (Figure 4.14) do not use any anti-spam software. Half of the respondents (53% in Figure 15) were not aware of Phishing and 71% (Figure 16) do not use the Phishing filter. Only 21% (Figure 17) were not aware of hacking and 27% (Figure 18) are not aware of identity theft. 15% (Figure 19) of the respondents do not use any antivirus software. Therefore, it can be concluded that a large portion of the respondents are not aware of

Figure 8. Perception towards online transaction (Information lost/stolen)

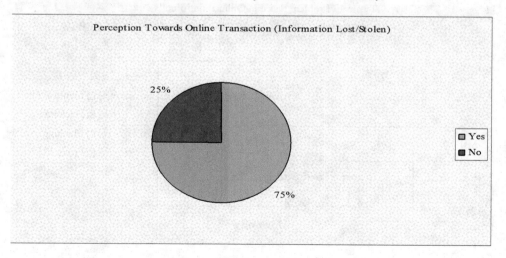

Figure 9. Problem faced in online shopping

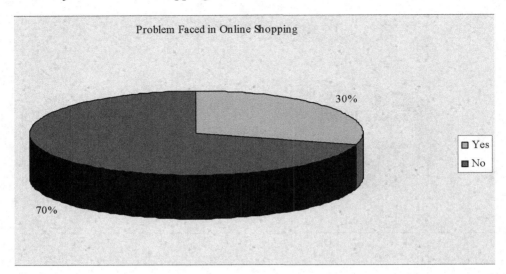

these security threats. As a result 29% (Figure 11) of the respondents were victimized by Internet fraud and 30% (Figure 9) faced problem while shopping online. Among them 17% faced identity theft problem, 19% were hacked, 10% faced Phishing and 54% faced other types of problem. So it justifies the hypothesis "Lack of awareness lead to information security risk".

Hypothesis 4: Regulation and Technology can help reduce information security risk.

Security policy by both government and the organization can help protect information. Advanced technology is also needed to establish security. 69% respondents consider that both security policy and advanced technology are needed

Figure 10. Types of problem faced in online shopping

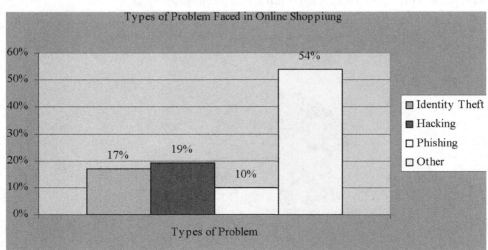

Figure 11. Victim of Internet fraud

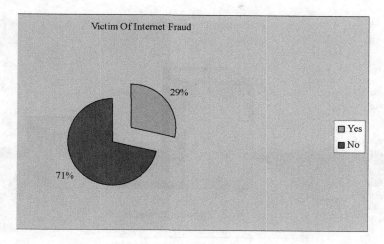

to minimize information security risk. Also only 16% voted for security policy and 15% suggested for advanced technology (Figure 24). Therefore, above hypothesis can be explicitly justified.

CONCLUSION AND RECOMMENDATIONS

Conclusion

The major purpose of this study was to examine consumers' perception on information security risk in relation to online shopping. The findings of the study confirm that the consumers' privacy and security concerns are strongly associated with consumers' purchase intention. The results suggest that Internet retailer should make efforts to better security mechanism in online shopping.

Nowadays information security is no longer a domestic issue. In this age of electronic commerce, information security certainly affects every business. For this reason, building a secured system is a vital need as the business customers demand an acceptable level of information security. Information security management standards can certainly

Figure 12. Online transaction from public place

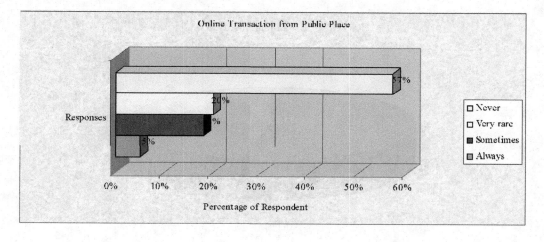

Figure 13. Perception towards spam mail

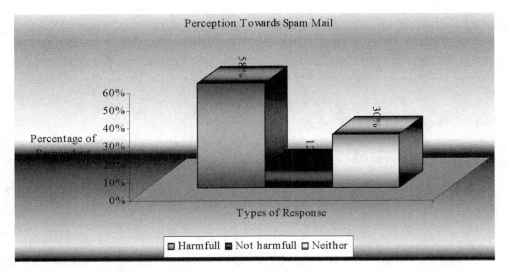

Figure 14. Use of anti-spam software

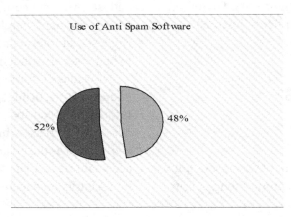

Figure 15. Phishing awareness

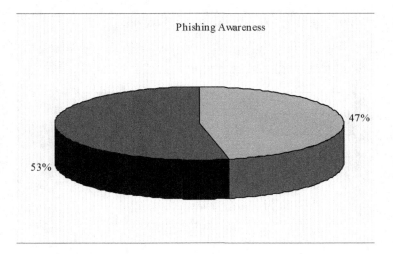

Figure 16. Use of Phishing filter

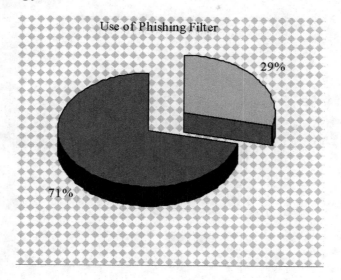

Figure 17. Hacking awareness

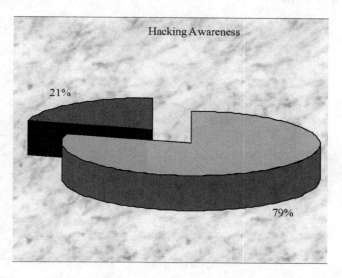

play a significant role in this regard. Information security is a core concern for all companies mainly in financial services. As the vague information security system can cause huge financial losses, this study analyzes the financial impact of losing information within the different organizations. Regular reviews of implemented information security arrangements are an essential feature of an organization's risk management program. The scope and frequency of security reviews should be based upon the requirement of a continuous assessment on security system by which ongoing maintenance of the entire security management system can be done effectively. However, technology can play an important role in increasing trust in the information security system and con-

Figure 18. Awareness of identity theft

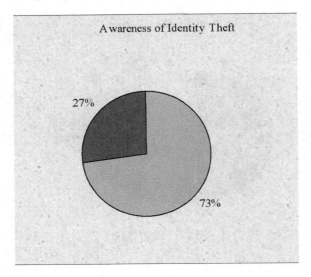

Figure 19. Use of antivirus software

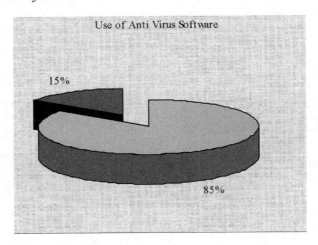

servation of consumer rights. So the organization should protect their clients' personal Information to make the e-commerce successful.

From the analysis part of the report it is obvious that the online shopping has huge market potential; 67% of respondents prefer shopping online. Among them 49% prefer both online and direct shopping. At the same time 69% of the respondents consider online shopping as risky and 29% of the respondents found it insecure. 75% of the respondents had the experience of losing personal information. 29% of the respondents were victimized of Internet fraud. But against all odds, 26% found it easier, 25% likes it and 20% found it quicker. Since customers found the online shopping easier and quicker solution, we can conclude that consumers prefer online shopping provided that their personal information will be totally secured. At the same time it can be predicted that usage of online shopping will also increase if customers consider it safe and secured.

Figure 20. Most vulnerable to data theft

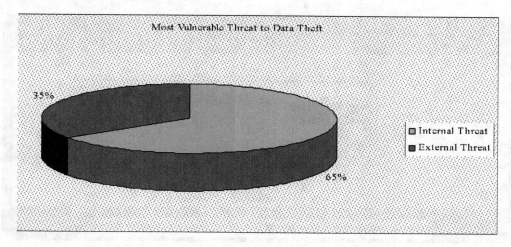

Figure 21. Customer awareness toward security threats

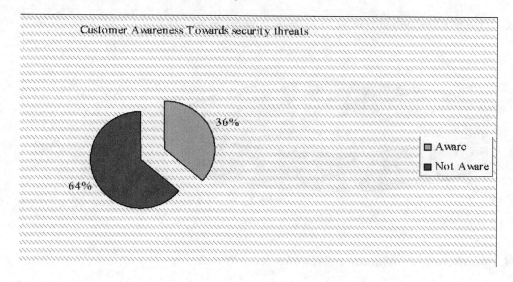

In today's competitive world, safe online shopping system will give customers comfort and convenience. If the marketers can bring the confidence back among them with regard to information safety issue, online shopping will become more popular although it is a big challenge for the marketers. A numerous customer education and awareness programs need to take up by them to ensure safety and protection of customer's personal information.

Future Recommendations

To minimize all types of threats (such as identity theft, hacking threat, phishing etc.), awareness-raising initiatives (like emails, pamphlets, leaflets, advertisements on the web pages and mouse pads, formal presentations) need to be taken. However, information security awareness training is also very important.

Security education and training for the employees can be arranged to increase security awareness

Figure 22. Customer opinion about minimizing security risk

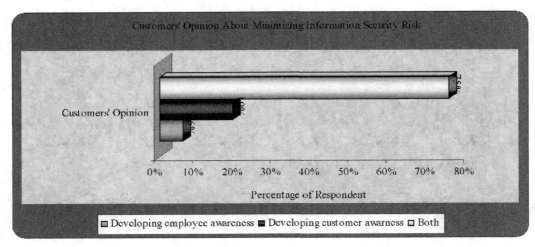

Figure 23. Use of education and training to minimize security risk

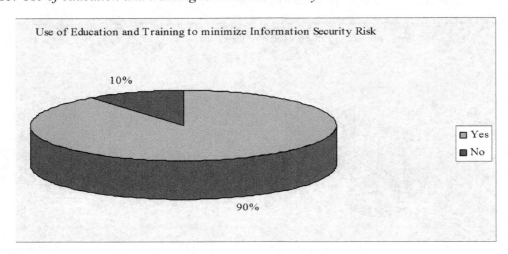

Figure 24. Effective tool to minimize information security risk

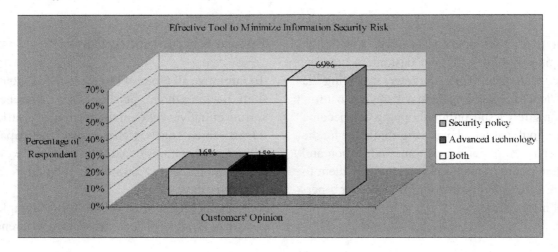

because appropriate training and education reduce human errors and ensure that users are aware of information security threats and concerns.

An effective information security system can be built which includes the biometrics, encryption, digital signature, intrusion detection system, virus control and compliance with data protection legislation and policy. Organizations need to make suitable policy by targeting not only their own view but also giving priority to the customers' choice to get customer's trust.

REFERENCES

Alder, G. S., Noel, T. W., & Ambrose, M. L. (2006). Clarifying the effects of Internet monitoring on job attitudes: The mediating role of employee trust. *Information & Management*, *43*(7), 894–903. doi:10.1016/j.im.2006.08.008

Aljifri, H. A., Pons, A., & Collins, D. (2003). Global e-commerce: A framework for understanding and overcoming the trust barrier. *Information Management & Computer Security*, *11*(3), 130–138. doi:10.1108/09685220310480417

Bagchi, K., & Udo, G. (2003). An analysis of the growth of computer and internet security breaches. *Communications of the Association for Information Systems*, *12*, 684–700.

Bort, J. (2000). The best-kept security secrets. *New World (New Orleans, La.)*, *17*(46), 109–114.

Butler, R. (2007). A framework of anti-phishing measures aimed at protecting the online consumer's identity. *The Electronic Library*, *25*(5), 517–533. doi:10.1108/02640470710829514

Chen, Y. H., & Barnes, S. (2007). Initial trust and online buyer behaviour. *Industrial Management & Data Systems*, *107*(1), 21–36. doi:10.1108/02635570710719034

Desai, M. S., Richards, T. C., & Desai, K. J. (2003). E-commerce policies and customer privacy. *Information Management & Computer Security*, *11*(1), 19–27. doi:10.1108/09685220310463696

Dhillon, G., & Backhouse, J. (2001). Current direction in IS security research: Towards socio-organizational perspectives. *Information Systems Journal*, *11*, 127–153. doi:10.1046/j.1365-2575.2001.00099.x

Durkan, P., Durkin, M., & Gillen, J. (2003). Exploring efforts to engender online trust. *International Journal of Entrepreneurial Behavior & Research*, *9*(3), 93–110. doi:10.1108/13552550310476184

Fleischer, P. (2007). *Google privacy chief calls for international data protection standards*. Retrieved February 8, 2009, from www.bespaci□c.com/mt/archives/015985.html#015985

Fletcher, N. (2007). Challenges for regulating financial fraud in cyberspace. *Journal of Financial Crime*, *14*(2), 190–207. doi:10.1108/13590790710742672

FSA report. (April 2008). Retrieved February 17, 2009, from http://www.fsa.gov.uk/pubs/other/data_security.pdf

Gauzente, C. (2004). Web merchants' privacy and security statements: how reassuring are they for consumers? A two sided approach. *Journal of Electronics Commerce Research*, *5*(3), 181–198.

Gauzente, C., & Ranchhod, A. (2001). Ethical marketing for competitive advantage on the Internet. *Academy of Marketing Science Review*, *1*(10).

Ghosh, K. A., & Swaminath, T. M. (2001). Software security and privacy risks in mobile e-commerce. *Communications of the ACM*, *44*(2), 51–57. doi:10.1145/359205.359227

Goan, T. (1999). A cop on the beat: Collecting and appraising intrusive evidence. *Communications of the ACM*, *42*(7), 46–52. doi:10.1145/306549.306569

Goodhue, D. L., & Straub, D. W. (1991). Security concerns of system users: A study of perceptions of the adequacy of security. *Information & Management, 20*, 13–27. doi:10.1016/0378-7206(91)90024-V

Grabner-Krauter, S., & Kaluscha, E. (2003). Empirical research in online trust: A review and critical assessment. *International Journal of Human-Computer Studies, 58*(6), 783–812. doi:10.1016/S1071-5819(03)00043-0

Gray, G. L., Debreceny, R., & Koreto, R. J. (2000). The electronic frontier. *Journal of Accountancy, 185*(5), 32–38.

Henari, T. F., & Mahboob, R. (2008). E-commerce in Bahrain: The non-technical limitations. *Education, Business and Society: Contemporary Middle Eastern Issues, 1*(3), 213–220. doi:10.1108/17537980810909832

Hirshleifer, J., & Riley, J. G. (1979). The analytics of uncertainty and information: An expository survey. *Journal of Economic Literature, 17*, 1375–1421.

Hopwood, W. S., Sinason, D., & Tucker, R. (2000). Security in a web-based environment. *Managerial Finance, 26*(11), 42–54. doi:10.1108/03074350010766981

Hu, Q., & Dinev, T. (2005). Is spyware an internet nuisance or public menace? *Communications of the ACM, 48*(8), 61–66. doi:10.1145/1076211.1076241

Karakaya, F., & Charlton, E. T. (2001). Electronic commerce: Current and future practices. *Managerial Finance, 27*(7), 42–53. doi:10.1108/03074350110767286

Kesh, S., Ramanujan, S., & Nerur, S. (2002). A framework for analyzing e-commerce security. *Information Management & Computer Security, 10*(4), 149–158. doi:10.1108/09685220210436930

Kierkegaard, S. (2005). Privacy in electronic communication- Watch your e-mail: Your boss is snooping. *Computer Law & Security Report, 21*(3), 226–236. doi:10.1016/j.clsr.2005.04.008

King, L. (2008). Ulster Bank loses 10 laptops/ *Computer World*. Retrieved February 10, 2009, from http://www.computerworlduk.com/management/security/ cybercrime/news/index.cfm?newsid=9165

Martin, W. (1995). *The global information society*. Aldershot, UK: Aslib/Gower.

McCrohan, K. F. (2003). Facing the threats to electronic commerce. *Journal of Business and Industrial Marketing, 18*(2), 133–145. doi:10.1108/08858620310463060

McCusker, R. (2006). Transnational organized cyber crime: Distinguishing threat from reality. *Crime, Law, and Social Change, 46*, 257–273. doi:10.1007/s10611-007-9059-3

McGuire, B. L., & Roser, S. N. (2000). What your business should know about Internet security. *Strategic Finance, 82*(5), 50–54.

Merrilees, B., & Frye, M.-L. (2003). E-trust: The in☐uence of perceived interactivity on e-retailing users. *Marketing Intelligence & Planning, 21*(2), 123–128. doi:10.1108/02634500310465461

Miyazaki, A. D., & Fernandez, A. (2001). Consumer perceptions of privacy and security risks for online shopping. *The Journal of Consumer Affairs, 35*, 27–44. doi:10.1111/j.1745-6606.2001.tb00101.x

Nelson, T. D. (2001). *E-business*. Retrieved February 17, 2009, from http://searchcio.techtarget.com/ sDefinition/0,sid182_gci212026,00.html

O'Rourke, M. (2003). Cyberattacks prompt response to security threat. *Risk Management, 50*(1), 8.

Papazoglou, M. P. (2003). Web services and business transactions. *World Wide Web: Internet and Web Information Systems, 6,* 49–91.

Pennanen, K., Tiainen, T., & Luomala, H. T. (2007). A qualitative exploration of a consumer's value-based e-trust building process: A framework development. *Qualitative Market Research: An International Journal, 10*(1), 28–47. doi:10.1108/13522750710720387

Raja, J., & Velmurgan, M. S. (2008). E-payments: Problems and prospects. *Journal of Internet Banking and Commerce, 13*(1), 1–17.

Ratnasingam, P. (2007). A risk-control framework for e-marketplace participation: The findings of seven cases. *Information & Computer Security, 15*(2), 149–166. doi:10.1108/09685220710748029

Reinsch, R. (2005). E-commerce: Managing the legal risks. *Managerial Law, 47*(1-2), 168–196. doi:10.1108/03090550510771377

Saunders, M., Lewis, P., & Thornhill, A. (2007). *Research methods for business students* (4th ed.). Harlow, UK: Pearson Education.

Schneider, G. P. (2004). *Electronic commerce: The second wave,* 5th ed. Wadsworth, UK: Thomson Learning.

Sharma, S. K., & Gupta, J. N. D. (2002). Securing information infrastructure from information warfare. *Logistic Information Management, 15*(5-6), 414–422. doi:10.1108/09576050210447118

Shifrin, T. (2007). *Halifax apologizes after 13,000 customer records stolen from the employee's car.* Retrieved February 13, 2009, from http://www.computerworlduk.com/ management/ security/ data control/news/index. cfm?newsid=2373

Smith, H. J. (1994). *Managing privacy: Information technology and corporate America.* Chapel Hill, NC: University of North Carolina Press.

Straub, D. W., & Welke, R. J. (1998). Coping with systems risk: Security planning models for management decision making. *Management Information Systems Quarterly, 22*(4), 441–469. doi:10.2307/249551

Symantec. (2005). *Operational risk management and the financial services sector.* (Published in 2005). Retrieved February 8, 2009, from http://www.symantec.com/business/library/ article.jsp?aid=IN_110705_operational_risk_management

Symantec. (2006). *Symantec Internet security threat report: Trends for January 06–June 06.* Retrieved March 5, 2009, from http://www.symantec.com/specprog/threatreport/ent-whitepaper_symantec_Internet_security_threat_report_x_09_2006.en-us.pdf

Symantec. (2008). *Symantec report on the underground economy.* Retrieved February 15, 2009, from http://www.symantec.com/business/ theme.jsp?themeid=threatreport

Thietart, R. A., et al. (2001). *Doing management research: A comprehensive guide* (pp. 58-79). SAGE Publication ltd.

Tran, E., & Atkinson, M. A. (2002). Security of personal data across national borders. *Information Management & Computer Security, 10*(5), 237–241. doi:10.1108/09685220210446588

Udo, G. J. (2001). Privacy and security concerns as major barriers for e-commerce: A survey study. *Information Management & Computer Security, 9*(4), 165–174. doi:10.1108/EUM0000000005808

Van Slyke, C., & Belanger, F. (2003). *E-business technologies.* New York, NY: Wiley.

Whitman, M. E., & Mattord, H. J. (2003). *Principles of information security.* Boston, MA: Course Technology.

Wilikens, M. (2001). Cofidence and confidentiality: Stimulating e-commerce in Europe. *The Journal of Future Studies, Strategic Thinking and Policies, 3*(2), 135–139. doi:10.1108/14636680110803067

Wirtz, J., Lwin, M. O., & Williams, J. D. (2007). Causes and consequences of consumer online privacy concern. *International Journal of Service Industry Management, 18*(4), 326–348. doi:10.1108/09564230710778128

Worzala, E. M., McCarthy, A. M., Dixon, T., & Marston, A. (2001). E-commerce and retail property in the UK and USA. *Journal of Property Investment & Finance, 20*(2), 142–158. doi:10.1108/14635780210420034

KEY TERMS AND DEFINITIONS

Data Theft: Is an illegal act of gaining access (usually by office workers) to technology such as desktop computers and hand-held devices capable of storing digital information (such as flash drives, iPods and even digital cameras) and stealing that information for any specific purpose.

E-Commerce: The buying and selling of products and services by businesses and consumers through an electronic medium especially over the internet. However any transaction that is completed solely through electronic measures can be considered e-commerce.

E-Shopping/E-Marketing/Online Shopping: Electronic commerce, commonly known as e-commerce (also known as electronic marketing or online shopping), consists of the buying and selling of products or services over electronic systems such as the Internet and other computer networks.

Hacking: Is an act of gaining unauthorised access to computer systems and network resources to acquire knowledge about the system and how it works.

Identity Theft: Is a crime in which a person's confidential information is stolen for the purpose of fraud or other criminal activities.

Information Security: Means protecting information and information systems from unauthorized access, use, disclosure, disruption, modification, perusal, inspection, recording or destruction.

Phishing: Is an e-mail fraud scam conducted for the purposes of information or identity theft.

Chapter 5
Analyzing Information Security Goals

Ella Kolkowska
Örebro University School of Business, Sweden

Karin Hedström
Örebro University School of Business, Sweden

Fredrik Karlsson
Örebro University School of Business, Sweden

ABSTRACT

One of the problems highlighted within the area of information security is that international standards are implemented in organisations without adopting them to special organisational settings. In this chapter the authors analyse information security goals found in hospital settings. They found that the CIA-triad fails to cover organisational specific information security goals in hospital settings. They found also that information security goals held by information security managers and business managers are not the same, implying that both these groups should be involved in designing of information security goals, in order to find information security goals relevant for the organisation. Finally, the authors found goal maps used in this study for analysis of empirical data, to be a useful tool for analysis and communication of information security goals in an organisation.

INTRODUCTION

A strong trend in information security management in organisations under the last decade has been standardization, certifications and development of best practices (B. von Solms, 2000). Consequently, information security management standards are seen as a basis for successful security management

DOI: 10.4018/978-1-4666-0978-5.ch005

in organisations and have become widely used for security management (Siponen, 2006). The most known and widespread standard today is the ISO/IEC 17799 – Information Security Code of Practice (Freeman, 2007; ISO/IEC 17799, 2005).

Although there are obvious advantages of using international standard for security management, various researchers point out that applying such standards without enough consideration to the specifics of the organisation may be detrimental to effective management of information security (e.g. Hsu, 2009; Höne & Eloff, 2002; Siponen, 2006; B. von Solms & von Solms, 2004). Every situation requires different solutions while standards are more of a general baseline for information security. In each specific situation the special context of the IT environment have to be taken into account when the standards are applied, in order to establish unique information security requirements of an organisation (Gerber & von Solms, 2005; Hsu, 2009).

Furthermore, the literature emphasizes the importance of dialogue between information security professionals and business managers when deciding information security goals for an organization (McFadzean, Ezingeard, & Birchall, 2006; B von Solms, 2001). Information security professionals typically have technical backgrounds and focus on technical aspects of information security, while business managers are mainly concerned with managerial and organizational aspects of information security. These two different views are important to consider in establishing information security goals for a specific organisation (Rainer, Marshall, Knapp, & Montgomery, 2007). Unfortunately, many organisations apply the standards without addressing the actual security needs of the organisation (Hsu, 2009; Thomson, von Solms, & Louw, 2006).

A consequence of applying security standards without considering the organisational context is the focus on Confidentiality, Integrity and Availability (the CIA-triad) as the only objectives for information security management. This means running the risk of missing specific information security goals that an organization needs. The CIA-triad has been criticized in the literature for its technical focus and ignorance of the socio-organizational context of information security management (e.g. Anderson, 2002; Dhillon & Backhouse, 2000; Trompeter & Eloff, 2001). Moreover it has been pointed out that the CIA-triad are general objectives for information security management, while information security objectives should be related to the organisational context (B. von Solms & von Solms, 2004). Therefore researchers agree that the CIA-triad should be complemented and/or re-defined; including ethical, social, and organisational aspects of information handling (Dhillon & Backhouse, 2000; Dhillon & Torkzadeh, 2006; Trompeter & Eloff, 2001).

For health care organisations, secure information is central to effective and good health care and to ensure patient security (Leitheiser, 2001). However, although information security and protecting patient information have always been of high priority in the health care sector, the level of information security in this sector is still insufficient (Nanji, 2010; Prince, 2008). Various reports of information security breaches (PWC, 2008) and unintended information disclosures of confidential patient information (Prince, 2008) have raised the awareness about security issues of health information systems (HIS) (Luethi & Knolmayer, 2009). We need to develop better knowledge about what constitutes secure information and good information management in hospital settings. With this in mind, is the purpose of the study presented in this paper to analyse information security goals in a Swedish hospital. This will bring us a little bit further in our quest to develop a secure information environment in hospitals.

The introduction of HIS and patient electronic health records (EHR) are seen as possibilities for improved health care quality, lower costs and also as an important part of meeting the new challenges arising in the health care sector in today's society (Miettinen & Korhonen, 2008). However, without adequate information security, there will be no trust for the health care services and the hope for improved patient care and reduced health care costs will be in tatters (Nanji, 2010). Therefore information security is important in health care sector.

Management of information security in health care organizations is not easy. An important aspect of health care work, which influences information security, is the complexity in delivering health care services. Health care involves many different collaborating and communicating actors, prioritizing different goals in their work with information security (Hedström, 2007; Åhlfeldt, 2008). This complexity has to be taken into account when goals for information security are decided and policy is formulated (Blobel & Roger-France, 2001; Chalmers & Muir, 2003). If the policy does not address the specific tasks of the organisation it might be misinterpreted and not accepted by all actors (de Lusignan, Chan, Theadom, & Dhoul, 2007). Therefore in this study we analyze information security goals at a hospital as expressed by different actors and relate them to the traditional information security objectives pointed out in the international standard.

The chapter is structured as follows. The following section provides definitions and discussions of information security objectives in health care. Section three gives an overview of the research method, and presents the findings from our empirical studies of information security goals at a Swedish hospital. In section four we discuss our results and solutions, followed by, in section five, discussion of future research direction and in last section, we give a short conclusion.

BACKGROUND

The following section describes the CIA-triad, its problems, and development of additional information security objectives for the organisational management and also information security issues in health care.

The CIA-Triad

The standard describes information security as "preservation of confidentiality, integrity and availability of information" (ISO/IEC, 2005b). These three objectives have guided the development of security measures to avoid different security threats in organisations. Confidentiality

means that information is not accessible for unauthorized people. Integrity means that information is protected against undesired changes. The last concept, availability, means that information is accessible for authorized users within desired time (ISO/IEC, 2005b). However, both the notion of information security and the CIA-triad have been criticized as insufficient in response to the emerging information security challenges (Anderson, 2002; Dhillon & Backhouse, 2000; Dhillon & Torkzadeh, 2006). The critique concerns the definition as such and the objectives. The CIA-triad fails to relate information security to an organisational and business context, and there is insufficient emphasis on the organisational actors' roles in working with information security (e.g. Anderson, 2002; Dhillon & Torkzadeh, 2006; B. von Solms & von Solms, 2005). Two concepts that are suggested to replace the information security concept are business security (B. von Solms & von Solms, 2005), and information system security (Dhillon, 2007). Business security emphasizes how security work with other organisational processes (B. von Solms & von Solms, 2005). Information system security describes a holistic and contextual view of security by not only focusing information, but including the whole information system as a protection object (Dhillon, 2007). Consequently, due to the wider definition, researchers in the information security area argue that the traditional objectives should be complemented by additional objectives including ethical, social, and organisational aspects of information handling, which provide better support for the new challenges of business security and information system security (Trompeter & Eloff, 2001).

Dhillon and Backhouse (2000) discuss additional objectives for information security. They suggest that the traditional objectives should be complemented by four new principles; responsibility, integrity, trust and ethicality (RITE). These principles are not really objectives, but can be viewed as areas to consider when managing information security in organisations. Responsibility means having knowledge of rules and understanding of responsibilities. Based on that knowledge, members of an organisation are able to develop their own security practices when needed; practices that are in line with overall organisational rules. Integrity means being morally sound and loyal to the organisation. In an information security context trust means that relationships within organisations should be built on confidence rather than control. For example, employees have to be trusted to act according to the organisation's norms and accepted behavioural patterns. Furthermore, employees have to feel confident that their privacy will not be compromised by too strict security controls. Ethicality means that employees should act according to ethical principles instead of strictly follow formal rules. The latter principle is supported by Trompeter and Eloff (2001). They emphasize the importance of consideration of ethical principles when deciding on policies for information security. In addition, responsibility has later received a wider interpretation. A number of scholars have discussed the importance of considering both internal and external organisational contexts when discussing responsibility. This means, for example, that organisations are accountable to its partners and clients and to follow laws and regulations issued by the government.

Another attempt to improve the information security management is illustrated in a study by Dhillon and Torkzadeh (2006). They studied security managers' values related to information security and transformed them to objectives that are essential in protecting organisations' information resources. Their results show that the CIA-triad is only a small part of possible objectives addressed in the information security management. Objectives such as maximizing awareness, developing and sustaining an ethical environment, enhance integrity of business processes, maximizing data integrity, maximizing organisational integrity, and maximizing privacy are also important in managing information security. Many of the identified objectives are not only important to ensure information security, but are also part of the corporate governance. This is in line with other researchers who emphasize information security in relation to organisational governance and not as isolated processes in the organisation (McFadzean, et al., 2006; B. von Solms, 2006; B. von Solms & von Solms, 2005)

Information Security in Healthcare

Secure personal health information, i.e., available and correct information protected from unauthorized use, is an important issue for health care organisations. Deficient or insufficient information can lead to serious consequences for the patients, ruined reputation for the organisation (Miettinen & Korhonen, 2008) and mistrust for the health care services (Nanji, 2010). Effective information security management is therefore very important in the health care sector.

However, various scholars point out a number of barriers that might limit the ability of implementing information security policies and goals in health care organizations (e.g. de Lusignan, et al., 2007; Graunt, 2000; Scott, Mannion, Davies, & Marshall, 2003). The problems might, for instance, be related to a strong professional culture (Graunt, 2000; Scott, et al., 2003), the complexity in delivering health care services (Åhlfeldt, 2008) and the existing conflict between security and improved patient care outcomes (Fernando & Dawson, 2009). Therefore the formulated information security policy and goals need to meet these challenges. The policy needs to take into account the roles of the individuals and the complexity of the organisation (Blobel & Roger-France, 2001; Chalmers & Muir, 2003). The formulated goals need to be related to health care processes, and the tension between them has to be managed (Graunt, 2000). Otherwise there is a risk that the policy will be misinterpreted and the goals will not be followed (de Lusignan, et al., 2007).

International standards are widely used in health care organisations as a base in developing information security policies and goals (Luethi & Knolmayer, 2009). The CIA-triad is therefore often seen as the most important objectives for information security management in health care. Besides the CIA-triad, accountability is often added from health care context (Åhlfeldt, 2008). Accountability refers to the ability to distinctly trace performed activities to a specific individual (Harris, 2002; SIS, 2003). These four objectives can be related to patient safety and patient privacy that are the two most important aims for information security management in health care (Åhlfeldt, 2008). Patient safety means "protection against medical injury" (SOSFS 2005:12, 2005) and is "the right of individuals, groups, or institutions to determine for themselves when, how, and to what extent information about them is communicated" (Patient Privacy Right Foundation, 2007). Confidentiality and accountability are related to privacy since patient privacy is only achieved if the right person has access to patient information. Availability and integrity are both related to patient safety, since patient safety means that the users are able to access the correct information at the right time. In health care literature patient safety is also discussed in relation to information quality (Leitheiser, 2001; Miettinen & Korhonen, 2008) The above aspects can be seen as descriptions of information quality. Information quality is, traditionally, defined by a number of dimensions such as accuracy, precision and timeliness (Leitheiser, 2001) but other dimensions might also be added (see e.g. Heeks, 2006; Wang & Strong, 1996). Heeks (2006) defines information quality in e-governments system by five dimensions: completeness, accuracy, relevance, timeliness and appropriateness of presentation. Completeness means the degree of which all the data required by users is present in the e-government system. Accuracy means the level of errors/incorrect data within the overall system data. Relevance is the degree to which data is necessary in order to complete particular user decisions and actions. Timeliness emphasizes the degree to which data can be delivered by the e-government system within a required timeframe. Finally, appropriateness of presentation is the degree to which data produced by the e-government system is accessible and intelligible to the recipient. Our aim in this chapter is not to discuss the different definitions and relevance of the different interpretations of information quality; but we would like to point out that there are information quality goals existing in health care sector that are related to information security and maybe should be considered in information security management in this sector.

INFORMATION SECURITY GOALS AT A SWEDISH HOSPITAL

This section gives an overview of the research method, followed by a presentation of our findings from the case study. We present the information security goals we found in the hospital's policy and routine documents. The goals are analyzed in the form of goal-maps (Yu, 1993) where main goals are related to sub-goals. The sub-goals are means to achieve the main goals.

The main information security goals are 'Complete confidentiality,' 'Available information,' 'Traceability,' 'Reliable information,' 'Standardized information' and 'Follow laws, rules, and standards'.

Methodology

This study was carried out at a small Swedish county hospital in central Sweden. The hospital serves approximately 90,000 citizens. The hospital is situated in a county that is responsible for healthcare for 274,000 inhabitants. There are, apart from the studied hospital, two more hospitals and several primary care clinics in the county.

The purpose of this paper is, as we wrote in the Introduction, to analyse information security goals in a Swedish hospital. The analyzed information security goals are found in official documents related to information security and information handling. We decided to focus our study on information security goals related to patient information, as treating patients is hospitals' main activity. In addition, we used the county's overall goal for information security as our working definition of information security, and subsequently as demarcation in the analysis: 'Correct information to the right people, right on time, and to the right place.' The case study method is based on a research method used by Dhillon and Torzadeh (2006) with the purpose of identifying information security objectives. The qualitative research method can be divided into three steps (identifying information security goals, structuring goals, and organising objectives), which have been carried out iteratively:

1. *Identifying Information Security Goals:* the process began with document analysis, to identify information security goals, as represented by organisational policies, guidelines and routines on the county council level as well as hospital level. The different documents were chosen in order to capture different actors' goals related to information security and not just information security managers goals espoused in information security policy. The following documents were analysed:
   a. County council information security policy
   b. County council IT strategy
   c. Information to county council staff about information security
   d. Security instructions for county council IT users
   e. IT policy for the county council
   f. County council policy for information and communication
   g. Routines for handling medical records at the hospital

The documents 'County council information security policy,' 'County council staff about information security' and 'Security instructions for county council IT users' were created by the information security manager and were related to information handled by IT systems. The other documents were not developed by information security manager. 'County council IT strategy' and 'IT policy for the county council' regulated the usage of IT-systems for handling of information in the county. 'County council policy for information and communication' was related to all information handling and communication with different stakeholders, while 'Routines for handling medical records at the hospital' regulated handling of medical records at the studied hospital. Form the documents we identified 68 goals statements that were numbered and listed in a database.

2. *Structuring Goals:* first, we structured all statements in order to eliminate duplicates. Second, the goals were structured in clusters (categories) that dealt with a similar issue according to inductive qualitative categorisation (Silverman 2001). The emerging categories were continuously discussed and analysed with other researchers during seminaries. Then the categories of goals were labelled. For each cluster we elicited a main goal, which was used as the cluster's demarcation. For example goals such as 'provide user with only necessary information', 'only discuss patient in need of care', 'prevent unauthorized access' deal with similar issue, i.e., confidentiality. We labeled the cluster as 'complete confidentiality.' In one case we had to phrase a main goal to summarize the goals expressed in the documents. The goal 'Follow laws, rules and standards' was not found in the reviewed documents, but is a generalization of its underlying sub-goals. Six main information security goals and 63 unique sub-goals (the numbering in the Figures is not an unbroken sequence, since it

Figure 1. Goal map – complete confidentiality

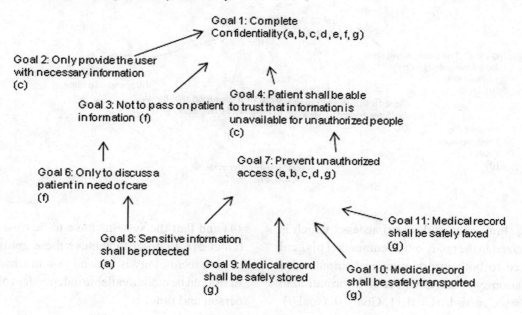

uses the numbers from the original analysis) supporting the main goals were identified in the study.

3. *Organizing Objectives:* in order to structure the goals we identified the relationships between the main goals and the sub-goals. We illustrated this using goal maps inspired by Yu (1993). During the analysis six goal maps were identified: 'Complete confidentiality', 'Available information', 'Traceability', 'Reliable information', 'Standardized information' and 'Follow laws, rules, and regulations'. The goal-maps were jointly developed by the researchers in order to minimize biases. To ensure traceability each goal was given an identifier (letter) and related to the specific document(s) where the goal was found. The letter(s) refers to the documents in the list above, and 'a', for example, relates to the 'County council information security policy.'

Complete Confidentiality

Figure 1 illustrates the main goal 'Complete confidentiality' (Goal 1). The purpose of 'Complete confidentiality' is to ensure that only authorized people can access sensitive information about a patient, and that only necessary healthcare information about the patient is shared and discussed.

The goal 'complete confidentiality' (Goal 1) is important in hospital settings and has been found in all analyzed documents. Confidentiality is in our setting related to information handled by the computer system, manual information handling as well as to spoken communication between staff. One part of the goal is related to protecting patients' information from disclosure to unauthorized people (Goal 4, Goal 7, Goal 11, Goal 10, Goal 9). The other part of the goal is related to handling of patient's information by authorized users (Goal 2, Goal 3, Goal 6, Goal 8). The central purpose of 'complete confidentiality' is respect to the patients and their privacy, as can be seen in goal g4 'Patient shall be able to trust that sensitive information is unavailable for unauthorized people.' This sub-goal is achieved by realizing

Figure 2. Goal map – available information

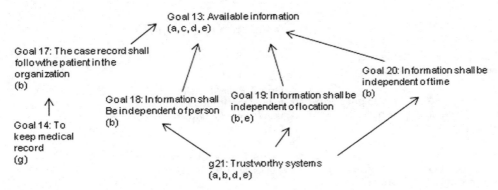

Goal 7, 'Prevent unauthorized access,' which is emphasized in the analyzed documents. This goal is related to both information in computerized information systems (Goal 8) and information in paper-based records (Goal 11, Goal 10, Goal 9). Suggested security measures are, for example, routines how to handle paper-based patients' records when they are used, stored, transported and faxed. Two other goals that support the main goal 'complete confidentiality' are Goal 2 and Goal 3. These goals are related to how authorized people should handle sensitive information about patients. The only information that should be communicated is information related to the health care.

Available Information

In Figure 2 we have illustrated the main goal 'Available information' (Goal 13). Available information means that healthcare professionals should have access to information when needed. This is crucial in a healthcare situation. Without access to relevant, as well as correct, information, there is a risk for the patient's health. The goal is emphasized in all analyzed documents.

According to the analyzed documents the goal 'available information' can be achieved when information is independent of person (Goal 18), time (Goal 20) and location (Goal 19) and when medical records follow the patient in the organisation (Goal 17). However, in order to achieve these goals the documents state two prerequisites: the hospital has to keep medical records (Goal

14) and that the systems have to be trustworthy (Goal 21). In order to achieve these goals information technology is viewed as a means, where EHRs can be made available independent of place, person and time.

Traceability

Figure 3 presents the main goal 'Traceability' (Goal 30). This goal means that actions and decisions concerning the flow of information, in the information system, shall be traceable through logging and documentation. This goal is mainly emphasized in two documents: the County council information security policy (a) and the Routines for handling medical records at the hospital (g).

The traceability goal is related to both manual handling of information and computerized information systems. Traceability related to computer systems emphasizes tracing performed actions in the systems to responsible actors (Goal 32). This is important in hospital settings because most of the users can access more information than they actually need for their work. The solution is a balance between security and flexible access to information. Thus to prohibit misuse of these rights in the system, traceability of user actions is extremely important. Traceability is in this case ensured by logging (Goal 32), supervision of the networks (Goal 33), and use of digital signatures (Goal 89). Another part of traceability in the hospital setting is related to tracing information. This mostly concerns paper-based medical

Figure 3. Goal map – traceability

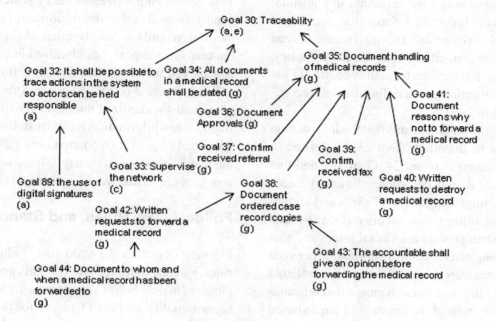

records, in order to know where the records are. Goals 37 to 43 concern the use of copies, the request of medical records and whether information have reached the desired destination and/or people.

Reliable Information

The main goal, 'reliable information' (Goal 15) is illustrated in Figure 4. Reliable information means that information should be correct; i.e., intact as well as updated. To have access to reli-

Figure 4. Goal map – reliable information

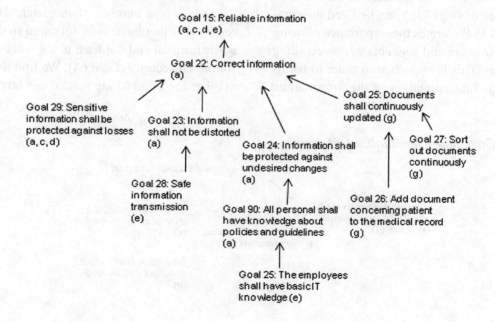

able information is very important in a hospital environment. Incorrect information could hurt patients, or even be fatal. This goal is emphasized in the County council information security policy, the Security instructions for county council IT users and the Routines for handling medical records at the hospital.

Intact information means that the information should not be distorted (Goal 23) by desired or undesired changes (Goal 24, Goal 28), and that information should be protected against losses (Goal 29). Improving users' IT skills and knowledge about information security (Goal 90 and Goal 25) shall prevent accidental losses and also by improving transmission of information between different receivers (Goal 28). In addition, reliable and correct information also means that information is kept updated. In the case of paper-based medical record it means that documents about the patient are added to the record (Goal 26) and the documents in the record are sorted continuously (Goal 27). Hence outdated documents are removed from the record and the documents are placed in a specific order.

Standardized Information

The goal map in Figure 5 describes the underlying structure of Goal 45: 'Standardized information'. Goal 45 illustrates the importance of using the same structure and concepts when recording information. This is important in order to facilitate a unified interpretation of the information.

This goal is emphasized in the IT policy for the county council and in the Routines for handling medical records at the hospital. According to our analysis the goal 'Standardized information' is achieved when medical records follow a pre-defined structure (Goal 46), when forms follow given and standardized templates (Goal 47) and finally when information is clearly defined (Goal 48). The last goal is elaborated even further stating that information is clearly defined when used concepts are shared by the personnel (Goal 49).

Follow Laws, Rules, and Standards

Figure 6 illustrates the main goal 'Follow laws, rules, and standards' (Goal 61). This goal is emphasized mainly in the County council information security policy and the IT policy for the county council. But it is mentioned even in other documents: 'Security instructions for county council IT users', and 'County council policy for information and communication'. This goal points at the importance of healthcare organisations following prescribed security information regulations, laws regulating healthcare and information use, as well as information security standards and classifications, as support for managing information security.

There are a number of important laws and regulations that have to be followed in the work at the hospital and not least in the work with information security (Goal 64). We find that goals number 5, 62 and 63 are related to a law on how

Figure 5. Goal map – standardized information

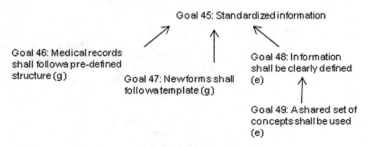

Figure 6. Goal map – Follow laws, rules, and standard

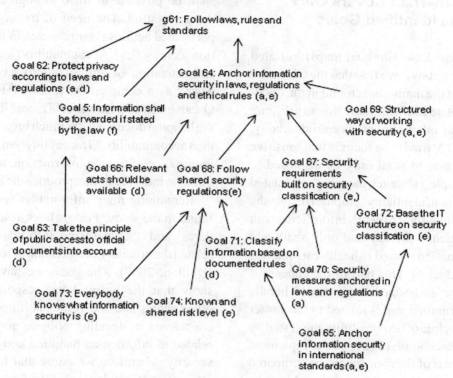

to handle privacy of patients and access to official documents. These goals influence the work with information security because they are related to how patient information has to be handled. Other sub-goals emphasized in the analyzed document stress structured work with information security (Goal 69) and the use of international standards (Goal 65). These standards should guide classification of information (Goal 67, Goal 71) and the implementation of security measures (Goal 70, Goal 72). Another important sub-goal in this context is that the rules and policies have to be known and followed (Goal 68). According to the analyzed document this will be achieved by distributing relevant acts (Goal 66), education about information security (Goal 73) and creating organizational risk awareness (Goal 74).

SOLUTIONS AND RECOMMENDATIONS

The purpose of this paper was to analyse information security goals in a Swedish hospital. Different strategic documents related to information handling and information security have been analyzed in the study to capture different actors' goals related to information security. It has been described earlier that one characteristic feature of hospital settings is a complex organisation with many different collaborating and communicating actors such as politicians, civil servants, healthcare professionals, administrators, patients, and managers. Many of the actors are responsible for creating policies and guidelines related to information security and information handling. Based on our empirical results, we will highlight four findings that have implications for management of information security in health care.

First, the CIA-Triad Covers Only a Part of the Identified Goals

If we take a closer look at the goal-maps illustrated in Figures 1 to 6 above, we find that the CIA-triad covers three of the main-goals found in the documents. 'Complete confidentiality' found in Figure 1, has a similar interpretation as confidentiality, found in the CIA-triad. The focus is that sensitive medical information shall only be disclosed to authorized people. However, the sub-goals related to 'Complete confidentiality' emphasize also the importance of handling patient's information with respect to patient's privacy and only share and discuss information related to health care matters (Goal 3 and Goal 6). This part of the concept is related to how authorized users should handle patient's information and is related to the earlier discussed principle of responsibility suggested by Dhillon and Backhouse (2000) as a complement to CIA. This part of the concept can be compared with the wider aspect of responsibility (Moulton & Coles, 2003) emphasizing organisational accountability to partners and clients, here patients in hospital settings. The second CIA-concept, integrity, is similar to the meaning of the main goal 'Reliable information' illustrated in detail in Figure 4. 'Reliable information' has in the hospital-setting, however, a wider definition than only to protect information against undesired changes. Here it also points at the importance of keeping information updated, understandable, and sorted. Finally, the third CIA-concept, availability, has the same meaning as the main goal 'Available information' in Figure 2. Both objectives aim to make sure that information is accessible irrespective of time or place.

But, the CIA-triad fails to cover the other information security goals we found in the formal documents from the studied hospital. These are 'Follow laws, rules and standards,' 'Traceability' and 'Standardized information'. 'Traceability' means that actions and decisions concerning the flow of information, in the information system, shall be possible to trace through logging and documentation. The need of tracing an actor's performed actions is emphasized in the information security field. Accountability (identification, authentication or authorization) has been suggested as a complement to CIA (Harris, 2002; Oscarson, 2007). However 'Traceability' found in the hospital document has much broader meaning than accountability. 'Traceability' emphasizes the importance of tracing information, and not only trace the individuals that produce the information.

Remaining main information security goals found in the study 'Follow laws, rules, and standards' and 'Standardized information' can be related the broader interpretation of responsibility (Dhillon, 2007). The goals we have identified show that the hospital has responsibilities to other actors and the responsibilities should be considered in deciding policies and guidelines related to information handling and information security. Therefore we argue that just applying international standards and the CIA-triad fail to satisfy all hospitals needs related to information security. Context specific information security goals are needed in this environment.

Second, Information Security Goals in Hospital Settings Correspond to Information Quality

The study shows that the CIA-triad fails to cover organisational specific information security aspects of a hospital. We have found that a number of information security goals, identified in a hospital setting clearly correspond to attributes of high quality of information, described earlier in this chapter. For instance, integrity in a hospital setting means that information is reliable, correct and updated, but also understandable and sorted. Such an interpretation of integrity corresponds to the information quality attributes: completeness, timeliness, relevance and accuracy. Completeness and timeliness are, for instance, achieved when all actors add the information to the medical records as soon as they have been with the patient (goal 26, main goals 'Reliable information'). Timeliness is also achieved when the medical records are updated (goal 25, main goal 'Reliable information'). Accuracy is achieved by protection of information against losses (goal 29, main goal 'Reliable information') and by protection of information against distortion (goal 23, main goal 'Reliable information'). Relevance is achieved when medical records are updated and sorted (goal 25 and 27, main goal 'Reliable information'). The examples above are mostly related to interpretation of integrity in hospital settings, but other information security goals identified in this environment clearly correspond to information quality. For instance 'available information' (goals 13) corresponds to timeliness, 'standardized information' (goal 45) is related to appropriateness of presentation and traceability, meaning that all notes in a medical record have to be approved (goal 36), read and evaluated for its accuracy.

Based on the discussion in this section, we argue that attributes defining information quality should be considered in designing and defining information security goals in hospital settings as complement to the CIA-triad.

Third, Information Security Managers and Business Managers Focus on Different Goals

The documents analyzed in this study were designed by different actors: information security managers and business managers. 'County council information security policy', 'Information to county council staff about information security' and, 'Security instructions for county council IT users' were created by the information security manager, while the other documents were developed by business managers. We found that the different actors focus different aspects of information security. While documents created by information security managers focus information handled by IT and clearly correspond

to the international standard and the CIA-triad, the other documents operationalize information security in a hospital setting and present them in context of business goals. For example even if goal 'complete confidentiality' is emphasized in all documents it is interpreted differently. While information documents created by security managers emphasize protection against unauthorized access and focus information handled by IT, the other documents define also how paper-based medical records should be handled and also how authorized people should handle sensitive information about patients. Similar differences can be seen in operationalizations of other goals such as: 'Available information', Reliable information', 'Traceability' and 'Follow laws, rules, and standards'. The goal: 'Standardized information' was identified only in documents created by business managers.

In the documents created by business managers we could also identify a number of business goals that make a context for information security goals at the hospital. These business goals are: 'Efficient healthcare,' 'Correct healthcare,' 'Empowered patients' and 'Individualized healthcare.' The information security goals contribute to the business goals. For example, 'reliable information' is strongly related to business goal 'correct healthcare', which means that the patient should receive the healthcare he or she is entitled to. In this context the goal 'reliable information' is related to responsibility that emphasizes organisational accountability to partners and clients, i.e., patients in hospital settings. 'Available information' aim to make sure that information is accessible irrespective of time or place and is also related to the business goal 'correct healthcare', but also to the business goal 'effective healthcare'. The goals 'Follow laws, rules, and standards' and 'Standardized information' are related to business goals 'efficient healthcare' and 'empowered patients.

We consider it important that the information security goals are associated to the business context in order to maintain the integrity of the organization. This is in line with earlier research that points out the importance of considering information security issues in relation to corporate governance (e.g. Baskerville & Siponen, 2002) due a to create information security goals and policies that are adopted to the special organisational settings (Graunt, 2000) and accepted in the organisation (de Lusignan, et al., 2007).

We argue also that information security managers' and business managers' views of information security complement each other, thus both these groups should be involved in designing information security goals in an organization. Information security managers, on one hand must understand the business context within the organisation and for that reason work closely with business managers. Business managers on the other hand have to understand the reasons behind information security goals to engage in its development and implementation and to adhere to it later.

Fourth, Goal Maps Are a Valuable Technique for Analysing Information Security Goals

In this study we have used goal maps inspired by Yu (1993) to illustrate relationships between information security goals identified from the different documents. We find goal maps supportive in analysis of our qualitative data. Based on our experiences we state that this technique provides a means of explaining and illustrating different views on information security in an organisation and the relationships between different goals. We can see a number of possible situations where this technique could be useful to improve management of information security. For instance, goal maps could be used as a technique for identifying information security goals in an organisation. We argue in the previous section that both information security managers and business managers should be involved in designing of information security goals in an organisation. We assert that goal maps could support communication in this process by

illustrating how information security goals emphasized by these two groups support each other or conflict with each other. Goal maps can be used to analyze and illustrate how information security goals support or conflict with business goals. This understanding is important in order to define information security goals that are integrated with business goals. Finally, we believe that goal maps can be used in awareness programs to explain how different goals support each other and how information security goals support business goals. Therefore we argue that maps of supporting and conflicting information security goals can serve as a tool for raising organizational awareness of security (the 'why' behind the 'how'), communication, and performance measurement.

FUTURE RESEARCH DIRECTIONS

Based on the results from this study we highlight three opportunities for future research. First, our study shows that context specific information security goals are needed in hospital settings and that applying the CIA-triad uncritically fail to support the development of high quality information security management. This finding is in line with research in the field arguing that in order to satisfy the unique information security requirements for an organisation, organisational context have to be taken into account when information security goals are established (e.g. Gerber & von Solms, 2005; Hsu, 2009; Höne & Eloff, 2002; Siponen, 2006; B. von Solms & von Solms, 2004). In this study we found a number of information security goals needed in hospital settings and also that attributes defining information quality in some cases can operationalize and complemented the CIA-triad. Our findings come from one hospital, and it would be interesting to do a follow-up study where we analyze information security goals at different hospitals. This would give us more data and make the results more robust. We believe that such a study would be a valuable contribution to an on-going research on information security challenges in the health care sector presented in the beginning of this chapter.

Second, we found that information security goals held by information security managers and business managers at the studied hospital are not exactly the same and focus different aspects of information security. We also argued that both the views are important in designing information security goals needed in the organisation. In a follow-up study we would like to further elaborate these findings and study how information security goals held by security managers and business managers support each other and/or conflict with each other in health care organisations. It is stated in the literature that information security management in health care sector is difficult because of the complexity of the organisations, where many different collaborating and communicating actors prioritize different goals in their work with information security (e.g. Blobel & Roger-France, 2001; Hedström, 2007; Åhlfeldt, 2008) (Hedström, 2007; Åhlfeldt, 2008). We believe such study, increasing understanding of different actors' information security goals would contribute to improved information security management in health care sector.

Finally, we would like to further elaborate usefulness of goal maps as a technique for analysing information security goals. In this study we used goal maps to analyse our empirical data and we found this technique supportive as a means for explaining both the different views on information security in an organisation and the relationships between different goals. We would like to study the usefulness of goal maps as a means for illustration and communication in designing information security goals and in awareness programs. We believe that goal maps have a potential to serve as a means for communication, and performance measurement and also as a tool for raising organizational security awareness (the 'why' behind the 'how').

CONCLUSION

The purpose of this paper was to analyse information security goals at a Swedish hospital. A critical view on the CIA-triad was taken in this study to see how it is related to a hospital setting. The main problem with the CIA-triad is that these goals are general, and as such not adapted to a specific organisation or type of organisation. Hence, the CIA-triad fails to cover organisational specific information security aspects of a hospital. Six main information security goals were identified in this study. These goals are 'Complete confidentiality,' 'Available information,' 'Traceability,' 'Reliable information,' 'Standardized information' and 'Follow laws, rules, and standards'. Three of the goals – 'Complete confidentiality', 'Available information', 'Reliable information' – correspond to the CIA-triad, although they have a somewhat broader definitions than the traditional definitions. The additional four objectives – 'Traceability', 'Standardized information', and 'Follow laws, rules, and standards' – are not at all found in the CIA-triad.

The study shows that special information security goals are needed in hospital settings and just applying the CIA-triad does not satisfy all hospitals needs related to information security. It seems to be more fruitful to start with employees' organisational responsibilities, and business goals to find specific information security goals for an organisation. In hospital settings information security goals could be compared with the attributes for good information quality (completeness, accuracy, relevance, timeliness and appropriateness of presentation), because different actors already interpret a number of information security goals in these terms. Our study indicates also that information security goals held by information security managers and business managers are not exactly the same, but complement each other, implying that information security goals should be designed by both these groups. Finally, we argue that goal maps used in this study for analysis of the empirical data can be used as a technique for analysing information security goals held by different actors in an organisation due to understand how these different information security goals support each other and/or how they conflict with each other.

REFERENCES

Åhlfeldt, R.-M. (2008). *Information security in distributed healthcare - Exploring the needs for achieving patient safety and patient privacy.* Doctoral dissertation, Stockholm University, DSV Report series No. 08-003.

Anderson, J. (2002). Why we need a new definition of information security. *Computers & Security, 22*(4), 308–313. doi:10.1016/S0167-4048(03)00407-3

Baskerville, R., & Siponen, M. (2002). An information security meta-policy for emergent organizations. *Logistics Information Management, 15*(5/6), 337–346. doi:10.1108/09576050210447019

Blobel, B., & Roger-France, F. (2001). A systematic approach for analysis and design of secure health information systems. *International Journal of Medical Informatics, 62*, 51–78. doi:10.1016/S1386-5056(01)00147-2

Chalmers, J., & Muir, R. (2003). Patient privacy and confidentiality. *British Medical Journal, 326*, 725–726. doi:10.1136/bmj.326.7392.725

de Lusignan, S., Chan, T., Theadom, A., & Dhoul, N. (2007). The roles of policy and professionalism in the protection of processed clinical data: A literature review. *International Journal of Medical Informatics, 76*, 261–268. doi:10.1016/j.ijmedinf.2005.11.003

Dhillon, G. (2007). *Principles of information systems security: Text and cases.* Hoboken, NJ: Wiley Inc.

Dhillon, G., & Backhouse, J. (2000). Information system security management in the new millennium. *Communications of the ACM, 43*(125).

Dhillon, G., & Torkzadeh, G. (2006). Value-focused assessment of information system security in organizations. *Information Systems Journal, 16*(3), 293–314. doi:10.1111/j.1365-2575.2006.00219.x

Fernando, J. I., & Dawson, L. L. (2009). The health information system security threat lifecycle: An informatics theory. *International Journal of Medical Informatics, 78*(12), 815–826. doi:10.1016/j.ijmedinf.2009.08.006

Freeman, E. H. (2007). Holistic information security: ISO 27001 and due care. *Information Systems Security*(16), 291-294.

Gerber, M., & von Solms, R. (2005). Management of risk in the information age. *Computers & Security, 24*, 16–30. doi:10.1016/j.cose.2004.11.002

Graunt, N. (2000). Practical approaches to creating a security culture. *International Journal of Medical Informatics, 60*, 151–157. doi:10.1016/S1386-5056(00)00115-5

Harris, S. (2002). *CISSP all-in-one certification exam guide.* New York, NY: McGraw-Hill/Osborne.

Hedström, K. (2007). The values of IT in elderly care. *Information Technology & People, 20*(1), 72–84. doi:10.1108/09593840710730563

Hedström, K., Dhillon, G., & Karlsson, F. (2010). *Using actor network theory to understand information security management.* Paper presented at the 25th Annual IFIP TC 11.

Heeks, R. (2006). *Implementing and managing egovernment.* London, UK: Sage Publications Ltd.

Höne, K., & Eloff, J. H. P. (2002). *Information security policy - What do international information security standards say?* ISO/IEC 17799 (2005). *International Organization for Standarisation* (ISO). Retrieved from www.iso.org

Hsu, C. W. (2009). Frame misalignment: interpreting the implementation of information systems security certification in an organization. *European Journal of Information Systems, 18*, 140–150. doi:10.1057/ejis.2009.7

ISO/IEC 27002. (2005). *Information technology - Security techniques - Code of Practice for information security management* (2005b).

Leitheiser, R. L. (2001, January). *Data quality in health care data warehouse environments*. Paper presented at the 34th Hawaii International Conference on System Sciences, Island of Maui, Hawaii.

Luethi, M., & Knolmayer, G. F. (2009). *Security in health information systems: An exploratory comparison of U.S. and Swiss hospitals*. Paper presented at the 42nd Hawaii International Conference on System Sciences 5-8 January, Big Island, Hawaii.

McFadzean, E., Ezingeard, J.-N., & Birchall, D. (2006). Anchoring information security governance research: Sociological groundings and future directions. *Journal of Information System Security, 2*(3).

Miettinen, M., & Korhonen, M. (2008, June). *Information quality in healthcare: Coherence of data compared between organization's electronic patient records*. Paper presented at the 21st IEEE International Symposium on Computer-Based Medical Systems, University of Jyväskylä, Finland.

Moulton, R., & Coles, R. S. (2003). Applying information security governance. *Computers & Security, 22*(7), 580–584. doi:10.1016/S0167-4048(03)00705-3

Nanji, F. (2010). The BP crisis and information security compliance in health care: Parallel disasters? *Journal of Health Care Compliance,* (September-October), 15-23.

Oscarson, P. (2007). *Actual and perceived information systems security*. Doctoral dissertation, Linköping University, Linköping, Sweden.

Patient Privacy Right Foundation. (2007). *Glossary right to privacy*. Retrieved from http://www.patientprivacyrights.org/site/pageServer?pagename=glossary_Right_to_privacy

Prince, K. (2008). *A comprehensive study of healthcare data security breaches in the United States from 2000 - 2007*.

PWC. (2008). *Security breaches survey 2008*. PricewaterhouseCoopers on behalf of the UK Department of Business. Retrieved from www.pwc.co.uk.

Rainer, R. K., Marshall, T. E., Knapp, K. J., & Montgomery, H. G. (2007). Do information security professionals and business managers view information security issues differently? *Information Systems Security, 16*(2), 100–108. doi:10.1080/10658980701260579

Scott, T., Mannion, R., Davies, H., & Marshall, M. (2003). Implementing culture change in health care: Theory and practice. *International Journal for Quality in Health Care, 15*, 111–118. doi:10.1093/intqhc/mzg021

Siponen, M. (2006). Information security standards focus on the existence of process, not its content. *Communications of the ACM, 49*(8), 97–100. doi:10.1145/1145287.1145316

SIS. (2003). *SIS handbok 550. Terminologi för informationssäkerhet*. Stockholm, Sweden: SIS Förlag AB.

(2005). *SOSFS 2005:12*. The National Board of Health and Welfare.

Thomson, K. L., von Solms, R., & Louw, L. (2006). Cultivating an organizational information security culture. *Computer Fraud & Security, 10*, 7–11. doi:10.1016/S1361-3723(06)70430-4

Trompeter, C. M., & Eloff, J. (2001). A framework for implementation of socio-ethical controls in infomration security. *Computers & Security, 20*(5), 384–391. doi:10.1016/S0167-4048(01)00507-7

von Solms, B. (2000). Information security - The third wave? *Computers & Security, 19*, 615–620. doi:10.1016/S0167-4048(00)07021-8

von Solms, B. (2001). Corporate governance and information security. *Computers & Security, 20*(3), 215–218. doi:10.1016/S0167-4048(01)00305-4

von Solms, B. (2006). Information security - The fourth wave. *Computers & Security, 25*, 165–168. doi:10.1016/j.cose.2006.03.004

von Solms, B., & von Solms, R. (2004). The 10 deadly sins of information security management. *Computers & Security, 23*, 371–376. doi:10.1016/j.cose.2004.05.002

von Solms, B., & von Solms, R. (2005). From information security to....business security? *Computers & Security, 24*, 271–273. doi:10.1016/j.cose.2005.04.004

Wang, R. Y., & Strong, D. M. (1996). Beyond accuracy: What data quality means to data consumers. *Journal of Management Information Systems, 12*(4), 5–33.

Yu, E. (1993). *Modeling organizations for information systems requirements engineering*. Paper presented at The IEEE International Symposium on Requirements Engineering.

ADDITIONAL READING

Björck, F. (2005). *Discovering information security management*. Doctoral dissertation, Stockholm University / Royal Institute of Technology.

Botha, R. A., & Gaadingwe, T. G. (2006). Reflecting on 20 SEC conferences. *Computers & Security, 25*, 247–256. doi:10.1016/j.cose.2006.04.002

Da Veiga, A., & Eloff, J. H. P. (2010). A framework and assessment instrument for information security culture. *Computers & Security, 29*, 196–207. doi:10.1016/j.cose.2009.09.002

Dhillon, G. (1997). *Managing information system security*. London, UK: Macmillan.

Dhillon, G. (2001). Violation of safeguards by trusted personnel and understanding related information security concerns. *Computers & Security, 20*(1), 165. doi:10.1016/S0167-4048(01)00209-7

Dhillon, G., & Backhouse, J. (2001). Current directions in IS security research: Towards socio-organisational perspectives. *Information Systems Journal, 11*, 127–153. doi:10.1046/j.1365-2575.2001.00099.x

Doherty, N. F., & Fulford, H. (2005). Do information security policies reduce the incidence of security breaches: An exploratory analysis. *Information Resources Management Journal, 18*(4), 21–39. doi:10.4018/irmj.2005100102

Furnell, S., & Thomson, K.-L. (2009). From culture to disobedience: Recognising the varying user acceptance of IT security. *Computer Fraud & Security, 2*, 5–10. doi:10.1016/S1361-3723(09)70019-3

Gerber, M., & von Solms, R. (2001). From risk analysis to security requirements. *Computers & Security, 20*, 577–584. doi:10.1016/S0167-4048(01)00706-4

Halliday, J., & von Solms, R. (1997). *Effective information security policies*. Port Elizabeth, South Africa: Port Elizabeth Technikon.

Harrington, S. (1996). The effects of ethics and personal denial of responsibility on computer abuse judgements and intentions. *Management Information Systems Quarterly, 20*(3), 257–277. doi:10.2307/249656

Herath, T., & Rao, H. R. (2009). Encouraging information security behaviors in organizations: Role of penalties, pressures and perceived effectiveness. *Decision Support Systems, 47*(2), 154–165. doi:10.1016/j.dss.2009.02.005

Herath, T., & Rao, R. (2009). Protection motivation and deterrence: A framework for security policy compliance in organisations. *European Journal of Information Systems, 18*, 106–125. doi:10.1057/ejis.2009.6

Kadam, A. W. (2007). Information security policy development and implementation. *Information Security Journal: A Global Perspective, 16*(5), 246-256.

Kankanhalli, A., Teo, H. H., Tan, B. C. Y., & Wei, K. K. (2003). An integrative study of information systems security effectiveness. *International Journal of Information Management, 23*(2), 139–154. doi:10.1016/S0268-4012(02)00105-6

Myyry, L., Siponen, M., Pahnila, S., Vartiainen, T., & Vance, A. (2009). What levels of moral reasoning and values explain adherence to information security rules? An empirical study. *European Journal of Information Systems, 18*, 126–139. doi:10.1057/ejis.2009.10

Sasse, A., Brostoff, S., & Weirich, D. (2001). Transforming the weakest link - a human / computer interaction approach to usable and effective security. *BT Technology Journal, 19*(3), 122–131. doi:10.1023/A:1011902718709

Siponen, M. (2000). Critical analysis of different approaches to minimizing user-related faults in information systems security: Implications for research and practice. *Information Management & Computer Security, 8*(5), 197–209. doi:10.1108/09685220010353178

Siponen, M. (2005). Analysis of modern IS security development approaches: Towards the next generation of social and adaptable ISS methods. *Information and Organization, 15*, 339–375. doi:10.1016/j.infoandorg.2004.11.001

Siponen, M., Pahnila, S., & At, A. (2007). Employees' adherence to information security policies: An empirical study. In H. Venter, M. Eloff, L. Labuschagne & R. von Solms (Eds.), *Proceedings of the IFIP International Federation for Information Processing, New Approaches for Security, Privacy and Trust in Complex Environments.*

Siponen, M., Wilson, M. R., et al. (2008). *Power and practice in information systems security research*. Paper presented at the International Conference on Information Systems 2008 (ICIS 2008)

Siponen, M., & Wilson, R. (2009). Information security management standards: Problems and solutions. *Information & Management, 46*, 267–270. doi:10.1016/j.im.2008.12.007

Stahl, B. C., Shaw, M., & Neil, D. (2008). *Information systems security management: A critical research agenda*. Paper presented at the SIGSEC Workshop on Information Security and Privacy (WISP) December 13, 2008, Paris, France

Stanton, J. M., Stam, K. R., Mastrangelo, P., & Jolton, J. (2005). Analysis of end user security behaviors. *Computers & Security, 24*(2), 124–133. doi:10.1016/j.cose.2004.07.001

Straub, D. W., & Welke, R. J. (1998). Coping with systems risks: Security planning models for management decision making. *Management Information Systems Quarterly, 22*(4), 441–469. doi:10.2307/249551

Thomson, K.-L., & von Solms, R. (2006). Towards an information security competence maturity model. *Computer Fraud & Security, 5,* 11–14. doi:10.1016/S1361-3723(06)70356-6

KEY TERMS AND DEFINITIONS

Goals Maps: A technique to analyze goals where main goals are related to sub-goals. The sub-goals are means to achieve the main goals.

Information Quality in Health Care: Information that is fit for use by information stakeholders. Information quality is often defined by a number of attributes such as accuracy, precision and timeliness.

Information Security Goals: Goals guiding work with information security in an organisation. Information security goals are included in information security policy.

Information Security Governance: The creation, management and maintenance of an environment handling the risks related to the Confidentiality, Integrity and Availability of information and its supporting processes and systems.

Information Security Policy: A document giving directions for information security within an organisation. Information security policy includes the most important goals for work with information security in the organisation.

Information Security: The protection of all information handling activities, may these be technical or non technical

International Security Standards: Collection of best practices and guidelines for management of information security in organisations. Information security standards offer guidance and requirements for writing an effective information security policy.

RITE: Responsibility, Integrity, Trust, Ethicality are principles suggested in the literature to complement The CIA-triad

The CIA-triad: Confidentiality, Integrity, Availability, the traditional objectives for management of information security in organisations

Chapter 6
Graphical Passwords

Luigi Catuogno
Università degli Studi di Salerno, Italy

Clemente Galdi
Università degli Studi di Napoli "Federico II", Italy

ABSTRACT

Authentication is probably one of the main security processes that almost everybody has at one point used. Currently, the most widespread authentication mechanism is based on textual passwords, a well-established approach that, with the growth of users and services, has increasing and serious drawbacks. With the rise of high quality displays and more ergonomic human computer interaction mechanisms such as mice, touch-pads and touch-screens, graphical passwords are credited as a valuable replacement to old-fashioned passwords. In contrast to alphanumerical passwords, graphical authentication mechanisms promise greater memorability and usability. In this chapter, an overview of the state-of-art of this topic is presented, introducing some of the main schemes proposed in current literature. The issues and concerns related to security and usability, which still challenge the researchers in this area, are also discussed.

INTRODUCTION

One of the key issues that every multi-user system has to manage is the identification of the users who are authorized to access its services. This problem has a long history in the field of computer security and its evolution has had a tremendous impact on user behaviour over the last few decades. Furthermore, it is not uncommon that the success of a service strongly depends on its ease of use, which includes the procedures that are needed to access it. From this point of view, crucial issues

that every identification system has to explicitly validate is, on the one hand, its security and, on the other, the effort that users will need to use it, i.e., its usability.

The problem of identification has many different aspects, depending on factors such as the specific application scenario in which it has to be solved, the technological constraints (or freedom), the security level of the information to be protected, the users expectations as well as their willingness to trade effort with security.

Nowadays, it is possible to assume that all the potential users of a service are used to Password or PIN based identification systems. This assump-

DOI: 10.4018/978-1-4666-0978-5.ch006

tion comes from the very simple fact that operations such as logging onto a personal computer or withdrawing money from an ATM are carried out by almost every human-being in developed countries on a daily basis.

These identification systems have the huge advantage of being (a) well known and (b) trusted by users. Such properties have clear benefits when deploying a new service in terms of user education and service acceptance. Nevertheless, password and PIN based authentication systems have well-known security issues such as guessing attacks, users problems in remembering different passwords and so forth. Moreover, user identification to distributed services poses the problem of securing the transmission of the user credentials through a potentially unprotected channel.

There have been many different improvements in password based authentication schemes over the years, including systems that prevent the selection of passwords "too easy to be guessed", one-time password schemes as well as biometric identification devices. When considering the most important and well-consolidated solutions, the impression is that they all aim at solving certain security issues by introducing some form of overhead to the user operation. In other words, any security improvement is often paid in terms of ease of use.

Graphical Password schemes have emerged as a possible security enhancing and user-friendly alternative to the old-fashioned password based authentication schemes. The key idea behind this new approach is that the operational overhead as well as the increased size and complexity of passwords, introduced to improve security, could be mapped to some type of information that humans can easily handle: images.

Among several "human affordable" authentication protocols, Graphical Password schemes have been studied since the early nineties. However, there have been significant developments over the last decade, due to the increasing availability of human-computer interaction technologies.

While earlier proposals were based on the idea of substituting letters and digits with images, more recent and sophisticated schemes have considered improving ergonomics by replacing classical interaction means such as the keyboard and screen with a plethora of new devices, including touchscreens, pointing devices at large or even devices capable of tracking user eyes movements as well as communicating through tactile stimulation.

This trend has had two significant consequences: (a) graphical identification systems are suitable for those pervasive computing devices (e.g., smart phones, PDAs) that no longer feature traditional human-computer interaction or have some computational constraint; (b) graphical identification systems can potentially outperform, in terms of user confidence and acceptance, the traditional identification systems in those applications where authentication and other security related tasks (e.g., stating authorization and access control rules) should be accomplished by poorly skilled users (e.g., elderly) or by people with impairments, someone who needs accessible interaction devices, for example, in the e-Health application scenario.

These considerations make graphical identification schemes a strategic research field that promises important innovations to ICT, especially to technologies for e-governance.

In this chapter, the world of Graphical Passwords will be reviewed. The review will not be a mere listing of existing schemes, it will extensively describe basic ideas that have been used by different systems, in order to try to evaluate how the different schemes deal with the two main concerns: security and usability.

BACKGROUND

It is commonly believed that password-based authentication systems are secure as long as the passwords are kept secret. This misconception is wrong due to a number of reasons.

Most of the time, users need to gain access to different services provided by different providers. Furthermore, passwords are often used to also protect private information, such as cryptographic keys or data files, stored on insecure devices. It is widely understood that it is impossible, even for the most skilled users to associate (and remember) a different password to every service or data they need to protect. Since service/data protection is essential, different users are likely to adopt simple strategies in order to make the password-remembering task easier.

Users might, for example, use the same password for all the services and data. This strategy has the clear advantage of eliminating the issue of remembering the per-service password recall problem but it has different drawbacks. If the password is compromised, an adversary has free access to every single piece of secured data/service. If the password is lost, the user can no longer access its data/services. It is worth noting that the last problem becomes an actual issue whenever, for example, one of the service providers requires its password to be changed. In this case, a subtler problem occurs. In fact, the user needs to change the password to every service and every piece of secured data and, if he forgets to do so for some of them, he will not be able to recall which password was associated to which service, i.e., he will "lose" the corresponding password.

Another common strategy is the one of selecting easy-to-remember passwords, e.g., dates, names, or words in a given language, or easy to remember "variations" (Bishop & Klein, 1995) of the above. It is not hard to see that the set of possible passwords that can be constructed using such a strategy is exponentially smaller than the set of all possible passwords of a given length. Different softwares (Openwall, 2010; Oxid, 2010) are therefore able to find-out the user password by executing a so-called dictionary attack, i.e., by simply trying to guess the password used by the user by selecting it among the ones in a given dictionary, e.g., the one containing all English words.

Different countermeasures have been adopted in order to reduce the problems related to the selection of easy-to-guess passwords. The first one consists of providing the user with a random password and forbidding to change it. This system is effective since every password held by every user is hard-to-guess. On the other hand, random passwords are hard to remember and, essentially, there is no chance that a user can use the same password for two different systems. The most successful solution is the one implemented by a proactive password checker (Bergadano, Crispo, & Ruffo, 1998; Ciaramella, D'Arco, Santis, Galdi, & Tagliaferri, 2006). This type of software filters easy-to-guess passwords and only allows the user to change the current password with a hard-to-guess one. The advantage with respect to the randomly generated password is that the user can select the passwords and, thus, is more likely to remember it.

Every solution that reduces the impact of guessing attacks cannot, however, overcome wrong user behaviour or more complex attack scenarios. For example, users might write down passwords on a piece of paper and store it in one of the drawers in their desk. In this way, everyone that has access to some specific physical object can gain access to all the service/data secured using the password therein stored. An adversary might observe the user while typing in the password. In this case, however complex the password is, a single observation compromises the security of the access. A more complex situation is associated to phishing attacks in which the adversary plays an active role by fraudulently convincing the user to reveal his password(s).

In summary, text-based password authentication systems have the huge advantage of being well-known, accepted and trusted by users with different technological abilities. On the other hand, they have a number of drawbacks that endanger service/data security.

Different approaches have been pursued in order to improve the security of password-based authentication systems.

One of the earliest examples of on this topic is presented in (Lamport, 1981), who proposed a one-time password scheme, i.e., an authentication method in which the user has to prove the knowledge of the password instead of providing it. This scheme belongs to the family of challenge and response protocols, where the system issues a challenge to the user, who has to compute a given function of the challenge as well as the secret password. The system successfully authenticates the user if the provided result is correct. The term one-time means that the same password can be used for several authentication rounds, but the response computed by the user is different for each round.

Several implementations of the aforementioned scheme were proposed in (Haller, 1994) and (McDonald, Atkinson, & Metz, 1995). The main drawback of this approach is that the user needs the help of a cryptographic device in order to compute the answer correctly.

Graphical password authentication systems constitute a step forward in classical password schemes, trying to maintain the benefits of classical schemes, while securing them against different attack scenarios.

GRAPHICAL PASSWORD: A REVIEW

Graphical passwords are a possible security enhancing and user-friendly alternative to the old-fashioned password authentication scheme, relying on the fact that humans remember images better than words (Grady, Mcintosh, Rajah, & Craik, 1998), (De Angeli, Coventry, Johnson, & Renaud, 2005), (Shepard, 2006). Among several "human affordable"' authentication protocols such as (Matsumoto & Imai, 1991), (Wang, Hwang, & Tsai, 1995), (Matsumoto T., 1996), (Hopper & Blum, 2000), (Hopper & Blum, 2001)

an authentication mechanism using graphical passwords was first proposed in (Blonder, 1996). Graphical passwords have been studied since the early '90s. However, there have been significant developments over the last decade, based on the increasing availability of human-computer interaction technologies.

There are different kinds of graphical password schemes. They differ from each other according to the way they deal with the two main concerns: usability and security.

Graphical Password Classification

Graphical password schemes are frequently classified according to the cognitive mechanism they are based on. Following the lead of (Raaijmakers & Shiffrin, 1992), the studies by Suo *et al.* (Suo, Zhu, & Owen, 2005) and (Hafiz, Abdullah, Ithnin, & Mammi, 2008) describe a classification of graphical password schemes composed of two groups: recall-based, and recognition-based schemes. Recall-based schemes rely on the user's ability in reproducing a pre-defined behaviour (e.g., reproduce a drawing). Recognition-based schemes are based on the user's ability to recognize, among a set of images, only those *pass-images* he previously selected as his secret.

This classification is essentially agreed upon (Monrose & Reiter, 2005) where, in addition, the authors introduce a third group: "Image interpretation" containing InkBlot (Stubblefield & Simon, 2004) as a representative scheme. This paper also evaluates the suitability of schemes from each class, for user authentication or key generation purposes.

In (Biddle, Chiasson, & van Oorschot, 2009) (Lashkari, Towhidi, Saleh, & Farmand, 2009) and (Towhidi & Masrom, 2009), recall based schemes are divided into: *pure* and *cued*. In a pure recall-based scheme, the user has to reproduce the secret without being given any hint, whereas in cued schemes, the system provides the user with some help in remembering precisely the secret.

Cued recall-based schemes are also known, in literature, as "Click-based" schemes. This is the classification adopted throughout this chapter.

In (De Angeli, Coventry, Johnson, & Renaud, 2005), (Renaud, 2009), graphical password schemes are grouped into three different sets according to the user's ability they measure, denoted respectively as: *cognometric*, *locimetric* and *drawmetric* schemes.

Cognometric schemes aim at measuring the user's ability to recognize target images amongst a set of distractor images. This group, which overlaps the recognition-based class defined above, has been refined further in (Renaud, 2009).

Locimetric systems are based on the user's ability to localize a point within a background image. The graphical password schemes of this class equally fit the cued recall-based, as well as *drawmetric* schemes, which measure the ability to reproduce a pre-selected image, coinciding with the pure recall-based system. One of the reasons for this class being renamed is the hypothesis that locimetric and drawmetric schemes actually measure two different mental processes, respectively: locating a place leveraging on a set of reference points, and reproducing the shape of an object by drawing it on a white sheet of paper.

In current graphical password literature, security and usability aspects of any scheme are evaluated according to metrics and qualitative criteria that are somehow common to every scheme belonging to the same class. Moreover, it is thought that schemes from different classes might perform differently if applied to the same problem. For example, recall based schemes are more suitable for user authentication on PDAs or systems equipped with pointing devices, while certain recognition-based schemes are more suited to authentication on keypad based interfaces (e.g., desktop computers, ATMs). Recently, to improve security, several multi-factor graphical password schemes have been proposed. These schemes put together different authentication paradigms (e.g., a graphical panel and a personal handheld device), with their overall classification, as well as the enumeration of evaluation criteria, not always being easy. Therefore, several multi-factor schemes are discussed separately.

Pure Recall-Based Schemes

In the *Draw A Secret (DAS)* scheme proposed by (Jermyn, Mayer, Monrose, Reiter, & Rubin, 1999), the user is required to paint a pre-defined two-dimensional picture in the same way he did during the registration phase (that is, drawing lines and points in the same order and on the same coordinates). A rather similar scheme is PassDoodles (Varenhorst, 2005).

One of the drawbacks of DAS is that the user choices, in creating the secret, are rather predictable and, in particular, symmetric drawings seems to be largely preferred. In order to overcome this problem, the BDAS scheme (Dunphy & Yan, 2007) shows a background image that encourages the user to break the symmetry in his paintings.

GrIDsure (GriIDsure Ltd, 2010) is a different kind of pure recall-based scheme, and is used to communicate a PIN code to the user of an ATM or similar devices. The user initially draws a pattern on a 5x5 matrix which is as long as the PIN. The user has to remember the pattern and the sequence of cells passed through when drawing it. During the authentication phase, the system challenges the user with a numeric 5x5 matrix. The user has to ideally re-draw the pattern on the matrix in the challenge and has to type, as a PIN, the numbers which appear in each cell in the pattern, following the same order as in the registration.

Cued Recall-Based Schemes

The archetype of a "cued recall-based" scheme is the one introduced in (Blonder, 1996). In this scheme, an image is displayed on the screen and the user is required to click on some previously chosen regions of the image, according to a certain sequence. The images, regions and sequences of the clicks are selected when the user registers.

The *PassPoints* system (Wiedenbeck, Waters, J.-C., Brodskiy, & Memon, 2005) improves the Blonder's scheme by allowing the user to select both the background image and the sequence of points to be clicked, during a preliminary user registration phase. The GPEX project, (Bicakci, Yuceel, Erdeniz, Gurbaslar, & Atalay, 2009), focuses on the design of an extension for the WEB browser, which features a graphical authentication system similar to PassPoints.

The Cued Click Points (Chiasson, van Oorschot, & Biddle, Graphical Password Authentication Using Cued Click Points, 2007) system, shows the user a sequence of images and the user is asked to click just one point for each image (instead of doing multiple clicks on the same background). The images are extracted from a pre-defined portfolio. If an incorrect click occurs, the sequence of images is altered and the images from different portfolios can be shown, giving the user an *implicit feedback* about the correctness of his answers.

In the Tell-a-Story system (Maets, Onno, & Heen, 2009), the user preliminarily builds his own secret by selecting a background image (the scene) and populating it with set of objects, each one placed in a certain position, according to the order given by a story, the user tells to himself. During the authentication, the user has to rebuild the scene following the same sequence as in the registration phase. The main aim of this scheme is to improve the authentication ergonomics as well as secret memorability.

Recognition-Based Schemes

As discussed later, Recall-based schemes present several drawbacks. They are particularly prone to the so-called Shoulder-Surfing attack, in which, any occasional observer, looking at the authentication session, may learn "which points the legacy users clicks on". In order to overcome

this problem, Graphical password schemes based on *pass-images* or *pass-icons*, challenge the user with scenes populated with dynamically generated arrangements of small icons, rather than static screenshots. The system generally has several sets of images among which the user chooses a subset of pass-images that constitutes the secret. In order to be authenticated, the user no longer replies with a sequence of clicks (i.e., the secret), but rather composes a responses that depends on which of his pass-images he sees on the screen that corresponds to proving he knows the secret.

In other words, the system challenges the human to play a kind of *cognitive game* in which, only who knows the secret can make the correct move. Under certain conditions (ranging from scheme to scheme), unaware observers could not (easily) learn the secret.

In the *Dèjá vu* system (Perrig & Song, 1999) (Dhamija & Perrig, 2000), the user, during the registration phase, is allowed to choose some images from a set of random pictures generated by the system. Later on, in order to be authenticated, the user has to recognize his pre-selected images in the set of images shown by the system.

Jansen *et al.* proposed an analogous paradigm in (Jensen, Gavrila, Korolev, Ayers, & Swanstrom, 2003), whereas, the ``Pass-Faces'' project by Real User Corp. (Real User Coorp., 1998) uses images of human faces instead of generic pictures. Sobrado and Birget (Sobrado & Birget, 2002) proposed a scheme where, during the registration phase, the user chooses a set of small pictures (pass-icons). When the user logs in, the system shows a screenshot populated by many different icons. In order to be authenticated, the user has to click any icon belonging to the convex-hull whose vertices are the pre-selected pass-icons. This scheme has been improved in (Wiedenbeck, Waters, Sobrado, & Birget, 2006).

In the scheme presented in (Weinshall, 2006), the user has to prove that he has recognized the path that connects all his pass-icons that the system has included in the challenge. The setup of this scheme is quite complicated. Users need to pass a training phase that spans over two days, and the login time can require up to several minutes.

The aim of the GraPE scheme (Catuogno & Galdi, 2008; Catuogno & Galdi, 2010) is to provide a graphical authentication scheme that is easily deployable over a wide range of equipment and, in particular, on computational constrained devices such as old-fashioned cell-phones, as well as devices with limited interaction capabilities such as smart cards or embedded systems in general. In GraPE, the challenge is a matrix of visual objects. The user has to enter, as a PIN, the row numbers of all the objects included in his secret. The paper presents two randomized protocols, which allow the user to arbitrarily introduce some errors in the response, in order to improve the resilience to shoulder surfing attacks.

Multi-Factor Schemes

TwoSteps (van Oorschot & Wan, 2009) is a hybrid scheme, which authenticates the user through both a textual and a graphical password. When registering, the user chooses his password, a portfolio of icons and, among them, he selects his own pass-icons. When the user logs in, he has to type the correct password and, recognize his pass-icons into the scenes the system shows him in a configurable number of rounds.

A two-factor enhancement of GraPE is described in (Catuogno & Galdi, 2010). More precisely, the authors improve their randomized protocol, by providing the user with a personal mini-device (which could possibly be embedded into a cell-phone or even in latest generation smart cards) that suggests to the user the errors to be made while typing the PIN, according to a random sequence generated by a secret seed, shared by the computer and the device.

Real User Corp. has recently enabled the "Pass-Faces" (Real User Coorp., 1998) scheme to be used as a "two-way" authentication scheme, by combining it with a server authentication mechanism.

A wide range of two-factor schemes, for mobile phones and hand held devices have been proposed. The two-factor improvement of a cued recall scheme such as PassPoints (Sabzevar & Stavrou, 2008) is discussed as a typical example.

SECURITY CONCERNS

In order to evaluate the security of an identification system, it is crucial to understand what possible threats have to be faced. For example, an identification system that needs to be used for an ATM machine has different requirements from one for accessing a service on the Internet. Thus, a scheme could be considered "secure" within a certain threat model, while unsuitable in a different scenario. A threat model is defined by security issues coming from: (a) the operational environment, e.g., "input device(s)", communication channel security, interaction with other identification schemes, etc, and (b) the identification scheme itself e.g., graphical password guessability/predictability, information leaking, suitability for passive/active attacks, etc. Unfortunately, to date, only a few papers describe several security models in detail. Among these papers, a few of them actually analyze the security of the presented scheme with respect to a specific security model. A taxonomy of security models is discussed in order to feasibly identify, for a specific application scenario, which might be the security threat that a graphical identification scheme should be able to withstand.

General Threat Models

The deployment and maintenance of every digital system that manages sensitive information are extremely hard tasks. Intuitively, the inherent complexity of such operations derives from the observation that the system needs to face *every practical threat* by properly combining secure subsystems that, most of the time, are (theoretically or empirically) validated against *specific attacks*.

Furthermore, whenever humans are involved in the system operations, physical security and user behavior need to be taken into account in order to prevent, or at least reduce, security issues due to user misbehavior.

It is the aim of this chapter to fully analyze the issues related to digital systems security, focusing on the threats that are specific to authentication systems. However, in order to clarify the discussion, a categorization of attacks that might constitute security threats to digital systems will be briefly presented.

The first step in analyzing the security of a system is the identification of the points of failure, i.e., the possible agents or parts of the systems that might be targets for an attacker. In an authentication system the possible points of failures are the user, the user terminal (including both hardware and software), the communication channel used by the terminal to route messages to the service provider and the actual system to which the user is gaining access (again, including both hardware and software).

In the context of this chapter, only the issues related to the first two points of failures, i.e., the user and the user terminal are considered. It is assumed that the communication channel and the digital system are secured using the proper countermeasures.

Every attack is defined by the goal that the adversary is willing to attain. Typical examples of attack goals might be secret extraction (e.g., extracting the user password from the password file) for a specific user or any user on a given system, authentication (without the knowledge of the whole secret information), denial-of-service, etc.

In principal, every attacker can be associated to one of the following categories: passive or active. A *passive adversary* is the one that tries to obtain information by simply observing the interaction among the agents in the system. For example, in the case of password authentication, a passive adversary is able to observe either the user display, or his keyboard (or both), and register

the interaction. An *active adversary* has the ability to interact with one or more agents and observes their response to (possibly maliciously modified) messages. For example, a forged smart-card reader might interact with the smart card by sending specific messages in order to gain information about the sensitive data therein stored.

Every attack can be classified as being either *off-line* or *on-line*. In an off-line attack, the adversary holds some data (e.g., password file, transcripts of communications, etc.) and analyzes them to obtain sensitive information. In an on-line attack, the adversary interacts with one or more agents in the system to reach the attack goal.

A *threat model* identifies the context in which the authentication system has been proved to be secure, i.e. the attack goal, the adversary type, attack type and attack context. As stated above, in this case the threat model does not include either the network connection or the system to which the user is authenticating.

Password-Related Security Issues

The purpose of every authentication mechanism is to allow legitimate users to properly access a given system and prevent, as much as possible, an illegal user gaining access to it. From this point of view, it is possible to identify different attack goals for an adversary. The most difficult task for an adversary is obtaining the secret information, e.g., password or graphical password, for a user on a given system. Whenever such goal is reached, the adversary can *always* log-in in place of the user using his secret information. A more relaxed goal might be the possibility to obtain *parts of the secret*. Intuitively, the latter attack, even if successful, might allow the attacker to impersonate a legitimate user with some probability strictly less than 1. Orthogonally, it is possible to consider attacks that are targeting *any* user, rather than *a specific user* for a given system. Clearly, the former attack goal appears to be easier than the latter.

Following the terminology in (Biddle, Chiasson, & van Oorschot, 2009), attacks to password and graphical password authentication schemes can be typically partitioned into *Guessing* attacks or *Capture* attacks. This classification does not correspond to the general *Passive/Active* one. In particular, some on-line guessing attacks might be considered, to some extent, *active*, in the sense they do need to be reactive to system responses. In the following, known attack strategies to graphical password schemes are described, with some of them directly deriving from a corresponding strategy known for the text-based password schemes.

Guessing Attacks

In Guessing attacks, the adversary tries to *guess* the user secret without any prior knowledge. The most intuitive example of such attacks is a *brute-force* attack corresponding to *trying every possible password*. These attacks can be successful if the number of possible keys, also known as the *key space*, is reasonably small. Clearly the adversary needs to have a way of realizing whether or not the password he is currently testing is correct. In an off-line attack, the adversary holds a file containing the passwords coded using *hash* function, i.e., a function that can be computed easily but for which, given a value in the co-domain, it is computationally infeasible to compute the pre-image. In the on-line version of the guessing attack, the adversary simply tries to authenticate to the service by providing a known username and the password he is testing. For the text-based password schemes, in current literature there is a number of techniques that try to reduce the probability of success for the adversary. Some of them are the extension of the password space obtained by forbidding the users to select easy-to-guess passwords, increasing the number of applications of the hash function required to validate a password or, for on-line attacks, doubling the response time or every unsuccessful login attempt, and so forth.

Although intuitively it might seem impossible to guess a secret in a graphical password scheme, this is completely wrong.

Brute Force: The Key Space

In the context of graphical passwords, the size of the key space is an important measure in preventing brute force attacks. There are schemes, e.g., (Catuogno & Galdi, 2008; Pass Faces, 1998) that, for specific values of several system parameters, induce a small key-space. These limitations make on-line guessing attacks feasible, with the known countermeasures, which include doubling response time for each unsuccessful trial or blocking the account after a small number of unsuccessful attempts, being a possible solution. However, it is worth noting that such solutions have costly side effects. In fact, on the one hand, the system becomes subject to denial-of-service attacks. An adversary might simply keep trying to authenticate random user accounts by blocking them in case they exist. A second, non trivial side effect, is the need to set up a sufficient customer-care help desk in order to restore legitimate user accounts when they have been blocked by an adversary. The deployment of authentication systems with a set of parameters that make them subject to brute force attacks should be avoided.

Password Predictability

A more refined class of guessing attacks is based on the observation that whenever the users are allowed to select their graphical passwords, similarly to what happens for text-based password, the selection is not done uniformly on the whole set of possible secrets. This characteristic makes user selected passwords predictable compared to with respect to randomly generated ones. In current literature, there are several papers dealing with password predictability.

Several studies address the fact that some click-points (hot-spots) can be chosen by the user, as part of his secret, more likely than the others (Thorpe & van Oorschot, 2007) (Salehi-Abari, Thorpe, & Oorschot, 2008) (Bicakci, Yuceel, Erdeniz, Gurbaslar, & Atalay, 2009) giving an adversary an advantage in *guessing* the secret. It is worth noting that password predictability is an issue in every class of graphical password scheme. Examples of these attacks include (Thorpe & van Oorschot, 2004; Thorpe & van Oorschot, 2004) for DAS (Davis, Monrose, & Reiter, 2004) for Passfaces, or (Thorpe & van Oorschot, 2007) for PassPoints.

Capture Attacks

In the context of graphical passwords, an active attack corresponds to an adversary that tries to gain either the whole secret or some information that can be used to reconstruct it. In this context, three major classes of attacks can be identified.

Shoulder Surfing

A shoulder surfing attack assumes that the adversary is able to observe the interaction between the user and the terminal while he is typing in the password. It is worth noting that in a classical text-based password scheme a single authentication by a legitimate user is sufficient for the adversary to obtain the whole password. As stated above, all recall-based schemes are typically subject to this type of attack since the user is required to reproduce some type of secret, just as for text-based password schemes. A slightly more complex discussion is necessary for recognition-based schemes. In this class of authentication mechanisms, the challenge to which the user has to answer is randomized and, thus, the mere imitation of the user behaviour, e.g., "clicking on the first image in the matrix" could not work. On the other hand, some schemes, e.g., Pass-Faces, require the user to select some pictures from a set of randomly chosen ones. In this case, an observer can register the set of faces selected by the user as part of the secret that might be used in subsequent fraudulent attempts. Thus, also in this class, some schemes cannot withstand shoulder surfing for "obvious" reasons.

It is worth noting that one of the main aims of early schemes was ergonomics. In addition, they did not feature any effective countermeasures against a malicious observer, who, in some cases, could learn the user secret just by observing a single or few authentication sessions. In order to deal with this threat, the following two strategies could be adopted.

The first strategy aims to make it difficult for the adversary to realize and understand what happens during the user log-in. In (Harada, Isarida, Mizuno, & Nishigaki, 2006; Hayashi, Dhamija, Christin, & Perrig, 2008), the system shows the user a distorted version of his pass-icons, based on the assumption that the legitimate user, being aware of the original pictures, is able to recognize them, whereas the adversary cannot. In (DeLuca, Denzel, & Hussmann, 2009; Kumar, Garfinkel, Boneh, & Winograd, 2007), the system gets the user response by means of a device that tracks his eyes movements, making it impossible for the adversary to capture the user's actions.

The second strategy assumes that the adversary is able to extract the transcripts of a certain number of authentication sessions and aims to lower the advantage that he can obtain from guessing the secret by processing the collected information.

Schemes described in (Roth, Richter, & Freidinger, 2004; Wiedenbeck, Waters, Sobrado, & Birget, 2006; Weinshall, 2006; Catuogno & Galdi, 2008) replace the simple image recognition with a cognitive game the user has to play in order to be authenticated and that he can easily answer correctly the challenge if aware of the secret. Although these schemes effectively contrast attacks mounted by transitory human observers (few memory, poor computation capabilities), they are still vulnerable to attacks by camera-equipped adversaries, i.e., an adversary that can record an unlimited number of interactions of the user with the terminal.

Sometimes, schemes that at a first glance appear to be secure against this type of attack have been proved to be unable to withstand it. In (Golle & Wagner, 2007), the authors present a simple attack that breaks the scheme presented in (Weinshall, 2006). They used information collected by observing a limited number of queries in building a system of boolean expressions, that could be solved in 102 seconds under the default parameters reported by the original paper after collecting just six-seven authentication transcripts.

Spyware and Malware

Malicious software installed on the user terminal might be used to gather information about user passwords. This type of software ranges from simple keystroke recording, in which the software simply records the sequence of keys used by the user to more complex mouse tracking or screen scraper software. It is worth making several considerations at this point. First of all, malicious software is typically installed *involuntarily* by the users on the terminals for which they have control, e.g., viruses, trojans on the user's PC or laptop. This means that, a *potentially secure* device can become an *insecure* one because of user behaviour. However, the user might be properly trained to avoid or reduce security issues, e.g., by frequently updating anti-viruses databases. The situation is completely different in the case in which the user/ the user organization does not have control over the terminal, e.g., while accessing a service from an Internet-point or while withdrawing money from an ATM.

Obviously, key loggers are sufficient for attacking a text-based password scheme. Typically, depending on the specific graphical password scheme, the adversary might need a combination of the aforementioned tools in order to collect the interaction between the user and the terminal.

Social Engineering

While malicious software targets the terminal used by the user, *Social Engineering* attacks target the user directly, trying to get him to reveal his password or information about it. The most celebrated form of social Engineering is *Phishing*, in which users are required to enter their passwords into websites that resemble the ones of the service providers. A typical phishing attack uses email messages to provide the user with the link of the malicious website. It is worth noting that search engines might also return fraudulent links. Countermeasures against such types of attacks are currently implemented by Email clients (Thunderbird, 2010), anti-spam software, web-browsers (Mozilla, 2010) and search-engines (Google, 2010).

Phishing is considered a *general* type of attack and simply requires the adversary to have an Internet connection. More complex attacks include *personalized* ones, in which a specific user is targeted. In a personalized attack, the adversary collects information about the target user in the hope that he can use it in order to gain the user password. A class of attacks requiring greater effort by the adversary consists of contacting the users using means of communication different form the Internet, e.g., phone calls, text-messages, mail, etc. One advantage of graphical passwords with respect to text-based ones, is that it is hard or even impossible to communicate the graphical password via phone or text-message.

USABILITY CONCERNS

Graphical Password schemes may look very different from each other, and act on different user cognitive abilities. Therefore, it is not easy to find a common way to measure and compare their performance. While some authors evaluate the ergonomics of their schemes by means of a statistical summary of the results of some usage trials, employing as measurement criteria those common parameters like the login time and the error rate, others place emphasis on the amount of information the user has to handle and remember. Finally, other relevant aspects of usability include user confidence and acceptance.

Definition of Usability

The standard document ISO 9241, entitled *"Ergonomics of Human-system interaction"* (International Organization for Standardization (ISO), 1998), defines usability as the *"extent to which a product can be used by specified users to achieve specified goals with effectiveness, efficiency and satisfaction in a specified context of use"*. Where *effectiveness* is defined in terms of *"accuracy and completeness with which users achieve the* specified goals", efficiency denotes "the resources expended in relation to the accuracy and completeness with which the users achieve their goals" and satisfaction is defined as the "freedom from discomfort and positive attitudes to the use of the product" from the user point of view.

This definition relates to interactive systems at large, and the subsequent parts of the standard contain specification and guidelines to design several components of both hardware and software interactive systems, including presentation of information (part 12), user guidance (part 13), accessibility guidelines for ICT equipments (part 20), and guidance on World Wide Web user interfaces (part 151).

In a graphical password scheme, effectiveness concerns the users' capacity for handling the authentication secrets and performing authentication tasks. On the one hand, this involves the users' ability to remember and recall the secret as well as the authentication procedure, while, on the other, how easily the scheme allows users to enter the secret correctly. In current literature, the first aspect is referred to as memorability, that is, "how easily a certain kind of secret can be remembered". The main technique to rate the effectiveness of a

scheme is to measure the average success/error rate of sets of authentication sessions over certain intervals of time. This measurement is obtained by means of trials that involve a significant sample of the scheme's target users for several months. The highest success rate is measured, with the best evaluating the scheme.

Another important index of the effectiveness is how resilient to *interference* the scheme is, that is, how it copes with negative effects that having to remember multiple secrets has on the user's capacity to recall one of them when it is requested (Wiedenbeck, Birget, Brodskiy, J., & Memon, 2005), (Everitt, Bragin, Fogarty, & Kohno, 2009), (Chiasson, Forget, Stobert, van Oorschot, & Biddle, 2009). Difficulties in correctly remembering the secret can occur when a user who normally authenticates to several services with the same scheme, is requested to insert a secret, which is quite similar to the one he uses to access another service. Interference is a critical issue for graphical password schemes and could be clearly become a serious problem whenever graphical authentication is widely adopted,

Efficiency is rated by assessing the resources that both the user and the system employ in order to implement the authentication tasks. From the user's point of view, it generally measures (by means of trials) the time spent for: registration and training, login, changing/resetting the secret. An efficient scheme holds these times as low as possible. On the system side, several considerations are made about the amount of computational resources required to handle the secret such as the disk space needed to store it, the size/resolution of the display needed for its visualization, computational time needed to recognize it, particular pointing devices, etc. This clearly drives the choice of deploying any scheme on certain platforms. For example, deploying a scheme that requires the visualization of huge images on devices with small-sized displays could require the user to waste time in repeatedly scrolling the display, in order to search for the click-points.

Satisfaction is related to the feelings of the users about the authentication scheme. In particular, the satisfactory evaluation of a scheme includes the user's attitude towards using the scheme and its perceived grade of security. These aspects are usually measured by means of qualitative user feedbacks collected by interviews or polls.

Comparing Schemes

Although, the usability evaluation measurements are nowadays rather well-defined, comparing the usability of different schemes is still a non-trivial task. In fact, plenty of studies dealing with the evaluation of graphical password usability have been presented. However, a convincing common framework that makes analytical comparisons of the measured performance possible has still to be created. In fact, even a standard definition of the usability of graphical password schemes is lacking.

Biddle, Chiasson and van Oorschot (Biddle, Chiasson, & van Oorschot, 2009) give a set of guidelines and recommendations that aim at facilitating the comparison among graphical password schemes. The authors argue that the usability of different schemes cannot be easily compared due to the fact that the evaluation should take into account several aspects that may vary according to: Target Users and Domain of application.

In fact, a certain operational complexity of a scheme can be rather acceptable to skilled users (e.g., IT or Security professionals), whereas it could be unaffordable for an uneducated class of users such as the elderly (Renaud, 2006), or people with impairments, that could make using the interface difficult such as people with limited capacity in moving or distinguishing colours (Hochheiser, Feng, & Lazar, 2008).

The suitability of a graphical password scheme, within a certain domain of application is widely believed to be a trade-off between security and usability. Users are more inclined to stand a certain level of complexity where the security requirements are higher, (e.g., in risky applications such as home banking, e-commerce), whereas they may not appreciate complicated schemes to authenticate themselves in more playful applications.

From a process point of view, graphical password schemes are mainly evaluated by measuring how users perform in the authentication-related tasks such as password management (creation, reset and change), and login. An additional parameter that the authors suggest is taking into accounts how performance of a scheme varies as long as the platform it is implemented on changes (portability). An example of non-trivial issues raised by applying the same scheme on two different platforms can be found in (Bicakci, Yuceel, Erdeniz, Gurbaslar, & Atalay, 2009).

CONCLUSION

The development of pervasive computational devices, the widening of services and environments that require user authentication, gives continual new proof of the increasing unreliability of traditional text based authentication mechanisms. Graphical password schemes, over the last decades, have been credited with being a valuable replacement of the old-fashioned password and PINs, due to their greater memorability and usability. Since the early nineties, plenty of schemes, based on the most sophisticated human-computer interaction devices, have been proposed. In this chapter, a comprehensive review of the main proposals and results in this area has been presented. Current literature dealing with important aspects such as classification, as well as security and usability evaluation criteria of graphical passwords schemes was also considered.

However, it is thought that this technology has yet to reach its maturity, since several aspects and effects of its wide deployment are either still unclear or have not been studied in sufficient detail.

Although most of the use studies carried out have highlighted how graphical passwords systems seem to outperform the text-based ones, convincing proof that supports this argument is still lacking, with this being mainly because both the schemes and the evaluation criteria used are often too diverse to be compared. Therefore, performance measurements cannot be easily aggregated and, moreover, the overall evaluation of any scheme largely varies according to the target users and application scenarios. In other words, these studies still does not give a clear view in a world where graphical passwords are the mainstream choice for authentication.

Therefore, further evolution of the graphical password technology urges researchers to investigate the definition of standard frameworks for security and usability evaluation as a necessary prerequisite to achieve more detailed and comparable use studies.

Multi-factor schemes constitute another interesting branch. In fact, coupling a graphical password scheme with a different identification mechanism, ranging from biometric measurements to personal devices such as cellular phones or RFID tags, could help in overcoming different security threats, without significant effects on the overall authentication ergonomics.

REFERENCES

Bergadano, F., Crispo, B., & Ruffo, G. (1998). High dictionary compression for proactive password checking. *ACM Transactions on Information and System Security*, *1*, 3–25. doi:10.1145/290163.290164

Bicakci, K., Yuceel, M., Erdeniz, B., Gurbaslar, H., & Atalay, N. B. (2009). Graphical password as browser extension: Implementation and usability study. *IFIP Advances in Information and Communication Technology*, *300*, 15–29. doi:10.1007/978-3-642-02056-8_2

Biddle, R., Chiasson, S., & van Oorschot, P. C. (2009). *Graphical passwords: Learning from the first generation*. Ottawa, Canada: School of Computer Science, Carleton University.

Bishop, M., & Klein, D. V. (1995). Improving system security via proactive password checking. *Computers & Security*, *14*, 233–249. doi:10.1016/0167-4048(95)00003-Q

Blonder, G. E. (1996). *Patent n. 5559961*. USA.

Blundo, C., D'Arco, P., Santis, A. D., & Galdi, C. (2004). HYPPOCRATES: A new proactive password checker. *Journal of Systems and Software*, *71*, 163–175. doi:10.1016/S0164-1212(03)00004-9

Catuogno, L., & Galdi, C. (2008). A graphical PIN authentication mechanism with applications to smart cards and low-cost devices. *Information Security Theory and Practices, Smart Devices, Convergence and Next Generation Networks, Second IFIP WG 1.2 International Workshop, WISTP, LNCS 5019*, (pp. 16-35). Seville, Spain: Springer-Verlag.

Catuogno, L., & Galdi, C. (2010). On the security of a two-factor authentication scheme. *Information Security Theory and Practices. Security and Privacy of Pervasive Systems and Smart Devices, 4th IFIP WG 11.2 International Workshop, WISTP 2010, LNCS 6033*, (pp. 245-252). Passau, Germany: Springer-Verlag.

Chiasson, S., Forget, A., Stobert, E., van Oorschot, P. C., & Biddle, R. (2009). Multiple password interference in text and graphical passwords. *Proceedings of the 16th ACM conference on Computer and Communication Security (CCS)* (pp. 500-511). ACM.

Chiasson, S., van Oorschot, P. C., & Biddle, R. (2007). *Graphical password authentication using cued click points. ESORICS 2007, LNCS 4734* (pp. 359–374). Dresden, Germany: Springer-Verlag.

Ciaramella, A., D'Arco, P., Santis, A. D., Galdi, C., & Tagliaferri, R. (2006). Neural network techniques for proactive password checking. *IEEE Transactions on Dependable and Secure Computing, 3*, 327–339. doi:10.1109/TDSC.2006.53

Davis, D., Monrose, F., & Reiter, M. K. (2004). On user choice in graphical password schemes. *Proceedings of the 13th USENIX Security Symposium,* August 9-13, 2004, San Diego, CA, USA, (pp. 151-164).

De Angeli, A., Coventry, L., Johnson, G., & Renaud, K. (2005). Is a picture really worth a thousand words? Exploring the feasibility of graphical authentication systems. *International Journal of Human-Computer Studies, 63*(1-2), 128–152. doi:10.1016/j.ijhcs.2005.04.020

DeLuca, A., Denzel, M., & Hussmann, H. (2009). Look into my eyes! Can you guess my password? *Proceedings of the 5th Symposium on Usable Privacy and Security,* (p. 7).

Dhamija, R., & Perrig, A. (2000). Dèjà Vu: A user study using images for authentication. *Proceedings of the 9th USENIX Security Symposium* (p. 4). Denver, CO: USENIX.

Dunphy, P., & Yan, J. (2007). Do background images improve draw a secret graphical passwords? *Proceedings of the 14th ACM Conference on Computer and Communications Security,* (p. 47).

Everitt, K. M., Bragin, T., Fogarty, J., & Kohno, T. (2009). A comprehensive study of frequency, interference, and training of multiple graphical passwords. *Proceedings of the 27th International Conference on Human Factors in Computer Systems* (p. 889-898). Boston, MA: ACM.

Golle, P., & Wagner, D. (2007). Cryptanalysis of a cognitive authentication scheme (extended abstract). *IEEE Symposium on Security and Privacy,* (pp. 66-70).

Google. (2010). *Report phishing site.* Retrieved from http://www.google.com/safebrowsing/report_phish/

Grady, C. L., Mcintosh, A. R., Rajah, M. N., & Craik, F. I. (1998). Neural correlates of the episodic encoding of pictures and words. *Proceedings of the National Academy of Sciences of the United States of America, 95,* 2703–2708. doi:10.1073/pnas.95.5.2703

GriIDsure Ltd. (2010). *GrIDsure: Strong authentication using one-time passwords.* Retrieved from www.gridsure.com

Hafiz, M. D., Abdullah, A. H., Ithnin, N., & Mammi, H. K. (2008). Towards identifying usability and security features of graphical password in knowledge based authentication technique. *2nd Asian Conference on Modelling and Simulation* (pp. 396-403). Kuala Lumpur, Malaysia: IEEE.

Haller, N. (1994). The S/KEY one-time password system. *Symposium on Network and Distributed System Security* (pp. 151-157). Washington, DC: IEEE Computer Society.

Harada, A., Isarida, T., Mizuno, T., & Nishigaki, M. (2006). A user authentication system using schema of visual memory. *Biologically Inspired Approaches to Advanced Information Technology: Second International Workshop, Bioadit 2006, LNCS 3853,* Osaka, Japan 26-27, (pp. 338-345). Springer.

Hayashi, E., Dhamija, R., Christin, N., & Perrig, A. (2008). Use your illusion: Secure authentication usable anywhere. *Proceedings of the 4th Symposium on Usable Privacy and Security,* (pp. 35--45).

Hochheiser, H., Feng, J., & Lazar, J. (2008). *Challenges in universally usable privacy and security.* Symposium on Usable Privacy and Security. Pittsburg, PA: ACM.

Hopper, N. J., & Blum, M. (2000). *A secure human-computer authentication scheme.* Carnegie Mellon Technical Report CMU-CS-00-139. Pittsburgh, PA: CMU.

Hopper, N. J., & Blum, M. (2001). *Secure human identification protocols. ASIACRYPT, LNCS 2248* (pp. 52–66). Gold Coast, Australia: Springer-Verlag.

International Organization for Standardization (ISO). (1998). *Ergonomics of human-system interaction.* ISO.

Jensen, W., Gavrila, S., Korolev, V., Ayers, R., & Swanstrom, R. (2003). *Picture password: A visual login technique for mobile devices.* Gaithersburg, MD: National Institute of Standard and Technologies Interagency Report.

Jermyn, I., Mayer, A., Monrose, F., Reiter, M. K., & Rubin, A. D. (1999). The design and anayisis of graphical passwords. *Proceedings of the 8th USENIX Security Symposium* (pp. 23-26). Washington, DC: USENIX.

Kumar, M., Garfinkel, T., Boneh, D., & Winograd, T. (2007). *Reducing shoulder-surfing by using gaze-based password entry.* Symposium on Usable Privacy and Security (SOUPS).

Lamport, L. (1981). Password authentication with insecure communication. *Communications of the ACM, 24*(11), 770–772. doi:10.1145/358790.358797

Lashkari, A. H., Towhidi, F., Saleh, R., & Farmand, S. (2009). A complete comparison on pure and cued recall-based graphical user authentication algorithms. *Proceedings of the 2nd International Conference on Computer and Electrical Engineering* (pp. 527-532). IEEE.

Maets, Y., Onno, S., & Heen, O. (2009). Recall-a-story, a story-telling graphical password system. *Proceedings of the 5th Symposium on Usable Privacy and Security* (p. 1). Mountain View, CA: ACM.

Matsumoto, T. (1996). *Human-computer cryptography: An attempt. Computer and Communication Security* (pp. 68–75). New Delhi, India: ACM.

Matsumoto, T., & Imai, H. (1991). *Human identification through insecure channel. EUROCRYPT, LNCS 547* (pp. 409–421). Brighton, UK: Springer-Verlag.

McDonald, D. L., Atkinson, R. J., & Metz, C. (1995). One time passwords in everything (OPIE): Experiences with building and using stronger authentication. *5th USENIX Security Symposium* (p. 16). Salt Lake City, UT: USENIX.

Monrose, F., & Reiter, M. (2005). Graphical passwords. In Crantor, L., & Garfinkel, S. (Eds.), *Security and usability: Designing secure systems that people can use* (pp. 157–174). Sebastopol, CA: O'Reilly Media.

Mozilla. (2010). *Firefox features, anti-malware, anti-phishing.* Retrieved from http://www.mozilla.com/en-US/ firefox/features/#anti-phishing

Openwall. (2010). *John the ripper.* Retrieved from http://www.openwall.com/john/

Oxid. (2010). *Available at Cain and Abel, password recovery tool for Microsoft operating systems.* Retrieved from http://www.oxid.it/cain.html

Perrig, A., & Song, D. (1999). Hash visualization: A new technique to improve real-world security. *Proceedings of the 1999 International Workshop on Cryptographic Techniques and E-Commerce.*

Raaijmakers, J. G., & Shiffrin, R. M. (1992). Models for recall and recognition. *Annual Review of Psychology, 43,* 205–234. doi:10.1146/annurev. ps.43.020192.001225

Real User Coorp. (1998). *Passfaces*. Retrieved from http://www.realuser.com

Renaud, K. (2006). *A visuo-biometric authentication mechanism for older users* (pp. 167–182). People and Computers XIX-The Bigger Picture.

Renaud, K. (2009). Guidelines for designing graphical authentication mechanism interfaces. *International Journal of Information and Computer Security*, 3(1), 60–85. doi:10.1504/IJICS.2009.026621

Roth, V., Richter, K., & Freidinger, R. (2004). A PIN-entry method resiliant against shoulder-surfing. *Proceedings of the 11th ACM Conference on Computer and Communications Security* (p. 236-245). Washington, DC: ACM.

Sabzevar, A. P., & Stavrou, A. (2008). Universal multi-factor authentication using graphical passwords. *Proceedings of IEEE International Conference on Signal Image Technology and Internet based Systems SITIS* (pp. 625-632). IEEE.

Salehi-Abari, A., Thorpe, J., & Oorschot, P. (2008). On purely automated attacks and click-based graphical passwords. *Proceedings of the 2008 Annual Computer Security Applications Conference*, (pp. 111-120).

Shepard, R. N. (2006). Recognition memory for words, sentences, and pictures. *Journal of Verbal Learning and Verbal Behavior*, 6, 156–163. doi:10.1016/S0022-5371(67)80067-7

Sobrado, L., & Birget, J. C. (2002). Graphical password. *The Rutgers Scholar, An Electronic Bulletin for Undergraduate Research, 4*.

Stubblefield, A., & Simon, D. (2004). *Inkblot authentication*. Microsoft Corporation.

Suo, X., Zhu, Y., & Owen, G. S. (2005). Graphical passwords: A survey. *Proceedings of the 21st Annual Computer Security Application Conference(ACSAC)* (pp. 101-202). Tucson, AZ: IEEE.

Thorpe, J., & van Oorschot, P. (2007). Human-seeded attacks and exploiting hot-spots in graphical passwords. *Proceedings of 16th USENIX Security Symposium.*

Thorpe, J., & van Oorschot, P. C. (2004). Graphical dictionaries and the memorable space of graphical passwords. *Proceedings of the 13th USENIX Security Symposium,* August 9-13, 2004, San Diego, CA, USA, (pp. 135-150).

Thorpe, J., & van Oorschot, P. C. (2004). Towards secure design choices for implementing graphical passwords. *20th Annual Computer Security Applications Conference (ACSAC 2004),* 6-10 December 2004, Tucson, AZ, USA, (pp. 50-60).

Thunderbird. (2010). *Thunderbird features, anti-malware, anti-phishing.* Retrieved from http://www.mozillamessaging.com/en-US/thunderbird/features/

Towhidi, F., & Masrom, M. (2009). A survey on recognition based graphical user authentication algorithms. *International Journal of Computer Science adn Information Security (IJCSIS)*, 119-127.

van Oorschot, P. C., & Wan, T. (2009). TwoStep: An authentication method combining text and graphical passwords. *E-Technologies: Innovation in an Open World, 4th International Conference, MCETECH* (pp. 233-239). Ottawa, Canada: Springer-Verlag.

Varenhorst, C. (2005). *Passdoodles: A lightweight authentication method,* (p. 15). Research Science Institute. Retrieved from http://people.csail.mit.edu/emax/ papers/varenhorst. pdf

Wang, C. H., Hwang, T., & Tsai, J. J. (1995). *On the Matsumoto and Imai's human identification scheme. EUROCRYPT, LNCS 921* (pp. 382–392). Saint-Malo, France: Springer-Verlag.

Weinshall, D. (2006). Cognitive authentication schemes safe agains spyware. *IEEE Symposium on Security and Privacy* (pp. 295-300). Berkeley, CA: IEEE Computer Society.

Wiedenbeck, S., Birget, J. C., Brodskiy, A. J. W., & Memon, N. (2005). Authentication using graphical passwords: Effects of tolerance and image choice. *Proceedings of Symposium on Usable Privacy and Security (SOUPS)* (p. 1-12). Pittsburgh, PA: ACM.

Wiedenbeck, S., Waters, J., Sobrado, L., & Birget, J. C. (2006). Design and evaluation of a shoulder-surfing resistant graphical password scheme. *Proceedings of Advanced Visual Interfaces, AVI, 2006*, 177–184.

Wiedenbeck, S., Waters, J. J.-C., Brodskiy, A., & Memon, N. (2005). PassPoints: Design and longitudinal evaluation of a graphical password system. *International Journal of Human-Computer Studies, 63*(1-2), 102–127. doi:10.1016/j.ijhcs.2005.04.010

KEY TERMS AND DEFINITIONS

Active Attack: An attack type in which the adversary can read, modify or even create messages between two parties.

Graphical Password Scheme: A human authentication mechanism in which the user needs to show the knowledge of some graphical password.

Graphical Password: A secret sequence of images, or parts of them, used for authentication purposes.

Guessing Attack: A passive attack in which an adversary tries to guess the Graphical Password of a user without any prior knowledge.

Passive Attack: An attack type in which the adversary can observe the communication between a user and a terminal without being able to modify the exchanged messages.

Social Engineering: Attack strategies in which an adversary tries to convince the users to perform specific tasks like reveal confidential information.

Threat Model: The definition of the operational environment and the security issues that a protocol considers.

Chapter 7
Assessing the Security of Software Configurations

Afonso Araújo Neto
University of Coimbra, Portugal

Marco Vieira
University of Coimbra, Portugal

ABSTRACT

Security evaluation is a complex problem. As more and more software systems become available, more diversity and alternatives can be found to accomplish the same tasks. However, there is still a lack of a standard approach that can be used to choose among the available alternatives or evaluate their configuration security. In this chapter, the authors present a methodology to devise security appraisals, which is based on the collection of widespread security knowledge for a specific domain. They demonstrate their methodology by devising two specific appraisals for the domain of transactional systems. The first one can be used to evaluate and assess the configuration of an already deployed database installation, while the target of the second one is to compare the capability of specific database brands concerning security aspects. The authors also present a real demonstration of both appraisals in real scenarios.

INTRODUCTION

In most software systems, security is dependent not only on the inexistence of software vulnerabilities, but also on the actual software capabilities and the configuration used. Configuring a system for high security is frequently addressed in an intuitive manner and its success depends on several aspects that, by definition, cannot be known in advance: Who are the attackers? What tools and knowledge do they have? What are their goals? These questions raise a major issue: what should the user look for in a given software in terms of security mechanisms?

When dealing with very complex software, like, for instance, a database management system (DBMS), selecting the best alternative and finding the best configuration are difficult and highly

DOI: 10.4018/978-1-4666-0978-5.ch007

time consuming tasks. This often leads to security vulnerabilities due to the use of inappropriate software or due to configuration problems (Bellovin & Bush, 2009). This way, we urge the definition of tools to assess and compare the security of software configurations and products.

Several security evaluation methods have been proposed in the past (Bertino et al., 1995; Castano et al., 1994; Department of Defense, 1985; Pernul & Luef, 1992; Schell & Heckman, 1987). However, to the best of our knowledge, none of the existing methods is oriented towards the comparison of software products or configuration alternatives. Furthermore, practical experience shows that these methods are very complex and cannot be easily used by system administrators to assess the security of real installations or to compare different software products. Thus, a common practice in large organizations is to hire security experts to analyze the systems and give their opinions and recommendations. Besides being a very expensive type of assessment (that may be out of the reach for small organizations), the results obtained are very dependent on the expertise of the person (or persons) performing the assessment, which is not easy to assess.

Medium and small enterprises have limited staff and, often, the administrators have very little knowledge and feedback regarding the security implications of their decisions. In fact, although information regarding the security of many systems is commonly available, it is hardly useful for administrators that cannot take a significant portion of time and resources to do research and specialize in the topic. In this chapter we present a practical and generic methodology to collect widespread security information about the most important configuration best practices for a particular application domain. Those security-related practices can then be used to define security appraisals for three scenarios:

- *Assessing software configurations.* The list of practices can be used to derive a list of

tests that allow an administrator (which may not be a security expert) to evaluate the environment he manages in terms of what are the best practices that the actual configuration of the system fulfills. This assessment allows not only a measurement of the distance of his configuration to an ideal one, but also makes him aware of important security factors (that he does not know about).

- *Assessing the capabilities of software products.* A list of security best practices associated with a particular domain allows deriving a list of security mechanisms that are expected to be part of the software that implements *some* functionality of that domain. Basically, the more security mechanisms a software product provides, the easier it is to carry out important security tasks. The idea is to create an appraisal able to evaluate how well the security mechanisms provided by a particular software help the administrator in the tasks of implementing the recommended security best practices.

- *Assessing the knowledge of system administrators.* In the very same way, a list of security practices can be used to devise tests to evaluate the security knowledge that an administrator has in a specific domain.

We present the main steps and difficulties involved in building such appraisals, and demonstrate their usefulness and feasibility by defining two specific appraisals for database installations (focusing the first two scenarios introduced above). The first one is targeted to assess the security of the configuration of a deployed database instance. We present the details of the appraisal and show its potential by evaluating, comparing and analyzing the configuration of four real installations based on four widely used DBMS (Oracle, SQLServer, PostgreSQL, and MySQL). The second appraisal is targeted to evaluate and compare out-of-the-box database software packages (which are combinations of a operating system and a DBMS engine) for database installations. In other words, this appraisal provides the ability to compare different combinations of operating systems and DBMS brands in terms of their ability to automatically provide out-of-the-box support for important database security best practices. We evaluate this appraisal by analyzing and comparing seven different software packages, based on a variety of combinations of open source and proprietary DBMS and operating systems.

BACKGROUND AND RELATED WORK

The vulnerabilities of a system may have origin in several distinct factors. In the literature, incorrect software design leading to software bugs that can be maliciously exploited is one of the most investigated sources of vulnerabilities, and ways to avoid them have been extensively researched (Fonseca & Vieira, 2008; Howard & LeBlanc, 2002; Zanero et al., 2005). However, vulnerabilities can also exist due to the incorrect configuration of the security mechanisms available in the system. While the system administrator cannot do much regarding the first problem, he is the one to blame for the second one. Therefore, a method to help administrators to assess their configuration settings is a very important and relevant contribution that has not been extensively researched yet.

The problem of configuration security is usually addressed in an ad hoc manner, following intuitive administration best practices learned in the field. A security best practice is a precaution, which can be a policy, a procedure or merely a choice for a configuration option that is widely known to improve the security of a particular system or scenario. For example, *"always check the type and length of an input parameter"* is a valid best practice for the development of any web application, which can prevent, depending on the circumstances, SQL injection and buffer overflow attacks.

One important aspect concerning best practices is that they can be provided in many forms (e.g., security books, software product manuals, specialized forums, etc.) by a large variety of sources (e.g., vendors, developers, system administrators, academics, etc.) and are usually based on field experience. When using a particular system for a long time, an administrator typically assembles knowledge about practices that tend to achieve good outcomes. In the end, these experts write books with recommendations, create checklists, issue advices and provide a lot of information that can be used in similar scenarios.

When someone employs security best practices in a system, the effect is that one or more known attack methods are being eliminated or reduced. Any particular method that an attacker has at his disposal as a way to carry out an attack (like an improperly programmed function that did not follow the best practice of "always check the type and length of an input parameter") is called an *attack vector*. The set of all *attack vectors* that are present in a system is called the attack surface of the system.

System administration requires a defense-in-depth approach (Howard & LeBlanc, 2002). Defense-in-depth assumes that any security precaution can fail, and therefore, security depends on several layers of mechanisms that compensate the failures of each other. Administrators are expected to apply the effort needed to put in place adequate security precautions that minimize the probability of successful attacks. Thus, they should minimize the attack surface of their systems as much as possible.

Several security evaluation methods have been proposed in the past. For example, the Orange Book (Department of Defense, 1985) and the Common Criteria for Information Technology Security Evaluation (Common Criteria, 1999) define a set of generic rules that allow developers to specify the security attributes of their products, and evaluators to verify if products actually meet their claims. Another example is the red team strategy (Sandia National Laboratories, 2010), which consists of a group of experts trying to hack its own computer systems to evaluate security. To the best of our knowledge, none of these security evaluation methods is oriented towards security comparison, and they are too complex to be used in real installations, where the administrators have limited resources and security knowledge.

The set of security configuration recommendations created by the Center for Internet Security (CIS) (Center for Internet Security, 2010) is a very interesting initiative. CIS is a non-profit organization formed by several well-known academic, commercial, and governmental entities that has created a series of security configuration documents for several commercial and open source systems, for areas such as DBMS, operating systems, and web servers. These documents focus on the practical aspects of the configuration of specific systems and state the concrete values each configuration option should have in order to enhance overall security of real installations. These documents are quite complex and meant to be used by highly experienced system administrators. The key advantage of the CIS approach is that the configuration settings are based on field experience.

In (Vieira & Madeira, 2005) the authors propose an approach to classify the security mechanisms of database systems. In this approach the DBMS are classified using a set of security classes. However, the list of mechanisms presented in the paper is limited as it is based only on the mechanisms implemented by DBMS engines. In our approach, we devise the security concerns from a field research which includes the whole environment where a database may be immersed, thus having a much more broad approach regarding the configuration aspects that may impact security.

GENERIC APPROACH FOR DEFINING APPRAISALS BASED ON SECURITY BEST PRACTICES

When security best practices are applied in a system, the effect is that one or more known attack vectors are being eliminated or reduced. In other words, the attack surface of the system is diminished. By taking advantage of this idea, it is possible to define a high level measure of how much a certain system of product complies with recommended security best practices, which we call *security best practices index* (SBPI). Depending on the scenario, this measure might represent one of the following:

- How far a system configuration is from the typical recommended configuration?
- How much the security mechanisms provided in a software product help in implementing typically recommended best practices for its application area?
- How much does a system administrator know about the correct security configuration of software of in a given domain?

In this section we present and explain a methodology that can be used to create security appraisals. More details about the methodology can be found in (Araújo Neto & Vieira, 2008; Araújo Neto & Vieira, 2009; Araújo Neto, Vieira & Maideira, 2009). The first steps of our methodology are independent of the target goal of the appraisal: 1) characterizing the application area; 2) collecting security recommendations; 3) defining security best practices; 4) weighting the best practices. Steps after these ones depend on the goal of the specific appraisal being designed. For example, the tests needed to assess if a given best practice in being fulfilled by a software configuration is completely different from the tests needed to evaluate if a system administrator understands that best practice. These are demonstrated in the two real examples in following sections.

Characterizing the Application Area

The division of the application spectrum into well-defined areas is necessary to cope with the huge diversity of systems and applications and to make it possible to make decisions during the definition of the appraisal. In fact, the best practices and the most common attacks are both very dependent on the specific area being targeted (e.g., database systems, operating systems, web servers, application servers).

Collecting Security Recommendations

After identifying the application area we need to collect information about security recommendations, practices, and policies. It is hard for a single person to exhaustively enumerate all relevant security recommendations applicable to all the systems in the application area under study, so the idea is to take advantage of the information multiple sources that are currently available. In the end, a multitude of books, web pages, checklists, white papers, and even interviews with security experts can be found about most topics.

This information gathering step results in an extremely long list with a mix of very clear statements (e.g., *"always do backups"*), very narrow suggestions about a particular software (e.g., *"after installing the software XYZ, delete the file XPTO. exe because some guy used it to see the system's password once, and we don't need this file"*), and very specific configuration values (e.g., *"it has always worked for me to set the web server timeout to 60 seconds"*). If comprehensive, this list should contain all information that is known about securing systems in a particular application area.

Defining Security Best Practices

The information gathered needs to be analyzed, filtered, and systematized into general security best practices. This requires the knowledge of a security expert or, better, a group of experts. It consists of analyzing the list of recommendations identified before in order to understand which attack vector(s) does each practice/policy/configuration sever, prevent or reduce.

Take, for instance, the following statement: *"it has always worked for me to set the web server timeout to 60 seconds"*. This suggests at least two obvious attack vectors: *"hijacking an idle connection"* and *"using an authenticated connection of an abandoned user console"*, and can be generalized in a best practice such as *"set the timeout to a prudent value"*. Obviously, additional knowledge about the target system would allow finding more attack vectors and writing this best practice in a more precise manner. However, as we can see, it can be easily done with very little context.

There are four key aspects to consider about this procedure. The first one is related to *conflicting recommendations*. In fact, as we are collecting information from a large set of sources, it might happen that different sources recommend contradictory approaches to tackle the same security problem. Expert judgment should then be used to determine which approach is the correct one (as contradictory solutions for the same problem means that one is incorrect). The second aspect is related to the fact that *several recommendations may be associated to a single best practice*, not only because different sources will probably mention similar things, but also because a lot of specific suggestions are related to the application of one practice in several different instances. The third aspect is related to the cases where a *given recommendation can be associated to more than one best practice*. In these cases, field experience and expert judgment can be used to determine if both are equally relevant or if there is a prevalent one. Finally, the last noticeable aspect is that *some best practices may be special cases of more general ones also considered*. The problem here is to decide when a specialization of a particular best practice is relevant enough to spawn a new one. Past experience on security tradeoffs is then required to evaluate and decide when such separation is important.

Weighting Security Best Practices

Although the identification of the list of best practices is the most relevant part of the process, it is necessary to address the fact that some practices are more efficient than others in terms of their contribution to the reduction of the attack surface. To be able to compute the *security best practices index (SBPI)*, it is necessary to estimate the weight each practice. This is not an easy problem, as the security perception might vary from one person to another. Additionally, although best practices can be identified from sources like books, forums, checklists, etc., their importance and contribution to the reduction of the attack surface is typically not addressed or unclear.

The idea is to use the consensual judgment of several experts. Here, the diversity of experiences becomes a relevant issue, thus it is very important to mix the input of experts from different fields. For example, when identifying the weights of security best practices for DBMS configurations, we include people with complementary backgrounds, namely: database administrators, database applications developers, operating systems experts, network specialists, and security experts. Ideally, this group of experts should include a large number of both practitioners and academics. The expectation is that, in average, the most important practices will be emphasized, even if there is no unanimity.

Although the process of obtaining weights is quite simple, there are a few caveats. As we want to capture the most of a person's experience and knowledge, the scale used for the classification of the best practices needs to be well defined, easy to understand, and include a short (but adequate) number of values. For example, an excessively detailed scale with 20 different values forces persons to make irrelevant considerations to decide

Table 1. Best practice importance key

Score	Importance to the system
4	Critical to the system
3	Important
2	Advisable to implement
1	Not much relevant

between close values (e.g., deciding between an 15 and a 16 is a very difficult task) and make the weighting process a lot harder without gaining much from it. On the other hand, a too vague scale (e.g., with 2 values) does not allow distinguishing and expressing the notion of importance of different best practices. In our work, we use a scale from 1 to 4, with a very specific semantic for each value (Table 1).

The weight of each best practice is the sum of all scores that each expert give to each best practice, but applied to a logarithm scale. This tries to stress the difference of the scores. Then, contribution of each security best practice to the reduction of the attack surface is then defined as the weight of the best practice divided by the sum of all weights. The attack surface of a system can be computed as the sum of the contribution of all best practices that are not implemented (meaning that their respective attack vectors are available for exploitation).

The *security best practices index* is the complement of the attack surface (i.e., one minus the attack surface). When considering the different implementation scenarios, this index has different interpretations. In each proposed case, it should be interpreted as follows:

- When *assessing software configurations*: 100% means that all known security best practices related to the system configuration are implemented and 0% means that no security best practices are implemented in the system. Values in between are an estimated measure of how important are the best practices implemented in the system (i.e., how much of the attack surface they cover).

- When *evaluating software products:* 100% means that the product provides security mechanisms to help implementing all important best practices, while 0% means that no support is provided. Values in between are an estimated measure of how important are the best practices that can be implemented.

- When *assessing administrators' knowledge:* 100% means that the person understand all the best practices of the domain and 0% means that he does not know any. Other values are an estimation of the importance of the practices known by the person.

It is important to emphasize that the *security best practices index* cannot be understood as an absolute measure of security. For example, when assessing a software configuration, a value of 100% does not mean that the system is 100% secure: it means that it implements all the security best practices considered relevant in the corresponding application area. Similar reasoning applies for software products evaluation and administrators knowledge assessment.

SECURITY BEST PRACTICES FOR DATABASE ADMINISTRATION

Databases play a central role in the information infrastructure of most organizations and it is well known that security aspects must be an everyday concern of a database administrator (DBA). A database environment is typically very complex, which makes database management systems suitable for our methodology. In this section we demonstrate how we defined and weighted a list of security best practices for databases that are the base for the appraisals presented in the following sections.

A key requisite is that the list of best practices should be applicable to any database. So, the best practices must come from different sources and consider several different engines. There is an enormous quantity of security recommendations for databases in the form of books, reports, papers, manuals, etc. However, due to the complexity and time needed to collect all this information, for this preliminary version we decided to narrow the collection of recommendations to two reliable independent sources: the Center for Internet Security (CIS) (Center for Internet Security, 2010) and the USA Department of Defense (Defense Information Systems Agency, 2001).

CIS has created a series of security configuration documents for several commercial and open source DBMS, namely: MySQL, SQLServer 2000/2005, and Oracle 8i/9i/10g. These documents focus on the practical aspects of the configuration of these DBMS and state the concrete values each configuration option should have in order to enhance overall security.

The other document we used is the Database Security Technical Implementation Guide (Defense Information Systems Agency, 2001), developed by the Defense Information Systems Agency for the use within the USA Department of Defense. This document contains a series of mandatory or recommended requisites that must be followed when installing a database. Although it is a generic document applicable to any DBMS, it enforces a very strict set of requisites that clearly follow a policy within the US government, and therefore makes it not suitable for general use.

Table 2 presents the final list of security best practices. This table is the result of a complex task of systematization of all the recommendations found in the CIS documents analyzed. The first column is a number that will be used to identify each best practice. The second is the statement of the security best practice. The last four columns show the number of recommendations from each CIS document that was associated to each practice. The column M is for the *MySQL Benchmark* document, O8 is for the *Oracle 8i Benchmark* document, O10 is for the *Oracle 9i and 10g Benchmark* document, and S is for the *SQLServer 2000 Benchmark* document.

A brief analysis of Table 2 raises some immediate considerations. The first aspect is that there are many best practices that appear only in a subset of the CIS documents. This is mainly due to two reasons. The first one is, of course, related to the fact that the documents are based on the empirical experience of different people. This results in different sensibilities of what are the most important security problems in each DBMS. The second reason is related to the fact that the documents are centered in the configuration mechanisms and parameters *available* in each DBMS, meaning that whenever a particular feature is absent or not configurable it is not shown in the documents.

Another aspect is that some best practices have a highly variable number of configuration settings across the four documents (e.g., best practice #1). That is the natural consequence of the fact that different people designed the documents. Thus, it can be seen as a side effect caused by the differences of how fine-grained the recommendations are specified.

The total number of recommendations in each document (last line of the table) suggests an interesting fact. Even though the commercial DBMS considered (Oracle and SQLServer) have a quite similar number of recommendations, the open source one (MySQL) has significantly less. This is understandable as the number of configuration settings presented in the CIS documents is obviously related to the number of functionalities and configuration options available. MySQL is an open source DBMS that provides a reduced set of functionalities when compared to more complex DBMS like Oracle and SQLServer.

After devising a set of best practices based on the analysis of the CIS documents, we turned to the analysis of the DoD document. We were able to find only a small number of complementary best practices that did not show in any of the CIS documents. All other advices in the DoD document can be generalized as at least one of the CIS related best practices shown in Table 2. The new best practices and corresponding groups are in Table 3.

With the list of best practices, we estimated the importance of each security best practice. We designed a spreadsheet and handed it to 9 experts with different backgrounds. This group of experts included five people from academia (three professors from a university, where two of them teach databases courses and the other teaches a security course, and two PhD students, one working on intrusion detection and the other working on security benchmarking for web servers) and four engineers from industry (three full time database administrators and one technical manager for the databases area in a medium size company).

The summarized weights are shown in Table 4. The practices presented in the second column of each row (see Tables 2 and 3 for the correspondence between the numbers and the description of the practices) are ordered by the computed weights, and have a relative importance in the interval presented in the first column. For example, all the practices presented in the third row of Table 4 (Class 2) have a relative weight between 1% and 2.5%.

From the analysis of the detailed results it is clear that each best practice typically falls into one of four distinct groups: 1) the ones that are unanimously critical, 2) the ones that are not critical but are important, 3) the ones that are advisable to implement, and 4) the ones that are unanimously not much relevant. This is very interesting and can be seen as a guide of which best practices should be implemented in a system according to its criticality.

Table 2. DBMS configuration security best practices devised from the analysis of the CIS documents

#	SECURITY BEST PRACTICE (CIS)	Recommendations in CIS documents			
		M	O8	O10	S
ENVIRONMENT					
1	Use a dedicated machine for the database	1	1	1	28
2	Avoid machines which also run critical network services (naming, authentication, etc)	1	1	1	1
3	Use Firewalls: on the machine and on the network border	1	3	3	1
4	Prevent physical access to the DBMS machine by unauthorized people				1
5	Remove from the network stack all unauthorized protocols		1	1	1
6	Create a specific userid to run the DBMS daemons	1	1	1	
7	Restrict DBMS userid access to everything it doesn't need	1	4	4	3
8	Prevent direct login on the DBMS userid account	2	1	3	3
INSTALLATION SETUP					
9	Create a partition for log information	2	1	1	1
10	Only the DBMS userid should read/write in the log partition	1			
11	Create a partition for DB data	1	1	1	2
12	Only the DBMS userid should read/write in the data partition	1			
13	Separate the DBMS software from the OS files	1	2	2	2
	Remove/Avoid default elements:				
14	Remove example databases	1			1
15	Change/remove user names/passwords	1	4	4	2
16	Change remote identification names (SID, etc...)		3	1	
17	Change TCP/UDP Ports		1	1	1
18	Do not use default SSL certificates	1			
19	Separate production and development servers		1	1	
20	No developer should have access to the production server		5	5	
21	Use different network segments for production and development servers		1	1	1
	Verify all the installed DBMS application files:				
22	Check and set the owner of the files	1	2	3	
23	Set read/running permissions only to authorized users	4	18	22	14
OPERATIONAL PROCEDURES					
24	Keep the DBMS software updated	3		1	1
25	Make regular backups	1			4
26	Test the backups	1		1	
SYSTEM LEVEL CONFIGURATION					
27	Avoid random ports assignment for client connections (firewall configuration)		1	1	
28	Enforce remote communication encryption with strong algorithms	1	1	11	3
29	Use server side certificate if possible	1		1	

continued on the following page

Table 2. Continued

#	SECURITY BEST PRACTICE (CIS)	Recommendations in CIS documents			
30	Use IPs instead of host names to configure access permissions (prevents DNS spoofing)		1	1	
31	Enforce strong user level authentication	2	6	8	4
32	Prevent idle connection hijacking		2	2	
33	Ensure no remote parameters are used in authentication	1	2	1	
34	Avoid host based authentication		1	1	
35	Enforce strong password policies	1	2		2
36	Apply excessive failed logins lock		1	1	
37	Apply password lifetime control		1	1	
38	Deny regular password reuse (force periodic change)		2	2	
39	Use strong encryption in password storage	3			
40	Enforce comprehensive logging	1	2	1	
41	Verify that the log data cannot be lost (replication is used)		2	2	1
42	Audit sensitive information		14	19	25
43	Verify that the audit data cannot be lost (replication is used)		1		1
	Ensure no "side-channel" information leak (don't create/restrict access):				
44	From configuration files		2	1	
45	From system variables	1			
46	From core_dump/trace files		8	8	1
47	From backups of data and configuration files		1	1	4
	Avoid the interaction between the DBMS users and the OS:				
48	Deny any read/write on file system from DBMS used	2	3	2	
49	Deny any network operation (sending email, opening sockets, etc...)		4	3	
50	Deny access to not needed extended libraries and functionalities	1	11	11	54
51	Deny access to any OS information and commands	2			
APPLICATION LEVEL CONFIGURATION AND USAGE					
52	Remove user rights over system tables	1	23	25	1
53	Remove user quotas over system areas		3	1	
54	Implement least privilege policy in rights assignments		9	10	6
55	Avoid ANY and ALL expressions in rights assignments	1	3	3	
56	Do not delegate rights assignments	1	3	3	3
57	No user should have rights to change system properties or configurations	3	4	4	2
58	Grant privileges to roles/groups instead of users		1	1	3
59	Do not maintain the DB schema creation SQL files in the DB server		1		
Total number of recommendations		48	166	183	177

Table 3. Complementary DoD best practices

#	Complementary Best Practices (DoD)	Group
1A	Monitor de DBMS application and configuration files for modifications	Operational Procedures
2A	Do not use self signed certificates	System Level Config.
3A	Protect/encrypt application code	Appl. L. Config./Usage
4A	Audit application code changes	Appl. L. Config./Usage
5A	Employ stored procedures and views instead of direct table access	Appl. L. Config./Usage

Table 4. Best practices ordered by relative weights

Class	Weight (W)	Ordered Best Practices (all 64 practices)
4	$5,26\% > W \geq 4\%$	4, 3, 19, 28, 57
3	$4\% > W \geq 2,5\%$	2, 24, 39, 35, 15, 1, 6, 52, 25
2	$2,5\% > W \geq 1\%$	20, 23, 18, 31, 8, 29, 51, 32, 36, 54, 33, 37, 10, 12, 42, 41
1	$1\% > W \geq 0,15\%$	22, 34, 5, 48, 21, 47, 38, 55, 46, 50, 7, 44, 45, 49, 26, 40, 43, 9, 4A, 11, 17, 13, 56, 30, 1A, 53, 58, 27, 2A, 14, 5A, 16, 59, 3A

A very important observation is that the 14 practices that ended up having the largest relative weights (the ones presented in the first two rows of Table 4) *account for exactly 51.61% of the security index* (which identifies the distance to the ideal configuration), while the other 50 best practices account for the remaining percentage. This shows that there is a subset of the best practices that is unanimously considered very important for any installation.

AN APPRAISAL TO ASSESS THE SECURITY OF DATABASE CONFIGURATIONS

With the list of security best practices and weights at hand, it is possible to create concrete and practical security appraisals. For database configurations, the last step consists of generating a list of security tests that will be used to verify the compliance or not with the recommended security best practices. These tests typically include two steps. The initial step is a procedure to obtain

specific information necessary to answer the test. This step is optional, in the sense that the DBA might obtain the knowledge in alternative ways (e.g., the system's manual). The second step is a series of yes/no questions that should be answered. One of the answers (yes or no) is defined as the failing answer. If, for any of the listed questions, the answer is the failing answer, then the test is considered as failed. Unknown answers must be treated as a failed test.

Table 5 presents some of the tests of our configuration appraisal. In this specific appraisal, the tests were designed in such way that they have to be answered by an experienced DBA with deep knowledge of the operating system in use, and some knowledge of computer networks, but may not be a security expert. For some of the tests, special security knowledge is required, which is defined by the figures of "security expert" and "experienced staff". In these cases, we provide references to bibliography where this security knowledge can be obtained (e.g., test #3). We also use the terms "reasonable" and "regularly" when a part of the test depends on particular bounds that

Table 5. DBMS configuration security tests

#	TEST	Fail
ENVIRONMENT		
1	If the machine is turned off, does any service other than the database become unavailable? Is there any process running on the machine which is not demanded by the DBMS, the OS or the machine maintenance/security?	Yes
2	If the machine is turned off, does any critical network service, like naming, directory or authentication services, becomes unavailable?	Yes
3	Is there a firewall on the network border? Is there a firewall running on the DBMS machine? Are both firewalls properly configured by experienced staff with solid network knowledge? [9, 14, 16]	No

* Only the first three tests are presented. The complete table is available in the appendix.

Table 6. Scenario details

	Case 1	Case 2	Case 3	Case 4
DBMS	Oracle 10g	SQLServer 2005	MySQL 5.0	PostgreSQL 8.1
OS	Windows 2003	Windows 2003	Windows XP	Windows 2000
Applications	3	54	3	2
DBAs	2	5	2	2
Test Duration	3 hours	1,5 hours	1 hour	1 hour

cannot be defined without taking into account the client applications that are using the database.

In order to demonstrate the usefulness and practicality of our assessment tool, we applied it to evaluate the security of four real DBMS installations using four distinct engines. Table 6 presents some relevant details about each installation, namely the DBMS engine used, the operating system running on the machine, the number of distinct applications currently using this database, the number of distinct database administrators and the number of developers that are not administrators, along with the duration of the tests execution. Results are presented in Table 7, table 8, table 9, and table 10.

We analyzed the number of *passed* (which identify the number of best practices that are implemented), *failed* and *unknown* tests, and computed the security best practices index (SBPI, in the last column) of each installation along with a partial index for each group, which indicates how close the system configuration is from an *ideal* configuration.

All four databases are used within academic contexts in two different universities, being mostly utilized to support administrative applications that have university staff, teachers and students as users. It is interesting to note that the relatively small number of unknown answers and the relative small time that it takes to apply the tests in all cases suggests that the tool is usable and relatively easy to apply.

Regarding the security best practices index computation, some details are important. The index made it possible to compare the four different installations and, although using completely different DBMS engines, we can affirm that Case 1 is more secure than Case 2, which is more secure than Case 3, and the least secure of all is Case 4. One aspect that strikes the eye is that even though Case 2 has one less passed test, it is still considered more secure than Case 3 because, according to our experts, the best practices it implements are more likely to improve security than the best practices implemented in Case 3. Also, in the light of the identification of the 14 most important databases

Table 7. Case 1, Oracle 10G installation

	Tests Passed	Tests Failed	Unknown	SBPI
Environment	6	2	0	83,89%
Installation setup	4	11	0	27,30%
Operational Proc.	1	3	0	34,76%
System level config.	16	8	2	55,53%
App. level conf./usage	7	4	0	92,07%
Total	34	28	2	58,44%

Table 8. Case 2, SQL server 2005 installation

	Tests Passed	Tests Failed	Unknown	SBPI
Environment	4	4	0	59,73%
Installation setup	5	9	1	30,43%
Operational Proc.s	2	2	0	85,56%
System level config.	12	13	1	39,20%
App. level conf./usage	3	8	0	50,84%
Total	26	36	2	46,63%

Table 9. Case 3, MySQL 5.0 installation

	Tests Passed	Tests Failed	Unknown	SBPI
Environment	3	5	0	44,30%
Installation setup	7	8	0	35,66%
Operational Proc.	1	3	0	50,80%
System level config.	12	13	1	38,78%
App. level conf./usage	4	7	0	65,74%
Total	27	36	1	43,07%

Table 10. Case 4, PostgreSQL 8.1 installation

	Tests Passed	Tests Failed	Unknown	SBPI
Environment	3	5	0	46,53%
Installation setup	4	11	0	26,02%
Operational Proc.	1	3	0	34,76%
System level config.	9	15	2	29,29%
App. level conf./usage	6	5	0	68,52%
Total	23	39	2	37,21%

best practices as presented in Section 3, we listed for each case the critical best practices that are missing. These are shown in Table 11.

It is important to emphasize that, despite the actual security index of the installation, the implementation of the best practices in Table 11 would guarantee that the index would stay above 50%, meaning that the configuration would be half-way from the ideal one (which is not the case of any of the systems assessed).

One interesting result is the low number of passed tests in the *Installation Setup* group in all cases (less than 50% in a 15-item group). Three things seem to contribute to these results: the default installation settings are kept and used, no file system partition planning for logs and data (which can lead to Denial of Service by exhaustion of disk space), and the use of an operating system that does not provide easy ways to keep track of file permissions and usually forces users to use administrative roles for several tasks.

SELECTING SOFTWARE PACKAGES FOR DATABASE INSTALLATIONS

Different software products offer different sets of security mechanisms that target diverse security concerns. This, adding to the fact that several software systems are needed to install a database environment (the minimum set is composed by an Operating System (OS) and a Database Management System (DBMS)), makes it very difficult for the database administrators to select the software package (i.e., set of software products) that best fits specific security requirements. This is quite complicate considering that, in many cases, a given database security concern needs several software components to provide specific security features, which calls for a concurrent assessment of the entire software package instead of an independent assessment of the different products.

In this section we demonstrate how to use the list of best practices to create an appraisal to

Table 11. Most important best practices to be implemented

Case	Missing critical best practices
1	19, 28, 24, 15, 6
2	3, 19, 28, 35, 6, 2
3	4, 19, 28, 35, 1, 6, 25
4	3, 19, 28, 24, 35, 1, 6, 2

systematically assess and compare the security features offered by different software packages in the context of database systems. Here, a software packages is defined by a set of operational system plus database management system. To actually create the appraisal, two additional steps are required: identify security mechanisms and weight them.

Identifying Security Mechanisms

The first step consists in using the list of security practices to extrapolate the mechanisms that can be used to implement those recommendations. If the list of recommendations is comprehensive and representative enough, then the list of security mechanisms derived from it shall also be representative. The process, however, is not straightforward and requires several steps of careful analysis.

We started by analyzing the list of 64 security recommendations for databases. Each recommendation was classified in terms of the type of support needed for its implementation, namely: *hardware support* (2 practices), *network support* (4 practices), *plain security policies* (10 practices), *OS support* (28 practices), *DBMS support* (38 practices), and *third party software* support (2 practices). This classification allowed us to focus on the practices that required at least some support for software components (a total of 51 out of 64 security practices).

The next step consisted of restating the practices in a way that allows identifying the security mechanisms needed to support them. Best practices are usually stated as actions that should be conducted on the system or environment to enhance security. However, these actions may define implicitly several factors, such as: what are administrators' responsibilities, what actions require software support, and what the environment dependent elements are. This way, instead of trying to identify security mechanisms directly from the best practices we propose the use of two intermediary steps that help in exposing hidden factors.

In the first step we restate each of the best practices as a *System State Goal* that represents the state of the system in a point in time when the practice is being correctly applied. For instance, one of the best practices related to the operating system is stated as follows: "*Remove from the network stack all unused/unauthorized protocols*". A potential system state goal for this best practice is: "*The OS network stack has no unused/unauthorized protocol active*". Notice that, although obvious in some cases, this rewriting step moves the focus from the action to the consequences of the action. This is extremely important to disclose the fundamental effects that are expected when applying a best practice. Additionally, as several practices can actually be applied in several software components at the same time (e.g., password related practices must be applied at both OS and DBMS levels), this rephrasing forces this distinction to be made clear, allowing to identify the practices for which more than one System State Goal should be defined (i.e., one for each of the components of the software package). When analyzing the *Systems States Goals* it becomes possible to start distinguishing the effects of the practice that are exclusively administrators' tasks (e.g., defining what are unauthorized protocols) and the ones that can be automated, and therefore can be supported by security mechanisms. From a high level perspective, any security practice is a policy that requires an action, implicit or explicit, from the administrator (in the sense that he can

always choose to not use it), and can typically be automated to a certain point.

In the second step, we rewrite again the *System State Goals*, but this time in terms of *Mechanisms Goals*. This additional step is used to define more precisely what are the steps needed to accomplish the System State Goal in terms of the software at hand (DBMS, OS, etc). In fact, the *Mechanisms Goals* can be seen as the *functions* that make the steps towards the accomplishment of the System State Goal as simple as possible (i.e., the complexity of the steps is hidden behind automation).

The identification of the security mechanisms based on the Mechanisms Goals is then quite straightforward. Note that, in some cases more than one mechanism may be required for the state goal to be accomplished. In other cases, different mechanisms may be used to accomplish the same goal, possibly with different amount of automation. Alternative ways of performing the same tasks are useful to suit different administrators, environments and requisites. Table 12 presents four examples of the mapping of security best practices into System State Goal and Mechanisms Goals. We summarize the process in three steps:

i. Restate the best practices in the form of *System State Goals* that describe the system when the best practice is correctly being applied. In this step it becomes necessary to clarify to which components of the software package (e.g., DBMS, OS, firewall) the goal refers to.
ii. Determine the *Mechanisms Goals*, which represents the steps required to achieve the System State Goal in terms of functions provided by the software.
iii. List exhaustively the mechanisms that can be used to implement (partially or fully) the Mechanisms Goals.

By following this process we have identified a total of 112 security mechanisms. Note that the mechanisms identified are generic and may (or

Table 12. Examples of the mapping between security best practices, system state goals, and mechanism goals

Security Best Practice	Component	System State Goals	Mechanisms Goals
Remove from the network stack all unauthorized protocols	OS	The OS network stack has no unused/ unauthorized protocol active.	Identify active protocols and disable unauthorized/unused ones.
Change default passwords	OS	No OS userid password is the default.	Prevent the installation of default passwords in the OS or allow identification and removal of default passwords.
	DBMS	No DBMS userid password is the default.	Prevent the installation of default passwords in the DBMS or allow identification and removal of default passwords.
Do not delegate privileges assignments	DBMS	Privileges a user have should not be delegated.	Prevent users from delegating their privileges or identify the use of privilege delegation operations.
Keep the software updated	OS	No patches provided by the OS vendor are unapplied.	Not allow an available OS patch to remain unapplied.
	DBMS	No patches provided by the DBMS vendor are unapplied.	Not allow an available DBMS patch to remain unapplied.

Table 13. Most important security mechanisms identified

Security mechanisms (automated support for...)	Target	Weight
Disabling access to extended functions.	DBMS	5
Configuring the system to always encrypt a remote connection to the DBMS.	DBMS	4
Encrypting the connection of native developer applications.	DBMS	4
Removing systems privileges of DBMS userids	DBMS	4
Restricting read/write privileges of a partition to a specific userid.	OS	4
Automated installation of DBMS pending patches.	DBMS	3
Automated installation of OS pending patches.	OS	3
Configuring the DBMS to store credential information using a reliable encryption scheme.	DBMS	3
Configuring the OS to store credential information using a reliable encryption scheme.	OS	3
Defining all DBMS passwords during the installation.	DBMS	3

may not) be present in a given software package. Additionally, the mechanisms are not tied to any specific product and are described in a broad way to allow a posterior assessment of their existence in specific software packages.

Table 13 presents the 10 most important security mechanisms. The first column of the table describes the mechanisms that a target software component (second column) is expected to facilitate. The mechanisms should be read as "*The software provides automated support for…*".

Note that, in practice, most of these mechanisms can be implemented manually or by using third party software, but their out-of-the-box support is invaluable to a DBA. The last column of the table represents the estimated importance for the mechanism in the whole software package. The computation of this estimated effort will be explained in the next section (identical weights indicate equivalent importance).

Table 14. Overall results of the experimental evaluation of 7 different software packages

DBMS Engine	Operating system	Package N.	MP	SBPC	SBPI(%)
SQL Server 2005	Windows XP	1	79	131,5	76%
Oracle 10g	Red Hat Enterprise Linux 5	2	74	118,5	68%
	Windows XP	3	73	118	68%
PostgreSQL 8	Red Hat Enterprise Linux 5	4	73	123	71%
	Windows XP	5	68	114,5	66%
MySQL Community Edition 5	Red Hat Enterprise Linux 5	6	66	110	64%
	Windows XP	7	66	110,5	64%

Establishing the Importance of Security Mechanisms

After devising the list of expected security mechanisms for a database software package, an obvious problem arises: some mechanisms are more relevant than others in terms of security. It is clear that this relevance is directly related to the security best practices each mechanism allows implementing, but other aspects must be addressed.

In the context of the appraisal, we must characterize the relevance of the security mechanisms from a usefulness perspective, which ideally is environment dependent. We want the appraisal to be as accurate as possible, but also as representative as possible, which means that taking too much environment assumptions into account would probably makes it less useful for a large number of scenarios (i.e., scenarios where those assumptions are not valid). To this end, we do not represent the exact importance of the mechanisms, but rather try to determine general classes of mechanisms that can justifiably be considered with the same relative importance. We therefore use the classes that can be found in Table 4 as the groupings of each security mechanism.

One of the problems is that security mechanisms may provide only partial support for best practices, and may need to be complemented. This should reflect in the weighting process. Two alternatives are possible: either we value

mechanisms that provide partial support only when their complementary counterparts are also present in the package or we count them always as providing half of the support (having half the weight of the original importance). In our work we decide for the second choice, assuming that half mechanism is usually better than no mechanism, even if it necessary to complement it with external methods in order to fulfill a best practice. Notice, however, that counting partial mechanisms as exactly "half" is also open for debate. The problem is that determining how much a mechanism actually fulfills of the best practice (e.g., 80% of the practice or 30% of the practice) is impossible as this depends also on other resources available to the administrator (which may vary from case to case). We decided that, for the purpose of the benchmark, partial mechanisms provide on average half the support, even if under the specific conditions of a real environment that might not be true.

Another issue is that some security mechanisms can be used to support multiple best practices. In this case the choice is between emphasizing these mechanisms or not. In other words, we had to decide if the importance of a given mechanism should be somewhat accumulated from different practices. In practice the question is: "*should a mechanism required to implement three not very important practices be considered more important than another mechanism that can be used to support a single very important practice?*" In this case we believe that yes, if a mechanism can be used in several best practices it should be emphasized. This is because we believe that security should be exhaustive, this choice follows a defense-in-depth approach. We are aware that this is open for debate, but the assumption appears to be reasonable. Anyway, this decision had little impact on the overall appraisal, as there are a very low number of mechanisms that are related to more than one security practice (3 to be exact). In fact, we performed several simulations on the calculation, and found that choosing differently would make little difference in the outcome.

The weight of each mechanism was computed by multiplying the best practice importance class (from 1 to 4) by the weight of the support of the mechanism (1 or 0.5). The individual weights (i.e., weights per best practice) for the mechanisms that contribute for more than one practice were then added, resulting, therefore, in weights ranging from 0.5 to 5. Table 14 presents the 10 most important security mechanisms.

Comparing Software Packages

We experimentally evaluated the proposed appraisal, by assessing a representative set of database solutions that can be found in the field. From the DBMS perspective, we selected two commercial DBMS engines, namely Oracle 10g and Microsoft SQL Server 2005, and two open source ones, namely PostgreSQL 8 and MySQL Community Edition 5. Oracle and SQL Server are two of the most widely used commercial DBMS, and these particular versions account for a representative number of installations. PostgresSQL and MySQL account for the majority of DBMS installations that use open source software, and are very popular alternatives to commercial software.

From the operating system perspective, we used the same rationale, therefore choosing Microsoft Windows XP and Red Hat Enterprise Linux 5. Both operating systems are widely representative

choices to support the DBMS mentioned above, but we are aware that several other alternatives would be interesting as well (e.g., Suse Linux and Microsoft Windows Server 2003, among many others). Excluding Microsoft SQL Server 2005, that is only available over Windows platforms, the other three DBMS could be installed over both operating systems.

We installed all software combinations and analyzed the documentation available. Basically, the process consisted in verifying, for each package, if it has native support for each of 112 security mechanisms defined by the appraisal. A fundamental difficulty was to determine what elements were provided by the software package as a whole (in contrast to determining the elements provided by each product individually). Password policies are one example where the platform influences the capabilities of the DBMS. For SQL Server 2005, some password policies can be inherited from the operating system only if it is installed over Microsoft Windows 2003, and not if the system is based on Windows XP due to the lack of interfaces for this system. On the other hand, PostgreSQL can use the Pluggable Authentication Module (PAM) features of Linux, which comes in the standard installation of the Red Hat Enterprise Linux 5, and therefore is available for the package at both the OS and the DBMS levels. This kind of details can make process to be relatively costly in terms of information gathering, though the outcome justifies the work.

Table 14 presents the overall evaluation of the packages. The first and second columns identify the components of each package and the third column presents an identification number for the package. The fourth column presents the total numbers of mechanisms present (MP) in the package, and the fifth column presents the security best practices compliance (SBPC), which is the sum of the importance of all mechanisms present. Finally, the sixth column presents the security best practices index SBPI, which is the percentage of mechanisms present.

Among the evaluated packages, the one that includes more security mechanisms is package 1. This means that it has more native support for implementing security best practices for databases. Notice that the plain number of mechanisms present does not say much about the importance of such mechanisms. As can be seen for packages 2 and 4, package 4 has security compliance metric higher than package 2, even though it has less security mechanisms available. This happens because the security mechanisms present in package number 4 are generically considered more important than the ones present in package number 2.

Based on the SBPC metric, the best package is Microsoft SQL Server 2005 over Windows XP. A key aspect that allows this result is an overall better integration with the operating system (allowing, for instance, utilizing the Windows Update mechanism for keeping the DBMS software up to date with little intervention). The feature of client applications roles (that allows to better support the development of applications with the ability to identify the end users behind database connections based on database authentication) and some extra backup features not present in the other DBMS also contributed to this result. However, the score for all the packages is not that different, which suggests that, in general, these packages (operating systems and database engines) tend to implement the same type of security features and mechanisms (despite being open source or not). The worst scored package was MySQL Community Edition over Windows XP.

Security Mechanisms Gap Analysis

Another type of analysis that can be done with this appraisal is the identification of the security mechanisms universally missing in most of the packages evaluated, but that are consistently required to facilitate the implementation of important security best practices. This can be done by conducting a gap analysis. This analysis reveals several very important aspects (see Table 16, in the appendix). As expected, several "common sense" mechanisms are present in all the packages. For instance, file system access privileges, partitioning, table level privileges, among others. However, several kinds of mechanisms that could be used to support the implementation of important security best practices are not available in any of the packages analyzed. Some examples include:

- Options for blocking the use or warning administrators about the use of not recommended commands.
- Backup testing and encryption.
- Testing of new patches before applying them to the system.
- Identification of actively available functions and extensions and their exact effects on the system (this information is usually buried under a heavy documentation).
- Identification of the presence of default configuration elements.
- Better identification and control of what elements are being installed.

As the analysis shows, there is a common set of security mechanism that is implemented by most DBMS and that several very important mechanisms have no support at all on the packages analyzed. The reasons are open for debate, but we can conjecture that it has to do with a tradition of simply copying what has already being proposed and has proven to work, without rethinking the whole features from scratch. When these systems are comprehensively analyzed from the perspective of our appraisal, then several missing elements become highlighted. We believe that this kind of analysis is of utmost importance for database administrators and could be of great interest for vendors to improve the security characteristics of future software products and packages.

CONCLUSION

This chapter presented a methodology to define new security appraisals based on security best practices. Security best practices are based on security recommendations collected from several sources and are classified based on experts' knowledge, which can be used to define security appraisals for software configuration, software capabilities and evaluate knowledge of an administrator. The methodology proposed has been used to define an appraisal to assess the effectiveness of database configurations. Our approach has been successfully applied to four real installations based on four distinct DBMS. Several problems have been disclosed and results clearly show that our approach is easy to apply and can be of extreme importance. Also, defined an appraisal to assess and compare software products and to evaluate administrators' knowledge. Results show that different packages allow system administrators to implement different security configuration, thus selecting the right packages is of utmost importance.

REFERENCES

Araújo Neto, A., & Vieira, M. (2008). *Towards assessing the security of DBMS configurations*. Intl Conf. Depend. Systems and Networks (DSN 2008), USA.

Araújo Neto, A., & Vieira, M. (2009). *Appraisals based on security best practices for software configurations*. Fourth Latin-American Symposium on Dependable Computing (LADC 2009).

Bellovin, S., & Bush, R. (2009). Configuration management and security. *IEEE Journal on Selected Areas in Communications*, 27(3), 268–274. doi:10.1109/JSAC.2009.090403

Bertino, E., Jajodia, S., & Samarati, P. (1995). Database security: Research and practice. *Information Systems Journal*, 20(7).

Castano, S., Fugini, M. G., Martella, G., & Samarati, P. (1994). *Database security*. ACM Press Books, Addison-Wesley Professional.

Center for Internet Security. (2010). *CIS benchmarks/scoring tools*. Retrieved August 24, 2010, from http://www.cisecurity.org

Common Criteria. (1999). *Common criteria for information technology security evaluation: User guide*.

Defense Information Systems Agency. (2001). *Database - security tech. implem. guide*, V8, R1.

Department of Defense. (1985). *Trusted computer system evaluation criteria*.

Fonseca, J., & Vieira, M. (2008). Mapping software faults with web security vulnerabilities. *IEEE/IFIP International Conference on Dependable Systems and Networks (DSN 2008)*, USA.

Howard, M., & LeBlanc, D. (2002). *Writing secure code* (2nd ed.). Redmond, CA: Microsoft Press.

João Pessoa, Brasil, Araújo Neto, A., Vieira, M., & Madeira, H. (2009). *An appraisal to assess the security of database configurations*. 2nd Intl Conference on Dependability, DEPEND 2009, Greece.

Pernul, G., & Luef, G. (1992). Bibliography on database security. *SIGMOD Record*, 21(1). doi:10.1145/130868.130884

Sandia National Laboratories. (2010). *The information design assurance red team*. Retrieved August 2010 from http://idart.sandia.gov

Schell, R., & Heckman, M. (1987). Views for multilevel database security. *IEEE Transactions on Software Engineering*, SE13(2).

Vieira, M., & Madeira, H. (2003). *A dependability benchmark for OLTP application environments*. 29th International Conference on Very Large Data Bases, VLDB2003, Berlin, Germany.

Vieira, M., & Madeira, H. (2005). *Towards a security benchmark for database management systems*. Intl Conf. on Dependable Systems and Networks, Yokohama, Japan.

Zanero, S., Carettoni, L., & Zanchetta, M. (2005). *Automatic detection of Web application security flaws*. Black Hat Briefings.

KEY TERMS AND DEFINITIONS

Appraisal: Act of judging the importance or condition of something.

Attack: Act or circumventing, taking unauthorized advantage or deforming the confidentiality, integrity, availability and authenticity attributes of a computer system.

Attack Surface: Collection of all attack vectors that exist in a computer system.

Attack Vector: System characteristic that can be used as leverage to attack a computer system.

Defense-in-Depth: Defensive philosophy which assumes that any security mechanism can fail, and therefore a system can only be protected by several layers of alternative security mechanisms that compensate the failures of each other.

Gap analysis: Analysis technique that allows understanding the differences between the current state of a system and a desired ideal state.

Security: Degree to which a computer system is immune to attacks.

Security Best Practice: policy, procedure or choice for a configuration option that is widely known to improve the security of a particular system or scenario.

Security Mechanism: Hardware or software element that helps employing security best practices in a system by automating tasks required to implement and maintain these practices.

APPENDIX

Table 15. DBMS security tests

#	TEST	Fail
ENVIRONMENT		
1	If the machine is turned off, does any service other than the database become unavailable? Is there any process running on the machine which is not demanded by the DBMS, the OS or the machine maintenance/security?	Yes
2	If the machine is turned off, does any critical network service, like naming, directory or authentication services, becomes unavailable?	Yes
3	Is there a firewall on the network border? Is there a firewall running on the DBMS machine? Are both firewalls properly configured by experienced staff with solid network knowledge? [9, 14, 16]	No
4	Is it possible to an unauthorized person to physically access the machine without supervision at any given time?	Yes
5	List the protocols available in the network stack in the OS of the DBMS machine. For each protocol, is there a clear justification for its availability?	No
6	List the DBMS processes in the OS. For each process, is the user running it used to run any other process at any time?	Yes
7	Locate the DBMS processes user. Does that user have administration rights? Does it can run applications not DB related? Does it have read rights on any file not necessary to the DBMS processes?	Yes
8	Locate the DBMS processes user. Can you login in the OS with it? (assume you know its password)	Yes
INSTALLATION SETUP		
9	Locate the log files of the DBMS and identify their file system partition. Are there any other files in this partition besides the logs?	Yes
10	Locate the log files of the DBMS and identify their file system partition. Does that partition have exclusive read/write rights for the DBMS user?	No
11	Locate the data files of the DBMS and identify their file system partition. Are there any other files in this partition besides the data files?	Yes
12	Locate the data files of the DBMS and identify their file system partition. Does that partition have exclusive read/write rights for the DBMS user?	No
13	List all OS users which work only with the DB. List all OS regular users (not DB users). List all DBMS applications and OS applications that are necessary for the OS users that work with the DB. Does any regular user can access any DBMS application listed? Does any DB user can access any application not in one of the lists?	Yes
14	List all DBMS databases. Install a fresh copy of the DBMS in a test machine without any customization and then list its DBMS databases. Is there any database in both lists which isn't required for the DBMS?	Yes
15	List all DBMS accounts. Install a fresh copy of the DBMS in a temporary machine without any customization and then list its DBMS accounts. Is there any account in both lists?	Yes
16	List any identification names a remote user must know to connect to the DBMS. Install a fresh copy of the DBMS in a temporary machine without any customization and then list the identification names a remote user must know to connect to this DBMS instance. Is there any name in both lists?	Yes
17	List any TCP/UDP ports a remote user must know to connect to the DBMS. Install a fresh copy of the DBMS in a temporary machine without any customization and then list the TCP/UDP ports a remote user must know to connect to this DBMS instance. Is there any port in both lists?	Yes
18	List all SSL certificates used with the DBMS. For each one, was it created by experienced staff with that specific purpose? [13]	No
19	Is there any kind of development or testing being done in the production server?	Yes
20	Does any developer have a valid DBMS account or OS account in the production server?	Yes

continued on the following page

Table 15. Continued

#	TEST	Fail
21	List the sub-net mask of the IP address of the production and the development servers. Are they the same? Are both servers reachable from one other through a path with only layer 2 network equipments (hubs, switches, etc…)?	Yes
22	List all files installed with the DBMS application. For each file, is its owner correctly set as the DBMS user?	No
23	List all files installed with the DBMS application. For each file, are its rights correctly configured according to its purposes?	No
OPERATIONAL PROCEDURES		
24	Check your DBMS version. Check the latest DBMS version available from the vendor which is an update to your version. Are they different? Is there any re-commendation from the vendor against the use of the version you are using?	Yes
25	Is a carefully thought out, documented backup procedure regularly executed? If the person in charge suddenly quit, is it easy for anyone else to resume its task?	No
26	Is the backup data regularly tested after it is generated? Is a recovery procedure regularly fully simulated? Is the backup data stored in a secure place other than the DB server?	No
1A	Is there any procedure (like checking the files hashes) employed to regularly identify if any of the DBMS application files or configuration files have been change by someone unauthorized?	No
SYSTEM LEVEL CONFIGURATION		
27	During a connection procedure, does the server assign a full range random local port for the remote user to connect?	Yes
28	Establish a connection from any remote user to the server, capture the underlying network traffic and ask for a security expert to analyze it. Is the connection being secured with a recognized encryption protocol like TLS?	No
29	Does the user connection require the knowledge of a server certificate?	No
30	List all configuration files/parameters of the DBMS. Is a host name used on any parameter?	Yes
31	For each registered DBMS user, was it created for a specific application/purpose/person? Is the authentication procedure used in the applications recognizably secure? Does it use a standard algorithm or protocol? [13, 14]	No
32	Establish a connection with the DBMS and let it stay idle. Is the connection severed in a reasonable amount of time?	No
33	Is any specific information other than a username and password obtained from the client host during the authentication procedure?	Yes
34	List all authentication methods used with the DBMS. For each one, does it depend only on the host?	Yes
35	Was a clear policy defined (and documented) about how passwords would be changed, when they must be changed, how they should be retrieved if lost and what rules they must obey? Does it comply with standard recommendations from security experts? [13, 17]	No
36	Try authenticating several times with a wrong password. Is there a try when the account becomes permanently locked?	No
37	Advance the server clock an unreasonable number of months. Authenticate to the server. Are you forced or recommended to change the current password?	No
38	Try changing your password to the same password. Did you succeed?	Yes
39	Locate the table or file where the passwords are stored and ask for a security expert to analyze it. Are the passwords stored as some recognizably standard hash algorithm? [13, 14]	No
40	Is logging turned on? Is the log level set to report at least database errors and client connections? Is there a clearly justified reason for it not to be set to a higher level?	No
41	Are the logs periodically checked? Are the logs also included in the backup procedures? Is the space of the partition where the logs are written monitored?	No
42	Are the following operations traceable: creation and destruction of users, objects and sessions, failed and successful logins, rights assignments and data changes on critical tables?	No
43	Is the trace data stored in a different area than the database? Does that area have its read/rights permissions correctly set? Is the space of the partition where it is stored monitored?	No
44	For each configuration file, analyze its permissions. Is it readable only by authorized users?	No

continued on the following page

Table 15. Continued

#	TEST	Fail
45	For each system variable, does it contain sensitive information (any which should be private) and can be seen by all OS users?	Yes
46	Are core_dump or trace files being generated for failed processes and are they generally visible in the OS?	Yes
47	Does the editor used to update configuration files generate backups of the edited files and do they remain available for reading afterwards?	Yes
48	For each function and extended functionality available, does it allow a user to access a file on the file system?	Yes
49	For each function and extended functionality available, does it allow a user to do any kind of network operation?	Yes
50	For each function and extended functionality available, is its availability clearly required? Is it impossible to do the same task without it?	No
51	For each function and extended functionality available, does it allow a user to gather any information about the OS? Does it allow a user to run any OS command?	Yes
2A	For each certificate used in the servers, is it bought from a trusted company, which has root certificate already installed in the most common browsers and operating systems?	No
APPLICATION LEVEL CONFIGURATION AND USAGE		
52	Make a list of all system tables (not created for use with applications). For each one, check if there is any user with some permission (read or write) over it. Are those permissions clearly justified and necessary?	No
53	Make a list of all system databases. For each element on the list, check if there is any user with some permission over it. Is this permission clearly justified and necessary?	No
54	For each non-DBA user, list all its permissions. For each permission, does it have a clear justification? Is it impossible for the user to work without it?	No
55	For each non-DBA user, list all its permissions. For each permission, is it of type ANY or ALL, which would automatically propagate to other objects of the same type?	Yes
56	For each non-DBA user, list all its permissions. For each permission, does it allow that user to grant it to another user?	Yes
57	For each non-DBA user, list all its permissions. For each permission, does it allow that user to change some system configuration which is either critical or valid to the whole DB?	Yes
58	For each non-DBA user, list all its permissions. For each permission, does the user inherit it from a group or role he is assigned to?	No
59	List all documents and files that contain any schema information. For each one, is it stored in the DB server?	Yes
3A	Is the production application code being stored in a trusted repository (like a Concurrent Versioning System), with proper authentication, or being closely controlled and checked against malicious modification (e.g. encrypted)?	No
4A	Is it possible to identify unequivocally, at all times, for all application code, who made each modification and programming?	No
5A	Are all data modification operations being applied through carefully programmed stored procedures instead of direct updates? When reading data from critical tables, are the unnecessary data fields being filtered through views or other means?	No

Table 16. Complete gap analysis matrix of the 7 packages

Security Mechanism (The package offers support for...)	Component Target	Package 1	Package 2	Package 3	Package 4	Package 5	Package 6	Package 7
Disabling access to extended stored procedures and functions	DB	X	X	X	X	X	X	X
Config. the system to always encrypt a remote connection to the DBMS	DB	X	X	X	X	X	X	X
Encrypting the connection of developer applications	DB	X	X	X	X	X	X	X
Removing system privileges of DBMS userids	DB	X	X	X	X	X	X	X
Restricting read/write privileges of a partition to a specific userid	OS	X	X	X	X	X	X	X
Automated installation of DBMS pending patches	DB	X						
Automated installation of OS pending patches	OS	X	X	X	X	X	X	X
Configuring the DBMS to store credential information using a reliable encryption scheme	DB	X	X	X	X	X	X	X
Configuring the OS to store credential information using a reliable encryption scheme	OS	X	X	X	X	X	X	X
Defining all DBMS passwords during the installation phase	DB	X	X	X	X	X	X	X
Defining all DBMS userids in the installation phase	DB	X						
Defining all OS passwords during the installation phase	OS	X	X	X	X	X	X	X
Defining all OS userids during the installation phase	OS					X		
Relying the DBMS on an outside specialized authentication mechanism	DB	X	X	X	X	X	X	
Relying the OS on an outside specialized authentication mechanism	OS	X	X	X	X	X	X	X
Removing all privileges of users over all systems tables.	DB							
Warning DBMS users, in a password change operation, that their new passwords are weak and cannot be accepted	DB				X			
Warning OS users, in a password change operation, that their new passwords are weak and cannot be accepted	OS	X	X	X	X	X	X	X
A DBMS authentication procedure that requests only credential information to the remote users	DB	X	X	X	X	X	X	X
An authentication procedure for remote clients that identify individual end users instead of individual applications	DB	X						
An OS authentication procedure that requests only credential information to the remote users	OS	X	X	X	X	X	X	X
Configuring the DBMS so only administrators have access to log information	DB	X	X	X	X	X	X	X
Configuring the OS so only admins. have access to log information	OS							
Configuring the system to drop idle connections after a specific period of inactivity	DB	X	X	X	X	X	X	X
Configuring the system to require that remote clients have the correct server certificate installed	DB	X			X	X	X	X

continued on the following page

Table 16. Continued

Security Mechanism (The package offers support for...)	Component Target	Package 1	Package 2	Package 3	Package 4	Package 5	Package 6	Package 7
Denying login into the DBMS from a credential with more than a specified number of failed authentication attempts	DB				X			
Denying login into the OS from a credential with more than a specified number of failed authentication attempts	OS		X		X		X	
Forcing the DBMS users to change their passwords when they're older than a specified time frame	DB				X			
Forcing the OS users to change their passwords when they're older than a specified time frame	OS		X		X		X	
Identifying systems privileges of DBMS userids	DB	X	X	X	X	X	X	X
Setting read/write/execution privileges over files	OS	X	X	X	X	X	X	X
Setting that a userid cannot login	OS	X	X	X	X	X	X	X
Setting who can change configuration files	OS	X	X	X	X	X	X	X
Setting who can change environment variables	OS	X	X	X	X	X	X	X
Specifying privileges in a row/value level	DB		X	X				
Using custom defined SSL certificates for encrypted connections	DB	X	X	X	X	X	X	X
Changing DBMS userids already in use	DB	X			X	X	X	X
Changing OS userids already in use	OS	X	X	X	X	X	X	X
Changing passwords of DBMS userids already in use	DB	X	X	X	X	X	X	X
Changing passwords of OS userids already in use	OS	X	X	X	X	X	X	X
Creating an OS userid with limited privileges	OS	X	X	X	X	X	X	X
Creating file systems partitions	OS	X	X	X	X	X	X	X
Identifying DBMS userids with default passwords	DB							
Identifying default DBMS userids	DB							
Identifying default OS userids	OS							
Identifying OS userids with default passwords	OS							
Identifying users with privileges over systems tables	DB	X	X	X	X	X	X	X
Making a backup copy of the database	DB	X	X	X	X	X	X	X
Making a backup copy of the OS which can be used to restore the environment to its current state	OS	X	X	X	X	X	X	X
Storing the backup in a custom storage place	DB	X	X	X	X	X	X	X

continued on the following page

Table 16. Continued

Security Mechanism (The package offers support for...)	Component Target	Package 1	Package 2	Package 3	Package 4	Package 5	Package 6	Package 7
Testing the installation of DBMS new patches	DB							
Testing the installation of OS new patches	OS							
Using a privilege limited userid to successfully install the DBMS.	OS		X		X		X	
Using a privilege limited userid to successfully load a DBMS process.	OS	X	X	X	X	X	X	X
Warning the admin that the last data backup is not up-to-date anymore	DB	X						
Warning the administrator that the last OS backup is not up-to-date anymore	OS							
Warning the administrator that there are DBMS vendor patches remaining to be applied	DB	X						
Warning the administrator that there are OS vendor patches remaining to be applied	OS	X	X	X	X	X	X	X
Allowing the DBA to not use ANY and ALL expressions	DB	X	X	X	X	X	X	X
Allowing to explicitly state that a particular privilege cannot be delegated	DB	X	X	X	X	X	X	X
Auditing a variety of important DBMS events	DB	X	X	X				
Auditing data changes	DB	X	X	X				
Blocking non-DBAs from delegating their privileges	DB							
Blocking privileges not inherited from groups/roles	DB							
Blocking the usage of ANY and ALL expressions in privileges granting	DB							
Changing listening TCP/UDP ports	DB	X	X	X	X	X	X	X
Changing remote identification information already in use. (e.g., SID)	DB	X	X	X	X	X	X	X
Config. the DBMS so only DBAs have access to audited information	DB	X	X	X				
Configuring the system to always establish connections through the same TCP/UDP ports during the installation phase.	DB	X		X	X	X	X	X
Configuring the system to always establish connections through the same TCP/UDP ports.	DB	X	X	X	X	X	X	X
Defining all remote identification information during the installation phase	DB	X	X	X	X	X	X	X
Defining listening TCP/UDP ports during the installation phase	DB		X	X	X	X	X	X
Disabling the generation of core_dump files	OS	X	X	X	X	X	X	X
Disabling the generation of trace files	DB	X	X	X	X	X	X	X
Encrypting backups with a reliable encryption algorithm	OS							
Identifying available functions that interact with the operating system	DB							

continued on the following page

Table 16. Continued

Security Mechanism (The package offers support for....)	Component Target	Package 1	Package 2	Package 3	Package 4	Package 5	Package 6	Package 7
Preventing specifying sensitive information in configuration files. (e.g., not require specifying password in configuration files, etc.)	OS	X	X	X	X	X	X	X
Preventing the general use of sensitive information in systems variables	OS	X	X	X	X	X	X	X
Preventing the installation of a database example during installation	DB		X	X	X	X	X	X
Removing quotas over systems areas	DB	X	X	X				
Setting and discarding a complex password for a userid	OS	X	X	X	X	X	X	X
Setting privileges to groups or roles	DB	X	X	X	X	X		
Setting the owner of files	OS	X	X	X	X	X	X	X
Specifying important events which occur in the DBMS that should generate a finger print	DB	X	X	X		X		
Specifying important events which occur in the OS that should generate a finger print	OS	X	X	X	X	X	X	X
Specifying privileges in a column level	DB	X						
Specifying privileges in a database level	DB	X	X	X	X	X	X	X
Specifying privileges in a table level	DB	X	X	X	X	X	X	X
Warning DBMS users that their passwords are older than a specified time frame	DB				X			
Warning OS users that their passwords are older than a specified time frame	OS	X	X	X	X	X	X	X
Warning the administrator if any important configuration or file was modified	OS							
Writing procedures that generate a trace for data changes	DB	X	X	X	X	X	X	X
Creating stored procedures	DB	X	X	X	X	X	X	X
Creating views	DB	X	X	X	X	X	X	X
Disabling a network protocol	OS	X	X	X	X	X	X	X
Identifying active protocols in the network stack	OS	X	X	X	X	X	X	X
Identifying available extended functions in general	DB							
Identifying available functions that can be used to perform network operations	DB							
Identifying available functions that can be used to read/write in the file system	DB							
Identifying example databases	DB							
Identifying users with quotas over systems areas	DB	X	X	X	X			
Removing a database	DB	X	X	X	X	X	X	X

continued on the following page

Table 16. Continued

Security Mechanism (The package offers support for...)	Component Target	Package 1	Package 2	Package 3	Package 4	Package 5	Package 6	Package 7
Selecting a different partition for OS log information	OS	X	X	X	X	X	X	X
Selecting a different partition than the main OS partition for auditing info	DB	X	X	X				
Selecting a different partition than the main OS partition for DBMS log information	DB	X	X	X	X	X	X	X
Selecting a different partition than the main OS partition for the data files	DB	X	X	X	X	X	X	X
Setting/unsetting access privileges over peripherals	OS		X		X		X	
Setting/unsetting read/write/execute privileges over files	OS	X	X	X	X	X	X	X
Testing if a recently created backup correctly restores the database data to its corresponding state	DB							
Testing if a recently created backup correctly restores the system to its corresponding state	OS							
Warning administrators of ANY and ALL expressions used in privileges assignments	DB							
Warning admin of users with the power of delegating their privileges	DB							

Chapter 8
A Decision Support System for Privacy Compliance

Siani Pearson
Cloud and Security Research Lab, HP Labs, UK

Tomas Sander
Cloud and Security Research Lab, HP Labs, USA

ABSTRACT

Regulatory compliance in areas such as privacy has become a major challenge for organizations. In large organizations there can be hundreds or thousands of projects that involve personal information. Ensuring that all those projects properly take privacy considerations into account is a complex challenge for accountable privacy management. Accountable privacy management requires that an organization makes sure that all relevant projects are in compliance and that there is evidence and assurance that this actually is the case. To date, there has been no suitable automated, scalable support for accountable privacy management; it is such a tool that the authors describe in this chapter. Specifically, they describe a privacy risk assessment and compliance tool which they are developing and rolling out within a large, global company – called HP Privacy Advisor (HP PA) – and its generalisation and extension. The authors also bring out those security, privacy, risk, and trust-related aspects they have been researching related to this work in particular.

INTRODUCTION

The tool discussed in this chapter is an intelligent online decision support system that assesses privacy compliance and risk, guiding employees in their decisions on how to handle different types of data. Employees access the tool via a web-based interface and answer a dynamically-generated

DOI: 10.4018/978-1-4666-0978-5.ch008

questionnaire; the tool compares the answers against the company's policies and standards, local laws and requirements, and other guidance. It assesses a project's degree of compliance with corporate privacy policy, ethics and global legislation, and the privacy promises the company makes. It generates a compliance report for each project that is retained in a central database and, if appropriate, notifies an appropriate member of the corporate Privacy Office. It also provides checklists, reminders, customized help and warnings to users. The major areas of technical innovation are in knowledge representation and inference and in simplifying knowledge management. The core technology that underpins this tool is the result of a joint effort by HP Labs and the HP Privacy Office.Organizations are currently finding it very challenging to be compliant to regulations, particularly in areas such as privacy. Contributing factors to this challenge include a growing number of privacy regulations around the world, outsourcing and transborder data flow concerns and novel technologies such as cloud computing that challenge existing governance and security frameworks for handling personal information.

Organizations processing personal data need to ensure that their operations are in compliance with applicable privacy regulations as well as with consumer expectations. Many larger organizations have a Chief Privacy Officer and privacy staff in order to implement compliance in their organizations. However a privacy staff is typically small, making effective oversight over hundreds or possibly thousands of projects per year difficult. Smaller organizations often do not have the resources for hiring qualified privacy experts.

Both large and small organizations can benefit from automated solutions (such as decision support tools) that help them take privacy concerns properly into account for all relevant projects. Both large and small organizations will benefit from broad privacy knowledge encoded in the knowledge base of such decision support tools as this knowledge is becoming increasingly complex. In addition, for large organizations, tools – unlike manual processes – can scale up to handle hundreds or thousands of projects. Tools can thereby achieve a better level of assurance that *most or all* their projects are in compliance with regulatory standards and an organization's policies.

Unfortunately up to this point no automated tools existed that comprehensively support privacy management within organizations. In this chapter we describe a decision support tool that we have developed for privacy as well as its generalization to other compliance domains. One of the key contributions of this work is to show that global privacy policies and laws can be successfully represented within a user-friendly tool. Although the knowledge base (KB) content we developed was specific to one company, we are confident that the KB is detailed and generic enough to make it highly likely that a similar approach can be taken for other companies (although some of their specific policies will surely differ). From initial modeling exercises for other compliance domains we conclude that their knowledge is not intrinsically more complex than that which we have encountered in the domain of privacy policies, suggesting that our approach to automating compliance can be utilized in these other domains as well.

BACKGROUND

In this section we review the most relevant decision support technology as well as formalized approaches for expressing privacy and security policies.

The tool we have built is a type of expert system, as problem expertise is encoded in the data structures rather than the programs and the inference rules are authored by a domain expert. Techniques for building expert systems are well known. A key advantage of this approach is that it is easier for the expert to understand or modify statements relating to their expertise. We are able to use a relatively simple underlying representation, as it was not necessary to use confidences, nor to schedule many rules that are eligible for execution at the same time through the use of a 'conflict resolution' strategy, as a one-step reasoning process sufficed. Issues with expert systems include:

1.   The 'frame problem', i.e. having to be narrow in the domain of knowledge, and so being prone to making errors that humans would easily spot.
2.   It is easy to write 'rules' that contradict each other in subtle ways. If the KB contains a contradiction this is an issue because anything follows from a contradiction.

We try to avoid these problems by involving humans within the reasoning process. Another issue we faced is that general expert systems are too generic to prove properties that we wanted for our system such as determinism.

Our system can also be viewed as a decision support system. Again, there is a large body of preceding research. Many different DSS generator products are available, including (Dicodess, 2006; XpertRule, 2006; Lumenaut, 2006; OC1, 2006). All use decision trees or decision tables which is not suitable for our use as the reasoning in our system needs to be more complex than a simple decision tree. When we tried to represent the reasoning with a decision tree, we ran into problems quickly because of the large number of possible answers, the need to duplicate information in many places within the tree, the huge size of resultant trees and the need to perform additional computation outside the decision tree (e.g. to decide if a country is part of EMEA), and in addition because of the need to conjoin output and not just stop once an output could be given. Decision trees are used to select the best course of action, but in our case we want to have a collection of independent rules that have to be tested and the result must be the output generated by *each one* of the checked rules. In summary, decision trees make it too cumbersome to express scenarios in which follow-up questions should be triggered based on Boolean combinations of previously given answers rather than on single answers.

In conclusion, existing technology turns out not to be appropriate to implement the highly dynamic, customised questionnaire generation process that we need. Thus we opted to build a strictly controlled rules engine environment which is expressive enough for our purposes yet still simple enough to prove determinism and completeness.

The other main area where there has been previous work is in the specification of privacy requirements and the translation of these into machine-readable policies.

Existing policy specification, modelling and verification tools that can be used as a basis for privacy policy representation include EPAL (IBM, 2004), OASIS XACML (OASIS, 2010), W3C P3P (Cranor, 2007; W3C, 2002) and Ponder (Damianou *et al*, 2001). These policies are formulated at a different level then the ones we are dealing with, as for example they deal with operational policies, access control constraints, etc. and cannot comfortably express context-specific privacy requirements for business processes such as marketing or software development. In circumstances where policies are specified by one party and enforced by another, the meaning must be agreed: this is achievable for example via standardization or via ontologies. There has been prior work to allow automated checking of user side policies with service side policies, e.g. via P3P (Cranor, 2007; W3C, 2002), and the Privacy and Identity Management in Europe (PRIME) project (PRIME, 2008).

Privacy policies such as EPAL (IBM, 2004) and XACML (OASIS, 2010) are low level privacy policy languages that can be machine executed but they are not well suited for human user understanding, which is what we need. In the Sparcle project, see e.g. (Vaniea *et al*, 2008), IBM Research built an editor to support transforming natural based policies into XML code that can be utilised by enforcement engines. This makes it easier for non-experts to input rules into the system, but the output format itself is not user friendly. The REALM project (IBM, 2006) from IBM Research translated high level policy and compliance constraints into machine readable formats but suffered the same shortcomings.

OASIS LegalXML (OASIS, 2007) has worked on creation and management of contract documents and terms, but this converts legal documents into an XML format that is too verbose. Travis, Breaux and Antón have also carried out some work on how to extract privacy rules and regulations from natural language text (Travis, 2008). Their work has a different focus, but could be complementary for helping to populate the knowledge base (KB) more easily.

Translation of legislation/regulation to machine readable policies has proven very difficult, although there are some examples of how translations of principles into machine readable policies can be done. Notable examples include: the Privacy Incorporated Software Agent (PISA) project (Kenny and Borking, 2002) (where privacy principles derived from (OECD, 1980) were modelled and used as a backbone in conversations between agents (Borking, 2006)), P3P (Cranor, 2007) (where user privacy preferences were matched against web site privacy statements) and PRIME (PRIME, 2008) (involving the definition and usage of various types of user and service side privacy policies). Other languages and frameworks aimed specifically at legal representation and reasoning include (Francesconi, 2009; Waterman, 2009; Förhécz et al., 2009). The amount of detail in policies and regulatory documents varies considerably between different domains, and this makes the task harder. However our research did not have to address the problem of interpreting and modelling arbitrary laws and adding them into our KB.

With regard to provision of a privacy knowledgebase that encapsulates current legislation, there are some structured databases of privacy laws that are being developed. The Governance, Risk Management and Compliance Global Rules Information Database Initiative (GRC-GRID) (GRC-GRID, 2010) has begun to create a DB of international "rules, regulations, standards, and government guidance documents". However, unlike our project the GRC GRID does not provide customized front ends for business users to access this information from the context of their business processes. Similarly, Archer Compliance Management solution (Archer, 2010) allows creation of a personalized workspace to set up standard reports, but supports mostly static templates and is thus not well suited for tailoring detailed assessments to a specific project situation, which we need.

HP PRIVACY ADVISOR

Our solution is based on decision support technology the authors developed for the HP Privacy Advisor system (HP PA) that can provide privacy assessments in complex intra-company scenarios. This section describes our solution, and the following section provides more detail about the underlying knowledge representation.

Overview

HP PA is an intelligent online rule-driven system that assesses privacy compliance and risk for projects being conducted within HP. It guides individual employees in their decisions on how to handle different types of data and is an innovative technological solution that dynamically compares answers against HP policies and standards, local laws and requirements, and other guidance.

HP PA elicits privacy-relevant information about a project via a customized sequence of questions. Based on the answers given, HP PA:

- Assesses a project's degree of compliance with corporate privacy policy, ethics and global legislation, and the privacy promises the company makes
- Integrates privacy risk assessment, education, and guidance into the process
- Scores projects for a list of ten privacy compliance indicators including transborder data flows, compliance, business controls, security, transparency, and so forth

- Generates a compliance report for each project that is retained in a central database and, if appropriate, notifies an appropriate member of the corporate privacy team
- Provides checklists and reminders to users
- Provides customized help and warnings to users as they fill out the questionnaire

The scores for different rules in the output report and the compliance indicators can be green, yellow or red. Green signifies that are no privacy issues with this project. Yellow indicates that the project possibly contains some privacy risks. Red indicates that the project could violate a regulatory requirement or company policy. A yellow flag would be raised, for example, if a project does not implement best practices, if there is missing information or if the project engages in privacy risky areas (such as catering to children or the elderly, or behavioral advertising.)

As the assessment is designed to be detailed, a broad range of privacy risks within a project will be flagged up. The distribution of these risks and their severity as indicated by the yellow or red flags gives a good understanding about which privacy risk a project carries.

Additionally, HP PA provides knowledge base (KB) management via an Expert Mode and a user-friendly Simple Mode that both can be used by domain experts to flexibly customize several aspects of the tool. HP PA also provides a dashboard view to compliance officers which presents statistics about submitted projects based on business units and/or regions.

The tool contains a hard-coded workflow for the submission and approval process of projects.

Accountability is promoted through integrating HP PA into standard business processes—that is, key decisions must pass through the tool before project deployment. At predefined periods, users with non-compliant projects are reminded of their responsibilities to bring their project into compliance. In addition, formal HP Privacy Office analysis and review of project reports is undertaken. The user may be held accountable if any privacy incidents arise from the project in the future.

The major areas of technical innovation are in knowledge representation and inference and in simplifying knowledge management. In particular, we are able to provide an accurate representation of organisational privacy policies, ensure desirable system properties such as deterministic behavior of questionnaire and report generation, enable tailoring, and ensure completeness of the questionnaire generation (Pearson *et al*, 2009; Pearson *et al*, 2010). We have also encapsulated heuristics and usability techniques in order to aid non-trained users in creating the knowledgebase (KB) and have addressed complexity, including the ramifications of KB updates, KB versioning and quarantine of parts of the KB (Pearson, 2010). Furthermore, we have researched the usage of tagging and privacy ontologies to link the KB to external data sources (Bruckshen *et al*, 2010).

We were able to successfully express the 300-page HP privacy rule book within the knowledge base (KB) of HP PA and confirmed through extensive testing that it can be used to risk-assess projects within HP that might pose privacy risks. HP PA has been transferred into the HP Data Center and is available to all HP employees for privacy assessments and accountability within HP.

In the remainder of this section we provide more detail about our solution, considering in turn the system architecture, end user interactions, knowledge engineering, practical insights and feedback from user testing and the current status.

Architecture

This section describes the HP PA component architecture and functionality, as illustrated in Figure 1. HP PA is a standard three tier web application using Java Enterprise Technology (J2EE), where the client is a standard web browser, the application tier is a standard Java application server (Apache

Figure 1. Architectural overview of HP privacy advisor

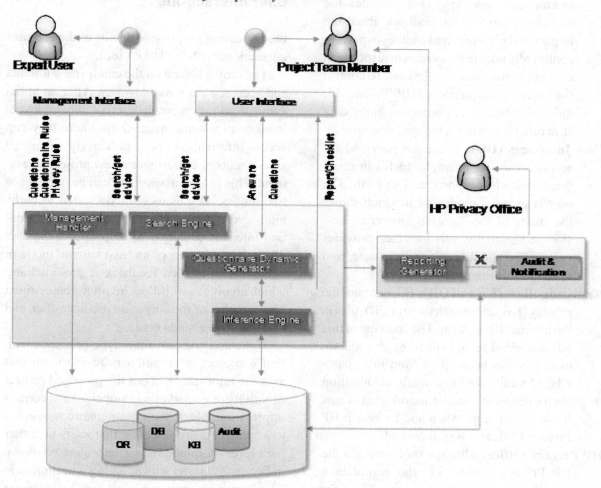

Tomcat), and the persistence layer is a standard relational database (Oracle 11g).

The main component parts are as follows:

Reasoning Engine: HP PA uses JBoss Drools 5 (JBoss, 2010), a forward chaining rules engine that uses the Rete Algorithm as the reasoning engine both for validating the user's responses against a set of privacy rules, and to dynamically tailor the user experience using a questionnaire generated by a set of questionnaire rules. JBoss is not an off-the-shelf product that can be directly used for this purpose. HP PA was developed

following considerable design, data structure definition, and algorithms work to leverage the capabilities of JBoss.

Management Interface: This is a central component of the HP PA architecture because it is tailored towards the (privacy) domain expert for creating and updating the underlying knowledge base. It allows the domain expert who is not well-versed in logic syntax to input complex rules and regulations into the questionnaire (QR) and privacy knowledge repository (KB). It also allows the expert to edit rules, both for accountability and generating questions, and test them against sample user sessions. This provides the domain expert instant feedback about the impact of their inputs and enables experts to continually update the system in response to changes in rules and regulations. To control the ordering of questions, HP PA uses additional formatting information in the data structure representing the questionnaire.

User Interfaces (UIs): These are provided for end users to, for example, to fill in questionnaires, view reports, and so forth. The user is shown a progress bar which shows the status of the question answering session. Additionally, this interface provides customized and rule driven assistance, tool tips, and warnings to users.

Knowledge Base (KB and QR): This contains the privacy (KB) and questionnaire (QR) rules in the internal JBoss form. The contents of this KB are added to and edited by the domain expert or can be adapted from third party KBs. 'Audit' contains audit information for the different compliance relevant events for a project, e.g., when and by which HP Privacy Officer it was approved.

HP Privacy Office: Through this interface the HP Privacy Office, i.e. the compliance organization with global responsibility for privacy, can review the projects that have been submitted, has manual approval and reject capabilities for projects possibly overriding system decisions (these events will be audited), and can access via a dashboard privacy compliance statistics for the organization, e.g., broken up by business unit or region.

Database/Persistence Layer (DB): This is the back end that stores questions and corresponding answers collected from the user (objects that are used by the rule engine). This layer uses Hibernate to remove the impedance between Java code and the database layer and to provide scalability.

User Interactions

In this section we provide details of the end user interactions with the HP PA tool.

The tool is hosted on the enterprise's intranet and accessed via a web browser. After an initial authentication process, the user (i.e. the employee) is taken to a home page, from where they can access information about previously submitted assessments or else trigger a new project assessment. This project assessment can be in either of two modes: a 'guidance' mode suited to early, high-level assessments of projects with information intended primarily to help inform the user of important issues, or an 'assessment' mode in which more detailed feedback is provided and which involves a workflow involving assessment by a member of the corporate privacy office and auditing of decisions made.

If the user triggers either type of assessment, first a project information page is shown that asks for information about the proposed project or activity (e.g. marketing campaign) and contact information. Next, the questionnaire moves on to a 'project profile' section that starts to gather high-level information about the project. As shown in Figure 2, it starts with a 'gating' question as to whether the program or project handles customer or employee information: if the answer is 'no' then there will not be any major privacy issues. The answers that the user gives to each question build the questionnaire, in the sense that they trigger the next questions to be asked. Hence, the questions shown in Figure 2 are not all generated at once, and appear in blocks. The user can navigate through the questionnaire using the section tabs that are shown at the top of the display.

As shown in Figure 3, informational messages (e.g. warnings) applicable to the question are highlighted using a circular icon containing an exclamation mark. Clicking the exclamation mark will display the message. Help associated with each question may be obtained by clicking on the underlined text next to each question: using

Figure 2. Example part of user questionnaire

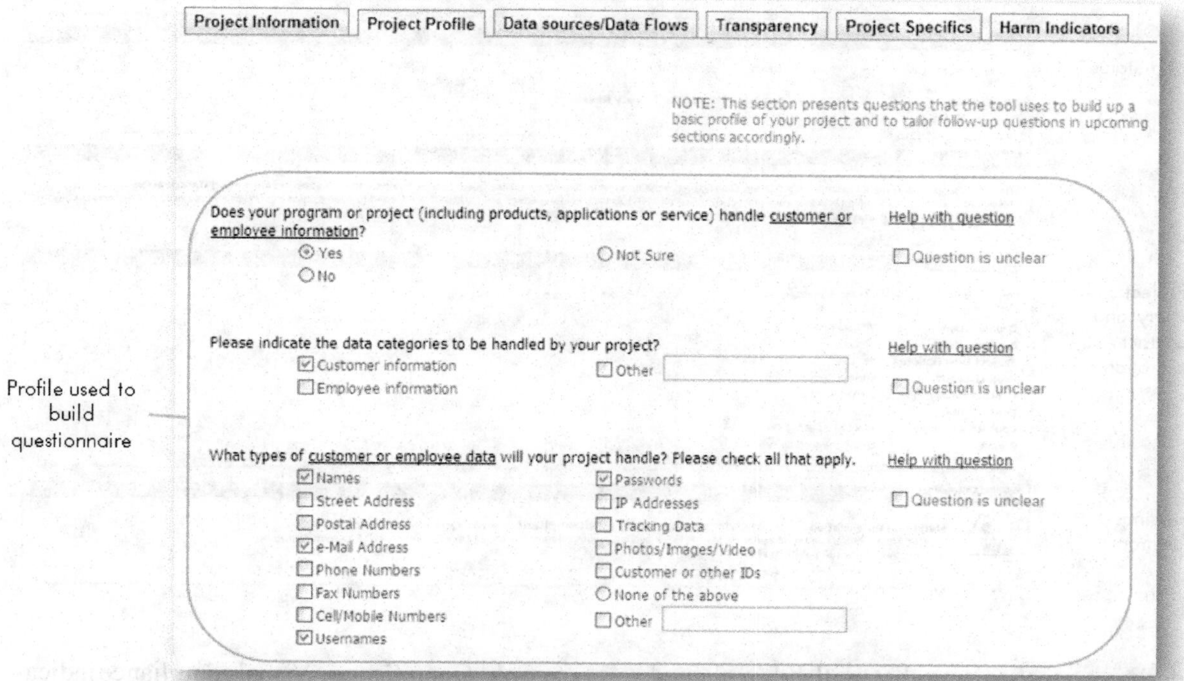

Profile used to build questionnaire

Figure 3. Informational messages

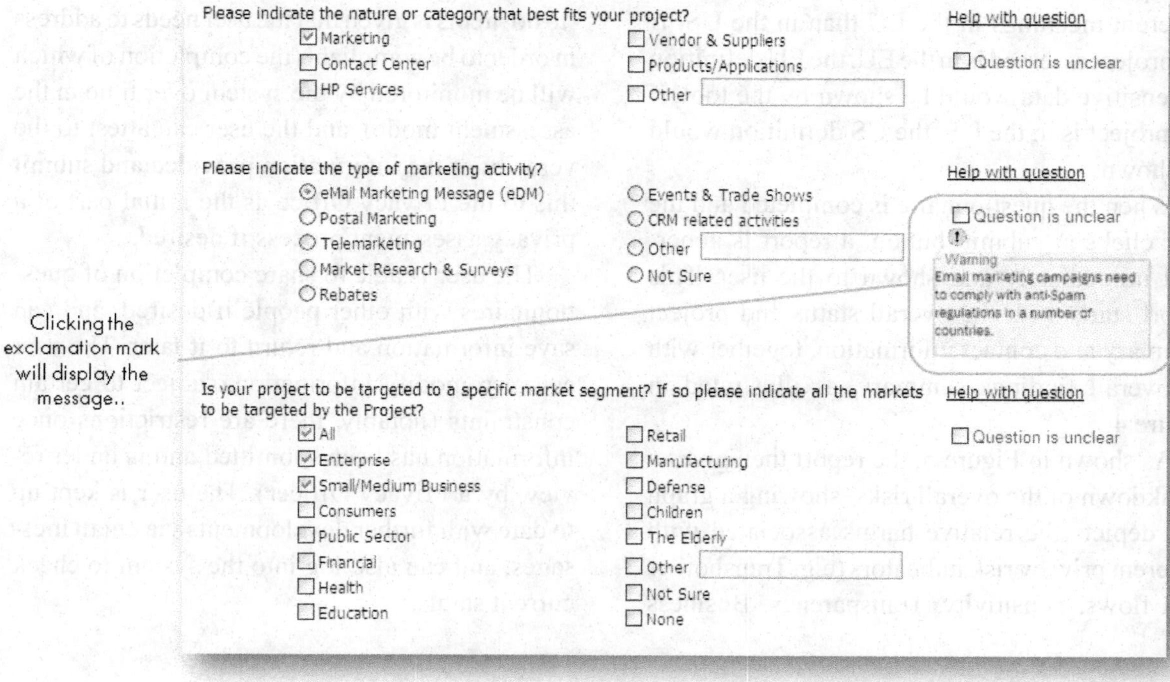

Clicking the exclamation mark will display the message..

Figure 4. Example report part 1

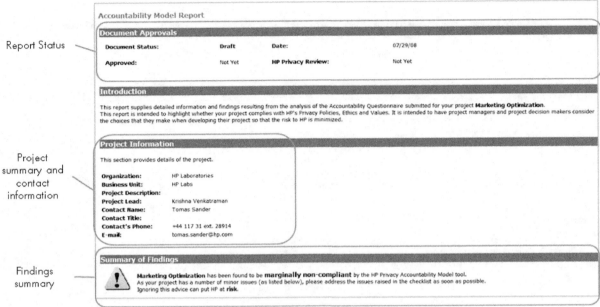

underlying mechanisms that will be explained further below, this help text can be customized according to the context in which this question appears, and so be more meaningful and useful for the user. An example for this is a help message to explain the term 'sensitive data' which has different meanings in the EU than in the US. If the project assessed is in the EU, the EU definition of sensitive data would be shown by the tool, if the project is in the US, the US definition would be shown.

When the questionnaire is completed and the user clicks a 'submit' button, a report is generated immediately and shown to the user. This report starts with the overall status and project summary and contact information, together with an overall findings summary, as illustrated in Figure 4.

As shown in Figure 5, the report then gives a breakdown of the overall risks, showing a graph that depicts the relative harms associated with different privacy risk indicators (e.g. Transborder data flows, Sensitivity, Transparency, Business controls, Compliance). Visual compliance indicators (compliance flags) give an overview of the status associated with each risk indicator, and detailed information is provided on the reasons for partial or non-compliance (see also Figure 6).

Finally, as shown in Figure 7, a checklist of 'to do' items is given that the user needs to address in order to be compliant (the completion of which will be monitored by the system over time in the assessment mode), and the user can attest to the veracity of the information provided and submit this to the Privacy Office as the initial part of a privacy assessment process if desired.

The user is able to share completion of questionnaires with other people if desired, and can save information and return to it later. The user can also modify information, subject to certain constraints (notably, there are restrictions once information has been submitted and is under review by a Privacy Officer). The user is kept up to date with further developments via email messages, and can also log into the system to check current status.

Figure 5. Example report part 2

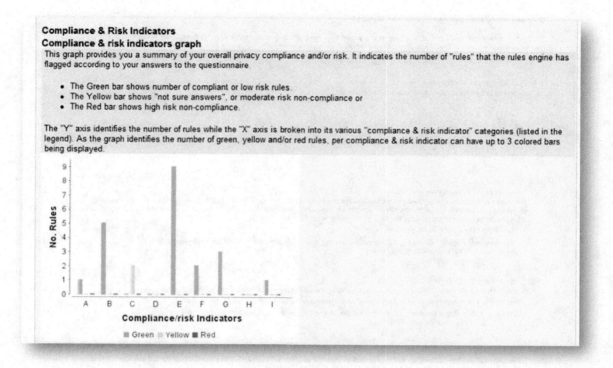

Another aspect of the system is the mechanism that allows experts to input knowledge into the system that then serves as the basis for deriving advice. This is considered further in the following section. In addition, there are UIs that allow setting of administrative constraints including access control, sharing of information (e.g. to allow collaboration in providing information within the questionnaire) and changing some workflow-related settings.

Practical Insights

Before describing the details of the knowledge representation in this section we share some insights from our user testing, and in particular what is important for end users and lessons learned. This will help motivate our system and knowledge representation design.

First, defining meaningful variables that capture important concepts is helpful for simplification of rule trigger conditions, and thereby makes the underlying question and domain rules easier to understand. Further explanation of these intermediate variables is given in the following section.

Questions and answers should have an effect on the report or other steps of the process, or else be dropped. Users do not like to be asked redundant questions or questions that seem irrelevant given what they have previously answered. Technical terms in questions and output require careful definition in order to be understandable to users, and jargon should be avoided. Asking *specific* questions is helpful to assess whether users do what they are supposed to do. Drill down questions (i.e. using depth-first mode in question rules, as explained further in the following section) are very helpful in order to specify scenarios, remove vagueness and enhance the quality of user input.

Figure 6. Example report part 3

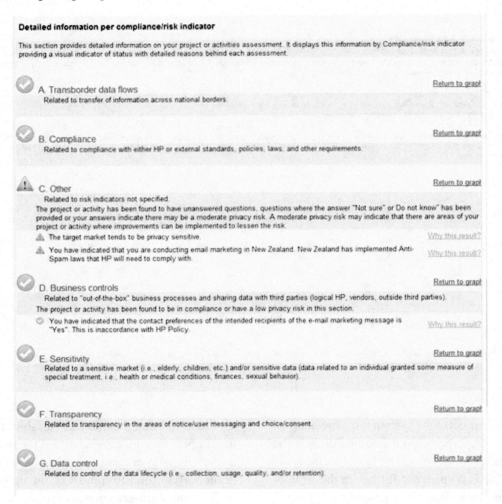

Figure 7. Example report part 4

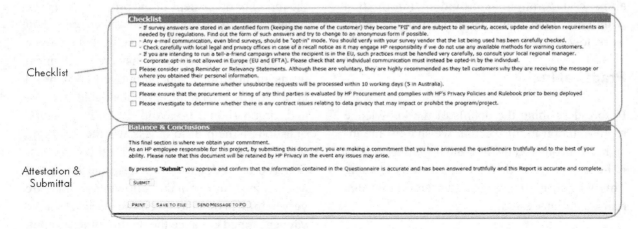

Users have a strong interest to have their project move forward and want to know what they can do concretely to bring their project into compliance – hence the need for and appreciation of the checklist within the report and being able to print that out. Users also appreciate positive output (i.e. the green flags in the report) so they know that they are doing something right, or if something is low risk.

Finally, we found that checklist entries should be specific and actionable and provide information on how a user can address remediation. It is important that a consistent notation is used throughout the tool, not only for terms, but also for activities and broader concepts. Reasons in the output report should be concise (but should link to more detailed information).

KNOWLEDGE REPRESENTATION AND INFERENCE

In this section we provide more detail about the knowledge representation and inference used in the system.

Dynamic Questionnaire and Report Generation

HP PA does both compliance checking and questionnaire generation within the same rule engine framework. The technique is questionnaire-based and adaptive with HP PA asking a dynamically generated set of questions. Based on user responses, HP PA generates an actionable report based on a set of compliance rules. HP PA uses question-generating rules to drive the questionnaire generation itself. HP PA groups related questions together, orders them logically, and allows drill-down—greatly enhancing the user-friendliness of the system.

HP PA considers three user types: the (privacy) domain expert who authors the compliance rule set and the questionnaire, the end user who will

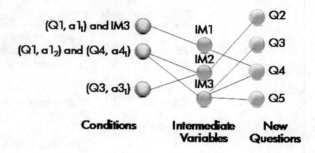

Figure 8. A representation of the questionnaire using tripartite graphs

be shown a subset of a list of questions and needs to answer them and the compliance officer

HP PA uses a set of intermediate variables (IMs) to simplify the authoring of the rule base. Intuitively, IMs are used to encode meaningful information about the project and to drive the questionnaire as shown in Figure 8. IMs can be thought of as flags. An example of an IM is 'project has transborder data flow', which indicates that the current context allows transborder data flow. For provability, we mandate monotonicity for the IMs, meaning that IM values cannot be retracted once they have been asserted.

The questionnaire allows a tripartite graph structure as shown in the previous figure. The left nodes are monotonic expressions involving (question, answer) pairs. The middle partition consists of intermediate nodes that are semantically meaningful IMs. The right set of nodes represents "new" question(s) that will be asked. In this way, the IMs give the domain expert an intuitive handle to control the flow of questions.

In summary, the IMs are conditions/variables within the tool that are set directly or calculated using the answers given whilst answering the questionnaire.

Privacy Knowledge Base

The system's knowledge base (KB) comprises:

Table 1. Rule structure

Rule type	Conditions	Actions
Privacy	Boolean combination of question/answer pairs and/or IMs	Generate output for the report
Question	Same as above	Generate questionnaire/ determine where questions are displayed
IM	Same as above	Set IM variables
Customised help	Same as above	Generate question help based on previous user answers
Intelligent warning	Same as above	Generate warnings

- *Information that domain experts author up-front*: questions and possible answers; semantically meaningful variables – IMs – with their different values; help content; rules for triggering questions to be displayed, output, customized help and warnings
- *Users' input*: project information and answers to questions
- *System analysis*: values of IMs, appropriate questions to display, output (reports, help, warnings, etc.), auditing records (including versioning)

The different types of rule that the domain expert can author are listed in Table 1.

For the *privacy rules*, our approach is to translate natural language phrases into an intermediate 'normal form' that is structured natural language; there are some similarities here with other approaches, including the Consequence project (Orlov, 2008). These allow the construction of valid trigger conditions, at an intermediate level. We use the UIs to constrain the domain experts into entering or editing rules using this format. An example of this format is given in Figure 9. The system then automatically translates this 'normal form' into the rules used by the inference engine.

Question rules generate the dynamic questionnaire. As discussed above, they follow the structure of a tripartite graph in order to trigger conditions from the answers that the user provides. Direct association from questions/answers to a new set of questions is allowed, but this relation can also be established using IMs.

The questionnaire can be formatted for user friendliness in the following way:

- Questions are organized within Sections
- Subsections can be used to group questions
- Follow up questions can be added in drill down mode or added at the current list of questions.
- The order of questions can be specified

In addition, help can be associated with each Section, and question help can be associated in a rule-driven way with each question. Warnings that are shown to the user when a user gives certain answers (as illustrated above in Figure 3) can be specified in a rule-driven way. 'Tooltips' – that appear as underlined terms and open when scrolling over them – are used to explain technical terms.

Figure 9. Example privacy rule

Rule name: eDM requirement
Categorization: use: secondary use: marketing
Risk level: very high
Risk indicator: harm to end user; missing information
Trigger conditions: IncludesFunctioningUnsubscribe = no or IncludesFunctioningUnsubscribe = unknown
Trigger condition description: Rule triggered when it is unsure if there is, or else there is not, a functioning unsubscribe
Applicability: eDM
Reason: HP must include a functioning unsubscribe mechanism or a simple means for the recipient to opt-out of receiving further messages
Checklist entry (in RCA: Action Record): Use appropriate opt-out for type of permission:
·   One-to-One Sales: If applicable, please let me know if you prefer not to receive these e-mails from me.
·   One-to-One Transactional: If applicable, please let me know if you prefer not to receive these communications through e-mail.
Include HP Privacy Statement and Physical Address.
For third-party messages where HP is the sole or primary content, use the following: HP is committed to respecting your privacy and occasionally works with opt-in, third-party subscription lists such as ours to share information about HP products and services with new audiences. HP intent is to work only with reputable opt-in partners and send messages to you only with your permission. To unsubscribe from (third party) communications, please follow the instructions below.
Link: http://intranet.hp.com/sites/privacyrulebook/2008/Pages/CustomerContactStandard.aspx#pref; http://intranet.hp.com/sites/privacyrulebook/2008/Pages/SPEC_EmailMarketing.aspx#examples
Origin:
•   Rulebook Customer Contact Standard 3.1; Rulebook Customer Contact Standard 3.2; Rulebook Customer Contact Standard 3.3; Rulebook Specification on Email Marketing 4

Adding tags assists the management of the KB. From the list of questions you can display tagged questions by selecting a tag. Tags can be attached to other KB objects as well. As shown in Figure 10, tags can be added to questions by filtering the list of questions by typing in the question ID or a search term to display one or more questions and then clicking on 'Tag Question Below'.

Rule Representation

The different types of rule in our system have already been introduced in Table 1. All the rules have the general form:

"when condition then action".

Question rules have as their conditions a monotonic expression (i.e. Boolean expression built up using $\&$ and v as logical operators) in intermediate variables (IMs) and/or (question,

answer) pairs and as actions, directives to ask the user some questions or else to set some IMs.

The privacy rules' condition is similarly a Boolean expression in a set of IMs and answers to questions and they generate as their actions the content of the output report (i.e. risk levels and other information). Some of the privacy rules encode the enterprise policies; others encode regulatory privacy requirements.

All the rules in the system are based upon the production rule system Drools (JBoss, 2010); this rules engine is run after each question is answered by the user. For provability, we mandate monotonicity for the IMs, i.e. they cannot be retracted once they have been asserted. In this way we ensure that there is no circularity in the dynamic questionnaire generation, where questions are triggered and later again retracted, possibly leading to infinite loops. Thereby we can prove termination and also determinism in the sense that the output report obtained does not depend on the order in which questions are answered.

Figure 10. Tagging

Note that the DSS only asks the user a subset of all the questions in its knowledge base. We call a selection strategy for a subset of questions *complete* if for all evaluations the output report on the selected subset of questions is the same as if all the questions had been asked. We have designed an algorithm in (Pearson *et al*, 2009) that implements a provably complete strategy for question selection.

Example

Let us now consider a simple example of the underlying representation, in Drools Rule Language (DRL) format (although the rules can automatically be converted to Extensible Markup Language (XML) format) (JBoss, 2010). Assume that an employee is answering a questionnaire, and that the question *"Will data be stored in encrypted form?"* is answered "Yes". Assume this question has identifier number 48 in the system. This (question, answer) pair is added to working memory and as a consequence the following question rule is triggered asserting a new IM "Encrypted storage":

```
rule "IMR21"
 when QA (id == 48, value == "Yes")
then insert(new IM("Encrypted
storage","Yes")); end
```

When the previous IM is asserted to the working memory it triggers the following question rule which adds new questions to the questionnaire:

```
rule "QR17"
when IM (name == "Enc", value ==
"Yes")
then AddToDisplayList_DF(current,
currentQuestion, new long[] {49});
end
```

Question 49 is "What encryption mechanism is being used?" In other cases, blocks of questions are added to the questionnaire just by adding them to the set in the rule above. The questionnaire generation procedure then iterates through the questionnaire. The initial (question, answer) pair will also generate a new parameter instance: "Encryption used in storage" with value "Yes". If we require this to trigger an output, then this can be captured within a output rule. For the example above, when this parameter instance is added to the working memory of the privacy engine it triggers the following privacy rule:

```
rule "Encrypted storage"
when ParameterInstance (name == "En-
cryption Used in storage", value ==
"Yes")
then report.addRule(new RuleFacade().
findById(50));  end
```

This rule adds a *Rule* object to the list of rules of the report. The rule can show a flag (to indicate the seriousness of the issue), a reason and a link to more information or other items to be included within the report.

Knowledge Engineering

There are two modes available for Privacy Office staff with HP PA KB access to add, update or delete content from the KB. One of these modes (the Simple Mode) involves simplified screens, and is targeted at staff who do not normally use the tool or else as a convenient way of achieving some basic functionalities for more expert users.

The Expert Mode is available directly from the Knowledgebase Management left-hand menu (that is only accessible to pre-authorised domain experts) and provides comprehensive options for adding, updating or deleting the following: sections, questions, question rules, privacy rules, question help, warnings, tool-tips and rule-based help. In addition, a 'Test Questionnaire' option allows testing of new KB content. This mode of KB input sometimes exposes the rule representations described above and is rather complex for a non-trained person.

The Simple Mode is similarly accessible to the domain expert, but as the last item under the Knowledgebase Management taskbar menu. It is designed in particular for untrained users and provides a reasonably simple means to updates rules in the KB that works for the majority of cases. Analysis of our KB helped focus attention on the 'simple' tasks which make up the majority of the rules which are actually likely to be written by domain experts (such as most questions having answers 'yes', 'no' and 'do not know', and most question rules setting IMs and privacy rules having the form for the trigger condition 'when QA(id==ID, value==Value)'). The Simple Mode uses heuristics and artificial intelligence techniques to hide the complexity of the underlying representation for such tasks from the domain expert and make choices on their behalf; it also tries to optimise usability. To do this, we decided to retrict the interface to a small set of possible constructs and actively fought against 'feature-creep'. Our goal was an interface that is restrictive, since such restrictions are balanced against the increased ease of learning and use, and users can always enlist help or undertake training to achieve more complex goals.

In the Simple Mode there is a closer linkage between authoring and the finished questionnaire, in that the authoring environment resembles the questionnaire in layout, and the authoring vocabulary is closer to the vocabulary of use, i.e. instead of rules and variables it talks about questions and answers and uses expressions like 'if you answer

A then you are asked the follow up question B' etc. In addition to a home page, screens are provided for adding new questions, listing questions, editing existing questions, adding follow-up questions (to determine where questions are displayed within a questionnaire), editing follow-up questions, adding report content, editing report content and listing privacy rules. This mode was found very useful by domain experts when building up the KB that corresponds to our internal corporate policies, and was improved in an iterative manner based upon feedback. Some example screens are shown in Figures 11 to 12. For more information see (Pearson, 2010).

Figure 11. Adding a question rule in simple mode

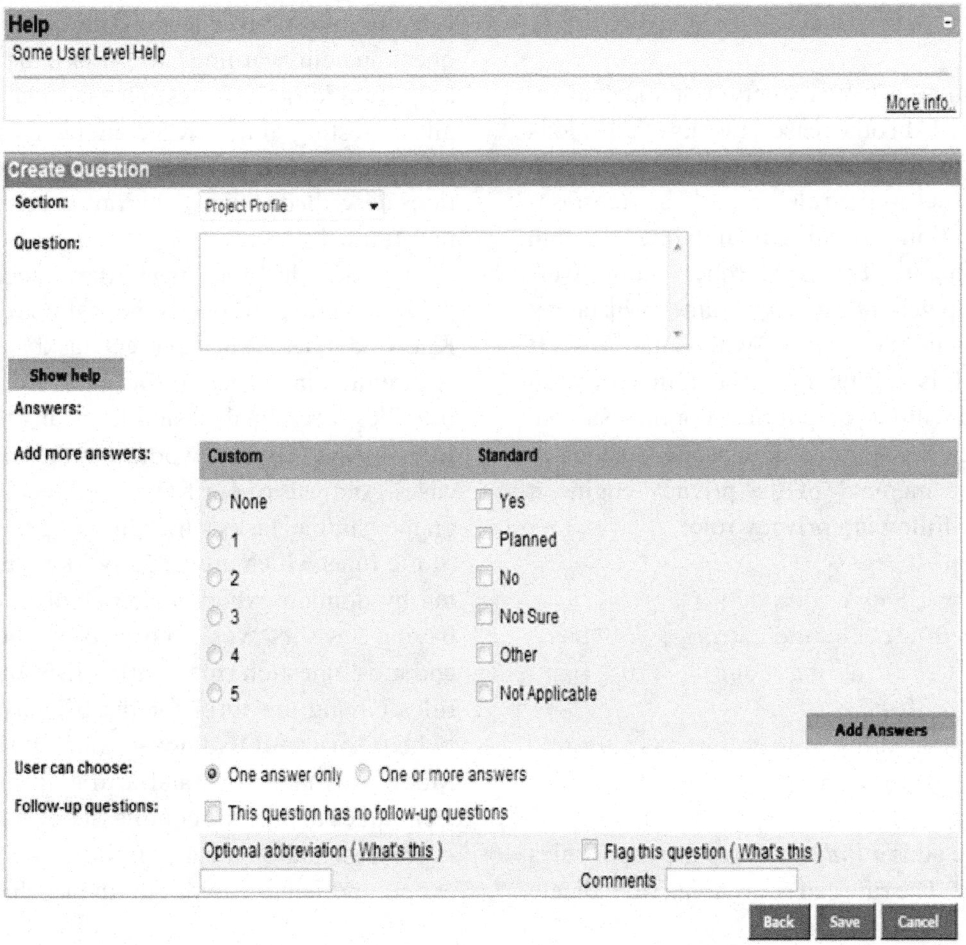

Figure 12. Editing a follow-up question in simple mode

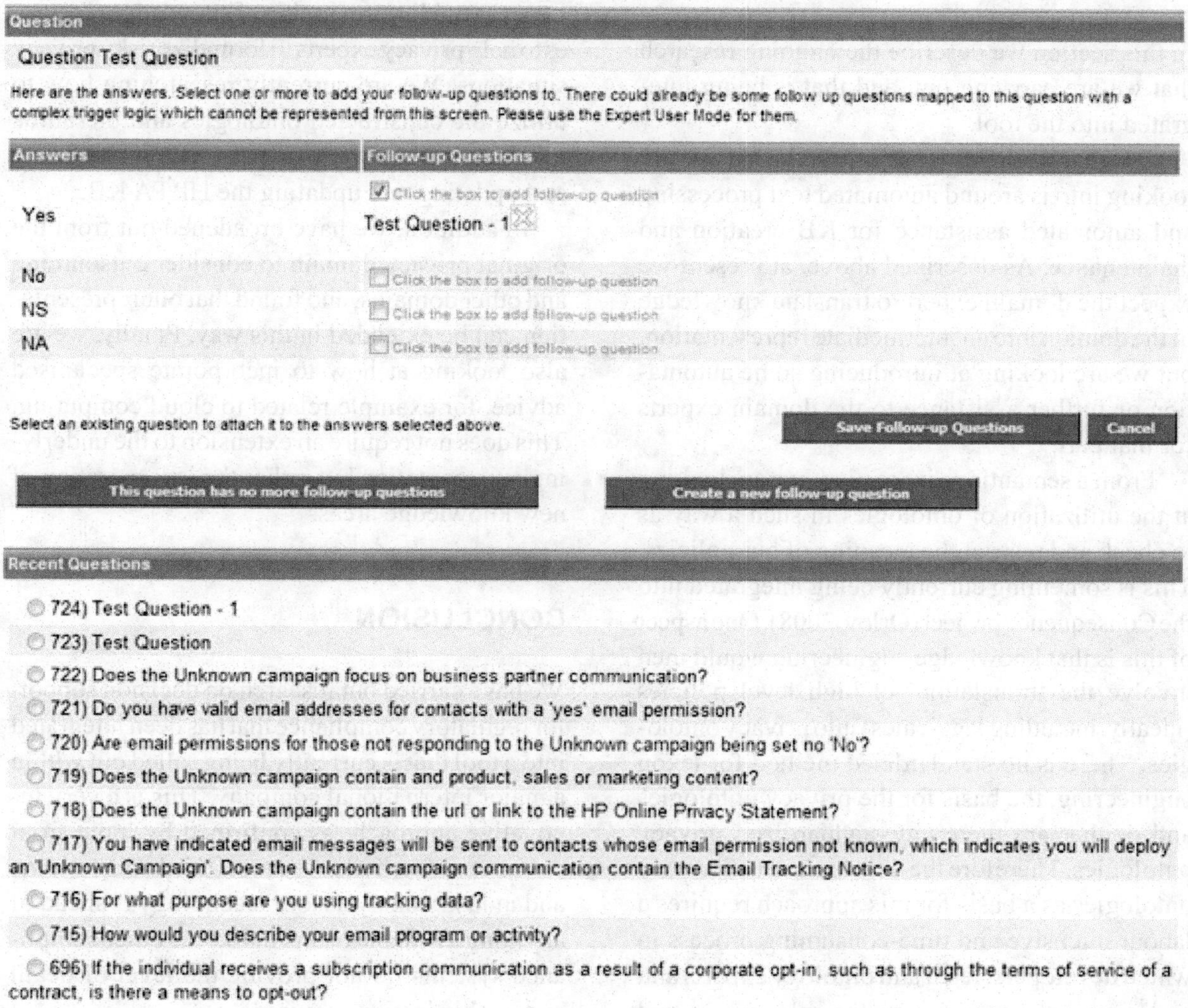

Knowledge Maintenance

Regulations and company policies are not static. Thus the questions and rules in the knowledge base have to be updated accordingly. As one of the requirements for the HP Privacy Advisor is to allow to reconstruct (and to demonstrate e.g., to regulators) how compliance decisions at a particular point in time were arrived at a simple deletion of rules from the knowledge base is problematic as that can break the audit trail. Instead we decided to deactivate rules rather than to delete them entirely. In this way old rules are still conveniently available when needed. For end users as well as expert users the experience of updates to the KB is smooth as the tool will make all the necessary modifications of rules automatically in the background. For example if a user logs to an existing project assessment after the KB has been updated he will be alerted to that fact. If there are additional questions to be answered this will be shown to him. He will also be asked to rerun the tool on his answers to produce an output report based on the latest rule set.

FUTURE RESEARCH DIRECTIONS

In this section we describe the ongoing research that we are carrying out, and that is being integrated into the tool.

One interesting area of research that we are looking into is around automated text processing and automated assistance for KB creation and maintenance. As described above, at present we expect the domain expert to translate knowledge of the domain into an intermediate representation, but we are looking at introducing some automation or further assistance to the domain experts for that part.

From a semantic point of view, we are looking at the utilization of ontologies in such a way as to check and restrict the meaning of our policies. This is something currently being integrated into the Consequence project (Orlov, 2008). One aspect of this is that knowledge engineering would then involve the 'translation' of high level policies (ideally, including legal rules) into privacy ontologies. There is no standardized method for lexon engineering, the basis for the privacy ontologies and neither are there any standardized privacy ontologies. Therefore the development of privacy ontologies as a basis for this approach requires a labour intensive and time-consuming process in which developers, legal and ontology experts and end users have to agree on the rule system and the ontology before the decision tool can be built. Hameed, Sleeman and Preece (Hameed et al, 2002) consider this process as inevitable – otherwise the validity of the developed privacy ontologies will be contested and that will decrease the trust in the working of the decision tool.

If a legal researcher delivers legal input and then technologists interpret and translate that input into triples and lexons, such an approach will lead to serious errors as has been demonstrated by Spyns & Hogben (Spyns et al. 2005). One approach would be to adopt the privacy ontologies developed in the EU PRIME project (PRIME, 2008).

In another research thread (Vieira *et al*, 2010) we are providing a mapping of knowledge resources to help privacy experts to formalize risky privacy situations. We are currently researching how to utilize the constructed ontologies and thesaurus to assist a privacy expert user with maintaining and updating and updating the HP PA KB.

In addition, we have broadened out from the original privacy domain to consider outsourcing and other domains, and found that our representation can be extended in this way. Finally, we are also looking at how to incorporate specialised advice, for example related to cloud computing. This does not require an extension to the underlying representation but rather the incorporation of new knowledge areas.

CONCLUSION

We have carried out research on decision support for regulatory compliance that has been integrated into a tool that is currently being rolled out within a major international company. This is a very innovative approach: as confirmed by input from customers, internal resources, third party views, and industry analysts, our technology is ahead of anything available on the market as other compliance systems do not provide the level of detail and sophistication required.

ACKNOWLEDGMENT

We would like to acknowledge the other members of the team involved in producing the HP Privacy Advisor, without whom this tool would not be a reality. This includes in particular the HP Privacy Office, HP Labs Research Engineering and HP Best Shore Application Services.

REFERENCES

W3C. (2002). *The platform for privacy preferences*, v1.0. Retrieved November 3, 2010, from http://www.w3.org/TR/P3P/

Archer. (2010). *Compliance management solution*. Retrieved November 3, 2010 from http://www.archer-tech.com

Borking, J. (2006). *Privacy rules: A steeple chase for systems architects*. Retrieved November 8, 2010, from www.w3.org/2006/07/privacy-ws/papers/04-borking-rules/

Bruckschen, M., Northfleet, C., da Silva, D., Bridi, P., Granada, R., Vieira, R., & Sander, T. (2010). Named entity recognition in the legal domain for ontology population. In *Proceedings of SPLeT-2010*. LREC.

Cranor, L. (2002). *Web privacy with* (p. 3P). O'Reilly & Associates.

Damianou, N., Dulay, N., Lupu, E., & Sloman, M. (2001). The ponder policy specification language. In *Policies for Distributed Systems and Networks, LNCS 1995/2001*, (pp. 18-38). Springer.

Dicodess. (2006). *Open source model-driven DSS generator*. Retrieved November 11, 2010, from http://dicodess.sourceforge.net

Förhécz, A., Kőrösi, G., Millinghoffer, A., & Strausz, G. (2009) Emerald: Legal knowledge engineering using OWL and rules. In G. Governatori (Ed.), *Proceeding of the 2009 Conference on Legal Knowledge and Information Systems: JURIX 2009: The Twenty-Second Annual Conference*, (pp. 53-58). Amsterdam, The Netherlands: IOS Press.

Francesconi, E. (2009). An approach to legal rules modelling and automatic learning. In In G. Governatori (Ed.), *Proceeding of the 2009 Conference on Legal Knowledge and Information Systems: JURIX 2009: The Twenty-Second Annual Conference*, (pp. 59-68). Amsterdam, The Netherlands: IOS Press.

GRC-GRID. (2010). *The governance, risk management and compliance global rules information database*. Retrieved November 3, 2010 from http://www.grcroundtable.org/grc-grid.htm

Hameed, A., Sleeman, D., & Preece, A. (2002). Detecting mismatches among experts' ontologies acquired through knowledge elicitation. *Knowledge-Based Systems, 15*, 265–273. doi:10.1016/S0950-7051(01)00162-9

IBM. (2004). *The enterprise privacy authorization language (EPAL), EPAL specification*, v1.1. Retrieved November 3, 2010, from http://www.zurich.ibm.com/security/enterprise-privacy/epal/

IBM. (2005). *Sparcle project*. Retrieved November 3, 2010, from http://domino.research.ibm.com/comm/research_projects.nsf/pages/sparcle.index.html

IBM. (2006). *REALM project*. Retrieved November 3, 2010, from http://www.zurich.ibm.com/security/publications/2006/REALM-at-IRIS2006-20060217.pdf

JBoss. (2010). *Drools*, v5. Retrieved November 3, 2010 from http://jboss.org/drools/

Kenny, S., & Borking, J. (2002). The value of privacy engineering. In *Journal of Information, Law and Technology (JILT), 1*.

Lumenaut. (2006). *Decision tree package*. Retrieved November 24, 2010, from http://www.lumenaut.com/decisiontree.htm

OC1. (2006). *Oblique classifier 1*. Retrieved November 11, 2010, from http://www.cbcb.umd.edu/~salzberg/announce-oc1.html

OASIS. (2007). *eContracts specification*, v1.0. Retrieved November 3, 2010, from http://docs.oasis-open.org/legalxml-econtracts/legalxml-econtracts-specification-1.0.html

OASIS. (2010). *eXtensible access control markup language* (XACML). Retrieved November 3, 2010, from http://www.oasis-open.org/committees/tc_home.php?wg_abbrev=xacml

Organization for Economic Co-operation and Development (OECD). (1980). *Guidelines governing the protection of privacy and transborder flow of personal data*. Geneva, Switzerland: OECD.

Orlov, A. (2008). Project consequence. *Science and Technology Magazine, 1*, 62–63.

Pearson, S. (2010). Addressing complexity in a privacy expert system. In E. Hüllermeier, R. Kruse, & F. Hoffmann (Eds.), *Proceedings of IPMU 2010, Part II, CCIS 81*, (pp. 612–621). Berlin, Germany: Springer-Verlag.

Pearson, S., Rao, P., Sander, T., Parry, A., Paull, A., & Patruni, S. ... Sharma, P. (2009). Scalable, accountable privacy management for large organizations. In *Proceedings of INSPEC09, 2nd International Workshop on Security and Privacy Distributed Computing, Enterprise Distributed Object Conference Workshops (EDOCW 2009)*, IEEE, (pp. 168-175).

Pearson, S., Sander, T., & Sharma, R. (2010). Privacy management for global organisations. In Garcia-Alfaro, J. (Eds.), *Data Privacy Management and Autonomous Spontaneous Security, LNCS 5939* (pp. 9–17). Berlin, Germany: Springer-Verlag. doi:10.1007/978-3-642-11207-2_2

PRIME. (2008). *Privacy and identity management for Europe*. Retrieved 3 November, 2010, from http://www.prime-project.org.eu

Spyns, P., & Hogben, G. (2005). Validating an automated evaluation procedure for ontology triples in the privacy domain. In *Frontiers in Artificial Intelligence and Applications: Vol. 134; Proceeding of the 2005 Conference on Legal Knowledge and Information Systems: JURIX 2005: The Eighteenth Annual Conference*, (pp 127-136).

Travis, D., Breaux, T. D., & Antón, A. I. (2008). Analyzing regulatory rules for privacy and security requirements. *Transactions on Software Engineering, 34*(1), 5–20. doi:10.1109/TSE.2007.70746

Vaniea, K., Karat, C., Gross, J. B., Karat, J., & Brodie, C. (2008). Evaluating assistance of natural language policy authoring. In *Proceedings of SOUPS '08: Vol. 337.*

Vieira, R., Agustini, A., Castilho, F., Bruckschen, M., Pizzinato, P., Bridi, P.,... Rao, R. (2010). *Representation and inference of privacy risks using Semantic Web Technologies*. Poster at EKAW 2010 - Knowledge Engineering and Knowledge Management by the Masses.

Waterman, K. K. (2009). *Pre-processing legal text: Policy parsing and isomorphic intermediate representation*. Association for the Advancement of Artificial Intelligence. Retrieved November 8, 2010, from http://dig.csail.mit.edu/2010/Papers/Privacy2010/ kkw-preprocessing/waterman. PRIVACY2010. parsing_privacy.pdf

XpertRule. (2006). *Knowledge builder*. Retrieved November 24, 2010 from http://www.xpertrule.com/pages/info_kb.htm

ADDITIONAL READING

American Institute of Certified Public Accountants. ("AICPA") in collaboration with the Canadian Institute of Chartered Accountants ("CICA"). (2010). *Generally accepted privacy principles ("GAPP") – A global privacy framework*. Retrieved November 24, 2010, from http://www.aicpa.org/InterestAreas/ InformationTechnology/Resources/Privacy/ GenerallyAcceptedPrivacyPrinciples/Pages/Generally% 20Accepted%20Privacy%20Principles.aspx

Asia Pacific Economic Cooperation. (n.d.). *The APEC privacy principles*. APEC.

Barth, A., Datta, A., Mitchell, J. C., & Nissenbaum, H. (2006). Privacy and contextual integrity: Framework and applications. In *IEEE Symposium on Security and Privacy*, Berkeley/Oakland, CA, (pp. 183-198).

Benjamins, V. R., Casanovas, P., Breuker, J., & Aldo, G. (Eds.). (2005). *Law and the Semantic Web: Legal ontologies, methodologies, legal information retrieval, and applications. LNAI 3369*. Springer.

Bermann, S., & Swire, P. (2010). *Information privacy: Official reference for the certified information privacy professional (CIPP)*. IAPP Publications.

Bourcier, D. (Ed.). (2003). Legal knowledge and information systems. *Proceedings of the 16th JURIX Conference 2003*. IOS Press.

Breuker, J., Casanovas, P., Klein, M. C. A., & Francesconi, E. (Eds.). (2009). *Law, ontologies, and the Semantic Web: Channelling the legal information flood. Frontiers in Artificial Intelligence and Applications*. Amsterdam, The Netherlands: IOS Press.

Cannon, J. C. (2005). *Privacy: What developers and IT professionals should know*. Addison-Wesley.

Casanovas, P., Sartor, G., Casellas, N., & Rubino, R. (Eds.). (2008). *Computable models of the law: Languages, dialogues, games, ontologies. LNAI 4884*. Springer.

Cloud Security Alliance. (2009, April). *Security guidance for critical areas of focus in cloud computing*. Retrieved November 24, 2010, from http://www.cloudsecurityalliance.org/csaguide.pdf

Davies, J., Grobelnik, M., & Mladenić, D. (Eds.). (2009). *Semantic knowledge management: Integrating ontology management, knowledge discovery, and human language technologies*. Springer.

ENISA. (2009). *Cloud computing: Benefits, risks and recommendations for information security* (D. Catteddu & G. Hogben, Eds.). Retrieved November 24, 2010, from http://www.enisa.europa.eu/act/rm/files/ deliverables/cloud-computing-risk-assessment

Kumaraswarmy, S., Latif, S., & Mather, T. (2009). *Cloud security and privacy: An enterprise perspective on risks and compliance*. O'Reilly.

Lam, P. E., Mitchell, J. C., & Sundaram, S. (2009). A formalisation of HIPAA for a medical messaging system. In *Proceedings 6th International Conference on Trust, Privacy & Security in Digital Business*, Linz.

Maxwell, J. C., & Anton, A. (2010). *A refined production rule model for aiding in regulatory compliance*. North Carolina State University CSC Technical Report, #TR-2010-3.

Microsoft. (2008). *Privacy guidelines for developing software products and services*. Retrieved November 24, 2010 from http://www.microsoft.com/downloads/en/

Russel, S., & Norvig, P. (2003). *Artificial intelligence – A modern approach* (2nd ed.). Englewood Cliffs, NJ: Prentice Hall.

Schweighofer, E. (1999). *Legal knowledge representation: Automatic text analysis in public international and European law*. The Hague, The Netherlands: Kluwer.

Stufflebeam, W. H., Anton, A., He, Q., & Jain, N. (2004). Specifying privacy policies with P3P and EPAL: Lessons learned. In *Proceedings 2004 Workshop on Privacy in the Electronic Society (WPES'04)*, ACM.

KEY TERMS AND DEFINITIONS

Accountability: Accountability is one of the Fair Information Practices. A data controller should make himself accountable for his collection and use of personal information. The recent Galway Project Plenary session Introduction" April 28th, 2009 (page 5) defines more broadly: "Accountability is the obligation to act as a responsible steward of the personal information of others, to take responsibility for the protection and appropriate use of that information beyond mere legal requirements, and to be accountable for any misuse of that information."

Decision Support System (DSS): A DSS is an interactive computer-based system that supports decision makers in their decision making processes. Examples where DSSs are used are medical diagnosis and sales forecast.

Governance: Corporate data governance is the management of the availability, usability, integrity and security of the data used, stored, or processed within an organization.

Personal Information: Information that can be used to positively identify an individual such as name, address, phone number, e-mail address, etc. Personal information is also referred to as personal data or personally identifiable information. The precise definition of personal information can vary among jurisdictions.

Privacy Management: For a corporation, privacy management includes all the activities,

processes and technologies for the application of laws, policies, standards and processes to the collection and use of personal information.

Privacy Policy: An organization's standard pertaining to the user information it collects and what is done with the information after it is collected.

Privacy: The fundamental right of an individual to decide about the processing of his/her personal data as well as to protect his/her intimate sphere.

Risk: Combination of the probability of an event and its consequence (i.e. threats plus vulnerabilities).

Sensitive Personal Data: Sensitive personal data includes information relating to racial or ethnic origin, political opinions, religious beliefs, trade union membership, health, sex life and criminal convictions. Under the EU directive 95/46 the processing of such data is subject to much stricter conditions.

Chapter 9
Information Security Management Based on Linguistic Sharing Techniques

Marek R. Ogiela
AGH University of Science and Technology, Poland

Urszula Ogiela
AGH University of Science and Technology, Poland

ABSTRACT

Secure information splitting is used in many tasks of the intelligent sharing of secrets and key data in business organisations. The significance of information splitting depends on its nature, while the significance of information sharing may depend on its importance and the meaning it has for the organisation or institution concerned. This chapter presents models for multi-level information splitting and information management with the use of the linguistic approach and formal grammars. Such methods constitute a secure enhancement of traditional secret splitting algorithms and introduce an additional stage at which information is coded using the appropriately defined regular or context-free grammar. The many possible applications of such methods include their use for the intelligent management of important or confidential information in government institutions or businesses. Algorithms of multi-level information splitting allow information that is not available to all employees of a given organisation or its environment to be securely split or shared.

INTRODUCTION

Matters of data acquisition, its flows, as well as the control and analysis of threats to the confidentiality and integrity of that data are among the fastest developing topics associated with applying modern

DOI: 10.4018/978-1-4666-0978-5.ch009

IT technologies to intelligently manage information within government institutions or commercial organizations. Scientific research in this direction is interdisciplinary in nature, and as the topic has become well known, it was possible to distinguish a new direction of research called Information Security. This field of scientific research on the above problems was seen as the one in which to include a new subject: the ability to intelligently divide important strategic data and the techniques of its management in various data flow structures. The subject of information classification and protection originates from cryptography, mainly dealing with algorithms for ensuring data confidentiality and information division techniques, as well methods of reconstructing it.

This is why intelligent information sharing and reconstruction will form the central subject of this publication. In particular, we will present new solutions aimed at developing so-called intelligent threshold schemes for information sharing. The introduction of new types of data sharing protocols implemented using so-called linguistic threshold schemes will also represent a significant novelty.

This publication will also attempt to demonstrate how such schemes can be used to develop new models of shared information management, e.g. in various organizational structures. Special emphasis will also be put on multi-level dividing algorithms. What characterizes such a division is the possibility of reconstructing information from sets containing various numbers of shares in the divided secret. This subject has not been fully explored in scientific research yet, while it seems very significant from the point of view of the future development of modern systems for information classification (as secret) or management.

The new solutions based on linguistic threshold schemes put forward by the authors will make it possible to depart from purely mathematical models of information dividing, or to use them only in dedicated, specialized tasks of cryptographic information sharing, and instead to use such techniques more widely for managing information designated for larger user groups. Such information can be utilized in practice in any commercial organizations or state institutions, and its meaning can be used only if it is accessed as authorized by appointed groups of persons participating in the secret division. This is why we will attempt to define a model structure of the flow and assignment of information shares to individual groups of interested persons (regardless of their number). The proposed model could then be rolled out in practice in any commercial organization or institution based on the information system it has.

INFORMATION MANAGEMENT METHODS

Today, information management processes are found in all types of organizations, which carry out various operating processes and management functions. This is because data acquisition and collection processes depend on, and are strongly correlated with, the constant development of information technology, serving inter alia to collect, analyze and transmit the processed information.

Information is now managed at all levels of the organization, and has the form of a set of rules, techniques, systems and devices which define the information/communication structure of the enterprise. Key information management tasks within an enterprise include:

- Planning, designing and implementing the institution's information strategy;
- Controlling information flows through the communication network;
- Planning capital expenses for developing information systems;
- Ensuring the effective operation of information systems;
- Information quality management;
- Creating conditions to keep the collected information secure (defining rights to access information);
- Ensuring effective forms of training and development for the IT staff and system users;
- Creating conditions for the institution or enterprise to have effective links to the information market;
- Integrating information systems used at various levels.

Areas of information management in a given institution depend on the internality and externality of the streams of information collected by this institution. The internality of information streams applies mainly to processing, transmitting and analyzing information inside the organization, whereas the term 'externality' is used if information originating inside the organization is exchanged with its environment, or, conversely, if information originating from the environment is exchanged for information originating within the organization. If this is the process of information management, the type of information related to its character should be defined. In general, for the purposes of information management within a commercial organization, two types of information are distinguished:

- Information of operations - informing;
- Information for cooperating – communicating.

In practice, these processes must inseparably harmonize and complement each another and also constitute processes of overall information management.

TYPES OF INFORMATION SPLITTING AND SHARING TECHNIQUES

Algorithms of intelligent secret splitting or sharing are a relatively new field of informatics, but one increasingly important in today's world (Menezes, 2001). They relate to splitting important information in a way that allows a certain group of n authorized persons (participants of the secret splitting protocol) cooperating to decipher the secret, to reconstruct the original message. At the same time, no group of participants less numerous than n should be able to decipher (reconstruct) this message.

Information splitting and sharing algorithms make it possible to split information into parts called shares or shadows, which are then distributed between protocol participants so that by combining the shares of certain subsets of users it becomes possible to reconstruct the original secret.

There are two groups of information division algorithms:

1. Secret splitting;
2. Secret sharing.

In the former, the message is split between protocol participants, and in order to reconstruct it, all users must combine their shares. In contrast, sharing techniques offer a more universal method of dividing secrets, in which the message is also divided among protocol participants, but to reconstruct it, a certain number of shares specified when the scheme is created is sufficient. Both methods are used in real-life tasks of secure information management. One example of such an application can be an electronic signature which allows a certain group of authorized persons to sign an electronic document after they combine their shares.

The first of the techniques mentioned, i.e. message splitting, consists in dividing the message into parts which are meaningless in isolation, but if they are put together into one whole, they yield the original message (Ogiela, 2009). This way, information can be split between any n people. All of them together can reconstruct the secret after combining the shares of information which they received. On the other hand, none of the split out shares allows the original message to be reconstructed without being combined with the remaining shares.

The other type of techniques, i.e. information sharing methods, are a more complex way of dividing information. Secret sharing algorithms are frequently referred to as threshold schemes.

Using such a scheme, any information can be divided into n unbound parts called shadows in such a way that any m ($m < n$) of them can be used to reconstruct the message.

This is referred to as an (m, n)-threshold scheme. The threshold scheme of message sharing was developed independently by A. Shamir (Shamir, 1979) and G. Blakley (Blakley, 1979), and was also intensely studied by G. Simmons (Simmons, 1992).

One of the purposes of this publication is to define new types of secret division schemes, namely linguistic threshold schemes, whose security will also be based on the use of linguistic formalisms to create new representations of shared data.

HIERARCHICAL INFORMATION DIVISION AND MANAGEMENT

Information is divided within institutions or organizations regardless of its type or the purpose for which the organization collects it. The significance of information splitting may depend on the method of its splitting, the purpose of splitting it and the type of information. The significance of information sharing, on the other hand, may depend on its importance and the meaning it contains for the specific organization. If information is important and of great materiality for the organization or for e.g. external organizations, then it makes sense to attempt sharing this information to protect it and secure it from disclosure to unauthorized persons (or organizations). When defining the type of information to undergo the splitting or sharing process, we should consider its 'character' determined by its confidentiality, significance and importance, because only important information justifies applying the method of its division and the effort to do so.

This chapter presents and characterizes models of multilevel information division and information management suggested for the purposes of commercial organizations. The significance of these models stems from the right choice of techniques used for the multilevel splitting and sharing of information that are appropriate for a specific commercial organization. The appropriate

methods for secret sharing to be chosen for the specific type of an organizational structure will be identified depending on this structure.

Multi-level information division algorithms are named after the type of division applied. This division can be hierarchical or by layers. The principal difference between the presented types of divisions concerns the method of introducing the division itself. When a division is made within homogenous, uniform groups of layers, then it is a layer division, whereas if the division is made regardless of the homogeneity of the group or layer but by reference to several groups ordered hierarchically, it is a hierarchical division.

A layer division is thus a division made relative to a given layer, while a hierarchical division accounts for the hierarchy (dependency) of the structure or more structures relative to one another.

Information can be divided both within the entire structure in which some hierarchical dependency is identified, within a given group, or within any homogenous layer. This is why, depending on the type of information divided, it makes sense to identify correctly selected information dividing algorithms.

The division of information between the members of a given group in which every one has the same privileges is a layer division. It is worth noting that the layer division may refer to the following types of divisions:

- Of various secrets divided in the same way within various layers - this situation means that the secret is divided in the same way (in the sense of the method), regardless of the layer which this secret concerns. What changes is the information constituting the secret being divided in the specific layer.
- The same secret divided in different ways depending on the layer – in this case, the same information is divided in different ways depending on the layer and the number of protocol participants in individual layers.

A hierarchical division is characterized by the ability to make any division of secret information in the way determined by the access rights at individual levels of a hierarchical structure. In the most general case, this can be the division of various secrets within various layers.

THE IDEA BEHIND LINGUISTIC THRESHOLD SCHEMES

This chapter presents new solutions in the field of secret data sharing based on the concept of mathematical linguistics. The essence of the presented approach is the use of linguistic formalisms originating from the formal language theory.

The proposed algorithm facilitates extending the functionality of traditional information splitting and sharing schemes by generating an additional information share in a linguistic form. This share will be necessary to reconstruct the whole secret. The general methodology of using formal languages to enhance traditional threshold schemes is as follows:

1. Select the basic secret sharing scheme from among known information division techniques;
2. Convert the shared data (text or image) into a bit representation;
3. Define a formal grammar coding bit blocks of various lengths;
4. Linguistically convert the bit sequence into a new representation in the form of a series of grammar production numbers;
5. Divide the new secret representation using the previously selected threshold scheme;
6. Distribute shadows to particular participants of the protocol.

These stages represent the basic steps necessary to generate the components of shared information which can be communicated to all who participate in the entire procedure of allocating the secret shares of the shared data.

However, it is worth noting that depending on the way of generating and assigning the secret shares and the information on the used grammar, two more options of subsequent procedure can be distinguished. These options are as follows:

1. If the rules of the grammar are known only to the instance which generates and distributes the shadows, then we have defined an arbitration protocol, in which a trusted arbiter or instance must also be involved to reconstruct the secret;
2. However, if the rules of the defined grammar are disclosed, then in practice we are dealing with the implementation of a pure threshold scheme in which the set of grammar generation rules constitutes another shadow.

Lower down, we will present a generalized grammar for converting a bit representation of the input secret into n-bit blocks and further transforming them into a new representation having the form of a series of numbers of productions of the defined grammar. Such a grammar can be defined as follows:

$G_{n-bit} = (N, T, P, STS)$

where:

N = {SECRET, BB, 1B, 2B, 3B, 4B, 5B, 6B, ..., NB} – set of non-terminal symbols,

T = {1b, 2b, 3b, 4b, 5b, 6b, ..., nb, λ} – set of terminal symbols, which defines n-bit blocks,

{λ} –an empty symbol,

STS = SECRET – grammar start symbol,

P – set of grammar rules defined in following manner:

1. SECRET → BB BB

2. $BB \rightarrow 1B \mid 2B \mid 3B \mid 4B \mid 5B \mid 6B, ... \mid NB$
   {BIT BLOCKS WITH VARIOUS LENGHT}
3. $BB \rightarrow \lambda$
4. $1B \rightarrow 1b \{0, 1\}$
5. $2B \rightarrow 2b \{00, 01, 10, 11\}$
6. $3B \rightarrow 3b \{000, 001, 010, 011, 100, 101, 110, 111\}$
7. $4B \rightarrow ...$
8. $5B \rightarrow 5b$
9. $6B \rightarrow ...$
10. ....
11. $NB \rightarrow nb$
12. $b \rightarrow \{0, 1\}$

A generalized grammar introduced in this way can make it quicker and briefer to re-code the input representation of the secret, which will then be divided among protocol participants. A benefit of grouping bits into larger blocks is that during the following steps of the secret sharing protocol we get shorter representations for the data that is divided and then reconstructed. This is particularly visible when executing procedures that use excessive bit representations, i.e. when single-bit or several-bit values are saved and interpreted using codes in 8 or 16-bit representations.

The methods of multi-level information splitting or sharing presented in this chapter, which use bit blocks of various lengths (one-, two- or n-bit), show how information division algorithms can be significantly enhanced by adding elements of linguistic and grammatical data analysis. This is a novel solution. The length of bit blocks has a major impact on the speed and the conciseness of the stage at which the input information representation is coded, at which stage information to be coded as a secret is prepared.

USING THRESHOLD SCHEMES IN HIERARCHICAL STRUCTURES

The significance of information splitting and sharing in a given organization or institution seems indisputable, as it results from the very nature of the correct use of information. Information held by an organization determines its strength and acts as its driving force. On the contrary, if significant information is not identified in a given organization, this forms its weakness.

Information splitting and sharing processes of institutions or organizations should account for the materiality of information, understood as its importance and significance, its degree of accessibility and thus confidentiality, the type of organization in which the process of information classification is performed, the structure of the organization within which the data will be divided, as well as the method of data division, i.e. hierarchical or layered.

Methods of information sharing in commercial organizations may differ, and their type depends mainly on the method of information division, i.e. on the selection of the algorithm for splitting and sharing the data. For every type of commercial organizations, there is one best information division algorithm, however we can also identify methods of data splitting and sharing which are universal. Such models will be presented lower down for modern structures of information management, i.e. process structures and virtual structures (virtual teams).

Information Division in Process Structures

A process structure operates mainly based on a layered division, although to some extent, a hierarchical division can also be introduced in this kind of structure. A hierarchical division refers to the relationship between task forces and their supervisors, as shown in Figure 1.

The formal grammatical notation of information division in process structures is presented by grammar G_{SECpr} with the form of:

$$Gsec_{pr} = (VN_{pr}, VT_{pr}, SP, STS)$$

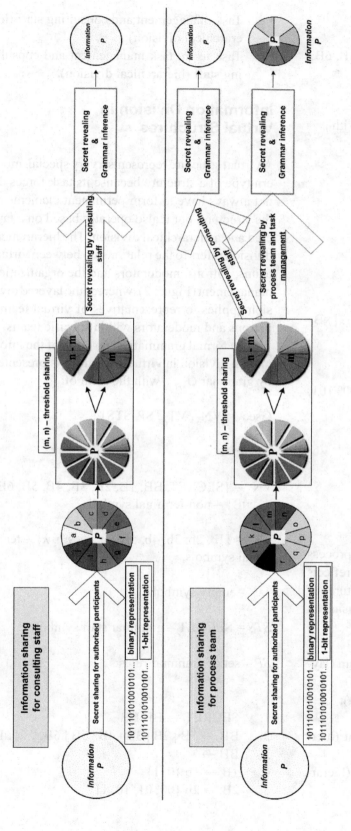

Figure 1. Hierarchical information division in process structures

where:

VN_{pr} = {SECRET, BB, 1B, 2B, 3B, 4B, 5B, 6B, ..., NB} – set of non-terminal symbols,

VT_{pr} = {1b, 2b, 3b, 4b, 5b, 6b, ..., nb, λ} – terminal symbol set defining bit blocks with various length

{λ} – an empty symbol,

STS = SECRET – grammar start symbol,

SP – set of grammar rules:

1. SECRET → BB BB
2. BB → 1B | 2B | 3B | 4B | 5B | 6B, ... | NB
3. BB → λ
4. 1B → 1b {0, 1}
5. 2B → 2b {00, 01, 10, 11}
6. 3B → 3b {000, 001, 010, 011, 100, 101, 110, 111}
7. 4B → ...
8. 5B → 5b
9. 6B → ...
10. ....
11. NB → nb
12. b → {0, 1}

The presented information division in process structures is based on an approach which reflects the subordination relations found in structures of that type. So information can be divided using an (m, n)-threshold division between:

- Members within a given process team (layered division);
- Task management (layered division);
- Consulting staff (layered division);
- Process team and task management (hierarchical division);
- Process team and consulting staff (hierarchical division);

- Task management and consulting staff (hierarchical division);
- Task team, task management and consulting staff (hierarchical division).

Information Division in Virtual Structures

A virtual structure represents a very special, modern type of a structure because its task forces do not always have to form permanent elements of the structure, but it also operates based on a layered and a hierarchical division. The hierarchical division refers to the relationship between virtual teams, patrons, moderators and the organization management (Figure 2), whereas the layered division applies to representatives of virtual teams, patrons and moderators within specific teams.

The formal grammatical notation of the information division in virtual structures is presented by grammar G_{SECpr} with the form of:

Gsec$_{pr}$=(VN$_{pr}$, VT$_{pr}$, SP, STS)

where:

VN_{w} = {SECRET, BB, 1B, 2B, 3B, 4B, 5B, 6B, ..., NB} – non-terminal symbols,

VT_{w} = {1b, 2b, 3b, 4b, 5b, 6b, ..., nb, λ} – terminal symbols,

{λ} – empty symbol,

STS = SECRET – grammar start symbol,

SP – set of grammar rules:

1. SECRET → BB BB
2. BB → 1B | 2B | 3B | 4B | 5B | 6B, ... | NB
3. BB → λ
4. 1B → 1b {0, 1}
5. 2B → 2b {00, 01, 10, 11}

Figure 2. Hierarchical information division in virtual structures

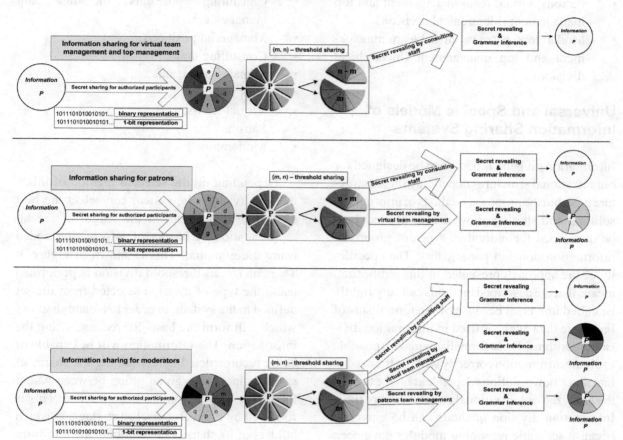

6. 3B → 3b {000, 001, 010, 011, 100, 101, 110, 111}
7. 4B → ...
8. 5B → 5b
9. 6B → ...
10. ....
11. NB → nb
12. b → {0, 1}

The presented information division in virtual structures is based on an approach which reflects the subordination relations found in structures of this type. So information can be divided using an (m, n)-threshold division between:

• Moderators (layered division);
• Patrons (layered division);

• Virtual team management (layered division);
• Moderators and patrons (hierarchical division);
• Moderators and the virtual team management (hierarchical division);
• Moderators and top management (hierarchical division);
• Patrons and the virtual team management (hierarchical division);
• Patrons and top management (hierarchical division);
• Virtual team management and top management (hierarchical division);
• Moderators, patrons and virtual team management (hierarchical division);
• Moderators, virtual team management and top management (hierarchical division);

- Patrons, virtual team management and top management (hierarchical division);
- Moderators, patrons, virtual team management and top management (hierarchical division).

Universal and Specific Models of Information Sharing Systems

Information division models can be designed for organizational structures depending on the structure type, but the proposed methods of information splitting and sharing allow universal models to be developed for individual types of groups of information division participants. The specificity of the approach presented in this publication means that the described methods can very rightly be called universal because of the formalisms of linguistic data analysis used in information division algorithms. These formalisms make it possible to divide information correctly without the need to introduce new solutions dependent on the type of the analyzed organizational structure every time. Information division methods can be universal because semantic reasoning modules have been used to design the algorithms (Figure 3).

The essence of the universality of the presented method is that depending on the type of institution or organization within which the information is divided, the types of information division are selected. These may include divisions between:

- Executive positions;

- Consulting positions including top management;
- Managerial positions;
- Consulting units;
- Management teams;
- Task forces;
- Virtual teams;
- Patrons;
- Moderators.

Depending on the selected method of information division, the system can select the best algorithm, depending on the length of the bit representation of blocks of information coded using the grammar. This is shown in Figure 3. Then, an (m, n)-threshold division is performed using the type of division selected from the set defined in the system, in order to isolate shadows which will form the basis for reconstructing the information. The information will be capable of being reconstructed by combining the shares of secret holders in a given group between whom the secret/information has been divided. This is followed by the secret disclosure stage, at which holders of its shares may combine them to form the basis on which, after the grammatical reasoning stage, the information constituting the secret can be combined and declassified.

The information division method discussed is significantly universal as the correct information division, its combination, reconstruction and disclosure are determined by the appropriately defined data splitting and sharing algorithms as well as grammatical reasoning algorithms based on

Figure 3. Universal information division in organizational structures

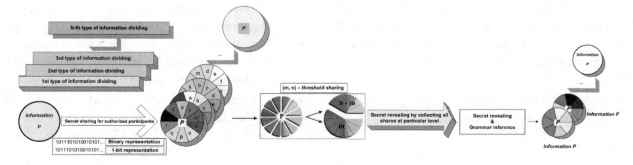

mathematical linguistics methods. The selection of the right secret division algorithms also represents a specific solution of the problem of classifying information within commercial organizations, as the literature of the subject currently does not mention this type of applications of mathematical linguistic formalisms to information division/secret classification.

PROPERTIES OF LINGUISTIC THRESHOLD SCHEMES

The algorithmic solutions proposed in this publication for splitting and sharing data have the following properties:

- Cryptographic threshold algorithms for information sharing are suitable for dividing important strategic data and assigning its shares to members of the authorized group;
- The algorithms introduced can handle any digital data (text or image) which needs to be intelligently divided among authorized persons and then possible to secretly reconstruct;
- There are numerous opportunities for using classical cryptographic information division techniques (i.e. (m, n)-threshold schemes) in these protocols;
- Introducing additional safeguards against the unauthorized reconstruction of the information and the possibility of implementing two independent versions of the protocols for assigning the created shadows to individual protocol participants: the option with a trusted arbiter as an intermediary in assigning and reconstructing the information and the option without an arbiter (an additional trusted party), but only with assigning the introduced grammar as an additional part of the secret;
- The level of security achieved does not depend on the length of blocks converted using the rules of the introduced grammar;

- The computational complexity of the proposed schemes is polynomial.

The above characteristics of the proposed linguistic algorithms of information division form their advantages and show how universal these proposed methods for splitting and sharing secret or strategic information are.

CONCLUSION

Methods of dividing information and techniques of its linguistic sharing are now emerging as new solutions that can contribute to processes of classifying information/data not accessible to a broader group. Thanks to them, confidential or secret information of any sort can be effectively encrypted, divided between the confidants of the secret, and then these confidants or a selected group of them can reconstruct it using the appropriate algorithms and grammatical rules specified during the definition of formal grammars.

The effectiveness of such solutions is measured by the degree of security of the applied algorithms, which are classified as secure and difficult to crack.

These kinds of solutions can therefore be used not just to split and share data in commercial organizations, but can be employed no less successfully by military units, medical institutions, state administration of any level, research institutes, government organizations etc., that is any organization which needs to apply effective methods of classifying information consisting in not just encrypting it, but primarily in its correct division between authorized groups or teams of people who may hold and reconstruct such important data. The essence of the approach presented is that it is not always right and justified to release strategically important information to one entity. This is because that entity may be unreliable and may become a weak link if an attempt is made to crack the secret.

It should be remembered that information management systems currently use various techniques and methods to acquire data, order it, search for it semantically, classify it as secret, or compile semantic tables etc. They are designed to simplify the access to and improve the effectiveness of finding information with specific meaning. Cryptographic algorithms for threshold information sharing are among such techniques. They can be used to divide important, strategic data and to assign its shares to people from an authorized group. Such authorized, selective access to information is used when it is necessary to safely manage strategic information. In the context of the globalization of the world economy, commercial organizations use important information on their market situation, achievements, development plans, strategic operations, new implementations and patents, usually classifying it and thus making selected information inaccessible to ordinary people. Within the structure of the specific organization or company, there are individuals at the appropriate management levels who have access rights to the data addressed to them. Such rights are very often exercised in hierarchic or layered structures, usually connected with the office held. In practice, this means that higher-placed individuals have access to more confidential data, and people at lower levels to less information. Consequently, the flow of information within such structures may require implementing hierarchical threshold schemes for secret division, which schemes assign the appropriate levels of rights to individuals who want to access secret data at particular levels. It is also possible to make layered divisions within a given staff group, which, when it has certain information, can assign its selected element/parts to individual employees, but without any selected employee from this group being able to view the complete information. Obviously, when talking of information management, we refer to data stored on digital media or in computer databases. For such data, there is a need to intelligently divide it between the authorized individuals and then to reconstruct it in secret.

This publication has presented the methodology of using threshold techniques of information sharing for multilevel management of data in digital form. A general model was shown for sharing important information using known mathematical formalisms including protocols of its reconstruction, and we also defined an original method of the linguistic sharing of information, which can play useful functions in various models of managing this information.

REFERENCES

Blakley, G. R. (1979). Safeguarding cryptographic keys. *Proceedings of the National Computer Conference,* (pp. 313–317).

Blakley, G. R. (1980). One-time pads are key safeguarding schemes, not cryptosystems: Fast key safeguarding schemes (threshold schemes) exist. In *Proceedings of the 1980 Symposium on Security and Privacy*, (pp. 108-113). IEEE Press.

Chomsky, N. (1957). *Syntactic structures*. London, UK: Mouton.

ElGamal, T. (1985). A public key cryptosystem and a signature scheme based on discrete logarithms. *IEEE Transactions on Information Theory*, 469–472. doi:10.1109/TIT.1985.1057074

Ingemarsson, I., & Simmons, G. J. (1991). *A protocol to set up shared secret schemes without the assistance of a mutually trusted party. Advances in Cryptology – EUROCRYPT'90 Proceedings* (pp. 266–282). Springer-Verlag.

Mackenzie, O. J. (Ed.). (2006). *Information science and knowledge management*. Berlin, Germany: Springer-Verlag.

Menezes, A., van Oorschot, P., & Vanstone, S. (2001). *Handbook of applied cryptography*. Waterloo, Canada: CRC Press.

Ogiela, M. R., & Ogiela, U. (2009). Linguistic cryptographic threshold schemes. *International Journal of Future Generation Communication and Networking, 2*(1), 33–40.

Ogiela, M. R., & Ogiela, U. (2009). Security of linguistic threshold schemes in multimedia systems. In Damiani, E., Jeong, J., Howlett, R. J., & Jain, L. C. (Eds.), *New directions in intelligent interactive multimedia systems and services – 2: Studies in computational intelligence* (pp. 13–20). Berlin, Germany: Springer – Verlag. doi:10.1007/978-3-642-02937-0_2

Ogiela, M. R., & Ogiela, U. (2009). Secure information splitting using grammar schemes. In Nguyen, N. T., Katarzyniak, R., & Janiak, A. (Eds.), *New challenges in computational collective intelligence: Studies in computational intelligence* (pp. 327–336). Berlin, Germany: Springer-Verlag. doi:10.1007/978-3-642-03958-4_28

Ogiela, M. R., & Ogiela, U. (2009). Shadow generation protocol in linguistic threshold schemes. In Ślęzak, D., Kim, T.-H., Fang, W.-C., & Arnett, K. P. (Eds.), *Security technology: Communication in computer and information science* (pp. 35–42). Berlin, Germany: Springer-Verlag. doi:10.1007/978-3-642-10847-1_5

Seberry, J., & Pieprzyk, J. (1989). *Cryptography: An introduction to computer security*. Englewood Cliffs, NJ: Prentice-Hall.

Shamir, A. (1979). How to share a secret. *Communications of the ACM, 22*(11), 612–613. doi:10.1145/359168.359176

Simmons, G. J. (1992). An introduction to shared secret and/or shared control schemes and their application. In *Contemporary cryptology: The science of information integrity*, (pp. 441–497).

Simmons, G. J. (1993). The subliminal channels of the US digital signature algorithm (DSA). *Proceedings of the Third Symposium on: State and Progress of Research in Cryptography*, Rome (pp. 35–54).

Tang, S. (2004). Simple secret sharing and threshold RSA signature schemes. *Journal of Information and Computational Science, 1*, 259–262.

Zheng, Y., Hardjono, T., & Seberry, J. (1994). Reusing shares in secret sharing schemes. *The Computer Journal, 37*, 199–205. doi:10.1093/comjnl/37.3.199

KEY TERMS AND DEFINITIONS

Cryptographic Threshold Schemes: Cryptographic techniques used for secret sharing, and allowing to reveal secret having a special subgroups of the total number of shares.

Flow of Information in Organization: Some decencies between information and the way of its distribution in particular organization.

Hierarchical Structures: An organizational structure where every entity in particular institution or organization, except one, is subordinate to a single other entity.

Mathematical Linguistic: A discipline which objective is the development ideas and basis of a formal apparatus for the description of the structure of natural languages. Now also formalism used in syntactic pattern recognition, and compiler construction.

Secret Splitting and Sharing: Algorithms allowing dividing secret information for particular number of parts (shares).

Secure Communication Protocols: Protocols allowing for secure voice or data transmission, usually based on cryptographic algorithms.

Secure Information Management: Solutions which can help find, classify and control how information is used based on content and identity, across physical, virtual and cloud environments. These solutions also enable to protect critical information, and guarantee integrity.

Chapter 10
SQL Injection Attacks Countermeasures

Kasra Amirtahmasebi
Chalmers University of Technology, Sweden

Seyed Reza Jalalinia
Chalmers University of Technology, Sweden

ABSTRACT

Due to the huge growth in the need for using Web applications worldwide, there have been huge efforts from programmers to develop and implement new Web applications to be used by companies. Since a number of these applications lack proper security considerations, malicious users will be able to gain unauthorized access to confidential information of organizations. A concept called SQL Injection Attack (SQLIA) is a prevalent method used by attackers to extract the confidential information from organizations' databases. They work by injecting malicious SQL codes through the web application, and they cause unexpected behavior from the database. There are a number of SQL Injection detection/prevention techniques that must be used in order to prevent unauthorized access to databases.

INTRODUCTION

Web applications basically work by getting some input/information from outside users. Using string operations, this information is later used and serialized into a textual representation and ultimately, a database-specific command is created and sent to the database for execution. The input from outside users is the basis of SQL injection attacks and can be malicious; therefore they must be monitored and controlled thoroughly. The 2002 Computer Security Institute and FBI revealed that on a yearly basis, over half of all database experience at least one security breach and an average episode results in close to $4 million in losses (C.S. Institute. Computer crime and security survey. http://www.gocsi.com/press/20020407.jhtml, 2002). As a result, input-validation vulnerabilities which are incorrect assumptions of input data must be carefully considered and monitored in order to reduce the risk of injection attacks.

Pietraszek and Berghe (2005) classify input validation vulnerabilities into the following categories.

DOI: 10.4018/978-1-4666-0978-5.ch010

- Buffer overflow vulnerabilities are caused by incorrect assumptions on the input's maximum size. As a result, buffer's boundary will be overrun and an attacker will be able write to the adjacent memory space.
- Integer overflow vulnerabilities are a result of insufficient assumptions on the range of the input. In this case, the result of an arithmetic operation will be larger than the memory space provided for the aforementioned variable.
- Injection vulnerabilities result from invalid assumptions on the type of input provided by the users. A user can enter syntactic content in his/her input and cause the database to perform unauthorized operations.

We have presented six SQL injection prevention techniques in this chapter which will cover a wide range of SQL injection attacks. A combination of these prevention techniques may lead to a more secure and reliable database system.

BACKGROUND

Many web pages ask users to input some data and make a SQL queries to the database based on the information received from the user i.e. username and passwords. By sending crafted input a malicious user can change the SQL statement structure and execute arbitrary SQL commands on the vulnerable system. Consider the following username and password example, in order to login to the web site, the user inputs his username and password, by clicking on the submit button the following SQL query is generated:

```
SELECT * FROM user_table WHERE user_
id =    'john' and password = '1234'
```

Now consider what will happen if the user input the following password:

```
' or 1=1 -
```

The SQL query will become:

```
SELECT * FROM user_table WHERE user_
id = 'john' and password = '' or 1=1
--'
```

The "or 1=1" will result in returning all the records in the "user_table" and the "--" comments out the last ' appended by the system. Therefore, the query will return a non-empty result set without any error. SQL injection problem can be solved by checking all SQL statements before sending them to the database; however, with respect to dynamic generation of SQL queries by web applications, each statement might be different, so we are not able to predefine the allowable SQL statements (Sam, 2005).

A LEARNING-BASED APPROACH TO DETECT INJECTION ATTACKS

Intrusion Detection Systems (IDS) are a common way of protection against malicious behavior and unauthorized access in regular desktop IT systems. An ID plays an important part in detecting and preventing attacks in regular desktop IT systems. Extensive research has been conducted on developing efficient and effective Intrusion Detection Systems. They can become handy when there are no prevention techniques defined for special types of attacks. In this case, intrusion detection systems can alert administrators about the attack so that appropriate measures can be taken.

In typical desktop IT, Intrusion Detection System is categorized as network based or host based IDS. Host based IDS monitors the activities on end systems such as system threads and processes. Network based IDS, on the other hand, monitors and analyzes traffic on the whole network by e.g. packet inspection to find attacks and malicious behavior (Hoppe, 2009).

Regardless of type, IDS must compare its existing data with some reference data in order to be able to perform intrusion detection. Hoppe, Kiltz and Dittmann (2008) present two different approaches to intrusion detection are presented. In the first approach, Signature-based detection, a number of predefined actions, behaviors and combinations are stored in a signature/rule database and network traffic will be compared with the values in the database. If a match between intrusion database and captured network traffic is found, IDS will notify the administrator about the possible malicious behavior. The second approach, Anomaly-based intrusion detection, is based on anomaly from the normal behavior. Normal actions are predefined for the IDS and an action will be considered malicious if it is deviating from the normal behavior (Hoppe, 2009). Some commercial companies such as Snort have developed hybrid detection mechanism which is basically a combination of rule based and anomaly based detection mechanisms.

IDS database must be updated regularly in order to detect new attacks. In a typical computer network, the administrator must update the database by either downloading new patches or adding new entries manually otherwise the IDS will not be able to detect malicious behavior and may result in increased false positive or false negative rates.

The Learning-Based System

As mentioned earlier, intrusion detection systems can be anomaly-based or signature-based. In order for an intrusion detection system to be able to detect and raise warnings on the condition of injection attacks, anomaly-based Intrusion detection system will be more robust and will be able to react with less rate of false positives or false negatives. Since generated SQL statements (by the web application) have an ad hoc nature and are not centralized, by using signature-based intrusion detection systems, it will not always be possible to identify injection attacks. Furthermore, due to large and different usages of web applications through the Internet, customized services must be developed in order to fulfill different needs from web applications. As a result, there will be no modeled signatures for all customized services and companies usually won't go through the time and resource consuming process of developing new signatures for their intrusion detection systems.

This learning-based approach is an anomaly based intrusion detection system which utilizes multiple anomaly detection models in order to detect injection attacks on SQL databases (Valeur, Mutz, and Vigna, 2005). Since it is learning-based, a training phase must be developed in order to prepare the system to function correctly. The training phase is consisted of two main sub-phases. In the first sub-phase, attack-free data will be sent to the database. By doing so, the system will be able to build profiles associated with models' parameters and also, it will learn normal statements as well. A profile is a collection of models and feature selector will decide which profile is best suited for a given query. In the second sub-phase, an anomaly score will be calculated based on the processed features. For each model, the maximum anomaly score is stored and used to set an anomaly threshold (Valeur, Mutz, and Vigna, 2005).

Upon completion of learning phase, the system will be ready to work in the detection mode. In this mode, the system works by intercepting SQL queries which are generated by applications; intercepted queries will be sent to the IDS for analysis prior to execution. The intrusion detection system will parse SQL statements and will provide a sequence of tokens. Next, a feature selector will assign queries to their appropriate profiles. After the analysis in the profile, an anomaly score will be generated for the processed query. The generated anomaly score will be compared to a standard anomaly score of the selected profile. If the score exceeds the maximum anomaly score associated with the query, a warning will be raised and sent to the administrator. Otherwise, the query will be passed for execution (Valeur, Mutz, and Vigna, 2005).

Structure

This learning-based system is consisted of 3 main components.

- Event provider: This component is responsible for intercepting generated SQL queries and sending them to the next IDS component for analysis. It must be on the application server since the server has access to information about the processes and can log security-relevant information (Valeur, Mutz, and Vigna, 2005).

- Parser: This component is responsible for processing incoming SQL queries in order

to be able to analyze them and provide a high-level view of the query (Valeur, Mutz, and Vigna, 2005). The result will be a sequence of tokens with flags which indicate whether the token is user-provided or not.

- Feature selector: This component is in charge of transforming queries into a form which will be suitable to be processed by models. It selects which profile each query applies to as well (Valeur, Mutz, and Vigna, 2005). Feature selector is the most important component in the implementation of this intrusion detection system. Figure 1 below describes different phases of the IDS and the appropriate steps to be taken.

Figure 1. Learning-based IDS

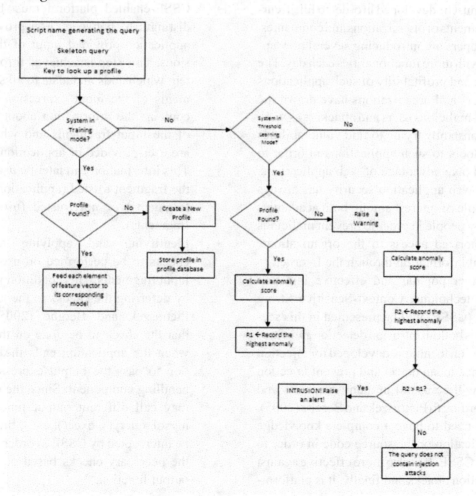

In order to for the system to find the appropriate profile, a skeleton key which is basically in charge of capturing the structure of SQL query must be generated. This is done by generating all occurrences of constants in the query with an empty place holder token (Valeur, Mutz, and Vigna, 2005). The skeleton query along with the script name which has generated the query will be a base to find the appropriate profile for analysis.

CONTEXT-SENSITIVE STRING EVALUATION (CSSE)

Since the need for Internet-based business and sales are increasing dramatically, proper web applications must be developed in order to fulfill current requirements of organizations and companies. Web developers are introducing several new applications with more functionalities each day. The importance and profitability of such applications to developers and organizations have drawn the attention of malicious users and attackers as well. They are constantly trying to find vulnerabilities and back doors to such applications in order to exploit and take advantage of web applications. Therefore, web application security has always been the topic of interest among both academics and industry people in order to prevent malicious and unauthorized access to the organizations' confidential information through the Internet.

As another popular and effective injection prevention technique, Context-Sensitive String Evaluation (CSSE) will be presented in this section. CSSE is both an intrusion detection and intrusion prevention technique developed for injection attacks. Since it can detect and prevent injection attacks, it will be useful in many scenarios and areas. According to Pietraszek and Berghe (2005), there is no need to have a complete knowledge of the application or the source code in order to implement CSSE. It is also more effective against many injection attacks and finally, it is platform-independent and can be implemented in different platforms (Pietraszek and Berghe, 2005).

CSSE Logic

CSSE assumes that all the user-provided input is the root cause for injection attacks and should not be trusted. As a result, CSSE works by separating user-provided input from application-provided input which is called channel separation.

Before the generated expression is sent to the database for execution, CSSE applies a series of checks to make sure that user-provided parts of the generated expression is not vulnerable against SQL injection attacks. According to Pietraszek and Berghe (2005) this is done in two major steps:

- CSSE-enabled platform must be able to distinguish between user-provided and application-provided input of the expressions. This step is achieved through a system which adds metadata to all string fragments of the input expression. Metadata contains the information about the origin of the input fragments and whether they are user-provided or application-provided. This information can later be used to make the fragment trusted (application-provided fragments) or not trusted (user-provided fragments).
- Identifying and applying appropriate checks to be performed on user-provided input fragments. This condition is achieved by deferring the checks to the last checks. Pietraszek and Berghe (2005) suggest that the check to be done on the moment when the application calls the API function to pass the output expression to the handling component. Since the expression may call different output functions (e.g. mysql_query(), exec(), etc.), the call must be intercepted by CSSE in order to perform the necessary checks based on the called output function.

By doing these steps, CSSE will learn the complete context. It will learn user-provided input from the metadata information, and will apply the appropriate checks by intercepting API calls. Therefore, CSSE can make an informed decision to check unsafe and malicious fragments. On the condition of detecting a malicious behavior, CSSE can whether prevent the expression to be executed (intrusion prevention) or can alert the administrators of the ongoing malicious behavior (intrusion detection).

CSSE IMPLEMENTATION

In order to be implemented properly and also in order to be able to test the functionalities of CSSE, Pietraszek and Berghe (2005) have chosen PHP as their implementation platform. The reason is because PHP applications are prone to injection attacks and also there exists several applications to test CSSE implementation due to PHP's open source nature (Pietraszek and Berghe, 2005).

Metadata Representation

As mentioned earlier, in CSSE, the origination of a fragment is identified by the use of metadata. The metadata will be attached to fragments and will travel with them through the application. Therefore, Pietraszek and Berghe (2005) have used a central metadata repository in their implementation. This repository is implemented as a hash table which is indexed by Zval pointer.

In this implementation, only user-provided fragments will receive a metadata which means that application-provided fragments of the expression will not carry a metadata alongside with them. This will culminate in both increased run-time performance and memory efficiency.

Metadata Assignment

In web applications, HTTP input will be the potential for injection attacks since user-provided data will be sent with HTTP commands. In order for CSSE to assign the appropriate metadata to the input from the users, the instrumented platform API will ensure that received variables are provided with the right metadata. During the importing of user input into the PHP variable space, proper metadata will be associated with the variables. Furthermore, in order to prevent second-order attacks, all the strings read from the database will be marked as untrusted as well (Pietraszek and Berghe, 2005).

Metadata-Preserving String Operations

Since the final output expression contains user-input and application constants merged together by a set of string operations, CSSE should be able to "preserve" the metadata assigned to user-input so that metadata will "survive" the string operations. Therefore, some string functions must be metadata-aware and must update their operands' metadata during string operations. According to Pietraszek and Berghe (2005), 92 out of 3468 functions of PHP need to be updated and instrumented in order to update their operands' metadata.

Context-Sensitive String Evaluation

This step is the final step in CSSE and is in charge of determining and performing appropriate checks to make sure strict channel separation is performed.

In the implementation by Pietraszek and Berghe (2005), MySQL is the basis for analysis. Since some of the functions are instrumented to recognize and update metadata, they will perform necessary checks on the executed expressions. Upon function call, the function will be intercepted by CSSE to be checked for correct association of metadata with SQL expression.

Figure 2. Variable normalization

SELECT * FROM assets WHERE price > 5000 and category = 'computer'

Normalized SQL	SELECT * FROM assets WHERE price > 0 and category = 'a'		
Variable 1	Position 37	Integer type	Original value: 5000
Variable 2	Position 65	String type	Original value: "computer"

It is also worth mentioning that the first three steps in the implementation is intended for metadata tracking system while the last step is intended for determining and performing appropriate checks on generated expressions.

VARIABLE NORMALIZATION

Here we introduce a method that uses a virtual database connectivity drive along with a special method named "variable normalization" using these methods we can determine the basic structure of a SQL statement therefore we will be able to decide if a SQL statement is legal or not. This method does not require changing the source code of database applications and can also be used for auto-learning the allowable list of SQL statements. There is also a very minimal overhead in the system due to the fact that determining whether a SQL statement is allowable or not is done by checking the existence of normalized statement in the ready-sorted allowable list.

Goal

The goal of variable normalization is try to take away the variables and get the basic structure of the SQL query, so that although the supplied variables differ every time, the basic structure remains the same. In the case of a SQL injection, the injected code will change the structure of the SQL statement, and hence we will be able to detect it.

In order to normalize variables in a SQL statement, this method converts all single quoted strings to a single character such as "a" for instance, and all positive or negative integer, or floating point numbers to single digit "0". Then the normalized SQL statement is stored in a data structure, called a "rule", along with its corresponding normalized variable information, including their types, positions and the original values. The only parameters which will be modified by the normalization process are variables, and everything else including SQL comments, carriage returns, white spaces, or character cases will remain unmodified (Sam, 2005) as shown in Figure 2.

Defining Allowable List

We will need to define an allowable list in order to verify if a normalized SQL statement is allowed. This list is a set of rules which were discussed before, but somehow different, because here the variable requirements are stored instead of variable values. This list can be defined manually by defining the normalized SQL statement along with the requirements of its variables. By running the system in "learning" mode, in which the system will not verify if a SQL statement is allowed, but recording all the SQL statements that go through it. We can have it "learn" the allowable list by itself because defining it manually is very tedious and error probing.

In this mode the variable value is stored as the expected value. This assumption is true until

Figure 3. Two stages of "learning" an SQL statement

SELECT * FROM jobs WHERE completed = 0 and start_day > '1/1/2009'

SELECT * FROM jobs WHERE completed = 0 and start_day > 'a'			
Variable 1	Position 39	Integer type	Expected value: 0
Variable 2	Position 58	String type	Expected value: "1/1/2009"

A similar SQL statement:

SELECT * FROM jobs WHERE completed = 0 and start_day > '1/1/2008'

SELECT * FROM jobs WHERE completed = 0 and start_day > 'a'			
Variable 1	Position 39	Integer type	Expected value: 0
Variable 2	Position 58	String type	Expected value: "1/1/2008"

another SQL statement with the same normalized form but with different variable value is found. Therefore, theoretically we need to "learn" each SQL statement twice; otherwise, all variables will be assumed to be static. Figure 3 shows the two stages of "learning" an SQL statement.

Since both normalized SQL statement expect value 0 for variable 1, this expectation is kept. But for variable 2 we have two different expected values ("1/1/2009" and "1/1/2008"), now we can perform more analysis on these two expected values in order to form a new requirement with say, character set constrain, or simply do not have any requirement. Without any extra analysis we will be formed as shown in Figure 4.

SQLBlock Implementation

In order to check the authorization of the executing SQL statement, we need a way to get it. This can

be done by implementing a proxy driver which is simply another database connectivity driver. This proxy driver calls another database driver as a client instead of passing the database query to the database server directly. This proxy driver also hides the error messages so the attacker will not be able to benefit from the information about the database schema contained in these error messages. After normalizing the SQL statement, the proxy driver will search the ready list to see if that particular normalized SQL statement exists or not. In case of existence, if the variables are within expected bounds this SQL execution is allowed and otherwise not. To provide the system with the ability of handling exceptional case which is not compatible to the current algorithm, the system checks the normalized SQL statement against another user supplied list of regular expressions. This will stop attackers from by passing the authorization process since the mentioned check

Figure 4. New Formed Rule

SELECT * FROM jobs WHERE completed = 0 and start_day > 'a'			
Variable 1	Position 39	Integer type	Expected value: 0
Variable 2	Position 58	String type	No requirement

Figure 5. SQL block implementation

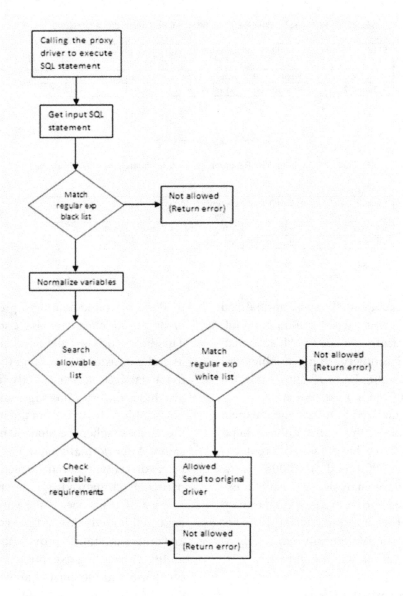

occurs after variable normalization (Sam, 2005). SQLBlock implementation stages are shown in Figure 5.

AMNESIA

AMNESIA implements a new technique for detecting and preventing SQL injection attacks. This technique detects illegal queries before be-ing executed on the database using a model-based approach. This technique consists of a static part in which it automatically builds a model of legal queries using program analysis, and also a dynamic part in which it inspect and checks the dynamically-generated queries against the statically built model using runtime monitoring. Queries violating the model are potential SQLIAs and are prevented from execution. The technique is consisted of four steps which we will go through respectively.

Algorithm 1.

```
public class Show extends HttpServlet {
    ...
  1.    public ResultSet getUserInfo(String login, String password)
       {
  2.         Connection conn = DriverManager.getConnection("MyDB");
  3.         Statement stmt = conn.createStatement();
  4.         String queryString = " ";

  5.         queryString = "SELECT info FROM userTable WHERE ";
  6.         if ((! login.equals(" ")) && (! password.equals(" "))) {
  7.           queryString += "login=' " + login + " ' AND pass=' " + pass-
word + " ' ";
             }
  8.         else {
  9.             queryString+="login='guest' ";
             }
  10.       ResultSet tempSet = stmt.execute(queryString);
  11.       return tempSet;
                    }
    ...
  }
```

Step1: Identifying Hotspots

Hotspots are some particular places in the application program which generate SQL queries to the database. In this step a simple scanning is performed to identify these points in the application code. For instance the statement at line 10 of the following code in Algorithm 1 is a hotspot (Halfond & Orso, 2005).

Step2: Building SQL Query Model

In this step a SQL-query model is built for each identified hotspot in order to compute the possible values of the query string passed to the database. Using the Java String Analysis (JSA) (Christensen, Moller & Schwartzbach, 2003) library a flow graph is constructed which abstracts away the control floe of the program represents the operations performed on string variables. This technique analyzes the flow graph for each desired string and simulates the string manipulation operations that are performed on the string resulting in a Non-Deterministic Finite Automata (NDFA) which represents all the possible values the considered string can take. A depth first traversal on the NDFA for the hotspot is performed in order to build the SQL-query model for that particular hotspot. Variable strings are presented using symbol β e.g. the value of password. Figure 6 shows the two possible branches followed if the statement for SQL-query model based on the hotspot at line 10 of the example illustrated in step 1 was executed (Halfond & Orso, 2005).

Figure 6. SQL query model for servlet in step 1

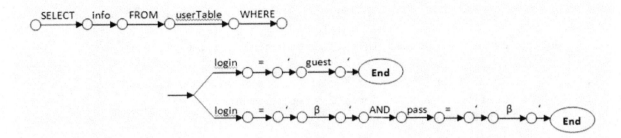

Step3: Instrument Application

In this step, we instrument the application in such a way that, there will be a call to the monitor before the call to the database, so the queries will be checked at runtime. By the time of calling the monitor, a string that contains the query and also a unique identifier for the hotspot are passed to it as its parameters. This unique identifier is used by the runtime monitor in order to relate the hotspot with the specific SQL-query model generated for that point. The code below shows how the mentioned technique can be applied to the example code on step 1; here the hotspot at line 10 is protected by a call to the monitor.

```
10a.    if (monitor.accepts (<hotspot
ID>, queryString))
{
10b.        ResultSet tempSet =
stmt.execute(queryString);
11.            return tempSet;
                    }
```

Step4: Runtime Monitoring

While executing normally when an application reaches a hotspot, the query will be sent to the monitor where it is parsed to a sequence of tokens according to SQL syntax. Empty string constants are identified by their syntactic position and are

presented using ε. An example of how a query can be parsed during runtime monitoring is as follows:

```
(a). SELECT info FROM users WHERE
login = 'doe' AND pass = ' xyz '
(b). SELECT info FROM users WHERE
login = ' ' OR 1=1 -- 'AND pass = ' '
```

The important issue about this technique is that, it interprets the query the same way as the database does according to the SQL grammar, therefore it does not result in false positives and problems with user input caused by a simple keyword matching.

After parsing the query, the runtime monitor checks it against the SQL query model associated with the hotspot from which the monitor has been called. To check whether a query is compliant with the model, the runtime monitor can check whether the NDFA accepts the query or not. In case of acceptance the monitor lets the query to be executed, otherwise considers it as an SQLIA.

Now remember the two queries mentioned in the example, where the first one was a legal query and the second one was a SQLIA.

The Checking of Query (a)

The method will start with matching the SELECT token and forming the initial state of the SQL-query model. Since the token matches correctly the automaton proceeds to the next state where again, INFO token matches the only transition from the current state, therefore the automaton will proceed to the next state. The automaton continues proceeding through states until it reaches the state labeled with "=" where it will proceed along both transitions. On the upper branch, the automaton does not reach an accept state, so the query is not accepted, whereas on the lower branch the automaton will reach an accept state since all the tokens in the query are matched with labels on transitions.

The Checking of Query (b)

Similar to query (a), checking will proceed until it reaches the OR token. Since it does not match the only out going transition from the current state (AND), the query is identified as a SQLIA.

SQL DOM

One of the most common interaction mechanisms between applications and databases is a call level interface (CLI) such as ODBC and JDBC. This mechanism has some advantages (power and performance) and disadvantages. The disadvantage is that for communicating through this mechanism, applications construct strings that contain SQL statements and these statements are only checked at runtime for correctness which is vulnerable for SQL injection attacks.

CLIs provide a low level interface to the database engine. By using a CLI for interfacing with a database engine, SQL statements will be constructed by concatenating and substituting strings that let the developer to create very powerful and flexible queries. The result of the queries won't be checked for correctness until the runtime when they are sent to the database engine (McClure & Krüger, 2005).

Therefore by constructing SQL statements in this way many errors and problems such as bad syntax, misspelled column and table names and data mismatches can arise. Also by changing the database schema, SQL strings that contain SQL statements will be problematic. The number of SQL strings can be large in medium or large sized projects so by changing an application and the database schema, maintaining the SQL strings becomes difficult therefore SQL strings make an application vulnerable for SQL injection attacks by inserting a malicious code into a web form. The result of the execution of these malicious codes is adding and removing data from the database.

This problem can be solved by applying a set of classes that are strongly-typed to a database which is called SQL DOM [6]. These classes are used to generate SQL statements instead of manipulating strings. This solution involves with an executable sqldomgen which is performed against a database. Sqldomgen generates a Dynamic Link Library (DLL) that includes SQL DOM. By applying this method, the compiler is secured to remove the possibility of SQL syntax, data type mismatch and misspelling problems. By using class names or enumeration members, names of tables and column are associated into the SQLDOM and also types of constructor and method parameters are extracted from data type of columns.

For enhancing the maintainability of the application, the compiler is needed to be support because during the life of an application the database schema alters. Sqldomgen is re executed if the database schema alters and then a modified SQL DOM is generated. When the application is rebuilt with the modified SQL DOM, some compiler errors will be arisen such as (McClure & Krüger, 2005):

- Data type conversion error: If the data type of a column was changed this error would occurred.
- No such class exists: If a table or column was renamed or eliminated this error would occurred.
- Missing constructor parameter: If a new column was added to a table this error would occurred.

By applying SQL DOM, the compiler would be able to help in the sustainment process. Hence the reliability of the application will be increased and also developers can change the database schema easily according to the requirements of their customers. If the SQL DOM is employed an application will be secured because SQL DOM constructs all the SQL statements and remove all syntax and data type mismatch bugs, and as a consequence, all known SQL injection attacks will be omitted. While in an application that uses SQL strings, it is difficult to prevent SQL injection attacks.

In order to show how SQL DOM is generated from the database schema automatically, sqldomgen must be analyzed. Sqldomgen performs three main steps. The first step is to get the schema of the database. This step is fulfilled by applying some methods provided by an OLEDB (Object Linking and Embedding, Database) provider. OLEDB is an application programming interface for accessing various types of data stored in a consistent manner. The second step is to repeat through the tables and columns included in the schema and obtain a number of files encompassing a strongly-typed instance of the abstract object model. The third step is to compile these files into a dynamic link library (DLL). To guarantee that changes to the database schema happen in compile time errors, we can imagine that sqldomgen being implemented daily as a part of the build of an application.

Benefits of SQL DOM

Since SQL DOM encapsulates the entire database schema, the schema will be analyzed by SQL DOM and as a result, developers can rely on the IDE to find the appropriate column names in the database.

SQL DOM has a direct effect on maintainability and testability of the overall code-base and because the transition from one database schema to another is guaranteed by the compiler and corresponding IDE, maintenance is promoted.

Due to the existence of class names which are created by the database schema the code accessing of the data base will be more readable (McClure & Krüger, 2005).

SQL DOM uses encapsulation of database queries to provide a safe and reliable way to access the database. These encapsulation techniques offer an effective way to avoid SQL Injection Attacks by changing the query-building process from unregulated processes (which uses string concatenation) to systematic processes (which uses a type-checked API) (McClure & Krüger, 2005). SQL DOM will remove the coding practice that causes an SQL Injection Attack by altering the development paradigm in which SQL queries are generated. Even though this technique is useful and effective, developers that use this technique need to learn and apply a new programming paradigm or query-development process and also they cannot supply any type protection or amended security for legacy systems.

SQL RAND

Many applications take the user input and will generate a pre-defined SQL query based on this input and send the resultant query to the database. An attacker can gain access to private and confidential information by having the knowledge of SQL language and the logic behind it. There have been numerous prevention techniques which try to prevent the attackers from gaining access to confidential information. As another prevention technique, SQLrand can be discussed. SQLrand assumes that SQL commands are provided by the web application and users should not enter SQL commands as their input data. The basic idea behind SQLrand is randomizing SQL commands in which the template query inside the application will be randomized. Before sending SQL commands to the database, it will encode the commands in the application. A de-randomizing proxy will interpret these encoded commands to original SQL commands later. In this way SQL commands which are injected by a malicious user will not be encoded, therefore the proxy will not recognize the injected commands and the attack will not be successful.

SQL Rand Architecture

SQLrand uses the logic of Instruction-Set Randomization (Kc, Keromytis & Prevelakis, 2003; Boyd & Keromytis, 2004); the SQL keywords are manipulated by appending a random integer to them which the attacker cannot easily guess (Boyd & Keromytis, 2004). By doing so, the SQL keywords which are pre-defined in the web application are randomized. Before entering the database, the manipulated SQL keywords are decoded into standard SQL commands by a proxy. The random integers will not be appended to any other SQL commands (which are injected by malicious users); therefore the proxy will not recognize these injected commands and will lead to invalid expressions.

The proxy in SQLrand is an independent module which can be placed anywhere. Having a separate proxy which is not an internal part of the database and is in charge of decoding the randomized SQL commands will culminate in flexibility, simplicity and security (Boyd & Keromytis, 2004).

A few benefits of having a separate proxy can be mentioned as follows:

- There can be multiple proxies to decode the SQL commands with different random keys and they can all send their decoded keywords to the same database.
- Since the randomized integers are removed in the proxy, the database will never be aware of the randomized integers and won't generate any error messages to reveal the information about the random integers.
- The proxy can be used in order to filter the error messages that are generated by the database. Attackers usually try to inject some SQL commands so that the database generates an error message; these error messages can reveal invaluable information about the database and its tables and column names. By having a proxy, database generated error messages will never return to the web application.
- The proxy has a simple structure which makes it possible and easy to protect it against the attacks.

SQL Rand architecture is shown in Figure 7 on a high level.

Figure 7. SQL rand architecture

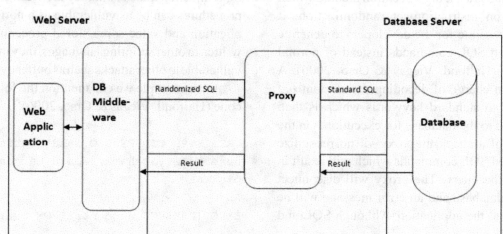

207

The following simplified example shows how the SQLrand works. First let's assume that the web application has generated the following SQL query (Boyd & Keromytis, 2004):

```
SELECT gender, avg (age) FROM cs101.
students WHERE dept = %d GROUP BY
gender
```

If the random integer would be 123 then the randomized query which will be sent to the proxy will be:

```
SELECT123 gender, avg123 (age)
FROM123 cs101.students WHERE123 dept
= %d GROUP123 BY123 gender
```

Since the proxy is in charge of receiving the randomized keywords from the application, the application must connect to the proxy instead of the database. The application must set its port number to the port number in which the proxy is using. Upon receiving a connection, the proxy will connect to the database and will transmit the commands sent by the client after having them decoded. If the proxy could not decode the received query, it will send an error message back to the application and will disconnect from the database. If the query was legitimate, the proxy will decode the randomized keywords and will transmit the standard query to the database.

SQLrand is a useful prevention method which is based on instruction-set randomization. It makes it possible for the developers to generate randomized SQL commands instead of normal keywords (Halfond, Viegas & Orso, 2006). A proxy is in charge of decoding the randomized keywords to standard keywords which is then transferred to the database for execution. On the condition of an attack, the proxy will not recognize the injected SQL commands which will result in rejecting the query. The proxy will disconnect from the database and an error message will be sent back to the application. Although SQLrand needs key management, developer training and proxy creation, it will have little overhead on the applications and systems.

STORED PROCEDURES

Stored procedures are subroutines in the database which the applications can make call to. They are becoming more widespread due to the fact that they add an additional abstraction level to the database which means that the underlying database structure can easily change if the interface on the stored procedure stays the same. SQL queries can be built at runtime based on user inputs which leads to flexibility. However, this feature will make the SQL injection attacks possible in stored procedures.

SQL Injection Attacks in Stored Procedures

Recently, database vendors contain a set of predefined stored procedures in their databases with the intention of increasing the functionality of database. If an attacker is able to identify the database type used by the company, he will be able to call these stored procedures (which some of them interact with the operating system) through SQL injection attacks. Some might think that stored procedures in the database are not exposed to SQL injection attacks but they are wrong. Stored procedures can be as vulnerable as a normal application and since some stored procedures are written in other scripting languages, they might be vulnerable to other attacks such as buffer overflow.

As an example we can mention the following code (Halfond, Viegas & Orso, 2006):

```
CREATE PROCIDURE DBO.isAuthenticated
@userName varchar2, @pass carchar2, @
pin int
AS
EXEC ("SELECT accounts FROM users
```

```
WHERE login =' " +@userName+ " ' and
pass =' " +password+ " ' and pin = "
@pin);
GO
```

Since the stored procedure is parameterized, a malicious user can inject SQL commands into the stored procedure and exploit the stored procedure. The attacker can enter the " ' ; SHUTDOWN; -- " phrase instead of username or password in the application. The result would look like the following:

```
SELECT accounts FROM users WHERE
login ='doe' AND pass = ' ';SHUTDOWN;
-- AND pin =
```

As we can see, stored procedures can be open to SQL injection attacks like the normal applications. We will now discuss a prevention technique which identifies SQL injection attacks in stored procedures. This technique is consisted of two phases and has little computational overhead.

SQL Injection Attack Prevention

The SQL injection attack prevention in stored procedure works by combining static analysis with runtime validation (Wei, Muthuprasanna & Kothari, 2006). The static analysis uses a stored procedure parser which identifies the commands that build the SQL statement. In the runtime analysis, a new function (SQLIAChecker) will identify the user input. If the input does not conform to the standard SQL commands, then the query will be marked as SQLIA.

Static Analysis

In this technique, there exists a stored procedure parser which extracts the control flow graph from the stored procedure (Wei, Muthuprasanna & Kothari, 2006). Static analysis is an offline procedure and is done by analyzing the stored procedure's source code. In this phase, an SQL graph will be generated and all the user input will be marked. These user inputs will be checked further at run time to compare the final generated statement with the original SQL statement. The SQL graph will contain queries (Q) and user input (I). The relationship (R) between two nodes is indicated by an undirected link between them. A dependency (D) is defined when a query is dependent to another one. In this case, a directed line shows the flow in the graph. It should also be mentioned that SQL statements which do not require user input, are not included in the SQL graph because they are not vulnerable to SQL injection attacks. Figure 8 shows the SQL graph from the stored procedure we mentioned before. Q1 is the query in the stored

Figure 8. SQL graph from a stored procedure

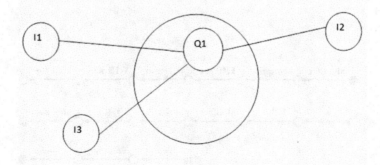

procedure and I1, I2 and I3 represent username, password and pin respectively.

The static analysis phase helps reducing the overhead in runtime analysis.

Runtime Analysis

In this phase, a function named SQLIACHECKER () will identify the user input and a finite state automaton will be built. After that, the user input will be checked with the finite state automaton. If the user input does not match with the original SQL statements which were identified by the finite automata, they will be flagged as a potential SQL injection attack; otherwise, the query will be valid and will be passed through.

An approach to reduce the computational overhead would be to track user inputs. If a user input passes through the SQLIACHECKER () function, it can be concluded that the input is not malicious and can be used over and over again on the condition of not being exploited. By doing so, the overhead will be reduced dramatically while SQL injection attacks are still detected and managed. Figure 9 below shows the finite state machine which is built based on user input. The first finite state machine corresponds to a normal

user and the second state machine corresponds to a malicious user (Wei, Muthuprasanna & Kothari, 2006).

Although some may think that stored procedures are secure and reliable, they are open to SQL injection attacks. A malicious user can perform denial of service attacks, execute remote commands and perform privilege escalation attacks. A prevention technique has been presented here which builds an SQL graph. The graph will be validated later at the runtime analysis against different user inputs in order to detect malicious activities. In conclusion, this technique has proved to be useful with little computational overhead which is able to detect tautologies, additional SQL statements and second-order injection attacks.

DISCUSSION

There have been a number of SQL injection detection/prevention techniques mentioned in this chapter. Each technique might not be useful itself, but we strongly believe that a combination of these prevention techniques alongside with an up-to-date intrusion detection system will improve the robustness of web applications dramatically.

Figure 9. SQL injection attack detection

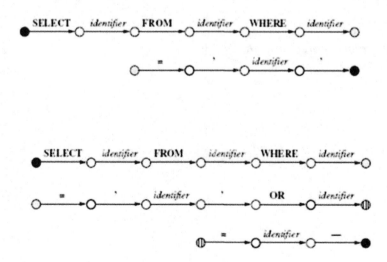

This chapter is a survey of different SQL Injection prevention techniques. First we started by studying different attacks which were more common and advanced. The research continued with organization and classification of different prevention techniques which we found and finally a summary of the best SQL injection prevention techniques were presented. The paper discusses the appropriate SQL prevention techniques for a given attack.

The learning-based system which acts as an intrusion detection system is the first injection detection technique introduced here. Since it is an anomaly based IDS, it is very suitable for detecting injection attacks and can have fairly low false positive rate if implemented carefully. It has a fairly simple logic and structure with little overhead in terms of resource exhaustion. The only drawback is the learning phase which we believe might take some time to complete. In addition, improper and incomplete learning phase will result in increased false negative or false positive rates which will ultimately be to the detriment of the web application.

Context-Sensitive String Evaluation is a useful and effective technique which can both detect and prevent injection attacks in web applications. There are some drawbacks though. First and foremost, this technique is highly platform-dependent which will affect implementation dramatically. With new platforms, CSSE must be implemented from scratch which can be time and resource consuming. On the other hand, Pietraszek and Berghe (2005) mention that a number of functions in the platforms must be instrumented in order for CSSE to fully function. Again, we are of the conviction that this approach will affect the scalability of CSSE and might even affect its functionality. An incomplete implementation of CSSE will result in false negatives or false positives which mean that some injection attacks will eventually succeed. Therefore, scalability is the main drawback of this injection prevention technique.

At the very beginning we started with introducing Variable Normalization technique which extracts the basic structure of the SQL statement, so in case of a SQL injection which alters the original structure of the SQL statement, we will be able to detect it. The introduced SQLBlock has a minimal overhead and works with all database servers without requiring any change in the client source code. The auto-learning option for the allowable list makes the system very convenient to setup for clients that issue many different SQL commands. There exist some cases that cannot be handled by Variable Normalization effectively. Imagine a website which allows the user to select different types of a particular product form a multi-line selection box. The normalized SQL command may be something like this:

```
SELECT * FROM Product_Tbl WHERE Product_name LIKE 'a' AND Product_type in ('a', 'a', 'a')
```

The SQLBlock will be able to handle these kinds of queries only by learning all different variants of the SQL statement. This is possible only in case that there are limited and also expected numbers of items in the selection box. (Sam, 2005)

AMNESIA is a fully automated technique for detecting and preventing SQL injection attacks. A web application code contains a policy which helps to differentiate between legitimate and illegal queries. This technique uses static and dynamic analysis to obtain the mentioned policy and use it to distinguish illegal SQL queries. It is important to mention that this technique targets SQLIAs, which happen when an attacker attempts to inject SQL statements into a query which is sent to the database. SQLIAs do not include other types of web-application related attacks. (Halfond & Orso, 2005)

Most of the existing techniques to deal with SQLIAs are focusing on queries generated within the application. Enabling the techniques to embody the queries that are executed on the database is

Table 1. A comparison between AMNESIA, SQL DOM, and SQL Rand

Technique	Tautology	Illegal	Piggy-Back	Union	Stored Procedure	Inference	Alternate Encoding
AMNESIA	✓	✓	✓	✓	X	✓	✓
SQL DOM	✓	✓	✓	✓	X	✓	✓
SQL Rand	✓	X	✓	✓	X	✓	X

a complex task. For this reason attacks based on stored procedures and also alternate encoding are problematic and difficult to handle. Only three techniques, AMNESIA, SQLCheck, and SQL-Guard explicitly address these types of attacks and that is because they use the database parser to interpret a query in the same way that the database would. (Halfond, Viegas & Orso, 2006)

The degree of success in finding the real SQLIAs by this technique is dependent on the accuracy of the generated query models which takes place in the static analysis phase. Depending on the precision of this step, the technique might result in both false positives and false negatives. (Halfond & Orso, 2005)

SQL DOM is an approach in which changes the process of query-building to a systematic process of API type-checking. SQL DOM creates new SQL commands instead of generating a string of SQL keywords that will later be sent to the database. By doing so, there are no more SQL string generations in the applications which are the main target of SQL injection attacks. SQL DOM offers protection against tautologies, illegal/logically incorrect statements, piggyback and union queries as well as protection against inference attacks and alternate encodings (Halfond, Viegas & Orso, 2006). On the other hand, it does not have any protection against attacks in stored procedures. While SQL DOM seems like an effective prevention technique against SQL injection attacks, it has the drawback which requires new programming paradigms that may not be desirable for developers.

SQLrand is a useful prevention method which is based on instruction-set randomization. It makes it possible for the developers to generate randomized SQL commands instead of normal keywords (Halfond, Viegas & Orso, 2006). A proxy is in charge of decoding the randomized keywords to standard keywords which is then transferred to the database for execution. On the condition of an attack, the proxy will not recognize the injected SQL commands which will result in rejecting the query. The proxy will disconnect from the database and an error message will be sent back to the application. Although SQLrand needs key management, developer training and proxy creation, it will have little overhead on the applications and systems. Apart from its advantages, SQLrand requires a complex setup which will make it harder for developers to use this prevention technique. From security point of view, SQLrand uses a secret key in order to change the instructions. On the condition that the secret key is revealed, the attacker will have access to randomized queries. SQLrand provides protection against tautology and piggyback queries as well as union query and inference attacks. However, this technique does not have any protection against illegal or logically incorrect queries, stored procedure attacks and alternate encodings (Halfond, Viegas & Orso, 2006).

Although some may think that stored procedures are secure and reliable, they are open to SQL injection attacks. A malicious user can perform denial of service attacks, execute remote commands and perform privilege escalation attacks. A prevention technique has been presented here which builds an SQL graph. The graph will be validated later at the runtime analysis against different user inputs in order to detect malicious activities (Wei, Muthuprasanna & Kothari, 2006). In conclusion, this technique has proved to be useful with little computational overhead and as the name implies, it provides protection in stored procedures.

CONCLUSION

SQL Injection Attacks are prevalent in web applications. There are numerous attackers and hackers who will try their utmost to gain unauthorized access to an organization's database. Web application developers might sometimes be unaware of security vulnerabilities of their applications and the consequences of these vulnerabilities. In order to help protect web applications from SQL injection attacks, numerous detection and prevention techniques have been introduced. In this chapter, we have introduced seven of the most popular techniques which will help to improve robustness of web applications.

REFERENCES

Boyd, S. W., & Keromytis, A. D. (2004). *SQLrand: Preventing SQL injection attacks*, (pp. 292-302). Columbia University. Berlin, Germany: Springer.

Christensen, A. S., Møller, A., & Schwartzbach, M. I. (2003). Precise analysis of string expressions. In *Proceedings of the 10th International Static Analysis Symposium, SAS 03, LNCS 2694*, (pp. 1–18). Springer-Verlag.

Halfond, W. G., Viegas, J., & Orso, A. (2006). A classification of SQL injection attacks and countermeasures. In *Proceedings of the International Symposium on Secure Software Engineering*.

Halfond, W. G. J., & Orso, A. (2005). *AMNESIA: Analysis and monitoring for neutralizing SQL injection attacks,* (pp. 174-183).

Hoppe, T. (2009). *Applying intrusion detection to automotive IT- Early insights and selected short term countermeasures.*

Hoppe, T., Kiltz, S., & Dittmann, J. (2008). Security threats to automotive CAN networks practical examples and selected short-term countermeasures. In *Proceedings of the International Conference on Computer Safety, Reliability and Security* (SAFECOMP), (pp. 235–248).

Kc, G. C., Keromytis, A. D., & Prevelakis, V. (2003). Countering code-injection attacks with instruction-set randomization. In *Proceedings of the ACM Computer and Communications Security (CSS) Conference,* October 2003, (pp. 272-280).

McClure, R. A., & Krüger, I. H. (2005). *SQL DOM: Compile time checking of dynamic SQL statements.* IEEE Explore.

Ng, S. M. S. (2005). *SQL injection protection by variable normalization of SQL statement.* Retrieved from www.securitydocs.com/library/3388

Wei, K., Muthuprasanna, M., & Kothari, S. (2006). Preventing SQL injection attacks in stored procedures. *Proceedings of the 2006 Australian Software Engineering Conference* (ASWEC'06), IEEE, Australia, (pp. 1-7).

Chapter 11
Security and Authentication Issues of an Embedded System Designed and Implemented for Interactive Internet Users

Siddhartha Baruah
Gauhati University, India

Anjana Kakoty Mahanta
Gauhati University, India

Kanak Ch Sarma
Gauhati University, India

ABSTRACT

Though embedded applications were originally built on standalone devices, nowadays these devices require a growing integration with other systems through their interconnection with TCP/IP networks. Web Services, which provide a service oriented distributed architecture for the interconnection of systems through TCP/IP networks, have been widely adopted for the integration of business applications, but this sort of integration is still not widely provided by embedded applications. The present work aims to demonstrate the feasibility of using Web Services for the integration of embedded applications running on heterogeneous architectures. This is achieved through the provision of a support for the development and deployment of web services for embedded applications. Basic objective of the system developed is to monitor and control Humidity and Temperature through Internet using interactive computer front end. The feasibility of this approach in terms of security and authentications of its Internet users is demonstrated by developing an mail server along with application deployed. Mail server keeps track of authorised users' with login password and email ID in a database table. This information is used to identify authorised users who are allowed to make changes in control parameters of the stated embedded application.

DOI: 10.4018/978-1-4666-0978-5.ch011

1. INTRODUCTION

System developed for the stated study is a micro-controller based embedded system for monitoring and controlling of parameters temperature and humidity. Microcontroller based embedded systems designed for monitoring and controlling of parameters like temperature and humidity is very essential in some industrial as well as research setups (National Instruments, n.d.; Mazidi & Mazidi, 2007). Developed system can be implemented using simple client server technology as well as web technology (Baruah, Kakoti Mahanta, & Sharma, 2009; 2010). Embedded hardware circuit is fabricated in to two separate digital circuits connecting to two com ports of Embedded server. First circuit will monitor temperature and humidity and display same in LCD. Application program executed in computer reads COM port and display the same in monitor and store in database. This program also continuously monitor the sense values against some user entered control values of humidity and temperature at which controlling action has to be carried out. User entered control values are stored in a separate database table so that time to time different values can be set as per requirement. Display of stored value and generation of graph can be also obtained as per choice of user. Second digital circuit will provide necessary hardware control of devices for controlling of temperature and humidity automatically when sense value reaches control value of temperature and humidity stored in database. As a web enable system monitoring and controlling of the system made feasible through web clients anywhere from web with necessary interactive front end and browser configuration. Figure 1 depicts Hardware configuration of boards with Embedded Server.

2. SCHEMATIC DESCRIPTION OF THE FUNCTIONING COMPONENTS

2.1. Power Supply Section

The regulated power supply section made with full wave rectifier (with IN 4007 diodes) using

Figure 1. Hardware configuration of boards with embedded server (Computer with database + Application To send / receive data to/from database)

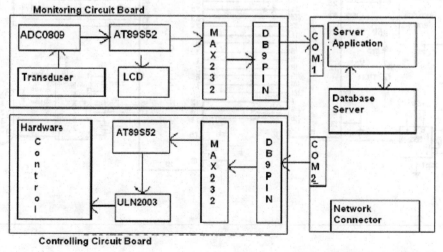

(Computer with database + Application To send / receive data to/from database)

215

Figure 2. Schematic diagrams; A) Monitoring circuit board; B) Controlling circuit board

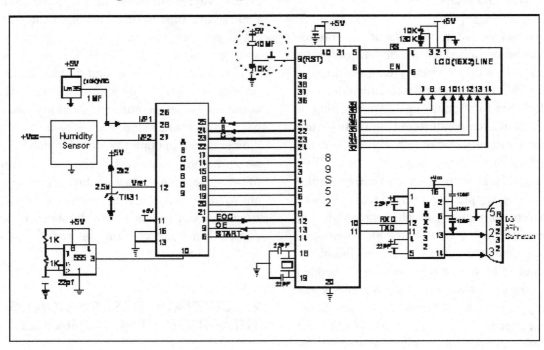

Schematic Diagram(Monitoring Circuit Board)

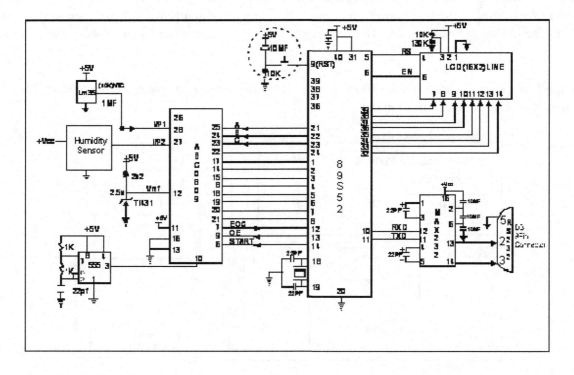

Schematic Diagram(Monitoring Circuit Board)

voltage regulator IC 7805 and IC 7812 which provide a constant voltage of 5V to the circuit as well as constant 12V to relays.

2.2. Analog to Digital Conversion Section

Analog parameters temperature and humidity are converted into digital by ADC 0809 which is a 8 channels microprocessor compatible ADC with easy availability (National Semiconductor Corporation, 2005). It will convert the analog signal of the transducer to digital value with respect to the reference voltage which is 2.5V in proposed system. This reference voltage is obtained using TL431, which is a programmable shunt voltage reference with output voltage range of 2.5V to 36V and works like zener diode (ST Microelectronics, 2002). For the conversion ADC requires a reference frequency which is supplied from 555 IC in the form of astable oscillator. The conversion frequency is kept around 150 kHz.

2.3. Sensor Used

Sensor used for temperature measurement is *LM 35*. LM 35 is calibrated in °C and is linear in +10 mV/ °C scale factor with 0.5°C accuracy (National Semiconductor Corporation, 2000) and no external calibration is needed. It uses humidity sensor LM324DG (Atmel Corporation, 2000) Amplifier circuit is used to amplify the electrical characteristic obtained through the transducer to raise the strength sufficiently.

2.4. Controller Section

The analog value is converted to digital value by ADC and is picked up by microcontroller AT89S52 which is a 40pin device. The AT89S52 is a low-power, high-performance CMOS 8-bit microcomputer with 8K bytes of Flash programmable and erasable read only memory (EPROM) (Wikipedia, n.d.).

2.5. Display Section

In addition to continuous display of sense temperature in the front end screen of computer in hardware circuit(a) on board 44780 LCD is used which is a 2x16 line display (8052.com, n.d.; Kalsi, 1999).

2.6. Temperature Control Section

This section consists of a 12V relay to control hardware to start cooling for maintaining temperature as set by the user (Wikipedia, n.d.).

2.7. Data Transfer

Displayed temperature is transferred to RS 232 which is interfaced with microcontroller through MAX232 (Dietikon, 2001; Maxim, n.d.). In this implementation monitoring board can be considered as transmitter as after converting the sense temperature into digital form it will transmit the same to RS232. A program executed simultaneously in computer will read and display the same in the front-end designed in the monitor. Additionally front-end will display temperature set value and status(on/off) of hardware device and enable user to enter new value of temperature in the database generate curve of temperature with respect to time. Controlling board will continuously compare sense data with set value and run hardware device for controlling temperature and humidity. Microcontroller of controller board is connected with relay through ULN2003(AllDataSheet.com, n.d.) to amplify the required current necessary to drive the relay.

3. OVERALL HARDWARE SETUP WITH INTERNET IMPLEMENTATION

Proposed system is connected the LAN with its own IP address making it accessible from Internet (from any location) (Comer, 2005). Mail server is

Figure 3. Experimental setup

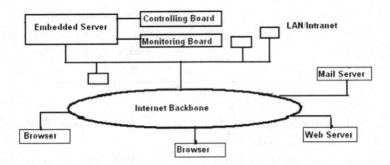

implemented to check the authenticity of Internet user when try to make change the limit values of parameters. It keeps track of authorized mail addresses in a database.

A Web Client is also called a web browser which send/receive and display data and web pages in a computer by sending request to a web server, generally a computer, kept at a remote location. A web browser is the software program used to access the World Wide Web, the graphical portion of the Internet.

Web server is installed for providing web services as required by the system. Figure 3 below depicts the experimental setup and as deployed in Web

4. SOFTWARE DEVELOPED FOR THE PROPOSED SYSTEM

Four different software modules work simultaneously to achieve the defined goal of the proposed system. These programs are divided into four modules.

4.1 Module 1

This module is burnt into the microcontroller of monitoring board. This program is developed in Keil-C and responsible for displaying sense values of temperature and humidity (Lewis, 2003).

It also makes the values available in RS232 port which itself is connected with the one COM port of the computer.

Algorithms Implemented in Monitoring Board

Initialize microcontroller registers P0, P1, P2, P3, TL1, TH1, TH0, IE, SCON and baud rate fixed at 9600 baud.

ADC is used for converting two different sensor values belonging to ZONE1, and ZONE2 which stands for Humidity and Temperature respectively

Procedure Initializing the Monitoring System

1. Initialize LCD port P0, P1, P2, P3.
2. IE (Interrupt Enable) register is set for masking and unmasking the interrupts.
3. SCON (Serial Control) register is set for start bit, stop bit, and data bits of data framing
4. TMOD (Timer mode) register is set. C/T bit is zero to indicate that the timer is used as a delay generator. Mode is set to 2 for Timer 1 which means 8-bit auto reload timer and mode 2 for serial com port. Set the TH1 for baud rate. Make the Timer 0 to operate in mode 1 for delay. TH0 and TL0 are loaded some initial values and are cascaded.

Reading Data from ADC Chip

Different channels are used to read appropriate sensor data from ADC. The channel A,B are assigned to different pins for sending data to by this procedure for humidity and temperature respectively.

Main Procedure of the Monitoring Board to Display and Transfer Data Serially

1. Call the Procedure initializing the monitoring system
2. Call the LCD initialization procedure
3. Initialize parameters for ZONE1
4. Read data for ZONE1. The character byte is serially written to SBUF register and store in a variable
5. The TI flag is monitored continuously by the timer interrupt, TF0, to see if the character has been transferred completely.
6. Call the procedure sending data to LCD for display
7. Repeat step 4 to 6 for a fixed period(millisecond) until user-defined external interrupt, INT1, forces to switch to ZONE2
8. Initialize parameters for ZONE2
9. Read data for ZONE2. The character byte is serially written to SBUF register and store in a variable
10. The TI flag is monitored continuously by the timer interrupt, TF0, to see if the character has been transferred completely.
11. Call the procedure sending data to LCD for display
12. Repeat step 9 to 11 for a fixed period(millisecond) until user-defined external interrupt, INT1, forces to switch to ZONE1
13. Repeat step 3 to 12 infinite number of times

Table 1.

Analog channel	A	B
IN0	0	0
IN1	0	1

Procedure for Interrupt Service Routine to Transfer Data Serially

1. TI is initially set to 0.
2. RI is initially set to 0.
3. The TI flag is raised at the beginning of stop bit to indicate that 8051 is ready to transfer another byte. If raised, make TI = 0;
4. RI flag is raised halfway through the stop bit and indicates that a byte has been received and places the byte in the SBUF register. If raised, make RI = 0;

Procedure for Interrupt Service Routine for Delay in a Zone

To generate time delay using timer 0 mode 2,so that each ZONE remains for a fixed number of delays, the following steps are taken:

1. Load the TMOD value register indicating which timer is used. This is done during system initialization procedure.
2. Load TH and TL registers with initial count value
3. Start the timer.
4. Keep monitoring the timer flag (TF0) to see whether it is raised. This is done using external interrupt (INT1)
5. Clear the TF flag.
6. Go Back to step 3 since mode 2 is auto-reload. Each reload should decrement a fixed unsigned value until it reaches 0. When it reaches zero, the 8051 should switch to different zone.

4.2 Module 2

This module is burnt in to the microcontroller of the controlling board. This program is also developed in Keil-C and responsible for carrying out necessary control action by starting some hardware devices through relays.

Main Procedure of Controlling Board Algorithm

Insert variables used in vb prog. For controlling

1. If received value is 1 then switch on relay for voltage
2. If received value is 2 at com port switch off the relay for voltage
3. If received value is 3 then switch on relay for voltage
4. If received value is 4 at com port switch off the relay for voltage
5. Repeat steps 1 to 4 whenever received interrupt is generated

Procedure for System Initialization of Controlling Board

1. Initialize LCD port P0.Also initialize P1,P2,P3 to FFH
2. IE register is set for masking and unmasking the interrupts. All interrupts will be acknowledged by unmasking the EA (IE.7) bit. The ES(IE.4) bit is unmasked for serial port interrupt and the ET0(IE.1) bit is enabled for Timer 0 overflow interrupt.

IE=0x92

3. SCON register is set for start bit, stop bit, and data bits of data framing. Mask the SM0(SCON.7)bit and unmask the SM1(SCON.6)bit for serial mode 1,8-bit data,1 stop bit,1 start bit to make data framing compatible to COM port of the computer.

SCON=0x50

4. TMOD register is set. C/T bit is zero to indicate that the timer is used as a delay generator. Mode is set to 2 for Timer 1 which means 8-bit auto reload timer and mode 2 for serial com port. Set the TH1 for baud rate. Make the Timer 0 to operate in mode 1 for delay. TH0 and TL0 are loaded some initial values and are cascaded.

TMOD= 0x21
TH1=0xFD
TH0 = 0x3C
TL0=0xB0

5. Stop timer 0 and start the timer 1

Procedure for Interrupt Service Routine of Serial Communication

The following steps are executed to receive character bytes serially.

1. The TMOD register is loaded with value 21H indicating the use of Timer 1 in mode 2 (8-bit auto reload) to set to baud rate.
2. TH1 is loaded with value FDH to set the baud rate (taking XTAL = 11.0592 MHz)
3. The TH0 and TL0 are loaded with 3CH and B0H to check TF0 flag periodically.
4. The SCON register is loaded with value 50H,indicating serial mode 1,where 8-bit data is framed with start and stop bits and receive enable is turned on.
5. TR1 is set to 1 to start Timer 1.
6. RI is cleared with instruction RI = 0.
7. The RI flag bit is monitored by the Timer interrupt 1 to see if an entire character has been received yet.
8. When RI is raised, SBUF has a byte. Its contents are moved to a save place.
9. The moved contents of SBUF are set to appropriate relay.

10. To receive the next character, go to step 6.

4.3 Module 3

This module is stored in computer, COM ports of which is connected with monitoring and controlling boards. Program written in Visual basic will read the values of COM port connected with monitoring board and display the same in interactive front end of the computer (Boehm & Lowe, 2008; Prince & Lowe, 2005). MySQL database server is installed in the computer which stores the sense values in Temperature and Humidity tables of database with corresponding Date and Time (Welling & Thomson, 2004). Another table MAXVALUES is constructed with corresponding limits of Temperature and Humidity at which control action has to be initiated. Program continuously monitor sense values with set values stored in MAXVALUES table. If it finds the sense values exceeding set value it passes signal through COM port of controlling board to start appropriate hardware device through relay to bring the parameter within the limit set. Update button provided in the interactive front end will enable users to change the limit value at desired level. Clients of the LAN will be provided with the same front end with all the features similar to server. Clients can monitor continuously sense values at its front end as per constant request for same to server at a regular interval. Client is capable of doing it as it is configured as fat client.

Algorithm: Embedded Standalone VB Controlling System

1. Establish database connection and create recordset for limit data. Also populate the limit recordset.
2. Set the control devices to a saved state and display the status of the controlling devices
3. Update the the limits for Humidity and Temperature, if required and display in appropriate text box.

4. Open com port 2 to write control data to controlling device to control the monitoring device parameters
5. Check if the current zone data exceeded the zone limit. If exceeded, send control data to the com port 2 to control the appropriate sensor device
6. Repeat step 2-5 after fixed time intervals.

System creates following database tables for keeping track of different sense values and limit values using MySQL database server installed the computer whose COM ports are connected with embedded boards (i.e. monitoring and controlling boards)

As per user request as given in interactive front end system can display graph based on value stored in Humidity and Temperature database tables. X–Y graph is plotted with respected time and value of the parameters Humidity and Temperature. Algorithm for implementing the graph given below.

Algorithm: XY-Data Graph for Humidity and Temperature

*   x, y = data to be plotted
*   x value is generally the time
*   y values can be the values of Temperature, Humidity.
*   xmin, ymin, xmax, ymax = mininimum and maximum values of x and y
*   n = number of data points

Table 2. Table for controlling parameter Table name: Maxvalues

Attribute Name	Function
Humidity	Stores the maximum humidity value
Temperature	Stores the maximum temperature value

Table 3. Table for keeping humidity values Table name: Humidity

Attribute Name	Function
Humidity	Stores the sense humidity value
Date	Stores the current date
Time	Stores the current date

Table 4. Table for keeping temperature values Table name: Temperature

Attribute Name	Function
Temperature	Stores the sense Temperature value
Date	Stores the current date
Time	Stores the current date

This procedure takes information on minimum, maximum values, major divisions (ticks) and minor divisions (sub-ticks) in the x and y axes of plot.

1. Connect to database and select any date of a particular recordset.
2. Populate the recordset for that date
3. Select minimum and maximum values of x.and y for that date.
4. calculate the values of x and y as

```
ticks = (Difference of min. and max
values) /10
subticks = (Difference of min and max
values)/100
```

5. Save the minimum, maximum, ticks and subticks of x and y values in a file temp.txt.
6. count the number of records, n, and write it to file, temp.txt
7. Take out all x and y values from the recordset and write it to file,temp.txt

4.4. Module 4

This module of the system is responsible for implementation of the system over Internet. It contains software for providing web services. It consist of IIS web server with.NET framework and web application, database server and a browser as a client. The web application is implemented in C#.NET (Howell, 2004; Boehm & Murach, 2008). It sends requests to the database server to send updated data for sending the same to client. Client may send HTTP request to Web server for getting updated values of temperature and Humidity or control data for change of new set values of temperature and humidity. Next Web server send request to Embedded server for retrieving updated values from database or setting new values of temperature and humidity for initiating control. Embedded server send updated values or new set values to web server. Web server in the form of HTTP response send the same to client. The advantage provided by such a web service is that the user can view and change the necessary values from any location. Above modules can combinedly represent in the following functional diagram of the overall system given in Figure 4.

Designed system is implemented in such a way, its users from both Internet and Intranet can access it simultaneously. Interactive front-end for both users designed separately. Figure 5 with user and system interface can depict the simultaneous working of the system from Intranet and Internet

Controlling is carried out through relay based on the set value of temperature and humidity and stored in database of computer. Developed system enables its Intranet and Internet users to set new controlling values of temperature and humidity based on client server and web technology. Both technologies work in a different manner. In client server technology users continuously receive the updated values of sense temperature and humidity as per constant request of client to server for updated values. Internet users using the web

Figure 4. Functional diagram of embedded server process

```
                        ┌──────────────┐
                        │ Front-end Display│
                        │  of Server   │
                        └──────┬───────┘
                               ▲
                               │
  ┌─────────────┐        ┌──────────────┐
  │ Temp Sensor │  Sensor Data  │ Monitoring   │
  ├─────────────┤─────►  │ & Controlling│ ──────────────┐
  │Humidity Sensor│        │   Process    │              │
  └─────────────┘        └──────┬───────┘              ▼
                               ▲                  ┌──────────┐
                               │                  │  Relay   │
                         ┌─────┴──────┐           │  ON/OFF  │
                         │Database Server│        └──────────┘
                         └─────┬──────┘
                               ▲
                               │
                         ┌──────────────┐         ┌──────────┐
                         │  Generate    │ ──────► │ Display  │
                         │ Graph process│         │  Graph   │
                         └──────────────┘         └──────────┘
```

technology will avail the same implemented in a three tire system of web browser, web server and embedded server. Due to stateless nature of web Internet users will not receive continuous updated data. Users of the system must send a HTTP request from web browser to web server then same will be forwarded to embedded server for retrieving the updated values. This phenomena is depicted in the following three tire model.

5. MONITORING AND CONTROLLING FROM INTRANET AND INTERNET

Intranet as well as Internet users can set the control values of temperature and humidity through their respective front ends at which necessary control will be initiated by controller board through relays. Hardware control will be initiated when sense values of temperature and humidity will

Figure 5. Overall functionality of software processes

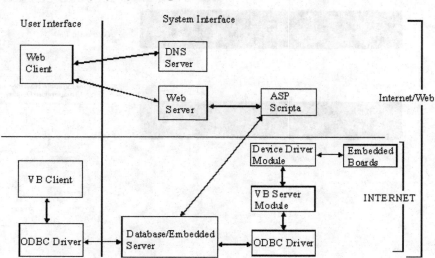

Figure 6. Three tier model of Web implementation

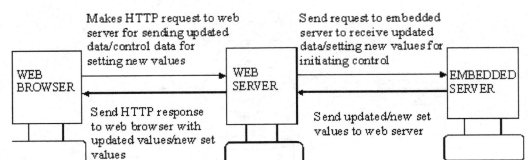

exceed the set values stored in limit value table by running some devices like cooler, dryer etc. Following Interactive front end of Figure 7 will be displayed in monitor for Intranet users.

Being fat client Intranet front end will continuously display sense values of parameters with respect to its date and time. Generate report and plot buttons enable users to generate report and graph based on temperature and humidity of a particular day as chosen by user. These will be retrieved from the database with corresponding date and time of recorded. Using update button user can change the limit values of parameters for controlling Humidity and Temperature at desired level. Front end also displays continuously the status (on/off) of hardware devices.

Interactive front end for Internet users is a thin client. It can't display sense values continuously.

Figure 7. Interactive front-end from Intranet displayed in monitor

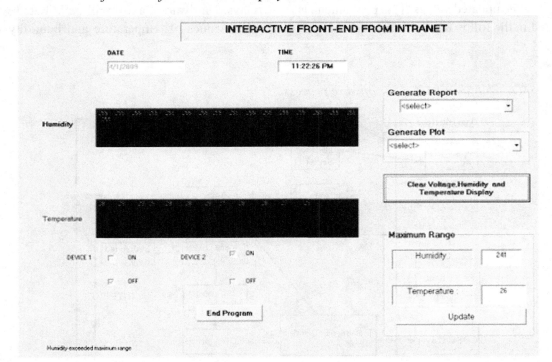

It works based on HTTP (details as given in 4.4). User as a web client select a particular date from available list and click on submit button for getting maximum temperature and humidity recorded for that particular date. Refresh date will enable user to refresh date. Clicking on get current values browser will sent request to web server for getting updated data of humidity and temperature. It will display the existing limit values of temperature and humidity in the space provided along with set temperature limit and set humidity limit when user click on show limit button.

To prevent unauthorized users from unwanted updation by setting new values of temperature and humidity system checks the authentication of users. System will allow user to set new control, for which user has to login with valid user-id and password as given in login form below. This is implemented by designing a mail server where database server keeps track of information with login-id, password and email-id of authorized users in a separate table. Administrator of the system will issue login-id and password to inter-net users of system authorized to set new values of temperature and humidity. These authorized

users can also change the existing password as given in the screen. If the user forgets his login-id password, he can use forgot password form by clicking on forgot password link of the web page. The user is then taken to the forget password web form, where he submits his e-mail id. E mail id if found correct on verification, then the password will be sent to the same email id. Any machine in the net can be configured as mail server. Mail Transfer Agent (MTA) used for sending mail, Sendmail is used for sending message for mail server. This facility is provided in ASP.NET by Send() method of mail class.

In order to enhancing the security measures forms are also provided for authorized users in case it is required to change the existing password.

6. IMPLEMENTATION OF AUTHENTICATION ISSUES AND LOGIN PAGE

Authentication is needed to secure a web page. The updation of controlling limits is granted to authorized users. Authorized user ids along with

Figure 8. Interactive front-end from Internet displayed in monitor

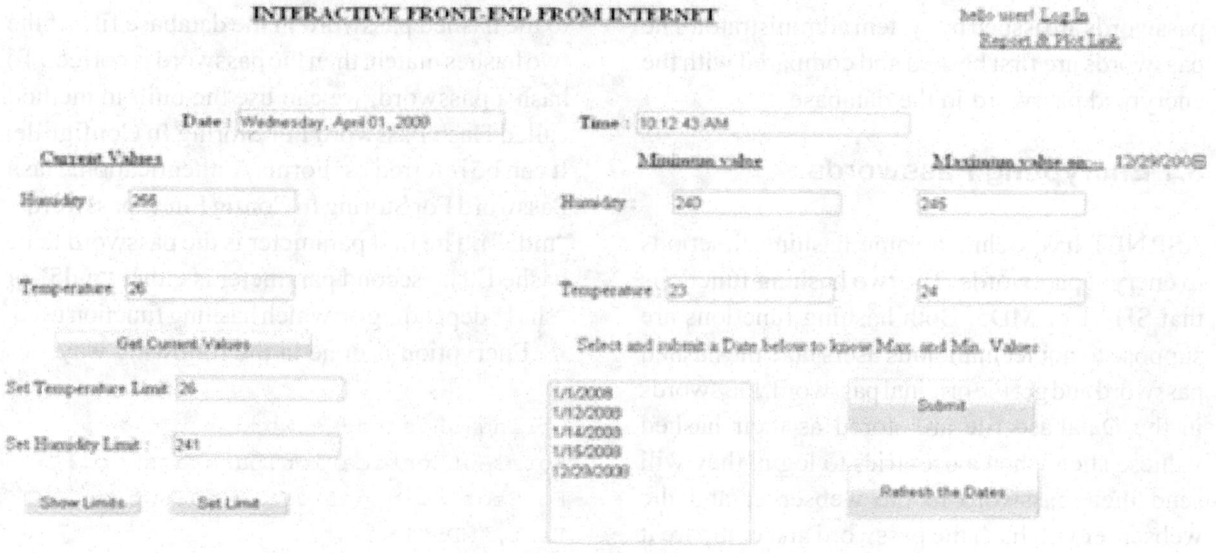

Figure 9. Login page

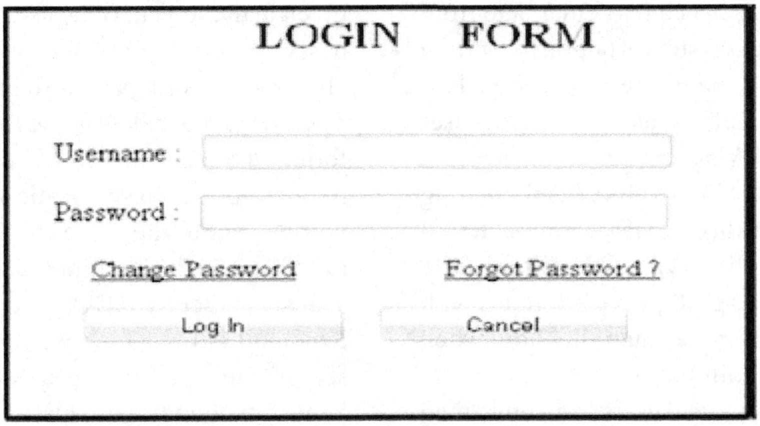

Figure 10. Forgot password form

passwords are issued by system administrator. The passwords are first hashed and compared with the encrypted password in the database.

6.1 Encrypting Passwords

ASP.NET has included some hashing functions to encrypt passwords. The two hashing functions that SHA1 or MD5. Both hashing functions are suppose to not let malicious users take the hashed password and get the original password. Passwords in the Database file are stored as their hashed values. Then when a user tries to login, they will send their password to the webserver and the webserver will hash the password and compare it to the hashed password in the database file. If the two hashes match, then the password is correct. To hash a password, we can use the built in method called Hash Password For Storing In ConfigFile. It can be referred as: Forms Authentication. Hash Password For Storing In Config File ("password", "md5"). The first parameter is the password to be hashed. The second parameter is either "md5" or "sha1" depending on which hashing function used.

Encryption is done in the following way:

```
String sHashedPassword =
FormsAuthentication.HashPassword
ForStoringInConfigFile(password.
Text,"MD5");
```

Figure 11. Change password form

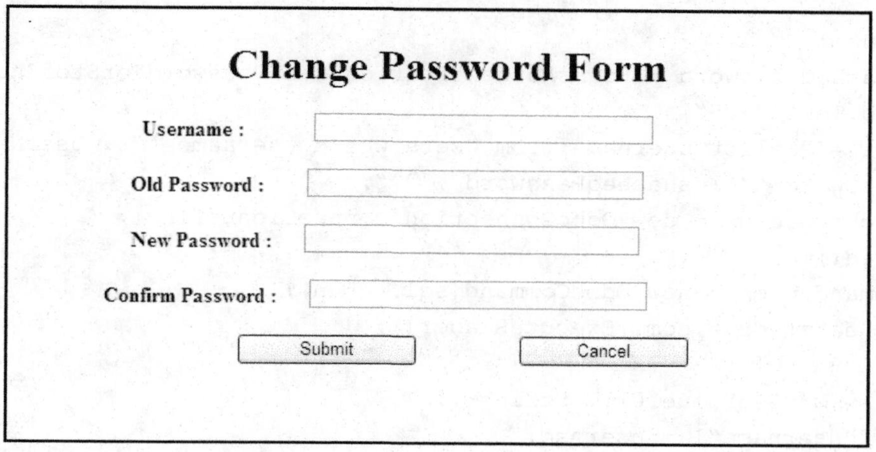

Change Password Form

Username :

Old Password :

New Password :

Confirm Password :

[Submit]   [Cancel]

User Accounts Stored in MySQL Database.

Storing user accounts in the web.config file has it's limitations. A lot of larger website will prefer to store the passwords in an SQL database or maybe a seperate XML/text file. So in this case, we won't have those optional <credential> and <user> tags in web.config file.

Authorization of user is saved in a session variable. The code for authorizing such login is shown in Algorithm 1.

Where "username" is the session parameter set for a user session. Each user will have a separate session value.

Once login is successful, the user is redirected back to the index webpage. The HashPassword-ForStoringInConfigFile method (described in the section above for encrypting password) is used. This function is used because the database will have the passwords hashed.

6.2 Implementation of Change Password Form

The sole purpose of granting authority to the web application lies in the administrator. The administrator has to insert a new user id (generally an email) into the users table database. He then gives a password to the inserted user(s) through user's email-id or through any communication media and request the users to change their password, (so as not to suspect the administrator putting wrong data on their behalf).

The user should be a registered/authorized user and should have his session set prior to changing his password. He should insert his old password which is required for further verification and security enhancement. If the old password match with the password in the database, the updation of password field takes place.

The procedure for changing password is given in Algorithm 2.

6.3 Implementation of Forgot Password Form and E-mail Process

If an authorized user forget his password same can be retrieved by using forgot password form. Developed System implements a mail server for sending an email message with authentication using ASP.NET 2.0 and C#.NET.

In the first step it is necessary to import the System.Net.Mail namespace.

The System.net.Mail namespace contains the SmtpClient and MailMessage classes which is

Algorithm 1.

```
String usernam;
  String sHashedPassword = FormsAuthentication.HashPasswordForStoringInConfigF
ile(password.Text,"MD5");
  String sql = "Select username from Users where username='" + UserName.Text +
"' and    password='" + sHashedPassword + "'";
  OdbcConnection conn = new OdbcConnection(connectionString);
    conn.Open();
    OdbcCommand comm = new OdbcCommand(sql, conn);
  OdbcDataReader dr = comm.ExecuteReader();
dr.Read();
    usernam = dr.GetValue(0).ToString();
    Session["username"] = usernam;
    if (usernam == "0")
      Response.Redirect("./login.aspx");
    else
      Response.Redirect("./index.aspx");
```

In this function, the FormsAuthentication.Authenticate function is used with some SQL code that will query the database for a username/password pair. If such a pair if found, then the credentials are correct and the user session parameters are set and saved in web server main memory for an entire user session and remains there until the user invalids the session parameter by logging out.

The session can be abandoned by writing:

```
if (((string)Session["username"] == "1"))
   {
     Session.Abandon();
     lbnlogin.Text = "Login";
     btnSetLimit.Text = "Set Limit";
     ......
     .......
   }
```

needed to send the email and specify the user credentials necessary to send authenticated email.

Using System.Net.Mail;

Email Client is called to, send the message using the variables from ASP.NET coded page. Next instantiate a System.Net, network Credential object with the necessary authentication info and assigning that object to the Credentials property of SmtpClient object.

For a user to be able to read his mail, it is required to connect his mail server. This is generally not the same machine as the web server. A mail server has to design to interact with the user's mailbox.

Algorithm 2.

```
string count;
String sHashedPassword = FormsAuthentication.HashPasswordForStoringInConfigFil
e(password.Text,"MD5");
    conn = new OdbcConnection(connectionString);
    conn.Open();
    sql = "select count(*) from users where username='" + UserName.Text + "'
and passwords='" + sHashedPassword + "'";
    comm = new OdbcCommand(sql, conn);
    dr = comm.ExecuteReader();
    dr.Read();
    count = dr.GetValue(0).ToString();
    conn.Close();
    dr.Close();
    comm.Dispose();
    conn.Dispose();
```
The TextBox3 and Textbox4 are new password and confirm new password respec-
tively as in change password web page.Update new password now:
```
    if (TextBox3.Text == TextBox4.Text)
    {
       if (count == "1")

        sql = "UPDATE users SET passwords= '" + TextBox3.Text + "' where user-
name ='" + UserName.Text + "'";
        conn = new OdbcConnection(connectionString);
        conn.Open();
        comm = new OdbcCommand(sql, conn);
        comm.ExecuteNonQuery();
        conn.Close();
        comm.Dispose();
        conn.Dispose();
```
There is no way to change the email-id or userid of a registered user. If ses-
sion is not set, the change password form will redirect the user to the login
page and request the user to authenticate with the web application first.
The following code performs this:
```
 if ((string)Session["usernam"] == "0")
    Response.Redirect("./login.aspx");
```

Details of Email Implementation

When password of a particular user is forgotten, the password can be recovered by sending the password to the user's email account. The user's email id is registered by the creating a new user for the application.

The user on entering the valid email-id in the email Text box gets a password in his email account. Mails are not sent to invalid email-id or that are not registered.

The protocol used for sending mail is Simple Mail Transfer Protocol. A Mail Transfer Agent (MTA), generally SendMail is used, for sending messages to the mail server. System uses the ASP. NET send() method of the Mail class.

The code behind the implementation is as follows in Algorithm 3.

7. CONCLUSION AND LINES FOR FUTURE WORK

Each day, our lives become more dependent on 'embedded systems', digital information technology that is embedded in our environment. Embedded systems are nowadays omnipresent and make it possible for creation of systems with a functionality that cannot be provided by human beings. Example application areas are consumer electronic products (e.g. CD players, microwave ovens), telecommunication (e.g. mobile phones), medical systems (e.g. pacemakers), traffic control (e.g. intelligent traffic lights), driving and car control (e.g. ABS), airborne equipment (e.g. fly-by-wire), and plant control (e.g. packaging machines, wafer steppers). The term embedded system thus encompasses a broad class of systems, ranging from simple microcontrollers to large and complex multi-processor and distributed systems.

Developed system can have a variety of uses in different applications. Monitoring and controlling of temperature and humidity has widest application requirement in areas ranging from industry to research. It has been also implementing in stated areas with different feasibility criteria with available technology and equipment for a long time. Available hardware and technology is having a great impact on its implementation. This work mainly focuses on use of readily available item and existing hardware set, at the same time making the system user friendly as well as reliable. This will certainly help in achieving economic feasibility. Considering the above facts in the developed system, it uses microcontroller AT89S52 from Atmel. Variety of microcontrollers in this category with some advanced features are produced, those products generally not made available everywhere due to some financial and some other constraints. Referring the same in the developed system AT89S52 does not have its in built ADC circuitry and direct interfacing features with USB port but it is readily available and cheap. Adding an extra ADC and Interfacing with COM port which provides a good solution with more reliability and making it more economically feasible with acceptable performance.

Considering the other criteria use of existing hardware setup and making it user friendly, system is interfaced with computer in the LAN. Considering the fact of availability of LAN in almost all the organizations will enable the organizations to implement such an application for remote monitoring and controlling. Use of computer will make it possible to provide users with interactive front end in monitor replacing push button keys of embedded boards with computer keyboard. With different application software it will be possible to store huge data in required format with adequate security. Representation of data in the form of report and graph also generated as per choice of user.

Performance of any system depends on accuracy. Here Performance is monitored in two levels, one being the performance of monitoring boards and other the performance of network or web. Performance of monitoring boards indicates how closely the sensor can measure the actual or real world temperature and humidity value. The more accurate a sensor is, better will be its performance. To achieve this, calibration is done with the values of appropriate devices comparing the sensor value displayed in LCD. Acceptable result is observed. The relays are also works properly at any set temperature and humidity automatically. Performance of the system from the remote client either Intranet or Internet depends on Network speed which is directly dependent on allotted bandwidth and congestion level of

Algorithm 3.

```
 Private bool SendMail (string to, string subject, string message, string
senderName)
{
Try
    {
    System.Net.Mail.MailMessage mail = new System.Net.MailMessage();
     Put the username and password of your mail server account
      System.Net.NetworkCredential cred = new
      System.Net.NetworkVCredential("jecmca@mail.com","myPassword");
      Mail.o.Add(to);
      Mail.Subject = subject;
      Put the sender address here
      Mail.From = new System.Net.MailAddress ("jecmca@mail.com", senderName);
      Mail.IsBodyHtml = true;
      Mail.Body = message;
      System.Net.Mail.SmtpClient("mail.com");
      Smtp.UseDefaultCredentials = false;
      Smtp.EnableSsl = false;
      Smtp.Credentials = cred;
      Finally send the mail
      Smtp.Send(mail);
    }
Catch (Exception)
  {
  Return false ;
  }
  Return true;
}
```

route. If required bandwidth is dedicated for the system, seamless online performance will be observed. Required performance is achieved during the testing of the application as Intranet as well as Internet (installing and configuring IIS in the LAN). Such a system will be feasible in applications where monitoring and controlling of temperature and humidity is very much essential such as Green Houses where this can be made possible from remote locations. However to make it flawless more experiments as well as

testing in real environment will be required (Sun & Wan Zhong, 2009; Spasov & Kakanov, 2004).

System can be further enhanced by using higher word length (16 bit) microprocessor/microcontroller with more accurate/sensitive sensors. This may be required in applications where more accuracy is desired. System can be further enhanced by assigning it more tasks for controlling like voltage, light etc. In such an application different levels of priority can be dynamically assigned. Task switching will be an important feature in such an application. It can be implemented easily in platforms like Linux. There are different types RTOS (Real Time Operating Systems) are commercially made available. However task switching can be implemented in attached computer in Linux like operating system using similar type of hardware. If processor like ARM is used for such application, Whole application may be possible to burn in to the processor's ROM with necessary RTOS enabling task switching depending on priority.

REFERENCES

AllDataSheet.com. (n.d.). Retrieved from www.alldatasheet.com/ULN2003/TEXAS/

Atmel corporation. (2000). *AT89S52 data sheet, 8-bit microcontroller with 8k bytes flash.* Atmel Data book, 2000 update.

Baruah, S., Kakoti Mahanta, A., & Sharma, K. C. (2009). A comparative study on client server technology and Web technology in design and implementation of an embedded system used for monitoring and controlling of physical parameters. *Proceedings of 4th International Conference for Internet Technology and Secured Transaction* (IC-ITST-2009, London, UK, 9-12 November 2009.

Baruah, S., Kakoti Mahanta, A., & Sharma, K. C. (2010). A review of designing and implementing an embedded system using client server and Web technology for monitoring and controlling of physical parameters. *International Journal for Infonomics, 3*(1), 273-282. *ISSN, 1742,* 4712.

Boehm, A., & Lowe, D. (2008). *Murach ASP. NET 3.5 web programming with VB 2008.* New Delhi, India: SPD.

Boehm, A., & Murach, J. (2008). *Murach's ASP. NET 3.5 web programming with C#2008.* New Delhi, India: SPD.

8052com. (n.d.). *Introduction to LCD programming tutorial by Craig Steiner Copyright 1997 -2005 by Vault Information Services LLC.* Retrieved from http://8052.com/tutlcd.phtml

Comer, S. (2005). *Internetworking with TCP/IP (Vol. 1-3).* New Delhi, India: Pearson Education.

Dietikon, P. L. (2001). *RS232 interface using MAX232, written by Peter Luethi Dietikon,* Switzerland, Revision-1.03.

Howell, N. (2004). *Using Internet information server.* New Delhi, India: PHI.

Kalsi, H. S. (1999). *Electronic instrumentation.* New Delhi, India: Tata McGraw-Hill Ltd.

Lewis, D. W. (2003). *Fundamentals of embedded software- Where C and assembly meet.* New Delhi, India: Prentice Hall of India.

Maxim. (n.d.). *Home page.* Retrieved from www.maxim-ic.com

Mazidi, M. A., & Mazidi, J. G. (2007). *The 8051 microcontroller and embedded systems.* Pearson Education Ltd.

Microelectronics, S. T. (2002). *Data book.* Retrieved from http://www.st.com

National Instruments. (n.d.). *A review of PC-based data logging and recording techniques.* Retrieved from www.ni.com/dataloggers

National Semiconductor Corporation. (2000). *LM35 datasheet, precision centigrade temperature sensors.* Atmel data book, November 2000 update.

National Semiconductor Corporation. (2002). *ADC 0809 data sheet, 8-bit microprocessor compatible A/D converters with 8-channel multiplexer.*

Prince, A., & Lowe, D. (2005). *Murach VB.NET 3.5 database programming with ADO.NET.* New Delhi, India: SPD.

Spasov, G., & Kakankov, N. (2004). CGI based applications for distributed systems for monitoring temperature and humidity. In *Proceedings of 5th International Conference on Computer Systems and Technologies-Compsys Tech* 2004, Rousse, Bulgeria, (pp. 1-6). ISBN 954-9641-38-4

Sun, R. A., & Wan Zhong, S. D.-C. (2009, January). Based on embedded database greenhouse temperature and humidity intelligent control system. *WSEAS Transactions on Circuits and Systems 8*(1), 41-52. ISSN: 1109-2734

Welling, L., & Thomson, L. (2004). *PHP and MySQL Web development*. Pearson Education.

Wikipedia. (n.d.). Liquid crystal display. Retrieved from http://en.wikipedia.org/wiki/Liquid_crystal_display

Wikipedia. (n.d.). Temperature measurement. Retrieved from http://en.wikipedia.org/wiki/temperature-measurement

KEY TERMS AND DEFINITIONS

Calibration: Calibration is the validation of specific measurement techniques and equipment. At the simplest level, calibration is a comparison between measurements-one of known magnitude or correctness made or set with one device and another measurement made in as similar a way as possible with a second device.

COM Port: Is a 9 or 25 pin serial port through which information transfers in or out one bit at a time.

Front-End: Front-end and characterize program interfaces and services relative to the initial user of these interfaces and services.

Intranet: An intranet is a private computer network that uses Internet Protocol technologies to securely share any part of an organization's information within that organization. The term is used in contrast to internet.

LAN: A local area network (LAN) is a computer network that connects computers and devices in a limited geographical area such as home, school, computer laboratory or office building.

Mail Server: A mail server also known as a mail transfer agent or MTA, a mail transport agent, a mail router or an Internet maile) is an application that receives incoming e-mail from users and forwards outgoing e-mail for delivery. A computer dedicated to running such applications is also called a mail server.

Web Server: A web server can be referred to as either the hardware, the computer or the software, the computer application that helps to deliver content that can be accessed through the internet.

Chapter 12
Distributed Key Management Scheme Based on CL-PKC in P2P Networks

Zhongwen Li
Chengdu University, China

Zhibin Xu
Xiamen University, China

Chen Liang
Xiamen University, China

ABSTRACT

P2P networks have characteristics of decentralization, autonomy, and dynamicity. The security problems caused by these characteristics have seriously affected further development of P2P networks. The authors did research on CL-PKC key management schemes. (1) They propose a certificateless-based key distribution scheme with multiple trusted centers that fits the characteristics of P2P networks, and analyzed its security. (2) They also propose an improved interactive key agreement protocol across multiple domains, and then compare it with some existing key agreement protocol from aspects of security and computational efficiency. (3) The authors have implemented the proposed key management schemes, then verified their correctness and tested their computational efficiency. Combined with master key share management and key management of nodes, this system constructed a complete certificateless-based key management model, which is an exploration to solve security problems in P2P networks.

BACKGROUND

P2P (Peer to Peer) that is peer computing or peer networks, is a new network technology. Pure P2P network does not have any client or server. Thousands of computers connected to each other

are on the equal status, while serving as a client (resource requestor) and server (resource provider) role. With the development of P2P networks, complete anonymity of the safety problem has seriously affected the further development of P2P networks. For example, in file-sharing system, the selfish users only enjoy the service refused

DOI: 10.4018/978-1-4666-0978-5.ch012

to provide services for other users ("freeriding" phenomenon) (Dinger & Hartenstein, 2006). This series of problem's solution is to build a reputation system in P2P networks. To get the nodes' reputation value, it needs authenticate the identity of the node at first. Therefore, the study on highly robust certification P2P system becomes one of the hot current P2P studies.

Traditional PKI needs a certificate to bind an identity and its public key, and certificate management in PKI is very complicated, including certificate distribution, certificate storage, certificate verification, certificate update, and certificate revocation. These processes need to consume a large amount of CPU resources and bandwidth resources. These problems prevent the implementation of PKI in the P2P network efficiently. The identity of public key cryptography (ID-PKC, Identity-based Public Key Cryptography) (Shamir, 1984), not only have the specific problem of key escrow, but also generally only is fit for small networks which do not ask for demanding security, but not fit for P2P networks which need for secure authentication (Aberer & Despotovich, 2002).

At Asiacrypt 2003, Al-Riyami and Paterson first proposed the notion of certificateless public key cryptography (CL-PKC, Certificateless Public Key Cryptography) (Al-Riyami & Pasterson, 2003). As CL-PKC does not need certificates to authenticate public keys, therefore there is no certificate management problem, and it also avoids the key escrow problem in ID-PKC. Therefore, CL-PKC is considered as more suitable for P2P network authentication scheme.

The existence of single trusted center limits the network scalability, also causes risks of single-point failure. Therefore, many authentication schemes without trusted center in P2P networks have been proposed. However, those schemes are only applicable to applications which do not need high-level security, and the signature of node can not provide a true non-repudiation feature. In fact, all schemes without trusted center have the similar disadvantages. Using Multi-KGCs in P2P networks can avoid the shortcomings:

1. The number of trusted KGCs P2P network can dynamically adjust accoding to the number of nodes to improve the scalability of P2P networks.
2. Multi- trusted KGCs can avoid single-point failure, to improve the robustness of P2P networks
3. It distributes the power of trusted KGCs to prevent the attacker to steal the master key, which can improve the security of P2P networks.

In summary, research on the certificateless-based multi-KGCs key distribution schemes that are fit for the characteristics of P2P networks is currently one of the problems needed to be solved. We apply the key generation schemes to the large-scale P2P networks, and study the corresponding session key generation and key management issues, thereby establishing a complete and reliable distributed key management system.

THE KEY DISTRIBUTION SCHEME WITH MULTIPLE TRUSTED CENTERS

In this section, we propose a certificateless-based key distribution scheme with Multi-KGCs that fits the characteristics of P2P networks, and analyzes its security.

A. Design Goals and Design Model

*   **Design Goals:** The existence of single trusted center limits the network scalability, also causes risks of single-point failure. If the security of authentication can not be guaranteed, let along the security of signature and reputation systems. For the above reasons, our design will introduce a

(t, n)-threshold CL-PKC scheme to avoid bottlenecks and security risks caused by these problems. Our system will achieve the following goals:

- KGCs only participate when nodes apply for partial private keys, and mutual authentication between nodes does not require KGCs' participation. In addition, there are n KGCs in the system totally, each time a node applies for the partial private key only needs t KGCs to participate. So it greatly reduces the load of KGCs and fits large-scale P2P networks.
- As long as there are at least t KGCs accessible, users can apply for the partial private key. So it avoids risks of single-point failure.
- Only if the adversary obtains at least t KGCs' keys or at least t KGCs collude, entities' partial private keys can be computed. So it greatly increases the difficulty of collusion, and improves the security of the system.
- System Model

Reference (Wang et al., 2005) proposes a certificateless-based (t, n)-threshold scheme, but the scheme needs a KGCs manager called KGC-clerk and an organization manager called organization-clerk. The security of the scheme relies on the honesty of the two managers. If the two managers collude, they can generate the partial private key of any entity. In addition, because it needs KGC-clerk to generate partial private keys for nodes, single-point failure of KGC-clerk will cause the whole key distribution system in P2P network paralyzed.

Our Scheme no longer needs organization-clerk, and KGC-clerk is only necessary in the setup phase. KGC-clerk generates the master key, then uses threshold technology to divide the master key into n secret shares, and sent them to n KGCs separately. After the setup phase, KGC-clerk destroys the master key, all secret shares and all parameters used in the setup phase. And then KGC-clerk will be involved neither in partial-private-key-extract phase, nor in any other activity. In partial-private-key-extract phase, the user applies to KGCs group for partial private key. Then at least t KGCs generate the partial private key shares separately, and send them to the user. After receiving at least t partial private key shares, the user can compute its partial private key, and then generates its private key by combining with the secret value he chose. In this way, compared with the scheme in (Wang et al., 2005), our scheme has effectively solved security problems and risks of single-point failure caused by the two centers (KGC-clerk and organization-clerk). So it can ensure security and robustness of the key generation process.

B. A Certificateless-Based Multi-KGCs Key Distribution Scheme

- **Key Distribution Scheme:** Next, we give our certificateless-based multi-KGCs key distribution scheme which fits the characteristics of P2P networks:

Let G_1 denote an additive group of large prime order q and G_2 denote a multiplicative group of the same order. We let P denote a generator of G_1. Assume e: $G_1 \times G_1 \to G_2$ be a bilinear pairing map. Define a hash function: H: $\{0, 1\}^* \to G_1$.

[Setup]

- KGC-clerk does the followings:

```
For 0 ≤ i ≤ t - 1, randomly choose r_i
∈_R Z_q.
Set s = r_0 as the master key, comput-
er P_0 = sP ∈ G_1, and publish params=<
G_1, G_2, e, q, P, P_0, H > as the system
public parameters.
Set R(x) = r_0 + r_1x + r_2x² + ...+ r_{t-1}x^{t-1}
(mod q) ∈ Z_q[X]. For 1 ≤ i ≤ n, com-
```

pute $s_i = R(i) \in Z_q$, and send s_i to the corresponding KGC_i via secure channels.

To prevent the master key leaking, KGC-clerk must destroy the master key s, all s_i and all r_i.

- When receiving s_i, each KGC_i computes $P_0^i = s_iP \in G_1$, then publishes P_0^i and keeps s_i secret.

[Set-Secret-Value]

- Node A randomly chooses a secret value $x_A \in_R Z_q$.

[Set-Public-Key]

- Node A computes its public key $P_A=<X_A, Y_A>$, where $X_A = x_AP$, $Y_A = x_AP_0$, and then send P_A to at least t KGC_i.

[Partial-Private-Key-Extract]

- When receiving node A's public key P_A from node A, each KGC_i computes node A' partial private key share $D_A^i = s_i \cdot Q_A = s_i \cdot H(id_A \| P_A) \in G_1$, where $Q_A = H(id_A \| P_A) \in G_1$. And then KGC_i sends D_A^i to node A
- After receiving D_A^i from KGC_i, node A check the validity of D_A^i (D_A^i is valid Iff the equation $e(D_A^i, P) = e(Q_A, P_0^i)$ holds). When node A has received at least t valid A's partial private key shares from KGC_i (without loss of generality, assume they are $D_A^1, D_A^2, …, D_A^t$ respectively), node A computes its partial private key $D_A = \sum_{i=1}^{t}$

$\lambda_{0,j}D_A^i = s \cdot Q_A$, where $\lambda_{x,j} = \prod_{\substack{i=1 \\ i \neq j}}^{t} \frac{x-i}{j-i}$

(mod q). Then node A computes $Q_A = H$

$(ID_A \| P_A) \in G_1$ and check the validity of D_A (D_A is valid Iff the equation $e(D_A, P) = e(Q_A, P_0)$ holds).

[Set-Private-Key]

- Node A combines partial private key D_A and the secret value x_A to obtain its private key $S_A=<D_A, x_A>$.
- Security Analysis

Current CL-PKC security models generally consider two adversary attack models: public key replacement attack and attack on the master key. Next, we consider these two attacks separately:

Public Key Replacement Attack:

In traditional PKI, the authenticity of public keys is guaranteed by certificates. In ID-PKC, public keys are derived from certain aspects of users' identities directly. In CL-PKC, entity A's public key is not only related to A's identity, but also related to system public parameters and the secret value A chose. So the public key replacement attack must be considered in CL-PKC.

In CL-PKC, the forms of public/private keys we use is (They're also the forms which are recognized secure): Entity A's public key $P_A = <x_AP, x_AP_0>$ and its private key $S_A = <D_A, x_A>$, where $D_A=sH(ID_A \| P_A)$ denotes partial private key. The identity information ID_A contained in the partial private key is the foundation to resist to public key replacement attack in CL-PKC. Assume node A want to send message m to node B, then A send $<ID_A, P_A, m, Sign(m)>$ to B. Node B can verify the signature by using A's public key P_A, A's identity ID_A and system public parameters params. If node C want to personate A, C chooses a secret value x_A' and replace P_A with P_A', where $P_A'= <x_A'P, x_A'P_0>$. Then C sends $<ID_A, P_A', m, Sign'(m)>$ to B. Assume that the signature algorithm used is unforgeable. So C must have the private key S_A' corresponding to P_A', if C wants to generate a signature which can be verified by P_A'. The form of S_A' should be $<D_A', x_A'>$, where $D_A' = sH(ID_A \| P_A')$. But node C can not obtain partial private key D_A', because KGC will refuse to generate the partial private key which contains node A' identity for node C. Therefore, even if C replaces A's public key, C can not get valid corresponding private key. Of course, whether the certificateless signature can resist to public key replacement attack depends on the specific signature scheme. A secure signature scheme must guarantee that only if one node has the legitimate private key, it can generate the signature which can be verified by the corresponding public key.

Attack on the Master Key

Our scheme introduces the secret sharing scheme based on Lagrange interpolating polynomial (Pedersen, 1992) and let n KGCs share the master key s. For a polynomial of degree t-1, it needs at least t points to reconstruct the polynomial by solving linear equations. If there are less than t points, no information of the polynomial can be got. Only if the attacker obtains at least t s_i or at least t KGCs collude, the master key s can be recomputed. So it greatly reduces the possibility of leakage of the master key.

C. Dynamic Adjustment of (t,n)- Threshold

- The generation of master key share

In the hybrid P2P networks, when the nodes gradually increase and the super peers providing services are overburdened, the scheme can choose some nodes with higher reputation in the P2P network, upgrades them to be super nodes, and then the nodes provide the KGC services for new peers. To get more details about the credibility models in P2P networks and the credit value, you maight as well refer to (Xi & Wang, 2009) (Aberer & Despotovich, 2002) (Li & Liu, 2003).

According that a non-super-node can be upgraded to a super node, we can consider that the original (t, n) threshold is adjusted to (t, n +1) threshold, which will enhance the self-adaptability of nodes expansion in the hybrid P2P network, and greatly increase the hybrid P2P network scalability.

When a new node is required to upgrade to be a KGC, the scheme need generate a new master key share for it. The node need have a unique KGC number, which is greater than or equal to 1, and is different from any existing KGC. We assume that the number of nodes is p (called the node KGCp). At the time, to generate a new master key share, it at least needs t KGCs.

More than t KCG_i computes the partial master key share s_{ip} and send the node P:

$$s_{ip} = s_i L_i(p), \text{ which}$$

$$L_i(p) = \sum_{j=1, j \neq i}^{k} \frac{p-j}{(i-j)}(\text{mod } q)$$

After the node P receive at least t partial master key shares, it can get the master key S_p

$$S_p = \sum_{i=1}^{k} S_{ip}$$

- Updation of the master key share

In the P2P network, when some KGC member quit the newwork, if the master key is all the same, the master key shares of that KGC can be used to participate in the conspiracy attack. So when a certain number of KGC exit (for example, $r \geq \left\lceil \frac{t}{2} \right\rceil$), in order to ensure the system's ability to tolerate evil KGC, we can update the KGC's master key share. Note that the update does not change the system master key share of the master key, so the node has the shares can continue to use them and does not need to update them. Share of the new master key systems still constitutes a master key (t, n) threshold secret sharing. KGC remove the old master key share, to use the new master key share. Master key share of the update process all the KGC does not need to participate, as long as t a KGC can be done in updating theshare of the master key, and do not need to restore the system master key. The new master key share is completely independent from the old master key shares, so opponents can not be combined with the new master key share and the old master key shares to restore the system's master key. The t KGCs will do the following things:

KGC$_i$ randomly select t-1 random number (r_{i1}, $r_{i2} \dots r_{it}$), which $R_i(x) = 0 + r_{i1}x + r_{i2}x^2 + \dots + r_{i(t-1)}x^{t-1} \in Z_q[X]$. For $1 \leq j \leq n$, it compute $S_{ij} = R_i(j)$. Then, KGC$_i$ sends S$_{ij}$ to the corresponding KGC$_j$.

After KGC$_j$ recevie S$_{1j}$, S$_{2j}$, \dots S$_{tj}$, it can calculate the new master key share

$$S'_j : S'_j = S_j + \sum_{i=1}^{t} S_{ij}$$

If there is enough time, the adversary may get enough master key shares reaching the threshold number t. To prevent this, using the same method, we can also update the master key shares regularly, to eliminate the dishonest KGC and ensure system security and reliability. Thus, the adversary needs to update this key period of a master key for at least t shares, greatly increasing the difficulty of an adversary attack. Now there are some verifiable secret sharing schemes (Chor et al., 1985) (Feldman, 1987) (Pedersen, 1992), and you can learn from these programs and identify the KGC.

D. Revocation and Updation the Node Key

- Revocation of the master key

In P2P networks, some nodes may be malicious or dishonest behavior. For the malicious nodes, we need some appropriate revocation mechanisms to present them from interacting with normal nodes.

Node key consists of three steps: the report of a malicious act, the certificate generation of removing the master key and the validation of certificate for removing the master key.

- Update of the master key

In a traditional PKI model, the certificate contains a default validity period of its public key to control the validity of the certificate. Paper (Boneh & Franklin, 2001) proposes a model for ID-PKC, which joined the period of validity in the public key. ID-PKC system generally put the hash value of the identity of the entity as a public key, for example, assume Bob's identity as "bob@hotmail.com", then Bob's public key is H ("bob@hotmail.com"). Now, assume that the validity of the key is one day, then Bob's public key can be H (bob@hotmail.com||Current-Date), which Current-Date shows the current date. PKG generates the private key every day, and sends it to Bob. The way of generating the part of the private key in CL-PKC is similar with the generation type of private key in ID-PKC, so the control method of validity period of its public key in CL-PKC could be similar with ID-PKC.

KEY AGREEMENT PROTOCOL

This section divides the certificateless key agreement into non-interactive key agreement, non-interactive key agreement of cross-domain, interactive key agreement and interactive key agreement of cross-domain. Lacking of space, description and analysis of specific agreements can be found in the reference. Then we propose an improved interactive key agreement of cross-domain, the agreement allows different generator parameters of the public parameters in different domain, which has better applicability.

A. Key Agreement

Sang (2009) proposes two non-interactive authentication key agreements, within and across domains, and analysis the security of the two non-interactive key agreement protocol when they against the public key substitution attack and the master key leakage attack. One of the agreements is non-interactive key agreement, and the other is non-interactive key agreement of cross-domain. Two of the protocols require the same generator parameter P of the public parameters and the same hash function H1 and H2.

When Al-Riyami and Paterson firstly proposed the CL-PKC, they also gave an certificateless interactive key agreement, but the agreement required large amount of calculation, the two communicating parties need to calculate totally eight bilinears, and there are loopholes in security analysis, the agreement cannot resist the master key leakage attack (KCI, Key-Compromise Impersonation). Paper (Zhu & Dong, 2006) presented an interactive key agreement (Protocol III), the agreement only need to calculate six bilinears, and can resist the KCI attack.

Tarjei studied on authenticated key agreement protocols in his dissertation, and gave a certificateless interaction key agreement protocol of cross-domain (Mandt, 2006) (Protocol IV).

B. Key Agreement of Cross-Domain with Different Generator Parameter

- System Model

The interactive key agreements of cross-domain currently always assume that the two domains have different primary key (set to s1 and s2), but require the same generator parameter P of the public system parameters in the two domains. This section presents a new interactive key agreement of cross-domain, the agreement allows that the generator parameters P of the public system parameters in the field can be different (set to P

and P'). In addition, the hash function H2 of the public system parameters can also be different, the two interactive sides can use the hash function H2 which is used by the session initiator. The system public parameters of the group G1, G2, bilinear map e, and the hash function H1 must be the same.

Assume that the session Initiator is located in the domain F_1, and the recipient is located in the domain F_2. The master key for the domain F_1 is s_1, the public system parameters are <G1, G2, e, P, P0, H1, H2>, where $P_0 = s_1 P$. The master key for the domain F_2 is s_2, the public system parameters are <G_1, G_2, e, P', P_0', H_1, H_2'>, where $P_0' = s_2 P'$. Assume both parties know or interact with each other to get the public system parameters from each other.

- Agreement Description

Protocol V:

1. Node A selects a random number $a \in R$ Zq, calculates $T_A = a P'$, $W_A = aP$, and then sends T_A, W_A, P_A to node B.

Node B receives the T_A, W_A, P_A from node A, and verify the legality of the public key of node A:

$$e\left(X_A, P_0\right) = e\left(Y_A, P\right)$$

If the authentication is successful, node B selects $b \in_R Z_q$, calculates $W_B = b P'$, and sends T_B, W_B, P_B to node A, then node B calculates the Session key $K_{A,B}$:

$$Q_A = H_1(ID_A \parallel P_A)$$

$$K_B = e(x_B D_B, T_A)\, e(Q_A, Y_A)^b$$
$$= e(Q_B, P')^{as_2 x_B} e(Q_A, P)^{bs_1 x_A}$$

Table 1. Comparison of safety

protocol	security Property	authntication	KnSK	PFwS	KCI
I		Yes	Yes	No	No
II		Yes	Yes	No	No
III		Yes	Yes	Yes	Yes
IV		Yes	Yes	Yes	Yes
V		Yes	Yes	Yes	Yes

$$K_{A,B} = H_2\left(K_B \parallel bW_A \parallel bT_A\right) = H_2\left(K_B \parallel abP \parallel abP'\right)$$

After the node A received the T_B, W_B, P_B, it verified the legality of the public key of node B by:

$$e\left(X_B, P_0'\right) = e\left(Y_B, P'\right)$$

If the authentication is successful, calculates the Session key $K_{A,B}$:

$$Q_B = H_1\left(ID_B \parallel P_B\right)$$

$$K_A = e\left(x_A D_A, T_B\right)e\left(Q_B, Y_B\right)^a$$
$$= e\left(Q_A, P\right)^{bs_1 x_A} e\left(Q_B, P'\right)^{as_2 x_B} = K_B$$

$$K_{A,B} = H_2\left(K_A \parallel aT_B \parallel aW_B\right) = H_2\left(K_B \parallel abP \parallel abP'\right)$$

C. Analysis and Comparison of the Five Agreements

- Comparison of safety

Analysis and comparison of the security aspects of five agreements from authentication, KnSK, it is showed by Table 1.

- Comparison of computational efficiency

The main advantage of Non-interactive key agreement protocol is efficiency, because of the savings in communication overhead. But at the cost of its security properties Compared with the interactive key agreement (Do not have perfect forward secrecy, cannot resist the attack with a long fake key). It is showed by Table 2.

IMPLEMENTATION OF KEY MANAGEMENT IN P2P NETWORKS

This section designs and implements the multi-trusted distributed key generation scheme of Section III and the session key negotiation of Section IV to verify the correctness of these programs, and test their efficiency. In the Respect of the management of the KGC's master key, this section realizes the initialization about the system parameters, the generation, update and Revocation of the master key of KGC's group. In the Respect of the key management of nodes, this section realizes the generation of the private key of the node, and the generation of of the communication session key between the nodes. System model will be achieved by combining the management of the master key and the key management of nodes. We will construct a complete key management model based on certificateless.

D. Selection of System Scheme

1. Hardware environment:
    ◦ CPU: Intel(R) Core(TM) 2 Duo CPU T5750 @ 2.00GHz
    ◦ Memory: 2GB

Table 2. Comparison of computational efficiency

protocol \ security Property	Cross domain	interactive	amount of calculation about bilinears(Do not use pre computation)	amount of calculation about bilinears(use precomputation)
I	No	No	10	2
II	Yes	No	8	4
III	No	Yes	6	2
IV	Yes	Yes	8	4
V	Yes	Yes	8	4

2. Software Environment:
   ◦ Development environment:Microsoft Visual Studio 2008
   ◦ Development language:C++
   ◦ Operating system:Microsoft Windows Vista
   ◦ Elliptic Curve library:Miracl

E. Yes

• System Design and Implementation

KGC clerk firstly makes the system initialization, and shares the generated master key with the appropriate KGCi.KGCi_receives the master key portion, and then provides the private key generation services for nodes in the system or provides the master key generation services for the new KGCp. In addition, KGCs group can also update the master key if it is needed. Cluster nodes can apply the private key portion to the KGCs group. After gaining sufficient partial keys portion, the nodes can calculate their partial private key, and then combines with their secret values to form their private key. Two nodes which have gained the legal private key can communicate with each other by the key agreement protocol to generate a common session key for secure communications. System model shown in Figure 1.

1. Global parameters initialization for Miracl

Miracl library requires a global program initializes firstly, including the need for storage and output settings to the large binary integer, where we set it to 16 hex.

2. KGC initialization

All the certificateless schemes currently assume that the nodes in the network can successfully obtain the correct system public parameters. Therefore, in our experiments, we assume that the KGC clerks generate the public system parameters in the initialization of the system. and then share the master key portion si to KGCi while sending the system public parameters. Nodes in P2P network can always obtain the system public parameters from any KGCi.

First of all, KGC selects the master key s, generates the system public parameters and make them known to the public. Calculates the master key Portion si, and then sends the si to the appropriate KGCi through the secure channel. We call KGC_init function to make the system initialization, the function prototype is Big* KGC_init(CommonParameters& parameters, Big& s), the incoming parameter must be set to the required threshold parameter t, n. KGC_init makes the assignment for the other system public

Figure 1. System model (n=5, t=2)

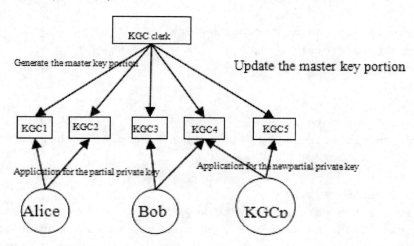

parameters, and s will be assigned to the selected master key. The return value of KGC_init are the n Portions of the master key generated by the KGC clerk si. After the KGCi received they own master key Portion si they calculate P0i[i] = si[i] * parameters.P and make P0i[i] known to the public. We can use the following code in Algorithm 1 to initialize the KGC:

After the node A receives the t partial private key portions from KGCi, it can call the function aggregate_partial_private_key to form the partial key. The prototype of the function is aggregate_ partial_private_key (CommonParameters parameters, ECn *DAi, int *choose, ECn *P0i, ECn QA). Firstly, the node A verifies the legitimacy of every DAi by e(DAi, P) = e(QA, P0i).and then calculates its partial key DA by Lagrange interpolation formula. Finally, it verifies the legitimacy of DA by e(DA, P) = e(QA, P0).

The Generation of Master Key Portion

When it comes to need to upgrade the node P to KGCp, the node P need to apply for master key portion sp. First, node P selectes t KGCi randomly and sends them the applications of the master key portion: choose = choose_t_from_n

(parameters.t, parameters.n). Each KGCi calculates the master key portion for node P. After receives the t master key portions, the node P can calculate its master key portion, and provide the private key portion generation services for nodes in the system. The node P can call the function aggregate_new_master_key_share to combine the t partial master key portion to form the master key portion sp: Big new_si = aggregate_new_master_key_share(parameters, sip).

Update the Master Key Portion

When it comes to need to update the master key portion, t KGCi generate the sij in accordance with the steps described in Section 3.2.2, and send it to the corresponding KGCj: sij[i]=renew_master_key_generate_sij(parameters);

When each KGCj has received t sij, they can update their own master key portion:

```
newsi[i]=enew_master_key_aggregate_
sij(parameters, si[i], sij, i);
```

• Analysis of experimental data

The time needed for each step of distributed multi-trusted key generation were showed in

Algorithm 1.

```
// KGC clerk initialize the System parameters
CommonParameters parameters;
parameters.t = 5;
parameters.n = 10;
Big s;
Big* si = KGC_init(parameters, s);
// KGCi receive the si,calculate P0i[i]=si[i]*P, and make them known to the
public
// P0i[i]
P0i[i] = si[i] * parameters.P;
(3) Nodes apply for the partial private key
After the KGCi Received the master key portion si, it can provide the private
key generation services for Cluster node.First, node A steps Set-Secret-Value,
chooses its own secret value xA, the secret value xA is a large integer less
than parameters.q chosen randomly:
PrivateKey sA;
sA.x = rand (parameters.q);
Then, node A steps Extract-Public-Key, calculate the public key PA = <XA,
YA>,which XA = xA * P,YA = xA * P0:
PublicKey PA;
PA.X = sA.x * parameters.P;
PA.Y = sA.x * parameters.P0;
Next, node A selects t KGCi randomly and  sends the partial private key por-
tion along with the PA. We can call the function choose_t_from_n(parameters.t,
parameters.n) to select t KGCi from n randomly.  The functions store the t KGCi
in the array and then return the first pointer of the array. After the t KGCi
receives the requests, they call the function extract_partial_private_key_shar
to form the partial private key Portion DAi[i] for node A, and then send it to
node A. The function comes true as follows:
ECn extract_partial_private_key_share(ZZn si,PublicKey PA, string idA, Common-
Parameters parameters)
{
        ECn QA = cal_QA(idA, PA, parameters);
        ECn DAi = si * QA;
        return DAi;
}
```

table 3. Because the KGC initialization, generate the master key portion and update the master key portion involve large integer arithmetic, so the computational overhead are small, and the time-consuming are short. But the process of the application for the partial private key for the node involves the elliptic curve operations specially the computing pairings, so it needs more time consuming.

Table 3. Time needed for distributed multi-trusted key generation

Operation	time
KGC initialization	32 ms
Form the partial private key	640 ms
Generate the master key portion	24 ms
Update the master key portion	16 ms

F. Session Key Agreement between Nodes

- System Design and Implementation

In non-interactive key agreement protocol, we can call the function bool check_public_key(PublicKey Pk, CommonParameters parameters) to verify the public key of the node, and call the function bool check_partial_private_key(ECn DB, ECn QB, CommonParameters parameters) to verify the partial private key of the node.

In the cross-domain key agreement protocol, each of the KGC clerks from the two domains executes the system initialization. For each part of the domain, KGC's group generates the private key portion. Subsequently, the Node A and Node B apply for the partial private key to the two parts of the domain KGCi, and then combine it with their secret values to form their private keys. After their private keys are generated, the node A and node B can perform cross-domain key agreement protocol.

- Analysis of experimental data

The interaction key agreement of cross-domain (protocol V) presented in this paper has similar time efficiency with the interactions key agreement of cross-domain (protocol IV) proposed by Tarjei. However, compared with the protocol IV, protocol V allows different generator parameters of the public parameters in different domain, which has better applicability (Table 4).

CONCLUSION

P2P network using is getting more and more widespread currently, it has received more and more attention about security problems, but the existing key distribution schemes are not well suited for P2P networks because of their security or the defects of robustness. This paper presents a certificateless key generation scheme based on distributed multi-trusted program adapt to the characteristics of P2P network, and then analyzes

Table 4. Session key agreement for nodes

Protocol \ Computational efficiency	Interactive	Cross-domain	Amount of calculation about bilinears (Do not use Pre-computation)	amount of calculation about bilinears (use Pre-computation)	time (Do not use pre computation)	Time (use Pre-computation)
I	No	No	10	2	405ms	124ms
II	Yes	No	8	4	359ms	234ms
III	No	Yes	6	2	312ms	172ms
IV	Yes	Yes	8	4	369ms	250ms
V	Yes	Yes	8	4	375ms	234ms

the security of the scheme. The scheme has the following advantages: (1) the introduction of threshold technology can effectively avoid the single point failure and the master key leakage exists in the single trusted system. (2) Using hybrid super-node in the P2P network as KGC consistent with the characteristics of hybrid P2P network. Because the super-node is not entirely credible, the scheme also uses the threshold technique to limit the right of the super-node to ensure the security of the system. (3) In addition to key distribution process, there is no need of the KGCs group (super nodes), reducing the load of the KGCs group. (4) One single trusted center only exists in the system initialization phase, reducing the risk of attack. In addition, we also discuss how to share and update the master key generation.

This paper also classifies and compares the present several certificateless key agreement protocols, and then presents an improved interactive key agreement of cross-domain that allows different generator parameters of the public parameters in different domain, which has better applicability.

REFERENCES

Aberer, K., & Despotovic, Z. (2002). Managing trust in a peer-2-peer information system. *Proceedings the Tenth International Conference on Information and Knowledge Management.*

Al-Riyami, S. S., & Paterson, K. G. (2003). Certificateless public key cryptography. In Laih, C. S. (Ed.), *ASIACRYPT 2003, LNCS 2894* (pp. 452–473).

Boneh, D., & Franklin, M. (2001). Identity-based encryption from the Weil Pairing. In Kilian, J. (Ed.), *CRYPTO 2001, LNCS 2139* (pp. 213–229). doi:10.1007/3-540-44647-8_13

Chor, B., Goldwasser, S., Micali, S., & Awerbuch, B. (1985). Verifiable secret sharing and achieving simultaneity in the presence of faults. In *Proceedings of 26th IEEE Symposium on Foundations of Computer Science*, Portland, OR, USA, (pp. 151–160).

Dinger, J., & Hartenstein, H. (2006). Defending the Sybil attack in P2P networks: Taxonomy, challenges, and a proposal for self-registration. *Proceedings of the First International Conference on Availability, Reliability and Security (ARES'06).* ISBN: 0-7695-2567-9/06

Feldman, P. (1987). A practical scheme for non-interactive verifiable secret sharing. In *Proceedings of 28th IEEE Symposium on Foundations of Computer Science*, Los Angeles, CA, USA, (pp. 427–437).

Li, X., & Liu, L. (2003). A reputation-based trust model for peer-to-peer e-commerce communities. *ACM Conference on Electronic Commerce*, (pp. 228-229). New York, NY: ACM Press.

Mandt, T. K. (2006). Certificateless authenticated two-party key agreement protocols. Gjovik University College, 2006.

Pedersen, T. (1992). Non-interactive and information-theoretic secure verifiable secret-sharing. In Feigenbaum, J. (Ed.), *CRYPTO 1991, LNCS* (*Vol. 576*, pp. 129–140). Heidelberg, Germany: Springer.

Sang, X. S. (2009). *Study on some topics of certificateless public-key cryptography.* Xiamen University, 2009.

Shamir, A. (1984). Identity-based cryptosystems and signature schemes. In *Proceedings of CRYPTO 1984, LNCS 196*, (pp. 47–53). Springer.

Wang, L., Cao, Z., Li, X., & Qian, H. (2005). Certificateless threshold signature schemes. In Hao, Y. (Eds.), *CIS 2005, Part II, LNAI 3802* (pp. 104–109).

Xi, Q., & Wang, Y. (2009). *P2P reputation model based on trust and recommendation.*

Zhu, Q. Z., & Dong, X. L. (2006). *Efficient and secure certificateless key agreement protocol*, 2008.

Chapter 13
A Privacy Service for Comparison of Privacy and Trust Policies within SOA

David S. Allison
The University of Western Ontario, Canada

Hany F. EL Yamany
Suez Canal University, Egypt

Miriam A. M. Capretz
The University of Western Ontario, Canada

ABSTRACT

Privacy for Service-Oriented Architecture (SOA) is required to gain the trust of those who would use the technology. Through the use of an independent Privacy Service (PS), the privacy policies of a service consumer and provider can be compared to create an agreed upon privacy contract. In this chapter, the authors further define a metamodel for privacy policy creation and comparison. A trust element is developed as an additional criterion for a privacy policy. The authors define the PS, outline what operations it must perform to accomplish its goals, and present how the PS operates in different scenarios. They believe the PS, combined with the enhanced metamodel, provides a strong solution for providing privacy in an SOA environment.

INTRODUCTION

The definition of privacy continues to evolve along with the times it inhabits. In 1888, Justice Thomas M. Cooley famously defined privacy as "the right to be left alone" (Cooley, 1888). Almost a hundred years later, privacy was viewed as the ability to control the release of information about oneself (Parent, 1983). In the digital world of the 21st century, releasing information about ourselves is often a necessity of communication, which is done in many cases without our knowledge. For this reason, we extend the definition of privacy to include not only the ability to control information about ourselves that has not been released, but to also retain some measure of control over the information that has.

DOI: 10.4018/978-1-4666-0978-5.ch013

Service-Oriented Architecture (SOA) offers the policies, practices and frameworks required to provide and consume services (Sprott & Wilkes, 2004). SOA provides a solution to finding, utilizing and integrating many different services to meet the business requirements of a consumer. The usefulness of services in providing business solutions is directly linked to the amount of interactions that exist between different services. This property of services poses a challenging problem for dealing with privacy protection. As an increasing number of services are composed together, often from multiple parties, it becomes easier for a consumer to unwittingly expose private information. A common approach to protecting consumers from this exposure is to provide pseudonyms to identifying information. However this solution is incomplete as even hidden identities can be deduced by tracking patterns of usage (Kanneganti & Chodavarapu, 2008). As services can provide complex and confidential actions such as Internet banking (Shan & Hua, 2006) and business-to-business (B2B) commerce (Vitvar et al., 2007), the protection of consumer data is of the utmost importance.

A privacy policy allows both the service consumer and provider to outline their preferences and concerns pertaining to their private data. We describe an expansion to our previously defined metamodel (Allison, EL Yamany, & Capretz, 2009) that will provide the consumer with greater input into how their data is used. This will be done through the introduction of a trust element to give the consumer a measure of control over the Privacy Service (PS) which acts as the negotiator of a privacy contract. The PS uses specific operations to compare the privacy policies of a service consumer and provider.

When discussing the entire security of SOA, privacy is often one of the smallest aspects highlighted (Kanneganti & Chodavarapu, 2008; Nakamura et al., 2005). Due to this, it is important to examine privacy both in and out of an SOA environment. In this chapter relative works are discussed which deal with privacy and trust issues. These works provide insightful comparisons to the research presented in this chapter.

This chapter will also present an outline of how privacy elements are selected to create a comprehensive SOA privacy solution. These elements outline what each party, the consumer and provider, are comfortable with providing to each other in a privacy contract. Together these elements create a privacy metamodel consisting of six elements: collector, what, purpose, retention, recipient and trust.

The sixth element, trust, is presented in greater detail. The addition of trust to the selection of privacy elements emboldens the consumer with a degree of control over what PS oversees the negotiation of their privacy contract. Without this ability, the consumer would have nothing to ensure themselves that the policy comparison is completed without bias.

Furthermore, this chapter will illustrate each of the elements that together create privacy rules, including the element of trust. It will be explained why the element trust is required, and how trust is defined. A Privacy Service will also be introduced to be used as a third party between the service consumer and provider. The Privacy Service will be outlined and the operations it can perform will be explained.

Finally, this chapter will present a proof of concept to outline how the Privacy Service performs and the interactions it creates in different scenarios.

At the end of this chapter, we will introduce some scenarios for establishing the interactions among the described services within an SOA security framework in order to provide the sufficient and necessary security dimensions for an SOA environment.

BACKGROUND

The Platform for Privacy Preferences (P3P) project is a standard created by the World Wide Web Consortium (W3C) (Cranor, Langheinrich, Marchiori, Presler-Marshall, & Reagle, 2002) that provides websites with a standard format for stating their privacy preferences. P3P was defined around the Fair Information Practices developed by the Organisation for Economic Co-operation and Development (OECD, 1980). It is from these same practices and principles that the metamodel presented here was developed. P3P is designed in XML and uses the OECD principles to create eight top level tags (Beatty, Reay, Dick, & Miller, 2007): category, data, purpose, recipient, access, retention, disputes and remedies. As P3P was not designed for an SOA environment, this specific set of tags differs from the values we have selected to deal with services. Another difference between our work and P3P is that P3P does not accept comparisons between the values for each tag. No option is considered more or less secure than another. This is a problem that must be addressed in a suitable SOA privacy metamodel due to the different perspectives each consumer will have on their own privacy.

There has been work (Yee & Korba, 2005) that created a privacy policy specifically for e-services which could be used in an SOA environment. The policy is derived from the Canadian Standards Association's (CSA) Model Code for the Protection of Personal Information (CSA, 1996). This Canadian model was based on the OECD guidelines and therefore has a similar list of principles (Bennett, 1997). From the CSA's guidelines, Yee and Korba (2005) extract five privacy elements: collector, what, purposes, retention time, and disclose-to. These five elements represent the same information as five of the six elements we describe, with trust being the exception. Beyond some examples of what a document containing these elements would look like, we were unable to find any definition for the possible values of the

elements presented. From the examples presented it seems their work envisions specific values for whatever system is using the policy rather than a more general set of definitions. A goal of this chapter is to create policies that can be specific when the situation warrants it, or can be general enough to cover the privacy requirements of many situations.

Another work (Yee, 2009) outlines an approach for estimating the privacy protection capability of a Web service provider. It explains what types of data and equations are required to estimate privacy in a provider. This provides an example to how estimation of privacy can be done for a provider service.

PRIVACY METAMODEL STRUCTURE

In this chapter we outline a privacy metamodel consisting of six elements: collector, what, purpose, retention, recipient and trust. The first five elements are needed to fulfill the Fair Information Practices of the Organisation for Economic Co-operation and Development (OECD, 1980) and have been introduced previously (Allison et al., 2009). These five elements will be briefly described to provide the background of what information a privacy policy contains. The sixth element, trust, is a new element that is being introduced to help provide consumer control and confidence. The six privacy elements together create a single privacy rule. A policy may have one-to-many rules. The total set of privacy rules combined with an identifying owner tag creates a single privacy policy.

Collector Element

The collector element states the name of the organization or party who will be collecting the data. As the provider is the one collecting the information, this element on the provider side will simply consist of the name of the provider. The consumer will use this element to list the collectors they are willing to have gather their information. Therefore, the element on the consumer side will consist of a set of names, or the general term "Any".

What Element

The what element allows the privacy policy to outline what types of private information will be collected. In order to provide a criterion for comparison in an otherwise subjective category, we allow individuals to rank their information according to four ordered levels: Top Secret, Secret, Confidential and Unclassified. This ranking is based on the levels of classification used by the government of the United States of America (Office of Security Management and Safeguards, 2003). Though these levels are the same as the Bell-La Padula (BLP) model (Bell & La Padula, 1973), they do not share the same properties as BLP, such as no write-down. This scheme of classification was selected because it is in use throughout the world and the vocabulary used is such that a layperson could easily discern the order in which the levels are ranked.

A service consumer would be required to sort a list of the most common types of private information into the four levels according to their own preferences. This information would be stored on the consumer side in a document called What Element Ranking (WER). A service provider would not require a WER and simply states the types of information they wish to collect.

Purpose Element

The purpose element is important in determining if a service consumer and service provider should be allowed to interact and share information. Purpose can be interpreted in two different ways. The first is to consider the purpose to be the goal of the service, such as for "Record Keeping". The second interpretation is for purpose to outline the operational reasons for needing data access, such

as for "Collection and Distribution". We create a purpose element that consists of two parts, a goal and an operation. The goal is required from the service provider in order to inform the consumer and to satisfy the OECD guidelines. If the consumer wishes to limit their data to a particular goal they have that option, or they can choose "Any" and allow any purpose as long as it satisfies the second criterion. This second criterion is the operation, which consists of four ordered levels outlining the possible operational uses of data: "No Collection and No Distribution" ("NC&ND"), "Collection and No Distribution" ("C&ND"), "Collection and Limited Distribution" ("C&LD"), and "Collection and Distribution" ("C&D").

Retention Element

Retention allows the consumer to outline how long they wish their data to be stored. Conversely, it allows the provider to outline how long they wish to store any data. Retention consists of an integer, -1 or greater, representing the number of days a provider may retain a consumer's information. The value of -1 is used to represent an unlimited amount of time. This unlimited value is useful for the situation where a consumer is not concerned with how long a particular piece of information is held. The value of zero states that any information gathered is deleted immediately upon completion of the service.

Recipient Element

The recipient element outlines who is permitted to have consumer information passed to them. This element is only used by the provider since the consumer specifies who may receive their data with the collector element. For the provider, recipient will consist of a set of names, listing each party who could possibly receive data.

Figure 1. Levels of trust

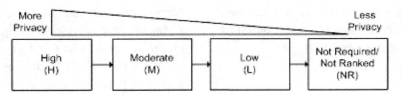

Trust Element

The trust element gives the consumer a degree of control over what PS can be used to negotiate the privacy contract. Without this ability, the consumer would have nothing to ensure them that the policy comparison is done without bias. The service provider uses this element to list the PS it wishes to use. There are four levels of trust a consumer can select for a PS to have. These levels are shown in Figure 1. For the comparison of this element to be successful, the trust level of the PS the provider supplies must be at least as high as the level chosen by the consumer.

TRUST AND THE PRIVACY METAMODEL

In this section we expand upon the sixth privacy element: trust. We focus on how it fits into our previously defined process, why it is important, and how it can be carried out.

Using Trust during Contract Agreement

We utilize a five stage process for reaching a privacy contract agreement, as seen in Figure 2. In the first stage, the service provider publishes itself to a service broker. In the second stage, the service consumer searches the broker for a suitable provider. In the third stage, the consumer inquires to the provider about comparing their privacy policies. This leads to a fourth stage where a third party PS compares the policies of the provider and consumer, and a contract is created. The fifth and final stage consists of the consumer and provider binding and interacting.

Previously, the consumer had no option but to use a PS suggested by the provider. With a trust element now defined by the consumer, there is

Figure 2. Contract agreement steps

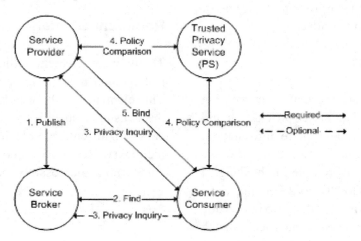

the chance that the PS suggested by the provider does not meet the consumer's desired level of protection. This leads to an expansion of the third stage, Privacy Inquiry. This expansion is highlighted as a dotted line in Figure 2. Since the PS is itself a service, it can and will be published to the service broker (a cataloguing service which allows for the publishing and discovery of other services). If the provider's PS is unacceptable to the consumer, they can search the broker for a suitable PS and present its details to the provider, otherwise the transaction is terminated. If the provider for some reason rejects the consumer proposed PS, it can provide a counter offer or terminate the transaction. The risk of the provider rejecting the consumer proposed PS should be low, as the main reason for rejection of the original PS by the consumer would be its low privacy ranking. Therefore any counter proposal should be of a PS that has a greater trust ranking, which also benefits the provider. However the provider does retain the option of rejection, at the risk of consumer and revenue loss.

How Trust is Defined

To classify each service into the three levels (low, moderate and high), statistics and ratings of the services will be used. The forth level (not required/not ranked) is used by services that do not participate. These four levels are shown in Figure 1. Ratings are given to each PS by consumer or provider services that have previous experience using the PS. These ratings can be used to develop a trust metric. Trust metrics are algorithms that are able to predict the trustworthiness of an unknown user (Massa & Avesani, 2007), or in the case of SOA, an unknown service. The selection and use of a trust metric falls outside of the scope of this chapter as there are many different trust metrics available for use (Massa & Avesani, 2007), each of which should be considered in greater detail.

The question of who will carry out the trust classification is an important one. The classi-

fication can be carried out either internally by the company or party that provides the PS, or externally by an outside organization. Internally would require no extra party be involved and therefore less work, but ultimately will be too unconvincing to a consumer. If each PS simply rates itself, the consumer would be unconvinced of the rating's authenticity.

Therefore the second option is required, that being an external organization which would gather the ratings and generate a trust metric. Such an organization could be a trusted institute such as the W3C, OECD or local government. Ultimately there must be some motivation for services to not provide the governing organization with false information. This must come in the form of legislation that provides punishment for losses of privacy and for knowingly providing false data. A government acting as the trusted organization is the best solution as they can enact laws and provide enforcement. Such legislation has already been enacted by many countries around the world (Treasury Board of Canada Secretariat, 2003; Office of Public Sector Information, 2003). If a service resides outside the jurisdiction of a government that performs privacy trust rankings and therefore cannot be ranked, it will remain at the NR level. If a consumer wishes to use one of the NR ranked services they can knowing they are at further risk, otherwise a more local and ranked service can be used.

The organization in charge of creating trust metrics would also notify consumers if the trust ranking of a particular PS has been changed. This notification can be done through direct communication where available, or through the posting of an alert to a designated website. The service consumer would then have the option to terminate a privacy contract if the PS who negotiated it has had their trust ranking reduced to a level no longer suited to the consumer. These contracts would then be renegotiated with another more suitable PS. Through this proactive approach, the suggested

Figure 3. Policy documents

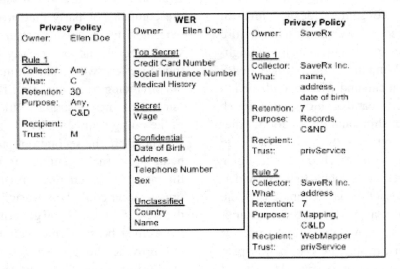

monitoring system would increase the level of trust among service consumers and providers.

PRIVACY SERVICE STRUCTURE

The purpose of the Privacy Service (PS) is to act as an intermediary between the service consumer and provider, and negotiate a privacy contract that both sides can agree on. The PS works in conjunction with a service provider, consumer and broker. In this section we will detail a number of operations the PS will perform in this comparison process.

Negotiate Policies Operation

In this operation, the PS is the recipient of two messages, one from the service provider and one from the service consumer. The message sent by the service provider contains a copy of its privacy policy, while the message sent by the service consumer contains its privacy policy and a copy of its WER. Examples of these three documents can be seen in Figure 3. The PS uses these three documents by comparing each element of the provider's rules to a corresponding consumer rule. If any problems in the matching process occur,

a resolveConflict message is sent to the service consumer. This message informs the consumer of the problem and suggests changes required to its privacy policy or WER. If the consumer replies with a new privacy policy and WER, this operation is repeated using these new documents and the previous service provider privacy policy. An example of the comparePolicies operation working without a conflict is shown in Figure 4a, while an example of it working with a conflict is shown in Figure 4b.

Create Contract Operation

The create contract operation is performed by the PS once the negotiate policies operation has completed. In this operation a privacy contract is first generated by taking the value provided by the service consumer, or the service provider if the provider's option is more secure. A message is sent to both the service consumer and provider stating that an agreement has been met and that a final signature is required. This requestSignature message also contains a copy of the agreed upon privacy terms for both parties to observe if they so require. The two parties sign the contract through the use of a secure identifiable process, such as

Figure 4. Policy comparison situations

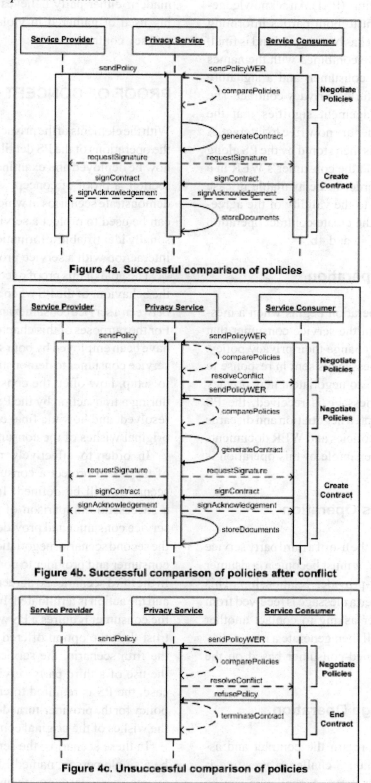

Figure 4a. Successful comparison of policies

Figure 4b. Successful comparison of policies after conflict

Figure 4c. Unsuccessful comparison of policies

Public Key Infrastructure (PKI). An acknowledgement message is sent to both parties informing them that the contract has been signed and is final. The privacy terms are combined with the names of the provider and consumer, and a signature from both parties to form a privacy contract. The signature acknowledgement signifies that the provider and consumer are now free to interact. A copy of the contract is then stored by the PS along with both policies and the consumer's WER in a secure database in order to be available in case a challenge is made to the validity of the agreement. Examples of the create contract operation are shown in Figure 4a and 4b.

End Contract Operation

The end contract operation begins when a message is received from the service consumer that states they refuse to change their privacy policy. This refusePolicy message is sent in response to an attempt by the PS to negotiate a new privacy policy. Once this message is received, the PS terminates the attempted negotiation and discards the current privacy policies and WER documents it has gathered. An example of this operation is shown in Figure 4c.

Convert Policies Operation

If a provider requires the use of a third party service to accomplish a goal, it must become a consumer in a new consumer-provider relationship. This operation begins when a message is received from the original provider asking to contact another provider. The PS will then generate a new policy for the provider-turned-consumer based on the original agreement.

Handle Challenge Operation

This operation will return the contract and associated policies when a challenge message is received from either party. A challenge can be made if either party believes information is being used or gathered in violation of the signed privacy contract.

PROOF OF CONCEPT

With the elements of the privacy policy defined and the operations of the PS detailed, the service must now be deployed and examined. In the following section, a proof of concept will be presented to demonstrate scenarios in which a Privacy Service can be used to protect a service consumer's personally identifiable information (PII) during their interaction with a service provider.

The goal of this proof of concept is to examine the behaviour of the PS when a transaction occurs between a service consumer and a service provider. For the purposes of this chapter, multiple policies have been employed by both service provider and service consumer to demonstrate how simple it is to setup, how often the consumer is interrupted during a transaction by the PS, how conflicts are resolved, and how the final contract satisfies the original wishes of the consumer.

In order to effectively monitor the ability of the PS to protect a consumer's privacy, five scenarios will be defined. In the first scenario a successful comparison of policies between a service consumer and provider will take place. In the second scenario, negotiation is required for the consumer and provider to come to an agreement. In the third scenario, no agreement can be reached and the action is terminated. In the fourth scenario the consumer requires a PS with a higher level of trust than the option offered by the provider. In the fifth scenario, the service provider requires the use of a third party service provider. In this case, the PS is required to create a new privacy policy for the provider-turned-consumer that takes the wishes of the original consumer into account.

In these scenarios, the service consumer will be a single person, named Ellen Doe, who is an average personal computer user. Ellen has owned a personal computer for more than 5 years, has had no formal training, and uses it primarily for communication through instant messengers, word processing, surfing the World Wide Web, and occasionally makes online purchases. Ellen has set up a WER document outlining how she ranks her PII using the WER Creator software, as shown in Figure 5.

The WER Creator is designed to be as user friendly as possible and to assist consumers who may not be aware of the importance of different types of PII. The graphical user interface (GUI)

contains a message bar at the bottom which informs the user any information they need to know and the cause of any errors they may encounter. The WER Creator includes statistics on what types of PII are generally considered to be of high importance. This allows the application to alert the consumer with a warning if they attempt to place such PII into a lower level. When the 'Create!' button is selected, the WER XML file is created automatically.

Ellen has also established a privacy policy using the privacy rule creator, shown in Figure 6. The

Figure 5. WER Creator GUI

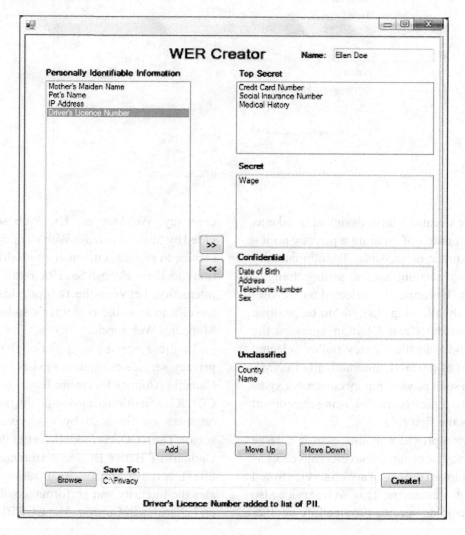

Figure 6. Privacy rule creator GUI

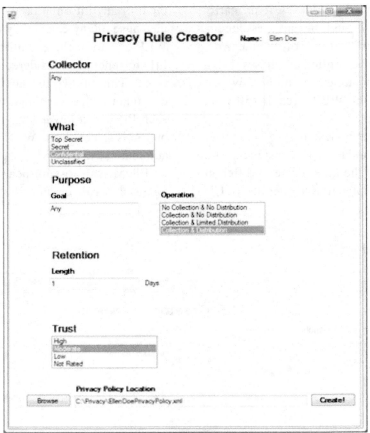

Privacy Rule Creator is also designed to take as much of the burden of creating a privacy policy off the consumer as possible. It automatically takes rules into account, such as setting 'Length' to ''0' when 'Unlimited' is selected as the 'Period', and only allowing 'Length' to be positive integers. When the 'Create!' button is pressed, the rule is appended to the privacy policy selected at the bottom of the GUI, automatically in XML format. If no such privacy policy currently exists, a new privacy policy is created, using the current selections as the first rule.

The service provider in this case is a large retail pharmacy store named SaveRx. SaveRx has recently employed the use of a Web service to sell products to its customers. This Web service also links to a mapping service provided by another company, WebMapper. The Web service provided by SaveRx can use WebMapper's mapping service to provide customers with driving directions to their closest SaveRx retail store. This interaction between the two providers requires SaveRx to send the customer's address to Web-Mapper's Web service.

In these scenarios, a fictional database of privacy service evaluations exists hosted by the Canadian Council for Online Rights (CCOR). The CCOR is a fictitious, not-for-profit, public service organization financed by the private business sector. The CCOR is modelled after the Canadian Council of Better Business Bureaus (CCBBB, 2011), a not-for-profit organization that evaluates the integrity and performance of businesses and charities in Canada. The CCBBB allows the public to inquire about a business or charity before engaging with that business or charity directly. In a similar fashion, the CCOR allows consumers to inquire about the trustworthiness of a PS before agreeing to use that particular PS to negotiate a privacy contract. This inquiry to the CCOR can be done manually by the consumer, or automatically for the consumer by software during the privacy contract negotiation process.

Each scenario begins with Ellen searching a UDDI registry for a drug store available in her city and discovering the service provided by SaveRx. Ellen interacts with SaveRx's Web service through a Web application.

Scenario 1: Successful Creation of a Privacy Contract

In the first scenario Ellen has discovered SaveRx and begins an interaction by requesting a privacy service. The policies used by both Ellen and SaveRx in this scenario can be seen in Figure 3. SaveRx replies to Ellen's query with the name of a privacy service, privService, and its location. An automatic search of the CCOR database of privacy services finds that privService has been given a ranking of High, which meets the standard Ellen has set of Moderate.

With the privacy service agreed upon, Ellen sends her WER and privacy policy to the privService PS as a SOAP message. Similarly, SaveRx sends their privacy policy to privService as a SOAP message.

The PS now stores the three documents with the date and begins its comparison. Based on the three documents received, the service provided by SaveRx meets the privacy levels outlined by Ellen. A contract is created based on the two policies, and sent to both consumer and provider as a SOAP message. A final signature is sent by the consumer and provider, indicating that the contract has been agreed upon and is now binding. The digital signatures can be sent as SOAP messages automatically to minimize consumer

interruptions. An acknowledgement message is sent to both Ellen and SaveRx, informing each that both parties have signed the contract. A copy of the contract is also saved by the PS along with the previously saved policies and WER. Ellen is now aware how SaveRx will use her PII, has agreed to its use, and is free to begin interacting with the service provider's service.

Scenario 2: Negotiation of a Privacy Contract

The second scenario begins in the same manner as scenario one using the same documents as shown in Figure 3 with one exception. In this scenario Ellen has specified one day as her retention time, which is now lower than the provider specified retention time of seven days. According to the retention time rules, these two policies are no longer compatible for the creation of a privacy contract. Since no other rule exists in Ellen's policy which covers this privacy rule of the provider, negotiations must take place. The PS in this case will query the consumer for a solution. The negotiation is done with the consumer rather than the provider, due to the number of consumers a single provider may have at any given moment. If negotiations were carried out on the provider's side, a large number of simultaneous conflicts could overwhelm any single provider. The consumer is notified of the cause of the failure and given two options: compromise or terminate. In this scenario the consumer chooses to compromise and change their privacy policy rule by lengthening the allowed retention time. The consumer will have the option to save this rule permanently in their policy so a similar conflict in the future will not occur and require their attention, or to allow the exception this single time. With this change in place, the policy comparison will continue and a contract will be created. Figure 7 demonstrates the prompt the consumer is given when negotiation is required.

Figure 7. PS Negotiation GUI

Scenario 3: Failure of a Privacy Contract

The third scenario uses the same policies outlined in scenario two; however in this case Ellen is uncomfortable and unwilling to compromise by raising her retention time. Ellen then chooses to terminate rather than compromise and the transaction between consumer and provider is concluded unsuccessfully. The consumer can then search the UDDI for a different provider offering a similar service.

Scenario 4: Privacy Service Trust Failure

In the fourth scenario the policies are identical to the policies shown in Figure 3. In this scenario an automatic search of the CCOR database of privacy services finds that the recommended PS, privService, has been given a ranking of Low. This PS does not meet the standard Ellen has set of Moderate. Ellen now has the option to terminate the transaction, similar to scenario three, or to search a service broker for a suitable PS. Any PS Ellen has used previously will be saved in a list of recommended Privacy Services, allowing Ellen

to automatically suggest an alternative. If no such list exists, due to a recent purge of a previous list or this being the first use of a PS, a search of a service broker for a suitable PS can be performed.

Scenario 5: Conversion of Policies

In the fifth scenario, the provider SaveRx wishes to call upon a third party service hosted by the company WebMapper. Ellen was informed of this possibility through Rule 2 in the privacy policy of SaveRx, as seen in Figure 3. In order to interact with this new party, SaveRx has the PS convert their provider policy into a consumer policy, taking the original wishes of Ellen into account. Each element in the privacy policies is directly comparable, allowing for this process to take place. With hierarchies developed between elements, the most secure option can be selected. For example, comparing the purpose elements in the policies in Figure 3, SaveRx's "C&LD" is more secure than Ellen's "C&D" and therefore the "C&LD" level is chosen. The rest of the conversion process is carried out in a similar, most-secure-wins format, with the results shown in Figure 8.

As can be seen in Figure 8, SaveRx now becomes a consumer negotiating with WebMapper, the provider. Thanks to the transitive nature of the policies, the converted policy can be compared to WebMapper's privacy policy.

FUTURE RESEARCH DIRECTIONS

The future work for this framework can be summarized in several basic directions. The first direction involves extending the privacy and trust SOA model presented in this chapter into a complete SOA security framework. This SOA security framework will include other services that are capable of handling the remainder of the SOA security aspects, including authorization, authentication, and auditing.

Figure 8. Converted privacy policies

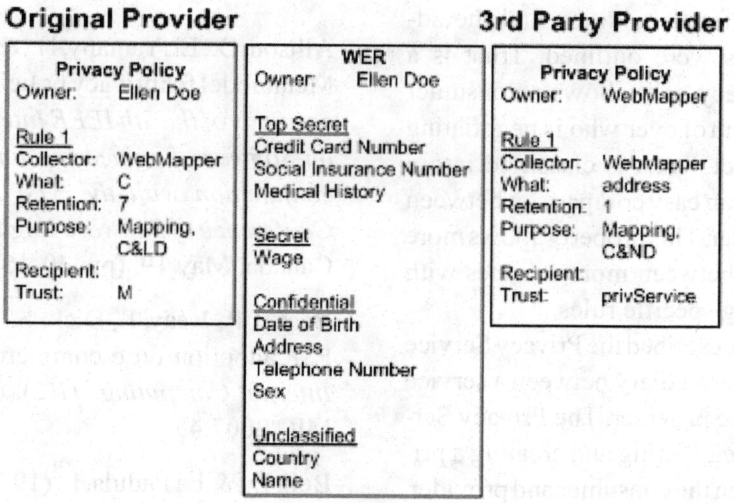

The creation of a unique Enterprise Service Bus (ESB) is planned. The ESB will be itself a service, and will work as an interface between the many service consumers and the Privacy Service. The ESB will be required to route each incoming message to a PS, and messages from the PS to their correct destinations. When the Privacy Service is put into public use, the demand from even a moderate amount of consumers will overwhelm any single PS. The ESB will be used to overcome this issue of traffic. The ESB will contain an intelligent engine that will be able to replicate the PS as many times as is needed to meet the current consumer demand. The ability to dynamically replicate the PS will provide assurance that each SOAP message sent by a consumer is processed within an appropriate amount of time. Replication will also improve the accessibility and performance of the Privacy Service, as the ESB's intelligent engine will predict the number of Privacy Services that are required to process the current number of SOAP messages. This prediction process will ensure a PS is always available for any consumer who wishes access to one. When the Privacy Service is placed within a larger security framework, the ESB will also have the task of interfacing the Privacy Service with the other security services, including an Authentication Service, Authorization Service and Auditing Service.

Another research direction involves improving the PS through the addition of an intelligent core. An intelligent core would allow the service to make better decisions when collecting attributes, converting policies and resolving conflicts. Also the selection and execution of a proper trust metric statistics will be carried out in future work. This will allow for the generation of a set of trust ratings that can be applied to each PS that is available.

The final piece of future research will involve deploying this privacy framework in a business environment. This deployment will allow for the determination of the framework's accuracy, ability and performance as well as to optimize its features and functionalities.

CONCLUSION

In this chapter we presented six privacy elements that form the foundation of a comprehensive SOA privacy solution: collector, what, purpose, retention, recipient and trust. These elements outline what each party, the consumer and provider, are comfortable with providing to each other in a privacy contract.

The element of trust was presented in greater detail. The reasons for its addition and the advantages it provides were outlined. Trust is a requirement of privacy as it allows a consumer to have a level of control over who is negotiating their privacy contract. Trust is classified into a hierarchy to provide an easy comparison between consumer and provider. This property allows more contracts to be met between more services with less work in defining specific rules.

This chapter also described the Privacy Service that will act as an intermediary between a service consumer and service provider. The Privacy Service is tasked with negotiating and creating a privacy contract between the consumer and provider. It was shown that the Privacy Service must also be able to terminate contracts, convert policies to facilitate the use of third party services, and handle challenges from the consumer or provider.

A proof of concept was also presented in this chapter. This proof of concept outlined how an average user would interact with the Privacy Service, and how software assists in the creation of a privacy policy and any issues that occur during the negotiation process. Several scenarios were presented to demonstrate how the Privacy Service acts in different situations. These scenarios were important in understanding how the Privacy Service reacts to both successful and unsuccessful attempts at creating a privacy contract.

Finally, this chapter concluded with future research directions. These directions showed how the Privacy Service can be improved, and how it can be combined with other components to form a larger SOA security framework.

REFERENCES

Allison, D., EL Yamany, H., & Capretz, M. (2009). Metamodel for privacy policies within SOA. *Proceedings of the 5th IEEE International Workshop on Software Engineering for Secure Systems in conjunction with the 31st IEEE International Conference of Software Engineering*, Vancouver, Canada, May 19, (pp. 40-46).

Beatty, P., Reay, I., Dick, S., & Miller, J. (2007). P3P adoption on e-commerce web sites. *IEEE Internet Computing*, *11*(2), 65–71. doi:10.1109/MIC.2007.45

Bell, D., & La Padula, L. (1973). Secure computer systems: Mathematical foundations. *MITRE Technical Report, 2547*, 1.

Bennett, C. (1997). Arguments for the standardization of privacy protection policy: Canadian initiatives and American and international responses. *Government Information Quarterly*, *1*(4), 351–362. doi:10.1016/S0740-624X(97)90032-0

Canadian Council of Better Business Bureaus. (2011). *Canadian BBB*. Retrieved February 11, 2011, from http://www.bbb.org/canada

Canadian Standards Association. (1996). *Model code for the protection of personal information* (Q830-96). Retrieved February 11, 2011, from http://www.csa.ca/cm/ca/en/ privacy-code/publications/view-privacy-code

Cooley, T. (1888). *A treatise on the law of torts or the wrongs which arise independent of contract* (2nd ed.). Chicago, IL: Callaghan & Co.

Cranor, L., Langheinrich, M., Marchiori, M., Presler-Marshall, M., & Reagle, J. (2002). *The platform for privacy preferences 1.0 specification*. Retrieved February 11, 2011, from http://www.w3.org/TR/P3P/

Kanneganti, R., & Chodavarapu, P. (2008). *SOA security*. Greenwich, CT: Manning Pub. Co.

Massa, P., & Avesani, P. (2007). Trust-aware recommender systems. *Proceedings of the 2007 ACM Conference on Recommender Systems*, Minneapolis, MN, USA, October 19-20, (pp. 17-24).

Nakamura, Y., Tatsubori, M., Imamura, T., & Ono, K. (2005). Model-driven security based on a web services security architecture. *Proceedings of the 2005 IEEE International Conference on Services Computing*, Orlando, Florida, USA, July 11-15, (pp. 7-15).

Office of Public Sector Information. (2003). *The privacy and electronic communications (EC Directive) Regulations 2003.* Retrieved February 11, 2011, from http://www.legislation.gov.uk/uksi/2003/2426/contents/made

Office of Security Management and Safeguards. (2003). *Further amendment to EO 12958, as amended, classified national security information.* Retrieved February 11, 2011, from http://nodis3.gsfc.nasa.gov/displayEO.cfm?id=EO_13292_

Organisation for Economic Co-operation and Development. (1980). *OECD guidelines on the protection of privacy and transborder flows of personal data.* Retrieved February 11, 2011, from http://www.oecd.org/document/18/0,3343,en_26 49_34255_1815186_1_1_1_1,00.html

Parent, W. (1983). Privacy, morality and the law. *Philosophy & Public Affairs, 12*(4), 269–288.

Shan, T., & Hua, W. (2006). Service-oriented solution framework for internet banking. *International Journal of Web Services Research, 3*(1), 29–48. doi:10.4018/jwsr.2006010102

Sprott, D., & Wilkes, L. (2004). Understanding service-oriented architecture. *The Architecture Journal, 1,* 10–17.

Treasury Board of Canada Secretariat. (2003). *Canadian privacy legislation and policy.* Retrieved February 11, 2011, from http://www.tbs-sct.gc.ca/pgol-pged/piatp-pfefvp/course2/mod1/mod1-3-eng.asp

Vitvar, T., Moran, M., Zaremba, M., Haller, A., & Kotinurmi, P. (2007). Semantic SOA to promote integration of heterogeneous B2B services. *Proceedings of the 4th IEEE Conference on Enterprise Computing, E-Commerce and E-Services*, Tokyo, Japan, Jul. 23-26, (pp. 451-456).

Yee, G. (2009). Estimating the privacy protection capability of a Web service provider. *International Journal of Web Services Research, 6*(2), 20–41. doi:10.4018/jwsr.2009092202

Yee, G., & Korba, L. (2005). Semi-automated derivation and use of personal privacy policies in e-business. *International Journal of E-Business Research, 1*(1), 54–69. doi:10.4018/jebr.2005010104

ADDITIONAL READING

Allison, D., EL Yamany, H., & Capretz, M. (2009). Privacy and trust policies within SOA. *Proceedings of the 4th International Conference for Internet Technology and Secured Transactions*, London, UK, November 9–12, (pp. 382-387).

Anderson, A. (2004). *The relationship between XACML and P3P privacy policies.* Retrieved February 11, 2011, from http://labs.oracle.com/projects/xacml/XACML_P3P_Relationship.html

Anderson, A. (2005). *A comparison of two privacy policy languages: EPAL and XACML.* Retrieved February 11, 2011, from http://labs.oracle.com/techrep/2005/ smli_tr-2005-147/TRCompareEPALandXACML.html

Ashley, P., Hada, S., Karjoth, G., Powers, C., & Schunter, M. (2003). *Enterprise privacy architecture language* (EPAL 1.2). Retrieved February 11, 2011, from http://www.w3.org/Submission/2003/SUBM-EPAL-20031110/

Atkinson, B., Della-Libera, G., Hada, S., Hondo, M., Hallam-Baker, P., Kaler, C., et al. (2002). *Web services security (WS-Security).* Retrieved February 11, 2011 from http://msdn.microsoft.com/en-us/library/ms951257

Buecker, A., Ashley, P., Borrett, M., Lu, M., Muppidi, S., & Readshaw, N. (2007). Understanding SOA security design and implementation (2nd ed.). Retrieved February 11, 2011, from http://www.redbooks.ibm.com/redbooks/pdfs/sg247310.pdf

Cavoukian, A., & Hamilton, T. (2002). *The privacy payoff: How successful businesses build customer trust.* Whitby, Canada: McGraw-Hill Ryerson Limited.

Cheng, V., Hung, P., & Chiu, D. (2007). Enabling Web services policy negotiation with privacy preserved using XACML. *Proceedings of the 40th Hawaii International Conference on System Sciences,* Waikoloa, HI, Jan. 3-6, (p. 33a).

EL Yamany, H., & Capretz, M. (2008a). An authorization model for web services within SOA. *Proceedings of the 3rd IEEE International Conference on Digital Management,* London, UK, Nov. 13-16, (pp. 75-80).

EL Yamany, H., & Capretz, M. (2008b). Use of data mining to enhance security for SOA. *Proceedings of the 3rd IEEE International Conference on Convergence and Hybrid Information Technology,* Busan, Korea, November 11-13, (pp. 551-558).

Epstein, J., Matsumoto, S., & McGraw, G. (2006). Software security and SOA: Danger, Will Robinson. *IEEE Security & Privacy, 4*(1), 80–83. doi:10.1109/MSP.2006.23

Erl, T. (2005). *Service-oriented architecture: Concepts, technology, and design.* Upper Saddle River, NJ: Pearson Education, Inc.

Garcia, D., & de Toledo, M. (2008). A Web service privacy framework based on a policy approach enhanced with ontologies. *Proceedings of the 11th IEEE International Conference on Computational Science and Engineering - Workshops,* São Paulo, Brazil, July, (pp. 209-214).

Guermouche, N., Benbernou, S., Coquery, E., & Hacid, M. S. (2007). Privacy-aware web service protocol replaceability. *Proceedings of the IEEE International Conference on Web Services,* Salt Lake City, Utah, USA, July 9-13, (pp. 1048-1055).

Yamany, EL, H., Capretz, M., & Allison, D. (2010). Intelligent security and access control framework for service-oriented architecture. *Journal of Information and Software Technology, 52*(2), 220–236. doi:10.1016/j.infsof.2009.10.005

Yee, G. (2006). *Privacy protection for e-services.* Hershey, PA: IGI Publishing. doi:10.4018/978-1-59140-914-4

Yu, W., Doddapaneni, S., & Murthy, S. (2006). A privacy assessment approach for serviced oriented architecture applications. *Proceedings of the 2nd IEEE International Symposium on Service-Oriented System Engineering,* Shanghai, China, October 25-26, (pp. 67-75).

Yu, W., & Murthy, S. (2007). PPMLP: A special modeling language processor for privacy policies. *Proceedings of the 11th IEEE International Symposium on Computers and Communications,* Aveiro, Portugal, July, (pp. 851-858).

Zhang, X., Wong, H., & Cheung, W. (2006). A privacy-aware service-oriented platform for distributed data mining. *Proceedings of the 8th IEEE International Conference on and Enterprise Computing and the 3rd IEEE International Conference on Enterprise Computing, E-Commerce, and E-Services.* San Francisco, CA, USA, June 26-29, (pp. 44-48).

KEY TERMS AND DEFINITIONS

Contract: A contract between two parties is a declaration of what services both parties have agreed to perform.

Policy: A policy allows a single party to state their preferences in a standard format.

Privacy: The ability to control information about oneself that has not been released, and to also retain some measure of control over the information that has been released.

Security: An overarching concern of software to keep it safe from danger. Security includes topics such as authorization, authentication, auditing and privacy.

Service-Oriented Architecture (SOA): SOA is a growing paradigm in the world of IT that uses services as the basis for building enterprise applications. Services act as an application front-end and encapsulate the logic required to accomplish a specific task. Services, together with a directory to locate them, known as a service broker, and a means for services to communicate, known as a service bus, form the foundation of SOA.

Trust: The more trust a third-party service provider has, the more assurance a consumer will have that the provider will do only the actions the consumer has agreed to.

Web Service: An autonomous software system which allows for networked, machine-to-machine interaction.

Chapter 14
Creating and Applying Security Goal Indicator Trees in an Industrial Environment

Alessandra Bagnato
TXT e-solutions, Italy

Fabio Raiteri
TXT e-solutions, Italy

Christian Jung
Fraunhofer Institute for Experimental Software Engineering IESE, Germany

Frank Elberzhager
Fraunhofer Institute for Experimental Software Engineering IESE, Germany

ABSTRACT

Security inspections are increasingly important for bringing security-relevant aspects into software systems, particularly during the early stages of development. Nowadays, such inspections often do not focus specifically on security. With regard to security, the well-known and approved benefits of inspections are not exploited to their full potential. This book chapter focuses on the Security Goal Indicator Tree application for eliminating existing shortcomings, the training that led to their creation in an industrial project environment, their usage, and their reuse by a team in industry. SGITs are a new approach for modeling and checking security-relevant aspects throughout the entire software development lifecycle. This book chapter describes the modeling of such security goal based trees as part of requirements engineering using the GOAT tool dedicated plug-in and the retrieval of these models during the various phases of the software development lifecycle in a project by means of Software Vulnerability Repository Services (SHIELDS, Software Vulnerability Repository Services) created in the European project SHIELDS (SHIELDS, SHIELDS - Detecting known security vulnerabilities from within design and development tools).

DOI: 10.4018/978-1-4666-0978-5.ch014

INTRODUCTION

Software security is still a challenging problem that affects software producers from small developer teams up to big vendors. The increasing complexity of software systems makes handling security ever more difficult. In addition, most software developers have insufficient knowledge regarding security aspects and use immature quality assurance techniques for preventing security defects across the entire software development lifecycle (SDLC), which aggravates the problem of secure software engineering.

Current quality assurance techniques for ensuring software security are, e.g., testing methods such as fuzzing (Sutton, Greene, & Amini, 2007), (Takanen, DeMott, & Miller, 2008), penetration testing (Arkin, Stender, & McGraw, 2005), or software inspections (Howard, 2006). Inspections – the systematic manual checking of a piece of software for certain defects – are one of the most effective and efficient quality assurance techniques (Runeson, Andersson, Thelin, Andrews, & Berling, 2006), (Wiegers, 2002). However, inspections often do not focus on security. Thus, the well-known and approved software inspections do not exploit their full potential regarding security. Adapting them to security needs is a challenging and time-consuming task, which requires appropriate security knowledge.

Detecting security-relevant defects too late in the development often leads to expensive corrections. Even worse is the deployment of faulty and insecure software, which may result in a bad reputation. Hence, interest in improving security inspections is widespread (Evans & Larochelle, 2002). In order to improve security inspections, a method for supporting inspections early in the SDLC has been developed. The approach provides structured reading support for the inspector during the inspection of a development artifact.

Security Goal Indicator Trees (SGITs), which are introduced in (Peine, Jawurek, & Mandel, 2008), were developed to improve guidance for

focused security inspections. SGITs are tree-structured models in which the root node defines the general security goal. This goal is hierarchically decomposed into indicators that can be inspected independently. These indicators guide the inspector through the inspection process by subdividing complex security goals into a set of simple aspects that can be verified more easily. Best practices or principles of secure software engineering can be modeled as an SGIT. In order to achieve a specific security goal, the inspector has to map indicators of the model onto individual parts of the software or relevant parts from the specification documents in order to decide whether they have been fulfilled or not. Thus, our new inspection approach provides well-defined criteria that either have to be avoided in case the indicator might violate the achievement of the security goal (traditional inspection focus) or have to be fulfilled to reach the security goal (expanding the traditional inspection focus).

An inspector with little security background (e.g., a software developer) is able to perform security inspections by using this approach, due to the fact that the security knowledge is covered by the model (i.e., the SGIT). This reduces the burden on security experts and still permits to ensure security in software products. Thus, the approach using SGITs bridges the gap between security experts and software practitioners without any specific security expertise.

This book chapter discusses initial experience collected during the creation phase of new SGITs and describes the elicitation and modeling of new SGITs during the requirements analysis phase in an industrial environment. Furthermore, experiences gained from the process of deriving security goals and their indicators in the requirements engineering phase are discussed by TXT e-solutions S. p. A.

The book chapter outlines the approach using SGITs as reading support during inspection, the e-tourism project in which the technique was applied, the description of the software vulnerability repository service (SVRS) for storing the developed models, and their application in the development. Lessons learned are described at the end of the chapter.

BACKGROUND

Using Software Inspections to Address Security Issues

Software inspections provide a formal process for the software development lifecycle to address quality assurance issues relating to the software product. The main objective of software inspections is to find as many defects as possible, especially critical ones. Furthermore, inspectors gain experience with the inspection, the artifacts, or certain qualities when they perform an inspection. For example, inspectors can inspect software artifacts with a special focus on certain defect classes or qualities (e.g., security) and try to identify defects that violate this predefined aspect (Porter & Votta, 1998). The inspectors are supported by reading techniques and have reading support such as scenarios or checklists. Most inspection techniques suggest marking potential defects in the software artifacts and documenting them. At the end, the quality of the entire software product should be improved.

Since the work of Michael Fagan (Fagan, 1976), much research has been conducted in the area of software inspections, resulting in software inspections often being treated as an integral part of software quality assurance strategies (Strooper & Wojcicki, 2007). The biggest benefit is the detection of defects during early stages of the software development lifecycle (e.g., requirements specification, architecture, and design), because no executable source code is needed for performing this manual task, contrary to traditional testing approaches such as unit testing.

However, a systematic approach that supports the inspector with customized (i.e., for a limited type of software artifacts, such as requirements specifications, only) and focused (i.e., for a specific quality attribute) guidance is still lacking (Denger, Ciolkowski, & Lanubile, 2004). For security, most descriptions contain bad practices such as lists of functions from the C library not to be used. The example already shows two problems. First, nearly all support is developed with a focus on source code. Second, security is expressed as bad practice (i.e., something that should be avoided), like a blacklist approach for a firewall. However, taking a whitelisting approach and hence limiting it to firewall rules that are explicitly allowed provides more security than forgetting some entry points in the blacklist.

Furthermore, what to analyze in the considered software artifacts and how to find evidence for the indicators is often not explicitly defined, leading to the situation that security issues are often insufficiently addressed. The financial damage can be immense if defects are detected after delivery or during late phases of the software development lifecycle. Assuming a huge and complex software system, inspectors do not know on which parts they should focus in the source code, for example. Hence, where to find what is another challenge when it comes to performing efficient software inspections.

Taking a Positive View

Achieving certain security goals is the ultimate aim of software development from a security point of view. There are two main categories of goals. The first category includes goals originating from the application or business domain (e.g., the group 'reader' can only view, but not edit or delete entries). The application under development needs to implement security measures that ensure a healthy business. This includes functionality-dependent security such as an implementation that ensures secure communication, auditability, or different authentication services. The second category includes requirements stemming from various proven principles, best practices, and patterns of secure software engineering (e.g., provide only the least privilege to each component that is still sufficient for its task). The first category should be addressed in the requirements specification, whereas the second category may be implemented in the software system, but is not mentioned explicitly anywhere (with the exception of the source code). Software developers may have taken part in special security training and are aware of such security principles.

As part of the software development lifecycle and especially for the inspection part, it is necessary to elicit security requirements and define security goals. Security goals can be derived from a list that addresses fundamental qualities such as confidentiality, integrity, and availability (CIA). When CIA qualities are used, the security of a software system can only be handled on an abstract level. The list does not directly lead to detailed criteria that could be checked to ensure security requirements in different development artifacts.

Threat modeling (Swiderski & Snyder, 2004) is another method for identifying security goals in a more detailed way and is closer to the needs of the software system. By taking the view of an attacker who wants to get the valuable assets of interest, security goals can be derived from these potential attack models by demanding suitable countermeasures. The approach models possible attacks and uses negative verbalizations for defining the security goal (e.g., preventing the mail system from reading user credentials).

In contrast, the Security Goal Indicator Trees (SGITs) approach (Peine, Jawurek, & Mandel, 2008) uses positive verbalizations (e.g., the system stores the password in a non-recoverable way) as indicators for expressing security knowledge in a checkable manner. In addition, these indicators can be enriched by further information for supporting the developer (who is not necessarily a security expert) in his decision making. The above mentioned indicator example "the system stores the password in a non-recoverable way" can be enriched by the following text: "The sys-

tem should use established one-way functions such as the secure hash algorithm sha-2 (md5 is outdated and should be replaced by sha-2) to store the password. Storing the password in plain text is inadequate. It is also recommended to use a salted hash for protecting against simple dictionary attacks with rainbow tables." The aim is to improve the inspection process (especially defect detection) by defining indicators that can be ruled out during defect detection. Thus, the SGIT's indicators advise the inspector to perform adequate inspection steps in order to check the overall security goal.

SGIT Composition

An SGIT (Peine, Jawurek, & Mandel, 2008) is a codified security goal that can be used for constructive support during development or as part of the quality assurance process. SGITs provide versatile support for different application scenarios. They are not limited to specific problem domains, a specific programming language, or specific hardware.

An SGIT consists of one root node (i.e., the security goal) and multiple positive and negative indicators that are structured by using the logical operators "AND" and "OR". The idea is to decompose the security goal into checkable indicators. Every indicator has to be phrased such that the inspector can decide whether it is fulfilled or not. Due to the kind of security issues that are addressed by SGITs, the approach mainly focuses on inspecting requirements and design documents. The difference between positive and negative indicators is their influence on the overall result of the tree. A negative indicator found during defect detection has a bad impact on the achievement of the security goal. In general, the use of positive indicators is recommended, if possible. However, in some cases it is better to use negative indicators for identifying actions or system functions that are counterproductive for security. For example, a system component that provides the function to recover a lost password should be modeled as a negative indicator.

SGIT Construction

This section provides the principles behind the creation of SGITs. In order to make it possible to express security knowledge using indicator labels, an appropriate level of security expertise is recommended. Furthermore, for the development of an SGIT it is beneficial that the modeler has some practical experience in security and maybe also in software inspections.

The first step in the development of an SGIT is to gather security requirements (e.g., provided by stakeholders and/or already refined by the requirements engineer) in order to determine the scope of relevant security goals. It is often necessary to get additional information about the domain and its specific requirements (e.g., data confidentiality has higher relevance in financial transactions than the availability of the system). Thus, the requirements analysis phase is a strategic starting point for getting initial information.

It is the quality assurance engineer's task to decide which security goals should be expressed as SGITs. Repositories such as the Software Vulnerability Repository Service (SVRS) (SHIELDS, Software Vulnerability Repository Services) as well as local storages may already provide some suitable models or can give further information.

After the relevant security goals have been identified, the corresponding models representing the goal have to be derived. There are multiple starting points from here. First, the quality assurance engineer finds an appropriate model in a local storage or in a repository that fits the needs of the software system, respectively the assumed needs of the quality assurance engineer. Hence, it is not necessary to model a new SGIT. Second, the responsible person finds a model that fits only parts of the needs and has to adapt, extend, or merge the model(s). Third, no suitable model exists, which leads to the construction of a new one.

After the decision has been made to create a new SGIT, the security goal (i.e., the root node of the SGIT) has to be refined by a tree structure. This is done by identifying indicators that can check whether the desired security goal can be achieved or not. For example, one indicator may be the existence of certain system components or system functions. Established best practices can be modeled as positive indicators (i.e., a property that should hold to meet the security goal), known problems as negative ones (i.e., a property that should be avoided to meet the security goal, such as a password recovery function). All indicators have to fulfill the following condition: They must clearly specify what to look for and where to look. In particular, each indicator must specify in which artifact type the indicator can be found best (e.g., **M**anual / **R**equirements / **D**esign / **S**ource Code). The reviewer should be able to decide which component or part of the software system is responsible for the required security aspect. Again, the indicator labels have to be phrased such that they can be either confirmed or refuted during the security inspection. This can result in a complex and time-consuming task. In order to mitigate complexity problems, the indicators can be combined logically. If several prerequisites have to be expressed, an AND node can be used. If the goal is to express several alternatives (e.g., several implementation possibilities of the same concept), the use of an OR node is recommended.

Sometimes a newly modeled SGIT has dependencies on other SGITs. This is visualized by a directed link "Depends on" to the dependent SGIT.

SGITs have to be modeled by security and domain experts, who need to express their knowledge in a tree structure, but they can be applied by users who have no security background and limited knowledge in this area. Thus, SGITs enable their user to act as the security expert in the software inspection. They close the gap between security experts and software developers in defect detection.

APPLYING SGITS IN PRACTICE

The e-Tourism Project

The project in which the SGIT models were created and used aimed at developing a new user-centric distributed repository of cultural heritage content. The project includes a software architecture for enabling customized content access and providing integrated access to European cultural destinations to facilitate virtual access and stimulate learning experience (Megliola & Barbieri, 2008).

The project was developed at TXT e-solutions. TXT e-solutions is a private software vendor and system integration company with more than 500 employees and an annual turnover of more than 50 million euros. TXT is a market leader in products and solutions for supply chain and content management. Local branches exist all over in Europe (Italy, France, Germany, UK, Spain) and the USA. It operates through three divisions: Supply Chain and Customer Management (providing modular products – the TXT Perform suite – that cover Supply Chain needs, Corporate Research Division, and Professional Services (real-time, safety-critical, embedded systems and SW testing and QA).

TXT intended to develop a distributed repository for storing digitalized cultural data provided by users such as tourists. Thus, the e-tourism system had to provide a complete mobile e-tourism information system for travelers and tourists. Within the scope of the development project, the five developers involved in the project at TXT were taught to use SGITs and, subsequently, started creating SGITs for their own context sharing the models among each other, taking advantage of a centralized model repository (SHIELDS, Software Vulnerability Repository Services).

The same models were applied throughout the entire software development lifecycle, during the requirements phase by the SGIT modelers, during the design and development phases by the developers, and during the testing phase by the test engineers.

The e-tourism system allowed contributing users to share their impressions and experiences by exchanging content with other users via chat, forums, blogs, image and video sharing in regard to points of interest (e.g., monuments and places). Taking advantage of the underlying web-based site, this information can be used by other people when planning their itinerary. The system also allowed suggesting location-based information and included an ad-hoc itinerary planning functionality. All information was collected and presented via web technologies. The main requirements of the SGIT models were related to two needs: 1) enhancing the security of the very important user management system behind the e-tourism site, which was a mandatory requirement in order to prevent misuse, and 2) guaranteeing that users will obtain reliable and secure information on geographic coordinates (i.e., geo-referential data) concerning all nearby locations with points of interest.

Information managed by the system comprises personal information and sensitive data. Consequently, security models have been introduced to cover security issues in the described scenario, such as confidential user data (e.g., privacy issues).

SGIT applications in the e-tourism project included the introduction of the following activities in the SDLC. The objective was to try out these new innovations in industrial settings, provide feedback, and highlight the real benefits of using SGIT resources stored in and retrieved from the SVRS repository.

The following sections describe how the approach was pursued in practice. First, the GOAT plug-in (SHIELDS, GOAT Modelling Tool) was used to build and upload SGITs. This included the process of creating new SGITs during the requirements phase of the project. The SVRS was used as a central repository for storing new SGITs and getting additional models. The models were applied during the design, development, and testing phases of the e-tourism project.

Using the GOAT Plug-in to Build and Upload SGITs

In order to provide a platform for creating SGITs, a plug-in for GOAT was developed. GOAT was developed within SHIELDS as a security modeling tool that can be customized to the user's needs via plug-ins, on the one hand, and can be connected to the SHIELDS repository (SVRS) on the other hand.

The tool should be used by security experts for creating security models. It can be used on any system that supports the Java Runtime Environment.

As shown in Figure 1, the tool consists of a painting pane, a tool bar, and a property area. The tool bar has the following buttons from left to right: green indicator; red indicator; and-node; or-node; three buttons for zooming, activating, and deactivating automatic numbering; and a final button for converting an SGIT into a guided checklist (GC) (Elberzhager, Klaus, & Jawurek, 2009). Depending on the active node, the modeler can edit the label text and add additional text as a description. Furthermore, the modeler has to

choose the corresponding document type (i.e., requirements, design, source code, or manual).

After the modeling is finished, the user can store the model locally or upload it to a repository like the SVRS, which is described in the following section.

SGIT Creation

Based on the TXT scenario described above and on the initial input from the TXT requirements documents, TXT created SGITs for their application software. To this end, they focused on the following critical requirements of the application:

- The system must ensure complete security of the user subscription process (i.e., non-repudiation, data integrity, data validity).
- The integrity of stored geo-referential data must be ensured and access to geo-referential data must be restricted to read-only for all registered users but the owner, who has read-write permission. Hence, the system must ensure that only authorized users have write access on sensitive geo-referential data.
- The system must ensure that user credentials (i.e., data for authentication purposes)

Figure 1. GOAT screenshot

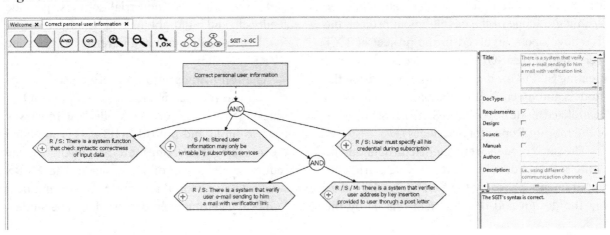

are stored securely and that all relevant data are not accessible to unauthorized parties.

The last requirement is very important in the analyzed context, since information entered by users is to be shared and trusted by the whole e-tourism community, and it is mandatory that the information provided on the site originates from a person with essential knowledge of the subject.

Prior to the creation of any SGIT models, a phone conference was held to introduce the general SGIT approach. After a basic understanding of the approach had been established, additional information was gained by studying SGIT-related publications and existing SGITs.

After gaining basic knowledge about SGITs, the security experts focused on the security priorities of the e-tourism application. Five internal meetings and additional refinements added by the research partner were necessary to define the following three security goals:

"Correct Personal User Information" aims at storing valid personal user information.

"Secure Geo-Referential Data" aims at preserving the integrity of stored geo-referential data.

"Secure User Authentication" aims at unimpeachable user authentication. This goal depends on the existing SGIT "Secure Password Management." In this chapter, the SGIT "Correct Personal User Information" is described.

The security goals were expanded into three SGITs by defining indicators for the achievement of specific root nodes. Using the SGIT approach, a detailed analysis was performed of the actions that must be implemented (positive indicators modeled as green boxes) and the conditions that must be avoided to reach the security goal (negative indicators modeled as red boxes).

Correct Personal User Information

Figure 2 shows the SGIT for "Correct Personal User Information", which aims at ensuring that the system forces the user to enter correct personal information such as address data during the subscription process. The model was created for the e-tourism project, but it is not limited to this project. Hence, the SGIT can be used as initial input for other software products with similar security requirements.

After establishing the security goal "Correct Personal User Information", it was necessary to analyze the available document types and determine which parts of them may be affected by the root node. The identified indicators for the achievement of the security goal are as follows.

Figure 2. SGIT for "correct personal user information"

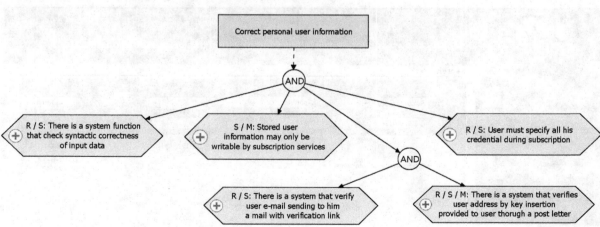

273

The first indicator stems from the requirement that user input has to be validated before being stored. Hence, user-provided input has to be checked for syntactic correctness. This indicator ensures syntax checking on every user input.

The second indicator stems from the requirement that the registration/subscription system has to avoid data modification due to injections. This requirement was added after the design documents had been analyzed.

In order to minimize the interaction between the frontend and the backend, the third indicator was introduced, which ensures that all relevant credentials must be provided by the user during the subscription process. Therefore, insert calls to the database and the number of forms in the graphical user interface should be reduced, which reduces the probability of malicious injections.

Address verification is essential for the credibility of the provided information. Any information about any point of interest in the e-tourism-maps uploaded by a contributor can be mapped to the address entry from the subscription process. In addition, the fourth indicator ensures the fulfillment of the requirement that address information must be verified.

The fifth and final indicator addresses the verification of the user's email address by sending an email with a confirmation link to the registering user as part of the subscription process. This procedure is best practice and quite common in registration processes on websites for ensuring the validity of the email address.

The combination of different communication channels (items 4 and 5) ensures high reliability in the subscription process. The five indicators are linked by an "AND" connector (as can be seen in Figure 2) because all indicators have to be met in order to achieve the desired security goal (Jung, Elberzhager, Bagnato, & Raiteri, 2010).

Using the Security Vulnerability Repository Service to Search SGIT Models

Many potential security vulnerabilities exist and are known to security experts. But developers often fail to avoid these vulnerabilities and make the same mistakes over and over again. One of the core reasons for this is missing information about vulnerabilities in a convenient form that is accessible to them while they are working on software design and development (SHIELDS, SHIELDS - Detecting known security vulnerabilities from within design and development tools). The Security Vulnerability Repository Service (SVRS)

Figure 3. SGIT search in SVRS

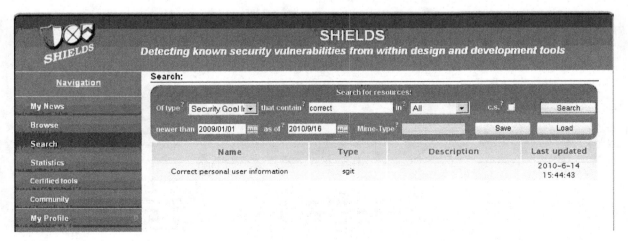

was developed as a service during the European project SHIELDS.

The repository was used during the entire SDLC of the e-tourism project to store, manage, and retrieve SGIT security-related content. In the context of the project, it served as a central repository where modelers, developers, and test engineers could access their models and where security experts could upload new models (SHIELDS, Software Vulnerability Repository Services).

Application

Three developers from TXT e-solutions were involved in the creation process of the three SGITs during the e-tourism requirements phase, one with a lot of security expertise, two with little security-specific expertise. The experienced par-

ticipant led the modeling of the SGITs, whereas the other participants mainly contributed relevant application-specific information, which resulted in additional indicators. The developers used the GOAT plug-in and uploaded the models into the SVRS. The modelers of the SGIT provided training on the approach to two developers involved in the design and development phases and three test engineers involved in the testing phase of the project.

The created models were retrieved by the two developers involved in the design and development phases; they downloaded the SGIT models from the SVRS and used them as a guide while developing their code without any supporting tool. The model was used as a kind of inspiration tool to guide the design and development efforts.

Three test engineers were involved in the testing phase; they downloaded the SGIT models

Figure 4. Download SGIT from SVRS

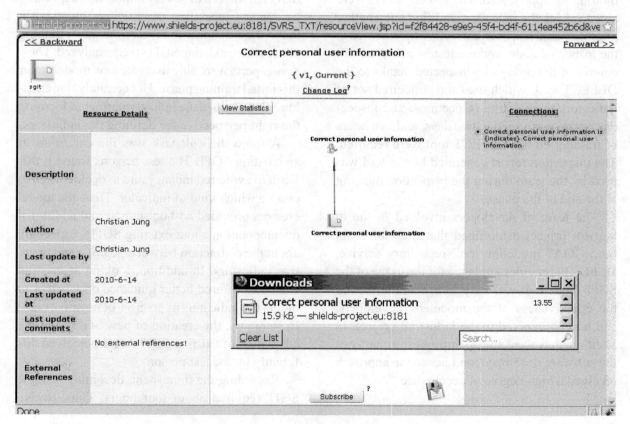

from the central repository and used them for code inspections supported by the SHIELDS Testing Tool DEFECT (SHIELDS, DEFECT – Dependability focused inspection tool).

DEFECT – Dependability focused inspection tool[1] – aims at supporting the inspection process by guiding the inspecting software practitioner through the defect detection phase of an inspection. The necessary instructions are provided by security models (which serve as reading support) from the SVRS. The DEFECT tool was considered very beneficial since it exactly followed the usual behavior of the inspectors and allowed to easily navigate through the SGITs models. Finally, DEFECT provides a report, which can be exported as HTML. No defects were found in the code by the test engineers, which proved how handling security errors much earlier in the software development lifecycle can save resources in later phases. The potential of a tool such as DEFECT for spotting defects that may have been missed was thoroughly appreciated. The test engineers were able to check the indicators and find out whether a security goal had been correctly implemented in the inspected code, and the testers achieved full control of the code to be inspected thanks to the DEFECT tool, which uses the structured set of indicators to guide the inspections. The inspections were performed in two days, and two hours of training on the DEFECT tool were required. The inspection report generated by the tool was used by the team during the inspection meeting at the end of the phase.

The team of developers involved in the e-tourism project determined that the tool chain (i.e., GOAT modeling tool, repository service, DEFECT) provides guidance for the usage of the SGIT models. It was easy to use and improved the effectiveness of the modelers, developers, and testers involved in the industrial project. In addition, they were able to improve the quality of the software developed, and hence the approach received a high degree of acceptance.

The SHIELDS Approach Guide (SHIELDS, 2010) was used as a reference during the various phases of the project.

RESULTS AND FUTURE RESEARCH DIRECTIONS

Lessons Learned from the e-Tourism Project

The process of defining general security goals was found to be rather straightforward. It boils down to gathering essential information about the scenario from the requirements specification. Thus, the assets and processes that affect the economic viability of the business supported by the e-tourism application have to be identified. Each security goal results from the security needed by one of these assets, respectively processes.

While following the new approach using SGITs, it was felt to be very important – especially for the two unskilled practitioners involved in the SGIT creation – to invest time into a training phase where existing SGITs were analyzed. Thus, non-experts were able to create new models after this initial training phase. Hence, analyzing existing SGITs helped the industry partner to focus on the right perspective for defining the indicators.

A more difficult task was the extension of an existing SGIT. The test persons found it difficult to avoid redundancy and to decide when to choose which kind of indicator. Thus, the model creators provided ad-hoc support and additional documentation about existing SGITs, especially about the distinction between positive and negative indicators. In addition, looking at existing examples offered better guidance on whether to model the indicators as positive or negative ones. In summary, the creation of new SGITs and the adaptation of existing SGITs were perceived differently by the test persons.

Regarding the time spent, designing a single SGIT required about four hours. Thus, twelve hours were spent on creating the three new models. An additional 16 hours were needed for training on existing SGITs. In summary, the test persons from TXT generally approved the SGIT approach and the responsible person considered the required time of 28 hours for learning and modeling as adequate. Hence, the application experts were able to learn and create SGITs within a reasonable amount of time.

In summary, the experience of SGIT creation within the e-tourism project has led to the following recommendations:

- Developers involved in the project should thoroughly examine the SGIT formalism and existing examples in order to obtain a better feeling for the use and combination of indicators; this greatly facilitates comprehension of the SGIT syntax and language. Furthermore, developers should browse existing SGITs in order to learn when to reuse existing SGITs by referencing a dependency in their own creations.

- Security experts involved in the creation of SGIT models and in their refinements should logically dissect their specific security goal into a combination of more generic security goals suitable for reuse by others. For example, the verification of the address data by sending a postal letter to the address entered could be formulated in a generic indicator that enforces the use of two-factor verification.

- Developers using SGITs combined with the DEFECT tool were able to perform inspections more effectively, particularly due to the quality of the DEFECT inspection report.

- The DEFECT tool was used by the test engineers for the first time during the e-tourism project and was greatly appreciated by the test engineers, indicating that an inspection that makes use of DEFECT

is easy to perform. One of the comments received from the users was: "The report has a very helpful HTML structure, and it is very beneficial that the indicators within the model have direct links to their related step in the report."

Future Work

One enhancement suggestion that emerged during the application of the approach was to improve the training mechanisms in order to provide better guidance for the modeling process by providing templates, guidelines, and more assistance. This could be done via appropriate tool support providing suggestions and alerts to the user during the indicator definition phase. The usage of templates could generally improve the creation phase. Future work will address the feasibility of SGIT models during inspection and their defect detection capability (effectiveness and efficiency).

The application of SGITs is supported by the DEFECT tool. At the moment, this is limited to defect detection. Further development will address support for the entire inspection process, including planning, resource allocation, meetings, etc. Hence, the tool will be enhanced to provide support for all phases of the inspection. The support for defect detection and the services provided will also be improved.

CONCLUSION

This book chapter summarizes the experiences gained from introducing and developing security goal indicator trees (SGITs) in an industrial environment. SGITs provide security knowledge, especially in early phases of the software development lifecycle. In addition, they have been used in the e-tourism project throughout the entire software development lifecycle to address security-relevant aspects. One very important aspect was the analysis of indicators from the corresponding security goal including design, development, and testing.

The security goals were expanded into three SGITs by defining indicators for the achievement of a specific root node. Using the SGIT approach, a detailed analysis was performed of the actions that must be implemented (positive indicators modeled as green boxes) and the conditions that must be avoided to reach the security goal (negative indicators modeled as red boxes).

By modeling and using SGITs, the TXT team involved in the project improved their focus on security aspects and maintained it during all the various phases of the project. The identification of previously unconsidered security-relevant requirements was improved during the modeling phase of the three SGITs. Furthermore, introducing SGITs at the beginning of the project helped to ensure better code quality in later phases of the software development lifecycle. The approach was found to be very useful and code quality and team efficiency were perceived as improved.

This book chapter highlighted how SGITs were developed and used in the context of an industrial project (even if only one example is shown in this book chapter due to space restrictions, all models are available by consulting (Jung, Elberzhager, Bagnato, & Raiteri, 2010)), and feedback from the practitioners was gathered. In the scenario described, the SGIT approach was perceived as very helpful. It will be applied in other projects in the future.

NOTE

Portions reprinted, with permission, from (Jung, Christian; Elberzhager, Frank; Bagnato, Alessandra; Raiteri, Fabio, Practical Experience Gained from Modeling Security Goals: Using SGITs an Industrial Project (Jung, Elberzhager, Bagnato, & Raiteri, 2010)). © 2010 IEEE.

REFERENCES

Arkin, B., Stender, S., & McGraw, G. (January 2005). Software penetration testing. *IEEE Security and Privacy*, (pp. 84-87).

Denger, C., Ciolkowski, M., & Lanubile, F. (2004). Does active guidance improve software inspections? A preliminary empirical study. *IASTED International Conference Software Engineering*. Innsbruck, Austria: ACTA Press.

Elberzhager, F., Klaus, A., & Jawurek, M. (2009). Software inspections using guided checklists to ensure security goals. *Conference on Availability, Reliability and Security*, (pp. 853-858). Fukuoka.

Evans, D., & Larochelle, D. (2002). Improving security using extensible lightweight static analysis. *IEEE Software*, 42–51. doi:10.1109/52.976940

Fagan, M. E. (1976). Design and code inspections to reduce errors in program development. *IBM Systems Journal*, 38(2-3), 182–211. doi:10.1147/sj.153.0182

Haley, C. B., Moffett, J. D., Laney, R., & Nuseibeh, B. (2006). *A framework for security requirements engineering*. International Workshop on Software Engineering for Secure Systems. Shanghai, China: ACM.

Howard, M. (2006, July/August). A process for performing security code reviews. *IEEE Security and Privacy*, 4(4), 74–79. doi:10.1109/MSP.2006.84

Jung, C., Elberzhager, F., Bagnato, A., & Raiteri, F. (2010). Practical experience gained from modeling security goals: Using SGITs an industrial project. *International Conference on Availability, Reliability, and Security* (pp. 531-536). Krakow, Poland: IEEE.

Megliola, M., & Barbieri, L. (2008). *Integrating agent and wireless technologies for location-based services in cultural heritage*. Digital Cultural Heritage - Essential for Tourism, 2nd EVA Conference, 2008, Vienna.

Peine, H., Jawurek, M., & Mandel, S. (2008). Security goal indicator trees: A model of software features that supports efficient security inspection. *High Assurance Systems Engineering Symposium, HASE* (pp. 9-18). Nanjing, China: IEEE.

Porter, A., & Votta, L. (1998, December). Comparing detection methods for software requirements inspections: A replicated experiment using professional subjects. *Empirical Software Engineering, 3*(4), 355–379. doi:10.1023/A:1009776104355

Runeson, P., Andersson, C., Thelin, T., Andrews, A., & Berling, T. (2006). What do we know about defect detection methods? *IEEE Software, 23*(3), 82–90. doi:10.1109/MS.2006.89

SHIELDS. (31. May 2010). *SHIELDS Project - Detecting known security vulnerabilities from within design and development tools*. Retrieved from http://www.shields-project.eu/files/docs/D1.4%20Final%20SHIELDS%20Approach%20Guide.pdf

SHIELDS. (n.d.). *DEFECT – Dependability focused inspection tool*. Abgerufen am 11. November 2010 von http://www.shields-project.eu/?q=node/119

SHIELDS. (n.d.). *GOAT modelling tool*. Retrieved from http://www.shields-project.eu/?q=node/32

SHIELDS. (n.d.). *SHIELDS - Detecting known security vulnerabilities from within design and development tools*. Retrieved from http://www.shields-project.eu/

SHIELDS. (n.d.). *Software vulnerability repository services*. Retrieved from https://www.shields-project.eu:8181/SVRS/

Strooper, P., & Wojcicki, M. A. (2007). Selecting V&V technology combinations: How to pick a winner? *International Conference on Engineering Complex Computer Systems*, (pp. 87-96). Auckland.

Sutton, M., Greene, A., & Amini, P. (2007). *Fuzzing: Brute force vulnerability discovery*. Amsterdam, The Netherlands: Addison-Wesley Longman.

Swiderski, F., & Snyder, W. (2004). *Threat modeling*. Washington, DC: Microsoft Press.

Takanen, A., DeMott, J. D., & Miller, C. (2008). *Fuzzing for software security testing and quality assurance*. Artech House Publishers.

Wiegers, K. (2002). *Peer reviews in software: A practical guide*. Boston, MA: Addison-Wesley.

KEY TERMS AND DEFINITIONS

Security Checklist: A list of items to be checked or performed as a part of technique to improve the security.

Security Goal: A goal that, when met, contributes to meeting some other security goal or ensures that one or more security properties desired by some stakeholder holds.

Security Indicator: A feature of a system development artifact that constitutes a certain evidence for or against some security goal being realized.

Security Inspection: A set of security instruction that checks system development artifacts (e.g., requirements specification, source code) for correct implementation of certain security goals or for presence of certain vulnerabilities. A security inspection may or may not be based on checking security indicators.

Security Model: A description of a phenomenon or behavior related to security, often simplified by abstracting certain details.

Security Objective: A term closely related to high level security requirements and security goals. Also often used to define the level of security your application should comply with.

Security Pattern: An established and well understood solution to a recurring security problem.

Security Requirement: A detailed requirement that implements an overriding security policy. Security requirements differ from high-level security goals, because they detail "who can do what, when".

SVRS: SVRS is an abbreviation for the SHIELDS Security Vulnerability Repository Service, which is a repository used for sharing of security knowledge (e.g., security models and artifacts).

ENDNOTE

[1]   The tool name recently changed to DETECT.

Chapter 15
Security Enhancement of Peer-to-Peer Session Initiation

Xianghan Zheng
Fuzhou University, P.R. China

Vladimir A. Oleshchuk
University of Agder, Norway

ABSTRACT

Today, Peer-to-Peer SIP based communication systems have attracted much attention from both the academia and industry. The decentralized nature of P2P might provide the distributed peer-to-peer communication system without help of the traditional SIP server. However, the decentralization features come to the cost of the reduced manageability and create new concerns. Until now, the main focus of research was on the availability of the network and systems, while few attempts are put on protecting privacy. In this chapter, we investigate on P2PSIP security issues and introduce two enhancement solutions: central based security and distributed trust security, both of which have their own advantages and disadvantages. After that, we study appropriate combination of these two approaches to get optimized protection. Our design is independent of the DHT (Distributed Hash Table) overlay technology. We take the Chord overlay as the example, and then, analyze the system in several aspects: security & privacy, number-of the hops, message flows, etc.

1. INTRODUCTION

Peer-to-Peer (P2P) computing has attracted great attention in both academia and industry. Compare with traditional server-based system architecture in which most of functionality is executed in server side, P2P-based computing allocates computing task to all participating peers. This might eliminate/

DOI: 10.4018/978-1-4666-0978-5.ch015

reduce functionality of server and therefore provides better robustness on system level. Today, P2P computing has been widely implemented in many kinds of networking systems and applications.

In communication field, one of the most well-known P2P applications is Skype ("Skype official website - download Skype free now for free calls and internet calls,"), which offers free Voice-over-IP (VoIP) and Instant Messaging (IM) services for computer-to-computer and charged services for computer-to-PSTN. Additionally, Skype service has been extended to mobile world. Many mobile platforms today (e.g. Symbian S60 ("Nokia - Nokia on the Web,"), iPhone OS (*Apple*), Android (*Android.com - Android at Google I/O*), Windows Mobile (*Mobile Phones | Choose the Best Phone for You | Windows Mobile*), etc), have been embedded with Wi-Fi/3G connection based Skype application. According to eBay statistics ("eBay Inc. Corporate Fact Sheet: Q3 2009,"), the number of Skype users has reached 521 million until Q3, 2009, and it is still growing fast.

However, Skype protocol has been monopolized and made unpublic. Although part of its functionality (e.g. login, NAT traversal, media transfer, codec, etc) has been understood via analyzing Skype network traffic (!!! INVALID CITATION !!!), researchers (outside Skype project) are still uncertain about its core technical specification, disadvantages, and required improvement. Besides, Skype does not provide interoperability with other open applications, such as SIP based WLM (Windows Live Messenger) (*Windows Live Messenger*), Yahoo IM ("Yahoo! Messenger - Chat, Instant message, SMS, Video Call, PC Calls,"), etc. This is partly because of

technical difficulty in seamless interconnecting among different protocols, and partly because of unwillingness of cooperation with its competitors.

The success of Skype greatly inspired the research on peer-to-peer based communication systems. Researchers were trying to find an alternative solution where on one hand, decentralized nodes are capable to auto-configure themselves in IP-based Ad-Hoc style; and on the other hand, the designed protocol supports fast location of nodes, optimized route selection, secure and reliable service delivery. Let us take a look at Figure 1, which illustrates an example of P2P based communication paradigm. Each node in the system has a few connections with its neighbours, and these neighbours act as intermediate nodes to deliver requests and responses. A few routing mechanisms, negotiation protocols are supposed to be implemented so that session between source peer (for instance, A in the figure) and destination peer (B) can be established in optimized way. The designed protocol is assumed to be an open standard so that everyone could develop applications on it.

However, reality is different. After a few studies, researchers began to recognize that it was not

Figure 1. P2P based communication

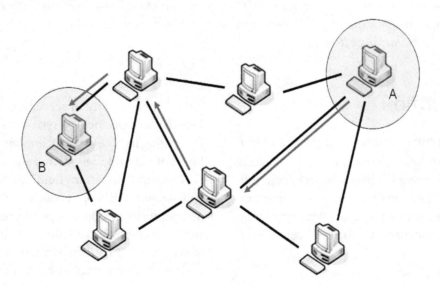

trivial to realize this type communication paradigm. P2P protocol lacks of session level description and negotiation mechanisms, which make some functionalities (such as optimized route selection, media codec negotiation, etc) difficult to achieve. At this moment, Session Initiation Protocol (SIP) comes into the sight.

Session Initiation Protocol (SIP) is a transaction-oriented, text-based protocol that inherits the simplicity from Hypertext Transfer Protocol (HTTP) and Simple Mail Transfer Protocol (SMTP) (Sparks, 2007). It is designed to create, modify, and terminate sessions with one or more participants. Because of its characteristics (e.g. Simplicity, extensibility, flexibility, etc), SIP is chosen by 3rd Generation Partnership Project (3GPP) as the main protocol for the IP Multimedia Subsystems (IMS)-based future All-IP network ("The SIP Center - A portal for the commercial development of SIP Session Initiation Protocol,"). SIP to telecommunication systems is regarded as important as HTTP to Internet.

Therefore, researchers began to study the approaches that combine decentralization nature of P2P with efficiency of SIP protocol. In 2003, the SIPpeer project at University of Columbia (Kundan Singh & Schulzrinne, 2005; Kundan Singh & Schulzrinne, Jan, 2005) and the SOSIMPLE project at William & Mary College (David. A Bryan, Lowekamp, & Jennings, 2005) were the first attempts in the study of P2PSIP communication systems. In the following years, the P2PSIP research has attracted great attention both from academia and industry (e.g. Cisco, Nokia, Ericsson, HuaWei, etc). IETF P2PSIP Working Group defines the motivation of P2PSIP ("P2PSIP,") as following: "The concept behind P2PSIP is to leverage the distributed nature of P2P to allow for distributed resource discovery in a SIP network, eliminating (at least reducing) the need for centralized servers".

A lot of possible solutions have been proposed in recent publications (D. A Bryan, Lowekamp, & Zangrilli, April, 2008; Cao, Bryan, & Lowekamp,

Feb, 2006; Fessi, Niedermayer, Kinkelin, & Carle, July, 2007; Matuszewski & Kokkonen, Jan, 2008) and Internet-drafts (D. A Bryan, Matthews, Shim, Willis, & Dawkins, July, 2008; Jennings, Lowekamp, Rescorla, Baset, & Schulzrinne, July, 2010; Maenpaa & Camarillo, July, 2010; H. Song, Jiang, Even, & Bryan, July, 2010). However, P2PSIP is still far from mature. Many technical questions are waiting for urgent answers. One of most critical questions is security.

As a originally designed algorithm for file sharing, P2P protocol does not focus much about system efficiency. For instance, the delay in P2P applications (e.g. BitComet (*BitComet - A free C++ BitTorrent/HTTP/FTP Download Client*), BitTorrent ("BitTorrent,"), etc) can be from a few seconds to even minutes. This is unacceptable in real-time multimedia services. Therefore, conventional peer/resource lookup algorithm is required to be improved or replaced.

Besides, the decentralized nature of P2P comes to the cost of less or decentralized management, which might also create security problems. In such scenario all participating nodes may distrust each other due to lack of centralized credential mechanism. It is possible that some malicious nodes create negative experience to the other nodes (for example, modify the received message and forward it out) or the overlay. Therefore, data transactions from beginning to end are regarded as not trusted.

In this chapter, we investigate on P2PSIP security issues and introduce two enhancement solutions: central based security and distributed trust security, both of which have their own advantages and disadvantages. After that, we study appropriate combination of these two approaches to get optimized protection. Our design is independent of the DHT (Distributed Hash Table) overlay technology.

2. SECURITY CHALLENGES

Security is one of biggest challenges in P2PSIP systems. The decentralized nature of P2P comes to the cost of reduced manageability and therefore causes security problems, e.g. distrust, privacy leaks, unpredictable availability, etc. In the following, we introduce security problems, including general security problems and P2P specific problems.

2.1 Generic Security Problems

Generic security problems are vulnerabilities existed in most of networking systems. In the following, we specify three kinds of generic security problems.

Denial-Of-Service attack

Denial-Of-Service (DoS) attack is an attempt to make a computer resource unavailable to its intended users (Needham, 1993). Generally, DoS attack is implemented by either forcing the target to reset or consuming its resource so that the victim is not able to offer intended services. In P2PSIP network, a malicious peer could flood a multitude of P2PSIP request to one or more peers. This might consume the computing resource or prevent legitimate network traffic. The flooding can be also overlay maintenance packets, which might endanger overlay performance.

Distributed Denial-Of-Service (DDoS) (Mirkovic, Prier, & Reiher, 2002) is the evolution of DoS when a multitude of compromised systems are involved into the attack. DDoS attack depends on a wide range of victim machines remote controlled by malicious program, called "Trojan horse" (*Trojan Horse - Wikipedia, the free encyclopedia*). The "Trojan horse" can be remotely activated and direct an attack to a certain peers or a part of overlay network.

DoS and DDoS attacks are big issue to most of network systems. Efficient credential mechanism

is able to reduce this attack; however, it is difficult to eliminate it.

2.1.1 Man-in-the-middle Attack

Man-in-the middle (MIM) attack (Ornaghi & Valleri) is a form of active eavesdropping. It might happen when an attacker impersonates enough sensitive information (e.g. IP, port, secret, etc) of endpoints that are talking each other. The attacker splits a normal connection into two separate tunnels, however, makes victims believe they are talking over a private connection, as illustrated in Figure 2. After that, the attacker M is capable to intercept all the messages going between two victims and send whatever response he wants.

In P2PSIP network, each participating peer must help each other in routing and storage. This gives great opportunity for malicious intermediate peer to study sensitive privacy of other peers. The information can be used to initiate MIM attack during the connection of victims.

Appropriate authentication mechanisms should be implemented to reduce the impact of this attack.

2.1.2 Worm Propagation

Worm (Spafford, 1989) is a self-replicating malware computer program. It spreads by exploiting vulnerabilities in software or operating systems. Worms propagating through P2P systems and applications might be disastrous. Since all the computers in P2P network are running the same (or similar) software, an attacker might compromise the entire overlay by finding only one exploitable security breach. Besides, it is much easier to propagate worm application because each P2P peer maintains a list of neighbouring peers, and these peers are considered trusted each other. Moreover, most peers are personal computers in real life, therefore, worm program is more likely to catch person private data (e.g.

Figure 2. Man-in-the-Middle Attack

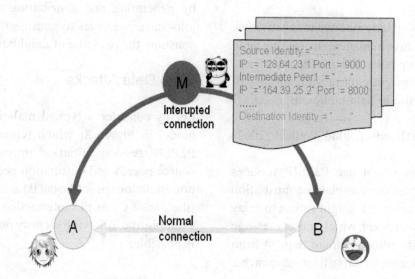

credit card numbers, user name, passwords, etc), which is attractive to attackers.

2.2 P2P Specific Security Challenges

Besides generic secure threats, P2PSIP systems also face specific security problems caused by P2P decentralized nature. Security problems include identity attack, overlay attack, data attack, Spam over Internet (SPIT), and other malicious behaviour. In this section, we specify these attacks.

2.2.1 Identity Attacks

Before participating the overlay, each peer needs to apply a unique identity (for instance, apply from an E&A centralized server). However, identity might be misused.

1.   Sybil attack (Douceur, 2002)

Since peer identifier is free to apply, a malicious attacker could create many identities and use them to join the overlay network. If these identities become valid, they can gain control on a part of network. These malicious entities are capable to compromise the network through malicious behaviours (e.g. compromise message routing, delete storage, etc).

2.   Eclipse attack (A. Singh, Ngan, Druschel, & Wallach, 2006)

Eclipse attack is closely related to Sybil attack. Intermediate peers can conspire to hijack and dominate the neighbour set of correct peers by controlling the data traffic through routing.

3.   Identity hijack (Seedorf, 2006)

Source peer sends out a request by forwarding the request to its neighbour peer who is nearest to the destination. However, a malicious neighbour is capable to intercept request message and responds to source that he is the destination peer. By pretending to be destination peer, the attacker can hijack a connection at setup time.

2.2.2 Overlay attacks

Overlay functions include maintenance activities, such as peer join/leave management, routing table construction and updates, link management, etc. A malicious peer might exploit vulnerability of these operations and initiate malicious attacks.

1.   Free ridding (Seedorf, 2006; Wallach, 2002)

Malicious peer might use P2PSIP services while refuse to provide reasonable contribution to overlay. For example, it might refuse to relay message for the other peers, which causes message lost. Also, it might refuse storage request from other peers by reducing/deleting its storage cache.

2.   Join-leave attack (Seedorf, 2006)

Joining and leaving overlay would generate a series of maintenance messages to neighbouring peers (for example, notification to successors and predecessors to update their routing table).

A malicious peer might compromise the overlay by generating and distributing a multitude of join-leave messages to confuse the overlay, and consume the resource of neighbouring peers.

2.2.3 Data Attacks

Let us consider a typical malicious behaviour model in Figure 3, which represents a typical P2PSIP session initiation interaction between source peer A and destination peer D. There are non-malicious peer (the cat B) and malicious peer (the panda C) as the intermediate peers. In this example, the following security related behaviour is possible.

1.   Data Temper

For example, peer C is capable to drop, misroute, and modify the message it received.

2.   Replay Attacks

Figure 3. A Malicious Behaviour Model

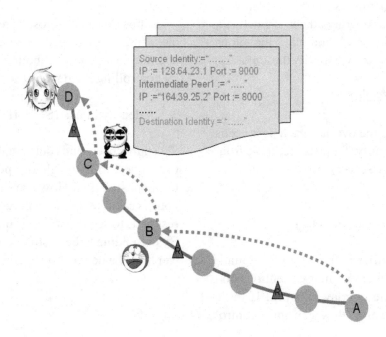

Figure 4. Potential P2PSIP Request

```
INVITE 80000000000000000000000000000001 SIP/2.0
Via: SIP/2.0/TCP client.example.com:5060
  ;branch=z9hG4bK74bf9
Max-Forwards: 70
From: 40e0f000a000b000r000r0000f000e01; tag=9fxced76sl
To: 80000000000000000000000000000001
Call-ID: 3848276298220188511
CSeq: 1 INVITE
Contact: 40e0f000a000b000r000r0000f000e01; transport=tcp
Content-Length: 0
```

The malicious peer can retransmit the previous message to confuse the overlay or replace newer data with old information.

3.   Privacy leaks

Let us take a look at a potential "P2PSIP INVITE" message presented on Figure 4. The "From" header indicates the source peer identity; the "To" header shows the destination peer identity; the "Via" header stores the identity/address of previous intermediate peers. These information may cause privacy violation. For instance, malicious peer C is capable to record a profile of source and destination peers (e.g. Identifier, IP, Port, etc.) through parsing the incoming P2PSIP messages. This information can be used to initiate a DoS attack to a peer or overlay network. It might also be sold to illegal advertisement parties, which results in much spam messages and calls.

2.2.4 SPIT Attacks

Similar with junk mail (or SPAM), SPAM over Internet Telephony (SPIT) (Schlegel, Niccolini, Tartarelli, & Brunner, 2006) greatly degrades user experience. SPIT can be initiated by an advertising agent who randomly selects a party to call for advertisements. The impact of this attack primarily depends on the size of advertising agency (e.g. the number of employees, etc). Another type of SPIT

is generated by computer software. It systematically or randomly selects one or more parties and transmits pre-recorded advertising message once connection is established. This annoys users because P2PSIP based devices might ring anytime.

As a type of synchronous communication, SPIT is more difficult to prevent than traditional asynchronous E-mail systems because there is not as much time to apply filter mechanism before communication establishment.

2.2.5 Other threats

Anonymity (Seedorf, 2006)

P2P systems allows for anonymity during communication. The easiest way to do this is just hide source identifier in P2PSIP request. However, the destination peer, who does not know the source, might regard it as malicious and refuse to receive it.

Lawful interception (Seedorf, 2008)

A Lawful Interception activity gets triggered by a Law Enforcement Agency (LEA) which authorises a Network Operator, Access Provider, or Service Provider to intercept traffic for a target identity. Lawful interception in P2PSIP systems, to some degree, damages the privacy because all information, including source identity, destination identity, call duration, and other signalling is intercepted.

3. SOLUTIONS

3.1. Proxy based security

Proxy based architecture is commonplace used in a huge variety of networking systems and applications. A proxy is an intermediary entity that intercepts communication and performs necessary services on behalf of network system. In most cases, proxy acts as a protocol translator, content adapter, security and privacy provider.

The original intention of P2PSIP is to eliminate the need of centralized entities. However, researchers begin to realize that this is not trivial, especially when considering security issues. Due to the distrust among participating peers, the session initiation process from the beginning and the subsequent data traffic are distrusted and insecure.

In this section, a possible proxy based security framework is proposed. The proposed proxy solution should, on one hand protect security and privacy, and on the other hand do not add much burden in system efficiency. Proxy entities MUST be assumed pre-configured and pre-exist at the backbone of overlay.

3.1.1 Proxy-based Architecture

Our proposed architecture involves three main parts: P2PSIP Peer, Resource, Chord Secure Proxy (CSP), as shown in Figure 5.

P2PSIP peer, which can be a mobile phone, laptop, PC, etc., is connected into the Internet. Resource is the data value stored in a particular peer. Each peer and resource is identified by an integer ID. Chord Secure Proxy (CSP) is the secure and trusted proxy server as well as a preconfigured P2PSIP peer in the overlay.

For locating a peer/resource in the overlay, the source peer first sends P2PSIP request to a specific CSP that is nearest to the destination. We logically regard this part of the network as source network (Step 1). The CSP acts as a proxy server to probe the existence of the destination peer and

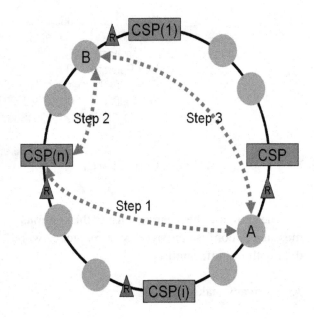

Figure 5. Architecture Overview

securely forward P2PSIP request message to the destination peer (Step 2). We logically consider this part of network as the destination network. After locating the destination peer, the connection can be established (Step 3).

Note that all the connections are SSL/TLS secured.

Chord Secure Proxy (CSP) is the key inter-working unit, acting as a bridge between source peer and destination peer. It is deployed as P2PSIP application server with the functionality of a normal P2PSIP peer. There are four main components inside a CSP unit (see Figure 6):

- Source inter-working. This part receives P2PSIP request from source peer. Based on security requirement in the request, source inter-working component chooses corresponding handling strategy.
- Policy management. This part is the decision center to decide which type of secure service should be handled. Inside this component, there is a policy database recording all the policy items.

Figure 6. Chord Secure Proxy Internal

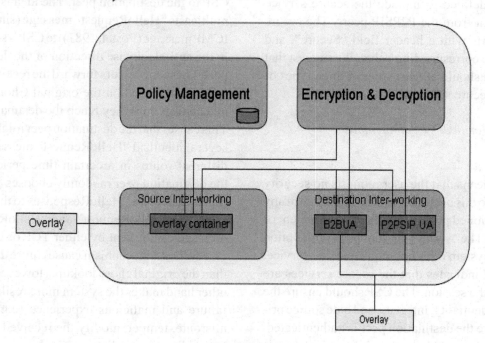

- Encryption & Decryption. This component helps CSP to encrypt the outgoing message and decrypt the incoming message.
- Destination Inter-working. Destination inter-working component is the portal function that probes destination peer, and forwards the P2PSIP request. The UA sub-component acts as normal P2PSIP peer; B2BUA subcomponent handles the secure services in the destination network.

3.1.2 Security

The communications in the source network and the destination network should be securely encrypted. P2PSIP WG (D. A Bryan et al., July, 2008) has suggested PKI-based certificate approach to provide security guarantees and functionality such as encryption, decryption, digital signature, etc. This can be reused in our proposed system.

3.1.3 Source Inter-working

Source Inter-working component contains an overlay container for receiving P2PSIP requests. With the assistance of Encryption & Decryption component, it is able to encrypt the outgoing response and decrypt the arriving requests. Besides, based on secure requirement from the message, Inter-working component turns to Policy Management component for the corresponding handling mechanism and delivers the message to the corresponding component in destination Inter-working component. Moreover, source inter-working component is responsible to response with the error code if exception happens in source network (e.g. the request message is in bad format; secure service request is not understood, etc).

3.1.4 Policy Management

Policy management contains a policy database that stores requirement items of how to handle the secure services. A new P2PSIP extension header is defined to include the secure service requirement from the P2PSIP peers. The secure header starts with a header field "Secure", and follows the corresponding value. We suggest that the system should at least support three types of different secure services:

"none" / "critical" / "anonymous"

where

none means that the user requests no security functions to this message request regardless of any pre-provisioned profile or default requirement of the device. The overlay peer can specify this option when the system does not require secure service.

critical indicates that the secure services are critical in the session. The CSP should ensure the data confidentiality, integrity, and hide source privacy before the destination peer is authenticated. The request should be rejected if service can not be supported.

anonymous value requests that the CSP should hide all the source sensitive privacy information to the other peers, including the destination peer. The request should be rejected if service can not be supported.

3.1.5 Destination Network

We logically define destination network that represents the connections from the specific CSP to the destination peer. The idea is that CSP multicasts "HelloRequest" message (similar with ICMP message (Postel, 1981)) to CSP's successors in the anti-clockwise direction of the destination peer. These successors forward the received "HelloRequest" based on the original Chord lookup mechanism until they reach the destination peer. This causes that the destination peer might receive several identical "HelloRequest" messages from different routes in a certain time period. Then, the destination peer randomly chooses one of the routes and return "HelloResponse" to the specific CSP. The "HelloRequest" and "HelloResponse" message can be sent by either TCP or UDP.

Multicast mechanism causes more data traffic than the original chord lookup. However, it on the other hand makes the system more resilient to the failure and malicious experience (e.g. discard, misroute, temper, modify the received message, etc) of the intermediate peer.

We define the structure of "HelloRequest" and "HelloResponse" messages (See Figure 7 and Figure 8) that include three fields (TOS, Code, Checksum) and five fields of P2P information (Call-ID, CSP Identifier, CSP public address and port, Destination Identifier). In the "HelloResponse" message, two more fields (Destination peer public address and port) are added. The descriptions of these fields are as following:

Figure 7. "HelloRequest" Message Format

Type of Service (8)	Code (8)	Checksum (16)
Call-ID (32 bits integer)		
Chord Secure Proxy Identifier (128/160bits)		
Chord Secure Proxy Public IP address		
Chord Secure Proxy port		
Destination Peer Identifier		

Figure 8. "HelloResponse" Message Format

Type of Service (8)	Code (8)	Checksum (16)
Call-ID (32 bits integer)		
Chord Secure Proxy Identifier (128/160bits)		
Chord Secure Proxy Public IP address		
Chord Secure Proxy port		
Destination Peer Identifier		
Destination Peer Public IP Address		
Destination Peer port		

TOS: describes the service type of this message. For instance, we can define 8 as the "HelloRequest" and 0 as the "HelloResponse".

Code: this is the further specification of the "Hello" message. For example, an unreachable destination might have this field set from 1 to 15. Each different number represents different error types.

Checksum: this field contains error checking of data from the whole "Hello" message.

Call-ID: a random number for identify "Hello" message.

CSP Identifier: an Integer ID of CSP.

CSP Public IP Address: public accessible address of CSP.

CSP port: public accessible port of CSP.

Destination peer Identifier: P2PSIP ID of destination peer.

Destination Public IP Address: public accessible address of destination peer.

Destination port: public access port of the destination Peer.

3.1.6 Use Scenarios

Use case 1 (see Figure 9) describes the P2PSIP communication establishment process between

source peer A and destination peer B. Possible messages flows are:

1. Source peer sends the P2PSIP "INVITE" message to a specific CSP that is clockwise nearest to the destination peer.
2. CSP multicasts a "HelloRequest" message to a few successors before the destination. Intermediate peers forward the "HelloRequest" to the next hop, step by step, until the destination.
3. Destination peer receives several identical "HelloRequest", and randomly chooses one of them. Then a "HelloResponse" is returned to CSP.
4. CSP forwards P2PSIP "INVITE" message to the destination peer.
5. Destination peer returns a P2PSIP "180 Ringing" to the source peer.
6. Session negotiation and establishment.

Figure 10 shows a use scenario with a malicious or compromised peer sitting in the destination network to interfere the message flow. Malicious/compromised peer (represent as a panda) is capable to discard, misroute, temper, and eavesdrop the data received. However, CSP-based system is tolerant to the malicious behaviour and guarantees

Figure 9. A Normal Use Scenario

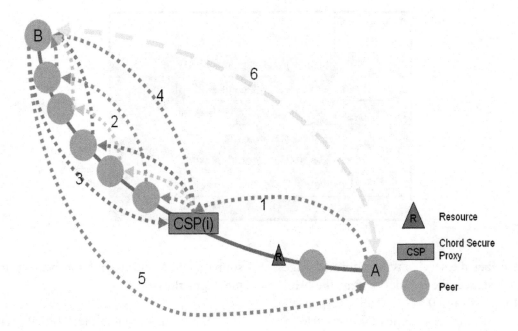

Figure 10. Malicious Interference Scenario

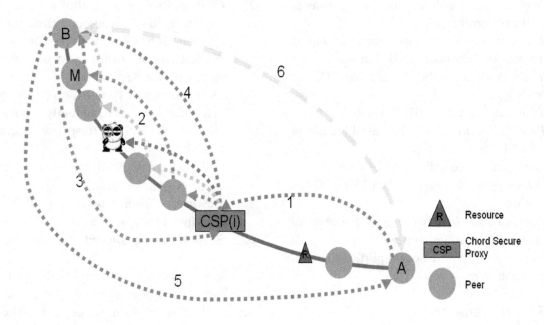

the system availability because CSP multicast mechanism increases the surviving rate of "HelloRequest" messages. Possible interaction can be as following:

1. Source peer sends the P2PSIP "INVITE" message to a specific CSP that is responsible for the destination peer.

2. CSP multicasts "HelloRequest" message to probe the destination. A few messages might be received by the malicious intermediate peer and thus is possible to be discarded, misrouted, tempered, etc. However, the others are routed to the destination peer B.

3. Destination peer receives several identical "HelloRequest", and randomly chooses one of them for handling. Then a "HelloResponse" is returned to the specific CSP.

4. CSP forwards P2PSIP "INVITE" message to the destination peer.

5. Destination peer returns a P2PSIP "180 Ringing" back to the source peer.

6. Session negotiation and establishment.

3.1.7 Evaluation

We evaluate the proposed system from several aspects: theoretical analysis, delay testing, and the implementation of a typical malicious use scenario.

Theoretical Analysis

In Chord-based system, the average number of hops is ½ $log N$ (Stoica et al., 2003), where N is the number of peers in the overlay. Assumed that there are S CSPs, splitting the overlay into S parts evenly. Therefore, the average number of hops between CSP and destination peer (for instance, CSP(i) to peer B in Figure 5-5) is

$$\frac{1}{2} \log(N / S)$$

Adding one hop connection to source network, the average number of hops in CSP-based overlay is:

$$\frac{1}{2} \log(N / S) + 1$$

The comparison in Figure 11 (We select S=16 and S= 32 for illustration) shows that CSP-based

Figure 11. Comparison of Number of Hops

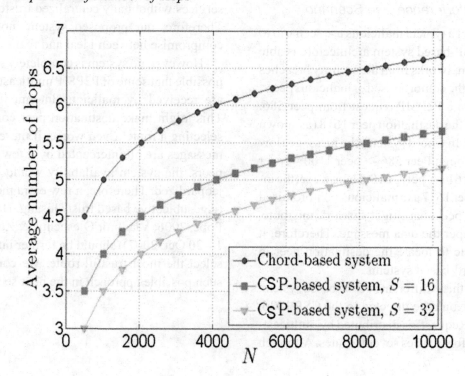

system reduces the number of hops comparing with original Chord-based system. Besides, the more CSPs in the overlay, the less hops needed (in average).

Delay Measurement

We also measure the delay in CSP based overlay. Peer 586 is set to be the source peer which sends out P2PSIP request to 100 random destination peers. We measure the time period between sending out request "P2PSIP INVITE" and receiving the response "180 Ringing", and get the average delay 62ms. This is much higher than Chord-based overlay (16ms as described in (Zheng & Oleshchuk, Oct, 2009)).

We believe this is because destination peer in CSP-based system should wait a certain period of time for receiving multiple "HelloRequest" requests (For instance, we set it to 30ms). Besides, the data traffic caused by multicast might increase the burden of the system and therefore enlarge the delay.

Malicious Interference Use Scenario

We implement a typical malicious use scenario to show that CSP-based system architecture is able to protect the networks from the security breaches coming from the compromised or malicious peers.

We initiate a P2PSIP request from peer 586, searching for the destination peer 1618 (as shown in Figure 12). In Chord system, the message flow should go through Peer 586 -> peer 1100 -> peer 1613 -> peer 1617-> peer 1618. Then, we set the intermediate peer 1617 as a malicious/compromised intermediate peer that might discard, misroute, revise or temper the data message. Therefore, it is not possible to locate the destination peer in original Chord-based systems.

However, this is different in CSP-based system. The request would be directed to the CSP 1536. Then "HelloRequest" is distributed by multicasting and therefore causes several routes. Although

one of the routes is interfered by malicious peer 1617 (the red route in Figure 5-9), two others (Green and black routes) can still reach the destination peer. Finally, the destination peer could randomly pick up the black or the green route for handling.

3.1.8 Summary

In this section we have proposed a proxy-based secure architecture for P2PSIP session initiation. The system architecture resolves several issues including security, source inter-working, policy management, message transaction, destination inter-working. We use the implementation to show feasibility of this solution. Also, the evaluation shows that this system offers protection of the network from the compromised/malicious peers.

P2PSIP aims to build decentralized communication systems without (or with limited) help of centralized server. However, the proposed system model breaks (slightly) the original concept of P2PSIP. During the research, we realize that it is difficult for P2PSIP system to provide secure services without any centralized trusted entities. Therefore, our proposed system model is the compromise between ideal and reality.

However, no system is completely secure. It is possible that some of P2PSIP multicast messages are received by malicious intermediate peers. This might make destination peer confusing in selecting a route. Even worse, if these multicast messages are all intercepted by a few malicious peers, the system availability would be greatly jeopardized. Therefore, a few extra mechanisms (e.g. subjective based trust (Josang, Hayward, & Pope, 2006; Vladimir Oleshchuk & Zadorozhny, 14-20 Oct, 2007)) should be further integrated to select the most trustful route. We consider one such possible approach in the next section.

Figure 12. A Malicious Interference Use Scenario

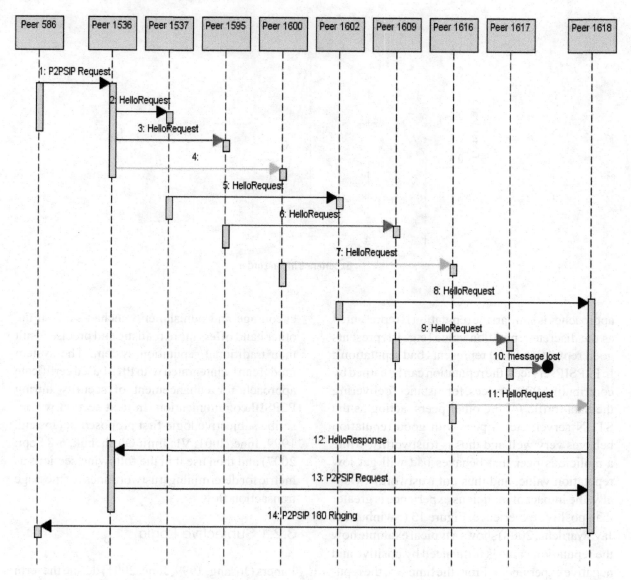

3.2. Trusted based Security Approach

Research efforts to improve P2PSIP trustworthiness are mostly based on PKI-based certificate approaches that have been proposed in the literature (D. A Bryan et al., April, 2008; Jennings et al., July, 2010). In this approach, certificates are issued by a Certification Authority (CA).

Certificates proves the existence and legitimacy of the specific peers.

Reputation system can be another approach to provide distributed trust. A reputation system collects, distributes, and aggregates feedback about participants' past behaviour. Several typical approaches for P2P distributed system are described in (Kinateder, Terdic, & Rothermel, 2005; Sepandar, Mario, & Hector, 2003; S. Song, Hwang, Zhou, & Kwok, 2005). The idea of these

Figure 13. Trust based Security

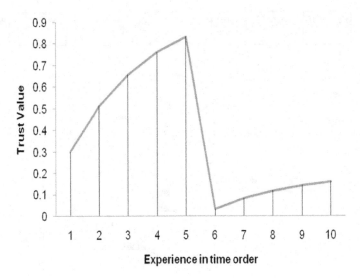

approaches is similar: the reputation is represented as the discrete reputation value (e.g. 1 represents good reputation and 0 represents bad reputation). In P2PSIP services, the reputation can be earned by contributing P2P services, for instance, delivering the data traffic for the other peers, acting as the STUN server, etc. A peer with good reputation behaves very well and thus is trustworthy, while a malicious peer that behaves bad will get low reputation value, and thus not trustworthy. Usually, the impact of malicious experience is greater than positive experience. Figure 13 (Swinburn & Jayawardena, 2008) shows a typical example how the reputation value is influenced by positive and negative experiences. From the time 1-5, the reputation value increases due to the good behaviour. However, the value decreases a lot (more than the sum of the previous 5 steps) in time 6 when the peer makes bad experience. Step 7-10 shows the positive experiences, however with lower increasing rate in the value than step 1-5.

In this section, we propose a novel trust-awareness based security enhancement approach. The proposed solution is based on subjective logic trust calculation, which on one hand absorbs advantages of reputation system (for instance,

encourage and punishment mechanism), on the other hand offers more realistic and precise result than traditional reputation system. The system model can be integrated with PKI-based certificate approach for enhancement of security during P2PSIP communication. In next section we describe subjective logic first proposed in (Josang, 1999, June, 2001; Vladimir Oleshchuk, 6-8 Sept, 2007) and then use it in the following sections as metric for determining trustworthiness of message transaction flow.

3.2.1 Subjective Logic

Papers (Josang, 1999, June, 2001) define the term opinion, denoted ω, which expresses an opinion about trustworthiness level. Let t, d and u be such that, $\{t, d, u\} \in [0, 1]$ and $t + d + u = 1$ Then a triple $\omega = \{t, d, u\}$ called an opinion where components t, d and u represent levels of *trust*, *distrust* and *uncertainty* respectively. The level of trustworthiness can be defined based on several elements, For example, trustworthiness level associated with distrust could be expressed as opinion $\omega_1 = \{0, 0.95, 0.05\}$, but trustworthiness level associated with high level of trust could be expressed as opinion $\omega_2 = \{0.89, 0.00, 0.11\}$. By varying these parameters one can express several levels of trust. Expressing trust by using three parameters instead of one simple trust level gives more adequate trust model of real world since when different opinions are combined these parameters are treated differently.

The subjective logic defines a set of logical operators for combining opinions such that conjunction, recommendation, consensus, etc (Josang, 1999, June, 2001). Let $\omega_p^B = \{t_p^B, d_p^B, u_p^B\}$ denote an opinion of peer B about logical statement p. In context of this section B is a P2PSIP peer in the overlay and statement p may be a statement that "data received by B are unchanged".

Assume that a peer A has an opinion $\omega_B^A = \{t_B^A, d_B^A, u_B^A\}$ about trustworthiness of recommendations given by B. Since entity A does not have any direct opinion ω_p^A when the message goes to peer B, it will try to deduce the indirect opinion about trustworthiness of p, denoted ω_p^{AB}, based on recommendation (opinion ω_p^B) given by B. For this purpose the recommendation operator $\otimes$ is introduced as follows.

$$\omega_p^{AB} = \omega_B^A \otimes \omega_p^B = \{t_p^{AB}, d_p^{AB}, u_p^{AB}\}$$

where

$$t_p^{AB} = t_B^A t_p^B, \quad d_p^{AB} = t_B^A d_p^B \text{ and}$$

$$u_p^{AB} = d_B^A + u_B^A + t_B^A u_p^B.$$

3.2.2 Subjective Logic based Architecture

In this section we propose an subject logic based trust architecture. The proposed architecture involves three main parts: P2PSIP Peer, Resource, and Secure Opinion Server (SOS), as shown in Figure 14. P2PSIP peer is connected to the Internet. Resource is the data value stored in a specific peer. Secure Opinion Server (SOS) is the trust management server that stores and computes the dynamic opinion for each P2PSIP peer.

To locate a peer/resource, the source peer first multicasts P2PSIP request to a certain number of successors which is in the anti-clockwise direction of the destination peer. Intermediate peers forward the received request step by step until the destina-

Figure 14. Subjective Logic Trust Model

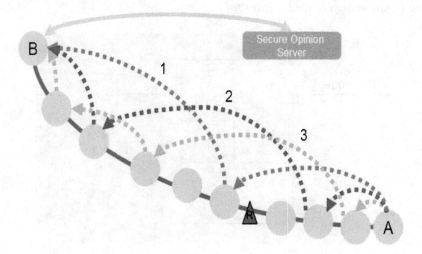

tion peer. Finally, the destination peer might receive multiple request messages, and it turns to the SOS server for selecting the most trustful one. After that, the session between source peer and destination peer could be securely established.

Secure Opinion Server (SOS) is the key interworking unit, acting as a decision maker for the destination peer. Note that SOS can be either collocated inside the Enrolment and Authentication (E&A) server or as a separate unit. It contains three components (See Figure 15):

- Connection handling receives the RPC (Remote Procedure Call) request message (that contains a list of route options), and generates the corresponding response.
- Opinion computation is responsible to calculate the opinion of each message flow based on the subjective logic rules. Besides, it updates the opinion for each peer periodically (according to the rules defined in section 3.2.4).
- Opinion DB is a component that stores current opinion about trustworthiness of each P2PSIP peer.

3.2.3 Opinion Calculation

The following will demonstrate opinion calculation based on subjective logic rules. Suppose that a request goes from the source peer A, through intermediate peers B_1, B_2, B_{n-1}, and to the destination peer B_n. Let p denote as "data received by B_n is unchanged". By applying the rules of subjective logic described in Section 2, the trustworthiness of this data delivered through this route can be calculated as following:

$$\omega_p^{AB_1B_2\ldots B_{n-1}B_n} = \omega_{B_1}^A \otimes \omega_{B_2}^{B_1} \otimes \omega_{B_3}^{B_2} \otimes \ldots \otimes \omega_{B_n}^{B_{n-1}} \otimes \omega_p^{B_n}$$

Where

$$t_p^{AB_1B_2\ldots B_{n-1}B_n} = t_{B_1}^A t_{B_2}^{B_1} t_{B_3}^{B_2} \ldots t_{B_n}^{B_{n-1}} t_p^{B_n} = t_{B_1}^S t_{B_2}^S t_{B_3}^S \ldots t_{B_n}^S t_{B_n}^S$$

$$d_p^{AB_1B_2\ldots B_{n-1}B_n} = t_{B_1}^A t_{B_2}^{B_1} t_{B_3}^{B_2} \ldots t_{B_n}^{B_{n-1}} d_p^{B_n} = t_{B_1}^S t_{B_2}^S t_{B_3}^S \ldots t_{B_n}^S d_{B_n}^S$$

$$u_p^{AB_1B_2\ldots B_{n-1}B_n} = 1 - t_{B_1}^A t_{B_2}^{B_1} t_{B_3}^{B_2} \ldots t_{B_n}^{B_{n-1}} t_p^{B_n} (1 - u_p^{B_n})$$
$$= 1 - t_{B_1}^S t_{B_2}^S t_{B_3}^S \ldots t_{B_n}^S t_{B_n}^S (1 - u_{B_n}^S)$$

Figure 15. Secure Opinion Server (SOS) Internal

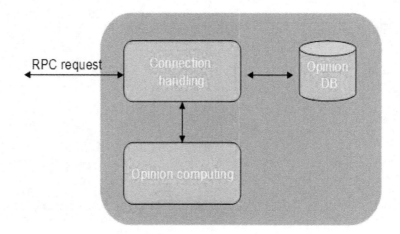

Based on the opinion result, we introduce another parameter v that represents the final score of a specific message transmission. The higher value of v, the higher trustworthiness of this message flow. We define v in the following:

$$v = t + (1/2)u - 2d$$

3.2.4 Opinion Maintenance

SOS is the secure server that stores the opinion for each peer in the overlay. We define the Initial Opinion (IOP) as the first opinion when peer joins the overlay for the first time. The Secure Opinion Server (SOS) assigns the IOP based on the system capabilities of the peer, such as available processing power (p), memory (m), bandwidth (b), etc. For instance, the rule could be as following:

- Initiative distrust value is: *0*.
- If the available processing is larger than *200MHZ*, $p=(1/6)$; otherwise, $p = (1/6)*(processing/200M)$.
- If bandwidth is larger than 300k, $b = (1/6)$; otherwise, $b = (1/6)*(bandwidth/300k)$.
- If memory is larger than *100M*, $m = (1/6)$; otherwise, $m = (1/6)*(free\ memory/100M)$.
- Initial trust value $t=p+b+m$, if $p+b+m<0.5$, otherwise, $t=0.5$.
- Initiative uncertainty value is: *1-t*.

The opinion is dynamically updated according to the behaviour of each peer. It may increase in some rate according to the contribution of the overlay (e.g. act as the intermediate peer to relay the traffic, etc) or degrades when have no contribution (for example, do nothing at some time period). The encouragement rules could be as following:

When the peer acts as an intermediate peer that relays the data traffic, the trust t increases and

the uncertainty u decreases if the peer behaves as expected:

$$t = t_{prev} + (1/200)d_{prev} + (1/200)u_{prev}$$

$$d = d_{prev} * (199/200) \text{ and}$$

$$u = u_{prev} * (199/200)$$

Periodically, the SOS server inspects the opinion DB. If the peer does not contributes in the time period (e.g. 10 minutes, etc), it is suspected to be malicious or faulty peer. Therefore, the distrust d increases while the trust t and the uncertainty u decrease. We define the rule as followed:

$$d = d_{prev} + (1/50)t_{prev} + (1/50)u_{prev}$$

$$t = t_{prev} * (49/50) \text{ and}$$

$$u = u_{prev} * (49/50)$$

Usually, the impact of negative experience is greater than the impact of positive experience. In our system model, we define that degrading rate based on negative experience is four times faster than increasing rate based on positive behaviour.

3.2.5 A Typical Use Scenario

We implement a typical use scenario to show that proposed approach provides better availability and security than traditional Chord-based system. Our implementation is based on previous implementation of Chord-based P2PSIP system with 512 peers in the space size 2048 (introduced in chapter 3.8). We modify several functions (e.g. one-hop multicast, semi-recursive routing, etc) to realize the proposed system. We also assume the system contains most of the normal P2PSIP peers (for example, 99 percent of overlay peers) and a few malicious / faulty peers.

We also implement a Secure Opinion Server by using Java as the programming language, Apache Derby as the opinion database, and Apache tomcat as the background HTTP container.

In this case, we initiate a P2PSIP request from peer 668, searching for the destination peer 1616. In original Chord system, the message flow goes through Peer 668 -> peer 939 -> peer 1030 -> peer 1110-> peer 1116. Then, we set the intermediate peer 1110 as a malicious/fault intermediate peer that might discard, misroute or temper the data message. The testing in original Chord-based system shows unability to locate the destination peer. However, this is different in the current approach. Because of the one-hop multicast function in the source peer, the destination peer might be able to receive multiple P2PSIP requests, as represented in Figure 16. Although the red one is misrouted/ blocked by the malicious intermediate peer 1110, the other two routes (Black one and Green one) can still reach the destination.

Then, we assume in a certain period, the opinions of related peers are:

We simulate this by manually modifying the opinion database. According to subjective logic rule specified before, the opinions of two routes are:

$$\omega_p^{Red} = \{0.392, 0.016, 0.592\} \text{ with } v\textit{=0.656}$$

$$\omega_p^{Black} = \{0.645, 0.027, 0.328\} \text{ with } v\textit{=0.755}$$

After the opinion calculation, SOS returns the most trustful route (the black one) to the destination peer 1116. And the session can be established in the most trustful situation.

3.2.6 Summary

Subjective logic based trust model provides secure services via selecting the most trustful message route. The system resolves several issues including opinion calculation, opinion maintenance, message routing, and NAT traversal. Our approach improves the trustworthiness in the P2PSIP session establishment and protects the system from security breaches caused by misbehaviour of the malicious or faulty peers.

However, some issues are still remaining. For example, source peer in this solution multicast session layer "P2PSIP INVITE" messages to the overlay. This might increase load within overlay network. Besides, the malicious peer who receives multicast messages is capable to collect sensitive privacy information. That creates new security concerns. Additionally, it might happen, in the worst case, multicast messages from source peer are all intercepted by a few malicious peers. In this case, the request fails.

3.3. Combining Efficiency and Security

Two security solutions proposed above have their limitations. Appropriate combination of these two solutions might provide solution that is both efficient and sufficiently secure. In this section, we study use case that combines both centralized proxy model and subjective logic trust model. Besides, we also combine two efficiency improvement approaches: cache mechanism and hierarchical layer division. According to previous study, cache mechanism is efficient in reducing chord lookup delay. Hierarchical layer division, according to theoretically analysis in (Le & Kuo, 2007), is capable to increase the overall capability of the overlay and reduce the system delay. On the other hand, computationally strong devices (with strong CPU power, big memory, and stable connection) have generally better protection (e.g. anti-virus software, firewall, etc) against security

Figure 16. A Typical Use Scenario

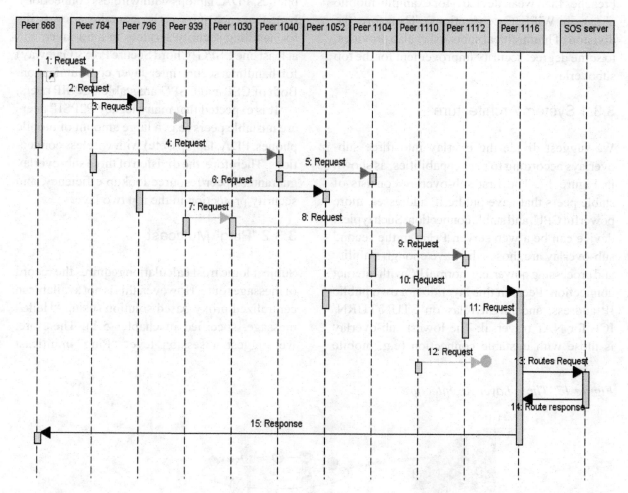

Table 1. Peer Opinion Table

Peer ID	Trust	Distrust	Uncertainty
668	0.9	0.05	0.05
784	0.8	0.1	0.1
796	0.82	0.08	0.08
1040	0.75	0.15	0.1
1052	0.92	0.04	0.04
1104	0.85	0.1	0.05
1112	0.9	0.05	0.05
1116	0.95	0.04	0.01

breaches than weak devices (for example, mobile phones in WiFi/3G connections). Therefore, the division of hierarchical suboverlay also provides, to some degree, security improvement for the top suboverlays.

3.3.1 System Architecture

We suggest divide the overlay into three sub-overlays according to peer capabilities, as shown in Figure 17. The first sub-overlay consists of stable peers that have public IP addresses, more powerful CPU, and stable connection. Such typical device can be a web server. Peers in the second sub-overlay are those who have enough stability and processing power, e.g. normal PC with Internet connection. Peers in this layer do not own public IP address, and might relay on STUN/TURN/ICE for NAT traversal. The lowest sub-overlay is those with unstable connection (e.g. mobile phones, PDA, laptops with wireless connection). Note that each sub-overlay contains a few CSPs for handling security services in intra-layer, and at least one CSPG (Chord Secure Proxy Gateway) for handling secure inter-layer communication. Both of CSP and CSPG are stable P2PSIP peers.

It is expected that many legacy P2PSIP peers are unstable peers (e.g. a large amount of mobile phones, PDA, laptops, etc) with wireless connections. Therefore, the division of three sub-overlay guarantees peer/resource lookup efficiency, and security protection in the top two layers.

3.3.2 "Ping" Multicast

Subject logic trust calculation requires the record of message route. However, this is not available in centralized proxy based solution (using "Hello" message, specified in chapter 5.1). Therefore, we suggest a session level "Ping" multicast

Figure 17. Three Layer Architecture

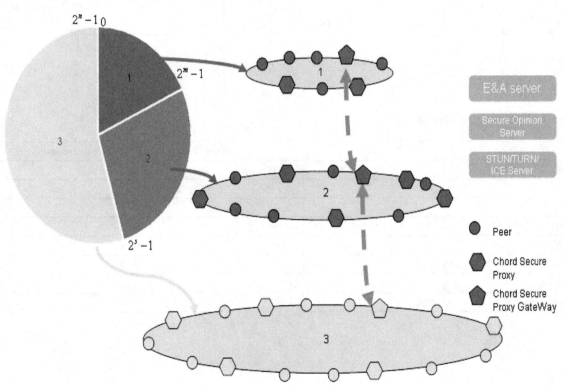

mechanism, which contains "PingRequest" and "PingResponse". "PingRequest" message consists of a "Via" header for recording the profile (e.g. peer ID, IP, port, etc) of each intermediate peer. An example is represented below:

```
P2PSIP PingRequest
Via: 586 158.36.228.48:9000; 612
128.39.189.61:8080
Call-ID: 9849303
CSP-ID: 512
CSP-IP: 158.36.228.48
CSP-Port: 9512
Dest-ID:586
```

When destination peer receives multiple "PingRequest" messages, it selects the most trusted route for handling (based on subjective logic trust calculation) and replies with a "PingResponse". An example of Ping Response is:

```
P2PSIP PingResponse
Call-ID: 9849303
CSP-ID: 512
CSP-IP: 158.36.228.48
CSP-Port: 9512
Dest-ID: 586
Dest-IP: 69.0.128.30
Dest-Port: 9001
```

3.3.3 Use Cases

Figure 18 illustrates inter-layer P2PSIP session initiation process between source peer A and destination peer B. Possible messages flows are:

1. Source peer sends P2PSIP "INVITE" message to the CSPG in its sub-overlay.
2. CSPG forwards "INVITE" to another CSPG in destination sub-overlay.
3. The "INVITE" is forwarded to the CSP that is clockwise nearest to the destination peer.

Figure 18. Inter-Layer Session Initiation

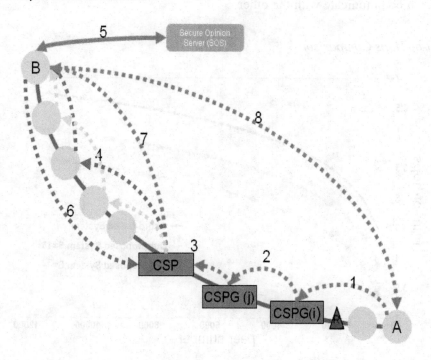

4. CSP multicasts a "PingRequest" to a few successors. Intermediate peers forward "PingRequest" step by step until the destination.

5. Destination peer receives several identical "PingRequest". It asks SOS server via sending all possible routes. After trust calculation, SOS replies with a best route.

6. Destination peer returns a "PingResponse" to CSP.

7. CSP forwards original P2PSIP "INVITE" message to destination peer.

8. Destination peer returns a P2PSIP "180 Ringing" to source peer.

3.3.4 Efficiency Study

We first analyze the lookup algorithm without the consideration of cache mechanism. We assume that the number of peers and CSPs in the overlay is N and S respectively, where N_1, N_2, N_3 are the number of peers in each sub-overlay from top to bottom and S_1, S_2, S_3 are number of CSPs in each suboverlay from top to bottom. Besides, we assume that peer in communicate with the other peer in the same suboverlay in a probability of p_1, p_2, p_3 ..Also, we assume that peers and CSPs are evenly distributed in the overlay space.

Based on Chord routing protocol (Stoica et al., 2003), the average num-of-hop of "PingRequest" multicast is $\frac{1}{2}^{1/2\log(N_i/S_i)}$, where i represents each suboverlay. Therefore, the complexity of intra-suboverlay is $(1/2)\log(N_i/S_i)+1$ due to the addition of one CSP; the complexity of inter-suboverlay is $(1/2)\log(N_i/S_i)+3$ due to addition of two CSPGs and one CSP (see Step 1-3 in Figure 5-16).

According to the Mean rule (Snell), the average hop number is:

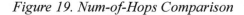

$$\sum_1^3 \{p_i * (1 + \tfrac{1}{2}\log(N_i/S_i)) + (1-p_i)*(3+\tfrac{1}{2}\log(N_i/S_i))\} = 3 - \frac{2(p_1N_1 + p_2N_2 + p_3N_3)}{N} + \frac{1}{2}\log_2(\frac{N}{S})$$

After that, we assume $p_1 = p_2 = p_3 = 0.8$, based on the concept that most communication session are geographically related to each other

Figure 19. Num-of-Hops Comparison

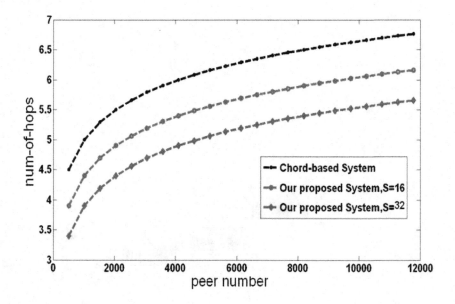

(in Section 3.3). Therefore, the average num-of-hops is:

$$1.4 + \frac{1}{2}\log_2(\frac{N}{S})$$

Figure 19 shows the improved result (we set S=16 and S=32 separately) compare with conventional chord-based system. We get the conclusion that our proposed lookup mechanism is more efficient than conventional Chord lookup approach. Besides, the more S, the better lookup efficiency will be.

In order to evaluate the impact of cache mechanism, we measure the system delay. We choose one peer (we use peer 586 for example) as the source peer, and randomly select 100 peers (which are divided into 10 groups, each of which contains 10 peers) in each suboverlay as the destination peer. We initiate P2PSIP request from source peer and measure the latency between request and response. After that, we calculate the average delay in each group (shown in Figure 20).

In the beginning, the delay in three sublayers is more or less similar (between 250-300ms). However, the latency in layer 1 (Green one) and layer 2 (red one) is greatly reduced with the increasing of the group number. We believe this is the contribution of cache mechanism.

4. CONCLUSION

P2PSIP is a promising future trend. It is supposed to be a communication protocol that supports a set of real-time multimedia services, such as presence, instant messaging, Voice over IP (VoIP), etc. Unfortunately, P2PSIP is far from mature and still needs time for solving critical technical challenges. In the chapter, we mainly investigate the P2PSIP security issues and propose a few possible approaches to enhance the security level.

Solutions begin with centralized proxy based approach, and follow by subjective logic based trust enhancement. Both of solutions contain centralized proxy/server elements for management of security functions and parameters. Although this is conflict with decentralization requirement of P2PSIP, we believe they are necessary for security and privacy concern. We also combine two solutions to achieve optimized security protection.

Figure 20. Delay Testing

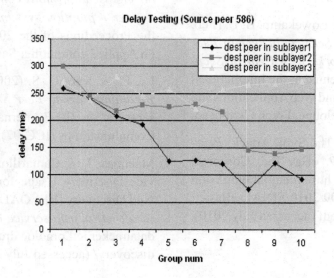

REFERENCES

P2PSIP. http://www.p2psip.org (accessed July 2010).

Android.com - Android at Google I/O. Apple.

BitComet - A free C++ BitTorrent/HTTP/FTP Download Client. BitTorrent. http://www.bittorrent.com.

Bryan, D. A., Lowekamp, B. B., & Jennings, C. (2005). *SOSIMPLE: A Serverless, Standards-based, P2P SIP Communication System* Paper presented at the First International Workshop on Advanced Architectures and Algorithms for Internet Delivery and Applications (AAA-IDEA'05) Orlando, USA.

Bryan, D. A., Lowekamp, B. B., & Zangrilli, M. (April, 2008). *The Design of a versatile, secure P2PSIP communications architecture for the public internet.* Paper presented at the IEEE international Symposium on Parallel and Distributed Processing, Miami, USA.

Bryan, D. A., Matthews, P., Shim, E., Willis, D., & Dawkins, S. (July, 2008). Concepts and Terminology for Peer to Peer SIP. *IETF Internet Draft (draft-ietf-p2psip-concepts-02)*, http://www.p2psip.org/drafts/draft-ietf-p2psip-concepts-02.html (accessed July 2010).

Cao, F., Bryan, D. A., & Lowekamp, B. B. (Feb, 2006). *Providing Secure Services in Peer-to-Peer Communications Networks with Central Security Servers.* Paper presented at the International Conference on Internet and Web Applications and Services (ICIW), Guadeloupe, Frech Caribbean.

Douceur, J. R. (2002). The Sybil Attack. *Peer-To-Peer Systems, 2429.* eBay Inc. Corporate Fact Sheet: Q3 2009. http://ebayinkblog.com/wp-content/uploads/2009/2010/FINAL-eBay-Inc-Fact-Sheet-Q2309.pdf (accessed July 2010).

Fessi, A., Niedermayer, H., Kinkelin, H., & Carle, G. (July, 2007). *A cooperative SIP Infrastructure for Highly Reliable Telecommunication Services.* Paper presented at the Proceedings of the 1st international conference on Principles, systems and applications of IP telecommunications (IPT-COMM'07), New York, USA.

Jennings, C., Lowekamp, B., Rescorla, E., Baset, S., & Schulzrinne, H. (July, 2010). REsource LOcation And Discovery (RELOAD) base Protocol. *IETF Internet Draft (draft-ietf-p2psip-base-09)*, http://tools.ietf.org/html/draft-ietf-p2psip-reload-00 (accessed June 2010).

Josang, A. (1999). *An Algebra for Assessing Trust in Certification Chains.* Paper presented at the Proceedings of the Network and Distributed Systems Security (NDSS'99).

Josang, A. (2001, June). A Logic for Uncertain Probabilities. *International Journal of Uncertainty, Fuzziness and Knowledge-Based Systems, 9*(3), 279–311. doi:10.1142/S0218488501000831

Josang, A., Hayward, R., & Pope, S. (2006). *Trust network analysis with subjective logic.* Paper presented at the Proceedings of the 29th Australasian Computer Science Conference, Hobart, Australia.

Kinateder, M., Terdic, R., & Rothermel, K. (2005). *Strong pseudonymous communication for peer-to-peer reputation systems.* Paper presented at the Proceedings of the 2005 ACM symposium on Applied computing, Santa Fe, New Mexico.

Le, L., & Kuo, G.-S. (2007). *Hierarchical and Breathing Peer-to-Peer SIP System.* Paper presented at the IEEE International Conference on Communcations (ICC'07), Glasgow, Scotland.

Maenpaa, J., & Camarillo, G. (July, 2010). Service Discovery Usage for REsource LOcation And Discovery (RELOAD). *IETF Internet Draft (draft-ietf-p2psip-service-discovery-01)*, https://datatracker.ietf.org/doc/draft-ietf-p2psip-service-discovery/ (accessed July 2010).

Matuszewski, M., & Kokkonen, E. (Jan, 2008). *Mobile P2PSIP - Peer-to-Peer SIP Communication in Mobile Communities*. Paper presented at the 5th IEEE Consumer Communications and Networking Conference (CCNC), Las Vegas, USA.

Mirkovic, J., Prier, G., & Reiher, P. (2002). *Attacking DDoS at the source*. Paper presented at the Proceedings of 10th IEEE International Conference on Network Protocols, Paris, France.

Mobile Phones | Choose the Best Phone for You | Windows Mobile.

Needham, R. M. (1993). *Denial of service*. Paper presented at the Proceedings of the 1st ACM conference on Computer and Communication Security, Fairfax, USA.

Nokia - Nokia on the Web. http://www.nokia.com/ (accessed July 2010).

Oleshchuk, V. (6-8 Sept, 2007). *Trust-based Framework for Security Enhancement of Wireless Sensor Networks*. Paper presented at the 4th IEEE Workshop on Intelligent Data Acquisition and Advanced Computing Systems: Technology and Applications (IDAACS 2007), Dortmund, Germany

Oleshchuk, V., & Zadorozhny, V. (14-20 Oct, 2007). *Trust-Aware Query Processing in Data Intensive Sensor Networks*. Paper presented at the International Conference on Sensor Technologies and Applications (SensorComm), Valencia, Spain.

Ornaghi, A., & Valleri, M. *Man in the middle attacks*.

Postel, J. (1981). Internet Control Message Protocol. *RFC 792*.

Schlegel, R., Niccolini, S., Tartarelli, S., & Brunner, M. (2006). *SPam over Internet Telephony (SPIT)*. Paper presented at the Global Telecommunications Conference (GLOBECOM 06), San Francisco, USA.

Seedorf, J. (2006). Security Challenges for P2P-SIP. *IEEE Network Special Issue on Securing Voice over IP, 20*(5), 38-45.

Seedorf, J. (2008). Lawful Interception in P2P-Based VoIP Systems. *Principles, Systems and Applications of IP Telecommunications, 5310,* 217–235.

Sepandar, D. K., Mario, T. S., & Hector, G.-M. (2003). *The Eigentrust algorithm for reputation management in P2P networks*. Paper presented at the Proceedings of the 12th international conference on World Wide Web, Budapest, Hungary.

Singh, A., Ngan, T. W., Druschel, P., & Wallach, D. S. (2006). *Eclipse attacks on overlay networks Threats and defenses*. Paper presented at the Proceedings of 25th IEEE International Conference on Computer Communications (INFOCOM 06), Barcelona, Spain.

Singh, K., & Schulzrinne, H. (2005). *Peer-to-peer internet telephony using SIP*. Paper presented at the Proceedings of the international workshop on Network and operating systems support for digital audio and video, Stevenson, Washington, USA.

Singh, K., & Schulzrinne, H. (Jan, 2005). *SIP-peer: A Session Initiation Protocol (SIP) based Peer-to-Peer Internet Telephony Client Adapt*.

Snell, J. L. *Expected Value and Variance*. Paper presented at the Introduction to Probability.

Song, H., Jiang, X., Even, R., & Bryan, D. A. (July, 2010). P2PSIP Overlay Diagnostics. *IETF Internet Draft (draft-ietf-p2psip-diagnostics-04)*, http://tools.ietf.org/html/draft-ietf-p2psip-diagnostics-04 (accessed July).

Song, S., Hwang, K., Zhou, R., & Kwok, Y.-K. (2005). Trusted P2P Transactions with Fuzzy Reputation Aggregation. *IEEE Internet Computing, 9*(6), 24–34. doi:10.1109/MIC.2005.136

Spafford, E. H. (1989). The internet worm program: an analysis. *SIGCOMM Comput. Commun. Rev., 19*(1), 17-57. doi: http://doi.acm.org/10.1145/66093.66095

Sparks, R. (2007). SIP: basics and beyond. *Queue, 5*(2), 22–33. doi:10.1145/1229899.1229909

Stoica, I., Morris, R., Liben-Nowell, D., Karger, D. R., Kaashoek, M. F., Dabek, F., & Balakrishnan, H. (2003). Chord: a scalable peer-to-peer lookup protocol for internet applications. *IEEE/ACM Transactions on Networking, 11*(1), 17-32. doi: http://dx.doi.org/10.1109/TNET.2002.808407

Swinburn, M., & Jayawardena, A. (2008). Co-operative Trust Model for a Decentralised Peer-to-Peer E-Market. *Innovations and Advanced Technologies in Systems, Computing Sciences and Software Engineering*, 330-335.

The, S. I. P. Center - A portal for the commercial development of SIP Session Initiation Protocol. http://www.sipcenter.com (accessed July 2010). Skype official website - download Skype free now for free calls and internet calls. http://www.skype.com/intl/en/ (accessed June 2010).

Trojan Horse - Wikipedia, the free encyclopedia.

Wallach, D. S. (2002). *A survey of peer-to-peer security issues*. Paper presented at the Proceedings of the 2002 Next-NSF-JSPS international conference on Software security: theories and systems, Tokyo, Japan.

Windows Live Messenger. Yahoo! Messenger - Chat, Instant message, SMS, Video Call, PC Calls. http://messenger.yahoo.com/ (accessed June 2010).

Zheng, X., & Oleshchuk, V. (2009, Oct). Improvement of Chord overlay for P2PSIP-based Communication Systems. [IJCNC]. *International Journal of Computer Networks & Communications, 1*(3), 133–142.

ADDITIONAL READING

Zheng, X., & Oleshchuk, V. (Oct, 2009). A Secure Architecture for P2PSIP-based Communication Systems. Paper presented at the Proceedings of the 2nd international conference on Security of information and networks, Famagusta, North Cyprus.

Zheng, X., & Oleshchuk, V. (Nov, 2009). Trust-based Framework for Security Enhancement of P2PSIP Communication Systems. Paper presented at the The 4th International Conference for Internet Technology and Secured Transactions (ICITST-2009), London, UK.

Zheng, X., & Oleshchuk, V. (2009, Oct). Improvement of Chord overlay for P2PSIP-based Communication Systems. [IJCNC]. *International Journal of Computer Networks & Communications, 1*(3), 133–142.

Zheng, X., & Oleshchuk, V. (Jan, 2010). A survey on peer-to-peer SIP based communication systems. Paper presented at the Peer-to-Peer Networking and Applications.

Chapter 16
Towards a Framework for Collaborative Enterprise Security

Janardan Misra
Independent Researcher, India

ABSTRACT

The role of human behaviour in enterprise security is one of the little studied aspects. The author proposes a reinforcement model of collaborative security employing basic concepts from game theory, socio-psychology, and probabilistic model-checking. The proposed model aims towards solving the problem of inducing positive network effect to enable user centric monitoring of security violations, in particular, against violations related to "semantic manipulation" of context dependent logical resources. Preventing such violations using existing security enforcement mechanisms is neither feasible nor cost effective. The author defines a payoff mechanism to formalize the model by stipulating appropriate payoffs as reward, punishment, and community price according to reporting of genuine or false violations, non-reporting of the detected violations, and proactive reporting of vulnerabilities and threats by the users. Correctness properties of the model are defined in terms of probabilistic robustness property and constraints for economic feasibility of the payoffs. For estimating the payoff parameters, system and user behaviours are further modelled in terms of probabilistic finite state machines (PFSM) and likelihood of the success of the model is specified using probabilistic computation tree logic (PCTL). PRISM model checker based automated quantitative analysis elicits the process of the estimation of various parameters in the model using PFSMs and PCTL formulas.

INTRODUCTION

With the increasing size of today's organizations having dynamically changing asset base (physical and logical), designing appropriate security policies and their enforcement to maintain confi-

dentiality and integrity of these assets are becoming increasingly difficult. One of the noticeable limitations of the existing security frameworks is that user base of assets is differentiated from the security administrators who design and enforce the security policies. Therefore, it appears a natural proposition that if securing confidentiality and

DOI: 10.4018/978-1-4666-0978-5.ch016

integrity of certain types of assets is considered as a collective responsibility of the users and security administrators, the security enforcement would enhance positively. For example, a malicious user making destabilizing changes in a code base could be better monitored and reported for doing so by the associated team members, who have probably better knowledge of it or can better detect it than the centrally administered monitoring mechanisms.

To make users responsible for the security of the assets (in particular critical assets), a plausible approach may be to involve them in different aspects of security including threat perception and monitoring the violations of policies. Now-a-days, all these operations are mainly taken care by a limited group of administrators. They define security policies, devise means to enforce them, and monitor continuously to detect possible violations. However, a large enterprise-wide organization typically has tens of thousands of employees and many more roles/tasks/permissions, and even larger number of assets and contexts present at any point of time. Thus, under- standing the multitude of security requirements and their enforcement for a large organization is not only difficult but also error-prone. It would be a better solution, if different groups formed based upon business focus, roles, emerging contexts, and tasks also participate in defining security policies and are entrusted with collective monitoring of the policy violations. In early 90s, Greenwald (Greenwald, 1996) advocated similar philosophy in the context of distributed resource management and access control and proposed a Distributed Compartment Model, which allows users to manage resources across different administrative domains with increased independence from central system administrators. Also Vimercati and Samarati (Vimercati & Samarati, 1996) proposed a model with local user autonomy in access control for federated databases. Administrative Role Based Access Control (ARBAC) (Sandhu et al., 1999; Sandhu & Munawer, 1999) is yet another decen-

tralized framework for access control policies, where different administrators can define and change RBAC policies independently. However policy comparison, consistency checking, or more generally 'safety property analysis' of these policies when considered together arises as a natural problem in such distributed policy synthesis frameworks. For example, (Sasturkar et al.,2006; Stoller et al., 2007) consider the problem of formally analyzing reachability, availability, containment, and information flow properties for ARBAC policies.

In this chapter we consider the problem of collaborative enforcement and monitoring of security policies. To guide individuals and groups for this, there needs to be a well-defined framework. This framework should be easy to follow for devising measures to ensure overall implementation of such collaborative monitoring efforts. Also as an organization's policies change over time, the framework should be such that it can effectively adapt with the changes. Unfortunately existing models of security do not consider such collaborative aspects and thus there is a need to devise one such.

We present a formal framework for devising policies to enable collaborative monitoring against policy violations. Importantly, presented framework does not mandate that the employees take up the additional roles of security completely. Only in certain scenarios, where they could have more effective role in enforcing the policies and are directly impacted by the violations, it is indeed desirable that they take proactive participation as specified by the framework. For example, a discussion on the deliberate coding violations by programmers and IP theft appears in (Group, 2008) highlighting the potential loss which such violations may cause to the organizations especially in the context of safety critical applications.

In many cases, social groups within an organization can provide wider scope and depth for monitoring the violations than any existing monitoring infrastructure. This is especially true for the context dependent logical resources, i.e., some data, significance of which is realized only when considered with respect to specific contexts, e.g. design documents and source code having product specific interpretation and significance. Such resources are most vulnerable to 'semantic manipulations' and securing them using automated monitoring is either not feasible or would be very costly.

A special class of such threats is known as insider threat (Cole & Ring, 2006; Schultz, 2002; Iyer & Ngo, 2005; Bishop & Gates, 2008; Bishop et al., 2008), which is a pressing problem for most of the organizations today. Recent studies on insider threats in finance and banking sector indicate that often other users (85%) had some amount of prior knowledge of the possible threat (Randazzo et al., 2005). Indeed, in 61% of the cases, insiders responsible for the threats were actually detected by the people who were not responsible for the security. In another study, it was estimated that more than 25% of the frauds were actually reported by non-security users involving customers and other co-workers (Cappelli et al., 2006).

A collaborative monitoring could then be considered as a kind of social networking based monitoring mechanism whereby each member having access on shared resources is expected to monitor for the compliance and specifically report the instances of violations of the associated security policies or potential threats. The fundamental question, which arises in such a scenario, is as to how can such a collaborative monitoring framework be made effective since there may not exist any prior (latent) positive network effect for users to monitor against the security violations. The network effect is often considered a fundamental prerequisite for the success of any collaborative networking phenomenon. Network effect (Metcalfe, 1995; Kilkki & Kalervo, 2004; Odlyzko & Tilly, 2009.) is generally expressed as a utility function which determines some useful value compared to the price paid for an actively engaged user in a network in terms of the size of

the network. For a positive network effect such a utility function must be non-decreasing with respect to the number of users in the network for a sufficient range.

Drawing inspiration from the organic unity represented in the biological systems against attacks and socio- psychological studies on security and human motivation, in this work, we propose a reward-punishment based reinforcement model for enabling collaborative monitoring of policy violations by extrinsically inducing positive network effect in the system. To this aim, the model stipulates appropriate payoffs as rewards, punishments, and community price according to the reporting behaviour of the users on genuine or false violations, non-reporting of the detected violations, and proactive reporting of potential vulnerabilities and threats. We use a payoff matrix based mechanism (often used in Game Theory (Leyton-Brown & Shoham, 2008)) to formally specify the model. A probabilistic robustness property of the resulting system, which also corresponds to Nash equilibrium in the resulting game, and constraints for economic feasibility of the payoffs are further defined. We will extensively discuss the socio-psychological aspects in the resulting framework including key challenges in practical realization. Finally, for estimating the parameters in the payoff model, system and user behaviours are modelled in terms of probabilistic finite state machines (PFSM) and likelihood of the success of the model is specified using probabilistic computation tree logic (PCTL) (Hansson & Jonsson, 1994). PRISM model checker (Kwiatkowska et al., 2001) based automated quantitative analysis elicits the process of the estimation of various parameters in the model using PFSMs and PCTL formulas.

THE REINFORCEMENT MODEL

Before we discuss the model further, let us specify the underlying assumptions:

Assumptions

Observability: Proposed model assumes that all genuine occurrences of policy violations have an 'observable impact' on the system, which could be determined by the security administrators. Thus we only consider such violations, which affect the state of the system and do not consider other kinds of 'silent' violations not affecting the system as far as the observable state of the system is concerned. This in turn, implies that security administrators will always be able to identify and validate the occurrence of a violation even if it remains undetected by the users. This assumption thus avoids the cases of false positives as further discussed in the Section on 'Challenges for Collaborative Security'.

Detection: A violation is considered to be detected only when it is reported to be done so (either by users or some monitoring device). Therefore if a violation occurs and is not reported by any of the witnesses (or captured by the monitoring device), it would be considered undetected.

Policy Synthesis: Model assumes that security policies are defined a priory. Nonetheless, it is possible that as a by product of the monitoring process, existing policies are refined or new policies may potentially be integrated into the framework as determined by the existing policy synthesis machinery. For example, certain sequence of events (each event is an operation on an object by some subject) might enable other access restriction violations, and therefore reporting the final access violation in terms of the scenarios consisting of these sequence of events might give rise to new set of access restrictions.

Policy Completeness and Consistency: Policies are also assumed to be contradiction free, mutually consistent, and complete. Lack of contradiction in a policy definition and mutual consistency among policies are required to avoid the cases of ambiguity in their interpretation by the users and for determining whether a scenario should actually be considered as a violation or not. On the other hand, the policy completeness requirement ensures that decisions could be made in all related scenarios. We will discuss further on this assumption in Section on 'Challenges in Collaborative Security'.

Policy Awareness: Model assumes that users have necessary knowledge of legitimate accesses/policies and capability to detect and report genuine violations. In the beginning, however, users may not have complete knowledge of the policies and with time, as violations would be reported, these would reinforce the awareness of the users. We will discuss further on this assumption in Section on 'Implementation Issues'.

Socio-Psychological Dimension

The justification to externally induced network effect comes from the numerous studies in social psychology on the role of extrinsic motivation in affecting individual and group attitudes and behaviours (Sansone & Harackiewicz, 2000; Petri, 2003; Daniel, 2005; Ernst & Armin, 1995). These studies provide insights into what are the usual behavioural effects of various kinds of rewards and punishments. Conclusions from these studies are significant as we discuss the mechanism for collaborative monitoring in the next section. These are discussed next:

1. Extrinsic rewards can be important motivator to start new (community) behaviours in the individuals.

2. Group punishment mechanisms usually play an important role in the continuation of the intuitively justified community behaviours. Individuals in groups tend to exert pressure (though not always explicitly) on other individuals to avoid themselves from pay-

ing community punishments owing to the violations caused by others.

3. Apart from rewards, punishments are also used as negative reinforcement tools for the individuals, who try to avoid such punishments by following the expected behaviours. Nonetheless, unless expected behaviours have been internalized by the individuals, the withdrawal of such negative reinforcements may put individuals at the risk of reverting to the old situation.

4. Sociological studies on the concept of locus of control (Rotter, 1966, 1990) reveal that individuals show increased motivation towards activities when they perceive better control over their environment. In essence collaborative security lets users have a say in designing policies and monitoring their violations, which would give them a sense of better control over the assets and policies they are using and in turn over the security environment against the current scenario where they have little or no say on these aspects.

Kabay (Kabay, 2002, Chap. 35) also discusses the importance of applying socio psychological understanding of individual and group behaviour while designing security policies. For example, he emphasizes on the need for having policies and environment of rewarding employees for reporting security violations.

Based upon this understanding, we will next formally define the payoff matrix model as an enabling mechanism for the collaborative monitoring.

THE PAYOFF MECHANISM

Let us consider a system consisting of subjects (processes/users) accessing shared resources according to specific (security) policies. The policies may specify that an object has some access restrictions (e.g. copy operation on a specific File not allowed) or may direct the behaviour of the subjects (e.g. a user must not share her password).

Formally, let the set of subjects be $S = \{s_1, s_2, \ldots, s_n\}$ and let there be finitely many ways to violate a security policy resulting into a set of violations $Vio = \{vio_1, vio_2, \ldots, vio_m\}$. We do not assume that policies remain fixed. If a policy changes, that would get reflected in the set of associated violations.

Let us associate with each subject, two types of time varying payoff matrices for each relevant policy violation. These are depicted in Figure 1 and Figure 2.

Notations: All the entries in the tables are functions of time implying that their actual value, at any time, might be dependent upon the previous events or past behaviours of the players. The time variable t, has the granularity of reporting occurrences. Further,

Figure 1. The payoff table for the reporting behaviour on primary violations

Primary Payoffs	True Violations	False Violations
Reported	$R_{ij}(t)$	$-P_{ij}(t)$
Non Reported + Undetected	$-CP_j(t)$	#
Detected + Not Reported	$-P'_{ij}(t)$	#
Threat Reporting	$\Theta_{ij}(t)$	#

Figure 2. The payoff table for the reporting behaviour on secondary violations

Secondary Payoffs	True Violations	False Violations
Reported	$r_{ij}(t)$	$-p_{ij}(t)$
Non Reported + Undetected	0	#
Detected + Not Reported	$-p`_{ij}(t)$	#
Threat Reporting	$\partial_{ij}(t)$	#

$R_{ij}(t)$: Reward for player s_i on reporting true primary violation vio_j

$CP_j(t)$: (absolute value) Community price associated with true primary violation vio_j.

$P_{ij}(t)$: (absolute value) The payoff for player s_i for not reporting true primary violation vio_j.

$\Theta_{ij}(t)$: Reward for player s_i on reporting potential violation (or threat) on vio_j.

$P_{ij}(t)$: (absolute value) The payoff for player s_i for false reporting on violation vio_j

$r_{ij}(t)$: Reward for player s_i on reporting true secondary violation on vio_j.

$cp_j(t)$: (absolute value) Community price associated with true secondary violation on vio_j.

$p_{ij}(t)$: (absolute value) The payoff for player s_i for not reporting true secondary violation on vio_j

$\partial_{ij}(t)$: Reward for player s_i on reporting potential secondary violation on vio_j.

$p_{ij}(t)$: (absolute value) The payoff for player s_i for false reporting of a secondary violation on vio_j.

#: Undefined value.

The first payoff matrix in Figure 1 defines the payoffs associated with the ith player s_i for her reporting behaviour on j^{th} policy violation vio_j.

We treat non-reporting of a policy violation itself to be a violation, which may invite punishment. We argue that in the absence of such treatment it might not be possible to give rise to a dynamically evolving and increasingly secure system. Therefore second payoff matrix in Figure 2, defines the payoffs associated with the ith player

s_i for the jth policy violation vio_j on the reporting behaviour of s_i for non reporting of vio_j by some other player.

Formally, let us consider the primary and secondary the payoff matrices for the subjects against each policy violation:

$$\langle(\overline{PT_1},\overline{ST_1})...(\overline{PT_n},\overline{ST_n})\rangle$$

In cases where *Vio* is an uncountable set, suitable equivalence relation needs to be defined which could partition *Vio* into finitely many classes such that all the violations in each class could be considered equivalent for defining payoffs.

Each player s_i is associated with primary payoff tables

$$PT_i = [T_{i1}^P, T_{i2}^P, ..., T_{im}^P]$$

and secondary payoff tables

$$ST_i = [T_{i1}^S, T_{i2}^S, ..., T_{im}^S]$$

such that T_{ij}^P, T_{ij}^S denote the payoff tables corresponding to policy violation vio_j.

In Figure 1 on Primary Payoffs, first column - *True Primary Violation* - represents the case when a genuine violation of a policy has occurred - impact of which is assumed to be observable later on. The second column - *False Primary Violation* - represents false violations where player si may act on the basis of a fabricated violation - a violation impact of which would never be observed. Such false violations might well be based on unreliable or unverified information sources. Reporting of these violations should invite punishment since they might be aimed toward falsely implicating others and being based upon non verifiable claims.

Rows categorize the reporting behaviour of the players. We consider the cases of reporting of violations after they have occurred and of potential violations reported in advance, which may occur if suitable measures on enforcing the policies are not kept in place.

When a violation occurs, either s_i would report such a violation (having detected it) [Row 1] or it will go unreported. The case of non-reporting is further classified into two categories: i) Row 2 represents the scenario where s_i did not report and violation remained undetected (that is, no one else also reported it.) ii) Row 3 represents the scenario where s_i detected a violation but did not report it, while some other player detected as well as reported it - to establish such a case - we need to consider another payoff matrix as depicted in Figure 2, which captures detection and reporting of such non reporting instances. The last row is meant to capture a potential violation or threat reported by s_i.

In the second table on Secondary Payoffs, first column - *True Secondary Violation* - represents that case, where player s_i detects a violation and also detects some other player(s) detecting the same violation though not reporting it. On the other hand, second column - *False Secondary Violation* - represents that scenario, where player s_i may act on the basis of a false or fabricated scenario and blame that such a scenario was witnessed by some other players but they did not report it. To elaborate these further, next we discuss each payoff entry in the tables.

In the following discussion, *PrimaryTable[m,n]* and *SecondaryTable[m,n]* would denote the cell in m^{th} row and n^{th} column in Primary Payoff Table

and Secondary Payoff Table respectively, where row/column indexing starts from 1.

Primary Payoffs

The reporting behaviour and corresponding payoffs for genuine (true) violations are represented in the first column and are discussed next:

PrimaryTable[1,1]: Represents the scenario where player si detects violation vio_j and duly reports it and is rewarded with $R_{ij}(t)$. Actual value of the rewards could be determined based upon the characteristics of the violation vio_j, reporting delay etc. and can very well vary over time. Increase in the clearance level for subjects as defined in various mandatory access control models (Bishop, 2003) can be considered as an example for such a reward.

In case majority of the players who detected and reported the violation also report that player s_i did not actually detect the violation but reported it only to get share in the reward, her reward could be withdrawn.

As discussed further in Section on 'Challenges for Collaborative Security', in this paper we limit our scope to only reporting of the violations and do not consider the aspect of who committed the violation. However there exists a special case of self-reporting, where a user reports a self committed violation. Since positive rewards for such self-reporting might give rise to instances of deliberate violations with reporting by the users for their advantage, we suggest that in such cases the rewards should be kept to 0 (e.g., intangible positive feedbacks.)

PrimaryTable[2,1]: Represents the scenario where a violation occurs but it is not reported by any of the associated players. This covers both the cases where violation was detected by some of the players but none of them reported it or when it remained undetected and hence was not reported. Note that owing to the assumption of observability, even if a violation remains undetected, the consequences of the violation will still be observed in the future and thus it would get identified by the system administrators.

In such a case, each player pays a community price for it as denoted by $-CP_j(t)$. In case, if violations occur repeatedly, value of $CP_j(t)$ might also increase. Otherwise if the frequency of similar violations decreases over time, value of $CP_j(t)$ might also decrease.

Consider, for example, a source code is being changed or copied and transferred by some of the members of the project team and none of those who had knowledge of it had reported it. Since its impact would be anyway felt at some stage later, all the associated players need to bear some loss for this.

Such a community price to be paid by each associated member is considered to be a critical component if such a model has to give rise to a dynamically evolving and increasingly secure system with collective responsibility. However in some cases, there might be legal constraints, which limit explicit community punishments (e.g., Geneva Convention.) In such cases value of $CP_j(t)$ could be set to 0 (or an intangible punishment like negative group feedbacks.)

PrimaryTable[3,1]: Represents the scenario where player si detects a violation but does not report it. We term it as secondary violation to distinguish it from the primary violation. Such a claim would be valid only when there exists some other player s_k, who also detects/witnesses the same violation vio_j and also detects that it has been witnessed by player s_i and s_k reports so. Note that s_k can also be a neutral monitoring device by which such a claim can be derived as well as verified. Therefore it is necessary to consider the cell *PrimaryTable[3,1]* for player s_i only in conjunction with the cell *SecondaryTable[1,1]* for some other player s_k.

$-P'_{ij}(t)$ denotes the price player s_i needs to pay for such non reporting of a violation. It can be argued that repeated occurrences of such nonreporting by a player must invite even harsher punishments, that is, $P'_{ij}(t)$ could be set as $P'_{ij}(t)$

$= c.P'_{ij}(t-1)$, where c is some constant greater than one.

The difficult part in such a scenario is to validate the correctness of the claim reported by player s_k that player s_i witnessed the primary violation! In general it would require environment specific proofs (e.g. audio-video recordings etc.) However we believe that bare difficulty of proving such should not exclude such a scenario from the discussion.

PrimaryTable[4,1]: Represents the scenario complimenting the scenarios considered in the earlier rows. Here player s_i proactively reports a potential violation and is therefore rewarded with $\Theta_{ij}(t)$.

Since a potential violation cannot be observed, it is assumed that it is logically possible to verify its truth by generating some hypothetical scenario where such violation would become possible. For example, for a newly created logical object, its owner subject/user might report potential access violations with the existing assess enforcement policies.

The reporting behaviour and corresponding payoffs for false violations are represented in the second column and are discussed next:

PrimaryTable[1,2]: Represents the scenario where player s_i falsely reports that violation vio_j has occurred in order to implicate other users, so need to be punished with $-P_{ij}(t)$. Again actual value of such punishment may depend upon the characteristics of the violation vio_j, past behaviour of the player s_i etc. For example, in case, s_i is found to be repeatedly reporting false violations for implicating other users, associated punishments could increase correspondingly. Notice that every genuine violation is assumed to have some observable impact hence falsity of any such reported violation is verifiable (see the assumption of Observability).

PrimaryTable[2,2]: Captures the scenario where violation vio_j has neither occurred nor has it been reported by s_i. It is associated with #, an undefined value.

PrimaryTable[3,2]: This cell is meant to complete the table which captures an inherently false scenario where player s_i does not report a false primary violation (which of course cannot be detected by anyone else!) It is also associated with undefined value #.

PrimaryTable[4,2]: Represents the scenario where player s_i reports a false potential violation. Similar to above, falsity of such a violation can be logically derived. We associate zero value for the corresponding cell since it might not possible to prove that player s_i reported such false potential violation only with malicious intentions and incomplete information or a faulty analysis might be the basis for such a conclusion by s_i.

Secondary Payoffs

The reporting behaviour and corresponding payoffs for genuine (true) secondary violations are represented in the first column and are discussed next:

SecondaryTable[1,1]: The first cell in the table represents the scenario where player s_i detects a violation and also detects that some other player(s) is(are) detecting the same violation but not reporting it. This cell event can be true only if for the same player, event corresponding to *PrimaryTable[1,1]* is also true: it is a consistency check which states that secondary violation can be detected (and reported) only in conjunction with primary violation and not in isolation. The reward associated with this as represented by $r_{ij}(t)$.

SecondaryTable[2,1]: Represents the scenario where a secondary violation occurs but it is not reported by any player. That means, there exists some user $_{sa}$, who detected the vio_j but did not report it. Also none of the other users having knowledge of this reported against $_{sa}$. Since it appears that in general independently establishing this is quite difficult and a secondary violation would not have serious negative impact on the whole community, we chose to give zero as the value in this cell.

SecondaryTable[3,1]: Represents the scenario where player s_i detects a secondary violation but does not report it. This is the case where it could be assumed from the context of the primary violation that with high probability several players must have detected such a violation but none of them reported it. In such a case, each player pays a community price for such complicity as denoted by $-cp_j(t)$.

This should be distinguished from the situation discussed in *PrimaryTable[2,1]*, where a primary violation occurs but is not reported. The crucial difference is that there might exist certain situations, where primary violation would be by nature undetectable (e.g. when a violation occurs in isolation), therefore would go unreported as well - this is the case for *PrimaryTable[2,1]*. On the other hand, there might also exist scenarios where primary violation must have been witnessed by or known to at least one player but was never reported (e.g. data manipulation on a shared document.), such cases are considered here.

Notice that we do not demand here that again some third player detects and reports such non-reporting of a secondary violation since we assume that it might not be possible in practice to continue to such an extent and such consideration might indeed lead to an indefinite regression.

SecondaryTable[4,1]: Represents the scenario where player si reports on a possible violation vio_j and also that some other player(s) would detect the same violation but would not report it. This basically means s_i would be characterizing the potential behaviour of certain other players who have greater probability of witnessing some violation vio_j. We associate some reward $\partial_{ij}(t)$ with it.

The reporting behaviour and corresponding payoffs for non existing false secondary violations are represented in the second column and are discussed next:

SecondaryTable[1,2]: Represents the scenario where player s_i (falsely) reports that some other user(s) witnessed violation voi_j but did not report it so s_i need to be punished with $-p_{ij}(t)$.

Notice that a false secondary violation cannot be considered in isolation and need to be considered only in conjunction with either true a primary violation or in conjunction with a false primary violation. This is because if s_i has to report that some other user s_k witnessed violation voi_j, s_i must also be reporting that violation vio_j occurred, which would imply that either *PrimaryTable[1,1]* or *PrimaryTable[1,2]* is also true for s_i.

SecondaryTable[2, 2]: Captures the scenario where no secondary violation has actually occurred and it has not been reported as well. # denotes an undefined value.

SecondaryTable[3,2]: This cell captures an inherently false scenario where player si does not report a false secondary violation (which of course cannot be detected by anyone else!) It is also associated with undefined value #.

SecondaryTable[4,2]: Represents the scenario where player si reports a potential false secondary violation. Such scenarios does not appear to have any serious relevance, hence we associate # with it.

CORRECTNESS PROPERTIES

A natural question which arises is the correctness and effectiveness of the model. This is important since collaboration by definition of the word cannot be guaranteed, in general.

Claim: Assuming that there does not exist any factor undermining the reporting behaviour of individuals, under the proposed design of the payoff matrix model, at any point, individual gains from reporting true primary violations are always positive.

Proof: The claim is based upon the following observation on the payoff matrix design: Suppose a player detects a primary violation. She would be faced with two choices – either she would proceed ahead and report the violation or she would not. In case of the former choice, she becomes entitled to receive the reward, which is a non negative value. Whereas, if she decides to

remain silent on the violation, she is taking a risk of either losing some value as a part of community price (provided no one else reports it either) or the risk of being punished for secondary violations in case there exist some other player who detected the violation and also detected that this player too had witnessed the same and the second player reports both of these violations.

So in case when there does not exist any factor, which counter these payoff matrix based rewards and punishments and motivate a player to remain silent on the violation, she would always be better off by reporting the violations detected.

This claim justifies the design of the model to be consistent with the motivation. The pay-off matrix model also discourages a user who understands the dynamics of the model not to falsely implicate another subject for a violation. Since the model only considers observable violations (ref. Section on 'Assumptions'), i.e., the violations impact of which can be observed, it rules out the possibility that a member of a group will be successful in alleging against a colleague by reporting a violation that has never occurred. Now it is possible that a subject may report an observed violation to be committed by someone who actually has not committed the violation. However, other users may also have detected the violation and reported the same. So by falsely implicating someone, the subject takes the risk of getting double punishment - one for not reporting the actual violation (violation committed by actual violator) and the other for reporting a false violation. Thus, by implicating a subject falsely for a violation, she always incurs the risk of getting punished.

In the pay-off matrix model, a subject is given reward for perception of a potential threat, but no punishment is given for wrong perception of a threat. There is a trade-off in giving and not giving punishment for reporting potential violation wrongly. If punishment is given for reporting an wrongly presumed potential threat (here we assume that the security administrators are able to determine if a reported potential violation is indeed possible to happen in future), then the subjects may not be willing to report a potential violation in the fear of getting it proved to be wrong, and getting punishment. On the other hand, there may be a many false positives among the reported potential violations. However, we have decided not to keep any punishment for reporting a wrong potential violation, as the pay-off matrix is defined for each group separately, and we assume that the members of a group have good judgments in identifying potential threats associated with the assets belonging to the group.

Economics of Payoffs

The idea that not reporting a violation would be treated as a violation could be a source of interesting social mechanisms. For example, it is possible that the system can apparently finance itself with no investment or revenue. This becomes possible when punishment for not reporting a detected primary violation, that is, $-P'_{ij}(t)$ is set at the same level as the reward for reporting the corresponding secondary violation, i.e. $r_{ij}^{(t)+} P'_{ij}(t) = 0$ and rest all other parameters are set to 0. Here a user reporting secondary violation would be earning at the cost of that user who did not report the primary violation. Therefore, we need to introduce additional constraints on the parameters to avoid the scenarios which are economically infeasible.

For an instance of voi_j at time t, let $MaxLoss_j(t)$ be the maximum possible loss, which could have happened if the violation remained undetected and let $ActualLoss_j(t)$ be the actual loss even after the violation was duly reported. Therefore the effective gain from reporting can be estimated as

$$\Delta_j(t) = [MaxLoss_j(t) - ActualLoss_j(t)]$$

In case when violation goes unreported, $\Delta_j(t) = 0$ otherwise $\Delta_j(t) > 0$. Next, for all $voi_j \in Vio$ and $\forall t$, we define the following constraints:

$$\sum_{s_i \in S} [R_{ij}(t) + r_{ij}'(t)] \leq \Delta_j(t) + \sum_{s_i} P_{ij}'(t) \tag{1}$$

Eq.(1) guarantees that for every violation voi_j, total rewards received by all the users who reported the violation or reported secondary violation on it are no more than the effective gain by reporting it plus the punishments meted out to those users who did not report the violation even having detected it.

$$\sum_{s_i \in S} P'_{ij}(t) \leq \Delta_j(t) \tag{2}$$

Eq.(2) guarantees that for every violation voi_j, total punishment for the secondary violation is not more than the effective gain which resulted by reporting it.

$$\sum_{s_i \in S} CP_{ij}(t) \leq MaxLoss_j(t) \tag{3}$$

Eq.(3) also similarly guarantees that total community punishment meted out to all the members is not more than the loss owing to the violation.

$$\sum_{s_i \in S} \Theta_{ij}(t) \leq MaxLoss_j(t) \tag{4}$$

Eq.(4) guarantees that for every reported threat, which might occur, the total rewards received by all the reporting users is no more than then maximum loss possible owing to the violation (assuming that it also goes undetected).

Robustness Property

Let $r_{vio}(t)$ be the number of violations per unit time distributed over t. Similarly, let $r_{rep}(t)$ denote the distribution of the number of cases reported for true violations and let $r_{false\_pri}(t)$ and $r_{false\_sec}(t)$ denote the distributions for the rate of occurrence of false primary and false secondary violations respectively.

In terms of these parameters, probability distribution for the occurrence as well as reporting of a true violation can be approximated as $r_{rep}(t)/r_{vio}(t)$. We define the following robustness property:

Probabilistic Robustness: A monitoring policy is termed as probabilistically robust if over a course of time the rate of detections and reporting of true violations reaches the rate of actual violations and the rate of reporting of false violations decrease. Formally,

$$\lim_{t\to\infty} \frac{r_{rep}(t)}{r_{vio}(t)} = 1 \text{ AND } \lim_{t\to\infty} r_{false\_pri}(t) = 0 \text{ AND}$$
$$\lim_{t\to\infty} r_{false\_sec}(t) = 0$$

Notice that the limiting point, where these conditions hold is also the point, where system would be in a state of *Nash equilibrium* (Leyton-Brown & Shoham, 2008) from Game theoretic point of view considering the set of users as the players of a multi-player cooperative game with utilities defined by the primary and secondary payoff matrices.

IMPLEMENTATION ISSUES

In case of users as actual subjects, implementation of the collaborative monitoring model demands suitable frame-work for dismantling the information on the proposed payoff matrices to all the users as well as mechanisms for reporting the primary or secondary violations. Actual reporting structure for various policies and associated violations may differ based upon the organization type, type of the policy, user base, nature of the violations, and other associated environmental factors. For example, a user on a managerial position might report a violation, might receive a report from other users, and also could be an authority to enforce payoffs. Also associated payoff need to be decided in a time varying manner to render the system adaptive together with adequate confidentiality measures for protecting the identities of the reporting users.

Deciding Rewards and Punishments

In general deciding appropriate rewards and punishments is critically dependent on the nature of the policy violations, their impact on the organization, ease of detecting them by the community members, and the nature of the groups associated with monitoring the policy violations etc. For example, with mandatory access control based security frameworks, employed for highly confidential assets (e.g. in military establishments), objects are differentiated according to their sensitivity levels, and the subjects are categorized based on their trust levels. Usually user accesses to different objects are limited according to their trust levels. There can be a number of schemes for defining the rewards and punishment criteria in terms of these levels. A simple scheme may be where a reward implies the increase in the trust level of a particular user, and punishment results into decrease in her trust level.

In reporting a violation, time is one of the important parameters. In general, the potential loss owing to a violation increases with increase in the reporting delay. So, reporting time may also play a role in deciding the reward for reporting a violation.

Let $\lambda(s)$ denote the trust level of subject s, and $\mu(o)$ denote the sensitivity level of an object o. The reward for reporting a violation of an access restriction on object o by subject s can be considered as follows:

$$\lambda(s) := \lambda(s) + f(\mu(o), r_t)$$

where $f(\mu(o), r_t)$ is any monotonically non-decreasing function of the sensitivity level o, and r_t, which denotes the reporting delay such that the value returned by the function increases with the increase in the value of $\mu(o)$ and decreases with the increase in the value of r_t. A reward can alternately be defined in terms of reduction in loss owing to the timely reporting the violation. For example,

$$Reward(s, o) = \alpha.(MaxLoss - ActualLoss)$$

where α is some constant in the interval [0..1].

Other parameters for rewards and punishments could also be defined accordingly for any given system set up. We next discuss some generic guidelines based upon the studies on extrinsic motivation.

1. Reward induced behaviours in individuals tend to stop once the rewards are withdrawn (*overjustification effect* (Greene & Lepper, 1976)). This fact places important constraints on deciding the rewards. For example, if rewards need to be withdrawn, it should be done gradually and also whenever intrinsic motivation is present, non tangible rewards (e.g., praise or recognition) should be preferred over tangible rewards.
2. Individuals evaluate the value of the rewards, which in turn determines their motivations for the tasks underlying the rewards, as compared to their current conditions (socio-economic status, responsibilities etc.) Hence rewards need to cater the satisfaction level of the individuals before they become effective.
3. Community price works as a negative reinforcement mechanism on the group level. Hence it would motivate people to monitor violations to avoid paying such price. Therefore for it to be effective, it is important that community prices are enforced strictly in the beginning though they should always be reduced as soon as reporting behaviour has been adequately reinforced within the community.
4. Punishments for false reporting and secondary violations also work as negative enforcement for the individuals.

As noted for the assumption of policy-awareness in Section on 'Assumptions', sometimes users may not have the complete knowledge of a policy and therefore they might not be able to interpret correctly a witnessed scenario as an instance of a violation of the policy and therefore

may fail to report it. Therefore it is suggested that for the first time, i.e., $t = 0$, if user does not report a witnessed violation, punishment for this (see *PrimaryTable[3,1]*) may be exempted if it turns out that the user was genuinely not aware that the witnessed scenario was a violation. Also it is possible that a user reports a false violation (see *PrimaryTable[1,2]*) because of the incomplete knowledge of the policy, that is, a user might presume a scenario as a violation though there is none, e.g., during an audit, people external to the group may be legally given some confidential information, however a user may presume it to be a violation and might falsely report this. In such cases also it is suggested that $Pij(0) = 0$.

EXPERIMENTAL ANALYSIS

For experimental analysis of the above system model we use PRISM model checker (Kwiatkowski et al., 2001) and express desired properties in terms of PCTL (Hansson & Jonson, 1994). PRISM is a tool for formal modeling and analysis of systems which exhibit probabilistic behaviour including MDPs and provides support for automated analysis of a wide range of quantitative properties of these models.

Probabilistic Model for Parameter Estimation

Dynamics of collaborative monitoring depends on various factors. Firstly, not all policy violations are equally likely to be detected. Moreover, if a user detects a violation, whether she would actually report the violation or not depends on different factors, for example, the rewards she would get for reporting, the punishment that she would invite if she does not report, and also any hidden incentives associated with not reporting the violation. Therefore, we model the system as a probabilistic system, more precisely as a basic Markov Decision Process (MDP without rewards), to estimate certain reporting probabilities and experimentally demonstrate how model checking based approach can help an administrator determine different parameters in the Payoff Matrix. In practice, the model needs to be initialized using Bayesian probabilistic estimates by the administrators using historical data or other associated analysis to support these estimates. However as we discuss later, some of these probabilities get refined iteratively as new data becomes available over time.

Let p_{det} be the probability that a violation *vio* could be detected by any user, which indicates the inherent difficulty in detecting the violation. Similarly let p_{det_sec} denote the probability that user *s* detects a secondary violation by any other user on violation *vio*. Further let probability p^{pri} denote that the user *s* will report the primary violation *vio*. Similarly let probability p^{sec} denote that *s* will report a secondary violation on *vio*.

We next define a motivation index, *m* for the user *s* to report a violation *vio*. Motivation index is a measure of the motivation a user has for reporting a violation. The motivation index can be considered to be determined by the following factors:

1. Individual gain from the reward.
2. Fear of Community price or punishment for secondary violation.
3. A number of factors that collectively can act as a deterrent for reporting the violation. For example, personal relationships with the violators or potential collusion, incentives offered by the violators, possible altruism, or delusional, consistent irrationality.

Even though quantitative measures for these factors are situational, we may consider the following approximate model for defining *m*:

$$m = |T^P[1,1]| + \max\{|T^P[2,1]|, |T^P[3,1]|\} - \Omega$$

where $T^P[1,1]$ is the reward, *s* would gain for reporting true violation *vio*, $T^P[2,1]$ is the corresponding community price if none of the subjects detecting the violation report it, and $T^P[3,1]$ is the punishment for the secondary violation, that is, the loss s_i would have in case she does not report the violation but in turn some other subject reports against him for doing so. Ω indicates the effect of the factors that collectively can act as a deterrent for reporting the violation (point 3 above). For simplicity, it is defined as a fraction $\delta \in [0, 1]$ of the *MaxLoss*, which is the maximum loss caused by the violation:

$$\Omega_j = \delta * MaxLoss$$

In this definition we assume that the factors which would work against reporting a violation could be indirectly considered as being related with the 'share' in the gain subject s_i may have by not reporting the violation. Under such formulation, a probabilistically weakly robust monitoring policy would require that violations by a group of users should be very difficult so that most of the users in the group other than the violator himself may become potential witnesses.

As a mathematical simplification, we also enforce that $m \le M$, where *M* is some large positive constant upper bounding *m*. We further assume that the probability of reporting a violation by *s* is related to *m* as follows:

$$p^{pri} = \begin{cases} \dfrac{m}{M} & \text{if } m \ge 0 \\ 0 & \text{if } m \le 0 \end{cases} \qquad (5)$$

Modeling with PRISM

For any model-checking activity the behaviour of the underlying system is abstracted as transition system. In order to construct and analyze a model with PRISM, it needs to be specified in the PRISM language, a simple, state-based language, based on the Reactive Modules formalism of (Alur & Henzinger, 1999).

The fundamental components of a PRISM model are modules. A model is composed of a number of modules which interact with each other. A module contains a number of local variables. The values of these variables at any given time constitute the state of the module. The global state of the whole model is determined by the local state of all modules. The behaviour of each module is described by a set of commands. A command is of the following form:

[ ]condition $\rightarrow$ p_1: update$_1$ + p_2: update$_2$ + . . . + p_n: update$_n$;

The condition acts as a guard which is a predicate over all the variables in the model (including those belonging to other modules). Each *update$_i$* describes a transition, which the module can make with probability p_i if the *condition* is *true*. A transition is specified by giving new values to the variables in the module, possibly as a function of other variables.

The PRISM model in this work consists of two kinds of modules: A module for the 'environment' considered to be generating violations and a module for a subject detecting either primary

violation or both primary and secondary violations. These modules are discussed next:

Environment Module

We capture the occurrence of a violation in an environment module in the PRISM model as depicted in Figure 3. The violations are assumed to be occurring independent of each other. Therefore, we consider only one violation in our experiments and study the consequences related to it. We will omit the subscripts for the violation in the following discussion.

States of environment module are denoted by *state_env* variable and the states of subject s_i are represented using *state_subi*. A violation may occur only when the system is in a stable state. When all the subjects complete their reporting activities related to the violation, the system again returns to the stable state. The state transition diagram of the model of environment is shown in Figure 3.

Module for a Subject Detecting only Primary Violations

Figure 4 depicts the transition diagram for a subject. Referring to the figure, a subject stays in a stable state when no violation occurs. When

Figure 3. State transition diagram for the environment module

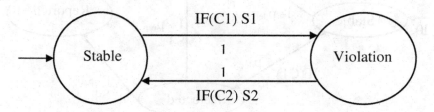

C1 :: state_sub1 = stable $\wedge$ state_sub2 = stable $\wedge$ ... $\wedge$ state_subn = stable;
C2 :: state_sub1 = end $\wedge$ state_sub2 = end $\wedge$ ... $\wedge$ state_subn = end;
S1:: state_env := violation; S2:: state_env := stable;

a violation occurs, as captured by the condition C1 in the Figure 4, a subject may or may not detect the violation based on detection probability. Therefore, from the *stable* state, the subject can go to state detected with probability p_{det} and to state end with probability $1 - p_{det}$. If the subject is in detected state, it can either report the violation with its reporting probability p_{rep} and transit to *reported* state, or it may not report the violation with probability $1 - p_{rep}$ and in turn may transit to the *end* state. After reporting the violation the subject finally moves to *end* state. When all subjects are in their *end* states and there are no more activities from the subjects regarding the violations, environment module can then move to its *stable* state. When environment is in *stable* state after a violation, all the subjects also move to their *stable* states.

We use a flag to distinguish two different possible behaviours of a subject after detecting a violation. In *stable* state, the flag is set to 0. If a subject reports the violation, its flag is set to 1 on taking a transition to the state *reported*. Otherwise if the subject does not report the violation after detecting it, its flag is set to 2. When the subject

moves from end *state* to the *stable* state, the flag is set to 0. This flag is used in writing PCTL properties and for modeling secondary violation, discussed next.

Module for a Subject Detecting both Primary and Secondary Violations

As depicted in the Figure 5, the module for a subject reporting only the primary violations can be extended to capture the activity of the subject related to secondary violations. The primary condition of detecting and reporting a secondary violation is that the subject has to report the corresponding primary violation also. So in the model of a subject for primary violation if the subject is in reported state, the subject may detect secondary violation by the other subject. We shall illustrate the model for two subject system. From the reported state, the subject may detect a secondary violation with probability p_{det_sec} and may move to *sec_vio_detected* state with probability p_{det_sec} and end state with probability $1 - p_{det\_sec}$. From *sec_vio_detected* state, the subject may move to *sec_vio_reported* with probability p_{rep_sec} or may

Figure 4. State transition diagram for a subject s_i detecting only primary violations

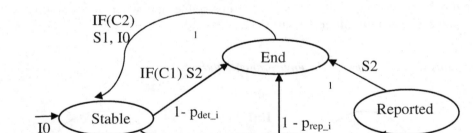

C1 :: state_env = violation; C2 :: state_env = stable; I0:: $flag_i := 0$;
S1:: $state\_sub_i := stable$; S2:: $state\_sub_i := end$; S3:: $flag_i := 2$;
S4::$flag_i := 1$;

Figure 5. State transition diagram for a subject detecting primary and secondary violations

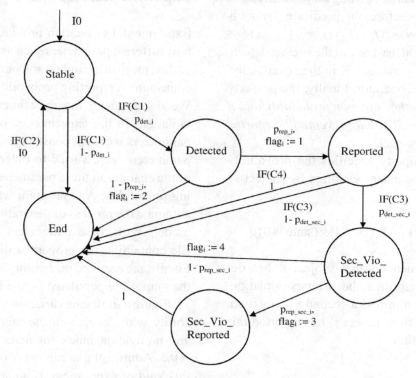

C1:: state_env = violation; C2 :: state_env = stable;
C3:: flag$_j$ = 2; C4 :: flag$_j$ ≠ 2; I0:: flag$_i$:= 0

move to the *end* state with probability 1- p_{rep_sec}. If a subject reports a secondary violation after detecting it, its flag is set to 3, otherwise the flag is set to 4. In Figure 5, *flag$_i$* denotes the flag for the subject, for which we are considering the model, and *flag$_j$* corresponds to the other subject.

The Combined System

The combined system can be represented as

$$Sys : \{\theta\}[Env \| Sub_1 \| \dots \| Sub_n]$$

where *Env* denotes the environment module used for generating violations. *Sub$_1$ . . . Sub$_n$* model the behaviour of the subjects $s_1, s_2, \dots, s_n$. θ specifies the initial values of variables.

Properties of Interest

In order to estimate the desired probabilities, we specify properties in PCTL. Since nondeterminism is involved, PRISM calculates the maximum and the minimum probability of a property being satisfied considering the best and worst cases after resolving all non-determinism. For primary violation, we are interested in estimating the probability of a violation to be reported by at least one subject. The following PCTL property specifies this:

$$P_{min} =?[(state = 1) \rightarrow F(Report \&(state = 0))]$$

where predicate (*state* = 0) checks if the environment module is in *stable* state and (*state* = 1) checks whether environment module is in *violated* state. $f_1, f_2, \dots, f_n$ denote the flags associated with subjects $s_1, s_2, \dots, s_n$. When value of a flag is 1, it indicates that the corresponding subject has reports the violation. Therefore, the predicate *Report* is defined as $Report \equiv ((f_1 = 1) \mid (f_2 = 1) \mid \ldots \mid (f_n = 1))$ denoting that at least one of the subject detects and reports the violation. **F** is the 'eventually' or 'in the future' operator. Finally, the property states that P_{min} is *the minimum probability that if a violation occurs, it would be eventually reported by at least one subject.*

The next property specifies the probability of reporting a secondary violation by subject s1 against subject s_2:

$$Pmin =?[(f2 = 2) \rightarrow F((f1 = 4)\&(state = 0))]$$

where $(f_2 = 2)$ denotes that subject s_2 has detected but not reported the primary violation, and therefore committed a secondary violation. $(f_1 = 4)$ denotes that subject s_1 has reported this secondary violation.

Experimental Results

Experimental evaluation provides insights as to how different parameters such as detection probability, motivation index, and number of subjects contribute to reporting probability of a violation. We discuss here the experiments on primary violation. In the experiments, one of the three parameters was kept constant and remaining two parameters were varied to determine the effect of the changes in these parameters on the reporting probability. A C program was developed to automate the process of generating these PRISM models with these parameters and a property file containing the properties discussed before. Finally, the required probability is extracted from the output file populated by the PRISM.

Figure 6 shows the variation of reporting probability with changes in the number of subjects and motivation index for detection probability = 0.5. Administrator can get useful insight from this kind of experiment. If an administrator can determine the detection probability for a policy violation from her experience, and if the number

Figure 6. The variation of reporting probability with changes in the number of subjects and motivation index for detection probability = 0.5

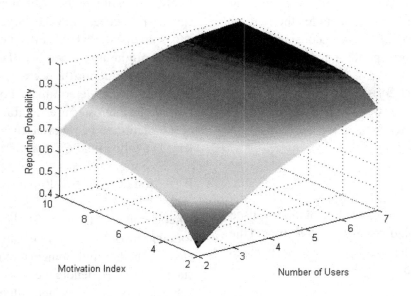

of associated subjects is also known, the required value of the motivation index can be assessed to achieve a particular reporting probability for the violation. This knowledge would in turn be used to determine the values for different entries in the payoff matrix for a subject-violation pair corresponding to the evaluated motivation index and associated reporting probability.

Figure 7 shows the variation of reporting probability with changes in the detection probability and the motivation index for number of users = 5. This is useful in the scenarios where a group of subjects are associated with an asset for which different violations are possible, and detection probabilities for these violations are also different. Figure 7 will give an administrator useful information about the motivation index for different violations for the same group of subjects.

Updating Detection Probabilities

While deploying the collaborative monitoring system, the administrator has to determine the

detection probability for a violation from her experience and historical analysis of the violations in past. This approach may get subjective, and sometimes the estimated values might be far away from the correct values. However to deploy the collaborative monitoring system, it is required to start with some values for detection probability. With some enhancement in the analysis, it is possible to have a better estimate of detection probability for some violation using the values for the total number of violations, the number of primary violations reported by a subject, and the number of secondary violation reported against the subject over a period of time.

Let us assume that the time period which is considered for estimating the detection probability of a subject s for violation vio_j is d time units. Let, in these d time instances, number of primary violations reported against violation vio_j is N. Also, the number of primary violation reported by subject s is n_p and the number of secondary violations reported against subject s is n_s. So, if

Figure 7. The variation of reporting probability with the changes in the detection probability and motivation index for number of users = 5

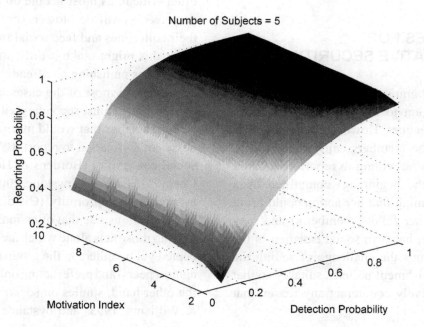

the actual detection probability of subject s for violation vio_j is p_{det_actual}, then

$$p_{det\_actual} \geq \frac{n_p + n_s}{N}$$

So, the administrator now has a new estimate for the detection probability of a subject for a violation. Let us estimate this new detection probability of subject s for violation vio_j as:

$$p_{det\_new} = \frac{n_p + n_s}{N}$$

Now the administrator needs to run the experiment again to get estimate of new reporting probability, or to estimate new motivation index for achieving the previous reporting probability. Note that the detection probabilities now may be different for different subjects. Though in our previous discussion, we have considered same detection probability for all the subjects, the model can be easily enhanced for different detection probability for different subjects, as the models for individual subjects are independent from each other.

CHALLENGES FOR COLLABORATIVE SECURITY

Success of collaborative security entails a member in an organization to report violations against her known colleagues. However, a member of a group, where the members enjoy camaraderie, may not always be willing to report a violation (especially in the beginning) committed by a colleague, assuming that her action could bring punishment to her fellow member(s) and may in turn endanger her own social isolation in the group. This brings the challenge of setting the reward and punishment policies suitably so that they can effectively counteract any reason that thwarts a member in a group to report a violation. Selecting the types of reward is yet another challenge. As the research in the area of motivational psychology demonstrates, individuals differ in their preferences for rewards - some people may be motivated by monetary rewards, while some others may be more interested in recognition, while others may aspire for career advancement, and on certain scenarios individuals may not even prefer having any explicit (or tangible) rewards and just an enabling framework for reporting and consequent reduction in the potential loss to the organization itself would be sufficient for them. Indeed a reward is an 'abstract token' working as a psychological catalyst for the motivation of the users. Similarly punishment is also an 'abstract token' to discourage users for not reporting the observed violations. The challenge present here is that since the same reward may not motivate all the members equally, this in turn might affect their reporting behaviours also.

Another challenge for collaborative security is setting up adequate regulatory controls so that the fundamental privacy rights of the members of the organization can be preserved. Maintaining anonymity of a person who reports a violation is often critical, as most people do not want to be perceived as whistle-blowers (or 'informers') by their colleagues and face social isolation. Sometimes this might make it difficult to punish the offender as punishing an offender would require an witness in most of the cases. In this respect, punishment against secondary violations should be beneficial as that would motivate all the witnesses of a violation to report it. Also studies on social conformity (Bordens & Horowitz, 2001, Chap. 7),(Martin & Hewstone, 2001) (also known as 'normative conformity' (Cialdini & Goldstein, 2004)) demonstrate that often individuals fear to get into those acts alone which are not so well accepted yet by others in the group (e.g., reporting against peers) and prefer acting only in groups. On the other hand, studies on social loafing (Karau & Williams, 1993) and bystander effect (Rowe et al., 2002) demonstrate that often individuals also feel a 'diffusion of responsibility' (Latene, 1981) when they are part of larger groups unless they are assigned clearly defined individual responsibilities. These conflicting factors demand that strong and effective initiatives to enforce collaborative security need to be adopted, which could counter the conformity biases, minimize negative peer influences (Felps et al., 2006), and motivate individuals to take leading roles in the process according to the prevailing socio-cultural environment in the groups/organization. In this respect consideration of secondary violations again could work as effective control for the individuals and could help reducing the bystander effect.

Next let us consider the assumption of policy consistency and completeness as described in Section on 'Assumptions'. In practice, it might be difficult to meet these requirements always. However, it turns out that these are critical for the success of the collaborative monitoring framework we discuss in this paper. To see this, consider the case of contradictions in policy definition. If a policy is not contradiction free, there would exist scenarios where it will be possible to interpret these scenarios both as a violation of the policy as well as in accordance with the policy. This may also imply an ambiguity in the interpretation of its observable impact on the system (ref. 'axiom of observability' in Section on 'Assumptions'). Therefore if a user reports it as a violation, she might expect due rewards, while system administrators might conclude otherwise and deny that reward to her. This in turn would negatively impact the motivation of the users to further report the violations in future. On the other hand, if a user concludes that the witnessed scenario does not constitute as a violation, she might not report on it, however some other users or the system administrators might interpret it differently and might impose punishment on her for non-reporting - which would again result in reduced motivation for further reporting. Therefore, it is absolutely necessary that policies are free from contradictions

and are mutually consistent. Wherever it is not possible, a balanced approach towards deciding rewards and punishments might possibly help in dealing with it.

In the collaborative monitoring model, as the users are involved in detecting and reporting a violation, it may give an impression that the reported violations may have many false positives - a member in a group may allege falsely against some other member in the group to gain personal advantage or to cause harm to the colleague. However, as the model only considers observable violations, i.e., the violations impact of which can be observed, this would rule out the possibility that the member will be successful in alleging against a colleague by reporting a violation that has never occurred. It is, though, possible that a user may report an observable violation to be committed by someone who actually has not. However, the payoff structure as stipulated in this paper, is limited to the reporting of the 'occurrence of the violation' and leaves it outside the scope as to 'who actually committed the violation?' and also 'who has been blamed for it by the reporting users?', though both these aspects are often tightly coupled. The primary reason for such a scope limitation is that the truth of who actually committed the violation can only be established through forensic investigation and even after using sophisticated and reliable mechanisms it is possible that non-violators are suspected as violators owing to various confounding circumstantial reasons. Therefore, we do not expect that reporting users would be able to always suspect/ identify correctly the actual violators and therefore do not stipulate any reward (or punishment) for merely reporting (correctly or falsely) who the violator(s) was (were) and leave such aspects to the pre-existing security enforcement mechanism. However, effectiveness of such post reporting investigations and enforcement of the punishment to the violators (or those who are proved to be framing non-violators knowingly) could also have an impact on the future reporting behaviour of the users (especially if the existing law and enforcement system is not so effective) since these would act as pointers for their justification towards determining the overall utility and effectiveness of the reporting actions. Indeed, for a concrete realization of the presented framework, it is important to decide who verifies the reported violation and who approves the payouts, which would be determined by the existing corporate governance structure and policies of the organization.

Finally, a big computational challenge for the proposed probabilistic model for parameter estimation (ref. Section on 'Experimental Analysis') is how to make it scalable to meet the needs of large organizations. The success of the payoff model largely depends on estimating the values of rewards and punishments properly. The experimental setup presented for estimating different parameters of a payoff matrix does not appear to scale well. However, our hope is that with the advancement of tools and techniques in the field of formal methods, we will be able to reason about larger systems in near future. Moreover, the collaborative security model is modular in the sense that the model considers individual groups separately. Therefore, we do not need to always think about scaling the framework up to the whole organization level, the framework needs to be capable of scaling up to the group levels. The size of different groups based on different context may be of varying size though.

DIRECTIONS FOR FUTURE WORK

Current model is only a step towards the larger goal of enabling social networking based collaborative enterprise security and there exist many challenges before this goal can be effectively realized in practice. For example, the proposed model only deals with the scenarios of collaborative monitoring and reporting and it is left to the existing centralized infrastructure to establish further details. As a next step, we need to extend the model to also deal with the scenarios where social networking (in particular transient social networking) based collaborative proof generation against security violations can also be enabled.

In our experiments, we implicitly assumed that individual motivation alone can determine the likelihood of reporting of a violation by a user as modelled by Eq. (5), which is still a high level abstraction and leaves the scope of further work in this direction. The objective of this work would be to relate human behaviour with intrinsic or extrinsic rewards and losses in a more detailed manner. Work in the direction of human behaviour modeling (Puleo, 2006) would contribute concretely toward this goal. Further analysis would require modeling the reporting behaviour of users for secondary violations in a general setting involving n players. This may in turn enable a derivation of closed form solutions for optimal estimates of parameters in the pay off model for various security scenarios. In practical situations distributed and collaborative strategies may also be required for such estimates. Also, we need to model more realistically the external environmental factors which could control the reporting behaviour of the users. Such modeling would give rise to extended game theoretic model for the overall system, equilibrium of which may shed further practical insights on designing policies for collaborative security.

The nature of emergent network effects (Kilkki & Kalervo, 2004; Metcalfe, 1995) under the proposed reward-punishment based reinforcement framework is yet another direction for future investigations. Currently when a new user joins a collaborative network/group, the detection probability for the violation(s) against the policies associated with the group would increase under the normal assumptions. This would in turn reduce the chances of other users fined for community price. This essentially induces positive network effect. Also on the other side, new members increase the overall probability of detecting secondary violations in the group, which may in turn have an effect on other users reporting the detected violations. These network effects become even more important in the presence other environmental factors e.g., community structure (Newman & Girvan, 2004; Newman, 2006). Development of analytical and/or experimental models to study the emergent macro level properties of the system e.g., plateau and reverse effects, small world effects, network resilience, and phase transitions (Newman, 2003) may potentially help in this direction.

User driven policy synthesis is an important aspect of collaborative security approach. In this work, we only consider users reporting violations and leave it upon the existing policy synthesis machinery to use these reported violations for defining new policies or refining existing ones. An important problem to be addressed when users are allowed to add new policies is the consistency checking and completeness analysis.

It is also interesting to analyze how learning could be enabled in the system. One way to introduce learning in the system is for deciding optimum values for the payoff parameters e.g., rewards and punishments. Modifying the system to learn about inconsistencies could also be considered as another direction for future work.

The framework could be further extended with *decoy violations*, which could be used to test the possible user and group response behaviours for detection and reporting. Also, if suitably designed, decoy violations could induce 'decoy-effect' (or 'asymmetric dominance effect') (Huber et al., 1982) in the system motivating users to prefer to reporting rather than not. Though decoy violations appear to have important role to play in the beginning, we need to understand if they also necessarily hold long term effects in the context of collaborative security. Also, the degree of correspondence between decoy violations and the Prisoner's Dilemma (Poundstone, 1993), in particular, iterated Prisoner's Dilemma needs to be further explored.

CONCLUSION

This chapter presents a principled approach to one of the many little-studied aspects of enterprise security which relate to human behaviour. Existing security frameworks often differentiate user base of assets from the security administrators who design and enforce the security policies. However, in many aspects of security, it is the user who is best suited to detect and prevent violations which currently lie beyond the scope of available security enforcement mechanisms. This is especially true for the violations on context dependent logical resources, e.g., some data, significance of which is realized only when considered with respect to specific contexts. Such resources are often vulnerable to 'semantic manipulations' and securing them using automated monitoring is either not feasible or would be very expensive.

In this respect, involving users, who usually have strong analytic ability to detect violations and threats, but are not primarily responsible for security, can be quite advantageous. In this work, we have presented a generic reinforcement framework for enabling monitoring and detection of (potential) violations by these users. The probabilistic analysis, associated state-transition model for PRISM, and the experiments demonstrate how specific parameters can be estimated for determining the reward-punishment based policies for collaborative monitoring. Influence

REFERENCES

Alur, R., & Henzinger, T. (1999). Reactive modules. *Formal Methods in System Design*, *15*(1), 7–48. doi:10.1023/A:1008739929481

Bishop, M. (2003). *Computer security: Art and science* (1st ed.). Addison Wesley.

Bishop, M., Engle, S., Peisert, S., Whalen, S., & Gates, C. (2008). We have met the enemy and he is us. In *Proceedings of the 2008 new Security Paradigms Workshop*. Lake Tahoe, CA.

Bishop, M., & Gates, C. (2008). Defining the insider threat. In *Proceedings of the 2008 Cyber Security and Information Infrastructure Research Workshop*. Oak Ridge, TN.

Bordens, K. S., & Horowitz, I. A. (2001). *Social psychology* (2nd ed.). Lawrence Erlbaum. *Detection of insider threats* (Tech. Rep. No. 2.1). Carnegie Mellon University, CyLab.

Cialdini, R., & Goldstein, N. (2004). Social Influence: Compliance and conformity. *Annual Review of Psychology, 55,* 591–621. doi:10.1146/annurev.psych.55.090902.142015

Cole, E., & Ring, S. (2006). *Insider threat: Protecting the enterprise from sabotage, spying, and theft.* Syngress Press.

Daniel, R. (2005). Monetary incentives, what are they good for? *Journal of Economic Methodology, 12*(2), 265–276. doi:10.1080/13501780500086180

di Vimercati, S., & Samarati, P. (1996). Access control in federated systems. In *Proceedings of the 1996 Workshop on New Security Paradigms* (pp. 87–99).

Ernst, F., & Armin, F. (1995). *Psychological foundations of incentives* (1st ed.). IEW - Working Papers, Institute for Empirical Research in Economics - IEW.

Felps, W., Mitchell, T., & Byington, E. (2006). How, when and why bad apples spoil the barrel: Negative group members and dysfunctional groups. *Research in Organizational Behavior, 27,* 181–230. doi:10.1016/S0191-3085(06)27005-9

Greene, B., Sternberg, D., & Lepper, M. R. (1976). Overjustification in a token economy. *Journal of Personality and Social Psychology, 34,* 1219–1234. doi:10.1037/0022-3514.34.6.1219

Greenwald, S. (1996). A new security policy for distributed resource management and access control. In *Proceedings of the 1996 Workshop on New Security Paradigms* (pp. 74–86).

Group, M. T. (2008, October). *Do you really know what your programmers are doing?* White Paper.

Hansson, H., & Jonsson, B. (1994). A logic for reasoning about time and reliability. *Formal Aspects of Computing, 6*(5), 512–535. doi:10.1007/BF01211866

Huber, J., Payne, J., & Puto, C. (1982). Adding asymmetrically dominated alternatives: Violations of regularity and the similarity hypothesis. *The Journal of Consumer Research, 9*(1), 90. doi:10.1086/208899

Iyer, A., & Ngo, H. Q. (2005). Towards a theory of insider threat assessment. In *Proceedings of the 2005 International Conference on Dependable Systems and Networks* (pp. 108–117). Washington, DC: IEEE Computer Society.

Kabay, M. (2002). Using social psychology to implement security policies. *Computer Security Handbook, 35,* 1–35.

Karau, S. J., & Williams, K. D. (1993). Social loafing: A meta-analytic review and theoretical integration. *Journal of Personality and Social Psychology, 65,* 681–706. doi:10.1037/0022-3514.65.4.681

Kilkki, K., & Kalervo, M. (2004, March). *Kk-law for group forming services.* Presented at 15th International Symposium on Services and Local Access.

Kwiatkowska, M., Norman, G., & Parker, D. (2001). Prism: Probabilistic symbolic model checker. In *Proceedings of PAPM/PROBMIV '01 Tools Session* (pp. 7–12).

Latene, B. (1981). The psychology of social impacts. *The American Psychologist, 36,* 343–356. doi:10.1037/0003-066X.36.4.343

Leyton-Brown, K., & Shoham, Y. (2008). *Essentials of game theory: A concise, multidisciplinary introduction.* Morgan & Claypool.

Martin, R., & Hewstone, M. (2001). Conformity and independence in groups: Majorities and minorities. In Hogg, M. A., & Tindale, S. (Eds.), *Blackwell handbook of social psychology (group processes)* (pp. 209–234). doi:10.1002/9780470998458.ch9

Metcalfe, B. (1995). Metcalfe's law: A network becomes more valuable as it reaches more users. *InfoWorld*, 17.

Newman, M. E. J. (2003). The structure and function of complex networks. *SIAM Review*, 45, 167–256. doi:10.1137/S003614450342480

Newman, M. E. J. (2006). Modularity and community structure in networks. *Proceedings of the National Academy of Sciences of the United States of America*, 103, 8577. doi:10.1073/pnas.0601602103

Newman, M. E. J., & Girvan, M. (2004). Finding and evaluating community structure in networks. *Physical Review E: Statistical, Nonlinear, and Soft Matter Physics*, 69, 026113. doi:10.1103/PhysRevE.69.026113

Odlyzko, A., & Tilly, B. (2009). *A refutation of Metcalfe's law and a better estimate for the value of networks and network interconnections.*

Petri, H. (2003). *Motivation: Theory, research and application* (5th ed.). Wadsworth Publishing.

Poundstone, W. (1993). *Prisoner's dilemma.* New York, NY: Doubleday.

Puleo, A. J. (2006). *Mitigating insider threat using human behaviour influence models.* Unpublished Master's thesis, Air Force Institute of Technology, School of Engineering and Management.

Randazzo, M. R., Keeney, M., Kowalski, E., Cappelli, D., & Moore, A. (2005). *Insider threat study: Illicit cyber activity in the banking and finance sector* (Tech. Rep. No. CMU/SEI-2004-TR-021).

Rotter, J. B. (1966). Generalized expectancies for internal versus external control of reinforcement. *Psychological Monographs*, 80(1), 1–28. doi:10.1037/h0092976

Rotter, J. B. (1990). Internal versus external controls of reinforcement. *The American Psychologist*, 45, 489–193. doi:10.1037/0003-066X.45.4.489

Rowe, M., Wilcox, L., & Gadlin, H. (2002, October). Dealing with – or reporting – "unacceptable" behaviour (with additional thoughts about the "bystander effect"). *Computers & Security*, 21(6), 526–531.

Sandhu, R., Bhamidipati, V., & Munawer, Q. (1999). The ARBAC97 model for role-based administration of roles. *ACM Transactions on Information and System Security*, 2(1), 105–135. doi:10.1145/300830.300839

Sandhu, R., & Munawer, Q. (1999). The ARBAC99 model for administration of roles. In *Proceedings of the 15th Annual Computer Security Applications Conference.*

Sansone, C., & Harackiewicz, J. M. (2000). *Intrinsic and extrinsic motivation: The search for optimal motivation and performance* (1st ed.). Academic Press.

Sasturkar, A., Yang, P., Stoller, S., & Ramakrishnan, C. (2006). Policy analysis for administrative role based access control. In *Workshop on Computer Security Foundations* (pp. 124–138).

Schultz, E. E. (2002, October). A framework for understanding and predicting insider attacks. *Computers & Security*, 21(6), 526–531. doi:10.1016/S0167-4048(02)01009-X

Stoller, S., Yang, P., Ramakrishnan, C., & Gofman, M. (2007). Efficient policy analysis for administrative role based access control. In *Proceedings of the 14th ACM Conference on Computer and Communications Security* (p. 455).

KEY TERMS AND DEFINITIONS

Collaborative Security: A model of enterprise security which prescribes mechanisms for enabling security services with the active help of the users of the system.

Computation Tree Logic: It is a temporal logic for specifying properties of branching-time futures, that is, its model is defined over temporal progression of states of a system in a tree-like structure in which the future is not unique - there are different possible states in the future from any given state, however any one of which might be an actual state that is realised by a system.

Markov Decision Process (MDP): A stochastic system in which for each action the system can take in a state, the probability that the system would reach a specific new state is determined only by the current state and the action taken and not by the past history of the system.

Model Checking: An automated technique for formally verifying user specified correctness properties of system designs.

Nash Equilibrium: In game theory, Nash equilibrium of a game with two or more players is a state in which no player has anything to gain by changing only his own strategy unilaterally assuming that all the players know others strategies.

Network Effect: Network effect is a utility function which determines some useful value compared to the price paid by an actively engaged user in a network in terms of the size of the network.

Reinforcement Learning: A study of techniques which an agent could apply for taking actions in an environment in order to maximize its (cumulative) reward.

Chapter 17
Privacy–Aware Organisation–Based Access Control Model (PrivOrBAC)

Nabil Ajam
Institut Télécom, Télécom Bretagne, France

Nora Cuppens-Boulahia
Institut Télécom, Télécom Bretagne, France

Fréderic Cuppens
Institut Télécom, Télécom Bretagne, France

ABSTRACT

In this chapter, the authors propose the expression and the modelling of the most important principles of privacy. They deduce the relevant privacy requirements that should be integrated in existing security policy models, such as RBAC models. They suggest the application of a unique model for both access control and privacy requirements. Thus, an access control model is to be enriched with new access constraints and parameters, namely the privacy contexts, which should implement the consent and the notification concepts. For this purpose, the authors introduce the Privacy-aware Organisation role Based Access Control (PrivOrBAC) model.

1. INTRODUCTION

The enforcement of a privacy policy is still an open issue. One challenge is the expression of a privacy policy in information systems using existing security policy models. It is not sure that proposing a new model for privacy will be commonly accepted because it will cause a huge

DOI: 10.4018/978-1-4666-0978-5.ch017

upgrade of existing solutions. Since privacy requirements are generally mixed with an ordinary access control, we aim to enhance existing access control models to include privacy needs.

Related works, which proposed a privacy-aware model, have the drawback of including only a subset of the privacy requirements. Even if we share the same objectives as (Ni et al. 2007), (Masoumzadeh and Joshi 2008), (Yang et al. 2008), and (Byun et al. 2005) in using an access control model to express privacy requirements, they mainly focused on purpose specification, explicit consent and obligation. They do not care about data anonymisation, for example. On other hand, sometimes they need to extend their language to express some contexts such as the owner age and the current time as it is done in (Ni et al. 2007). We propose the embedding of the most important privacy requirements within a single model, the OrBAC model, namely owner consent, data obfuscation, provisional obligation, and other environment contexts such as temporal, spatial and prerequisite ones (Ajam et al. 2009). Minimal modifications are introduced into it since we aim an easy upgrade of existing information systems, which use the OrBAC model, towards a privacy-aware model.

In this chapter, we thus propose to use the OrBAC model enhanced by some concepts to model privacy policies. First, we focus on modelling the requirements of the data owner consent before delivering the sensitive data. The subscriber defines that he must be notified before terminating the access. The access is delayed until the satisfaction of this condition.

Then, the accuracy of the sensitive data is usually underestimated within privacy models. We design an object hierarchy based on predefined accuracy levels. For this, we propose a derivation rule of sensitive objects. So, a data owner can define authorizations based on different object accuracies. Furthermore, access control models usually permit the access to the stored data based on the role of the requester. We propose to extend this concept to take into account the purpose of the access. For this, we take advantage of the OrBAC user-declared context. We also propose in this work to model the provisional obligations after accessing personal information.

Third parties must notify the data controller about further usage of collected data. Then, we extend OrBAC contexts to model the communica-

tion state between the subject and the data owner. This state indicates if the owner initiated a call to the service provider, so this fact can be considered as an implicit consent and the sensitive information can be authorized to be accessed. Also, we extend the spatial context to constrain the access based on the area of the object and not only on subject location. To validate our approach, we show how the resulting model can be used to model the privacy policy for a location-based service. This can be applied within a mobile operator organization.

This chapter is organised as follows. Section 2 lists the privacy requirements that will be deployed through access control models. Section 3 presents the OrBAC model. Section 4 is dedicated to our privacy-aware OrBAC model. Section 5 presents a use case of location service and how a privacy policy is specified through our privacy-aware OrBAC model. Section 6 details related works and the advantage of our proposal. And concluding remarks are presented in section 7.

2. MODELLING MOTIVATION

We illustrate in this section the issues related to private data management and how to use a privacy policy to specify privacy requirements. We assume that the private data are collected by mobile operator networks since we focus, in our work, on sensitive data such as location and presence of mobile subscribers that only the network operator can collect. At this stage we do not care about means used to collect data. Collected data concerns operator's subscribers.

The information is stored within operator's information system. The later should implement the OrBAC model to enforce the privacy policy defined by the subscribers. Service providers request that information to offer enhanced services. So, the operator should manage the access to services.

Figure 1. Privacy enforcement in mobile operator networks

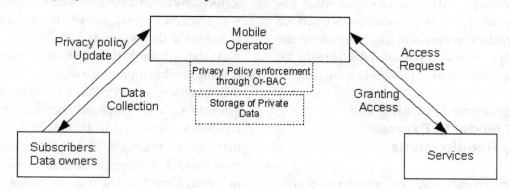

2.1 Privacy Requirements

We can identify the following goals of the privacy policy:

- The definition of purpose should be specified before delivering private data. Third parties should mention the purpose of the access request. This requirement corresponds to the purpose specification principle, which is required by OECD (OECD 1980),
- The definition of the accuracy of the private data by the data owner: the user can set its preferences by choosing the accuracy, which corresponds to the level of anonymity and/or to the level of the accuracy of the remaining data. This parameter enforces the principles of collection limitation and use limitation,
- The user consent about data owner preference: it is the requirements before delivering the personal data to third parties. The user notification is on the fly, so the access is pending until the consent of the data owner is given. These requirements are exclusively mentioned in the use limitation principle,
- Obligations, after the access, refer to the actions to be taken by the requestors. The data controller, who collects personal data

has to ensure the usage of personal data. This corresponds to some obligations to be fulfilled by third parties. Usage control is a relevant concept to enforce privacy requirements. It is closely related to the principles of use limitation and accountability.

- We consider a new OrBAC context to handle the current state between the data owner and the requestor. The data collector, which is the intermediary entity between them, has to verify if there is a current call between them and who initiates the call. This requirement is typically used for location-based service in mobile network. Standards require that the data owner can control the access to his private data if he was the initiator of a session call to the third party. In other terms, if the data owner initiates a call to a service provider, which then requests the location of the subscriber, the location information can be delivered to it without more privacy verification,
- We propose to extend the spatial context used in the OrBAC model to take into account the location of objects, because currently it is exclusively used to determine the location of subjects. It is used to control the subjects' access based on their positions. We aim to extend it by constraining the subjects' access based on the location

of objects. This issue is useful when objects are location information. So, service providers' access will also depend on the spatial context of objects, which are the location information of mobile subscribers.

2.2 Motivation for Using the OrBAC Model to Express Privacy Requirements

Integrating privacy requirements into a security policy, expressed through an access control model will permit an easy upgrade of existing information systems, which already implemented access control policies.

The OrBAC model presents some interesting characteristics. It supports environment and dynamic parameters through contexts. The OrBAC is based on the concept of organization so that different organizations can define their security policy. This corresponds to the fact that privacy practices usually apply to an organization on which data owners define their preferences. Users also specify obligations that requesters must perform after accessing sensitive information. For this, we chose the OrBAC model to include privacy requirements.

Other privacy models, such as P-RBAC, Purpose-BAC and Pu-RBAC focused on purpose entity and on few privacy requirements. This does not provide a complete set of concepts to specify privacy policies. They also propose major changes on existing models like the definition of new language extension to express access contexts. By contrast, in our privacy-aware OrBAC we suggest reusing most of the existing mechanisms implemented in OrBAC.

2.3 The Nature of Objects

Objects used in this chapter are a special kind of private data. We focus on the location information since we aim to define a privacy policy model to manage the privacy preferences of mobile sub-

scribers. We assume that each location is associated with some data owner, namely the subscriber that is located in that position.

Location information is sensitive information. It is the combination of the user identity and the user position. (3GPPa,3GPP) define location estimate as a geographical location of a user equipment expressed in latitude and longitude data. It can optionally contain the velocity. The coordinate shall be represented in a well-defined universal format. (ETSIb) specifies that location is expressed through a longitude, latitude and accuracy but altitude is optional. In this chapter, we are more concerned about the location information that can be provided by the mobile operator.

So, we consider that it is presented by a longitude, a latitude and an accuracy. The later assumption will impact the degradation algorithm to depreciate the location since, if we consider that a velocity can be provided, we can use more sophisticated algorithms to have k-anonymity and l-diversity (Gedik and Liu 2008). But, we aim to propose a flexible solution since the common attributes, provided by operator networks, include longitude and latitude.

On the other hand, we consider that the degradation algorithm is an input to our model. Given the two coordinates, the chosen algorithm will compute two new co-ordinates, say longitude' and latitude', so that the user is indistinguishable within a set of users. (Duckham and Kulika 2006) and (Krumm 2008) give a survey of the alternative algorithms that can be used.

The location information of subscribers constitutes the objects that we aim to protect the access to. We assume that each subscriber can have several pieces of location information. Each object has the following attributes: Data-owner, Longitude, Latitude, Accuracy.

3. OrBAC

The Organization-Based Access Control model (OrBAC) (Cuppens 2007) provides interesting mechanisms to express the security policy and enables making distinction between an abstract policy specifying organizational requirements and its implementation in a given information system.

Traditional models are based on subjects that have the right to make actions on objects. An abstraction level is offered by OrBAC to categorize subjects into role, objects into view and actions into activity. This abstract level is introduced to design implementation-independent policies. These entities are designed within an organization to control interoperability between organizations and enforce separation of duties. The organization is the central component. It groups a set of subjects and it is in charge of defining and enforcing the security policy applied to these subjects when they perform actions on objects controlled by the organization. So, the specification of the policy is parameterised by the organization. This is used to handle simultaneously several security policies associated with different organizations.

Privileges do not directly apply to subjects, they are assigned to roles within an organization (Cuppens 2007).

Abstract organization privileges, such as permission, are expressed through the predicate:

Permission(organization, role, activity, view, context)

OrBAC authorizes the use of four kinds of privileges: permission, prohibition, obligation and dispensation. They mean that a given role, is permitted, respectively prohibited, obliged or dispensed, to perform a given activity on a given view.

A privilege corresponds to a relation between roles, views and activities at the organizational level. The concrete policy is logically derived from abstract privileges, according to derivation rules.

The corresponding derived concrete privileges are Is_permitted, Is_prohibited, Is_obliged and Is_dispensed. They compute if a given subject, belonging to a role, can perform a given action, belonging to an activity, on a given object, belonging to a view.

In OrBAC, there are three built-in predicates, which specify conditions over subjects' role, actions' activity and objects' view. Let Org be the set of organizations:

- Empower is a predicate over domains Org ×S× R. If org is an organisation, s a subject and r a role, then Empower(org, s, r) means that org empowers s in the role r,
- Consider is a predicate over domains Org ×A× A. If org is an organisation, α an action and a an activity, then Consider(org, α, a) means that org considers that α is implementing the activity a,
- Use is a predicate over domains Org ×O× V. If org is an organization, o is an object and v is a view, then Use(org, o, v) means that org uses the object o in the view v.

Contexts are designed to take into account dynamic parameters of a security policy. A context is defined as an abstract condition that takes into account such environment parameters when specifying abstract organization privileges. So, contexts are designed to allow the definition of a dynamic security policy. Contexts are constraints that model extra conditions a subject, an action and an object must satisfy to activate a privilege. An OrBAC built-in predicate Hold permits linking those entities:

- Hold is a predicate over domains Org ×S×A×O×C. If org is an organization, s is a subject, α is an action, o is an object and c is a context, then Hold(org, s, α,o, c) means that context c holds between subject s, action α and object o within org.

Box 1.

$$\forall org \in Org, \forall s \in S, \forall \alpha \in Action, \forall o \in O, \forall r \in R, \forall v \in V, \forall a \in Activity, \forall c \in C,$$
$$Permission(org, r, a, v, c) \wedge Empower(org, s, r) \wedge Use(org, o, v) \wedge Consider(org, \alpha, a)$$
$$\wedge Hold(org, s, \alpha, o, c) \rightarrow Is\_permitted(s, \alpha, o)$$

The OrBAC model defines five types of contexts (Cuppens 2007): spatial context: that depends on the subject position, temporal context: that depends on the time of the subject request, user-declared context: that depends on parameters declared by the subject, prerequisite context: that depends on a application-specific relation between the subject, the action and the object, and provisional context: that depends on the previous actions of the subject.

Given the materials presented before, the rule, named concrete permission derivation, is modelled by the following in Box 1.

That means s is permitted to perform α on o, if (1) there is an abstract permission in organisation org, which allows the role r to perform activity a on view v within the context c, and (2) org empowers subject s in role r and (3) org uses object o in view v and (4) org considers that action α implements activity a and (5) within org, the context c holds between s, α and o. Similarly, the concrete privileges Is_prohibited, Is_obliged and

Is_dispensed, are derived from prohibition, obligation and dispensation, respectively.

To structure the set of entities and authorizations in OrBAC, hierarchies and inheritance mechanisms are introduced. Roles, views, activities, contexts and organizations may be structured according to hierarchies. In this case, privileges are inherited through this hierarchy. For this purpose, we define the predicate Sub_role to specify role hierarchies. Similar predicates for activity (Sub_activity), view (Sub_view), context (Sub_context) and organization (Sub_organisation) are defined for hierarchies.

4. THE PRIVACY-AWARE ORBAC MODEL (PRIVORBAC)

In order to add privacy requirements to the OrBAC model, we propose to model (Figure 2): the consent context, object's hierarchy based on the accuracy of objects, the purpose as a user-declared context,

Figure 2. The privacy-aware OrBAC model

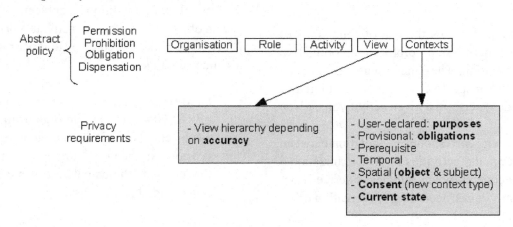

provisional obligation following the access to sensitive information, the current state context and the enhanced spatial context.

4.1 Consent

4.1.1 The Consent_Preference View

When the operator receives an access request from the service provider, we suppose that the operator should maintain a trace of the data owner's preference regarding the need for consent or not. This need depends on the data owner. The trace (or the history) of users preference is modelled by a view: consent_preference.

Each object of this later view has four attributes: Requestor, Target, Data-owner and NeedConsent. Requestor is the subject who requests the access to the object. Target is the requested object or view. Data-owner is the subscriber that the object or the view referred to. And, NeedConsent is a Boolean parameter, If it is true, this means consent must be given by the data owner before granting the access. Note, that each data owner can have several entries in this view.

By inserting this object into the consent_preference view, Alice informs the operator that no consent is needed for Bob:

Use(mobile-operator,Alice_preference_1, consent_preference)

This object must be inserted to the consent_preference to be effective:

Use(mobile-operator,Alice_preference_2, consent_preference)

Example 1. Assume that Alice and Bob are mobile subscribers. Alice permits Bob to see her coordinates without her consent. For this purpose, Alice defines the object:

Alice_preference_1:	
Requestor	Bob
Target	Alice-coordinates
Data-owner	Alice
NeedConsent	false

4.1.2 The Consent Context

The user consent is modelled in the OrBAC model thanks to new context type, named consent. Two cases are identified:

1. When NeedConsent attribute (of the corresponding object of consent_preference view) is true,
2. When NeedConsent attribute (of the corresponding object of consent_preference view) is false.

The first case is when the consent is needed. We need to model the data owner response before making the access decision. We model the data owner response by a built-in predicate Consent_response. If org is an organization, s is a subject, do is a data-owner, resp $\in$ {accept, deny}, then Consent_response(Org,do, s, resp) is the response returned by the data owner to the organization. It is a predicate over domains Org $\times$ S $\times$ S $\times$ {accept, deny}:

Figure 3. Consent preferences

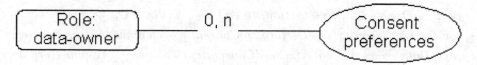

Example 2. Alice now would require her consent before the access of the service provider Advertiser to its coordinates. For this purpose, Alice defines the object:

Alice_preference_2:	
Requestor	Advertiser
Target	Alice-coordinates
Data-owner	Alice
NeedConsent	true

$\forall org \in Org, \forall do \in S, \forall s \in S$

$Consent\_response(Org, do, s, accept) \leftarrow true$

If the data owner accepts subjects request, and deny otherwise

The organisation can submit the consent request to the data owner through its specific communication means. For example, mobile operator organisation can send a short message to notify the mobile subscriber. The data owner will answer by accept or deny.

Note that this response cannot be evaluated in advance, so the Consent_response predicate is evaluated on the fly when a location request is received by the organization. The access decision must be pending for some amount of time until the response of the data owner is received. This corresponds to a pre-obligation to be fulfilled before taking the decision to accept the location request (Elrakaiby et al. 2010). If there is no response, an alternative policy can be applied. We can assume that the default Consent_response is deny, so the sensitive information cannot be accessed when the users does not give his consent explicitly.

However, to provide a fine-grained policy, the default value of the Consent_response can be set by the data owner himself. In other terms, the data owner can access to that attribute and set it to accept if he agrees to reveal his sensitive information when he does not respond to the consent notification.

On the other hand, the amount of time when the access decision is pending can depend on a timer whose value is fixed by the organisation. The two issues of the timer and the default value of the Consent_response are investigated in (Elrakaiby et al. 2010). By default, we assume that Consent_response is set to false.

The second case is when the data owner does not require his consent before revealing his location to the requestor. In this case, the NeedConsent(cp) attribute is false (and ¬NeedConsent(cp) is true). The access decision can be made without waiting the Consent_response.

The user consent context can now be specified for the two cases as show in Box 2.

The above formula means that if org is an organization, s a subject, α an action, v a view, cp is an object belonging to the Consent_preference view, and Consent_response is the built-in predicate detailed above then the Consent_context holds if there is an object cp, which has the attributes Requestor whose value is s, Target whose value is v and NeedConsent.

When the latter is false we do not need the consent of the data owner of the object o, which belongs to the view v. Else the predicate Consent_response is needed. By this means, the data owner can choose which view the subject can access.

Box 2.

$\text{Rule}_{consent} \quad \forall org \in Org, \forall s \in S, \forall \alpha \in Action, \forall o \in O, \forall v \in V, \forall cp \in O,$

$Hold(org, s, \alpha, v, Consent\_context) \leftarrow Use(org, cp, Consent\_preference) \land \text{Re}\,questor(cp, s)$

$\land T\arg et(cp, v) \land Data - owner(v, do) \land (\neg NeedConsent(cp) \lor Consent\_response(org, do, s, accept))$

When the service provider, who is the fleet manager, makes a request to the database to access the location information of that user, then the consent context will be evaluated. The mobile subscriber will be notified and its response is encoded into the Consent_response predicate. So, the Consent_response is activated only if Consent_response is accept.

4.2 Accuracy Attribute

Privacy enforcement requires the use of different levels of accuracy depending on the purpose and the subject requesting the access to the private data. That principle is consistent with the privacy directive of collection limitation since service providers cannot access more accurate objects than user preference and needed accuracy for the service.

We suggest that private objects, of each data owner, have different levels of accuracy. We propose to consider a hierarchy between the root view of one data owner that groups the initially collected objects, and sub-views of that data owner. These sub-views group the derived objects that have different accuracies. We recall that Sub_view is a relation over domains Org × V × V, if org is an organisation, and v1 and v2 are views (∈ V), then Sub_view(org, v1, v2) means that in organization org, view v1 is a sub-view of v2. So, data owner can define several access policies depending on accuracies of his location objects.

4.2.1 Accuracy Levels

Before defining the hierarchy of location data, we will propose an accuracy model for private data. We will focus on the special case of the location data. Each location object has four attributes: the identity of the data owner, the location information, composed of a longitude, a latitude, and the accuracy.

The data owner identity and the location are loosely coupled. Malicious third parties can hinder

Example 3. Let Alice be a mobile subscriber that defines the need of consent before granting access to her location information view, which is named ms-location-information. And, let fm be a fleet management service provider. Let us assume we have an object fm_preference belonging to the consent_preference view that has the following attributes:

fm_preference:	
Requestor	fm
Target	ms-location-information
Data-owner	Alice
NeedConsent	true

And Use(mobile − operator, fm_preference, consent_preference)

user privacy only if they can break the relation that binds the accurate position with the identity of the subscriber.

We define two kinds of accuracy. The accuracy of an object is specified by the couple (anonymity level, k). Anonymity level defines the accuracy of the identity attribute of location information. k determines the accuracy of the location attributes, which are the longitude and the latitude.

The anonymity level defines how the subscriber identity is masked. We identify three levels of anonymity: anonymous user, which means that no identity is used when delivering location data, pseudonymity, which means that a temporary pseudonym is used to identify the location information, and fair identity, which means that the subscriber chooses to use his identity (name or phone number) to identify the location information.

The k parameter can be used in several manners to introduce an obfuscation of the position depending on the operator policy. It may be used as an input to a k-anonymity algorithm. The subscriber is indistinguishable within some zone area between k-1 other subscribers. There is a plethora of such algorithms (Duckham and Kulika 2006,Krumm 2008,Gedik and Liu 2008).

The k parameter can be also used in another way. Independently from the positions of other users, the latitude and the longitude can be depreciated based on k. The returned values will be chosen randomly from (userLatitude − k, userLatitude + k) and from (userLongitude − k, userLongitude + k), where (userLongitude, userLatitude) is the real position of the subscriber.

The latter obfuscation is more suited for the LBS services. An LBS service depends on the accuracy of the location information and each service has an accuracy threshold. If the location accuracy is lower than that threshold the service cannot be provided. When using k-anonymity algorithms, the location obfuscation can be important because there are few users located by the operator. Then, the accuracy, for k-anonymity algorithms, can be lower than the threshold.

4.2.2 Accuracy-Based Object Hierarchy

When a data owner defines his anonymity preferences, we propose to create a view for each preference. This means that each view contains the sensitive objects of the data owner with specified anonymity preferences.

Figure 4 shows two levels in the hierarchy of the location views:

• The first one is computed by replacing the identity attribute by a pseudonymous, anonymous or the true identity itself,

• The second stage is computed by executing the k-anonymity or the k-degradation algorithm over location attributes (coordinates). The implemented algorithm depends on the operator choice.

Each subscriber defines his own private data hierarchy, composed of different views. Each view is described by the couple (anonymity level, k). The subscriber can then specify a different privacy policy and access control for each view. 'Permission privilege' is granted to the authorized service providers by subscribers.

Example 4. Let Alice be a mobile subscriber. She wants to subscribe to two LBS services. The first is a dating service, which needs the location information to let her talk with the nearest friends, and the second one is a yellow page service, which indicates to her the nearest points of interest within a zone area. She prefers to let the first service know her location with an accuracy of 10 kilometres. By contrast, Alice uses the second service to find the closest restaurants for example, so she sets the accuracy for the second service to 10 meters. For both services, she aims to stand anonymous. Based on our representation of accuracy, Alice defined two preferences:

	anonymity level	k parameter
preference1:	anonymous user	10 km
preference2:	anonymous user	10 m

4.2.3 Object Derivation Rule

We assume that the data controller implements a degradation algorithm $algo_k$, which depreciates the position of users. k is an entry parameter set by the data owner. Let $algo_k$(latitude, longitude) = (latitude', longitude'), where (latitude', longitude') is the depreciated position.

Location information, as presented in section 2.3, consists of a triple (identity, position, real-accuracy). Position is formed by the latitude and the longitude, and real-accuracy is the accuracy of the collected object before the degradation.

We define RV as the root view containing the collected location information of subscribers. The accuracy of this information is real-accuracy. And the DV is the view containing the location information after applying the degradation algorithm, so the accuracy of these objects is decreased. Accuracy, which is fixed by the data owner, is defined by the couple (anonymity_level × N) where anonymity_level = {fair, anonymous, pseudonymous}. Let ro be a root object belonging to the root view RV. The derived object dr,

Figure 4. Accuracy levels of location data

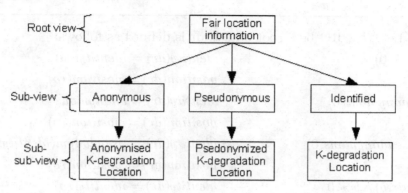

belonging to a derived view DV, is specified as follows in Box 3.

Example 5. Let Bob be a mobile subscriber. He defines two accuracies (anonymous, m) and (pseudonymous, 0). Based on his root location information ro and his preferences, anonymized-M-Degradation-view and pseudonymous-view are the two sub-views created within his mobile-operator's organization. We assume that the Bob's pseudonym is stored within a mobile operator database, say Bob-pseudonym. Based on the identity attribute of the ro object, the derived objects dr-M-anonym, belonging to anonymized-M-Degradation-view, and dr-pseudonym, belonging to pseudonymous-view, are defined as shown in Box 4.

4.3 Purpose as a User-Declared Context

We suggest modelling purpose as a user-declared context. In the OrBAC model, the definition of a user-declared context consists in two steps: the specification of roles that can declare this user-declared context, and the specification of roles that are permitted to fulfil a given activity when they declare the associated user-declared context.

The purpose specification is clearly a relevant requirement for the privacy policy. In other terms, the requestor should declare the purpose of its access before granting this access to the location information. This corresponds to the purpose specification principle of privacy practices.

Each purpose object has two attributes (Cuppens 2007). Recipient defines who takes advantage of the declared purpose (the service provider in our case), and declared_purpose is a predicate which associates the purpose value, such as route optimising, with the declared purpose. Purpose values represent the set of purposes recognized by the data collector and they can be viewed as a purpose ontology defined within the mobile operator. We aim to use this OrBAC capability to specify purpose enforcement.

4.3.1 Purpose Specification

We assume that purposes are grouped into a Purpose view. Each data owner defines objects belonging to his purpose sub-view, say data-owner-po. Purpose objects form a finite set denoted PO. They are used to describe the user-declared context activated by some data owners. So, data owners have to define these po objects, which have two attributes Recipient and Declared_purpose.

Recipient is a predicate over domains PO×S. So, if po is a purpose object belonging to PO, and s be a subject, then Recipient(po, s) states that s is the subject which takes advantage of the declared purpose po.

Declared_purpose is a predicate over domains PO × PV, where PV is the set of purpose values.

Box 3.

$\text{Rule}_{\text{derivation}}$: Let $ro \in RO$ be a root object, dr is defined as follows:

$$accuracy = (fair, 0) \quad \rightarrow \quad identity(dr) = identity(ro)$$
$$position(dr) = position(ro)$$

$$accuracy = (anonymous, 0) \quad \rightarrow \quad identity(dr) = anonymous$$
$$position(dr) = position(ro)$$

$$accuracy = (pseudonymous, 0) \quad \rightarrow \quad identity(dr) = pseudonym(identity(ro))$$
$$position(dr) = position(ro)$$

$$accuracy = (fair, b) \wedge b \succ 0 \quad \rightarrow \quad identity(dr) = identity(ro)$$
$$position(dr) = a \lg o_b(position(ro))$$

$$accuracy = (anonymous, b) \wedge b \succ 0 \quad \rightarrow \quad identity(dr) = anonymous$$
$$position(dr) = a \lg o_b(position(ro))$$

$$accuracy = (pseudonymous, b) \wedge b \succ 0 \quad \rightarrow \quad identity(dr) = pseudonym(identity(ro))$$
$$position(dr) = a \lg o_b(position(ro))$$

Box 4.

$$accuracy = (pseudonymous, 0) \quad \rightarrow \quad identity(dr - pseudonym) = Bob - pseudonym$$
$$position(dr - pseudonym) = position(ro)$$

$$accuracy = (anonymous, m) \quad \rightarrow \quad identity(dr - anonym) = anonymous$$
$$position(dr - M - anonym) = a \lg o_m(position(ro))$$

These values provide an ontology of possible purposes. For example if PV = {fleet-management, optimise-route} and po is a purpose object then Declared_purpose(po, optimise-route) means that optimise-route is the purpose value associated with the declared purpose po.

On the other hand, the service provider declares the purpose to be provided. user_declared is a function over the PV domain. It returns the value of the context entered by the service provider.

That is, in organisation org, subject s performs action α on object o, which has do as data owner, in the user declared context user_declared(pv), if there is a purpose object po used in the sub-view do-purpose by organisation org such that s is the recipient associated with po and pv is the declared purpose associated with po.

The view Purpose consists in objects which provide access to service providers. Each data owner, say do, has his own view do-purpose. The latter is a sub-view of the Purpose view. We need now to specify the relation between the declarant and the recipient. So, we will specify who can insert new objects in this view.

For instance, in mobile network, the declarant must have subscribed to the service, which is provided by the second subject. In other terms, the service provider can only request the access to the location information of users, who have subscribed to its service.

346

Box 5.

$$\mathrm{Rule}_{\text{purpose}} \quad \forall org \in Org, \forall s \in S, \forall \alpha \in Action, \forall o \in O, \forall po \in PO, \forall pv \in PV,$$
$$Hold(org, s, \alpha, o, user\_declared(pv)) \leftarrow data - owner(o, do) \wedge Use(org, po, do - purpose)$$
$$\wedge \operatorname{Re}cipient(po, s) \wedge Declared\_purpose(po, pv)$$

In the OrBAC model, we can use a prerequisite context to model the relation between the declarant of the context and the recipient. We define the subscription context to specify that the declarant must have subscribed to the recipient.

Then, subject empowered in role data-owner are permitted to access his purpose view, say data-owner-po, and declare new objects:

Permission(org, data-owner, declare, data-owner-po, subscription)

That is, in organisation org, the role data-owner is permitted to perform the activity declare on its purpose view data-owner-po in the prerequisite context subscription. This context is active if s' has subscribed to service provider s. This is modelled by the application-dependent predicate Subscribed.

To sum up, the specification of purposes has three steps. There are two actors, the declarant, who declares a purpose, and the recipient, who takes advantage of this purpose when it is declared.

The first step consists in granting the declarant an access to the Purpose view. This access allows

data owners to insert purpose objects inserted the purpose view.

The second step states that the access to the Purpose view is constrained by a prerequisite context. This context binds the recipient and the declarant by the subscription condition. The declarant must have subscribed to one or more services provided by the recipient. This step specifies this prerequisite context.

Third, the subject, who aims to access the sensitive information, has to declare a purpose value as a user-declared context. This value must correspond to a purpose object defined by the declarant in the first step.

4.4 Requirements beyond Granting the Access: Provisional Obligation

Since private data can be stored and reused for unauthorized purposes, we define usage control over private data. Basically, usage control is introduced thanks to obligation requirements. Thus obligations are introduced within the OrBAC

Box 6.

$$\mathrm{Rule}_{\text{purposeView}} \quad \forall org \in Org, \forall s \in S, \forall s' \in S, \forall \alpha \in Action, \forall po \in PO,$$
$$Hold(org, s, \alpha, po, subscription) \leftarrow Use(org, po, do - purpose) \wedge \operatorname{Re}cipient(po, s')$$
$$\wedge Subscribed(s, s')$$

Figure 5. Purpose preference

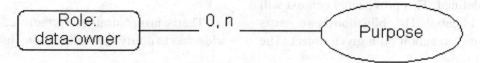

model (Cuppens 2007). For example thanks to provisional obligation, the operator can order service providers to perform certain actions following their access to location information. So, the obligation is automatically triggered as a counterpart of the access to the private information. The obligation is expressed thanks to two types of contexts Context_activation and Context_violation:

Obligation(org, role, activity, view,Context_activation,Context_violation)

This privilege means that in organisation org, the action α has to be performed by the subject s on the object o once Context_activation becomes true, and will be violated if Context_violation occurs before the activity is fulfilled.

For example, within mobile network organization, a service provider has to send details to subscribers about provided service before accessing location data. Context_activation will be providing location service, while Context_violation could be a time period of one day if details must be sent on the same day.

4.4.1 Provisional Obligation

The service provider cannot ignore the obligation because of an existing agreement between the service provider and the operator. Furthermore, the operator can order that an external legal entity will supervise the usage of the sensitive information.

Here, we assume that the trustworthy level requires that the service provider has to notify subscribers about further usage, such as deleting data or providing new service. The notification obligation is delivered to the operator that will hand it to the subscriber. We are only concerned about the notification to the operator.

The specification of a provisional obligation requires three steps. First, a provisional context should be defined. This provisional context will trigger the obligation. The obligation then consists in performing an action on a given object. The

second step consists in defining this action and this object. Third step defines the obligation privilege.

Hereafter, we further illustrate how obligation is specified. We take as an example an obligation triggered by a notification provisional context.

1. As defined in (Cuppens 2007), the history of access requests should be stored in the log view. Objects belonging to the log view have five attributes: Log_actor, Log_action, Log_target, Log_date and Log_context. These attributes represent the subject s who performs an action α on an object o at a given date d and in a given context notification, respectively. A reference monitor is responsible for inserting entries into log objects. The first step defines a provisional context notification within the operator organization shown in Box 7.

That is, in organisation mobile-operator, subject s performs action α on object o in the provisional context notification if there is an entry l in the history of access requests. l states that the subject s previously performed an action α', which is considered as a read activity, on the location-information object.

2. We then define a view Notification_list that groups the notifications received by the operator from service providers. Objects in this view have three attributes: sp-identity, content of the notification and subscriber to which the notification must be handed later. If n is an object belonging to the Notification_list view, then these attributes represent the service provider sp (sp-identity(n, sp)), which sends a notification (content(n, notification)) to a subscriber s (subscriber(n, s)). The content of the notification can be for example data deleted or the purpose of further usage.

3. Third, we define the obligation following the provisional context:

Obligation(org, Serviceprovider, notify, notification_list, notification, deadline)

That is, in organisation org, the role Serviceprovider has to notify the Notification_list when the

Box 7.

$\mathrm{Rule}_{provisional} \quad \forall s \in S, \forall \alpha \in Action, \forall \alpha' \in Action, \forall o \in O, \forall l \in O,$

$Hold(mobile - operator, s, \alpha, o, notification) \leftarrow Empower(s, Service\,Pr\,ovider)$

$\wedge Use(mobile - operator, l, \log) \wedge Log\_actor(l, s) \wedge Log\_action(l, \alpha') \wedge$

$Consider(mobile - operator, \alpha', read) \wedge Log\_t\arg et(l, location - \inf ormation)$

---

context notification becomes true and before the end of the deadline.

Example 6. Let fm be a service provider that has an agreement with the organization mobile-operator to provide a location-based service to mobile subscribers.

Alice is a mobile subscriber, who subscribed to that service. Alice requires to be notified if fm accesses and deletes her location information Alice-lo. The content of the notification will contain data-deleted. To illustrate provisional obligation for LBS, let us show the three steps modelled above.

1. mobile-operator stores the history of access requests in the log view.

The provisional context notification is triggered since there is an entry l in the log view where fm performed read action on the object Alice-lo:

Hold(mobile-operator, fm, read, Alice-lo, notification) ← Use(mobile-operator, l, log) ∧ Log_actor(l, fm) ∧ Log_action(l, read) ∧Log_target(l,Alice-lo)

2. fm builds the notification object no that has the attributes: sp-identity(no, fm), content(no, data-deleted) and subscriber(no, Alice).

3. Obligation privilege is expressed as follows:

Obligation(mobile-operator, fm, send, no, notification, 3600)

The mobile-operator requires that the notification object no is sent by the service provider fm when the activation context notification (step 1) is true. This action must be done no later than 3600

seconds or else the operator may undertake some sanctions (also called remedies by P3P) against fm.

4.5 Communication State as Context in Privacy-Aware OrBAC

The current state of the communication between the service provider and the user can express a relevant parameter for the privacy policy. For location service for example, if the user initiated a call to the service provider, so related-call is the current state, then the service provider can retrieve user's location without consent.

This context is used to describe privacy preference. For example a service provider can locate a user only if the user has initiate a call (or sent a SMS) to it. It describes the current connection or the state of the session between the requestor and the data owner.

4.5.1 Communication State Context

It is necessary to be able to evaluate the current state in this context. The communication state indicates if the user has initiated a call or a session to the service provider or not. We define that semantics for communication state contexts in location service. Let states={initiated_call, initiated_data_session, unrelated-call} be the set of possible current states. We define three sub-contexts of the communication state corresponding to each of these states: the initiated_call-context, the initiated_data_session-context, and the unrelated-call-context.

The organization shall be able to evaluate that state. For example, a mobile operator uses the call records to compute if the current state context is triggered or not. It receives this kind of information from the switching centre entity.

We assume that preferred-states view contains data owner's preferences regarding authorized current states. The data owner sets its preference by adding a new entry to that view. Objects belonging to that view have three attributes: calling, state-type and called. If ps is an object belonging to preferred-states view, c (calling(ps, c)) and cd (called(ps, cd)) have the state sType (state-type(ps, sType)).

That is, in organisation org, subject s performs action α on object o in the current state context initiated_call−context (respectively initiated_ data_session−context, unrelated−call−context) if there is a preferred state ps used in view preferred-states such that the calling subject is the data owner of the object o and the called subject is s and the state type is initiated_call (respectively initiated_data_session, unrelated−call).

Then, subject empowered in role data-owner is permitted to access preferred-states view and declare new objects:

Permission(org, data-owner, declare, preferred-states, subscription)

That is, in organisation org, the role data-owner is permitted to declare objects belonging to the preferred-states view in the prerequisite subscription. The latter is defined when a subject s performs action α on a preferred state ps belonging to the preferred-states view if this object ps has s' as called and where s' is subscribed to s. This is presented by the application-dependent predicate Subscribed as for purpose view shown in Box 9.

Example 7. Let Bob be a subscriber of the service provider Advertisement. Bob permits that his location Bob-location is delivered if he initiated a call to Advertisement. So, Bob inserts the object Bob-sp in the preferred-states that has the attributes: calling(Bob-ps, Bob), called(Bob-ps, Advertisement) and state-type(Bobps, initiated_ call).

Figure 6. Preferred states

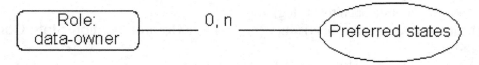

Box 8.

$Rule_{state}$ $\forall org \in Org, \forall s \in S, \forall \alpha \in Action, \forall o \in O, \forall ps \in preferred - states,$

− $Hold(org, s, \alpha, o, initiated\_call - context) \leftarrow Use(org, ps, preferred - states)$
   $\wedge calling(ps, Data - owner(o)) \wedge called(ps, s) \wedge state - type(ps, initiated\_call)$

− $Hold(org, s, \alpha, o, initiated\_session - context) \leftarrow Use(org, ps, preferred - states)$
   $\wedge calling(ps, Data - owner(o)) \wedge called(ps, s) \wedge state - type(ps, initiated\_data\_session)$

− $Hold(org, s, \alpha, o, unrelated\_call\_context) \leftarrow Use(org, ps, preferred - states)$
   $\wedge calling(ps, Data - owner(o)) \wedge called(ps, s) \wedge state - type(ps, unrelated\_call)$

Box 9.

$$\forall org \in Org, \ \forall s \in S, \ \forall s' \in S, \forall \alpha \in Action, \forall ps \in preferred - state,$$
$$Hold(org, s, \alpha, ps, subscription) \leftarrow Use(org, ps, preferred - state) \wedge called(ps, s')$$
$$\wedge Subscribed(s, s')$$

Box 10.

$$Hold(org, Advertisement, \alpha, Bob - location, initiated \_ call \_ context) \leftarrow Use(org, Bob - ps, preferred - state)$$
$$\wedge calling(Bop - ps, Bob) \wedge called(Bob - ps, Advertisement) \wedge state - type(Bob - ps, initiated \_ call)$$

So, Bob privacy preference can be modelled through the communication state context as shown in Box 10.

The context is triggered when the call is initiated by the subscriber.

4.6 Extension for Spatial Context

Spatial context in OrBAC concerns only the location of subjects that access sensitive information. But sensitive information also includes location information and privacy preference can depend on the zone area of that object. For this kind of data, the spatial context can indicate that the permission is valid only if the object, and not only the subject, is within the zone area referred by the context.

4.6.1 OrBAC Spatial Context

The location of subjects, who request the access to sensitive data, is modelled in OrBAC through a spatial context. There are two different types of it: the physical spatial context and the logical spatial context.

By physical context, we express the physical location of the user, namely his home, his office, a specific building, the country, etc. The logical one represents the "logical location" that the subject stands in, such as, a computer, a network, an IP address, etc. The logical location can change its physical location during time. But in general, the two contexts are correlated. The network IP address from which a user is connected probably corresponds to a specific physical place.

The OrBAC model assumes the existence of a set SO of spatial objects, according to the notation called spatial features suggested by the Open GIS Consortium. For example, Rennes and Hospital are spatial objects. One organization can belong to a spatial object. Spatial objects are associated with location functions to determine if a given subject is located in the area of a given spatial object. A built-in predicate Is_located is introduced. It is over domains Org×S ×SO, if org is an organization, s is a subject and so is a spatial object, then Is_located(org, s, so) says that the location function used in organization org can determine that the subject s is located in the area of spatial object so. Note that the truth value of the Is_located predicate depends on the organisation because the latter chooses its location functions (Cuppens 2007).

The location function applies to the set SO and returns a physical spatial context for subjects as shown in Box 11.

This means, in organisation org, the subject s performs the action α in the spatial context location(so) if this subject is located in the area of spatial subject so.

Like other objects, spatial objects are grouped into views. A view v is a spatial view if it contains spatial objects, and the set of spatial views is denoted SV. For example, if Office is a spatial view then Use(Hospital, office_3, Office) says that the organisation Hospital uses the spatial object Office_3 in the spatial view Office.

The location function can be generalized to apply to the set SV and so return a physical spatial context as shown in Box 12.

This means that in organisation org a given subject s is performing a given action α on a given object o in the spatial context location(sv) if this subject is located in the area of some spatial object so, which is used in the spatial view sv.

On the other hand, the logical spatial context depends on the host to which the subject is connected. So, it depends on the computer infrastructure of the organization. To describe this infrastructure, a set of predicates can be defined. For example, the predicate Login(s, h) determines the logical location of the subject s who logged on the host h, and the predicate Location_zone(h, net) models the computer infrastructure and means that the host h is connected to the network net. But in this work, we do not consider the logical locations.

4.6.2 Spatial Predicates for Geographical Data

Authors, in (Gabillon and Capolsini 2009), are interested in the authorisation model of spatial applications. They extend OrBAC with spatial attributes and spatial methods, geometric functions and some spatial predicates. They are based on geometric concepts introduced on the OpenGIS Geometry Model (OpenGis 2006). Their objective is to model contexts based on the position of users, the zoom level, the direction of moving objects, etc.

Based on the spatial objects defined by (OpenGis 2006), like point, curve, line, authors introduce eight spatial predicates to enrich the OrBAC model. Those predicates can then be applied to the spatial objects to evaluate if the spatial context is triggered or not. The added predicates are: Equal, Disjoint, Intersects, Touches, Crosses, Within, Contains and Overlaps.

To reason about object's motion, two attributes are defined: speed and direction. Objects that are stateless have not these attributes.

For example, the proposed taxonomy is able to mix conditions on user position and object position:

$$\forall s \in S, \forall \alpha \in Action, \forall o \in O, \forall d \succ 0,$$
$$Hold(Army, s, \alpha, o, radius(d)) \leftarrow distance(s, o) \succ d$$

Box 11.

$$\forall org \in Org, \ \forall s \in S, \ \forall \alpha \in Action, \forall o \in O, \forall so \in SO,$$
$$Hold(org, s, \alpha, ps, location(so)) \leftarrow Is\_located(org, s, so)$$

Box 12.

$$Rule_{spatialSubject} \quad \forall org \in Org, \forall s \in S, \forall \alpha \in Action, \forall o \in O, \forall sv \in SV, \forall so \in SO,$$
$$Hold(org, s, \alpha, o, location(sv)) \leftarrow Use(org, so, sv) \wedge Is\_located(org, s, so)$$

That is, in the organisation Army, the context radius, which is a function that takes d as an input, holds between subject s and object o if and only if the distance between s and o is less than d. This work is valuable for our topic since it provides us with a richer typology of spatial contexts. It allows us to model a fine-granular privacy policy. Subscribers can set more precise preferences regarding their positions. Also, this work introduces the concept of spatial context for private objects that we will detail in following section.

4.6.3 Using Spatial Context for Subjects and Objects

Physical and logical spatial contexts are relevant features for a privacy policy. In addition to using it to locate the subject who is asking for an access to the data, spatial context is also useful to locate objects. We propose to extend the semantic of spatial context to include the property to define the position of objects. The OrBAC model considers that only subjects can move from one location to another one, but objects also move along in time.

Let LA be the set of known location areas. Then, the predicate Is_within determines if a given object or subscriber, located through a positioning method, is within a location area or not. We illustrate this through the predicate Is_within over the domains Org ×O ×LA. So, Is_within(org, o, la) means that the object o is within the location area la. The spatial context can now be defined for objects within the OrBAC model using this new predicate.

This means that in organisation org a given subject s is performing a given action α on a given object o in the spatial context location(la)

if the object o is located in the area la. The position function applies to the set LA and returns the physical spatial context of objects. Like other objects, location areas are grouped into views. And, the set of location views is denoted LV.

We notice that spatial-preferences view contains data owner's preferences regarding the allowed locations where users can be localized. Owners set their preferences by inserting new objects to that view. Objects belonging to the spatial-preference view have three attributes: the location area, the data owner and the authorized service provider.

Example 8. Let Alice be an employee in the gas company gas_com. She allows other employees of gas_com, who have the role gas_com_employee, to access her location, named Alice-location, if she is at work. She specifies next privilege for mobile-operator, which collects her location:

Permission(mobile-operator, gas_com_employee, consult, Alice-location, position(gas_com_site))

The spatial context gas_com_site within the mobile-operator organisation is defined as follows in Box 14.

Alice aims now to permit only gas_com_employees, who are at work, to access her location, and if she is also at work. So, we need to combine the two kinds of spatial context. First, a spatial context must be defined for subjects, the employees who access the location information. Another spatial context must be defined for the object Alice-location. Alice authorizes the following policy:

Box 13.

$$\text{Rule}_{spatialObject} \quad \forall org \in Org, \forall s \in S, \forall \alpha \in Action, \forall o \in O, \forall la \in LA,$$
$$Hold(org, s, \alpha, o, position(la)) \leftarrow Is\_within(org, o, la)$$

Permission(mobile-operator, employee_company, consult, Alice, location(gas_com_site) &

position(gas_com_site)).

5. USE CASE

5.1 User Preference Scenario and Privacy Requirements

Based on the privacy policy for Location Service (LCS), we propose to study the sample of a privacy policy specified by a mobile subscriber to protect his location data. We assume that the mobile operator organisation is responsible for collecting the locations of its subscribers. Then, it enforces the privacy policy that controls the access of service providers to these locations. Mobile subscribers can define their preferences through the management of a contextual policy as we defined above.

Let fleet management 1 and fleet management 2 be two services providers that planned to offer the fleet management service to mobile operator's subscribers. The purpose of service is to optimise the route undertaken by mobile subscribers. Let Alice be a user that subscribed to that service. Alice has some preferences:

- She is afraid of being localized during holidays, her positioning is only permitted during working hours and within a predefined area. This area is within the city centre. The city centre is a location area that can be recognized by the organisation,

- Alice also distinguishes between the two service providers. The two service providers are associated with two accuracies. Fleet management 1 can access to the location Alice-location with accuracy 1 and fleet management 2 can access to the location with accuracy 2,
- When fleet management 1 requests for an access, the subscriber must give his consent before granting access and the location must be anonymized,
- When fleet management 2 accesses private data, a provisional obligation is defined to be fulfilled after the access. The service provider has to notify the operator when the location information is deleted,
- Alice prefers that access can only be done when she is at work.

The privacy requirements can be summarized as follows. Fleet management 1 and fleet management 2 are assigned to the role of fleet management service provider. These service providers must have contracted an agreement with Alice to offer the service. So, subscription is a prerequisite context. The first subject, who is the fleet management 1, can only access the anonymized location view of Alice, named anonymized-Alice-location. The purpose of the access is optimise route. This purpose is considered a user-declared context. Service providers mention it before accessing Alice's location views. The spatial temporal contexts specify that the access is granted only if Alice is at work and during working hours. Furthermore, a consent context is triggered before delivering location data for fleet management 1. An obligation

Box 14.

$$\forall s \in S, \forall \alpha \in Action, \forall o \in O, at\_work \in SO, at\_work \in LA,$$
$$Hold(mobile-operator, s, \alpha, o, position(gas\_com\_site)) \leftarrow Is\_within(mobile-operator, o,$$
$$gas\_com\_site)$$

has to be fulfilled by fleet management 2 when location data is accessed. The obligation specifies that location data deletion must be notified.

5.2 Specifying the Privacy Policy of the Use Case through the Privacy-Aware OrBAC Model

Now, we present how our use case can be specified using the OrBAC model. The policy is defined within the operator (mobile network) organisation to control the access of the service providers. We start by specifying the relevant contexts of the privacy policy.

To define the consent context, Alice inserts a new object Alice_preference into the consent_preference view. This view is maintained by the mobile-operator organisation to store when consent is needed:

Use(mobile-operator,Alice_preference, consent_preference)

The Alice_preference object has the following attributes: Requestor(Alice_preference, fleet management 1), Target(Alice_preference, Alice-location), Data-owner(Alice _preference, Alice) and NeedConsent(Alice_preference, true). That object models the need for consent by Alice when fleet management 1 requests its location. Alice needs not defining a new object for the second service provider since the need of consent is false by default. We recall that the consent context is triggered as shown in Box 15.

Then, Alice defines her preference according to the location accuracy. Assuming that the root object Alice-location is collected by the mobile-operator, Alice has to define the accuracy that fleet management 1 can access. She defines the accuracy (anonymous, 0). According to section 4.2.3, new objects are created with that accuracy, these objects are used in a new view anonymized-Alice-location. Alice has now two views: Alice-location, which groups the root objects collected by the operator, and anonymized-Alice-location, which groups anonymized objects.

Alice aims that only services with optimise route purpose are authorized to access her location. The Purpose view includes the purpose object optimise route. On the other hand, possible purpose values are grouped into PV within the mobileoperator. PV has to include this purpose to recognize it. We assume that Alice is already authorized to declare purposes within the mobile-operator organization (Permission(mobile − operator, subscriber, declare, optimise, subscription)).

The corresponding user-declared context is specified by the rule as shown in Box 16.

After that, Alice states that fleet management 2 is obliged to inform the mobileoperator about the deletion of the date. For that, she has to specify that the service provider must send an object no, containing the deletion information, within 3600 seconds:

Obligation(mobile-operator, fleetmanagement2, send, no, notification, 3600)

Where notification is a provisional context activated by the mobile-operator when the service provider access the location information.

Box 15.

$$\forall org \in Org, \forall s \in S, \forall \alpha \in Action, \forall o \in O, \forall cp \in O,$$
$$Hold(org, s, \alpha, o, Consent\_context) \leftarrow Use(org, cp, Consent\_preference) \land \mathrm{Re}\,questor(cp, s)$$
$$\land T\arg et(cp, o) \land Data\_owner(cp, do) \land (\neg NeedConsent(cp) \lor Consent\_response(org, do, s))$$

Box 16.

$$Hold(mobile - operator, fleetmanagement1, \alpha, Alice - location, user\_declared(optimiseroute)) \leftarrow$$
$$Use(mobile - operator, optimise, Purpose) \wedge \text{Re} \, cipient(optimise, fleetmanagement1)$$
$$\wedge Declared\_purpose(optimise, optimiseroute)$$

Furthermore, Alice prefers to be located by service providers only when she is at work. The spatial context is specified within the mobile operator as shown in Box 17.

Alice's privacy policy that enforces her preferences within the mobile-operator organisation can be summarized by the following permissions concerning the fleet management 1 and fleet management 2, respectively as shown in Box 18.

5.2.1 Compliance with Privacy Requirements

The proposed policy specification tends to enforce major privacy principles as they are required by OECD. We illustrate how these principles are implemented in our policy.

- Purpose specification principle is expressed through a user-declared context.

The service provider has to mention the objective of its access before processing the access request,

- Collection limitation principle is naturally defined through the use of different accuracies that limit the access of service providers,
- Data quality principle stipulates that collected data must be accurate but we proposed to let the choice to subscribers define a view hierarchy depending on the accuracy of objects,
- Accountability and use limitation principles are enforced by provisional obligations. From the service provider point of view, it is responsible for notifying the operator about further usage applied to the private information,
- Individual participation principle means that an individual can access his own data

Box 17.

$$\forall s \in S, \forall \alpha \in Action, \forall o \in O, \forall at\_work \in LA,$$
$$Hold(mobile - operator, s, \alpha, o, position(at\_work)) \leftarrow Is\_within(o, at\_work)$$

Box 18.

— $Permission(mobile - operator, fleetmanagement1, consult, anonymised - Alicelocation,$
  $consent\_context \& user\_declared(optimiseroute) \& location(at\_work))$

— $Permission(mobile - operator, fleetmanagement2, consult, Alicelocation, location(at\_work)$
  $\& user\_declared(optimiseroute))$
  $Obligation(mobile - operator, fleetmanagement2, send, no, notification, 3600)$

to modify, rectify and suppress them. It is easy to model that through new privileges where data owner can execute these actions in the context of "personal_information" meaning that a subject executes actions on objects that this subject owns. We omitted these privileges due to space limitation,

- Openness and security safeguards principles are omitted in our policy specification because they are implementation-dependent.

6. RELATED WORKS

Our privacy-aware OrBAC takes advantage of existing contexts, such as the user declared and the provisional ones, and specifies new ones. Our objective is to support privacy requirements with minimal extensions. Our approach is different from related models (Ni et al. 2007, Masoumzadeh and Joshi 2008, Yang et al. 2008) that require fundamental changes. We essentially integrate the privacy requirements in the OrBAC contexts. We benefit from the nature of contexts. The latter embed the dynamic parameters of the security policy, users can manipulate them by adding new objects in the preference views without impacting the whole policy.

Qui Ni et al. (Ni et al 2007) proposed RBAC extensions to incorporate constraints and conditions that are related to privacy. They define a family of privacy aware RBAC (P-RBAC) models. A user is a human being when a role is a job title or a job function. A customized language, LC0, allows the definition of conditions. Privacy permission explicitly defines: the intended purposes of the action, under which conditions, and what obligations have to be performed after the access.

So, the two main extensions are: an obligation definition and a dedicated language for conditions. In (Ni et al 2007) privacy policy is enforced by permission assignments.

The Purpose-Based Access Control model was proposed in (Yang et al 2008). It is more concerned on the formalization of purposes and obligations.

It provides proofs of privacy invariants. Authors aim to enforce privacy in non-trusted domains. Purposes are divided into two classes: intended purposes class, which groups the intended usage of data element, and access purposes class, which groups the intentions for which data are accessed. Access purpose should be compliant with intended purpose to authorise the access. The definition of role entity in RBAC was extended to include conditional role, which is based on role attributes and system attributes (Byun et al 2005). Also, a key characteristic of this work is that several purposes may be related to each data element. This model was deployed in relational databases.

In our proposal, our concept of role is different from conditional role. We argue that a role cannot be modified by some attributes after being assigned by the administrator.

A Purpose-Aware Role-Based Access Control model (PuRBAC) is proposed in (Masoumzadeh and Joshi 2008). It extends RBAC by modelling privacy requirements. Purposes are the central entities, they are the intermediate entities between role and permission entities. The model defines constraints and obligations as conditions on assignment of permissions to purposes.

In this model, users are assigned to roles, purposes are assigned to role, permissions are assigned to purposes, and conditions are assigned to permission. A user request is formed by a session, purpose and requested permission. Authorisation can be requested only for purposes related to the active role. There is another major difference with the RBAC model. When a user request is submitted to the Access Decision Function (ADF), it either denies access or defines a conditional authorization. Authors model three types of conditions:

- Constraints: they are used to check information based on data variables in the system. For instance, the consent of the data owner is considered a constraint,
- Pre-obligations: the system or the user has to exercise some actions before granting

the access. They include for example: the re-authentication of the user before accessing sensitive data, or the readjustment of the data accuracy,

- Post-obligation: they include for example a data retention policy that would schedule data deletion.

Cited works share our objective to model privacy within the access control policy since both policies manage access to the same resource. These models are based only on purposes. We argue that purpose is not sufficient for users to define their privacy preferences. We present limited changes in the OrBAC model that first include: a new context type: Consent context. We then showed that purposes and provisional obligations are expressed thanks to existing context types: user-declared and provisional contexts respectively. The accuracy is finally introduced by defining a view hierarchy of sensitive objects based on user preferences. These concepts are sufficient to conform with privacy principles and they take into account more privacy requirements than aforementioned models.

By contrast to (Ni et al. 2007), we do not define a condition language. The privacy constraints are integrated in OrBAC context using a first-order logic. In (Ni et al. 2007) purposes are introduced as a standalone component like objects and actions. In (Masoumzadeh and Joshi 2008), authors introduce some confusion between roles and purposes saying that they are different types of roles (roles are derived based on organisational positions and purposes have no relation to organizational structure). However, we suggest introducing the purpose parameter as a user-declared context. We argue that in doing so the OrBAC model keeps its fundamental structure of a role based access control model. We also benefit from the existing mechanisms in the OrBAC model to detect and manage conflicts without new issues.

Furthermore, we were interested in the collection and use limitations of the private data. So, we specified the accuracy levels of private data and how data owner can define different levels according to his preferences. Existing models do not bother with this parameter, which enforces the use limitation requirements, and consider it as a low-level mechanism. We differentiated between the high-level accuracy that should be specified within the privacy policy and the low-level mechanism, such as the obfuscation algorithm, to enforce that parameter.

We specified a privacy-aware access control model that integrates the major privacy requirements. By contrast, related works focused on a subset of them and they suggest fundamental changes on the access control model.

7. CONCLUSION

In this chapter, we have focused on the specification of privacy policies. Access control models provide a scalable solution to introduce a privacy policy. Related works mainly proposed an extended RBAC model based on the definition of purposes and obligations. They chose RBAC to integrate a privacy policy because it is a widely deployed model in information systems.

We chose to extend the OrBAC model due to the fact that few extensions are sufficient to specify privacy requirements in this model. It supports a privacy policy thanks to the expressivities of its contexts. And, we used first-order logic without fundamental changes. We then showed how privacy preferences could be integrated in the access control policy enforced by the operator.

REFERENCES

Ajam, N., Cuppens, N., & Cuppens, F. (2009). Contextual privacy management in extended role based access control model. *Workshop DPM, DPM-ESORICS, LNCS*, (pp. 121-135). Saint-Malo, France.

Cuppens, F., & Cuppens-Boulahia, N. (2007). Modeling contextual security policies. *International Journal of Information Security*, 7(4), 285–305. doi:10.1007/s10207-007-0051-9

Duckham, M., & Kulik, L. (2006). Location privacy and location-aware computing. In Billen, R., Joao, E., & Forrest, D. (Eds.), *Dynamic and mobile GIS: Investigating change in space and time* (pp. 34–51).

Elrakaiby, Y., Cuppens, F., & Cuppens-Boulahia, N. (2010*). From contextual permission to dynamic pre-obligation: An integrated approach*, (pp. 70-78). Paper presented at the ARES Conference.

European Telecommunications Standards Institute, ETSI. (2005). *Open service access (OSA): Parlay X web services: Par 9: Terminal location.* ETSI, ES 202 391-9.

Gabillon, A., & Capolsini, P. (2009). Dynamic security rules for geo data. *The Second International Workshop Autonomous Spontaneous Security (SETOP), LNCS*, (pp. 136-152). St. Malo, France.

Gedik, B., & Liu, L. (2008). Protecting location privacy with personalized k-anonymity: Architecture and algorithms. *IEEE Transactions on Mobile Computing*, 7(1), 1–18. doi:10.1109/TMC.2007.1062

Herring, J. R. (2006). *OpenGIS implementation specification for geographic information - Simple feature access - Part 1: Common architecture.* Open Geospatial Consortium Incorporation, OGC 06-103r3.

Krumm, J. (2008). A survey of computational location privacy. *International Journal of Personal and Ubiquitous Computing*, 13(6), 391–399. doi:10.1007/s00779-008-0212-5

Masoumzadeh, A., James, B., & Joshi, D. (2008). PuRBAC: Purpose-aware role-based access control. In *On the Move to Meaningful Internet Systems (OTM 08)*, (pp. 1104-1121).

Organisation for Economic Co-Operation and Development, OECD. (1980). *Protection of privacy and transborder flows of personal data.*

Qui, N., Trombetta, A., Bertino, E., & Lobo, J. (2007). *Privacy-aware role based access control*, (pp. 41-50). Paper presented at the 12th ACM symposium on Access control models and technologies, Session Privacy management.

3rd Generation Partnership Project, 3GPP. (2009). *Location service (LCS), service description, stage 1.* 3GPP TS 22.071, Release 9.

3rd Generation Partnership Project, 3GPP. (2010). *Functional stage 2 description of location service (LCS).* 3GPP TS 23.271, Release 9.

Yang, N., Barringer, H., & Zhang, N. (2008). A purpose-based access control model. *The Third International Symposium on Information Assurance and Security*, (pp. 143-148).

KEY TERMS AND DEFINITIONS

Access Control: Policy checking before granting the access to the information.

Context: Dynamic parameter that impacts the access control decision.

Data Owner: The subject or person to whom the private data refers to.

Location-Based Services (LBS): Applications that use the location information to offer enhanced services.

Obligations: Actions to be performed by the requesters after accessing the information.

Private Information: Pieces of data that permit to identify directly or indirectly a physical person.

Service Provider: Organisation or subject that requests the location information needed for their LBS.

Chapter 18
Can Formal Methods Really Help:
Analyzing the Security of Electronic Voting Systems

Komminist Weldemariam
Fondazione Bruno Kessler, Italy

Adolfo Villafiorita
Fondazione Bruno Kessler, Italy

ABSTRACT

In this chapter, first the authors discuss the current trends in the usage of formal techniques in the development of e-voting systems. They then present their experiences on their usage to specify and verify the behaviors of one of the currently deployed e-voting systems, using formal techniques and verification against a subset of critical security properties that the system should meet. The authors also specify attacks that have been shown to successfully compromise the system. The attack information is used to extend the original specification of the system and derive what the authors call the extended model. This work is a step towards fostering open specification and the (partial) verification of a voting machine. The specification and verification was intended as a learning process where formal techniques were used to improve the current development of e-voting systems.

INTRODUCTION

Modern electronic voting (e-voting) system started in the mid 90's as a system to support traditional voting in many ways and has since then evolved into a full-fledged system attempting to ensure

DOI: 10.4018/978-1-4666-0978-5.ch018

safe and secure elections. This has been made possible somehow by the introduction of a number of mechanisms such as the introduction of the direct recording electronic, DRE, (Cranor, 1996; Mercuri & Camp, 2004). These mechanisms are the basis to improve elections by over-performing of traditional voting systems, such as to allow accessibility and prevention of voter mistakes, let the visually impaired vote without assistance, and vastly simplify the ballot management using some kinds of memory cards instead of paper.

However, the effect of widespread deployment of e-voting systems is that the security perimeter of a typical modern government has also changed markedly. This is evident from much increased interest over the last few years in the study of the development process and security of e-voting systems. Numerous recent security studies revealed that most currently deployed DRE-based e-voting systems share critical failures in their design and implementation, which render their technical and procedural controls insufficiency to guarantee trustworthy voting. One of the main reasons for this is that the development of existing e-voting systems are directed almost exclusively at large scale known engineering disciplines and consequently a niche too small to drive significant adoption of e-voting technology into our democracy. Other factors contribute to make e-voting systems a less adopted for critical elections. For example, existing methodology for requirements structuring mostly provide high-level principles and recommendations for e-voting systems development, see, e.g., (McGaley, 2008; Volkamer, 2009). In one hand, this is due to the sophisticated nature of the requirements for e-voting systems. On the other hand, there is little or no tool to support the management and structuring of these requirements. Obviously, this would create further difficulty in realizing the links between legal regulations and technical requirements, as well as in realizing the requirements during development process.

Today, in fact, we now have a much better understanding of the issues that pose the development of a trustworthy e-voting system. However, it is not clear that which development process that we require to follow, that how requirements can be allocated during the execution and monitoring of the actual election, and that how incidents occurred during the election should be analyzed after election and then incorporating the analysis results in the next development cycle. Additionally, as

noted in (Oostveen & den Besselaar, 2004; Gardner et al., 2007), we have a long way to go in terms of providing a mean through which we convince how individual vote is really recorded and stored. However, to tackle some of these issues, a range of development trends and technological solutions have been explored and proposed (Sastry et al., 2006; Paul & Tanenbaum, 2009). Several standards and requirements development strategies have also been introduced in the literature for the development of trustworthy e-voting systems (Bryans et al., 2006; Anane et al., 2007; McGaley, 2008; Volkamer, 2009). Works that evaluate the security of e-voting systems have also been discussed, e.g., in (Kohno et al., 2004; Ansari et al., 2008; Aviv et al., 2008; Balzarotti et al., 2010; Wolchok et al., 2010).

We believe that the security of e-voting systems can be improved through a multidisciplinary approach that requires know-how in business process modeling (for understanding the context of elections), formal methods (for detailed formal analysis of critical security and safety requirements about the system and its procedures), and system or security engineering (for the adoption of rigor secure-aware development process). This chapter, though, will focus on the usage of formal methods in the specification and verification of e-voting systems. Existing works in formal methods present specification and verification of e-voting systems at different level of abstractions. These works particularly aimed to demonstrate the feasibility of formal verification of voting machine logic, thereby providing a higher level of assurance on the security of the system.

In this chapter, we particularly discuss where formal methods can be incorporated in e-voting systems development process using our past experiences as evidence. We applied formal modeling techniques where we felt they would add rigor to the development and evaluation of an e-voting system named ProVotE (Villafiorita et. al, 2009). In this case, the usage of the formal methods was intended to improve the development process of the ProVotE e-voting system. In contrast, we applied formal methods to formally specify and verify currently deployed e-voting machines in U.S.A. named the ES&S e-voting system (Weldemariam et al., 2009; Weldemariam et al., 2010). In this case, the usage of formal methods was intended as a learning process where we would use formal techniques as the need arose, say, as well as developing generic requirement specifications that would help us to build new generation e-voting systems. This would also help developing a better understanding of the role of the different formal methods that would help us to follow a more formal process in future development. We will only present the second usage scenario of formal methods as case study.

This chapter is structured as follows. First, we analyze the role of formal methods in the development of e-voting systems at different abstraction levels. Second, we present a case study that demonstrate the usage of formal methods in the development and engineering of e-voting system, by presenting sample of the specifications of requirements and system behavior, and their verification. Third, some lessons learned from these experiences are discussed paving relevant issues and pointing out some directions for future research. Finally, we conclude the chapter.

THE ROLE OF FORMAL METHODS IN THE DEVELOPMENT OF E-VOTING SYSTEMS

Table 1 shows trends in the development of e-voting systems. As you can see from the table, a lot of efforts are on going aimed at improving the current trends in the development of e-voting systems. In this chapter, we only focus on reviewing the contributions of formal methods in e-voting domain (the last row in Table 1). The trends in this area focus in three closely related directions: verifying cryptographic protocols, e.g., (Kremer & Ryan, 2005; Delaune et al., 2009), system behavior, e.g., (Tiella et. al, 2006;Sturton et. al, 2009), and procedures, e.g., (Bryl et al., 2009, Grimm et al., 2010).

The authors in (Kremer & Ryan, 2005;Delaune et al., 2009) present a framework for formal

Table 1. A brief summary of trends on the development of e-voting systems

Work	Brief Description
Requirement Engineering, e.g., (Bryans et al., 2006; Anane et al., 2007; McGaley, 2008;Volkamer, 2009; Weldemariam et al., 2009)	Contribute to the definition, development and structuring of requirements for e-voting systems with a clear separation between functional and not-functional requirements as well as the specifications for various hardware components' requirements.
Business Process (Re-) engineering (BPR), e.g., (Xenakis & Macintosh, 2005; Xenakis & Macintosh, 2007; Mattioli, 2006;Weldemariam et al., 2007)	Understand the effective implementation of e-voting procedures, namely by using BPR to understand what changes could be introduced to the conventional voting procedures to allow a safe and secure transition to electronic elections.
Design and Implementation, e.g., (Cramer & Franklin, 1995; Chaum, 2004; Karlof et al., 2005; Ryan et al., 2009)	Design of cryptographic schemes, protocols, and/or techniques to improve the design of voting systems or machines, as well as the actual implementation of the voting systems themselves.
Security Evaluation, e.g., (Kohno et al., 2004; Proebstel et al., 2007;Balzarotti et al., 2010; Aviv et. al, 2008;Wolchok et al., 2010;Schmidt et al., 2010)	Combine different security engineering techniques to test and/or analyze the security posture of e-voting systems. The works in this area mainly assessed the security of e-voting systems used in real-world elections, and identified procedures that may eliminate or mitigate discovered issues.
Formal Methods, e.g., (Kremer & Ryan, 2005; Tiella et al., 2006; Cansell et al., 2007;Heitmeyer et al., 2008;Delaune et al., 2009; Weldemariam et al., 2009; Sturton et al., 2009; Villafiorita et al., 2009;Gibson et al., 2010)	Apply formal techniques (such as theorem provers and model checkers) to analyze the security of e-voting systems, thereby ensuring the correctness of the voting process as well as the underlying infrastructure mathematically.

specification and verification of e-voting protocol properties, i.e., fairness, eligibility, individual/universal verifiability and coercion-resistance. These properties are vote-privacy, receipt-freeness, and coercion-resistance. Their work is about formally verifying the correctness of protocols with respect to these properties. The authors used applied pi-calculus to formalize these properties as observational equivalence, after being formalized the voting protocol as a set of processes using the same machinery. Their analysis was partially automated by the ProVerif tool. The authors in (Juels et al., 2005) defined a model for e-voting schemes that involves a more powerful adversary than previously proposed. Their schemes allow an adversary to demand coerced voters that they vote in a particular manner or disclose their secret keys. The authors also provide formal security definitions for essential properties of correctness, verifiability, and coercion-resistance. However, the paper does not consider a verification process using automated techniques.

The authors in (Campanelli et al., 2008) used a CCS like process algebra with cryptographic primitives to specify and analyze some properties of the e-voting system they built. More specifically, they presented a small mobile implementation of an e-voting system named M-SEAS (Mobile Secure E-voting Applet System) and used formal verification technique to validate the security property of the system. Their analysis goal is checking whether their system is free from Sensus vulnerability by using the Crypto-CCS language (Martinelli et al., 2002) and the PaMoChSA analysis tool (a software model checking tool with a particular for on verifying security related properties).

Simidchieva et al. (2008) demonstrate the usage of different technologies for specifying and verifying requirements for election processes, namely by reasoning rigorously about the presence or absence of errors during all phases of an election process. In particular, they used Little-JIL process definition language (Cass et al., 2000)

to formally define election processes and PROPEL tool to support the development of precise lower-level properties, which are then fed to the verification system called FLAVERS to check whether the process model satisfies these properties. If the process model violates a property, the FLAVERS system provides counterexample as traces. These traces are sequence of steps in the process model that may lead to the property violation as generated by the verification system. Such traces can then be used to guide the improvement of the process model iteratively. Similarly, Villafiorita et al. demonstrate the integration of formal methods in the development process of a voting system named ProVotE. In particular, the authors specified the behaviors of voting control logic using UML finite state machine and developed a tool named FSMC+ (Tiella et al., 2006) that automatically generates NuSMV code corresponding to the specified finite state machines. Then they performed the verification using the NuSMV model checker. The results of the model checker, presented in the form of counter-measurement, are then analyzed. This enabled the authors to incorporate the analysis results of the verification into the actual development process of the core application.

An approach for the design and analysis of an e-voting machine based on combination of formal verification and systematic testing is presented in (Sturton et al., 2009). They formally verify the correctness of each of the individual component of voting machine, as well as verifying some crucial correctness properties of their composition. Their work is targeted to the following verification goals: ensuring that each individual component of the voting machine and their composition should meet the specification of the individual components and their composition respectively; voting machine should be structured to enable sound systematic system testing; ensuring that the voting machine must behave and store votes according to the voters selection when configured with a particular election definition file. For each module, they construct a formal specification that fully characterizes the intended behavior of that component. A number of properties related to the structural and functional aspects that the machine should satisfy are identified, specified and verified accordingly.

The above works do not focus on the aspects related to procedures in their modeling and analysis. In that regard, we complemented such works by widening their scope of analysis with procedures analysis (Weldemariam & Villafiorita, 2008). An approach to reason on security properties of the to-be models (which are derived from as-is model) in order to evaluate procedural alternatives in e-voting systems is presented (Bryl et al., 2009). Additionally, the authors in (Grimm et al., 2010) presented a formal model for the correction and abort requirement of e-voting with some concepts borrowed from Protection Profile (Volkamer & Krimmer, 2007) of the Common Criteria (Common Criteria, 2009). More specifically, they first described a formal IT security model that allows the formalization of (some) basic security requirements for e-voting. Secondly, they modeled the corresponding security properties as secure system states using the same machinery. Thirdly, they specified state transition rules that control the voting behaviors. Finally, an attempt to mathematically prove that such function following the rules would transfer a secure state into a secure state.

In summary, among the broader benefits formal methods provide:

- *Ensuring the safety and security of critical components.* Critical components typically coordinate and control (all) the devices of the voting machine (touch-screen, smart-card reader, printer, etc) for trustworthy elections. Formal methods allow to analyze the correctness and integrity of such components in order to ensure that the e-voting machine correctly implements the procedures required by the electoral law, by formally and automatically verify that

the implementation satisfies high-level and low-level correctness properties during the development process. This would guarantee the design and development of e-voting machine with assurance that it will work correctly during Election Day.

- *Discovering missing critical requirements.* By reverse synthesizing currently deployed e-voting systems (using formal methods) one can verify that how the machine will behave on Election Day in a manner consistent with the voters' expectations of correct operation. Such reverse synthesis using formal methods are a step toward discovering missing critical requirements by the system and procedures.

THE USAGE OF FORMAL METHODS

Electronic voting has illustrated the importance of formal approaches (e.g., formal software engineering) in the development of complex systems: poorly engineered and poorly documented voting systems have had serious negative consequences for all system stakeholders (Gibson et al., 2010). It is clear that the formal verification of e-voting system models would help to address problems associated with certification against standards, and would improve the trustworthiness of the final systems.

Usage Scenario in Security Engineering

In this section, we present our experiences on using formal techniques for the specification and verification of ES&S e-voting system.

The most important components of the ES&S voting system from the formal specification viewpoint are the direct recording electronic voting machine (DRE), real-time audit log printer (RTAL), personalized electronic ballot (PEB), and compact flash cards (CF Cards). DRE is a touch-screen machine where the voter casts his or her votes by interacting with the machine. The information shown by the touch-screen changes in real-time to match the voter's choices. The RTAL is a continuous feed thermal printer that performs the function of VVPAT on the ES&S DRE machines. It produces a paper-based record of the choices selected by the voter. The (paper) voter's choices are under this transparent glass so that they cannot be modified other than through the normal voting procedure. The main purpose of collecting the paper records for each eligible voter is for auditing. The PEB is a palm-sized device used by the poll worker to load a ballot, initialize the next ballot, and collect tabulated data and audit information. The CF Cards, whereas are used to hold files too large to fit in the PEB flash storage as well as audio ballots and audit and

results data. The ballot data is accessed by the DRE on demand, but the presence of the CF card is checked periodically and the DRE will not boot without its presence. The card must be present to open and close the terminal. At poll closing, the audit data is automatically dumped into the card.

Figure 1 shows a high-level view of the voting process using the ES&S voting system. The figure shows after the poll worker activates the ballot (for qualified voter), the machine takes the voter through each contest. The ES&S DRE machines automatically forbid over-voting, but not under-voting. When a voter selects or cancels a candidate for a particular contest, an appropriate indication is printed on the RTAL record. If the voter selects a candidate, the RTAL record is marked as "Selected" and scrolled out of sight; otherwise, it is marked as "Canceled" and scrolled out of sight.

Figure 1. The normal voting process, i.e., election day voting process using the ES&S voting system. Once the polls are opened, a poll worker initializes the ballot for a qualified voter by inserting a supervisor PEB into the DRE machine.

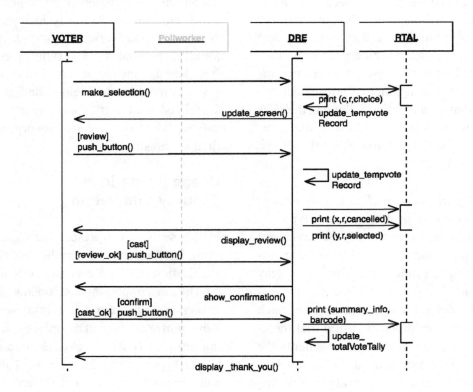

Table 2. A sample of informal description of critical requirements. In the table, the authors also linked specific requirements with abstract or generic voting system requirements.

Component	Requirement	Type
DRE	The same CF card must be present throughout the voting session.	Availability
DRE	The DRE must authenticate the PEB using the EQC, and the same master PEB must be used to open and close the terminal.	Eligibility
DRE	The DRE must automatically forbid an overvote.	Integrity
DRE	For each valid voter action (i.e., starting to vote, making a select or cancel, and finishing a vote) the DRE must enable the RTAL to record the action on the RTAL tape accordingly.	Integrity
RTAL	The RTAL should scroll up a minimum distance after the summary has printed, in order to out of sight the previous vote.	Privacy
RTAL	The RTAL must update the paper tape after the voter pushes the start button, makes a choice (select or cancel), confirms a vote, or when the poll worker rejects the ballot of a fleeing voter.	Accuracy/Integrity
PEB	At the end of the election, the copy of the ballot images down- loaded from the DRE must be the same as the ballot images that were loaded into the DRE prior to starting the election.	Integrity
CF Card	The poll closing procedures must copy the audit information (such as the event log) accumulated in the local storage to the CF card.	-
Global	No discrepancy should be observed among the following: (1) the individual cast ballot records (or ballot images) recorded by the machines; (2) the summary tape generated on Election Day at the close of polls on individual machines; (3) the totals that were accumulated and reported by the DRE and RTAL.	Accuracy/Integrity

The voter is eventually given the opportunity to review his ballot, and if the voter commits to it (confirms it), it is recorded to local storage. The process continues in this way for all qualified voters until the poll closing time.

A number of requirements that the ES&S system must satisfy are enumerated in the ES&S system manual (Inc. ES&S, 2007) (such as configuration instructions and the user's manual) and a corresponding video that describes how the system works on Election Day. Table 2 shows some of the most important critical security requirements that the ES&S voting system must meet. More properties that are essential building blocks for most DRE e-voting machines equipped with RTAL/VVPAT can be found in (California Secretary of State, 2007).

Besides specifying and analyzing the ES&S system under normal circumstances, we are also interested in specifying and analysis the systems in the presence of attacks. The attacks we have

considered are those that have been demonstrated in the EVEREST report. To make the attack realistic, it is natural to make some assumptions about the attack model. For instance, we assumed that some voters could leave the voting booth without checking the votes shown on the confirmation screen and/or on the RTAL screen do indeed accurately reflect their intentions. This assumption, in fact, is based on what happened in real scenario, i.e., even if the ES&S system offers (in general, any DRE-based machines) voters the opportunity to verify their vote, some voters leave the voting booth without completing the voting procedure. Moreover, like any other voting systems, the ES&S voting system can be subject to attack by a number of different types of attackers with different capabilities. An attacker can be outsiders (have no special access to any of the voting equipment), voters (have limited and partially supervised access to voting systems during the process of casting their votes), poll workers (have extensive access to polling place equipment), election officials (have extensive access both to the back-end election management systems and voting equipment), and etc.

An example of attack scenario: *Canceling or completing the vote for a fleeing voter*. In this scenario, the attacker takes advantage of a fleeing voter, a voter who does not complete the voting procedure, by intercepting the call to the routine that enables a chirping sound. In ES&S machine, this chirping sound alerts the poll worker that a voter has fled without completing the voting process. There are two possible scenarios depending on the voter's vote. The first scenario is if the fleeing voter voted against the attacker's candidate, then the attacker does nothing and lets the chirping routine perform as it should, see also Figure 2 (a). The poll worker then discards the ballot and there will be one less vote for the undesired candidate. The second scenario, whereas is if the fleeing voter voted for the attacker's candidate but s/he did not complete the voting process then the attacker completes the voting process, see also Figure 2(b). This results in another vote being cast for the attacker's candidate.

In the remaining of the section, we discuss how we specified the voting process, critical (security) requirements, and attacks' scenarios using ASTRAL language by giving sample specifications. We then discuss about the verification of these requirements both before and after extending the specification with attack scenarios. We did so, by verifying that each individual component must meet its specification when considered separately. Second, we analyze what happen when these components are all together. In addition, we specify attacks that have been shown to successfully compromise the system. With this information, we extend the original specification of the system and derive what we called the extended model. Using the PVS verification system, we analyze the same critical requirements do indeed hold in the extended model.

It is also worthy remarking our goals of the specification and verification of the attacks. The first point is if all of the proof obligations were to be proved, then the system specification must be missing some critical security requirements, since the modeled attacks have already been demonstrated to be successful. Therefore, it would be necessary to see what additional critical requirements are needed to disallow the threat actions and keep the extended specification from being proved. In contrast, not being able to prove the extended specification would indicate that one, or more, threat action violates at least one critical security requirement. However, since we know that attacks composed of these threat actions have been used to successfully compromise the system, it also indicates that there could be an implementation or specification error or an unsatisfied procedural assumption that results in the actual system or the environment not satisfying their respective formal specification. Second, analyzing the extended model would allow to derive mitigation or countermeasure strategies when the system behaves differently than it should. Finally, not being able to prove the extended model would indicate that one, or more, of the threat actions violates at least one critical security requirement. This indicates that there must be an implementation error or an unsatisfied procedural assumption that results in the actual system or the environment not satisfying their respective formal specification.

We have followed the following steps for the verification and specification of the ES&S system.

1. *Specify the Voting Process*. Here, we specify all the nominal behaviors corresponding to each component of the machine discussed above using the ASTRAL specification language;

2. *Specify Critical Requirements*. Here, we specify critical requirements (e.g., see Table 1), procedural requirements, as well as environmental assumptions about the system operation;

Figure 2. Canceling or completing the vote for a fleeing voter: (a) shows the canceling of the vote scenario and (b) shows the completing the voting process attack for a fleeing voter.

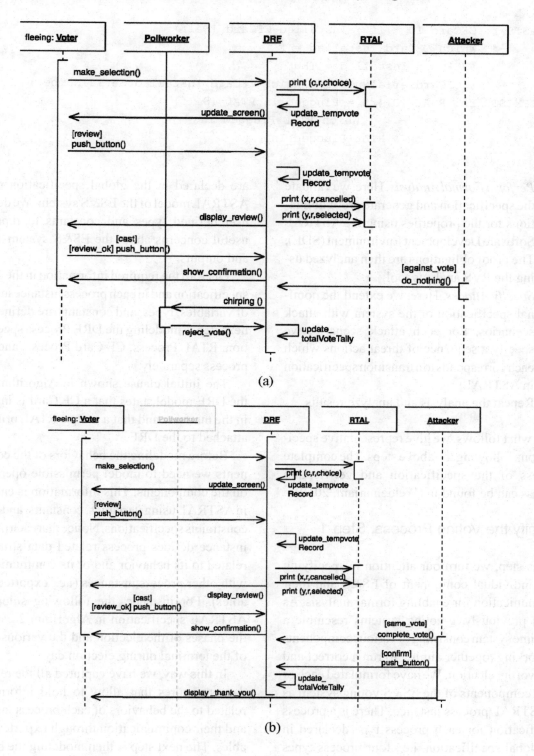

(a)

(b)

Algorithm 1.

```
INITIAL
  EXISTS f: CFCard_ID   (f = Installed_CFCard (Self)
        -> Which_CFCard_Installed = f
           & CFCard_Installed = TRUE
           & CFCardSerialNumber = Which_CFCard_Installed.SerialNumber)
    & EXISTS rt: RTAL_ID (rt = Plugged_In_RTAL (Self)
              ->          Which_RTAL_Plugged_In = rt
                 & RTAL_Plugged_In)
```

3. *Perform Formal Analysis.* Here, we validate the specification and generate proof obligations for the properties using the ASTRAL Software Development Environment (SDE). The proof obligations are then analyzed using the PVS analysis tool;

4. *Specify Attacks.* Here, we extend the nominal specification of the system with attack scenarios. For each attack scenario, we specify a sequence of threat actions which each corresponds to a transition specification in ASTRAL;

5. Repeat the analysis and analyze results.

In what follows, we give representative specifications following the above steps. The complete process of the specification and verification process can be found in (Weldemariam, 2010).

Specify the Voting Process, Step 1

In this step, we turn our attention in specifying each individual component of ES&S and their communication for enabling formal analysis. As noted previously, e-voting systems resemble a real-time system consisting of various components all working together aiming to run a correct and trustworthy election. We have formulated each of these components of the ES&S voting system as an ASTRAL process instance. There is a process specification for each process type declared in the global specification, i.e., four process types

are declared in the global specification of the ASTRAL model of the ES&S system. We defined user defined types and constants to represent useful concerns about the ES&S system inputs and outputs.

Once all the required information in the global specification and in each process instance in terms of variables, types, and constants are defined, the next step is modeling the DRE Process specification, RTAL Process, CF Card Process, and PEB process separately.

The initial clause shown in Algorithm 1 of the DRE model states that a CF Card is inserted in the machine and that a unique RTAL printer is attached to the DRE.

Before modeling the behaviors of the components we need to model permissible operations on the components. This information is encoded in ASTRAL using variables, constants, and initial constraints specifications. Notice that each process instance defines process related data structures related to its behavior and/or its communication with other process instances (i.e., exported variables). For instance, the following snippet of ASTRAL specification in Algorithm 2 captures the phases of the election and the various mode of the terminal during election day.

In this way, we have captured all the relevant data structures that allow to hold information related to the behaviors of each process instance and their communication through exported variables. The next step is then modeling the behav-

Algorithm 2.

```
VARIABLE
    Which_Phase: Voting_Phase,   //(pre-voting, during voting, and post-voting
phases)
    Terminal_Mode: Mode,    //(opening, opened, closing, or closed)
    DRE_State: Terminal_State,
```

ior of the components using ASTRAL transition specifications. That is, each operation that triggers behavioral change to the corresponding process instance is encoded as a transition in ASTRAL. Sixteen transitions are specified to model the possible operations of the components. Of these transitions twelve model the DRE machine behavior; two transitions are used to capture the behavior of the RTAL; and the behaviors of the CF Card and PEB are captured by one transition each accordingly.

An example of such operations is shown in Algorithm 3, which shows the insertion of PEB into the DRE by a poll worker changes the current state of the DRE to some other state.

Specify Critical Requirements, Step 2

In this step, we modeled the critical requirements for each individual component and the system as whole. These requirements should meet, given that the assumptions about the behavior of the system and the external environment that interacts with the system. In particular, we have specified two classes of requirements about the ES&S voting system: *environmental* or *procedural* assumptions and *security* requirements. The specifications of the security requirements correspond to those we discussed previously. We have formulated each of them as ASTRAL invariants, constraints, and/ or schedules formulas.

In addition, there are a number of behaviors we have specified that are related to external environment that the e-voting system relies on.

Algorithm 3.

```
TRANSITION Initialize_Ballot
    ENTRY        [ TIME: I_B_Dur ]
        DRE_State = Opened & Terminal_Mode = pollworker
        & EXISTS p: PEB_ID (Which_PEB_Inserted = p & PEB_Inserted))
        & Proceed_Ballot_Init & ~Ballot_Initialized
    EXIT
        FORALL R: Race (Displayed_Candidates (R) =
                        { SETDEF C: Candidate (C ISIN Race_Candi-
dates (R))})
        & FORALL R: Race, C: Candidate (C ISIN Displayed_Candidates (R)
        & ~Picked (Candidate_Name(C),Race_Title(R)))
        & FORALL R: Race (Number_Of_Selected(R) = 0)
        & Ballot_Initialized & ~Proceed_Ballot_Init & underVotedRaces =
EMPTY
```

The behavior of the people (voters, poll workers, and election officials) who interact with the system is outside the control ES&S voting system, but it influences how the system operates. In fact, the DRE cannot control the behavior of the voter when s/he interacts with the screen. For example, if the voter touches the candidate name faster then DRE can process the touches, since this could disrupt the normal functioning of the e-voting system. In addition, the procedures that control the voting process are completely outside of the system. For example, the poll worker has to wait for some amount of time to remove the PEB after loading the ballot, or after activating the ballot for the next active voter. However, they are equally important to carry out a correct and secure election. Therefore, we need to express these concerns in order to guarantee the critical requirements that the system should meet. Below we show a snippet of the code defines the fact that DRE must automatically forbid an overvote.

```
/* This specifies the second re-
quirement give in Table 1.
FORALL R: Race (
     Change (Number_Of_Selected (R),
Now)
     & Number_Of_Selected (R)  ~=
Number_Of_Selected' (R)
```

In this way, we have specified more than twenty-five critical requirements and a number of environment assumptions for each component.

Perform Formal Analysis, Step 3

In this step, the consistency of the specification has been validated using the ASTRAL validation engine. Then, the ASTRAL SDE automatically generated PVS proof obligations that enabled us to perform the formal analysis using the PVS system. Before invoking the theorem prover, the ASTRAL split engine was used to split and classify the ASTRAL specification into collections of simpler properties that infer the whole clause so

that the proof of each property could be tackled separately. The splitter can be invoked on any section of an ASTRAL specification that resolves to a boolean expression. After splitting and then generating the proof obligation, there are a total of 22 invariants, 10 schedules, and 8 constraints. We have discharged the ASTRAL specific proof strategies and PVS proof commands to prove these critical requirements. We have proved 16 of the 22 invariants, 5 of the 8 schedules, and 7 of the 10 constraints.

Specify Attacks and Repeat the Analysis, Step 4 & 5

While extending the system model (Step 4 above), we actually augmented the specification with new possible states that are the result of the execution of the threat actions. In particular, the attack scenarios are encoded to extend the original specification of the ES&S voting system using the following strategies:

- We defined new types, variables, and constants. There are two kinds of variables that we declare: those that provide additional information about the state of the system (e.g., the system is now about to display the review ballot) and those that hold information about the successful execution of a threat action (e.g., a fleeing voter has been faked). For example (see below), the *VoterType* is a type declaration representing the various kinds of voters (unattentive, careful, and fleeing), and the three variables respectively are declared to hold information about whether the voter's vote is changed (obviously, by a successful attack action), whether the fleeing voter is faked, and the name of the attacker's candidate.
- A transition is defined for each threat action, which is part of a given attack scenario. Note that one attack scenario can

be implemented using one or more threat actions.

- A transition may be split into two or more transitions, or a transition may be extended with more information to specify the attack scenario.

The below snippet demonstrates how we extended the data structures' definition to capture the attacks.

```
TYPE
    VoterType: (unattentive, care-
ful, fleeing)
VARIABLE
    vote_changed, Fleeing_Faked:
Boolean, attPickedName: Name
```

In the next page, we provide an example that shows how we extended the transitions according to the attacks' scenarios. The specification particularly shows the completing the voting process attack as discussed previously (see Figure 2 (a) also).

After extending the system specification with the threat actions following the above strategies, the ASTRAL SDE is used to generate the proof obligations for the extended specification. Because there are additional transitions, there are more proofs to be done. In addition, because some of the original transitions were split and/or extended, the corresponding proof obligations must be reproved. In order to prove the requirements, we followed the same procedure as before. However, the proofing process is very complex in the extended model. We started with the proof obligations that were unchanged to assure that they are still valid. We have reproved 6 of the 16 invariants and 2 of the 7 constraints. Most of these reproved properties in the extended model are not complex. For instance, "RTAL must scroll forward Min *ScrollForward* Position amount after the vote summary has printed." easily reproved with additional proof strategies that are discharged

to consider the added specification corresponding to the attack actions. By analyzing these obligations in the extended model, we have attempted to understand why they were proved. In most cases, to proof these obligations we just discharged few more steps. However, in the majority of the cases the current ASTRAL specific proof strategies are not sufficient for completing the proof. Sometime we also have faced heap storage problem although we assigned the maximum heap size for PVS Allegro Lisp. These are some of the reasons that we did not complete the remaining proof obligations. Hence, there are more complex proof obligations, which need additional more powerful proof strategies to complete the proof.

LESSON LEARNED AND FUTURE RESEARCH DIRECTIONS

Lessons Learned and Discussion

The main lessons we learned span from understanding the voting process followed in US, driving the specification, up to the usage of PVS. We started the specification by looking at the video about how to vote using the ES&S system, the various documentations about the system specification and machine usage scenario, and some known requirements recommendations. This allowed us to learn the various components' operating scenario, the underlying communication among them, and the kinds of data they exchange during the communication (e.g., DRE sends the "selection" information to the RTAL). Converting these concepts to formal language is very complex and demands a clear understanding the process, each component behavior, their combined behaviors, the properties/requirements as well as the specification language itself. In fact formalism these using ASTRAL was relatively easy as the language is closer to higher-level language. However, the difficulty arose when using the PVS system, as

Algorithm 4.

```
EXCEPT
 /* Complete voting process attack. */
 /*This attack assumes a fleeing voter. In this scenario the
   fleeing voter voted for the attacker's candidate*/ Which_Phase = During_
Voting
 & Terminal_Mode = voter_mode
 & vType = Fleeing
 & scrName = REVIEW_SCREEN
 & scrNumber = Number_Of_Race + 1
 & Now - Change (scrNumber)  >= 10
 & EXISTS R: Race   (vc ISIN Displayed_Candidates (R)
      & ac ISIN Displayed_Candidates (R)
      & Picked (Candidate_Name (vc), Race_Title (R) ) )
 & vc = ac  & Review_Displayed   & NormalVotingProcess
EXIT
 /*the attacker calls the confirmation function and complete the process.*/
 scrNumber = scrNumber' + 2
 & scrName = THANKYOU_SCREEN
 & EXISTS b: Button   (b = CONFIRM
      -> Button_Pushed (b)   BECOMES TRUE)
  & Min_Display (scrNumber)
       BECOMES Display_Info (Thank_You, NoButton)
 /*The normal voting process is intrupted by the attacker and the DRE is not
chirping for this voter.*/
   &~NormalVotingProcess
```

this requires understanding the different proof sketching and structuring techniques in PVS.

As said before, the PVS specification is very complex and required us to discharge a number of proof commands even for a simple property to prove. Thus, it makes sense to think of an approach that would allow a modular way of carrying on a proof, namely an approach to modularly proofing strategy and possibly by extending the ASTRAL specific PVS strategies. To make the specification modular, the ASTRAL language contains structuring mechanisms that allow one to build modularized specifications of complex systems. It is interesting to specify the attack scenarios in other specification and try to compose them

using the composition mechanism of ASTRAL. However, the combined specification obviously more complicated than individual specifications. Consider two ASTRAL specifications: each of these specifications contains one or more process type specifications and a global specification. Composing these specifications means to build a new specification, that is the specifications of a system obtained by making the processes of the original specifications interact. The behavior, the environment, and the properties of the new system are obtained from those of its components, once their interaction is formally described. In order to compose ASTRAL specifications one needs to define how to formally describe the interconnection between two or more specifications, how the resulting new specification can be built starting from the specification of its components and the description of their interaction, and under what conditions the properties verified about the components will still be valid in the composed system.

Additionally, the choice of modeling language poses many problems due to the complex mix of requirements that such an e-voting system is required to satisfy. In other experience, different modeling languages are more-or-less suited to the verification of different critical requirements. For instance, using ASTRAL/PVS we could specify and verify requirements related to environments (e.g., the behavior of the voter with the machine). Although, PVS can allow us to specify complex behaviors about the system and its environment, it is too mechanical and needs relatively deep technical understanding from the verification and usability point of views. Model checking systems, such as NuSMV (http://nusmv.fbk.eu), instead allow to perform automatic verification of specification but they suffer from being scalable for reasonable large specification such as the specification of an end-to-end e-voting system. Further research is essential to allow a mixed-model approach, i.e., expressing and verifying different types of critical requirements using different modeling languages in development strategies. Quoting from (Gibson et al., 2010), *"the main problem that could arises from such a mixed-model approach to architecture verification"*. In this case, ensuring that the different models are coherent when we integrate them in a final implementation is yet another challenge.

Future Research Directions

Based on different experiences, we draw the following lessons for future research. First of all, it is important to highlight the different dimensions of attacks since they allow to define the sequence of actions that can potentially lead to a particular attack under consideration. We can categorize attacks that target e-voting systems (elections in general) as: detectable verses undetectable, recoverable verses unrecoverable, and preventable verses detectable. In the first case, some attacks are undetectable no matter what practices are used while others are detectable in principle but are unlikely to be detected by the routine practices currently in place. In the second case, in some cases, if an attack is detected, there is an easy way to recover while other attacks can be detected, but there may be no good recovery strategy. In the third case, there is a trade-off between different strategies for dealing with attacks. One strategy is to design mechanisms to prevent the attack entirely, closing the vulnerability and rendering attack impossible. Thus, further studies on attack surfaces and dimensions will allow us to effectively characterize the effects of threats and would also provide a clear picture for the definition of a set of generic library of attack models corresponding to threat actions. In line with this, some preliminary results have already been obtained to model and analyze attacks, and indicate that it is indeed possible to devise an effective technique capable of allowing for systematic injection of threats into the nominal voting process specification. It would also be of interest to model side channel attack, since this has not been modeled for voting systems to the best of our knowledge. Notice, however, that prior to this we require to highlight those critical requirements that can be of interest of formal specification and verification, as discussed before.

It is clear that the use of formal methods would allow designers to prove, test, or otherwise examine interesting properties of a complex process whose behavior is specified abstractly, and then interactively refine the behavioral specification to be as close to an implementation as appropriate for a given assurance level. Since the technique has been recognized as powerful and effective approaches for improving the security and quality of complex systems (such as in flight systems), drawing straight connection with this could help making better the current development of e-voting systems. Within an initial investigation of requirements catalogues, it is possible to classify those requirements that are of interest of formal verification, by evaluating their relevance with respect to a particular e-voting system. Taxonomically detailing requirements will be a plus for the formal specification and verification activity. This is because that once requirements' are structured according to a given taxonomy, it will be much easy to correspond to the type of properties we wish to formally verify (such as, like safety related, security related, and procedural or organizational related).

Furthermore, the state of e-voting research (and also the technology itself) has not progressed to the point where it could be used effectively to address a wide variety of real problems we faced in the domain, such as making an e-voting system a fundamental service that can be used with acceptable security and privacy level. In particular, the lack of open source e-voting systems has precluded the kind of acceptance by the research and citizens that e-voting could have been received. Although this limits their usage in a larger scope, the research community should push work like (Adida, 2008) for wider acceptance of e-voting systems. Finally, sharing and studying experimental data about the e-voting machines' security, performance and their evolution with respect to the social and technical aspects are still relatively poor.

CONCLUSION

In this chapter, we presented our experiences on how formal methods could be effectively applied for the specification and verification of an e-voting system. More specifically, we discuss the lesson learned and good practices to deal with how to improve the current development trends in the area. Two main lessons can be draw from this work. The first one is that formal methods help get a better understanding of the security boundaries of e-voting systems. In the case of the ES&S, for

instance, various security requirements could not be proved without making assumptions about the procedures and about the environment. Notice that we expect this result to equally apply to other e-voting systems. Formalizing such hypotheses helps to delineate the necessary conditions for the secure use of systems. The second one is that of open specifications plays a pivotal role for the development of more secure e-voting systems. The formal specification of the ES&S, for instance, required the collection of information from different sources, such as configuration instructions, the user's manual, and videos. The adoption of an open-standardized specification could help simplify, extend, and generalize the results we have found to other systems.

Finally, we remark that any relevant effort in the development of e-voting should take into account pertinent issues such as measurement of impacts before and after deploying e-voting system. Hence, getting a clearer view of the research activities in the area, highlighting both positive and negative results, and emphasizing some trends could help, in our opinion, to draw a neater line between opinion and facts, and contribute to the construction of a next generation of e-voting machines to be safely and more confidently employed for elections. Thus, in order to achieve this we should adapt formal software engineering techniques. This means that while incorporating formal methods in the development and analysis phase, we should consider viewpoints related to technologies (that usually represent the system level) and related to public administration (that usually states how the procedure works).

REFERENCES

Abadi, M., & Fournet, C. (2001). Mobile values, new names, and secure communication. *SIGPLAN Notice*, *36*(3), 104–115. doi:10.1145/373243.360213

Adida, B. (2008). Helios: Web-based open-audit voting. In the *Proceedings of the 18th Conference on USENIX Security Symposium* (pp. 335–348). Berkeley, CA: USENIX Association.

Ansari, N., Sakarindr, P., Haghani, E., Zhang, C., Jain, A. K., & Shi, Y. Q. (2008). Evaluating electronic voting systems equipped with voter-verified paper records. *IEEE Security and Privacy*, *6*(3), 30–39. doi:10.1109/MSP.2008.62

Antoniou, A., Korakas, C., Manolopoulos, C., Panagiotaki, A., Sofotassios, D., Spirakis, P. G., & Stamatiou, Y. C. (2007). A trust-centered approach for building e-voting systems. In the *Proceeding of EGO* (pp, 366–377). Springer.

Aviv, A., C˘erny, P., Clark, S., Cronin, E., Shah, G., Sherr, M., & Blaze, M. (2008). Security evaluation of ES&S voting machines and election management system. *In Proceedings of the Conference on Electronic Voting Technology*. Berkeley, CA: USENIX Association.

Balzarotti, D., Banks, G., Cova, M., Felmetsger, V., Kemmerer, R., & Robertson, W. … Vigna, G. (2008). Are your votes really counted? Testing the security of real-world electronic voting systems. In *International Symposium on Software Testing and Analysis* (pp. 237-248). New York, NY: ACM.

Balzarotti, D., Banks, G., Cova, M., Felmetsger, V., Kemmerer, R., & Robertson, W. (2010). An experience in testing the security of real-world electronic voting systems. *IEEE Transactions on Software Engineering*, *36*(4), 453–473. doi:10.1109/TSE.2009.53

Bishop, M., & Wagner, D. (2007). Risks of e-voting. *Communications of the ACM*, *50*(11), 120–120. doi:10.1145/1297797.1297827

Blanchet, B. (2009). Automatic verification of correspondences for security protocols. *Journal of Computer Security*, *17*(4), 363–434.

Bryans, J. W., Littlewood, B., Ryan, P. Y. A., & Strigini, L. (2006). E-voting: Dependability requirements and design for dependability. In the *International Conference on Availability, Reliability and Security (ARES)* (pp. 988-995). Washington, DC: IEEE Computer Society.

Bryl, B., Dalpiaz, F., Ferrario, R., Mattioli, A., & Villafiorita, A. (2009). Evaluating procedural alternatives: A case study in e-voting. *Electronic Government, an International Journal*, *6*(2), 213-231

California Secretary of State. (2007). *Withdrawal of approval of Diebold Election Systems, Inc, Gems 1.18.24/Accuvote- Tswaccuvote-Os Dre & optical scan voting system and conditional re-approval of use of Diebold Election Systems, Inc., Gems 1.18.24/Accuvote-Tsx/Accuvote-Os Dre & optical scan voting system*. Retrieved April 20, 2008, from https://www.sos.ca.gov/voting-systems/oversight/ttbr/diebold-102507.pdf

Cansell, D., Gibson, J. P., & Mèry, D. (2007). Refinement: A constructive approach to formal software design for a secure e-voting interface. *Electronic Notes in Theoretical Computer Science*, *183*, 39–55. doi:10.1016/j.entcs.2007.01.060

Cass, A. G., Lerner, B. S., Sutton, S. M., McCall, E. K., Jr., Wise, A., & Osterweil, L. J. (2002). Little-JIL/Juliette: A process definition language and interpreter. In *Proceedings of the 22nd International Conference on Software Engineering*, pp. (754-757). New York, NY: ACM.

Cobleigh, J. M., Clarke, L. A., & Osterweil, L. J. (2002). FLAVERS: A finite state verification technique for software systems. *IBM Systems Journal*, *41*(1), 140-165. ISSN 0018-8670

Common Criteria. (2009). *Common criteria for information technology security evaluation*. Retrieved November 10, 2009, from http://www.commoncriteriaportal.org/

Cranor, L. F. (1996). Electronic voting: Computerized polls may save money, protect privacy. *Crossroads, 2*(4), 12–16. doi:10.1145/332159.332163

Delaune, S., Kremer, S., & Ryan, M. (2009). Verifying privacy-type properties of electronic voting protocols. *Journal of Computer Security, 17*(4), 435–487.

Gibson, J. P., Lallet, E., & Raffy, J. L. (2010). Engineering a distributed e-voting system architecture: Meeting critical requirements. In *ISARCS, LNCS* (pp. 89-108). Springer.

Grimm, R., Hupf, K., & Volkamer, M. (2010). A formal IT-security model for the correction and abort requirement of electronic voting. In *Electronic Voting* (pp. 89-107).

Heitmeyer, C. L., Archer, M., Leonard, I. E., & McLean, J. (2008). Applying formal methods to a certifiably secure software system. *IEEE Transactions on Software Engineering, 34*(1), 82–98. doi:10.1109/TSE.2007.70772

Jones, D. W. (2003). The evaluation of voting technology (Chap. 1). *Advances in information security* (pp. 3-16). Kluwer Academic.

Juels, A. Catalano, & D., Jakobsson, M. (2005). Coercion-resistant electronic elections. In *Proceedings of the 2005 ACM Workshop on Privacy in the Electronic Society* (pp. 61-70). New York, NY: ACM.

Kohno, T., Stubblefield, A., Rubin, A. D., & Wallach, D. S. (2004). Analysis of an electronic voting system. *Symposium on Security and Privacy,* (Vol. 27). IEEE Computer Society. Gardner, R., Garera, S., & Rubin, A. (2007). On the difficulty of validating voting machine software with software. In *Proceedings of the USENIX/Accurate Electronic Voting Technology on USENIX/Accurate Electronic Voting Technology Workshop*. Berkeley, CA, USA: USENIX Association.

Kremer, S., & Ryan, D. R. (2005). Analysis of an electronic voting protocol in the applied pi-calculus. *In ESOP '05, LNCS* (pp. 186-200). Edinburgh, UK, April 2005. Springer.

Martinelli, F. (2002). Symbolic semantics and analysis for crypto-CCS with (almost) generic inference systems. In *Proceedings of the 27th International Symposium on Mathematical Foundations of Computer Science* (pp. 519-531). London, UK: Springer-Verlag.

Mercuri, T. M., & Camp, L. J. (2004). The code of elections. *Communications of the ACM, 47*(10), 52–57. doi:10.1145/1022594.1022623

Oostveen, A. M., & den Besselaar, P. V. (2004). Security as belief user's perceptions on the security of e-voting systems. In the *Proceedings of Electronic Voting in Europe* (pp. 73-82).

Paul, N., & Tanenbaum, A. S. (2009). Trustworthy voting: From machine to system. *Computer, 42*(5), 23–29. doi:10.1109/MC.2009.169

Reinhard, K., & Jung, W. (2007). Compliance of POLYAS with the BSI protection profile - Basic requirements for remote electronic voting systems. In *VOTE-ID, LNCS* (pp. 62-75). Springer.

Sastry, N., Kohno, T., & Wagner, D. (2006). Designing voting machines for verification. In *Proceedings of the 15th Conference on USENIX Security Symposium*. Berkeley, CA: USENIX Association.

Schmidt, A., Volkamer, M., & Buchmann, J. (2010). An evaluation and certification approach to enable voting service providers. In *Electronic Voting* (pp. 135–148). LNI.

Simidchieva, B. I., Marzilli, S. M., Clarke, A. L., & Osterweil, J. L. (2008). Specifying and verifying requirements for election processes. In *Proceedings of the 2008 International Conference on Digital government research* (pp. 63-72). Digital Government Society of North America.

Smith, R. L., Avrunin, G. S., Clarke, L. A., & Osterweil, L. J. (2002). PROPEL: An approach supporting property elucidation. In *Proceedings of the 24th International Conference on Software Engineering* (pp. 11-21). New York, NY: ACM.

Sturton, C., Jha, S., Seshia, A. S., & Wagner, D. (2009). On voting machine design for verification and testability. In *ACM CCS* (pp. 463–476). ACM. doi:10.1145/1653662.1653719

Thomas, D. E., & Moorby, P. R. (1991). *The VERILOG hardware description language*. Norwell, MA: Kluwer Academic Publishers. doi:10.1007/978-1-4615-3992-6

Villafiorita, A., Weldemariam, K., & Tiella, R. (2009). Development, formal verification, and evaluation of an e-voting system with VVPAT. *IEEE Transaction in Information Forensic Security*, *4*(4), 651–661. doi:10.1109/TIFS.2009.2034903

Volkamer, M. (2009). *Evaluation of electronic voting: Requirements and evaluation procedures to support responsible election authorities: LNBIP*. Berlin, Heidelberg: Springer-Verlag.

Volkamer, M., & Krimmer, R. (2007). Independent audits of remote electronic voting – Developing a common criteria protection profile. In *Proceedings of EDEM'07*.

Weldemariam, K. (2010). *Using formal methods for building more reliable and secure e-voting systems*. PhD thesis, University of Trento, via Sommarive 18, Trento, Italy.

Weldemariam, K., Kemmerer, R. A., & Villafiorita, A. (2009). Formal analysis of attacks for an e-voting system. *In International Conference on Risks and Security of Internet and Systems* (pp. 26-34). IEEE.

Weldemariam, K., Kemmerer, R. A., & Villafiorita, A. (2010). Formal specification and analysis of an e-voting system. In the *International Conference on Availability, Reliability and Security (ARES)* (pp. 164-171). IEEE Computer Society.

Weldemariam, K., & Villafiorita, A. (2008). Modeling and analysis of procedural security in (e) Voting: The Trentino's approach and experiences. In *USENIX/ACCURATE Electronic Voting Workshop (EVT)*. Berkeley, CA: USENIX Association.

Weldemariam, K., Villafiorita, A., & Mattioli, A. (2007). Assessing procedural risks and threats in e-voting: challenges and an approach. In *VOTE-ID* (pp. 38–49). Lecture Notes in Computer Science Springer-Verlag. doi:10.1007/978-3-540-77493-8_4

Wolchok, S., Wustrow, E., Halderman, J. A., Prasad, H. K., Kankipati, A., & Sakhamuri, S. K. … Gonggrijp, R. (2010). Security analysis of India's electronic voting machines. In *Proceedings of the 17th ACM Conference on Computer and Communications Security* (pp. 1-14). ACM.

KEY TERMS AND DEFINITIONS

ASTRAL: It is a high-level formal specification language designed for reactive systems.

Direct Electronic Recording (DRE): A type of voting machine that allows the recording of votes by means of a ballot display provided with mechanical or electro-optical components that can be activated by the voter (typically buttons or a touch-screen). It allows the processing of data by means of software and the recording of voting data and ballot images in memory components such as Compact Flash Card.

Electronic Voting: One of the many forms of voting systems that allows a voter to record his or her secure and secret ballot electronically.

ES&S: ES&S is the acronym of "Election Systems and Software". The E&S e-voting system is one of the DRE-based e-voting systems with VVPAT/RTAL. (http://www.essvote.com/HTML/home.html)

Formal Methods: A mathematical and modeling approach applicable to the specification, design, and verification of software and hardware systems. The emphasis is on the creation of theories and tools to aid these activities.

PVS: It is a specification language integrated with support tools and a theorem prover. It is intended to capture the state-of-the-art in mechanized formal methods and to be sufficiently rugged that it can be used for significant applications. (http://pvs.csl.sri.com/)

VVPAT/RTAL: VVPAT is the acronym of "Voter Verified Paper Audit Trail" and RTAL is the acronym of "Real Time Audit Log". The terms are equivalent and refer to a kind of "vote receipt" printed by an electronic voting machine that shows the elector his/her vote as it is being entered into the electoral system. It is a mean to provide immediate assurance and confidence to a voter that his or her vote is accurately recorded by displaying behind a transparent glass.

Chapter 19
Countering Spam Robots:
Scrambled CAPTCHA and Hindi CAPTCHA

Aditya Raj
Netaji Subhas Institute of Technology, India

Tushar Pahwa
Netaji Subhas Institute of Technology, India

Ashish Jain
Netaji Subhas Institute of Technology, India

ABSTRACT

CAPTCHAs are employed on websites to differentiate between human users and bot programs that indulge in spamming and other fraudulent activities. With the advent and advancement of sophisticated computer programs to break CAPTCHAs, it has become imperative to continuously evolve the CAPTCHA schemes in order to keep the Internet network and website free of congestion and spam-bots. In light of these developments concerning information security, in this chapter, the authors introduce the novel concept of Scrambled CAPTCHA, which is a combination of OCR-based and Picture CAPTCHAs and exploits an inherent characteristic of human vision and perception. They also introduce Hindi CAPTCHA, developed in Hindi language (Devanagari script). This CAPTCHA will typically address spamming on Indian websites. It also contributes to the digitalization of books written in this script. The authors also discuss the features and security aspects of these schemes in detail, which, to the best their knowledge, had not been implemented earlier.

INTRODUCTION

The ever increasing use of Internet and web resources calls for strong security measures to prevent malicious activities like spamming (Siponen 2006), phishing (Dhamija 2005), credit-card

DOI: 10.4018/978-1-4666-0978-5.ch019

frauds and unauthorized access to information. One of the primary mechanisms of enforcing security and preventing misuse of online resources is the Human Interactive Proof (HIP) system. HIP system is a broad set of protocols to distinguish between computer programs known as 'bots' and human users. CAPTCHAs (Completely Automated Public Turing Test to Tell Human and

Computers Apart) are a form of HIP. CAPTCHAs are employed as means to prevent 'bots' (that pose as human users) from indulging in spamming and other unscrupulous activities. The essence of a CAPTCHA is that it should be identified easily by a human but not by a bot. Broadly, CAPTCHAs can be classified into two groups:

- OCR (Optical Character Recognition) based
- Non-OCR based

OCR-based CAPTCHAs are mainly text-based CAPTCHAs in which the user is shown distorted images of letters and/or digits and the user is required to recognize them and type the answer. The OCR-based CAPTCHAs have been employed on many popular websites such as Google, Yahoo!, Hotmail, Facebook etc. However, these CAPTCHAs have an inherent limitation. Since the strength of these CAPTCHAs significantly depends upon the degree of distortion in the displayed text, increasing security by increasing text distortion may lead to failure of recognition by humans (Yan 2008), thus making the CAPTCHA ineffective. Further, for mobile phones and devices like PDAs and palmtops, the use of keyboard may be infeasible or difficult thus making OCR-based CAPTCHAs inconvenient.

These weaknesses can be resolved by using Non-OCR based CAPTCHAs. Non-OCR based CAPTCHAs include audio (Tam 2008), logical (Shirali-Shahreza 2007), animated (Athanasopoulos 2006, Kluever 2009, Shirali-Shahreza 2008) and picture CAPTCHAs (Baird 2005, Chew 2004, Jain 2009, Shirali-Shahreza 2007, Shirali-Shahreza 2008, Shirali-Shahreza 2008) which basically test the audio/video sense capability associated with a human. Logical CAPTCHAs display questions, puzzles etc. which can be easily solved by humans but not by bots. In audio CAPTCHAs, users are required to recognize sounds played out to them. They are also beneficial to blind users (Shirali-Shahreza 2007) who otherwise cannot interact with OCR-based and video/animated CAPTCHAs. CAPTCHAs have also been designed for deaf users (Shirali-Shahreza 2008). In Picture CAPTCHAs, picture(s) of some object(s) is/are shown to the user. The user has to identify the displayed objects or recognize some properties associated with these pictures. This mechanism exploits two facts:

- The human eye is naturally very good in recognizing pictures of objects.
- The large variety of objects present in the world makes recognition of pictures highly infeasible for a computer.

In this chapter, we introduce two novel CAPTCHA schemes: Scrambled CAPTCHA and Hindi CAPTCHA. We also discuss their security implications and benefits. The following section discusses some broad associated definitions and the research already conducted in CAPTCHA generation and breaking.

BACKGROUND

Research Work Conducted in OCR-Based CAPTCHAs

The MSN CAPTCHA popularly used by Hotmail has been broken by Yan et al.(Yan 2008) with overall success of 60% by employing the technique of snake segmentation. They also broke CAPTCHAs from captchaservice.com (92% success) and register.com (47.8% success). Mori et al. (Mori 2003) employed object-recognition techniques to break the EZ-Gimpy (92% success) and the Gimpy (33% success) CAPTCHAs. Moy et al. (Moy 2004) estimated distortion and broke EZ-gimpy (99% success) and 4-letter Gimpy-r (78% success). K. Chellapilla et al. (Chellapilla 2004) achieved 34.4% success rate on breaking an improved version of Yahoo/EZ Gimpy CAPTCHAs. Moreover, they broke Google HIP which used only image warp as means of text distortion. STCs proposed by Gupta et al. (Gupta 2009) introduced the concept of 'Tagging'. von Ahn et al. (von 2008) introduced ReCAPTCHA which is being used by Facebook.

Research Work Conducted in Non-OCR based CAPTCHAs

Shirali-Shahreza et al.(Shirali-Shahreza 2008) proposed PIX CAPTCHA in which a number of pictures that have a similar subject are selected and shown to the user. The user is required to select the subject of these pictures. Baird et al. (Baird 2005) proposed Implicit CAPTCHAs which involve clicking in certain target areas in an image, for example, the glasses of a skier. Shirali-Shahreza et al. (Shirali-Shahreza 2007) proposed a picture CAPTCHA called Collage CAPTCHA. In this CAPTCHA, the user was shown pictures of some objects and was required to click on the picture of some specific object from among the displayed ones. They also proposed Advanced Collage CAPTCHA (Shirali-Shahreza 2008). This CAPTCHA was identical to Collage CAPTCHA but the user now had to identify the required picture from a group of pictures appearing on the right of the screen also. They also introduced Drawing CAPTCHA (Shirali-Shahreza 2006) which required the use of mouse/pointer device.

It is imperative to define here some terminology which will be used throughout this chapter. This terminology includes our own observations and those of other researchers (Chellapilla 2004, Chew 2004, Jain 2009, Mori 2003, Yan 2007, Yan 2008). We also present a concise summary of CAPTCHA breaking techniques so that the reader can comprehend the security analysis of our proposed schemes (presented later) much more clearly.

A typical CAPTCHA breaking attack follows this order:

- *Preprocessing the Image:* The background noise in the CAPTCHA image is either removed completely or reduced by filtering. In addition, if the CAPTCHA is colored, the text may be converted to monochrome format to facilitate breaking. Preprocessing may include connecting the disconnected components in the image and image reconstruction.
- *Segmentation of Characters:* Segmentation refers to separating the different characters in the CAPTCHA from the background noise and also from one another. This is done in order to know how many characters are present so that identification techniques can be applied on them. The currently proposed segmentation attacks are vertical segmentation (vertical scan lines), snake segmentation (vertical curved scan lines) and color-filling segmentation (CFS) (flood-filling) (Yan 2007).
- *Character Identification:* Typically, shape/geometric analysis is employed along with dictionary matching and pixel count to recognize the CAPTCHA words/characters.

The following two types of breaking attacks are relevant in context to this chapter:

- *Random Guessing Attack (Chew 2004):* We observed that the random guessing attack is the simplest attack that could be employed to break CAPTCHAs. It requires no computation time to solve the CAPTCHA and no significant resources on the hacker's part. Therefore, the random guessing attack can be used with a high frequency and even a low success rate results in a huge volume of spam. Hence, a robust CAPTCHA generation scheme must provide high security against this attack. Therefore, we have included this parameter in our comparison.

- *Pictionary-based Attack:* In this attack, the bot maintains a 'picture dictionary' (pictionary) or a 'look-up table' of object pictures along with their object names and any associated information useful in picture matching. Hence, whenever the bot comes across a picture, it searches for the picture by comparing properties like color/intensity, edge detected pattern, pixel pattern etc. with those of every picture it has in its table. If a match occurs, the bot simply 'looks up' the answer. If there is no match, this picture gets added in the table for future look-up.

Misspelling, mislabelling, polysemy and synonymy (Chew 2004) are inherent problems in case of Picture CAPTCHAs. They hamper the user-friendliness of the CAPTCHA. Mislabelling is a serious problem in the on-the-fly implementation mechanism which is discussed below. It leads to confusion and ultimately affects the user-friendliness of the CAPTCHA.

Implementation strategy – This refers to the strategy chosen for selecting the object pictures which will be displayed to the user in a CAPTCHA round. This is essential in the case of Picture CAPTCHAs. The selection of the object pictures is a matter of choice and policy. We consider two general selection mechanisms and discuss the advantages and disadvantages of both:

1. Database Mechanism: A huge number of pictures are collected from the Internet and other sources and stored in a database. Pictures are randomly chosen from this database for display in CAPTCHAs. The advantages of using this mechanism are:
   - High quality and clear pictures can be selected because the pictures are chosen and stored beforehand. Thus, the pictures do not pose any problem in user identification as each picture perfectly displays the required ob-

ject. Potential problems like mislabelling and low picture quality are eliminated.
   - Since the pictures are stored beforehand, SPC generation is time-efficient. It requires little time to retrieve and load the images as suitably designed hashing functions could be employed. Hence, the loading time of the CAPTCHA decreases which increases the user-friendliness of the website and causes little inconvenience to users.

However, the prime disadvantages associated with this mechanism are:

- The cost of updating the database with new pictures will be high. This is because it will be a time consuming process since each picture will be accompanied by a 'label' and associated information (used during look-up) that will have to entered manually or generated by some automated means. This process will have to be repeated periodically and hence will be costly.
- The costs associated with the storage of a large number of pictures and database maintenance may become too high and unacceptable.
2. On-the-Fly Mechanism: First the names of the objects to be displayed are selected out of a bank of N total object names. Then, random pictures of these selected objects are searched and selected from the Internet using standard search engines like Yahoo!, Google etc. These images are then displayed in the CAPTCHA. The benefits of this mechanism are:
- Since the pictures are obtained dynamically from the web, the costs associated with storage of a large number of pictures and maintenance of a database is eliminated.

- The web is completely dynamic and is updated constantly. Since in on-the-fly mechanism, pictures are being searched on the web, the effort required to keep a static database, updating it with new pictures constantly is not a factor here. Thus, the costs associated with constant upkeep of a database are eliminated

The disadvantages with this method are:

- Since the pictures are searched and chosen from the Internet, they may not completely match their object. Thus, mislabelling is present which reduces the user-friendliness of the CAPTCHA.
- This method is not time-efficient. Time required to search for pictures on the web and to include them in the CAPTCHA may be significant enough to adversely affect the loading time of the CAPTCHA. This decreases its user friendliness.
- If the website attracts high amount of traffic, pictures may start repeating themselves. This is because search engines only provide limited search results (1000 for Google). This may assist the hacker in breaking the picture CAPTCHA.

MAIN FOCUS OF THE CHAPTER

We analyzed a lot of CAPTCHAs and made the following observations:

- Segmentation is a critical phase during CAPTCHA breaking. Hence, in order to develop a robust CAPTCHA, it is essential to make the CAPTCHA highly resistant to segmentation attacks.
- A CAPTCHA scheme which exploits some inherent human ability will prove to be very convenient for humans. However, it will call for the development of very so-

phisticated computer programs to break the CAPTCHA scheme.

- There is a need to further study and develop a CAPTCHA scheme which clubs the benefits of both OCR-based and Non-OCR based CAPTCHAs as such a scheme promises to be very convenient for users, while at the same time, having high security. We felt little research work has been conducted in this direction.
- The growing number of computer users in India has motivated us to develop a CAPTCHA scheme in Devanagari script which will not only cater to the non-English speaking Indian population but also spark some research work in the field of Devanagari script recognition.

These motivations led us to introduce the schemes of Scrambled CAPTCHA and Hindi CAPTCHA which we discuss in this chapter.

Scrambled CAPTCHA

Scrambled CAPTCHA is a combination of OCR-based and non-OCR based CAPTCHAs. It consists of a number of object pictures. Each picture is accompanied by a Tag which is a text-based CAPTCHA. The object pictures are displayed to the user and the Tags are seen below their 'owner' picture. The text displayed in each Tag is either an anagram of the respective displayed object or some random irrelevant text. For solving Scrambled CAPTCHA, the user is required to determine the Tag which contains an anagram of its corresponding object name. If the final answer as selected by the user is correct, only then is the user authenticated. The beauty of this scheme lies in exploiting the natural ability of the human brain to rearrange and transform apparently meaningless text into meaningful words very quickly. Hence, this scheme is a fitting test to differentiate the human brain from a trained bot program.

Thus, Scrambled CAPTCHA scheme can be broadly divided into the following three stages:

- Displaying Object Pictures
- Generation of Tags
- Response Submission Mechanism

We now discuss these various stages in detail.

Displaying Object Pictures: Object pictures can be displayed by either the database implementation or by on-the-fly implementation.

Generation of Tags: Tags consist of jumbled words in English. For example, the Tag of the picture of an apple may contain the text – 'Aplpe'. Since this Tag contains the letters of the word 'apple' in a scrambled form, this Tag is the target Tag. It is customary to note that in a CAPTCHA round, only one Tag will be a target Tag. Thus, the Tags other than the target Tag will contain irrelevant text which will not be an anagram of their owner object's name. A sample target Tag is shown in Figure 1.

Response Submission Mechanism: In Scheme-I, after the user identifies the target Tag, the user is required to type the name of the owner object of the target Tag in correct order in a text box. In Scheme-II, after the user identifies the target Tag, the user is required to select the name of the owner object of the target Tag from a drop-down menu which also contains other object names as possible candidate answers.

Analysis of Scrambled CAPTCHA

The following types of attacks are possible on Scrambled CAPTCHA:

1. Random-Guessing Attack: The random guessing attack is infeasible for breaking Scheme-I as the response in this case should be in textual form. The probability of breaking Scheme-II evaluates to $1/n$ where n is the number of options for object name in the drop-down menu. Taking n=15, this comes out to be 6.7%. This is a significant improvement over other non-OCR CAPTCHA schemes.

2. Pictionary-based Attack: This attack is infeasible to break both the Scrambled CAPTCHA schemes because in the schemes, the Tags of the object pictures determine whether the object name is the Target answer. For eg., if the object apple has its Tag 'Aplpe', then this indeed is the target Tag and the name 'Apple' is the answer. However, suppose the Tag for the object apple appears as 'Aplon'. In this case, the Tag is not the target Tag and the name 'Apple' is not the correct answer. Hence, the Tags of the object pictures determine whether the object's name is the correct answer. Since the Tags are in the form of CAPTCHAs and difficult to break and vary in each round, there is no benefit to the hacker in storing the generated Tags in each round. Hence, Pictionary-based attack is rendered ineffective.

Resistance to Segmentation – We have designed Scrambled CAPTCHA such that it renders the segmentation attacks mentioned above ineffective. Transformation operations of translation, shearing, rotation and scaling and overlapping between characters are applied to each character in

Figure 1. A sample target Tag

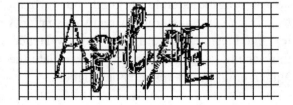

a word. These counter the first two segmentation attacks mentioned above. In addition, we employ fragmentation of pixels in the characters. This means that a character is not completely colored. Rather, it is only partially filled. This technique counters CFS attack as the continuous process of flood-filling a region keeps breaking frequently. Moreover, we attempted to break Scrambled CAPTCHA by recognizing the number of characters in a CAPTCHA word by recording vertical pixel densities along a horizontal scan line starting from the extreme left of the image. But the degree of overlap/touch between the individual characters was such that the attack was rendered unsuccessful as it could not locate the region of touching of characters. As a result, the density obtained along the horizontal axis was almost constant for the entire length of the challenge text.

Hindi CAPTCHA

Our method proposes a way to distinguish a human user from a bot using a CAPTCHA that uses Hindi language (Devanagari script). Hindi CAPTCHA is an OCR-based CAPTCHA in which we show Hindi words to the user. The user needs to identify the word or type the word depending on the CAPTCHA scheme being used. We propose three schemes in Hindi CAPTCHA. The first scheme (Hindi Baf)e-text) is OCR-based and the other two are Non-OCR based schemes. These are discussed below:

• Scheme - I (Hindi Baf)e-text Method): In this scheme, the word shown to the user is a Hindi word which is distorted and has noise present in the image. The user needs to type the displayed word as the answer with the help of a virtual Hindi keyboard which appears on the screen. A sample Hindi CAPTCHA image is shown in Figure 2.

• Scheme - II: In this scheme, the word displayed is the same as that displayed in Scheme - I. However, now, rather than typing the word as answer, the user is required to select the displayed word from a drop-down menu which contains

Figure 2. A sample Hindi CAPTCHA image

other incorrect choices as well. All these word names appear in Hindi language. These choices may be either incorrect words altogether or may differ in the spelling and hence, be incorrect. For a user well versed in Hindi, identifying the correct word from the options is a trivial task. Thus, the user is required to simply click on the required word in the menu. Hence, the need of keyboard is eliminated in this scheme.

• Scheme - III: In this scheme, the user is displayed a picture of a random object. A drop-down list is also provided which contains the name of the object along with other incorrect object names. All these object names appear in Hindi language. The user is required to select the correct object name from those in the menu. Here also, the user is required to simply click on the required word. Hence, the need of keyboard is eliminated in this scheme.

Analysis: Security Aspects of Hindi CAPTCHA

There are certain features of the Hindi language that have been exploited to improve the security of the Hindi CAPTCHA. We discuss these features and show how the CAPTCHA offers resistance during different stages in CAPTCHA breaking.

A. Pre-processing

Pre-processing of the CAPTCHA image is the first step performed by the bot during CAPTCHA breaking.

• Removal of symbols: We selected a standard MATLAB function medlfit2 to test the result of noise filtration on Hindi CAPTCHA. medfilt2 is a function which performs median filtering. It is a nonlinear operation often used in image processing to reduce noise. Median filtering is more effective than convolution when the goal is to simultaneously reduce noise and preserve edges. As a result, the characters were also significantly filtered and they became very hard to recognize. The further addition of noise in the CAPTCHA image makes detection of characters very difficult. This is because many of the Hindi words contain dots/curves. Pre-processing of noise may result in removal of these symbols of the word as well after being misinterpreted as noise. This eventually leads to false detection of characters.

• Removal of Characters: All the characters in Hindi words are connected together by a horizontal line which appears at the top of the word. Further, vertical and horizontal lines appear in many characters. These lines may be misinterpreted as noise during pre-processing and be subsequently removed. This effect, cumulated with removal of symbols, results in removal of a significant part of the CAPTCHA image. A sample image is shown in Figure 3.

• Grid lines: Grid lines may be interpreted as noise and removed. This is because the thickness of grid lines and some parts of the CAPTCHA characters is identical. Thus, removing grid lines also removes the characters.

B. Image Segmentation

Image segmentation is one of the most important and crucial stages in CAPTCHA breaking. Hence, we rigorously tested the results of currently employed segmentation techniques on Hindi CAPTCHA. We assumed that the challenge text had been extracted perfectly during pre-processing. The next step performed by a bot would be to segment the characters in the image and extract them. There

are three types of segmentation techniques which have been currently employed to break CAPTCHAs as mentioned earlier. Hindi CAPTCHA, due to its design intricacies, is resistant to all three segmentation techniques. As a result, the whole word is segmented into one block/incorrect number of blocks.

C. Character Recognition

Similarity between characters: An inherent feature of Hindi language that can be exploited to design a secure CAPTCHA is that the Hindi character set has many subsets of characters that are very similar to each other. Table 1 shows some of these characters. These similarities make the recognition of characters very difficult as they result in false detection of characters. This property of similarity amongst Hindi characters can be exploited in many ways; the most efficient way being partly disconnecting the characters. If a character is broken/disconnected in a suitable region, then while recognizing that character, there is a fair chance

Figure 3. Sample images showing pre-processing of Hindi CAPTCHA

Table 1. Table showing similar characters in Devanagari script

Similar Characters
व , व , क्र
ड , ड़ , ड
ट , ठ , द
इ , ई
प , फ , प , फ
ध , थ , भ
अ , आ
उ , ऊ
ए , ऐ
ज , ज , ञ
थ , श
भ , म

Table 2. Table showing analysis of scrambled captcha and hindi captcha

Similar Characters
व , व , क्र
ड , ड़ , ड
ट , ठ , द
इ , ई
प , फ , प , फ
ध , थ , भ
अ , आ
उ , ऊ
ए , ऐ
ज , ज , ञ
थ , श
भ , म

that the bot may misinterpret that character as some other similar character. This results in false detection of characters. However, the character set is such that such discontinuity does not result in misreading by a human.

• Resistance to Dictionary Attacks: The words displayed are random and do not form a dictionary word. Hence, dictionary attacks are rendered ineffective.

D. Random Guessing Attack

For Schemes-I and II, the probability of breaking the CAPTCHA by random guessing method is given by 1/n where n is the number of options in the drop-down menu. Taking n = 15, we obtain a probability of breaking as 6.7%. Thus, it can be observed that random guessing method is rendered ineffective. This attack is not feasible

in Scheme - I as the answer needs to be typed by the user in this case.

A summary of both Scrambled CAPTCHA and Hindi CAPTCHA is shown in Table 2.

FUTURE RESEARCH DIRECTIONS

In our extensive study on CAPTCHAs, we have observed the following as strong candidates for future research direction:

- The next breakthrough CAPTCHA scheme is most likely going to be one which has the benefits and subtle features of both OCR-based and Non OCR-based CAPTCHAs.
- Another CAPTCHA type not explored much is the video CAPTCHA which holds a lot of promise. The human brain is highly

capable of registering and remembering short videos/moving frames. Hence, the challenge is to tap this natural gift into a classic scheme which distinguishes a human from a trained bot.

- We feel that not enough research has been undertaken in the field of recognition of Devanagari script.
- Picture morphing is another field which has witnessed minimum research work. The combination of two or more pictures to result in a single yet comprehensible picture is a challenge and has the potential of a fitting HIP.

CONCLUSION

In this chapter, we introduced two novel CAPTCHA schemes – Scrambled CAPTCHA and Hindi CAPTCHA. Scrambled CAPTCHA is a non-OCR based CAPTCHA which exploits a natural ability of text perception of the human brain. Hindi CAPTCHA is an OCR-based CAPTCHA which will cater to the growing computer-literate Indian population. Both the schemes retain ease of use while providing high security and are practical, convenient and not resource-heavy.

REFERENCES

Athanasopoulos, E., & Antonatos, S. (October 2006). Enhanced CAPTCHAs: Using animation to tell humans and computers apart. *Proceedings of 10th Int. Conf. on Communications and Multimedia Security (CMS 2006), LNCS 4237*, (pp. 97–108).

Baird, H. S., & Bentley, J. L. (January 2005). Implicit CAPTCHAs. *Proceedings of SPIE-IS&T Electronic Imaging, Document Recognition and Retrieval XII, Vol. 5676 of SPIE Proceedings*, (pp. 191–196).

Chellapilla, K., & Simard, P. (2004). Using machine learning to break visual human interaction proofs (hips). In *Advances in Neural Information Processing Systems 17, Neural Information Processing Systems (NIPS)*, (pp. 265 – 272).

Chew, M., & Tygar, J. D. (September 2004). Image recognition CAPTCHAs. In *7th International Information Security Conference, (ISC'04)*, (pp. 268–279).

Dhamija, R., & Tygar, J. D. (May 2005). Phish and hips: Human interactive proofs to detect phishing attacks. In *Second International Workshop on Human Interactive Proofs, (HIP 2005)*, (pp. 127–141). USA.

Gupta, A., Jain, A., Raj, A., & Jain, A. (March 2009). Sequenced tagged CAPTCHA: Generation and its analysis. In *International Conference on Advanced Computing, (IACC'09)*, (pp. 1286–1291). India.

Jain, A., Jain, A., Raj, A., & Pahwa, T. (2009). Sequenced picture CAPTCHA: Generation and its strength analysis. *International Conference for Internet Technology and Secured Transactions, ICITST 2009*, (pp. 1 – 8).

Kluever, K. A., & Zanibbi, R. (July 2009). Balancing usability and security in a video CAPTCHA. In *Proceedings of the 5th Symposium on Usable Privacy and Security 2009*, Mountain View, CA, USA.

Mori, G., & Malik, J. (June 2003). Recognizing objects in adversarial clutter: Breaking a visual CAPTCHA. In *Conference on Computer Vision and Pattern Recognition, (CVPR'03)*, Vol. 1, (pp. 134 – 141).

Moy, G., Jones, N., Harkless, C., & Potter, R. (2004). Distortion estimation techniques in solving visual captchas. In *IEEE Computer Society Conference on Computer Vision and Pattern Recognition, (CVPR04)*, Vol. 2, (pp. 23–28).

Shirali-Shahreza, M., & Shirali-Shahreza, M. H. (January 2008). Online PIX CAPTCHA. *Proceedings of IEEE International Conference on Signal Processing, Communications and Networking (ICSCN2008)*, (pp. 582–585).

Shirali-Shahreza, M., & Shirali-Shahreza, S. (June 2006). Drawing CAPTCHA. *Proceedings of 28th Int. Conf. Information Technology Interfaces (ITI 2006)*, (pp. 475–480).

Shirali-Shahreza, M., & Shirali-Shahreza, S. (February 2007). Collage CAPTCHA. In *Proceedings of the 20th IEEE International Symposium Signal Processing and Application (ISSPA 2007)*, Sharjah, United Arab Emirates.

Shirali-Shahreza, M., & Shirali-Shahreza, S. (2007). Question-based CAPTCHA. In *ICCIMA '07: Proceedings of the International Conference on Computational Intelligence and Multimedia Applications (ICCIMA 2007)*, (pp. 54 – 58). Washington, DC: IEEE Computer Society.

Shirali-Shahreza, M., & Shirali-Shahreza, S. (December 2007). CAPTCHA for blind people. *Proceedings of 7th IEEE International Symposium on Signal Processing and Information Technology (ISSPIT 2007)*, (pp. 995–998).

Shirali-Shahreza, M., & Shirali-Shahreza, S. (April 2008). Advanced collage captcha. In *Proceedings of the 5th International Conference on Information Technology: New Generations (ITNG 2008)*, pages 1234 – 1235, Las Vegas, Nevada, USA.

Shirali-Shahreza, M., & Shirali-Shahreza, S. (May 2008). Motion CAPTCHA. *Proceedings of Conf. on Human System Interaction(HSI 2008)*, (pp. 1042–1044).

Shirali-Shahreza, S., & Shirali-Shahreza, M. (April 2008). A new human interactive proofs system for deaf persons. *Proceedings of 5th International Conference on Information Technology: New Generations (ITNG 2008)*, (pp. 807–810).

Siponen, M., & Stucke, C. (January 2006). Effective anti-spam strategies in companies: An international study. In *39th Annual Hawaii International Conference on System Sciences, (HICSS'06)*, Vol. 6, (pp. 127c – 136c).

Tam, J., Simsa, J., Hyde, S., & Ahn, L. V. (December 2008). Breaking audio CAPTCHAs. In *Advances in Neural Information Processing Systems 21, Proceedings of the Twenty-Second Annual Conference on Neural Information Processing Systems, NIPS*, (pp. 1625–1632). Vancouver, British Columbia, Canada.

von Ahn, L., Maurer, B., McMillen, C., Abraham, D., & Blum, M. (2008, September). Recaptcha: Human-based character recognition via web security measures. *Science Express, 321*(5895), 1465–1468.

Yan, J., & Ahmad, A. S. E. (December 2007). Breaking visual CAPTCHAs with naive pattern recognition algorithms. In *23rd Annual Computer Security Applications Conference, (ACSAC'07)*, (pp. 279–291).

Yan, J., & Ahmad, A. S. E. (October 2008). A low-cost attack on a Microsoft CAPTCHA. In *15th ACM Conference on Computer and Communications Security, (CCS'08)*, (pp. 543 – 554).

Yan, J., & Ahmad, A. S. E. (July 2008). Usability of CAPTCHAs or usability issues in CAPTCHA design. In *Symposium on Usable Privacy and Security, (SOUPS'08)*, (pp. 44 – 52).

ADDITIONAL READING

Baird, H. S., & Bentley, J. L. (January 2005). Implicit CAPTCHAs. In *Proceedings, SPIE/IS&T Conference on Document Recognition and Retrieval XII (DR&R2005)*, San Jose, CA.

Chan, T. Y. (November 2003) Using a text-to-speech synthesizer to generate a reverse Turing test. *Proceedings of 15th IEEE International Conference on Tools with Artificial Intelligence (ICTAI 03)*, (pp. 226–232).

Chew, M., & Baird, H. S. (2003). BaffleText: A human interactive proof. *Proceedings, 10th SPIE/IS&T Document Recognition and Retrieval Conference (DRR2003)*, Santa Clara, CA, (pp. 305-316).

Chow, R., Golle, P., Jakobsson, M., Wang, L., & Wang, X. (2008). Making CAPTCHAs clickable. In *HotMobile '08: Proceedings of the 9th Workshop on Mobile Computing Systems and Applications*, (pp. 91 – 94). New York, NY, USA.

Haichang, G., Liu, H., Yao, D., Liu, X., & Aickelin, U. (July 2010). An audio CAPTCHA to distinguish humans from computers. In *Third International Symposium on Electronic Commerce and Security*, (ISECS2010), (pp. 265-269). Guangzhou, China.

He, P., Sun, Y., Zheng, W., & Wen, X. (January 2008). Filtering short message spam of group sending using CAPTCHA. *Proceedings of Int. Workshop on Knowledge Discovery and Data Mining (WKDD 2008)*, (pp. 558–561).

Hoque, M. E., Russomanno, D. J., & Yeasin, M. (2006, March-April). 2D CAPTCHAs from 3D models. *Proceedings of IEEE SoutheastCon, 2006*, 165–170. doi:10.1109/second.2006.1629343

Jain, A., Raj, A., Pahwa, T., Gupta, A., & Jain, A. (July 28-31, 2009). *Overlapping variants of sequenced tagged Captcha (STC): Generation and their comparative analysis*. In The First International Conference on 'Networked Digital Technologies, (NDT'09), Ostarava, The Czech Republic.

Khan, B., Alghathbar, S. K., Khurram Khan, M., Al-Kelabi, M. A., & Al Ajaji, A. (2010). Considering students' emotions in computer-mediated learning environments. In *Security technology, disaster recovery and business continuity* (pp. 8–17). SpringerLink. doi:10.1007/978-3-642-17610-4_2

Lopresti, D. (May 2005). Leveraging the CAPTCHA problem. *Proceedings of 2nd International Workshop on Human Interactive Proofs (HIP 2005), LNCS 3517*, (pp. 97–110).

Misra, D., & Gaj, K. (2006). Face recognition CAPTCHAs. *Proceedings of Advanced International Conference on Telecommunications and Int. Conf. on Internet and Web Applications and Services* (AICT-ICIW 06), (p. 122).

Raj, A., Jain, A., Pahwa, T., & Jain, A. (2009). Analysis of tagging variants of sequenced tagged CAPTCHA (STC). *Science and Technology for Humanity (TIC-STH), 2009 IEEE Toronto International Conference*, (pp. 427 – 432).

Rusu, A., & Govindaraju, V. (2004). Handwritten CAPTCHA: Using the difference in the abilities of humans and machines in reading handwritten words. *Proceedings 9th International Workshop on Frontiers in Handwriting Recognition*, (pp. 226-231).

Shirali-Shahreza, M. (April 2006). Verifying spam SMS by Arabic CAPTCHA. *Proceedings of 2nd IEEE International Conference on Information and Communication Technologies: From Theory to Applications (ICTTA 06)*, Vol. 1, (pp. 78–83).

Shirali-Shahreza, M. (May 2008). Highlighting CAPTCHA. *Proceedings of the Conference on Human System Interaction (HSI 2008)*, (pp. 247–250).

Shirali-Shahreza, M. H., & Shirali-Shahreza, M. (2006, December). Persian/Arabic Baffletext CAPTCHA. *Journal of Universal Computer Science, 12*(12), 1783–1796.

Shirali-Shahreza, M. H., & Shirali-Shahreza, M. (November 2007). Localized CAPTCHA for illiterate people. *Proceedings of International Conference on Intelligent & Advanced Systems*.

Shirali-Shahreza, M. H., & Shirali-Shahreza, M. (October 2007). Multilingual CAPTCHA. *Proceedings of 5th International Conference on Computational Cybernetics*, (pp. 135–139).

Shirali-Shahreza, S., & Movaghar, A. (April 2007). A new anti-spam protocol using CAPTCHA. *Proceedings of 2007 International Conference Networking, Sensing and Control*, (pp. 234–238).

Shirali-Shahreza, S., Shirali-Shahreza, M., & Manzuri-Shalmani, M. T. (2007, July). Easy and secure login by CAPTCHA. *International Reviews on Computers and Software*, 2(4), 393–400.

Shirali-Shahreza, S., Shirali-Shahreza, M., & Movaghar, A. (April 2007). Exam HIP. *Proceedings of 2007 IEEE International Workshop on Anti-counterfeiting, Security, Identification (ASID 2007)*, (pp. 415–418).

Shirali-Shahreza, S., Shirali-Shahreza, M., & Movaghar, A. (July 2007). Restricted access to exam grades on the web by HIP. *Proceedings of 1st IEEE International Workshop on e-Activity (IEEE-IWEA2007)*, (pp. 967–971).

Von Ahn, L. (December 2005). *Human computation*. PhD thesis, School of Computer Science, Carnegie Mellon University, Pittsburgh, PA, USA.

Von Ahn, L., Blum, M., Hopper, N. J., & Langford, J. (May 2003). CAPTCHA: Using hard AI problems for security. *Proceedings of International Conference on the Theory and Applications of Cryptographic Techniques (EUROCRYPT 2003), LNCS 2656*, (pp. 294–311).

Von Ahn, L., Blum, M., & Langford, J. (2004, February). Telling humans and computers apart automatically. *Communications of the ACM*, 47(2), 56–60. doi:10.1145/966389.966390

Xu, S., Lau, F. C. M., Cheung, W. K., & Pan, Y. (2005, May). Automatic generation of artistic Chinese calligraphy. *IEEE Intelligent Systems*, 20(3), 32–39. doi:10.1109/MIS.2005.41

KEY TERMS AND DEFINITIONS

Bot: A sophisticated computer script/program developed to achieve a particular test by masquerading as a human.

CAPTCHA: Completely Automated Public Turing test to Tell Computers and Humans Apart is a test which distinguishes a human user from a computer program.

CFS (Color-Filling-Segmenation): The technique of flood-filling a closed region by starting from the interior of the region. Thus, a figure having multiple regions is filled with different colors, thus isolating the different regions.

Fragmentation: The technique of generating text which appears in broken form (not continuous). This is done to render techniques like CFS ineffective as the latter segments one actual block into multiple ones.

Pictionary: A picture-dictionary maintained by a hacker which stores the object pictures displayed in previous CAPTCHA rounds and also the names of the displayed objects for instant matching with pictures displayed in any future round.

Segmentation: The process of isolating the text characters in the CAPTCHA from background clutter as well as from each other.

Tag: An image which appears below an object picture. A Tag may be in the form of an OCR-based CAPTCHA and conveys information which is used by the user in his response to the CAPTCHA round.

Chapter 20
Embedded System Security Risk in a Green-House Environment

Trailokya Oraon
Jorhat Engineering College, India

ABSTRACT

Embedded systems are extensively used in the field of pervasive computing. These systems are used to such an extent that embedded systems are now controlled and monitored from remote locations by using Web services. Internet authorities are able to assign every device a unique Internet protocol address with the introduction of IPv6 on the Web. Peer-to-peer communication between Internet-enabled devices helped Web services to make performance improvement. On the worse side, it created new attacks on the components used in the embedded systems. The chapter discusses the details of security issues on a Web-enabled embedded system used in greenhouse environment. The devices used in greenhouse environment are monitored and controlled by different software components used in the entire system. Various vulnerabilities are introduced during entire development process of the greenhouse environment. The problem is to search the real threats, then define security policies and implement them during development process. The chapter discusses most of the vulnerabilities of a generalized greenhouse project and tries to find out possible security techniques to deal with the vulnerabilities. Instead of showing the design to build a greenhouse embedded system, it shows to introduce security policies at various levels of life-cycle, be it before development, during development, or after development.

1. INTRODUCTION

Our lives and our businesses depend unavoidably on computing systems and, increasingly, on embedded systems in particular. Applications of embedded systems to monitor and control the greenhouse environment has become a notion of pervasive computing and now these computing devices can be applied and are available anywhere and anytime. Embedded systems are generally hidden from the user (Marwedel, P., 2003). For example, proper use of greenhouse environment helps the crop-growers to maximize the productivity and better the quality of crops and seeds.

DOI: 10.4018/978-1-4666-0978-5.ch020

Embedded products and tools that growers have at their disposal to control the environment, are manipulated with respect to the important environmental influences on plant growth and development, for the actual optimization of the greenhouse environment. These embedded systems, which are ubiquitously used to sense, capture, store, process and transmit vital data used for control of the environment to maximize the photosynthetic process in the crop. Security observation is a basic requirement when an embedded system performs any of these tasks. As more and more embedded systems came to be accessed from remote locations, security became a major concern. Security of embedded systems employed in greenhouse environment provided new business opportunities and also prevents dangers of economical loss. For example, it prevents undue change of environmental changes and should help preserve grower's expectations. Examples of new business opportunities are secure embedded devices that are applied for use in timely production of crops. With the adoption of Internet Protocol version 6 (IPv6), network solutions for embedded devices, peer-to-peer communication is now possible and thereby giving easy access and control of such devices from remote locations. This has resulted an increasing number of security breaches, which have been detected in embedded systems in recent years, which also reveals the importance of fundamental security solutions. Security solutions, which are basically applied to embedded systems that also incorporate the concept of network model, are specific cryptographic algorithms, adding security functionality to the network security protocols or adding one more security layer to the embedded device (Summers, R., C., 1997). In general, most developers apply security 'patches' only at the beginning of implementation phase or only if a security faults is detected. The embedded system data processing itself is vulnerable to its own system as we shall see this in section 7. The chapter discusses the various embedded system security issues with reference to systems employed in greenhouse environment. A very specific concept of life-cycle of embedded products and the vulnerabilities is discussed in section 2 and 3 respectively. The section 4 and 5 discusses secure design policies and why secure design is needed. The reason and concept of greenhouse security is discussed in section 6. To design a highly secure system, different design strategies are proposed. This strategy consists of prevention, tolerance, removal and forecasting. Prevention and tolerance are basic security strategies while removal and forecasting are strategies for security assurance.

It is often argued for giving too much importance to security of embedded systems (Paar, C., & Weimerskirch, A., Jan. 2007). Security policies should be implemented to tackle real threats. Vulnerabilities arises when a system is connected to network and also when working as a single system. Mere encryption and decryption of incoming and outgoing data does not provide a complete integrated solution of security. Security should not be on short term benefits, but long-term benefits should be taken keeping the cost factors into account.

The security philosophy of almost all greenhouse embedded systems is quite same. The example project given in the chapter does not show how the system is designed, but it shows the real security threats, the security policies built on these threats and which security policies are can be applied for the greenhouse system. Since most embedded systems can be controlled and monitored through wired and wireless network.

2. LIFE-CYCLE OF EMBEDDED SYSTEM FOR GREENHOUSE ENVIRONMENT

In general, there are three phases of any embedded system: development, use and disposal.

• Development of the system for the environment

- Deployment and use of the system in the environment
- Disposal / Removal/ Transfer of the system from the environment

The "*Development of the system for the environment*" incorporates all activities starting from system requirement specification to acceptance testing. It also includes the activities until the final system is delivered. All activities are carried out only after proper study of the environment and various climatic factors that are going to affect the system. The various activities of this phase are Requirement specification, Design, Production, Product Shipment and Support/ Maintenance. The "*Deployment and use of the system in the environment*" starts when the system passes user's acceptance testing and the system is deployed in the environment. Deployment activities consist of installation of the system and configuring the system to match and create the greenhouse environment. Use phase consists of educating the users of the system, alternating periods of correct service delivery, service outage, service shutdown and maintenance. The "*Disposal / Removal/ Transfer of the system from the environment*" phase starts when the system no longer performs its activities. In such as case, the system may not be able to monitor and control the environment according to the requirement or the system may start malfunction under specific climatic changes. It can also start when the climate undergo an abrupt change or the device is transferred from one person to another. Activities of this phase include removal of the storage media, software, components and data stored on the device. The significant aspect of this phase is that it prevents release of vulnerable data, information or software. In maintaining greenhouse environment this phase will prevent flow or usage of data when the system is moved from one location to another. The security is needed to be considered in this phase to preserve and adhere to copyright, statutory and regulatory requirements, verify the authenticity, confidentiality and integrity of the system. We will further study this in later sections.

3. SOURCES OF VULNERABILITIES IN LIFE-CYCLE

In the previous section we have discussed the phases of life-cycle of embedded systems in greenhouse environment. Now let use analyze the vulnerabilities of each phase of life-cycle. Vulnerabilities and security threats can rise in every process and entities associated with processes created before, during or end of life-cycle of embedded system.

Vulnerabilities in Development Phase

The correct physical world phenomenon cannot be predicted at the start of a greenhouse environment project. Poor analysis of the environment conditions can be a source of vulnerability. In the development phase, the system and environment analyst who does not processes enough knowledge are a source of vulnerabilities. There are developers, who assist in this phase, but their aim is to harm the development phase with the available development tools, production tools and test tools, thus damaging hardware and software process, can be the source vulnerabilities.

Vulnerabilities in Deployment and Use Phase

When system was brought to the environment, the persons responsible for installation and configuration, the administrators, users responsible for providing service, service providers, entities associated with the service, climatic conditions, natural disasters of the environment and adversaries from other living things of the environment are the source of the vulnerabilities. Improper handling of the system by limited users of the system and lack of proper manual of running the system can be a source of vulnerability during the use phase. Though the basic source of new vulnerability during this phase is forcing the system to create the requisite environment even during the abrupt environmental climatic changes and conditions.

Vulnerabilities in Disposal/Removal/Transfer Phase

Security is not a major concern in design phase when the system is removed from the environment. A major source of vulnerability in this phase is when the system is transferred to another location with the information and data used in the previous location and the users are unaware about this fact. Availability vulnerabilities and threats are ignored during security analysis when there is a complete discard of the system from the environment.

In the next section, we will further study the reasons of doing security analysis to the design methodology of embedded systems.

4. SECURITY IN PRODUCT DESIGN METHODOLOGY

Our requirement defines the embedded system design, what product we are going to apply, whom we are asking for a solution. It may range from a least expensive thermostat to computer that uses microprocessors that controls variety of equipments used to perform specific task. For some, it is analog device that considers multiple sensors in a single environment when it performs control actions. But it is always a device with some RAM, ROM, storage media and some peripheral device performing some desired input and output. Design should support development process so that the result is outcome-oriented. Developers have enough flexibility to adopt new tools so that they can deliver the best to meet the governance criteria

and schedule tasks according to the design. Design methodology helps to analyze the requirements, conceptualizing, planning, developing, testing and supporting the components, products and solutions that respond to those requirements. So a product design advances through various levels down the completion and final delivery.

At the *Business level,* design process develops preliminary specifications for the proposed product and helps to enable investment risk. At the *operational level,* the product requirements are drawn in detail with adherence to plans and checkpoints. At the *schedule assignment, design, testing and debugging and delivery levels,* peer design reviews are conducted. The most critical stage in this process is testing and debugging where the test plans are executed. This is one area where the development process moves back to design. So the information assets need to be protected and the products developed to acceptable quality tolerance. At the *final release level,* the user manual and documentation are developed before taken to the deployment site. Here, the checkpoints help to test the quality of the product to acceptable conditions. Initial approaches to support security in product design methodology are described in (Uner, E., Sept. 2005, Jansen, W., Gavrila, S., Korolev, V., Heute, T., & Séveillac, C. June 2004, Verbauwhede1 I., & Schaumont, P., Jul. 2007, Arora, D., Ravi, S., Raghunathan A., & Jha, N., K., Aug. 2005).It is necessary to know the threat(s) of a product under consideration and then devise security policies. Threats help to define policies and a secure product is designed based on those policies.

The embedded product design is a combination of hardware and software. The hardware is generally selected based on current availability. The most critical module is the software module selection. Most system vulnerability arises from this module, and even more, if it uses the concept of network model, hence this is one area where security is a major concern. The existence of hardware and software on a common platform is an area of vulnerability. There are certain vulnerabilities that exist side-by-side. For example the information gained from power consumption, electromagnetic leaks, timing, sound, physical implementation of cryptosystem can make the system vulnerable (Weingart, S., 2000, Quisquater, J., J., & Samide, D., 2002). Vulnerability assessment in design process is mostly done in software. Vulnerabilities arises when the *scope is too big for software* (software modules are written for existing software), when there is *too much interaction between software modules* (execution of a sub-function which never really belongs to the main executing function), *when software modules are not clearly defined* (there is no cleanly defined interfaces and function use different schemes to achieve results), when there is *no establishment of communication protocols* (lack of usage of proper global variables and not adhering to module development rules) and *inflexible platform* (modules calling the remote procedures of different platform and presence of security loopholes on the executing platform).

Embedded software products that are designed on client-server paradigm are highly vulnerable to network threats. Designing the software around sockets and messages opens up potential security holes in the system to the network. We require high degree of security in software module design as the users of the system always thinks the network as secure and thus forgets to apply security policies. Applying the network security policies in modular design, like client-server, will give the developer and other users quite some time to be aware of security functionalities.

No system is ever 100 percent secure. Security is not a mixture of cryptographic algorithms and security protocols to the system. Security is a process, not a product. It changes from time to time depending on requirement. Why we require security in embedded products varies from user to user and depends on what we are going to use, where we are going to use and who will use it. The basic requirement of security for most users is to preserve the identity of the system and authenticate the system so that others cannot access it. Different security responses of analyst, developers, administrators, maintenance personnel, authorize users of system are generated during product design at any time, be it before development, during development, after development, during the use phase and during disposal phase. Good security policies will help the investors invest in the product confidently, thus making sure that their revenue is properly protected.

To remove some of the above vulnerabilities and threats of an embedded product, we need to enforce security to product design. Most of the security design discussions on removing vulnerabilities are at sections 9, 10, 11 and 12, which are explained with reference to a developed system. In the following section, we will see what basic necessities are required to develop a secure product. (Ravi, S., Raghunathan, A., Kocher, P., & Hattangady, S., 2004, Hwang, D., Schaumont, P., Verbauwhede, I., & Yang, S., 2006, Grand, J. 2004).

5. REQUIREMENTS FOR A SECURE PRODUCT DESIGN

Security in the design should be considered from the beginning. In the previous sections, vulnerabilities in different phases in life-cycle and the requirement of security in design has been emphasized, now we see the possible security solutions for the threats.

Security analysis is an initial requirement in designing a secure embedded system. Most threats and their counter-measures are studied for a long time(Ravi, S., Raghunathan, A., & Chakradhar, S., 2004). Security threats of and from both internal and external components should be considered. This will help to build a protected security policy. Generally, the security consideration of a system is frozen at the start, as development process for most products goes through adhoc approaches. There is always a need to hire a security specialist.

Security threats are analyzed by building threat models. A threat model is necessary to analyze the threats, assess the probability of potential harm and attack priorities. A hierarchical arrangements of threats in threat model helps to know the different attack goals of the attacker to the system. A few basic points that should be taken in security requirements are:

- Hardware and software involvement in an embedded system design incurs cost. Securing an embedded product on heterogeneous platforms still incurs bigger cost; so only the real threats of the system should be considered.
- External sources of power needed by an embedded product should undergo change or recharge. Powerless systems open-up disposal security threats and loss of data.
- There should be a requirement to hire a experienced security specialist as most developers use tools they apply generally to all products without knowing the real threats.
- Too much security is harm to the product design itself(Ravi, S., Kocher, P., Lee, R., McGraw, G., & Raghunathan, A., June 2004). So, equilibrium should be maintained between flexibility and security, thus saving resources.
- Violation of integrity should be checked so that components of the system do not behave abruptly under normal conditions.
- A system should learn to secure by itself. The example section of the chapter explains in detail on this point. A self-adaptive, self-configuring or self-restoring techniques preserves security.
- Present security solutions should pave the way for new security solutions with less computational requirements, smaller size and lower energy consumption.

- Applying security policies should not cause the development process to cross the deadline in delivering the final product. Time-to-market is an essential which increases the value the product. So organizations should make to invest more money on right security practices to deliver the product within specified deadlines.
- A mandate for continuous security improvement in technology and manufacturing drives accountability and action.
- A community of hardware and software engineers that innovate and share practices and tools for secure product development.
- Integration across products that is achieved through client use cases, scenarios, and end-to-end usage threads in concert with an architectural framework that enables componentization.
- Consumability analysis that looks beyond product defects to the client experience of using the offerings.
- Organizations should be responsible for implementing security awareness programs for their development teams. Persons working in development teams should have different roles to create *security awareness programs* so that they deliver the right information to each other and the impact of security issues on the clients. The key concern on the technical details on security issues lies in the hands of developers.

Security standards, security practices and security compliance criteria play an important role in supporting the product development process of organizations. In the overall requirement, hardware, software and services development are governed by four necessary factors: assets security, check points in product development, security and quality plans, product testing (Allan, D., Hahn, T., Szakal, A., Whitmore, J., & Buecker, A., Mar. 2010).

Resources used in development projects are always required by an organization. In fact, they are never isolated. *"Security of assets"* aims in protecting disclosure of user's privacy, location and personal information and other proprietary information. *"Checkpoints Product in Development"* help to review the development when the project moves from one level to the next. These checkpoints can be used as control points for assessing project risk, expense control, product quality, security issue review, and for synchronization of a secure project plan. The project development team should define and remove the vulnerabilities for the prior work before transition to the next level. If there is any change in scope or content, it should prove the change from a security level. Both *"security and quality plans"* are required within an organization. Security issues are discussed above while a *quality plan* highlights the technical and audit requirements for asset control, along with the standards and practices for quality engineering to be applied in the development process. The development checkpoint plan should help to review all of the security and quality plans, practices, and findings in the development phase. *"Product testing"* is required to verify the functionality of the various components of the product and whether it secures from the vulnerabilities in the product. It should go through all official design specifications of component, product, or solution. Security mecha-

nisms and services included into the component, product, or solution should be verified.

6. SECURITY PHILOSOPHY OF EMBEDDED SYSTEM DEVELOPMENT

In our embedded system development for green-house environment, focus is given on building security to real threats rather than trying to make the system fully secured. Hardware threats like theft of the device, threat of changing climatic influences on the material of the device are not considered in this design methodology. Security policies build on these threats can be implemented by *educating and creating awareness* of user of the device. Rather we keep our eye on the software threats, which generally occurs both internally and externally in the system.

With the introduction of Internet Protocol version 6 (IPv6) in the internet, peer-to-peer communication became possible, and data transmission of each device with another device become faster, thus open doors to new level of attacks. Mostly, these attacks are external. Everything now happens in the web. Every device transmitting data is stored on the web database, monitored and then controlled through the web. We just require a browser to open a web page and then request a web form from the web server, fill data in the

Figure 1. Components of a development process in our embedded system development

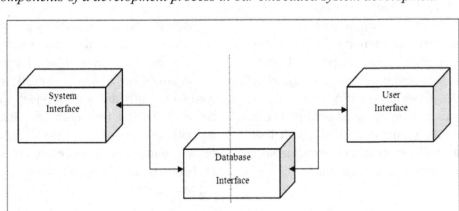

form, then send it to the web database via the web server. Designing a web system has become an assembly line job; no more complex algorithms to prove and no more costly project overruns. Our embedded system is monitored and control through web interface. Such a design requires a database to interface with the user interface and the system interface as shown in Figure 1.

The embedded system development process comprises the system interface development process and the user interface development process as the two main sub-processes. These sub-processes are connected to each other by the database server process. The database server process uses a connector, typically database driver software, which interfaces with the involved software modules, so that they can talk to each other efficiently without interfering each other task. This type of design establishes a client-server model, which makes us to think about security from a different angle. Security policy to stop the *interception* attacks, to stop *fabrication* attacks, to stop *modification* attacks, to stop *repudiation* attacks, to have strong *access control* and to stop *interruption* of resources, are built both at the system interface level and user interface level as shown in Figure 2.

Different components that are required for user interface design are scripting language, SQL queries, and HTML. All free software, that is, Linux, the popular open source operating system which makes use of the apache, the popular web server, MySQL database and PHP/Perl scripting languages can be is used to take the advantage of cost. Linux an operating system is itself secure. Other packages which are free are bind package for developing a DNS system, the sendmail package, which are installed on Linux by default; these give us an added security, which is cost. That does not mean that other software products, like the SQL server, Visual Studio.NET, IIS Web server, all from Microsoft, does not give that advantage. These proprietary products greatly help by reducing time needed during development.

The *system interface* includes a component in the form of device drivers. The device driver interfaces the devices with the software modules. A device driver generally uses the open, read, write and close functions to interface with device. As said earlier, a system should learn to protect by itself. A software system handling multiple parameters may violate integrity and system starts to respond unusual events. In our embedded system, integrity of the system can be maintained if some security

Figure 2. Security policies are inserted at the system interface and user interface

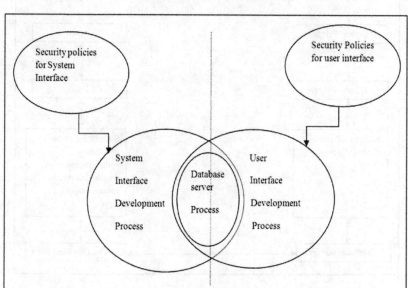

rules are inserted at the system interface level. There is certainly a modular concept involved in our embedded system design, where sockets, message queues, threads are different interprocess communication mechanisms that are used in client-server model for communication between modules. Not all security policies are applied in this kind of client-server design. A few security policies related to confidentiality, authentication, integrity, non-repudiation and access control are included into our embedded system development.

To make viewing of data on these web pages secure and to make sure that the user is viewing the correct data, and not a tempered data, the data can should be digitally signed by the server and sent to the client. The access control security policy determines read and write permission to and from the database by the users. If the client wishes to update any parameters of the system, it must first authenticate itself. Proof of identities is established using *authentication* mechanism. The authenticated information should be encrypted using cryptographic algorithms and sent to the server after signing the information.

An embedded system may have limited authorized users instead of a single user. A change made by one user may later refuse that he had done a change. The principle of non-repudiation defeats such possibilities of denying changes once sent.

We have incorporated the email system as a security measure of recovering authentication violation. Developing mail server and mail clients should be removed from the development process as these are very huge software modules and it would require designing a huge set of security policies which would stop us to deliver the final product in time. It would be wise to take an existing authenticated email server, a DNS server for our embedded system.

Unfortunately, there does not exist an exact definition of software engineering. There is no such hard and fast rules that certain security policies should exists at a certain level, otherwise this would make us overlook security rules, and end up making policies without actually implementing them. Figure 3 gives us a brief look at our final security design.

Figure 3. Insertion of security policies in the design levels

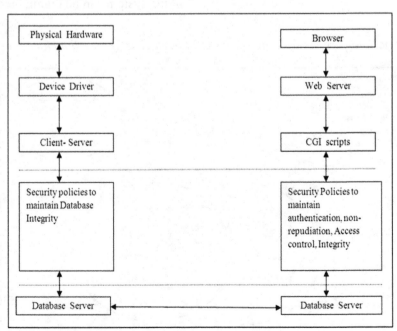

So our embedded system development has the system development process and the user interface development process. The client-server concept is used during design with the introduction of database server process as a middleware. The client-server is the application program that takes processes data to and from the database and communicates with the device via the device driver. Security policies are inserted between the client-server module and the database server module. Similarly, the security mechanisms are introduced between scripting languages and the database server when the user submits a filled out web form to the web server and the web server update the database. The system interface development process takes this update from database and sends requisite signals to the device to set the greenhouse environment. Let us see what security policies and be best in our project for greenhouse environment.

7. SECURITY AT SYSTEM INTERFACE LEVEL

As said in the earlier section, data of an embedded system is itself a threat to the system. The basic functionality of system interface module is to collect data of various environment physical parameters sent by the different sensors attached to the device. We are considering a generalized version of a greenhouse project where the device consists of two temperature sensors and two humidity sensors. All these sensors are connected to a microcontroller that processes data and sends it to a computer via a serial port. The device driver collects the data stores on the database after appropriate processing. There are also two temperature control units and two humidity control units. These control units are connected to a separate microcontroller that accepts signals from the same computer via a different serial port. So communication with the device and computer is done through serial port 1, say COM1, which is used for monitoring purposes, and serial port 2, say COM2, which is used for controlling purposes.

The microcontroller send all four sensor data to COM1, where the device driver further sends to the client-server module for processing and finally the data gets stored in the database. Microcontroller sends first temperature sensor data for a finite interval of time, followed by second temperature sensor, then the first humidity sensor followed by second humidity sensor data for the same finite interval respectively. This occurs in an iterative fashion as in Figure 4.

The computer system interface software comprises the monitoring process and the controlling process. A primary level of security is introduced in the microcontroller itself, for example, the Figure 4 shows that the device informs the monitoring process whenever it finishes sending a block of data for a particular sensor. This piece of information is the *critical data* for the system. The controlling device takes actions whenever the controlling process records parameter(s) that violates the climatic conditions of greenhouse environment. The threat factor is that the critical data send by the microcontroller after sending a block of monitoring data, is missed by the monitoring process, which results in violation of integrity of the database. This makes the controlling process to check the condition with respect to specified values set to control the greenhouse environment to send signals to the controlling device. This harms the environment and the entities associated with it.

The reason for violation of integrity can be explained by mechanism of process switching and the occurrence of event by the controlling process. The two processes are under the influence of various other processes, for example the scheduling process, the database process and the operating system itself. A signal may be sent by the controlling process at the moment when the critical data is sent by the device. It depends on the mercy of the scheduler as to which process it decides to give hold of the processor.

Figure 4. Flow of data from the microcontroller device to the computer system and occurrence of threats

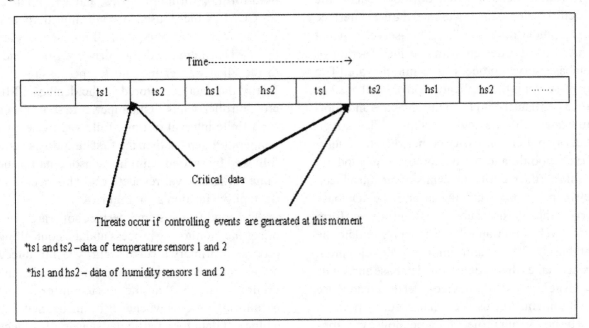

There can be three ways of dealing with this threat. Firstly, the critical data should be sent along the each temperature or humidity data. Second, process priority should be implemented with the process at system interface. The first method is not possible because 8-bits cannot be fragmented into two sections, for example, 2-bits for critical data and 6-bits for usual data. The second method may be feasible, as the monitoring process may be given higher priority compared to controlling process when such situations occur. But, such solution may introduce long delay for the controlling process and control devices may not be initiated on time. Finally, the only way to make the system adapt to itself by inserting some intelligence into the system. Just before inserting data into the database, the monitoring process can make the current data to be checked with the recent previous values (one or two values is sufficient) in the same database. If there is fractional or one or two units of change or no change from the previous value, the current data are inserted into the appropriate database table, otherwise it is discarded.

8. SECURITY AT USER INTERFACE LEVEL

The design in previous section showed that most user interface threats arises from the network and from the browser side. The two kinds of security generally applied at this level: the web security and the network security. The network security threats are beyond the scope of this chapter. The basic vulnerability at user interface level is modification of critical parameters needed to set up the environment, although there are other web security threats like interception, fabrication, modification and repudiation. Security policies are made at this level by understanding the threats.

Authentication

Authentication helps to establish identity of a person. The embedded system maintains a set of values of specific physical parameters needed to control the environment. The users want to set these parameters through the interface. So the users need to be authorized through authentication mechanisms. The general authentication mechanism used here is a login form where users are required to enter their username and password. Valid users are allowed to gain access to update the critical parameters of the embedded system. As database is updated, control actions specific to the update are taken by the controlling process. Mail server play and important role in authentication process. For example, if the user forgets his password or username or if he forgets some authentic personal information, such information are delivered to user email account on request.

Integrity

Violation of integrity means that the message is change before it reaches the intended recipient. The information that comes from the database through the web server may be changed and an authorized user may be viewing these values. Based on what the user view the data stored in the database on the user interface, the user can update the critical parameters, thus leading to threat for the entities associated with the environment. To counter attack such threat, the concept of digital signatures is used. The basic concept of digital signature is not to achieve confidentiality but achieve authentication and non-repudiation.

Non-Repudiation

Our embedded system consists of a limited group of users to run and control the system. On security analysis, it was found that due to some of the personal differences between users, some users develop intent of damaging the environment. They may update certain critical information in the system and try to repudiate that they are not responsible for such misdeeds. This kind of threat not only damages the system and the environment, but also hampers the confidence relationship with the developers, as the other user may continue to think to be some system defect. Security can be

given by creating an admin user, who is responsible for creating, deleting and managing users. When the user logs in, all the activities, for example the updating activity, of the user can be recorded in the log file or database.

Access Control

The access control security is applied in those greenhouse products where certain components of the system is used in one area belonging to an owner, and some components used in another belonging to another owner. Both having authority to monitor and control their respective areas, but uses the same web interface. The owner may have the intent to damage and access each other resources, thus affecting the objective of the system. In our project, if one part monitoring and controlling temperature and humidity belong one user, and the other part belong to another, then giving rights to access resources through the same web interface, each would suspect and blame the other if anything wrong happens during the working of the system. Even though they have monitoring rights to monitor each other system, the security of access control of their respective resources can help to develop healthy relationship and maintain assets in a better way.

Safeguards against SQL Injection Attack

When malicious SQL code is inserted into strings and then passed to an instance of database server for parsing and execution, it is called SQL injection attack. Since the database server executes any query, all possible SQL vulnerability assessment should be done. Injection vulnerability should be reviewed in any function that constructs SQL statements. The basic reason for such security is that the database instance will run all syntactically valid queries.

Basically, the primary form of SQL injection consists of direct insertion of code into user-input variables that are concatenated with SQL commands and executed. Malicious code that forms a less harmful injection attack is to insert data or metadata and fill up the storage space. When the stored strings are subsequently concatenated into a dynamic SQL command, the malicious code is executed.

The technique of filtering input is applied in applied in the greenhouse system to protect against SQL injection by removing escape characters. The number of input characters is not huge; this may not pose problems and provide a reliable defence.

9. PREVENTION: A SAFE STRATEGY

Vulnerabilities occur or are introduced during the development process. The best strategy to create a secure system is to prevent insecurities. Development process vulnerabilities and be stopped by means of prevention. There are various security policies and techniques adopted during development process. Identifying real threats help in improvement of the design and security policies applied in development methods from the beginning result in good strategies for preventing security vulnerabilities.

The embedded system developers work hard to present a secure system. But it seen that developing a fully secure system is not guaranteed, as the behavior of the system is quite unpredictable, and how the climatic conditions are going to behave during the use phase. After deploying our system, we can predict the network vulnerabilities from current network attacks on existing systems. So, there is a need to consider all undetectable vulnerabilities and the vulnerabilities that can arise from existing vulnerabilities, it is possible to built a safe prevention strategy.

10. TOLERANCE

Though there are defects and presence of vulnerabilities, the system continues tolerate faults and provide service. The techniques called tolerance techniques can be applied towards tolerance. There are three categories of applying tolerance techniques: Vulnerability detection, Recovery and Self-adaptive techniques.

Vulnerability Detection

Mechanisms exist to detect possible *vulnerability detection* in the system. Vulnerability detected during normal delivery of service is called *concurrent detection*. For instance, every file is checked for virus and other security rights before execution. The system may check for presence of vulnerability at any time. Due to this, the processes which are scheduled for execution are suspended. This is called preemptive way of detecting faults in the system. For example, the system may perform scanning operation to detect the existence of malicious files and take necessary precautions if any such files are detected.

Tolerance techniques do not simply mean vulnerability detection and vulnerability assessment. Tolerance techniques are also applied in a newly installed system, even though we know the system is free from insecurity. For example, we apply antivirus solutions in newly installed machine even though the machine is working in an isolated environment. There is always a general fear that there is some vulnerability. In fact we consider that there might be some vulnerability. We do not want that attack on the system should ever happen. The applied tolerance techniques should be capable enough to detect new threats. Therefore, we require these techniques as it prevents vulnerabilities from being activated again.

Vulnerabilities detected in the system can be collected for diagnosis purposes to prevent future vulnerability. However, the detected vulnerabilities should be isolated from the running process as it would create a new threat to the working system. For example, the vulnerabilities found in the computer system used in our greenhouse project running user interface process are isolated from the running process. This means that the processes used in the use phase can be prevented from the vulnerability by moving the vulnerability to a special container. If we want to physically isolate the vulnerability component from the process, we need an extra system with extra storage space, this may incur some additional cost on security research. This requires re-configuring the system, very similar to the existing working system in a similar environment. We need to build and initialize database tables, install and re-initialize the softwares or even re-initialize the registry of the operating system.

Recovery Safeguards

Though every possible technique is applied to detect vulnerability, we suppose an intruder detected vulnerability and performed an attack. What we can do in case of an attack? *Attack recovery safeguards* techniques are followed in these cases. Any attacks related to maintain confidentiality are hard to recover. Most of important data in our greenhouse system are not quite confidential. But these kinds of recovery safeguards can be taken during design if the system demands confidentiality. The usual way of recover from data integrity attacks is replace the data from backup. In our greenhouse system, the system interface process itself posed a threat to data integrity. If the mechanisms described in previous sections to counterattack this threat still cannot be removed, than techniques such as Rollback, Rollforward and Compensation can be applied. When the system is taken back to a saved state that existed prior to vulnerability detection, it is termed as *Rollback*; that saved state is a checkpoint. *Compensation* is replacing the redundant component to enable vulnerability elimination. For example, an old saved similar database can be used to activate the removal of vulnerability. *Rollforward* is setting the state without the detected vulnerability as a new state.

Self-Adaptive Techniques

Most greenhouse embedded systems have the capability to adapt themselves and the system develops the tendency to get fit itself to work in the given climatic conditions. In fact, recoverability should be an important security asset of the system. This gives us the idea that self-adaptive techniques should be a requirement of a secure design. The program should be self-configurable and necessary programs should re-execute by itself for total re-initialization to a saved state or start of the system. So, provisions to automatically recover might initiate some threats to the system. For example, if our greenhouse system hardware starts to malfunction, the whole hardware system functioning can be re-initialize to the start without affecting the other process of the system. The time required to undergo recoverability should be small so that the associated entities of the environment with the system remains unaffected. These security techniques are real challenges for the system employed in greenhouse environment.

It is not enough to make and qualify security test for a system. No doubt, the system can deliver secure information and deliver trusted service from all the security techniques applied at the system interface level and the user interface level and also applied to the system as a whole. Overall, prevention and tolerance techniques can fully make the system secure. But, assurance cannot be given by these techniques. An assurance technique helps to build confidence in the system by justifying the various applied security policies, the degree of accuracy of security specifications and thus increases the dependability on the system. The following sections discuss the assurance techniques that can help to qualify the security policies applied in the system.

11. REMOVAL OF VULNERABILITY

Vulnerabilities occurred during development process and use phase of the system is removed by applying vulnerability removal technique. This assurance technique can be performed during the entire life-cycle of the embedded system. There are three possible steps to remove vulnerability during development process of a system life-cycle: Verification, Diagnosis, and Correction

Verification is the process of checking whether security policies does not alter or restrict the behavior of the system. If it does, the other two steps follow: diagnosing the vulnerabilities that prevented the verification conditions from being fulfilled, and then performing the necessary corrections. After correction, the verification process should be repeated in order to check that vulnerability removal had no undesired consequences.

When verification process is applied without actual execution, it is referred as *static verification*. Inspection of the environment before installation of the greenhouse system, confirmed analysis of security algorithms used in development process of greenhouse system are kinds of static verification process. The other aspect of verification is *dynamic verification* which is done by actually executing the system. For example, there may exist some vulnerable files which are inserted into our greenhouse software system, which are safely removed during the use phase. So dynamic verification is an important concern to safety and security.

Vulnerability removal after deployment of the system in the environment is regarded as corrective and preventive measures. In our system, if a threat changes the values set by the user to control the environment to some unexpected value, say very large value, corrective measures help in removing these vulnerabilities. Preventive measures help to remove vulnerabilities by reporting and discovering the threat, before it changes the behavior of normal operation. For example, we have introduced some intelligence in security at the system interface level, as explained in previous section. Preventive measures try to find the fault based on preventive measures taken on the last fault detected. Preventive measures are also taken into account based on the threat model of other similar systems, for example, the preventive measures taken in the threat model of the controlling system applied in car cooling systems. The damage given by a threat in violating the integrity of the system can be separated patch by patch until the vulnerability is fully removed from the system.

12. VULNERABILITY FORECASTING

The security aspect of vulnerability forecasting is dependent on the applied security policies and behavior of the system. This type of forecasting increases the precautionary measures to be taken with respect to attack occurrence on the system. Our system is evaluated on two aspects:

- Running a host of processes on the operating system would lead to system attack.
- Evaluate the likelihood that an intruder in the network would interfere with the data changes in the database.
  Some recommendable issues where security forecasting is required for our system:
- There might be theft of the system or a component of a system.
- If the same computer is used to monitor and control more than one greenhouse environments, each having a separate software application to handle the data.
- Forecasting misuse of the system by humans.
- Forecasting possible threats in the system assets that create obstacles in achieving system objectives.
- Forecasting the attack of a common component, for e.g. a database component.
- Detecting the nature of attack in early stages

- Determine the severances of an attack on the associated entities with system's environment.

The above vulnerability forecasting issues can help to determine the assurance, thereby increasing the user confidence on the system.

13. CONCLUSION

Today, embedded systems are a part of life and their use determine the importance. The embedded system discussed in the chapter is controlled and monitored through a system interface and a web interface and such security of embedded systems is important. Focus is given on introducing strong security mechanisms to prevent damages so that new business opportunities can be developed. The chapter tries to formulate and implement new policies and keeping throughout the life-cycle of the system. It gives a new dimension of thinking of an existing product. There are a few security measures applied to our green-house project after understanding real threats such as accidental modification of data or violation of integrity, violation of access control methods and their implications on the system after applying appropriate security policies such as authentication, non-repudiation, access control and integrity. The chapter discusses the insertion of security policies at the design level and what policies are required to develop a secure system. The chapter stresses the point to hire a security analyst for a new-born system and how a simple vulnerability is can introduce major system setback and would result in deletion of the product from the market. Security policies are introduced into the design only after vulnerability assessment. The ensuing economical losses and the coming potential dangers pave the way to design a fundamental security solution. The chapter also discusses as how running multiple processes raises threats to the system and environment where the system is applied. The present security solution applied

to the project in such a way so that system can learn to apply security by itself. Further research is required in prevention and tolerance techniques so the vulnerabilities can be known before they appear in the system. Research is required to develop some kind of security intelligence into our system that will help to have assurance in security of the system.

REFERENCES

Allan, D., Hahn, T., Szakal, A., Whitmore, J., & Buecker, A. (March 2010). *Security in development: The IBM secure engineering framework.* Retrieved from http://www.redbooks.ibm.com/redpapers/pdfs/redp4641.pdf

Arora, D., Ravi, S., Raghunathan, A., & Jha, N. K. (August 2005). Architectural enhancements for secure embedded processing. *NATO Workshop on Security and Embedded Systems,* Vol. 2, (pp. 18-25).

Grand, J. (2004). Practical secure hardware design for embedded systems. *Proceedings of the 2004 Embedded Systems Conference,* San Francisco, California.

Hwang, D., Schaumont, P., Verbauwhede, I., & Yang, S. (2006). Multilevel design validation in a secure embedded system. *IEEE Transactions on Computers*, *55*(11), 1380–1390. doi:10.1109/TC.2006.184

Jansen, W., Gavrila, S., Korolev, V., Heute, T., & Séveillac, C. (June 2004). A unified framework for mobile device security. *Proceedings of the International Conference on Security and Management (SAM'04)*, (pp. 9-14).

Marwedel, P. (2003). *Embedded system design* (1st ed., pp. 1–8). Kluwer Academic Publishers.

Paar, C., & Weimerskirch, A. (2007, January). Embedded security in a pervasive world. *Information Security Technical Report*, *12*(3), 155–161. doi:10.1016/j.istr.2007.05.006

Quisquater, J. J., & Samide, D. (2002). Side channel cryptanalysis. *In Proceedings of the SECI 2002*, (pp. 179-184).

Ravi, S., Kocher, P., Lee, R., McGraw, G., & Raghunathan, A. (June 2004). Security as a new dimension in embedded system design. In *Proceedings ACM/IEEE Design Automation Conference*, (pp. 753-760).

Ravi, S., Raghunathan, A., & Chakradhar, S. (2004). Tamper resistance mechanisms for secure embedded systems. *In Proceedings of the International Conference of VLSI Design*, (pp. 605-611).

Ravi, S., Raghunathan, A., Kocher, P., & Hattangady, S. (2004). Security in embedded systems: Design challenges. *ACM Transactions on Embedded Computing Systems*, *3*(3), 461–491. doi:10.1145/1015047.1015049

Summers, R. C. (1997). *Secure computing: Threats and safeguards* (pp. 3–11). McGraw-Hill.

Uner, E. (September 2005). A framework for considering security in embedded systems. *Embedded.com*.

Verbauwhede1, I., & Schaumont, P. (July 2007). Design methods for security and trust. *Design, Automation & Test in Europe Conference & Exhibition*, (pp. 1-6).

Weingart, S. (2000). *Physical security devices for computer subsystems: A survey of attacks and defenses*. Workshop on Cryptographic Hardware and Embedded Systems.

KEY TERMS AND DEFINITIONS

Cryptography: Cryptography means computerized encoding and decoding of information in secret code or cipher. The encrypted messages are called cipher text. It is generally used to maintain confidentiality of a message.

DNS: The Domain Name System or DNS is a system that stores information about host names and domain names in a kind of distributed database on networks, such as the Internet. Most importantly, it provides an IP address for each host name, and lists the mail exchange servers accepting e-mail for each domain. The DNS provides a vital service on the Internet, because while computers and network hardware work with IP addresses to perform tasks such as addressing and routing, humans generally find it easier to work with host names and domain names, for example in URLs and e-mail addresses.

Email Server: Often referred to as simply "mail server", an e-mail server is a computer within your network that works as a virtual post office. A mail server usually consists of a storage area where e-mail is stored for local users, a set of user definable rules which determine how the mail server should react to the destination of a specific message, a database of user accounts that the mail server recognizes and will deal with locally, and communications modules which are the components that actually handle the transfer of messages to and from other mail servers and email clients. Email servers also store email data prior to delivery. It is a program running on a computer system that is constantly connected to the Internet.

IPv6: Internet Protocol Version 6 (IPv6) or Internet Protocol Next Generation (IPng) is a recent defined internet protocol. It is of 128 bits compared to its previous version IPv4, which is 32-bits. It is slowly covering most networks of the internet. The most important factor for replacement of IPv4 with IPv6 is the address depletion in the internet and IPv6 fills this space.

Microcontroller: It is a single purpose processing unit designed to execute small control programs, sometimes in real time. The program is frequently stored on the microcontroller in an area of nonvolatile memory. It is designed specifically for specific tasks such as controlling a specific system. Microcontrollers are electronic controls with added computer programming. They are often used by embedded systems working transparently for the user.

Chapter 21
Security in Wireless Sensor Networks with Mobile Codes

Frantisek Zboril Jr.
Brno University of Technology, Czech Republic

Jan Horacek
Brno University of Technology, Czech Republic

Martin Drahansky
Brno University of Technology, Czech Republic

Petr Hanacek
Brno University of Technology, Czech Republic

ABSTRACT

Security of wireless sensor networks (WSN) relates in many aspects to security of distributed systems. On the first sight WSNs form a large distributed ad-hoc system with lot of tiny devices that sense some phenomena and communicate wirelessly. Due to some limitations, among which the energy consumption problem is the most important one, security issues could demand different solutions than those used in the area of ordinary distributed systems. In this chapter, the authors briefly introduce the hardware and software approach to WSN design first, and then they define the main security aspects in such systems. Then some security mechanisms are presented, and their connection to possible countermeasures of the identified risks is described.

1 INTRODUCTION

Security of wireless sensor networks (WSN) relates in many aspects to security of distributed systems. On the first sight WSNs form a large distributed ad-hoc system with lot of tiny devices that sense some phenomena and communicate wirelessly. Due to some limitations, among which

the energy consumption problem is the most important one also the security issues could demand different solutions than these used in the area of ordinary distributed systems. In this chapter we briefly introduce the hardware and software approach to WSN design first and then we define the main security aspects in such systems. Then some security mechanisms will be presented and their connection to possible countermeasures of the identified risks will be described.

DOI: 10.4018/978-1-4666-0978-5.ch021

2 ARCHITECTURES OF WIRELESS SENSOR NETWORKS

Among architectures that relate to WSN belong those that relate to hardware realization of the WSN, especially realization of individual nodes. Also the architectures of software applications and their realization may influence security question of these kinds of systems. Communication protocols, which are used for interaction among particular node devices combine often both software and hardware aspects of WSN system realizations. These protocols will be also discussed in this section.

2.1 Hardware Realization of WSN Nodes

As mentioned earlier, WSN consists of a large number of tiny devices called sensor nodes. Some of the nodes are base-stations that serve as gateways between WSN and other network or just a control station and they gather data from the sensor network and send commands from the control system to the network. The WSN sensor nodes (except of the base-stations) should be able to sense, to communicate by wireless radio device and of course to make computations over sensed and received data. Architecture of a sensor node then consists of some sensor devices, microcontroller and a transceiver at least. Recently there are some solutions for scientific and commercial usage, among which predominate products of Sun and Crossbow (now MEMSIC) companies. Sun offers their SunSpots, which are based on 32bit ARM920T. They are programmable in Java and are more aimed to the networking. On the other hand the second company offers their nodes named Mica-2, MicaZ and IRIS (usually called simply as motes) that are programmable in C or nesC language and because of their lower-level background they are also probably more energy thrifty than the SunSpots. Motes are based on Atmel A128L and A1281 microcontrollers. In the following text we will be mostly concentrated on

the motes because the idea of simple device of extreme low energy consumption is more relevant for security questions in WSN as we will present them in this text.

2.2 Software Applications for WSN

In these days WSN programming often means to implement a program in a C-dialect called nesC. This language is such modification that enables to create the software as a hierarchic module structure. The lowest level modules are these working with device hardware and implement commands from higher level modules and on the contrary they propagate up the events raised on the hardware (data sensing, time clock events, message reception etc.). Along with nesC the programming environment contains also library known as TinyOS (Levis, 2006) that provides modules of various purposes ranging from hardware platform specific modules to general modules that can be used across the similar type of hardware. General modules provide hardware abstraction and we are using them mostly and only in some specific cases where we have to use hardware specific modules. Due to this fact we are able to build our application across similar platforms (for example MicaZ and IRIS) without changes. nesC/TinyOS applications are compiled to a binary file and the binary module then may be loaded into motes flash memories.

The second area that relates to the dynamism of the program code in the nodes uses mobile codes as the programming paradigm for the WSN. Mobile code usually consists of the control code, a state that means data, variables etc. and some attributes. The attributes are usually some meta-data describing the code itself, for example code owner, producer, trust level and so on. In general, mobile codes or mobile agents have been recognized as beneficial in many aspects. Lange and Oshima summarized these benefits in (Lang and Oshima, 1999) and had found seven arguments for mobile agents:

- *Reduce Network Load*: Data are processed on the place where they have been collected. Instead of sending them to a server, an agent that process the data and which is of smaller size then the data is transported to the node.
- *Overcome Network Latency*: Agents can act locally at a controlled device instead of controlling such real-time device remotely by messages and commands passing.
- *Encapsulate Protocols*: Agent can move to some nodes and establish communication channels between these nodes, which are based on proprietary protocols.
- *Execute Asynchronously and Autonomously*: They can better adapt on mobile systems that cannot rely on reliable and continuously available link connection. Agents may do their tasks autonomously and after they finish and find the connection open they send the result to the home device.
- *Adapt Dynamically*: Agents may autonomously distribute themselves in the network in such way that they constitute optimal configuration of solving of the given task.
- *Are naturally Heterogeneous*: From both perspectives – software and hardware – the computer network is heterogeneous. Agents are able to better adapt on various platforms and to complete their task in such heterogeneous environment.
- *Are Robust and Fault-tolerant*: They are able to resist against faults during communication and surrounding influences.

Nevertheless, the negatives of use of mobile codes or agents still prevail and they are not the mainstream in the area of WSN at the present time. The most significant reason against agents in the WSN is that the mobility of codes means considerable energy demands as radio communication between nodes means significant energy costs for the devices.

It is worth to mention that there have been recently also efforts to make the TinyOS system to be dynamic and reprogrammable as various modules of the program systems are added and deleted to/from the motes at WSN work time (Munawar et al., 2010). We understand that mobile codes are transported inside a distributed system and they are interpretable by some kind of virtual machines. The virtual machines are then implemented at the particular devices of the system. In WSN these devices are the motes. In our approach the dynamic codes are these that are interpretable on a virtual machine implemented in the motes. Mobile codes are usually referred as agents but due to the lack of some agent properties (e.g. reactivity or flexibility) we prefer to call them mobile codes. Among the systems supporting mobile codes paradigms belong Agilla (Fok et. al., 2009), ActorNet (Kwon et. Al., 2006) aimed to the motes and for example MAPS (Fortino et. al., 2009) designed for Java environment of SunSpots. Beside communication costs that take passing codes among particular nodes, it might be considered that the dynamic memory, in which the code is usually stored during its execution on a mote, is also limited. Another argument against the use of such paradigms in WSN programming brings some security problems that will be described later in this chapter.

2.3 Communication Protocols

At the physical and link levels the devices, or better their transceiver, are compatible with IEEE 802.15.4 specifications. To be concrete the DSSS (*Discrete Spectrum Spread Signal*) protocol is used at the physical layer. Communication is performed at 868 MHz, 915 MHz or IMS 2.4 GHz bandwidths. At the link layer the access to the physical channels, frame transmissions and possible network beaconing or CSMA/CA is guaranteed. More about 802.15.4 protocol specifications can be found for example in (Sastry and Wagner, 2004).

The higher layers are network and application layers that are known as ZigBee. In 802.15.4

specifications the device architecture divides nodes to full function devices and reduced function devices. At the network and application layers of the ZigBee specifications the devices are understand to be coordinators, routers or end devices. Only the end devices may be those with reduced functionality. Coordinators are responsible of network building, synchronization etc. The end devices can only communicate with a router and their meaning is to sense and collect data.

3 SECURITY THREATS IN SENSOR SYSTEMS WITH MOBILE CODES

The security analysis means the identification of risks in a system. Consequently identification of possible threads plays an important role in the process of risk analysis. For this reason we identify threads in the discussed systems from the point of WSN view as well as from the mobile code view. Both approaches provide then some common threat that should be sorted out by some appropriate countermeasures.

3.1 Security Threads in WSN

Computing in sensor networks pose problems to networking due to changing the physical location that requires continuous reconfiguration of the data links. If the connectivity cannot be always maintained, applications also have to handle extended off-line periods as well. The code in sensor network nodes generally runs in the hostile environment. From the security point of view there are a number of threats for the sensor network. The main threats include (Hanacek, 2005).

- *Eavesdropping of Communication*: The attacker can obtain all available information about the sensor network, including security relevant information and position of individual nodes from the eavesdropped messages.

- *Replay Attack*: The attacker is not able to break the cryptographic protection of messages but is able to re-send previously sent genuine messages.

- *Jamming the Communication*: Injecting noise in the radio channel can be used to make the communication within the network impossible. This attack could be made more difficult by using spread spectrum radio channels.

- *Denial of Service*: The attacker nodes can produce a large number of demands to fill-up network nodes or exhaust the node batteries.

- *Node Masquerade*: The attacker produces its own net nodes and attempts to connect these bogus nodes to the existing net.

- *Falsification of Sensor Data*: The attacker nodes can produce a counterfeit sensor data that they send to other sensor network nodes for distortion of sensor data.

- *Tampering with the Node Computer*: The attacker is able to use a direct logical or physical manipulation with the node to change the behavior of the node and, consequently perform further attacks to the rest of the network nodes. The attacker can also acquire the cryptographic keys stored in the node computer.

3.2 Security Threats of Mobile Codes

If we consider mobile code to be interpretable on a device, then threats are extended with these that relate to mobile agents security and were described e.g. in (Loureiro et. al., 2000). However, the mobile code suffers from considerable security problems. In general, security of mobile codes can be divided into security of device that receives possible dangerous code and security of the code that will be carried out by the device.

A mobile code, which is permitted and executed on a platform, may be dangerous in the following aspects:

- *Resource Wasting*: Code if properly executed may produce lot of messages that consequently can bring collapse of other devices or this can produce a lot of data to be stored on the mote or just to run inefficiently.
- *Spying*: If data resources are not protected and agent is able to access them then problem of platform data integrity and confidentiality arises.
- *Agent Masquerade*: Agent tries to persuade platform that its owner or sender is other than the really one. Then such platform can take an incorrect reputation of the presented owner or sender and treat the agent as trustworthy while it is not.

On the other hand there exist threats for a mobile interpretable code. Running mobile code in a hostile environment means that programs or program fragments are executed in computation devices that could have different interests in comparison to the author of the code. This problem can also arise when a (non-mobile) code is withdrawn from a device and put to another, hostile one. Threads of this kind may be categorized as follows:

- *Eavesdropping of Agent Code*: Mobile agent may intent to keep its code and data they carry confidential. But if the agent travels around the network in its open form there is no problem for any platform to read the agent code.
- *Modification of Agent Code*: Also when the agent code is not protected and its integrity is not ensured by some integrity supporting mechanism then there is no problem for any platform to modify the agent code.
- *Full and Proper Execution*: Agent supposes that soon or later it will be properly and completely executed on the platform. But it is difficult to ensure that an unreliable platform will always completely and correctly execute the code.

- *False Service Outputs*: Hostile platform may provide false data either in the form of false sensor data or it may provide false results of a service executed by the agent on the platform. Agent's behavior is then not correct even when the code is interpreted properly.
- *Correct Transport*: Codes are not transported as they desire. Malicious nodes may put the agents outside agent's area of interest or they can delete these codes from the system.

The first sort of problems could be reduced by a proper access policy of the note and it should be guaranteed that the agent code will not be attacked by the platform what is quite difficult task. In (Farmer, 1996), these threats were classified as impossible, possible but not easy and easy. Among impossible were classified threats that the interpreter will not execute the code correctly and completely, that the platform interpreter is tamper resistant, that data that are carried by the mobile code remains confidential and that platform must correctly transport the agent. The privacy of inter-agent communication and distinguishing code from its clone also belong among impossible tasks. Difficult but possible tasks are authorization of agents and agent senders by the interpreter, design of a secure agent language and design of mechanisms that may control that an agent is in a sage state. Finally, under the easy tasks are understood the following: authentication of code sender, checking of code integrity, agent's confidentiality during transmission and protecting interpret against malicious agents.

Both analyses show that the security countermeasures fall into three areas – protection of radio channel, protection of messages and protection of node hardware. Making the motes more tamper resistant is usually not economically viable. Therefore we must sometimes admit that the attacker could compromise the sensor nodes. Also to protect mobile code against malicious platform and against some threats that were discussed above is not possible unless we use trusted network of nodes where code integrity, confidentiality, correct execution and transport are ensured. Following sections discuss possibility of security improvement in some of the above mentioned points.

3.3 Security Countermeasures and Security Mechanisms

Above described problems may be solved by using security mechanism like cryptography or secure tamper-resistant devices. However other countermeasures may be considered, for example tracking of agent history and interpretation process, this text will go on with discussion how to use cryptography and tamper-resistant devices as countermeasures to the above risks.

First we discuss how recent specifications deal with the security issues and for this reason we start with the ZigBee protocols. It should be no surprise that ZigBee specifications pay close attentions how to secure communication inside the ZigBee-based network. Protection of a net based on ZigBee protocols includes security mechanism at every protocol level from physical through network to the application level. As a symmetric encoding algorithm the AES (*Advanced Encryption Standard*) with 128bits key is used. At the link layer the authentication of messages, their integrity and also replay protection should be guaranteed (Sastry and Wagner, 2004). Authentication and integrity is ensured by message authentication code (MAS) that is a checksum computed with shared secret key. Replay attack is avoided by adding a sequence number to every message and confidentiality is protected by encryption.

Beside this, other keys may be used as a link key that serves for security of a pair of nodes inside the network. Node that has the role of trust coordinator is responsible for ad-hoc creation of the network as just these nodes that know the shared secret in the form of the master key may be included in the network. In general it is supposed that network keys are distributed by trust center that is usually a coordinator and that for such

distribution the master key is used. In a secure mode also the communication between two nodes in the network is secured by an established link key. Question of key distribution is still matter of research. Reader is advised to see for example (Camtepe and Yener, 2005).

We should also address security of communication in such kind of systems. All agent platforms have to realize the most important demands for wireless sensor network protocols: low communication and computational cost, scalability and data integrity. Depending on the application and the use of WSN – motes are mostly scattered in a hostile environment – there could be also the additional requirement for security protocols: authentication (information is genuine and comes from declared source), data integrity (information cannot be modified without authorization), confidentiality (information cannot be read by an unauthorized subject), availability (information must be available when it is needed) and for some applications also non-repudiation (one party of transaction cannot deny having received a transaction nor can the other party deny having send the transaction).

Another question is how the security issues can be implemented when one built his or her own application with development tools like nesC/TinyOS. Conventional architectures, such as TinySec (Karlof et. al. 2004), are compromise between information security and limited resource requirements. Strong cryptography and algorithms used on the Internet are usually too computational consuming, so they had to be replaced by alternative solutions, mostly by symmetric ciphers and stream ciphers. These solutions could guarantee authentication, confidentiality and integrity at the expense of shared global cryptographic key. But usage of one shared key could be a problem, if the motes (sensor node) are placed in a hostile environment. Typical sensor motes are not tamper-resistant due to the cost factor. Also a key distribution schemes based on public key cryptography or elliptic curve cryptography are not suitable, due to their computational cost.

3.4 Role of Cryptography

Cryptography has an important role in the design of wireless sensor networks that usually work in a hostile environment with the different threats. The application of cryptographic mechanisms can help to achieve security objectives such as confidentiality, data integrity, authentication, and non-repudiation. The cryptographic mechanisms used in sensor networks systems include (Hanacek 2005).

- Secret key encryption/decryption
- One-way hash functions
- Challenge-response cryptographic protocols
- Digital signatures.

Secret key (symmetric) encryption methods provide confidentiality, authentication and data integrity. Asymmetric algorithms could provide all these objectives including non-repudiation but at the expense of much higher time and resource consumption. Therefore, symmetric algorithms are generally preferred. Data integrity and authentication are achieved by applying well-known hash and MAC algorithms, such as CBC-MAC and SHA.

Research highlights that public key cryptography, especially RSA algorithm, is not well suitable for wireless sensor networks. Much more suitable is the usage of ECC algorithm and 160 bit keys, that is as secure as RSA-1048 but at a lower power consumption. While the application of the stronger ECC-224 still seems to be feasible, the time and power consumption for the equivalent RSA-2048 is far beyond the acceptable level (Amin et. al. 2008).

3.5 Role of Tamper-Resistant Hardware

Most widely used kind of trusted device is a smart card. Smart cards offer very cheap implementation of the one of the security concepts, this concept is called "tamper resistant hardware". This term can be described like a hardware resistant against physical attack or as secure hardware. Secure hardware is hardware module (Anderson, 1972), (DoD, 1985) equipped with microprocessor, which contains some secured data and algorithms, which manipulate with these data. These features can be used in two main ways:

- Secure hardware contains data, with which can be manipulated by the specific way. As an example we can use telephone smart card, which contains impulse counter, which can be only decreased.
- Secure hardware contains secret cryptographic key, which can be used only for encrypting data and this key remains in the card and can't be read. As an example we can use authentication smart card, this card authenticates itself thanks to encrypting data with his secret key.

This secure hardware can't be cloned or emulated, because these features can't be replaced just by software without special hardware. For example: if we will simulate the telephone smart card, we can't ensure that someone wouldn't rewrite counter number in our program and as well we cannot ensure that in our software implementation of smart card someone wouldn't rewrite our secret key.

Tamper resistant devices are evaluated by means of FIPS PUB 140-1 or FIPS PUB 140-2, U.S. government computer security standards. FIPS 140-2 defines four levels of security – "Level 1" to "Level 4".

The lowest security is provided by Level 1, example of such device is a personal computer (PC). Security Level 2 enhances physical security mechanisms of Level 1 device by adding tamper-evidence properties. Security Level 3 has to have strong enclosures and tamper a detection/response circuit that zeroizes all plaintext sensitive data when the removable covers/doors of the cryptographic module are opened. The highest level of security is provided by Level 4, such devices are secured against compromise due to environmental conditions outside of the device's normal operating ranges of voltage and temperature.

Today smartcards offer security properties consistent with Level 2-3 of FIPS 140-2.

3.6 Architecture of Motes with Tamper Resistant Microcontrollers

There could be also made more secured motes for mobile code interpretation and we will discuss security of a code interpreter itself at this moment. An attacker may attack our code using his own interpreter that miss-interprets proper code to his or her purposes. To avoid such situation we also have to secure interpret the program, i.e. to run such interpreter in tamper-resistant mote. Memory where a code is stored, memory where an interpreter is stored and memory where data variables are stored have to be secured.

We searched the nowadays secured microcontrollers and we have found a few of them that can serve to our purposes. We choose for example AT90SC144144CT and AT90SO128 microcontrollers, which provide EAL4+ security certification. They provide environmental pro-

tection like voltage monitor, frequency monitor, light protection and temperature monitor. These microcontrollers are built around 8/16 bits AVR microcontroller like MicaZ motes based on ATmega128 MCU. Energy consumption is higher (around 20 mA against 6 mA on full workload), but working frequency is also increased (26 MHz against 8 MHz). So the performance/consumption comparison is also well balanced. Both secured MCU can be powered via 2 AA batteries and MCU contains some hardware accelerators like DES, 3DES, AES modules, random number generator and also checksum accelerator.

There could be two designs of connecting secured MCU to other WSN hardware. First one is done using a normal WSN node for sensing data and for communication purposes. Data from sensors can be modified as like as data from radio module. MicaZ mote should not contain any sensitive data like shared keys, the code itself and code interpreter. All such data should be stored in secured microcontroller!

MicaZ MCU works only like interconnecting bridge and resends data from sensors and radio to/from a secured MCU. Physical connection of both MCU can be done through SPI or I²C bus. Such solution can be seen in Figure 1.

Figure 1. First solution of secured WSN node (with MicaZ mote).

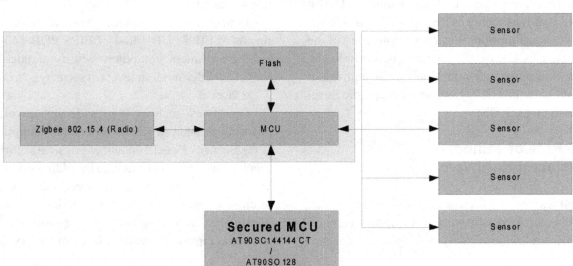

Figure 2. Second solution of secured WSN node (own mote design).

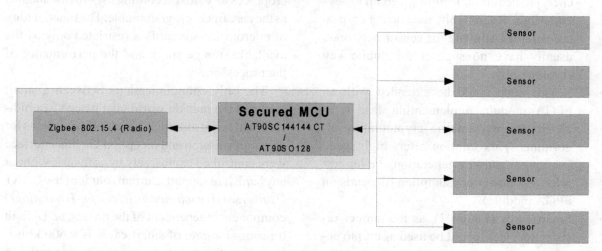

One of the main disadvantages of the first solution is energy consumption. We have to power both MCU, but only the secured one is there for computational purposes. We can reduce first solution from Figure 1 and we can move on to Figure 2. Our second solution uses secured MCU, which is directly connected to the radio module and sensors via SPI or I²C bus. Energy consumption of such solution is clearly lower. Main reason why we mentioned first solution is that an attacker can also put his MCU in the middle of secured MCU and sensors or radio module. So we have to always take into an account such possibility!

Design of the second solution doesn't contain an additional flash memory. We could connect such external memory but the use of such memory should be only for such purposes like storing data from sensors, storing unprocessed messages and so on. There must not be stored any sensitive data like program variables, the interpretable code etc. So usage of such external memory is disputable.

4 REALIZATION OF CRYPTOGRAPHY ALGORITHMS FOR WSN NODES

Agent platforms are usually based on a conventional hardware with no hardware or software cryptographic support. Cryptographic abilities of such platforms could be improved in several ways:

- Cryptography algorithms could be implemented into the firmware of sensor node. This least expensive solution provides usually only the private key cryptography at low speed. Performance of this cryptography could be sufficient for simple applications. Security of stored cryptographic keys is usually very low.

- Sensor nodes could be extended with an auxiliary microprocessor(s) implemented parallel computing of the cryptographic algorithms. Performance and security of this solution depends on auxiliary microprocessor(s).

- Sensor nodes could be improved by an add-on secure microcontroller with secure memory and hardware crypto engine supporting AES and 3DES encryption standards. The encryption engine increase encrypted communication speed up to several Mbps. Regrettably, the current crypto-accelerators, suitable for sensor networks, usually have no support for public key cryptography.

- Sensor node could be extended with an FPGA module implementing fast symmetric and asymmetric cryptography algorithms. This solution offers high speed encryption and key generation at a highest price and power consumption (depends on FPGA module).

- Smart cards (Figure 3), as the tamper resistant devices, could be used as crypto accelerators and also as a secure storage for cryptographic keys. These crypto-accelerators ordinarily support symmetric and asymmetric cryptography together with low power consumption. Smart card consumption can be also decreased powering them up only for cryptographic operations. Furthermore, cost of high-end smart cards is lower than cost of the same feature crypto-processors and FPGAs.

4.1 Smart Cards

As the smart card family consists of two broad categories – memory cards and microprocessor cards – we will be interested only in the contact microprocessor cards (according ISO 7816 standard) as they are freely programmable. The functionality of microprocessor cards is restricted only by the available storage space and the performance of the processor.

The only communications between a smart card and the outside world take place via a bidirectional serial interface. Originally, solutions for data transmission and reception via this interface were controlled exclusively by software, without any hardware support. Current solutions use UART (*Universal Asynchronous Receiver-Transmitter*) component independent of the processor. Default transmission rate of smart cards is 9,600 kbit/s, but most of the cards can transmit up to rate 115 kbit/s with a 3.5 MHz clock.

Smart cards can communicate by means of byte-oriented $T=0$ protocol or by block-oriented $T=1$ protocol. Other transmission protocols are not standardized and therefore they are not usually supported. There protocols transmit APDU (*Application Protocol Data Unit*) blocks. APDUs can be classified into (terminal → smart card) *command APDUs* (Table 1) and (smart card → terminal) *response APDUs* (Table 2) (Rankl and Effing, 2003).

Command APDU consists of instruction class (CLA), instruction code (INS) and two parameters (P1, P2) in the mandatory header. Optional body carries command data (Lc, Data) and maximum number of data expected in data field of response

Figure 3. Smart-card structure (Tiresias 2011); Typical smart-card contacts (SmartCardsBasis 2011).

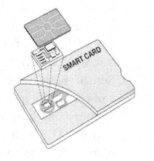
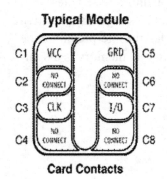

Table 1. Command APDU structure (EMVCo, 2000).

CLA	INS	P1	P2	Lc	Data	Le
← Mandatory header →				← Optional body →		

Table 2. Response APDU structure (EMVCo, 2000).

Data field	SW1	SW2
← Optional body →	← Mandatory trailer→	

(Le). Response APDU carries optional data and two mandatory status bytes (SW1, SW2).

Power consumption of smartcard is similar (or lower) to consumption of wireless sensor nodes – see Figure 4a and Figure 4b. Active supply current of ATmega128 could reach 10 mA. MICAz sensor nodes, we are using, consume 5 mA in an active state (Atmel, 2008).

4.2 Smart Card Interface and TinyOS

Firmware of sensor nodes is typically implemented using nesC/TinyOS system or even in the C lan-guage. Binary code compiled from the source language is then uploaded to the boot sectors of the sensor's flash memory.

Smart card is connected to the sensor node via UART (serial interface) and one auxiliary pin on the data bus for sending of a reset signal. Before using of connected smart card, it's necessary to send reset signal. If the smart card gets through this reset successfully, answer-to-reset (ATR) block is send to the sensor node. ATR describes supported transmission protocol, transmission rate, timing and other serial interface settings.

Box 1. Examples of commands of Gemplus GPK smart cards (GPK, 2001).

```
// Select application ("CRYPTO1")
00 A4 04 00 07 'C' 'R' 'Y' 'P' 'T' 'O' '1' FF      // PC -> Smartcard
90 00        // OK                                  // PC <- Smartcard
// Verify PIN (1111)
00 20 00 01 08 01 01 01 01 FF FF FF FF FF           // PC -> Smartcard
90 00        // OK                                  // PC <- Smartcard
// SelectCryptoContext (7)
80 A6 07 32                                         // PC -> Smartcard
90 00 // OK                                         // PC <- Smartcard
// PutCryptoData ("<data>")
80 DA 01 05 07 55 05 <data>                         // PC -> Smartcard
90 00 // OK                                         // PC -> Smartcard
// PK_Sign
80 85 00 00 80                                      // PC -> Smartcard
<response> 90 00 // Response & OK                   // PC <- Smartcard
```

Figure 4. **(A)** *Supply current of 3DES encryption using GemXpresso R4 smartcard (Pecho et. al. 2009);* **(B)** *Supply current of RSA-1024 signature using GemXpresso R4 smartcard (Pecho et. al. 2009).*

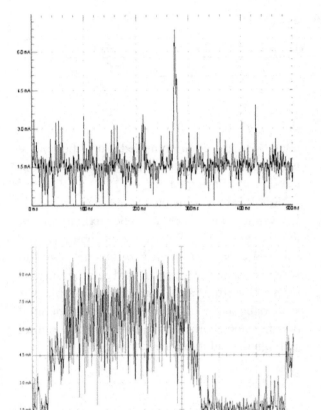

Described solutions was successfully tested on MICAz platform (ATMega128 processor) and Gemplus GemXpresso Pro R3 (E64 PK) smart card.

4.3 Resulting Architecture and Application

The above described parts could be combined into one wireless sensor network, using agents and smart cards as cryptographic processors for data transfer encryption – see Figure 5a.

As shown in Figure 5b, each sensor mote consists of two interfaces (communication with sensor(s) or actuator(s) and wireless communication with the outer world), microcontroller, agent(s) and a smart card. Each sensor mote is a separate unit, which communicates with other motes in the wireless sensor network, and performs the programmed tasks, which are either pre-programmed or delivered via other agents. The microcontroller is responsible for enabling the measurement and agent process, and sends data or code to the smart card. The smart card in each note includes a secret key (either for symmetric or asymmetric cryptography) and performs the encryption and decryption of data or interpretable code. The secret key is stored in secret memory and could not be copied out.

Figure 5. (A: left) Connection scheme of sensor node and smart card. (Pecho et. al. 2009); (B: right) Architecture scheme (Pecho et. al. 2009).

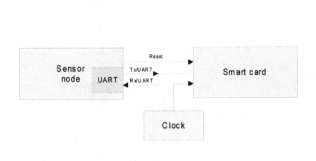

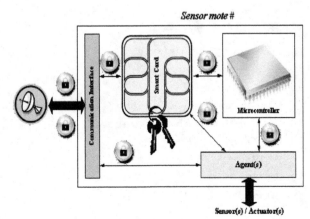

The agents have two main tasks – the first one is common for wireless sensor networks, i.e. to ensure measurement, data transfer and storage and furthermore they are responsible for feedback to actuators. If one node is inaccessible, agents restore the previous functionality of the whole network (ad-hoc solution), whereas the missing node (mote) is compensated through other sensor motes (bridge). The second task of agents could be the security assurance. Each agent could be a heuristic toll, which tries to find attacks or intrusions tries and stops the "suspicious" mote or makes a bridge that the "suspicious" mote is jumped over. Such heuristics is joined with the possibility to reconstruct the wireless sensor network in ad-hoc principle.

The communication inside the mote is unsecured, i.e. not encrypted. The communication with the outer world is done either encrypted or as a plain text. Agents, which are used for heuristic analysis of the WSN security, travel in the network in opened form – they could not be enciphered. On the other hand, all data and commands are send in enciphered form, because the security of them could be ensured only if these data are resistant against attacks.

Significance of such solution is in contemporary wireless sensor networks that are used in security relevant regions – (petro/bio) chemical, medicine and military industrial solutions. The use of wireless data transfer in such branches is pushing ahead by big industrial companies. Such solutions often do not offer any securing of data transfer. These networks are able to make an ad-hoc reconfiguration, but are not able to detect intruders and attacks. In addition, applications with very high security requirements (nuclear industry, poisons etc.) do not allow sending information from separate motes in their open forms, because only the information from these nodes could be used for extensive attack, based on social engineering.

5 CONCLUSION

Security aspects in the wireless network system are of significant importance as the WSN is a dynamic highly distributed system that uses communication and sometimes also interpretable code transferring during its work. To avoid main security risks some mechanisms like cryptography and tamper resistant hardware may be of useful. Then there is important how these mechanisms may be included in architectures of WSN nodes. There should be some special hardware and software modules that enable implementation of these mechanisms and they should respect usual demands to these sorts of devices. We presented some approaches to the realization of tamper-resistant data and code interpreter and we also showed how smart cards may be used for realization of cryptographic algorithms.

As we discusses above mentioned mechanisms we found that the use of mobile codes is quite problematic as their mobility is energy consumptive and also they means increased security risks in such systems. Nevertheless mobile codes and agents may find their place when trusted network is used especially in design, experimental and prototype analysis phases of the WSN applications development.

ACKNOWLEDGMENT

This research has been done under the support of the following grants: "*Security-Oriented Research in Information Technology*", MSMT-MSM0021630528 (CZ), "*The IT4Innovations Centre of Excellence*", MSMT-CZ 1.05/1.1.00/02.0070 (CZ), "*Advanced, secured, reliable and adaptive IT*", BUT-FIT-S-11-1 (CZ) and "*Automated attack processing*", MPO-FR-TI1/037 (CZ).

REFERENCES

Amin, F., Jahangir, A. H., & Rasifard, H. (2008). Analysis of public-key cryptography for wireless sensor networks security. *Proceedings of World Academy of Science, Engineering and Technology*, Vol. 31.

Anderson, J. P. (1972). *Computer security technology planning study*, ESD-TR-73-51, vol 1. ESD/AFSC, Hanscom AFB, Bedford, MA. (NTIS AD-758 206)

ATMEL. (2008). *ATMega128 datasheet: 8-bit AVR microcontroller with 128kBytes in-system programable Flash*. Retrieved from http://www.atmel.com/dyn/resources/ prod_documents/doc2467.pdf

Borselius, N. (2002). Mobile agent security. *Electronics and Communication Engineering Journal, 14*(5).

Camtepe, S. A., & Yener, B. (2005). *Key distribution mechanisms for wireless sensor networks: A survey*. Technical Report TR-05-07 Rensselaer Polytechnic Institute, Computer Science Department.

Department of Defense. (1985). *Trusted computer system evaluation criteria*. DoD 5200.28-STDm December 1985, US Department of Defense, December 26, 1985.

EMVCo. (2008). *EMV integrated circuit card specification for payment systems*.

Farmer, W. M., Guttman, J. D., & Swarup, V. (1996). Security for mobile agents: Issues and requirements. *Proceedings of the 19th National Information Systems*.

Fok, C. L., Roman, G. C., & Lu, C. (2009). Agilla: A mobile agent middleware for self-adaptive wireless sensor networks. *ACM Transactions on Autonomous and Adaptive Systems, Special Issue on Self-Adaptive and Self-Organising Wireless Networking Systems, 4*(3).

Fortino, G., Aiello, F., Gravina, R., & Guerrieri, A. (2009). MAPS: A mobile agent platform for Java Sun SPOTs. In *Proceedings of the 3rd International Workshop on Agent Technology for Sensor Networks (ATSN-09), jointly held with the 8th International Joint Conference on Autonomous Agents and Multiagent Systems (AAMAS-09)*.

GPK. (2001). *Gemplus reference manual.*

Hanacek, P. (2005). Problems of security in ad-hoc sensor network. *Proceedings of MOSIS '05*, MARQ, Ostrava.

Karlof, C., Sastry, N., & Wagner, D. (2004). TinySec: A link layer security architecture for wireless sensor networks. *SenSys '04: Proceeding of 2nd International Conference on Embedded Networked Sensor Systems*.

Koubaa, A., & Alves, M. (2006). Eduardo Tovar: IEEE 802.15.4: A wireless communication technology for large-scale ubiquitous computing applications. *Proceedings of Conference on Mobile and Ubiquitous Systems*, Guimarães, June 29-30.

Kwon, Y. M., Sundresh, S., Mechitov, K., & Agha, G. (2006). *ActorNet: An actor platform for wireless sensor networks*.

Lange, D., & Oshima, M. (1999). Seven good reasons for mobile agents. *Communications of the ACM*, 42.

Levis, P. (2006). *TinyOS programming*. Retrieved from http://csl.stanford.edu/~pal/pubs/ tinyos-programming.pdf

Loureiro, S., Molva, R., & Roudier, Y. (2000). Mobile code security. *Proceedings of ISPYAR Code Mobile*, Toulouse, France.

Munawar, W., Alizai, M. H., Landsiedel, O., & Wehrle, K. (2010). Dynamic TinyOS: Modular and transparent incremental code-updates for sensor networks. *Proceedings of ICC*, Cape Town, South Africa.

Pecho, P., Zboril, F., Drahansky, M., & Hanacek, P. (2009). Agent platform for wireless sensor networks with support for cryptographic protocols. *Journal of Universal Computer Science, 6.*

Rankl, W., & Effing, W. (2003). *Smart card handbook* (3rd ed.). John Wiley and Sons. doi:10.1002/047085670X

Sastry, N., & Wagner, D. (2004). Security considerations for IEEE 802.15.4 networks. *Proceedings of the 3rd ACM Workshop on Wireless Security.*

SmartCardsBasis. (2011). Retrieved from http://www.smartcardbasics.com/smart-card-types.html

Tiresias. (2011). Retrieved from http://www.tiresias.org/research/ guidelines/cards_and_smart_media.htm

Chapter 22
Grid of Security:
A Decentralized Enforcement of the Network Security

Olivier Flauzac
University of Reims Champagne-Ardenne, France

Florent Nolot
University of Reims Champagne-Ardenne, France

Cyril Rabat
University of Reims Champagne-Ardenne, France

Luiz-Angelo Steffenel
University of Reims Champagne-Ardenne, France

ABSTRACT

Network security is in a daily evolving domain. Every day, new attacks, viruses, and intrusion techniques are released. Hence, network devices, enterprise servers, or personal computers are potential targets of these attacks. Current security solutions like firewalls, intrusion detection systems (IDS), and virtual private networks (VPN) are centralized solutions, which rely mostly on the analysis of inbound network connections. This approach notably forgets the effects of a rogue station, whose communications cannot be easily controlled unless the administrators establish a global authentication policy using methods like 802.1x to control all network communications among each device. To the best of the authors' knowledge, a distributed and easily manageable solution for the global security of an enterprise network does not exist. In this chapter, they present a new approach to deploy a distributed security solution where communication between each device can be control in a collaborative manner. Indeed, each device has its own security rules, which can be shared and improved through exchanges with others devices. With this new approach, called grid of security, a community of devices ensures that a device is trustworthy and that communications between devices progress in respect of the control of the system policies. To support this approach, the authors present a new communication model that helps structuring the distribution of security services among the devices. This can secure both ad-hoc, local-area or enterprise networks in a decentralized manner, preventing the risk of a security breach in the case of a failure.

DOI: 10.4018/978-1-4666-0978-5.ch022

INTRODUCTION

The definition and deployment of security policies is a domain widely studied in the last years. Most solutions, like firewalls, intrusion detection systems (IDS), intrusion prevention systems and virtual private networks (VPN) are all centralized, being more adapted for traditional cabled networks than for wireless networks. Today, wireless devices are important elements on the access-layer network, and solutions to secure communications between devices require the deployment of complex solutions like wireless controllers, 802.1x authentication or virtual private network tunnels. While these solutions ensure that communications cannot be intercepted or modified, nothing prevents a virus, Trojan or malicious user to launch an attack on the network, from the inside.

In this paper, we first study existing solutions, proposing a new approach to ensure a fast and decentralized enforcement of the network security: *the grid of security*. This new approach can be described as the addition of each device security policies, creating a global security behavior. We define a community like a set of devices that share the same global policy. With this collaborative approach, devices in the community exchanges their local policy rules among each other, even if the final decision to accept or deny a new rule depends on the device's user. With this new approach, a user who wants to open a network service such as a file transfer service (FTP) will create a new local policy rule. This new rule will be exchange with other device on the community and other users must approve or refuse this new service. With this approach, we can quickly create a secure network without any centralized solution. While each device is independent of any centralized solution, a device may benefit from the mutual security enforcement from a community. In the same principle, different communities may arise as a result of different security levels authorized by the users.

Which differs our approach from other trustiness and recommendation-based approaches is that we structure our mechanisms around a middleware especially tailored for grid computing and peer-to-peer communication model. A grid-like approach offers the advantage to rationalize every resources of each device, like storage, computing resource or data analysis. With a peer-to-peer communication model, devices communicate without relying on a central server, improving therefore the system fault tolerance.

In this work, we first present current techniques to ensure security of a network. From this study, we observe that each solution needs a complex centralized administration device or service to manage global security. But now, with the mobility of each user, this solution is not appropriate. From these observations, we propose a new approach of information system based on grids and how to offer new distributed security services. Finally, we conclude this chapter giving some open tracks from this work.

THE SECURITY PROBLEM

Today, the Internet is far from being a secure environment. The continuous growth of security risks (intrusions, virus, spywares, information stealing) forces enterprises and network administrators to expend a considerable amount of time and money to improve security aspects from their networks, usually through the association of multiple techniques and tools. Despite the fact that defining and deploying security policies if a study field that rapidly advanced in the last years, most of the proposed solutions are still based on centralized servers.

In our approach, we try to better represent the constraints from the real world by starting our models with a typical enterprise network, connected to the Internet. In this model, all network devices connected to the enterprise network constitute what we call a "confidence zone". By default,

Figure 1. A typical Firewalled network

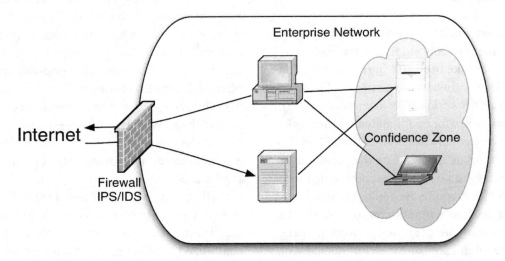

the confidence zone is delimited by the equipment directly connected to the Internet, i.e. those devices with a public IPv4 interface. Formally, a confidence zone includes all communicating devices in a network where the global security is under mutual control. Therefore, a confidence zone can be extended across a WAN link or reduced to a few devices if the devices find a common agreement on the security policies.

Security: Study Cases on Today Networks

In this section, we present three scenarios that represent typical situations where secure communications are required: (*i*) protection against intrusions, (*ii*) connection to the confidence zone from abroad and (*iii*) communication security inside the confidence zone. In all these cases we observe that current networks rely on centralized services. Indeed, inbound and outbound communications are usually filtered through firewalls, intrusion detection systems and VPN concentrators. Some companies like Cisco Systems and CheckPoint reinforce this centralized organization by integrating all security services in a single box. We believe however that reinforcing the central

role of a security box only increases the risks in the case of failures or attacks.

Intrusion Detection Systems

Networks hidden behind a firewall typically represent this scenario. Here, only authorized data flows may reach the internal network. Authorization policies include source and destination addresses, ports and even the protocol types. Usually at the enterprise network entry point (cf. Figure 1), firewalls are now found also installed in each user's computer.

According to their specifications and strategic location in the enterprise network, firewalls (personal or not) are good tools to block direct attacks coming from the outside of the confidence zone. At the other hand, data flows originated from the inside network are seldom analyzed by the firewalls.

Indeed, while a network administrator is able to control the connections that traverse the enterprise entry points, it has no control over alternative access points opened by an user, as for example a laptop computer connected to the Internet through the user's cellular phone. To ensure that all devices in the internal zone share the same security policies, it is important to implement an additional control over the internal exchanges. Due to the complexity of this task, the security policies coordination must be implemented through mechanisms that are transparent to the user.

Connection to a Secured Zone

A data flow authorized by a firewall allows a distant machine to exchange data with the secured zone but doesn't guarantee the confidentiality of the data that cross the Internet. Therefore, some additional properties must be ensured when connecting to a confidence zone: encryption, authentication and data integrity. These properties are provided, for example, by VPN "tunnels" connected to the enterprise network (Figure 2).

Indeed, some protocols individually provide some of these properties (SSL, SSH) but the Virtual Private Networks - VPN - have the advantage to integrate these properties while securing the totality of the data flows that are tunneled. Furthermore, VPNs create a virtual extension of the local area network, preserving the internal security appliances defined on the confidence zone and given access to internal services like

printer and mail servers. The problem, however, is that nothing prevents harming codes such as virus to flow through the VPN, compromising the internal security.

Also, accessing a VPN requires a centralized server (usually called a VPN server or VPN concentrator). As this central server must relay all the traffic, the available bandwidth is limited. Some companies integrate all functionalities from firewalls, IPS and VPNs in a single network device, which has the side effect of centralizing even more the network and limit the bandwidth. For instance, a high-end device like Cisco ASA 5585-X firewall can handle only 5Gbps if both VPN and firewall are active, against 20 Gbps in a firewall mode only[1]. In a mid-range device like Cisco ASA 5550, the firewall-only mode handles up to 1.2Gbps while the addition of a VPN drops this capacity to 425Mbps.

Establishing a Confidence Zone

To allow a machine to access a confidence zone is always a risky decision as virus or malwares may infect this machine. Similarly, some applications may not be adapted to the established

Figure 2. VPN usage in current networks

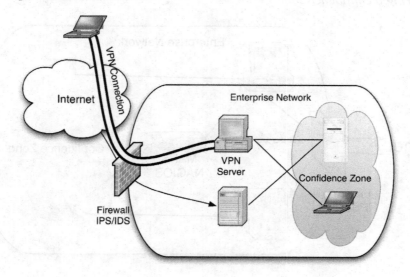

security policies (instant messaging, P2P and gaming devices for example). To reduce the risk and verify if a device complies with the security policies, some companies like Cisco Systems[2], Microsoft or Nortel Networks propose the use of *Network Access Control* - NAC – mechanisms. Also, *PacketFence*[3], an open-source implementation, is available. Basically, a NAC associates user authentication and verification of the user's machine, before allowing it to connect to the network. Among the elements a NAC may verify (or impose) there are:

• Antivirus status (activation, last update);
• OS security updates;
• Public key certificates;
• Firewall status and current rules;
• Authorized applications;
• Permission to activate WiFi or Bluetooth connections;

In addition to the previous controls, most NAC systems allow the analysis of the behavior of the network devices, looking for abnormal patterns. For example, if Cisco's NAC Appliance detects an IP phone establishing a *telnet* connection with a computer instead of exchanging information with the call manager, an alert will be thrown. Among the possible reactions, the NAC Appliance can alert the network administrator, the final user or even automatically isolate the incident zone, placing it in quarantine. The inconvenient of this approach relies on the fact that all connections (data, voice and video) must pass through the NAC server, with a potential performance bottleneck. In addition, several workarounds have spotted techniques to allow a machine to connect to a network bypassing NAC control.

In the same philosophy we found the network supervising systems (Figure 3). With functionalities going from the simple display of network statistics to a proactive network management (such as the Intrusion Detection Systems), these services are useful tools to identify the weaknesses in a network. As before, Cisco Systems proposes a solution called MARS[4] where information is exchanged among MARS agents, improving the behavioral analysis of the network. In spite of its interest, MARS has been discontinued and no replacement product was announced by Cisco.

All these approaches are centralized solution. We always have a centralized service that analyzes all other devices of the network. In our solution, NAC functionalities can be distributed

Figure 3. Monitoring a confidence zone

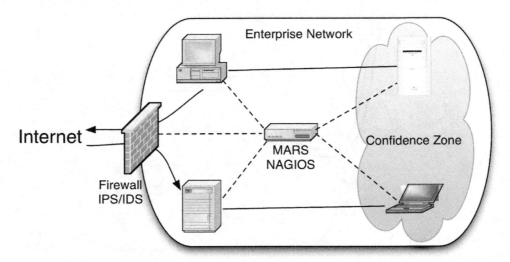

in many device of the network in order to avoid overload of only one device and to be fault tolerant.

A path to IPv6 secure Network

The gradual deployment of IPv6 represents a milestone on the security community. Indeed, IPv6 has a much larger address space (2^{128} for IPv6 against 2^{32} for IPv4) that allows every communicating device to hold a public IP address. While IPv4 still resists in many networks, the available IPv4 address blocks were depleted at the beginning of 2011[5]. For the matter of example, IPv6 allows roughly $3{,}4 \times 10^{38}$ addresses (the rest of the address space is reserved for now), which represents more than 6×10^{19} IP address per cm^2 on planet Earth. With this abundance of public IPv6 addresses, the use of private addresses inside a network will disappear.

However, once each network device (PC, cellular telephone, sensor and so on) uses a public IP address, it becomes more vulnerable to attacks. This is especially true with Mobile IPv6 (Ebalard, 2006; Valadon, 2008), as a mobile device will be able to roam from network to network keeping the connections previously opened. Different routers will exchange connection information in order to migrate transparently the user's connections. This new kind of service may be explored to allow an attacker to enter the enterprise network by piggybacking on the previously opened connections from the mobile device. Some works (HyunGon, 2008; Elgoarany, 2007) exist to secure Mobile IPv6 with IPSec but specific security functionalities need to be deployed.

Secure ad-Hoc Networks

An ad-hoc network is a network without fixed infrastructure in which each device can communicate with its neighbors. It differs from current enterprise solutions that were developed for networks with fixed infrastructure, even in a wireless environment. The security is done with secure communication link between the wireless client and the access point. For instance, the access to the access point is a major control point that cannot be neglected. Actual researches on security and ad-hoc networks are based on cryptographic solutions (Lidong, 1999; Castelluccia, 2007; Castelluccia, 2008). These solutions are enough to ensure confidentiality and data integrity but are not design to deploy the same security policies on the network. Other works (Ping, 2004) focus on data exchange to secure ad-hoc network but these solutions are similar to fixed infrastructure solutions.

Indeed, the problem is that while communication can be secured using cryptographic methods in and ad-hoc environment, this approach becomes too expensive in a complex enterprise network where only a part of the traffic flows through a VPN or cryptographic tunnel. At the opposite side, an extensive control on the access points of the network through firewalls only works on structured networks, not on an ad-hoc environment where nothing prevents a user to share its Internet access or to open a web or FTP service.

It becomes important therefore that secure communication between two devices can be implemented together with the deployment of security policies on each device of the network.

THE GRIDS: GENERAL PRESENTATION

The grids are one of the solutions to manage and share available resources on a network. Two types of grids are distinguished: grid computing and data grids. In grid computing solutions, like SETI@home (Anderson, 2002), BOINC (Anderson, 2004), XtremWEB (Cappello, 2004), Diet (Caron, 2006), Globus (Allcock, 2001), and CONFIIT (Flauzac, 2010), resources are associated to computing (processor, memory...). In data grid - OceanStore (Kubiatowicz, 2000), Freenet

(Freenet, 2011) -, resources are associated to data storage. Whatever the grid type, it is necessary to develop a middleware for management of the different resources: connectivity, resources monitoring, tasks scheduling in computing grid and data replication (or distribution) management in data grids. Today, most of grids are based on either centralized or hierarchical architecture. In both cases, they require several management tasks and each device must be specialized.

In parallel to this grid concept, peer-to-peer model have been developed. A P2P communication model uses fully decentralized architectures and is easily scalable. Moreover, it can tolerate dynamic networks like wireless or ad-hoc networks. At the end, the main objective of peer-to-peer systems is to allow communication between each device without any additional requirement (location server, proxy, etc.).

However, when we design a middleware or grid application, we must use a theoretical model. Like in a grid, each device have a specific function and we can have many device in the network (switch, firewall, personal computer, server...), the model must describe each function and each device in order to correctly study and evaluate our grid application. From this theoretical model and study, we can try to find solution to each problem.

To be most effective, a model must take into account the whole system. The grid model can be applied in an environment that is not necessarily dedicated. In this case, applications or mechanisms outside the grid can affect the overall effectiveness of the middleware or grid application. The model must also take into account the physical hardware if we want to make appropriate management mechanisms. However, the models proposed in the literature take only into account a sub-part of the overall system. That is why we proposed a new theoretical model.

In (Lacour, 2004), authors proposed a method focusing on the description of network components. Their model allows describing both protocols used and the network hardware such as

routers or switches. Thus, the physical network of the grid is represented as a graph where each node represents a network device or a particular type of network (*Ethernet, Myrinet…*). The interest of such model, close to the physical network, is to highlight the problems of network congestion or delay in transferring data.

In (Baker, 2002), a new approach is proposed, based on the concept of a factory. Components and architecture of the grid are organized into layers as shown in Figure 4. The lowest layer is close to the physical network and represents the physical resources of the grid. These resources are accessible via the local resource managers. The second layer represents the security and how to access the resources, aiming to ensure the security of connections. The third layer is the middleware that serves as an interface between the application and the access to resources. The last layer represents the application itself, in which operates the middleware. Contrary to the previous model, it does not highlight issues close to the physical network, but focuses on the problems of access to resources in terms of middleware and its services.

Figure 4. Grid model proposed in (Baker, 2002).

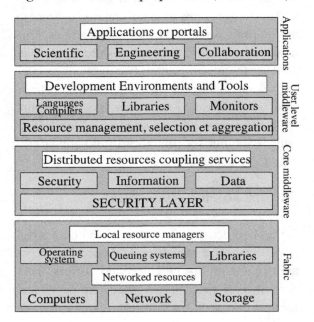

Figure 5. Grid model proposed in (Foster, 1997).

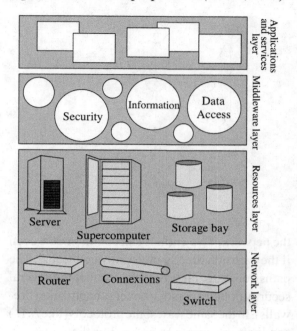

Figure 6. Theoretical model for grid applications designing

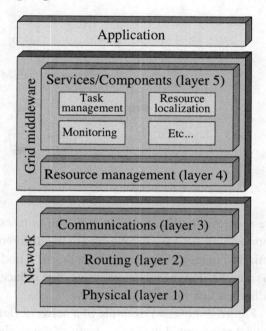

Another commonly used model is based on *Globus* from (Foster, 1997). It focuses on the material forming the grid as shown in Figure 5 and is composed by 4 layers. The first layer represents the physical network, i.e. physical connection and routing equipment. Over this layer, we find the resources of the grid: the computing resources, storage or applications shared. The third layer relates to components and middleware services that communicate with the resources. And the last layer is the application that uses the services provided by the middleware.

As these previous grid models do not consider all the resources of a network and a grid application, another model was proposed in (Rabat, 2006). In this new theoretical model, physical devices, communication link and each resource of the application are represented. This model is the most adapted to design the grid of security in which physical devices, communication links and their policies have a main role. It is structured in five independent layers: physical layer, routing layer, communication layer, resource manager

and finally all the components and middleware grid services.

Grid Design

In (Rabat, 2006), we have proposed a 5 layers model for grid or peer-to-peer applications design. This model is represented in Figure 6. It is used to model the network of a grid that interacts independently of the grid middleware. It also models the components of the grid middleware and interactions between them.

Layer 1: Physical Network Layer

The first layer concerns the physical network. The network is represented by a graph $G1=(V1,E1)$. $V1$ is the network nodes set. A node can be an *active* component (like desktop computers, servers...), or a *passive* component (like routers, switches...). $E1$ is the set of links that interconnect network nodes. We distinguish two kinds of links: wired and wireless connection. The wired connections

Figure 7. Example of a network representation in Layer 1

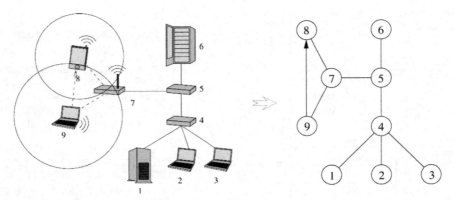

are naturally undirected. But with the wireless connections, we have to take care of the different emission ranges of the network nodes. If a node has a higher range than another one, this induces a directed link in *E1*.

Figure 7 shows an example of a network (left figure) represented in the first layer of the model (right figure). The nodes (*1* to *7*) are connected with wired connections: the links in the corresponding graph are undirected. For the two wireless nodes, we can remark that Node *9* has a higher range that Node *8* (ranges are represented by a circle on the figure). We obtain a directed link in *E1*.

Layer 2: Routing Layer

Over the physical network, a routing protocol builds and maintains paths between the nodes of the network. Two entities can communicate even if they are not directly physically connected. The paths construction takes into account the several security policies deployed over subnetworks (firewalls). In the same way, some protocols (like *NAT*) can limit the access to nodes. For these reasons, directed communication links are considered. In Layer *2*, the network is represented by the graph $G2=(V2,E2)$, where $V2=V1$ and *E2* is the set of paths between nodes of *V2*.

Figure 8 is based on the example of Figure 7 and shows the representation of the network in Layer *2*. To simplify, the paths that start or end from passive components (Nodes *4*, *5*, and *7*) are not displayed. We remark new links that represent the paths computed by the routing protocol. For the wireless entities (Nodes *8* and *9*), we remark

Figure 8. Example of a network representation in Layer 2

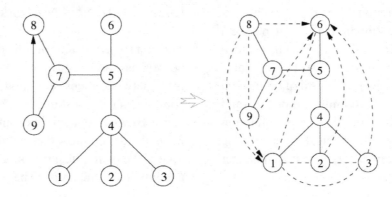

Figure 9. Example of a grid representation in Layer 4

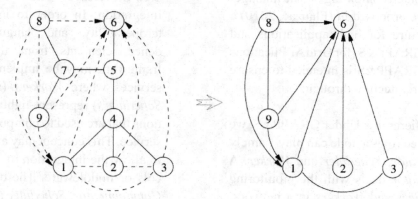

that the directed link *(9,8)* has been deleted: Node *8* can contact Node *9* through Node *7*.

Layer 3: Communication Layer

Over the paths built from the lower layer, it is possible to send data between two distant nodes that are not physically connected. The network is represented as a graph *G3=G2*. In this layer, we can have the message send and receive capabilities thanks to a given protocol or a protocol stack. Several mechanisms can be proposed to manage communication problems (loss or duplication of messages, data corruption). An acknowledgment mechanism can ensure that a sent message has been received. If a message is lost, it is sent again. Another mechanism can ensure the message integrity.

Layer 4: Resource Management

The two higher layers focus on the grid middleware. Layer 4 is the resources management layer that can be viewed as an interface between the components and the services of the grid and the lower layers. In this layer, we distinguish two kinds of nodes. The first ones, called the *active nodes*, are within the grid. These nodes share their own resources or use the grid resources. The others ones, the *passive nodes* are outside the grid such as routers or switches.

In this layer, the grid is represented as a graph *G4=(V4,E4)* where *V4* is the set of active nodes and *E4* is the set of communication links between active nodes. Passive nodes are not represented in the graph (*cf.* Figure 9) but they can influence the efficiency of the grid application (due to network overloads).

Layer 5: Grid Components and Services Layer

The last layer concerns the grid components and services including the tasks management and the resources monitoring service. The deployed components depend on the middleware: if it concerns the file sharing, it must have a component to transfer the files and maybe a component to manage access rights and queues for users.

The grid is represented by the graph *G5 = (V5, E5)* where *V5=V4* and *E5* is the set of communication links proposed by the topology layer. *E5* is not equal to *E4*: it depends on the protocol that manages the grid topology or the peer-to-peer overlay network.

FROM GRID TO NETWORK SECURITY ARCHITECTURE

From the previous observations, it is clear that a grid environment can be used to handle much more than distributed computing or data management. Indeed, we proposed in (Flauzac, 2010) a generic architecture for both applications and services, called GRAPP&S (for Grid APPlications and Services). GRAPP&S is intended to ensure a generic Grid architecture through:

- Modular Hierarchy: Under GRAPP&S, we defined three roles a node can play, namely *Communicator*, *Scheduler* and *Worker*. A *Communicator* deals with the monitoring of *Schedulers* and *Workers* in a network, as well as a message aggregator and message-relaying agent when dealing with other *Communicators*; a *Scheduler* manages the lists of tasks and services, while the *Workers* execute these tasks.

In the GRAPP&S architecture, these three roles must be played in different combinations according to the node capacity and needs. Therefore, a multiprocessor machine may instantiate several *Workers* that report to a single *Scheduler*, improving the system efficiency. A slow machine, at the other side, may decide to run only a *Worker* and report to a *Scheduler* in another machine, or implement both *Scheduler* and *Worker* but not a *Communicator*.

- Multi-Site Management: One of the problems when running on multiple sites is that all involved networks must be configured to bypass firewall restrictions. The GRAPP&S framework relies on the aggregator role of *Communicators*. A *Communicator* may act as a Rendezvous point if need to traverse a firewall, routing messages to other *Communicators*. It also acts as a local area "subscription desk" for nodes wanting to join the community, whose acceptation will depend on the agreement of the agents distributed in the network.

- Web-Services and Multi-Protocol Integration: In order to improve the interoperability and language independence, elements from the GRAPP&S framework may be implemented as Web services where *Workers* (and eventually *Schedulers*) represent lightweight applications that are used to compose a computing service. This concept may also be extended to allow the integration of different protocols or middleware. The distinct roles of *Communicator*, *Scheduler* and *Worker* and the intensive use of XML make GRAPP&S easily extendable. Therefore, a wrapper implemented on the *Scheduler* allows an existing service such as an IDS or a NAC Appliance to share tasks and results with each other and with native GRAPP&S tasks, while beneficing from a light and fast intercommunication structure represented by GRAPP&S.

Therefore, we propose a new security middleware based on GRAPP&S in which each device or user is an actor of the global security of the network. Thus, each user can manage its local security but also, through exchanges with its neighbor in his community, manage the global security policies. To prevent malicious users to attack the network, each exchange must be secure, controlled and validated by authorized users or authorized devices. An authorized user is a user who was already in the community and has exchanged some policy rules with another authorized neighbor. An authorized device is either a computer, a server or a network device who is considered to be secure and authenticated.

To form a "confidence zone", exchanges inside the network must be secured to prevent unauthorized actions that can compromise the security of the community. Our work, however, goes beyond the proposal of a simple security mechanism, as we can have specialized actors (a wireless LAN controller or network access controller) or distributed/replicated tasks. Indeed, a computer or a device, with our security middleware, can be specialized to control some particular services. For instance, a computer can administrate the anti-virus database, another can administrate authentication and another some firewall rules. From the specifications of each computer, we can choose which security function the computer must offer. In the case of an agent's failures, the own nature of the grid middleware allows the detection and transparent replacement of the faulty node by a backup agent or even a group of agents.

Therefore, in our security architecture, devices will be mutually monitored. If a device become "dangerous" because a virus or a Trojan is detected, it will be blocked and removed from the community (or confidence zone), as illustrated in Figure 10. Furthermore, a new user in a mobile environment must be authorized to enter the community. Nowadays, similar procedures can be implemented through the use of 802.1x authentication or VPNs but the configuration complexity and the technical knowledge required is high. In our solution, a new device can be added without any human manipulation, making the security of our network self-managed.

Figure 10. Grid of security example

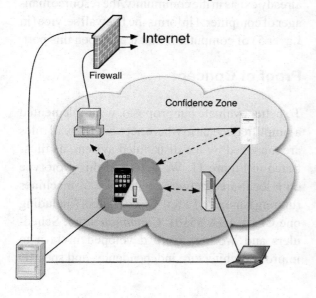

IMPLEMENTATION ISSUES

To achieve our objectives, we need to answer several questions: how to distribute the security functions on peers, how to exchange data, which communication protocols will be used between peer, how to distinguish different types of traffic. Also, we must define how to secure voice traffic, how to block communications from a peer... In the next section we analyze some of these implementations issues and point current techniques to bring these services. At the end of this section we also present a prototype scenario used to demonstrate our architecture.

Distributing Security Resource on Peers

From our middleware (in Layer 4), all data exchanged among peers in the same community are consider to be safe, so we don't need to verify each exchanged data. However, if a user wants to create a new community, he needs to control the traffic between this new community and his own community, which implies that new services must be installed on this peer. For instance, a similar approach is used on wireless environment with a wireless LAN controller, where the protocols LWAPP or CAPWAP are used. Data exchanges between wireless client and access point can be controlled either by the access point or the controller. With our middleware, the procedure is similar. A peer A can exchange information with another peer B in order to use a security service that A does not have but B has. From the technical specification of a peer, a user can define which service he wants and he can deploy it on his peer.

Control the Data Exchanged in a Community

Inside a community, if a peer receives too many messages during a small amount of time from one of its neighbor, it can decide to start an analysis on this neighbor. Therefore, a mechanism similar to the CONFIDANT protocol (Buchegger, 2002) can be used to control these exchanges. CONFIDANT is based in four components that can be distributed in a grid, namely (*i*) a controller, (*ii*) a reputation system, (*iii*) a path manager and (*iv*) a confidence controller. Using such approach in our middleware, a peer that detects a security anomaly may launch a security task in a distant node from the same community. One example is when a peer decides to run an anti-virus on one of its neighbor.

Joining an Existing Community

From the access network resource in layer 4 of our middleware, we can implement a network access service to control new peers. In this layer, we manage authentication exchange with the 802.1x protocol and in layer 5, a Radius service. When authentication is successful, exchanges can be made with other resource manager in order to control all services that must be present on the peers.

Removing a Peer from the Community

To exclude a peer from the community because this peer became untrusted, each of its neighbors can decide to change their firewall rules to block communication from this untrusted peer. This action can be commanded by a specific agent (that verifies the rules on the neighbors) or globally executed by all peers.

Deploying a Logical Secure Architecture on a Physical Existing Network

In many cases, users need to exchange data via secure communication link. But current solutions are not so easy to deploy. The right communication port must be open and we need to ask to the administrator to change the rules of the firewall only for this connection, perhaps for only a small amount of time. The approach "grid of security" can solve these problems. For instance, if a user in a community wants to create a VPN from his computer A to a server S, the middleware asks if an existing VPN from on computer of the community to this server exists. If a computer B has already established this connection, a simple connection between A and B can be establish and all data from A to B will be redirect to S. If no VPN connection to S exist in the community, the connection resource manager (in layer 4 of our model) will inform the firewall service (in layer 5) to open a given port to allow a VPN connection between A and S. In the same principle, several security services can benefit from this distributed management: firewall services, anti-virus, intrusion detection, system updating, network access control, virtual private network, etc. For each of these services, rules are defined for inbound and outbound connections. The resource manager (in Layer 4) exchange information between each service of each peer. For instance, if a user wants to open one communication port for an existing service on his computer A, the resource manager will contact all other peers in the community and look for a similar rule on each peers. If this rule already exists in the community, the resource manager of computer A informs the firewall service (in Layer 5) of computer A that it can open this port.

Proof of Concept

To better evaluate our proposal, we implemented a simplified scenario where network firewall rules are managed by the distributed system, as illustrated in Figure 11. We deployed this prototype on a local-area network composed of machines running Linux and a few Cisco routers (including one Cisco ASA 5510). *Communicators*, Schedulers and Workers were developed in Java to improve architecture independency, and specific

Figure 11. GRAPP&S for security

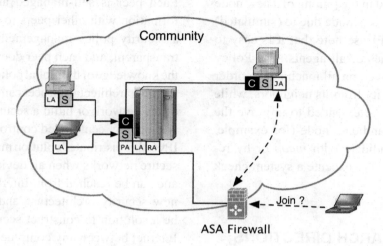

scripting interfaces allow our workers to control other devices that cannot run our agents:

- **Communicator:** Relays the messages to other communicators in the same network. When a node wants to join the community (trusted zone), it contacts the communicator that transmits its demand to the community. While the node negotiates its admission (i.e., through the exchange and application of security rules), the Communicator will act as a proxy for that node.

- **Schedulers:** Schedulers act as MOM (Message Oriented Middleware) servers, relaying messages between the agents. This choice allows agents to interact with the community without knowing exactly where a service is executed. Schedulers in the same community exchange messages (through the Communicators) in order to keep a replicated database.

- **Workers:** In our scenario, we implemented four different worker agents:
  - ◦ Local firewall agent (LA): These workers act on the local firewall, modifying the *iptables* on the machine.

- ◦ Remote firewall agent (RA): These workers execute distant actions on devices that cannot host a local firewall agent (for instance, we use them to control the Cisco routers ACL in our network).
- ◦ Policy agent (PA): When a new firewall rule must be implemented, this policy agent contacts both local and remote firewall workers in order to distribute the new rules. In our experiment the network administrator controls this Policy agent, but it could also be interconnected to an IDS/IPS, reinforcing the network security in the case of an attack.
- ◦ Join agent (JA): When a new node wants to join the community, this agent ensures the transition by transmitting the inner rules to the candidate node, verifying that these rules are implemented and contacting the Policy agent to allow the new node into the network.

Although simple, this scenario can be used as a testbed for the testing other mechanisms. For instance, we were able to test the coordination mechanism involved in the joining of a new node and the banishment of a node due to (simulated) security breaches. Please note that it is easy to extend functionalities of all agents: The Policy agent may be deployed on all machines in order to monitor the activity from its neighbors, while the Join Agent can be extended to improve the validation of the candidate node (for example, by probing the candidate with *nmap* or by requiring the candidate to execute a system check application).

FUTURE RESEARCH DIRECTIONS

In addition to the issues presented in the previous section, several other elements can be integrated in order to form a real distributed security grid. Therefore, problems like agreement and trustworthiness require special attention in a distributed system as to ensure *liveness* properties. Indeed, a real environment may be subjected to malicious attacks that can block the network if too many false-positive alerts are raised. Current solutions from the security community like authentication and cryptography are not enough to ensure *liveness* as they focus mostly on *safety* properties, so distributed systems researchers may contribute with distributed agreement mechanisms able to handle this problem that is quite similar to the Byzantine Generals' Problem (Lamport, 1982).

The P2P community can also contribute to this subject, as the MOM approach used in our testbed probably is not the best solution for a large-scale deployment. Hence, most aspects regarding service deployment and discovery are essential to deliver efficient and fault-tolerant solutions.

CONCLUSION

The new approach developed in this paper permit to easily create a confidence community in which each user communications are safe and secured.

Each peer is self-managed and exchanges information with other peers to mutually develop a security policy management. This process is transparent, and each peer does not need to have the knowledge of the global policy. Moreover from this new architecture, a peer can be easily excluded of the network or build a secure ad-hoc network without any centralized control. In the advent of IPv6, this distributed solution may help to establish secure networks when all devices have public IP and can be reached from Internet. The proposed new security architecture and middleware can be a solution to construct secure solutions over Internet between any computers.

REFERENCES

Allcock, W., Chervenak, A., Foster, I., Pearlman, L., Welch, V., & Wilde, M. (2001). *Globus toolkit support for distributed data-intensive science*. In International Conference on Computing in High Energy and Nuclear Physics (CHEP'01). IEEE Press.

Anderson, D. P. (2004). BOINC: A System for public-resource computing and storage. In *GRID'04: Proceedings of the Fifth IEEE/ACM International Workshop on Grid Computing* (pp. 4–10). Washington, DC: IEEE Computer Society.

Anderson, D. P., Cobb, J., Korpela, E., Lebofsky, M., & Werthimer, D. (2002). SETI@home: An experiment in public- resource computing. *Communications of the ACM, 45*(11), 56–61. doi:10.1145/581571.581573

Baker, M., Buyya, R., & Laforenza, D. (2002). Grids and grid technologies for wide-area distributed computing. *Software: Practice and Experience (SPE) Journal, 32*(15), 1437–1466.

Buchegger, S., & Leboudec, J. Y. (2002). Performance analysis of the CONFIDANT protocol (cooperation of nodes - fairness in dynamic ad-hoc networks). In *Proceedings of MobiHoc 2002*.

Cappello, F., Djilali, S., Fedak, G., Herault, T., Magniette, F., Néri, V., & Lodygensky, O. (2004). Computing on large scale distributed systems: XtremWeb architecture, programming models, security, tests and convergence with Grid. *FGCS Future Generation Computer Science, 21*, 417–437. doi:10.1016/j.future.2004.04.011

Caron, E., & Desprez, F. (2006). Diet: A scalable toolbox to build network enabled servers on the grid. *International Journal of High Performance Computing Applications, 20*(3), 335–352. doi:10.1177/1094342006067472

Castelluccia, C., & Spognardi, A. (2007). Rok: A robust key pre-distribution protocol for multi-stage wireless sensor networks. In *Proceedings of IEEE SecureComm, International Conference on Security and Privacy in Communication Networks*, Nice, France.

Castellucia, C., & Francillon, A. (2008). *Protéger les réseaux de capteurs sans fil*. Paper presented at the Symposium sur la Sécurité des Technologies de l'Information et des Communications (SSTIC), Rennes, France.

Ebalard, A., & Valadon, G. (2006). *La sécurité dans mobile IPv6*. Paper presented at the Symposium sur la Sécurité des Technologies de l'Information et des Communications (SSTIC), Rennes, France.

Elgoarany, K., & Eltoweissy, M. (2007). Security in mobile IPv6: A survey. *Information Security Technical Report, 12*(1), 32–43. doi:10.1016/j.istr.2007.02.002

Flauzac, O., Krajecki, M., & Steffenel, L. (2010). CONFIIT: A middleware for peer-to-peer computing. *The Journal of Supercomputing, 53*(1), 86–102. doi:10.1007/s11227-009-0349-7

Foster, I., & Kesselman, C. (1997). Globus: A metacomputing infrastructure toolkit. *The International Journal of Supercomputer Applications, 11*(2), 115–128. doi:10.1177/109434209701100205

Freenet. (2011). Retrieved February 23, 2011, from http://freenetproject.org/

HyunGon. K., & ByeongKyun, O. (2008) Secure and low latency handoff scheme for proxy mobile IPv6. In *Mobility '08: Proceedings of the International Conference on Mobile Technology, Applications, and Systems* (pp. 1-9). New York, NY: ACM Press.

Kubiatowicz, J., Bindel, D., Chen, Y., Eaton, P., Geels, D., & Gummadi, R. … Zhao, B. (2000). Oceanstore: An architecture for global-scale persistent storage. In *Proceedings of International Conference on Architectural Support for Programming Languages and Operating Systems (ASPLOS)*. ACM Press.

Lacour, S., Perez, C., & Priol, T. (2004). A network topology description model for grid application deployment. In *Proceedings of the Fifth IEEE/ACM International Workshop on Grid Computing (GRID '04)*, (pp. 61–68). Washington, DC: IEEE Computer Society.

Lamport, L., Shostak, R., & Pease, M. (1982). The Byzantine generals problem. *ACM Transactions on Programming Languages and Systems, 4*(3), 382–401. doi:10.1145/357172.357176

Lidong, Z., & Zygmunt, J. H. (1999). Securing ad hoc networks. *IEEE Network, 13*(6), 24–30. doi:10.1109/65.806983

Ping, Y., Yan, Y., Yafei, H., Yiping, Z., & Shiyong, Z. (2004) Securing ad hoc networks through mobile agent. In *InfoSecu '04; Proceedings of the 3rd International Conference on Information Security*. ACM Press. Rabat, C., Bui, A., & Flauzac, O. (2005). A random walk topology management solution for Grid. In *Proceedings of Innovative Internet Community Systems (I2CS '05), Lecture Notes in Computer Science 3908*, Paris, France. Springer.

Valadon, G. (2008). *Mobile IPv6: Architectures et protocoles* (PhD Thesis). Paris, France: Université Pierre et Marie Curie.

ADDITIONAL READING

Abd-El-Malek, M., Ganger, G., Goodson, G., Reiter, M., & Wylie, J. (2005). Fault-scalable Byzantine fault-tolerant services. In *Proceedings of the ACM Symposium on Operating Systems Principles*.

Bui, A., Flauzac, O., & Rabat, C. (2007). Fully distributed active and passive task management for grid computing. In *Proceedings of the Sixth International Symposium on Parallel and Distributed Computing (ISPDC '07)*, IEEE Computer Society.

Castro, M., & Liskov, B. (2002). Practical Byzantine fault tolerance and proactive recovery. *ACM Transactions on Computer Systems, 20*(4), 398–461. doi:10.1145/571637.571640

Clement, A., Wong, E., Alvisi, L., Dahlin, M., & Marchetti, M. (2009). *Making Byzantine fault tolerant systems tolerate Byzantine faults*. USENIX Symposium on Networked Systems Design and Implementation.

Cowling, J., Myers, D., Liskov, B., Rodrigues, R., & Shrira, L. (2006). HQ replication: A hybrid quorum protocol for Byzantine fault tolerance. In *Proceedings of the 7th USENIX Symposium on Operating Systems Design and Implementation*.

Hugues, L. (2010). *The Second Internet: Reinventing computing networking with IPv6*. Open-source book. Retrieved February 24, 2011, from "http://www.ipv6forum.org/dl/books/the_second_internet.pdf"

Kotla, R., Alvisi, L., Dahlin, M., Clement, A., & Wong, E. (2009). Zyzzyva: Speculative Byzantine fault tolerance. *ACM Transactions on Computer Systems, 27*(4).

KEY TERMS AND DEFINITIONS

Bizantine General's Problem: The Byzantine Generals' Problem is an agreement problem in which generals of the Byzantine Empire's army must decide unanimously whether to attack some enemy army. The problem is complicated by the geographic separation of the generals, who must communicate by sending messengers to each other, and by the presence of traitors amongst the generals. These traitors can act arbitrarily in order to achieve the following aims: trick some generals into attacking; force a decision that is not consistent with the generals' desires, e.g. forcing an attack when no general wished to attack; or confusing some generals to the point that they are unable to make up their minds. If the traitors succeed in any of these goals, any resulting attack is doomed, as only a concerted effort can result in victory. Byzantine fault tolerance can be achieved if the loyal (non-faulty) generals have a unanimous agreement on their strategy. Note that if the source general is correct, all loyal generals must agree upon that value. Otherwise, the choice of strategy agreed upon is irrelevant.

Grid Computing: Grid computing refers to the combination of computer resources from multiple administrative domains to reach a common goal. What distinguishes grid computing from conventional high performance computing systems such as cluster computing is that grids tend to be more loosely coupled, heterogeneous, and geographically dispersed. Although most grid environments focus on distributed computing, the grid computing paradigm is one of the basis of cloud computing – distributed data, services and infrastructure.

Intrusion Detection Systems: An intrusion detection system (IDS) is a device or software application that monitors network and/or system activities for malicious activities or policy violations and produces reports to a Management Station. Intrusion prevention is the process of performing intrusion detection and attempting to stop detected possible incidents. Intrusion detection and prevention systems (IDPS) are primarily focused on identifying possible incidents, logging information about them, attempting to stop them, and reporting them to security administrators.

IPv6 Security: Internet Protocol version 6 (IPv6) is a version of the Internet Protocol (IP) that is designed to succeed Internet Protocol version 4 (IPv4). IPv6 is designed to restore the end-to-end connectivity lost by IPv4 depletion countermeasures (RFC 1918, etc.), but also implements additional features not present in IPv4 such as simplified address assignment (stateless address autoconfiguration) and network mobility, which can menace bad designed networks.

MOM: Message-oriented middleware (MOM) is software infrastructure focused on sending and receiving messages between distributed systems. MOM allows application modules to be distributed over heterogeneous platforms, and reduces the complexity of developing applications that span multiple operating systems and network protocols by insulating the application developer from the details of the various operating system and network interfaces.

NAC: Network Access Control (NAC) is an approach to computer network security that attempts to unify endpoint security technology (such as antivirus, host intrusion prevention, and vulnerability assessment), user or system authentication and network security enforcement.

VPN: A virtual private network (VPN) is a computer network that uses a public telecommunication infrastructure such as the Internet to provide remote offices or individual users with secure access to their organization's network.

ENDNOTES

[1] http://www.cisco.com/en/US/products/ps6120/prod_models_comparison.html

[2] Cisco Network Access Control Appliance - http://www.cisco.com/go/nac

[3] http://www.packetfence.org

[4] http://www.cisco.com/go/mars

[5] http://penrose.uk6x.com/

Chapter 23
Effective Malware Analysis Using Stealth Breakpoints

Amit Vasudevan
CyLab, Carnegie Mellon University, USA

ABSTRACT

Fine-grained malware analysis requires various powerful analysis tools. Chief among them is a debugger that enables runtime binary analysis at the instruction level. One of the important services provided by a debugger is the ability to stop execution of code at arbitrary points during runtime, using breakpoints. Software breakpoints change the code being analyzed so that it can be interrupted during runtime. Most, if not all malware are very sensitive to code modification with self-modifying and/or self-checking capabilities, rendering the use of software breakpoints limited in their scope. Hardware breakpoints on the other hand, use a subset of the CPU registers and exception mechanisms to provide breakpoints that do not entail code modification. However, hardware breakpoints support limited breakpoint ability (typically only 2-4 locations) and are susceptible to various anti-debugging techniques employed by malware. This chapter describes a novel breakpoint technique (called stealth breakpoints) that provides unlimited number of breakpoints which are robust to detection and countering mechanisms. Further, stealth breakpoints retain all the features (code, data and I/O breakpoint abilities) of existing hardware and software breakpoint schemes and enables easy integration with existing debuggers.

INTRODUCTION

Malware -- a term that refers to viruses, trojans, worms, spyware or any form of malicious code -- is widespread today. Given the devastating effects that malware have on the computing world, detecting and countering malware is an important goal. Malware analysis is a challenging multi-step

DOI: 10.4018/978-1-4666-0978-5.ch023

process providing insight into malware structure and functionality, facilitating the development of an antidote. To successfully detect and counter malware, malware analysts must be able to analyze them in binary, in both coarse- (behavioral) and fine-grained (structural) fashions.

Microscopic malware analysis is a fine-grained analysis process that provides insight into malware structure and inner functioning. This helps in gleaning important information about a malware and facilitates the development of an antidote. With malware writers employing more complex and hard to analyze techniques, there is need to perform microscopic analysis of malicious code to counter them effectively.

Fine-grained analysis requires the aid of various powerful tools, chief among them being a debugger that enables runtime binary analysis at the instruction level. One of the important services provided by a debugger is the ability to stop execution of code being debugged at an arbitrary point during runtime. This is achieved using breakpoints, which can be of two types: Hardware and Software.

Hardware breakpoints are provided by the CPU and support precise breakpoints on code, data and I/O. They are deployed by programming specific CPU registers to specify the breakpoint locations and type. Software breakpoints on the other hand are implemented by changing the code being debugged to trigger certain exceptions upon execution (usually a breakpoint exception). However, both hardware and software breakpoints are severely limited in the context of malware.

Current CPUs however, contain support for only 2–4 hardware breakpoints. This imposes a serious restriction on the analysis process in the context of malware, most if not all of which carry complex polymorphic and metamorphic code streams (Szor, 2005). Further, many malware employ efficient anti-debugging primitives to prevent hardware breakpoints from being used altogether. For example, the W32/HIV virus uses CPU debug registers and the breakpoint exception for its internal computations while the W32/Ratos employs the breakpoint exception to handle its decryption in kernel-mode.

Current software breakpoint techniques either rely on the availability of program sources or entail modification to the executing code, both of which are unsuitable in the context of malware. Most malware exist in binary form and possess self-modifying and/or self-checking (SM-SC) capabilities. Further, software breakpoints do not

support I/O breakpoints. Also, there are speculations regarding the correctness of certain software breakpoint implementations. The combination of trap and single-stepping may result in missed breakpoints in a multithreaded program if not correctly implemented by the debugger (Ramsey, 1994).

In contrast, stealth breakpoints provide unlimited number of code, data and I/O breakpoints, which are robust to detection and countermeasures. While various ideas using virtual memory for breakpoint purposes have been explored in many debuggers (Beander, 1983; Loukides et al., 1996; Compuware Corp., 1999), they allow only data read and/or write breakpoints. Also none of them are specifically tailored for malware analysis and their breakpoint implementation can be easily detected and thwarted. In contrast, stealth breakpoints leverage virtual memory, single-stepping and CPU task state segments (TSS; used to store all the information the CPU needs in order to manage a task. This includes the processor registers, stack and the task's virtual memory mappings) to provide a stealth and portable breakpoint framework highly conducive for malware analysis. Further, the framework can be easily integrated into existing debuggers and its performance is within limits to suit interactive debugging.

This chapter starts with a brief background on breakpoints in general and discusses related work. This is followed by a detailed description of the design and implementation of stealth breakpoints. Following that is a discussion on analysis experiences with several real-world malware and the framework performance. The chapter concludes with a summary of stealth breakpoints and directions for future research in this space.

BACKGROUND AND RELATED WORK

Breakpoints — debugging aids that provide the ability to stop execution of code at an arbitrary point during execution — are primarily categorized into hardware and software. There are various designs and implementations of breakpoints. Several authors have speculated that efficient data breakpoints require special purpose hardware [Johnson, 1982; Cargill et al., 1987; Mellor-Crummey et al., 1989). There are also surveys (Paxson, 1990) which discuss the architectural support towards debugging that emphasize the need for special purpose hardware as a debugging aid. One such mechanism is called ICE breakpoints. ICE or in-circuit emulation is a specialized circuitry embedded within the processors, designed for debugging the internals of the processor. There are various approaches to embed the functionality of in-circuit emulation, in hardware, software and hybrid (Chen et al., 2002). ICE breakpoints require supporting hardware (Corelis Corp., 2005; American Arium Corp., 2009) and are typically used for processor core debugging than normal program debugging. Many processors also have built-in support for hardware breakpoint facilities. This involves a subset of the processor register set and exception mechanisms to provide precise code, data and/or I/O breakpoints albeit allowing breakpoints to be set on a limited number of locations (typically 2–4 locations).

Software breakpoints on the other hand provide an elegant, cost-effective and scalable solution with the existing hardware. There are various categories of software breakpoints. The first variety relies on program source code availability. This coupled with help from the compiler is used to insert data and/or code breakpoints. Practical data breakpoints (Wahbe, 1992; Wahbe et al., 1993) use efficient runtime data structures and ideas from compiler optimization to provide several methods of data breakpoints. The method involves checking all read and/or write instructions using complex data flow analysis with a segmented bitmap, reserving registers to hold intermediate values during address lookup.

The second variety of software breakpoints uses processor supported trap and/or breakpoint instructions to set desired breakpoints. There are a host of implementations as in GDB (Loukides, 1996), KDB (Buhr, 1996), Windbg (Robbins, 1999), DBX (Linton, 1990), and Softice (Compuware Corp., 1999). In this method, a debugger typically encodes a 1 byte trap instruction at the breakpoint location, while saving the byte that was replaced. When the breakpoint triggers by means of the trap exception, the debugger gets control and the original byte is replaced and the program is restarted to execute the instruction. While this method solves the problem of the number of breakpoints that could be active simultaneously, it does not support data and/or I/O breakpoints and is unsuitable for self-modifying and self-checking code. Also, there are speculations regarding the correctness of trap-based breakpoint implementations. The combination of trap and single-stepping may result in missed breakpoints in a multithreaded program if not correctly implemented by the debugger (Ramsey, 1994).

Fast breakpoints (Kessler, 1990) suggested a novel way to implement software breakpoints using instruction flow change. The idea is to encode a jump instruction to transfer control to the debugger at the breakpoint. While the idea is similar to that of a trap, this method, to some extent, avoids the problem of correctness of a breakpoint in a multi-threaded program. However, the mechanism supports only code breakpoints and is not applicable to self-modifying and self-checking code.

There are software breakpoint mechanisms which employ the virtual memory system. Vax debug (Beander, 1983), a source level debugger, implements data read and/or write breakpoints using page protection techniques. The attribute of the memory page containing the breakpoint is modified so as to trigger an exception when any location in the page is accessed. The debugger then performs a few checks to ensure the correctness of breakpoint triggering and responds accordingly. However, this idea was not studied or developed further to study the performance or to support code and I/O breakpoints. Popular debuggers such as GDB (Loukides, 1996) and Softice (Compuware Corp., 1999) and Poor Man's Watch-point (Copperman, 1995) also support data breakpoints via a similar mechanism.

Another category of software breakpoints is found in debuggers based on virtual machines. While complete virtual machine based interfaces such as Simics (Magnusson et al., 2002) and debuggers running on them can overcome many problems related to breakpoints and their robustness to attacks, they are seldom constructed in that fashion as they do not specifically target malware analysis and are not well suited for interactive debugging. The alternative of using debuggers based on compatibility layers such as TTVM (King et al., 2005), has its drawback since they do not run on commodity OSs and use offline techniques based on logging, replaying and check-pointing (Dunlap et al., 2002). Also, they only maintain a single or a subset of the execution traces which is unsuitable for self-modifying and self-checking code.

DESIGN AND IMPLEMENTATION

Overview

Stealth Breakpoints are realized through a combination of virtual memory, single-stepping, TSS (for applicable processors) and simple stealth techniques. The basic idea involves breakpoint triggering by manipulation of memory page attributes of the underlying virtual memory system (for code, data or memory-mapped I/O breakpoints) and I/O port access control bits in the TSS (for legacy I/O breakpoints). Note that virtual memory and single-stepping are common to most if not all processor architectures and, a TSS (or an equivalent) is typically found on processors supporting legacy I/O such as the IA-32 (and compatible) processors. Figure 1 illustrates the architecture of the stealth breakpoint framework.

The core of the framework is composed of a *Kernel-Mode Monitor* (KMM), a *Page-Fault Handler* (PFH), a *General Protection Fault Handler* (GPFH), and a *Single-Step Handler* (SSH). The KMM protects critical kernel-mode structures and OS regions from tampering and facilitates kernel-mode legacy I/O breakpoints. The PFH provides breakpoints to be set on code, data and memory-mapped I/O while the GPFH provides

Figure 1. Architecture of stealth breakpoints

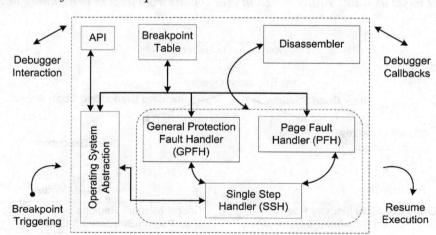

legacy I/O breakpoint support. Every breakpoint has an associated callback (provided by the debugger), a function to which control is transferred upon breakpoint triggering.

When a breakpoint triggers, the PFH or GPFH receive control, determine the type of breakpoint (by employing a disassembler) and invoke the callback to do the processing and resume execution. The single-step handler is employed by the framework for breakpoint persistence, a feature that allows a breakpoint to re-trigger automatically at a later time. A stealth breakpoint can be persistent (able to re-trigger) or non-persistent (one-shot) and can be active or inactive at any instant. A breakpoint-table contains the list of breakpoints set using the framework and is used to identify a breakpoint (and its callback) during breakpoint triggering and processing.

Kernel Mode Monitor (KMM)

The Kernel-Mode Monitor (KMM) performs two important functions: protects critical kernel-mode structures and OS regions from tampering and facilitates kernel-mode legacy I/O breakpoints. The KMM (Figure 2) employs three concepts for its functionality: Stealth Localized Executions (SLE), Execution Overlaying and Cloning.

Stealth Localized Executions

Stealth Localized Executions (Vasudevan et al., 2006) is a mechanism by which a code stream (or a group of code streams) is executed in a manner that allows monitoring/alteration while mimicking its normal execution. In other words, it allows dissecting an executing code stream at the instruction level while making it very difficult for the code stream to detect SLE in a deterministic fashion.

SLE begins at an overlay point and ends at a release point, a range within a code stream where analysis is desired. The basic idea behind the runtime dissection of a code stream involves dynamic binary translation. SLE begins by disassembling instructions at the overlay point to construct instruction blocks within a local code cache. The instruction blocks are then scanned to insert stealth-implants which prevent SLE from being detected by the executing code-streams. The instruction blocks are then executed within the least privilege level during which SLE handles various events that a block might cause, e.g., access to memory regions and CPU registers. Every instruction block terminates with an xfer-stub - a group of non-invasive instructions that transfer control to the next instruction block via SLE.

SLE is completely re-entrant and hence is multithreaded in both user and kernel mode. Further, it

Figure 2. Kernel mode monitor: Protects stealth breakpoints from attacks originating in either user or kernel-mode

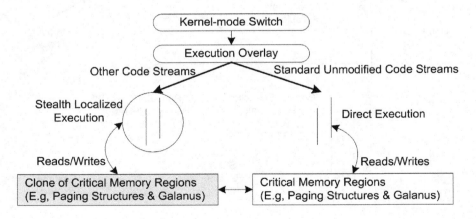

incorporates performance enhancement strategies which allow coalescing of instruction blocks as well as skipping standard OS code streams. Most importantly SLE runs on a real system at real time thereby allowing a malware to see the real system as it would normally.

Kernel-Mode Execution Overlaying

One way for the KMM to execute kernel-mode code under supervision, would be to set an overlay point on every entry into kernel mode and a release point into exit from kernel-mode. However, doing this would entail running the entire OS kernel code within SLE which would result in high run time costs. However, if we assume that we can trust the underlying OS and associated kernel mode components are not malicious to start off with, we can then employ SLE only on kernel-mode code that are not a part of this standard set. Note that this assumption is very realistic as malware analysis is typically carried out on systems which are clean in the first place.

There are only a fixed number of ways in which a nonstandard kernel mode code stream can execute within a commodity OS. As an example on all versions of Windows (XP, 2K, 2003) the kernel function KiSwapContext is the only function that can switch to a kernel-mode code stream for execution. The KMM sets a stealth breakpoint at the KiSwapContext function and executes the target nonstandard code stream using SLE.

Cloning

The KMM maintains clones of memory pages that correspond to critical memory regions such as page-tables, descriptor tables, OS code and data and supporting OS kernel-mode components. During initialization the KMM creates exact copies of such memory pages which are called clones. The KMM then sets up SLE in such a way that during block execution all the original pages are marked non-present. Further, SLE is setup to catch read/writes to such memory areas during block execution. Upon access to such regions, the KMM presents to the block the cloned version of the pages. Note that, standard code streams see the original critical memory regions, while the non-standard code streams always see the cloned copies.

Memory Breakpoints

Stealth breakpoints use the virtual memory system of the underlying platform to provide breakpoints on code, data and memory-mapped I/O. Support for virtual memory on most processors, is in the form of page directories and page tables. The memory addressing space is divided into chunks of equal size elements called a page (typically 4K or 8K bytes in size). Pages can have various attributes such as read, read/write, present, not-present, user, supervisor etc. These attributes along with a page-fault exception is used to provide virtual memory support and memory protection.

A page-fault exception is generated by the underlying processor when a reference to a page is inconsistent with the page attributes (e.g. a write is issued to a location in the referenced page, while the page attribute is read-only). The OS normally installs a handler for the page-fault exception, which implements a paging algorithm, provides protection and other features such as copy-on-write etc. The stealth breakpoint framework installs its own PFH (pseudo-code shown in Figure 3), replacing and chaining to the existing handler to implement breakpoints on code, data and memory-mapped I/O.

When a memory breakpoint is set, the attribute of the memory page corresponding to the breakpoint location is made not-present. This results in a page-fault exception when any location in that page is referenced. When the framework PFH gets control, it first checks to see if there is an active memory breakpoint on the page. If not, the PFH applies a clock patch (to hide its processing latency) and obtains the current PFH address from

Figure 3. Stealth breakpoints page-fault handler: Handles code, data and memory-mapped I/O breakpoints

```
1: linearAddr = linear address of the page-fault
2: mPfn = memory page corresponding to linearAddr
3: if no active breakpoints on mPfn then
4:    pfhPointer = current PFH from cloned IDT
5:    Apply clock patch
6:    If pfhPointer = OSdefault and OS regions unmodified then
7:       Resume execution at pfhPointer
8:    else
9:       Start SLE at pfhPointer
10:   end if
11: end if
12: Attributes of mPfn |= Present
13: eAddr = effective address of instruction that caused the fault
14: if eAddr = BreakpointAddress then
15:    bpType = get breakpoint type [read, write or execute]
16:    ProcessBreakPoint(linearAddr, eAddr, bpType)
17: end if
18: if CPUInstructionPointer in mPfn then
19:    CPUTrapFlag |= SingleStep
20:    Setup SSH in original IDT
21: end if
22: Apply clock Patch
23: End of Fault
```

the clone Interrupt Descriptor Table (IDT; a CPU data structure that contains pointers to various exception handlers). If the PFH address defaults to that of the OS and the OS regions are unmodified, the OS PFH is invoked directly. If the OS regions were modified in some form, then the PFH sets an overlay point on the OS PFH address and begins SLE. This is shown in lines 1–11.

If the framework PFH was invoked due to an active memory breakpoint on a memory page, the effective address of the instruction and the type of memory access causing the fault are obtained. If the effective address matches any breakpoint location and type, the breakpoint is triggered and processed (lines 12–17, Figure 3). The PFH then prepares to re-trigger any persistent breakpoints on the memory page by setting the CPU trap flag. It then applies a clock patch and returns marking the end of exception (lines 18–23).

Legacy I/O Breakpoints

Legacy I/O uses processor supported I/O instructions to read from or write to a I/O port. Legacy I/O breakpoints involve breakpoint triggering due to such I/O instructions attempting to read from or a write to a specific I/O port. Processors which support legacy I/O along with virtual memory, support legacy I/O protection or virtualization in the form of a Task State Segment (TSS) or an equivalent.

Stealth breakpoints enforce user-mode legacy I/O breakpoints by leveraging the CPU TSS. The TSS consists of a bitmap structure called the I/O Bitmap which is a bit array with 1 bit for every legacy I/O port in the system. If the bit corresponding to an I/O port is set to a 1, the processor causes a general protection fault (GPF) when I/O instructions referencing that I/O port are executed. The stealth breakpoint framework installs its own GPFH (pseudo-code shown in Figure 4), replacing and chaining to the existing handler to implement breakpoints on user-mode legacy I/O.

Figure 4. Stealth breakpoints general protection fault handler: Handles user-mode legacy I/O breakpoints

```
1: Obtain linear-address of the fault via TSS
2: Disassemble the instruction causing the fault
3: If not legacy I/O instruction
4:     Apply clock patch
5:     Chain to previous GPF handler
6: End If
7: Determine I/O port in disassembled instruction
8: If I/O breakpoint on I/O port
9:     Reset I/O bitmask for the port
10:     Find breakpoint type (read or write)
11:     Trigger breakpoint and process
12: End If
13: Setup re-triggering for persistent breakpoints on memory page
14: Setup single-step handler for breakpoint persistence
15: Apply clock patch
16: End of Fault
```

The GPFH semantics is very similar to the PFH. To set a breakpoint at the desired I/O location (read or write), the bit corresponding to the I/O port, in the I/O Bitmap array is set to 1. This results in a GPF when any access is attempted using that particular I/O port. When the GPFH gets control, it obtains the linear address of the fault via the TSS and disassembles the instruction causing the fault. If the instruction does not belong to the category of legacy I/O instructions, the GPFH applies a clock patch (if applicable) to hide its processing latency from the malware and chains to the original GPF handler as the fault was not due to the framework. This is shown in lines 1–6, Figure 4.

If the instruction causing the fault is identified as a legacy I/O instruction, the GPFH checks to see if the corresponding I/O port (extracted from the instruction) has a breakpoint set on it. If so, the corresponding I/O permission bit in the I/O Bitmap is set to a 0 to prevent recursive faults from accessing that port within the handler. The GPFH then obtains the breakpoint type (read or write) and processes the breakpoint. This is shown in lines 7–12, Figure 4. The rest of the GPFH processing (lines 13–16, Figure 4) is the same as described for the framework PFH.

To support legacy I/O breakpoints in kernel-mode, the stealth breakpoint framework uses the Kernel-Mode Monitor (KMM) as described pre-

viously. The KMM configures Stealth Localized Executions to implant xfer-stubs for all legacy I/O instructions that are found within all block corresponding to the instruction stream that is executed. On the x86 class of CPUs there are only 4 variants of the I/O instructions that need xfer-stubs (the IN, INS, OUT and OUTS instructions). The xfer-stubs transfer control to the breakpoint framework which then compares the destination port and triggers the breakpoint.

Breakpoint Persistence

Stealth Breakpoint persistence is achieved using the single-step feature of the CPU; a non-breakpoint instruction causing the fault is stepped over while temporarily disabling breakpoints. The framework Single-Step Handler (SSH) maintains a per-thread copy of the CPU trap flag. This is needed in order to invoke the SSH of the thread in case it installs one. Also, the SSH checks to see if the virtual CPU trap flag is set in the executing code-stream and if so invokes the thread SSH using SLE.

Figure 5 shows the SSH pseudo-code. When the SSH gets control due to a CPU single-step exception, the handler first makes sure that any effect of the CPU trap flag (indicator for single-step) is masked out of the instruction that has just been stepped over. This prevents the executing

Figure 5. Stealth breakpoints single step handler: Handles breakpoint persistence

```
1: remove effect of CPUTrapFlag and update virtualCPUTrapFlag
   of code-stream
2: for each activeBreakpoint do
3:    if activeBreakpoint is legacy I/O then
4:       IOBitmap[Port] = 0
5:    else
6:       mPfn = memory page corresponding to activeBreakpoint
7:       Attributes of mPfn |= Present
8:    end if
9: end for
10: if virtualCPUTrapFlag is SET then
11:    sshPointer = current SSH from cloned IDT
12:    Apply clock patch
13:    If sshPointer = OSdefault and OS regions unmodified then
14:       Resume execution at sshPointer
15:    else
16:       Start SLE at sshPointer
17:    end if
18: end if
19: Apply clock Patch
20: End of Fault
```

code stream from seeing the original value of the CPU trap flag. Any active breakpoints on the memory page are temporarily disabled by the SSH. For user-mode legacy I/O breakpoints, it clears the corresponding bit in the I/O Bitmap. This is shown in lines 1–9.

The SSH then checks the status of the virtual CPU trap flag of the executing code stream. If it is set, it obtains the current SSH address from the clone Interrupt Descriptor Table (IDT). If the SSH address defaults to that of the OS and the OS regions are unmodified, the OS SSH is invoked directly. If the OS regions were modified in some form, then the SSH sets an overlay point on the OS SSH address and begins SLE. The SSH then applies a clock patch (to hide its processing latency) and returns from the exception. This is shown in lines 10–20, Figure 5.

Security Analysis

The primary goal of stealth breakpoints is to ensure that it is undetectable from both user and kernel mode. The KMM employs SLE which in itself

cannot be deterministically detected (Vasudevan et al., 2006). Further, the KMM employs cloning to ensure that kernel mode code never sees the memory regions specific to the stealth breakpoint framework. Cloning also ensures that original critical memory regions such as page-tables and descriptor tables are the ones that are always used by the CPU whereas non-standard and modified standard kernel mode code streams read and write to their clones. Further, the clones do not contain values from the original structures that are specific to the stealth breakpoint framework (protection flags and exception handlers). Finally, the framework SSH maintains per-thread virtual trap-flags and will chain to the thread specific SSH handler in case one is installed. This prevents detection by querying the trap-flag status.

EXPERIENCES

This section describes experiences in analyzing real-world malware using stealth breakpoints. The discussions are based on analysis sessions involving the Troj/Feutel-S, W32/Wuke and W32/HIV malware. These malware contain sophisticated anti-debugging tricks which render traditional hardware and software breakpoints ineffective. The malware samples were obtained from Offensive Computing (Offensive Computing, 2010).

Troj/Feutel-S

Troj/Feutel-S is a key-logger running under the Windows OS and is usually installed by other rootkits or remote administration trojans. The malware is registered as a system service (usually named DriverCache) and includes a kernel mode component that installs a keyboard interrupt handler to record keystrokes. Troj/Feutel-S hides its critical files, configuration and process information and has the ability to inject its code into other processes to provide application specific key-logging. The following paragraphs describe

the key-logging mechanism of Troj/Feutel-S that was uncovered using stealth breakpoints.

Before the malware is executed, a code breakpoint is set on the OpenSCManager API. The breakpoint is immediately triggered to indicate that Troj/Feutel-S is loading a kernel-mode driver in the system. Following this, code breakpoints are set on the keyboard class driver dispatch routines to track keyboard I/O Request Packets (IRPs) originating from the malware kernel-mode driver. However, it is seen that no such IRPs are found. At this point, kernel-mode legacy I/O breakpoints are set on ports 0x60–0x64 (keyboard controller ports) with a hunch that the malware does key-logging by directly communicating with the keyboard controller. The breakpoints in this case successfully trigger on the code streams as shown in Figure 6a and Figure 6b.

Figure 6a shows part of the Troj/Feutel-S IRQ-1 interrupt handler. This interrupt is generated by

Figure 6. Trojan Feutel-S: (a) employs anti-hardware breakpoint techniques and performs direct keyboard I/O using IRQ-1 handler in kernel-mode, and (b) employs kernel-mode threads to conceal the location where keyboard I/O is done

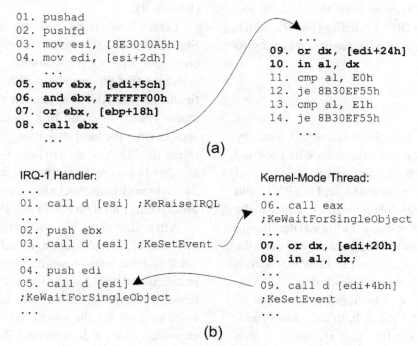

```
01. pushad
02. pushfd
03. mov esi, [8E3010A5h]
04. mov edi, [esi+2dh]
    ...
05. mov ebx, [edi+5ch]
06. and ebx, FFFFFF00h
07. or ebx, [ebp+18h]
08. call ebx
    ...
```
```
    ...
09. or dx, [edi+24h]
10. in al, dx
11. cmp al, E0h
12. je 8B30EF55h
13. cmp al, E1h
14. je 8B30EF55h
    ...
```

(a)

```
IRQ-1 Handler:
...
01. call d [esi] ;KeRaiseIRQL
...
02. push ebx
03. call d [esi] ;KeSetEvent
...
04. push edi
05. call d [esi]
;KeWaitForSingleObject
...
```
```
Kernel-Mode Thread:
...
06. call eax
;KeWaitForSingleObject
...
07. or dx, [edi+20h]
08. in al, dx;
...
09. call d [edi+4bh]
;KeSetEvent
...
```

(b)

the CPU as a result of any keyboard activity. As seen in lines 9–10, the malware uses the IN instruction to record the keystroke directly from the keyboard controller. Also, as seen in lines 5–8, the malware makes use of DR7 debug control register (operand of line 5) to check if any hardware breakpoints are set. If so, the target address of the CALL instruction in line 8 is computed to be a spurious one a leads to an irrecoverable fault in kernel-mode. Such checks are found scattered throughout the malware code streams precluding the use of traditional hardware breakpoints. Further, the code streams are metamorphic in nature which makes traditional software breakpoints ineffective.

Troj/Feutel-S also employs keyboard I/O in its kernel-mode threads (Figure 6b). This makes it difficult to find the exact location where the keyboard I/O is done. Let us consider Figure 6b. The kernel-mode thread waits on a kernel event that is set by the IRQ-1 handler (line 6). When IRQ-1 triggers as a result of a keyboard activity, it signals the corresponding event (lines 2-3), upon which the kernel-mode thread performs the I/O involving the keyboard controller (lines 7–8). Once the I/O is complete, the kernel-mode thread signals the IRQ-1 handler (line 9), which then performs an end of exception returning to the kernel.

W32/Wuke

W32/Wuke is a kernel-mode rootkit used by the W32/Wuke@MM worm to hide its files and processes. W32/Wuke incorporates low-level device access to the hard-disk and the BIOS and employs several anti-debugging tricks which make it difficult to analyze using traditional debugging primitives. The following paragraphs describe how the file access mechanism of W32/Wuke is documented using stealth breakpoints.

As a first step, code breakpoints are set on all filesystem related APIs in both user and kernel-mode to observe the files that are being created

or used by the worm. It is immediately observed that the W32/Wuke malware is being loaded by the worm. However, after that point the code breakpoints corresponding to the filesystem APIs are never triggered. The worm somehow bypasses the filesystem APIs and directly accesses the hard-disk using the W32/Wuke rootkit. Analysis proceeds by setting a code breakpoint on the DeviceIoControl API which is used to communicate with a kernel-mode driver from user-mode. One can immediately observe a series of breakpoints corresponding to the DeviceIoControl API issued to the W32/Wuke rootkit.

More code breakpoints are set on the disk driver dispatch routines to track any I/O request packet being sent directly to the underlying disk bypassing the flow of a normal file-system function invocation. However, no such I/O request packets are found. This shows the rootkit controls the hard-disk at a much lower level, possibly using direct I/O commands to the hard-disk controller. To ascertain this, a legacy I/O breakpoint is set on the command I/O port (0x1F7) being used by the primary hard-disk controller. The breakpoint is triggered in a region of code shown Figure 7 (lines 7–9).

Let us consider the code fragment shown in Figure 7. Lines 4-9 program the primary hard-disk controller in PIO (Programmed I/O) mode to select the first physical hard-disk. Further investigation into the RETN instruction in line 15 reveals that it results in a call to a function that reads sectors from the hard-disk using PIO commands (lines 16–33). Also seen in lines 1-2, is one of the anti-hardware breakpoint strategies employed by the malware which checks for any active hardware breakpoints and if so halts the CPU.

After several such investigations it is found that the W32/Wuke upon initialization copies itself and the worm towards the end of the root partition and erases details in the file allocation tables. Thus, the OS does not see any files specific to the worm. When the worm needs to read/write its supporting files, it does so via a DeviceIoControl

Figure 7. W32/Wuke Rootkit: employs anti-hardware breakpoint techniques and performs direct disk I/O using programmed I/O mode of ATA controllers

```
    ...
01. mov eax, dr0                16. ...
02. mov ebx, dr1                17. mov al, [esi]
03. or eax, ebx                 18. out dx, al
    ...                         19. inc dx
04. mov dx, 01f6h               20. inc esi
05. mov al, d0h                 21. loop 21
06. out dx,al                   22. mov dx, 01f7h
    ...                         23. mov al, 20h
07. mov dx, 01f7h               24. out dx, al
08. mov al, 08h                 25. dec dx
09. out dx,al                   26. in al, dx
10. in al, dx                   27. and al, 08h
11. and al, 60h                 28. jz 28
12. jz errordisk                29. in al, dx
    ...                         30. mov ax, 01f0h
13. mov ebx, [esp+20h]          31. mov cx, 512
14. push ebx                    32. les edi, [esi+20h]
15. retn                        33. rep insb
    ...                         ...
```

command to W32/Wuke, which in turn employs PIO mode to access the required information from the harddisk.

W32/HIV

The W32.HIV is a dangerous per-process memory resident Win32 subsystem virus that infects Windows executable and MSI (install) archives and corrupts certain important system files. The virus has a unique technique of upgrading itself from the internet and also possesses e-mail spreading abilities. Besides employing a stock encryption and polymorphic/metamorphic engine, the virus uses anti-debugging tricks to prevent itself from being analyzed. It also has mechanisms to halt the machine completely if a debugger is detected.

The W32.HIV virus and modified strains cannot be analyzed using traditional software breakpoints as we describe in the following paragraphs. Even hardware breakpoints fail to help in the complete analysis of the virus.

Consider a code fragment from the W32/HIV as shown in Figure 8a. This code fragment might not look interesting at a first glance. However, after

further analysis, it is found that this code fragment is in fact an example of the virus polymorphic/metamorphic engine kicking into action.

If a traditional software breakpoint is set on the second CMP instruction (line 13, Figure 8a), it is seen that the breakpoint is not triggered. Tracing back a few instructions manually, the problem is found to be the section of the code fragment (lines 6–11, Figure 8a), that generates new code (at runtime) overwriting existing code starting from the second CMP instruction (line 13, Figure 8a). This explains why the traditional software breakpoint is not triggered, as it is overwritten by the newly generated code. A manual work-around to this problem is achieved by tracing through the REP MOVSB instruction (line 11, Figure 8a) one step at a time and inserting a traditional software breakpoint after the new code is generated. However, since a majority of the virus code is littered with such code fragments, this process soon becomes a tedious task.

Now, consider the code fragment as shown in Figure 8b, which will be used to demonstrate the self-checking nature of the virus. The W32.HIV has the capability to detect any kind of modifica-

Figure 8. W32/HIV: (a) Self-modifying code fragment, (b) Self-checking code fragment, and (c) Anti-debugging code fragment. Lines in bold denote locations where a breakpoint is set

(a)

```
...
1.  xor eax, esi
2.  and eax, 38567fffh
3.  add eax, ecx
4.  cmp eax, edi
5.  jbe 10015000
6.  mov edi, eax
7.  mov ecx, [esi+3ch]
8.  xor ecx, [esi+30h]
9.  mov [esi+3ch], ecx
10. mov esi, [esi+40h]
11. rep movsb
12. mov eax, edi
13. cmp eax, 5
14. je 1001F0F0
15. cmp eax, 10
16. je 1001F1F0
17. cmp eax, 4F
18. je 1001F4F0
...
```

(b)

```
...
1.  xor eax, esi
2.  and eax, 38567fffh
3.  add eax, ecx
4.  cmp eax, edi
5.  jbe 100F5000
6.  mov edi, eax
7.  mov ecx, [esi+3ch]
8.  xor ecx, [esi+30h]
9.  mov [esi+3ch], ecx
10. mov esi, [esi+40h]
11. xor eax, eax
12. mov dl, [edi]
13. or dl, [esi]
14. movzx edx, dl
15. add eax, edx
16. inc edi
17. inc esi
18. loop 12
19. cmp eax, 5
20. je 100FF0F0
21. cmp eax, 10
22. je 100FF1F0
...
```

(c)

```
...
1.  sub esp, 8
2.  sidt [esp]
3.  mov eax, [esp]
4.  mov edx, [esp+2]
5.  mov eax, [edx+8]
6.  cmp eax, [esi+2bh]
7.  jb 11
8.  cmp eax, [esi+2dh]
9.  ja 11
10. jmp 12
11. jmp CA50D000h
12. mov dr0, edi
13. mov eax, esi
14. ror eax, 16
15. mov dr1, eax
16. mov ebx, dr2
...
```

tion done to its code and will act in a way that will confuse the individual analyzing the virus. The code fragment shown in Figure 8b is very well constructed to mislead someone who is trying to study the behavior of the virus. Though, at a first glance it is very similar to the self-modifying code fragment as shown in Figure 8a, it is just a plain sequence of instructions. When a traditional software breakpoint is set on the second CMP instruction (line 19, Figure 8b), it is found that the breakpoint triggers successfully. Everything appears normal, and there is no sign of any code changes etc. However, after further tracing, a section of code is reached that is garbage and leads to spurious faults. The problem is traced back to the section of the code fragment as shown in lines 11–18, Figure 8b.

Here we see an integrity check being attempted on the code starting from the CMP instruction on line 19, Figure 8b. Setting a traditional software

breakpoint on this CMP instruction causes the instruction to be overwritten with a breakpoint instruction. This causes the code fragment to compute a wrong checksum during the integrity check (lines 11–18, Figure 8b). Further, the virus is very intelligent in that, it does not terminate or branch to any location upon a failed integrity check. Instead, the checksum is the branch variable (stored in register EAX) itself. In other words, the virus uses the checksum as a representative of the target address of a branch that performs some processing pertaining to the functionality of the virus. Thus, on an incorrect checksum, it branches to a location where the code is nothing but garbage and on a valid checksum the code fragment performs the function it was designed for. To further complicate matters, the self-checking code fragments are generated at runtime with random predefined values for the branch variable (EAX) for each fragment. This precludes manual work-around by adjusting the branch variable values.

While it is possible to set hardware breakpoints on the code fragments discussed so far, further analysis reveals that the virus has efficient anti-debugging capabilities that prevent the use of hardware breakpoints too.

The hardware breakpoint mechanism on the IA-32 (and compatible) processors makes use of a set of debug registers named DR0–DR7 and an exception handler for breakpoint and single-step. Registers DR0–DR3 are 32-bit registers which contain the linear address in memory where a code, data or an I/O breakpoint should occur, providing 4 breakpoints in total to be active at a time. DR7 is a control register which is used to setup the breakpoints initially. When a breakpoint is triggered, the exception handler is invoked with certain status flags in the DR6 (status) register which describes the type of breakpoint and its attributes (code /data /I/O, read/write/execute).

Let us look at Figure 8c which shows a code fragment from the virus in the context of hardware breakpoints. The W32.HIV spawns (and eventually kills) several kernel-mode (privileged) threads in the system at arbitrary intervals. The code to spawn these threads is concealed within the virus polymorphic/metamorphic layers. The threads are different each time they are spawned, but have a common functionality as shown by the code fragment in Figure 8c.

The threads first check to see if the default single-step handler has been altered by checking the system interrupt descriptor table (IDT). It makes use of the SIDT instruction to grab hold of the single-step handler address. It then checks if the handler is pointing to something different from the expected system default range (e.g., for the Windows OS the range is C0000000h–C000FFFFh). If the handler address is out of range, the thread knows that there is a debugger installed, and behaves in a very unfriendly manner (using the JMP instruction) to throw the system into an unstable state as long as the debugger is active.

This is shown in lines 1–11, Figure 8c (the actual behavior is concealed behind the JMP instruction and is not shown here).

The second level of anti-debugging within the threads employ the debug registers themselves for computation and functioning as shown in lines 12–19, Figure 8c. The only work-around to this when using hardware breakpoints, is to manually compute the values in registers and trace them one at a time, while changing the instructions to hold registers other than debug registers. However, this is non-trivial as: (a) there are multiple threads one needs to change that are spawned and killed at regular intervals, and (b) the threads themselves have self-checking code fragments, which means one has to set the instructions back to what they were before proceeding to trace further.

However, since stealth breakpoints do not make use of any hardware specific debugging registers or change the code, it is possible to set breakpoints and trace through such code fragments with ease.

PERFORMANCE EVALUATION

The performance of a breakpoint framework such as stealth breakpoints depends heavily on the number and nature of code streams being debugged, and the way breakpoints are set. These factors are not easy to characterize and hence it is difficult to employ a representative debugging session for performance measurements. Therefore, we report the performance of stealth breakpoints on debugging sessions involving various real-world malware (W32/HIV, W32/MyDoom, W32/Ratos, Troj/Feutel-S and W32/Wuke).

We use our prototype debugger for performance measurements on an AMD 1.8GHz system with 512MB of physical memory running Windows XP SP2. Figure 9 shows the performance measurements of code, data and I/O stealth breakpoints, in the context of various arbitrary analysis sessions involving real-world malware. The code fragments within each session were chosen so that

Figure 9. Performance measurements for stealth breakpoints and comparison with traditional hardware breakpoints

	Malware	Mode	Stealth	H/w	Type
Memory Breakpoints (code and data on same memory page)					
1	Feutel-S	Kernel	0.314	NA	NS
2	Wuke	Kernel	0.412	NA	NS
3	Ratos	User	0.789	NA	S
4	Mydoom	User	0.397	0.026	S
Memory Breakpoints (code and data on different pages)					
5	Ratos	Kernel	2.122	NA	S,L
6	Doom	User	0.165	0.095	S,L
7	Ratos	User	0.864	NA	S,H
8	Wuke	User	0.102	0.019	NS,L
9	Doom	User	0.112	0.011	S,L
Kernel-mode Legacy I/O Breakpoints					
10	Wuke	Kernel	0.367	NA	DevIO
11	Wuke	Kernel	3.215	NA	Init
12	Feutel-S	Kernel	0.004	NA	Thread
13	Feutel-S	Kernel	1.785	NA	IRQ-1

their functionality remained the same with their structure being more or less constant for various deployments of the malware.

The latency shown represents the additional time that has elapsed (in seconds), between executing the code with the breakpoint set and breakpoint triggering. We use wall-clock time as our performance metric as our primary aim is to show that the framework latency is suitable for interactive analysis. Figure 9 also shows the corresponding performance measurements for traditional hardware breakpoints for each analysis session. We choose to omit software breakpoints from our performance measurements as they are rendered ineffective by all the malware.

Performance measurements of code and data breakpoints are divided into two broad categories: (a) where the executing code and breakpoint fall on the same memory page, and (b) where the executing code and breakpoint fall on different memory pages.

In general, the latency of code and data breakpoints is strictly governed by the intensity of data access to the memory page containing the breakpoints. E.g., analysis session 7 has higher latency than analysis ranges 6, 8 and 9. Further, in user-mode, the latency is lower when the executing code and breakpoints are on different memory pages (analysis sessions 6, 8 and 9) than when they are on the same memory page (analysis sessions 3 and 4). This is due to breakpoint persistence that results in multiple invocations of the SSH when the code and breakpoint are on the same memory page.

In kernel-mode, when the executing code and breakpoints are on the same memory page, the performance overhead is comparable to that of user-mode since the SSH latency in user-mode and the KMM SLE latency in kernel-mode balance themselves (analysis sessions 1 and 2). In kernel-mode, when the executing code and breakpoints are on different memory pages, the performance overhead is higher than user-mode due to the KMM SLE latency (analysis session 5). In all cases, the latency is well suited for interactive analysis.

To measure the performance of kernel-mode legacy I/O stealth breakpoints, we set breakpoints on ports 0x60–0x64 and 0x1F0-0x1F7 in our analysis sessions involving the Troj/Feutel-S and W32/Wuke malware respectively. As seen from Figure 9, the latency in analysis sessions 10 and 12 are quite small when compared to the rest. Session 10 involves I/O during DeviceIoControl requests from the W32/Wuke worm to the rootkit while session 12 involves I/O performed within kernel-mode threads of the Feutel-S trojan. Since I/O in both cases is performed soon after the SLE overlay, the KMM only executes a small number of instructions via SLE before triggering the I/O breakpoint. Sessions 11 and 13 on the other hand result in relatively higher latencies. This is due to the polymorphic and metamorphic code-streams in the case of Wuke and Feutel-S respectively. The KMM in this case executes a large number of instructions via SLE before triggering the I/O breakpoint. In all the sessions, the latency of legacy I/O breakpoints in kernel-mode is found to be within limits to suit interactive debugging.

CONCLUSIONS, LIMITATIONS, AND FUTURE RESEARCH

This chapter discussed Stealth Breakpoints that overcome the limitations of current hardware and software breakpoints in the context of malware analysis. Stealth breakpoints are robust to detection and countering mechanisms and provide unlimited number of breakpoints to be set on code, data, and I/O with the same precision as that of hardware breakpoints. This makes stealth breakpoints highly conducive for microscopic analysis of current generation malware that are increasingly becoming hardened to analysis. This chapter also discussed experiences using stealth breakpoints to analyze several real-world malware, demonstrating the efficacy of the framework. The performance of stealth breakpoints is suited for interactive debugging and the framework can be integrated into existing debuggers with ease.

While stealth breakpoints are a powerful primitive, they are currently ineffective against malware that use hypervisors such as Blue Pill (Rutkowska, 2006) or System Management Mode (Wojtczuk, 2009) for execution. However, malware which employ such techniques are extremely difficult to realize and very rare in practice. Further research in the area of hypervisor-based binary-code debugging and analysis can seek to overcome this limitation.

REFERENCES

American Arium Corp. (2009). *Itanium ITP: Intel ICE kit.*

Beander, B. (1983). *Vax debug: An interactive, symbolic, multilingual debugger*. In ACM SIG-SOFT/SIGPLAN Software Engineering Symposium on High-Level Debugging.

Buhr, P. A., Karsten, M., & Shih, J. (1996). *Kdb: A multithreaded debugger for multithreaded applications*. In SIGMETRICS Symposium on Parallel and Distributed Tools.

Cargill, T., & Locanthi, B. (1987). *Cheap hardware support for software debugging and profiling*. In Second International Conference on Architectural Support for Programming Languages and Operating Systems.

Chen, H., Kao, C., & Huang, I. (2002). *Analysis of hardware and software approaches to embedded in-circuit emulation of microprocessors*. In 7th Asia Pacific Conference on Computer Systems Architecture.

Compuware Corp. (1999). *Debugging blue screens*. Technical Paper.

Copperman, M. & Thomas, J. (1995). Poor man's watchpoints. *ACM SIGPLAN Notices, 30*(1).

Corelis Corp. (2005). *EMDT/K5 boundary-scan (JTAG) emulator for the AMD K5 processors.*

Dunlap, G. W., King, S. T., Cinar, S., Basrai, M., & Chen, P. M. (2002). *Revirt: Enabling intrusion analysis through virtual-machine logging and replay.* In Symposium on Operating Systems Design and Implementation (OSDI).

Johnson, M. S. (1982). *Some requirements for architectural support of software debugging.* In Symposium on Architectural Support for Programming Languages and Operating Systems.

Kessler, P. (1990). *Fast breakpoints: Design and implementation.* In Conference on Programming Language Design and Implementation.

King, S. T., Dunlap, G. W., & Chen, P. M. (2005). *Debugging operating systems with time-traveling virtual machines.* In Usenix Annual Technical Conference - General Track.

Linton, M. A. (1990). *The evolution of DBX.* In Usenix Summer Conference.

Loukides, M. & Oram, A. (1996). Getting to know GDB. *The Linux Journal, 29.*

Magnusson, P. S., Christensson, M., Eskilson, J., Forsgren, G., Hallberg, G., & Hogberg, J. (2002). Simics: A full system simulation platform. *IEEE Computer Society, 2*(35), 50–58. doi:10.1109/2.982916

Mellor-Crummey, J. M., & LeBlanc, T. J. (1989). *A software instruction counter.* In Third International Conference on Architectural Support for Programming Languages and Operating Systems.

Offensive Computing. (2010). *Community malicious code research and analysis.* Retrieved December 15, 2010, from http://www.offensive-computing.net

Paxon, V. (1990). *A survey of support for implementing debuggers.*

Ramsey, N. (1994). *Correctness of trap-based breakpoint implementations.* In 21st Symposium on Principles of Programming Languages.

Robbins, J. (1999). Debugging Windows based applications using windbg. *Microsoft Systems Journal, 1999.*

Rutkowska, J. (2006). *Subverting Vista kernel for fun and profit.* SyScan and Black Hat Presentations.

Szor, P. (2005). *The art of computer virus research and defense.* Addison-Wesley and Symantec Press.

Vasudevan, A., & Yerraballi, R. (2006). *Cobra: Fine-grained malware analysis using stealth localized-executions.* In IEEE Symposium on Security and Privacy.

Wahbe, R. (1992). *Efficient data breakpoints.* In 5th International Conference on Architectural Support for Programming Languages and Operating Systems.

Wahbe, R., Lucco, S., & Graham, S. L. (1993). *Practical data breakpoints: Design and implementation.* In Conference on Programming Language Design and Implementation.

Wojtczuk, R., & Rutkowska, J. (2009). *Attacking SMM memory via Intel CPU cache poisoning.* Invisible Things Lab.

ADDITIONAL READING

Szor, P. (2005). *The art of computer virus research and defense.* Addison-Wesley and Symantec Press.

Vasudevan, A. (2009). *Reinforced stealth breakpoints.* In 4th IEEE Conference on Risks in Internet Systems (CRiSIS).

Vasudevan, A., & Yerraballi, R. (2005). *Stealth breakpoints.* In IEEE 21st Annual Computer Security and Applications Conference (ACSAC).

Vasudevan, A., & Yerraballi, R. (2006). *Cobra: Fine-grained malware analysis using stealth localized-executions.* In IEEE Symposium on Security and Privacy.

KEY TERMS AND DEFINITIONS

Anti-Debugging: A set of techniques that are designed to thwart code debugging and analysis.

Breakpoint: Debugging aids that provide the ability to stop execution of code at an arbitrary point during execution

Malware: A piece of code specifically designed for malice.

Metamorphic: A code stream that is capable of mutating the order of instructions while retaining the same functionality.

Polymorphic: A set of code fragments that can be arranged in any given combination while achieving the same functionality.

Self-Checking Code: A code stream that checks its own integrity (for potential modifications) during runtime.

Self-Modifying Code: A code stream that modifies itself during runtime.

Chapter 24
A Dynamic Cyber Security Economic Model:
Incorporating Value Functions for All Involved Parties

C. Warren Axelrod
Delta Risk LLC, USA

ABSTRACT

One cannot develop effective economic models for information security and privacy without having a good understanding of the motivations, disincentives, and other influencing factors affecting the behavior of criminals, victims, defenders, product and service providers, lawmakers, law enforcement, and other interested parties. Predicting stakeholders' actions and reactions will be more effective if one has a realistic representation of how each of the various parties will respond to internal motivators and external stimuli. In this chapter, reactions of involved parties are assumed to be based on "personal utility functions." However, it is not sufficient merely to develop static utility functions, since the net value of security and privacy changes dynamically. External events, such as the announcement of a new threat, also have a significant effect on both subjective and objective net value. Knowing how such value functions vary over time helps determine the overall dynamic impact of security and privacy measures on the behavior of various participants and ultimately on the economic model that describes these behaviors. Also in this chapter, the authors enumerate the many factors that affect all the various parties and examine how these factors affect the responses of all those involved due to the economic impact of particular exploits and situations as they affect different groups.

INTRODUCTION

In large part, the failure of current cyber economics models is a result of attempting to use macro-economic methods to control the behavior of individuals and groups (together "subjects"), without having a good understanding of the motivations, threats and other influences affecting the economic actors, which include criminals, victims, service providers, lawmakers, etc. As behavioral economists have demonstrated, one is much better able to accurately predict subjects' actions and reactions using a realistic representation of how

DOI: 10.4018/978-1-4666-0978-5.ch024

subjects respond to external and internal factors based on their utility functions.

If the SQL Slammer worm[1] had hit during the business week, rather than early Saturday (January 25, 2003) at 5:30 am UTC, and if IT (information technology) and IS (information security) departments had not spent all or part of that weekend remediating the extensive problems that arose,[2] the damage and costs would have been orders of magnitude greater, likely in the many billions of dollars. Apart from the good fortune that SQL Slammer was launched on a weekend rather than on a weekday, the costs of remediation clearly paid off handsomely in most cases.[3]

The Y2K date rollover also happened to take place over a weekend. As a result of this good fortune, many potentially damaging issues were resolved without having the additional pressure of regular weekday workloads. The vast majority of systems were up and running in time for Monday morning start-of-business. This excellent record can be attributed to the years of preparation and remediation and to organizations having staff at hand or on call. Also, many Web-facing systems were shut down, so that greater damage was either avoided or addressed on the spot.[4]

Furthermore, probing by attackers was mostly unsuccessful over the Y2K weekend. Ironically, attempts at major DDoS (Distributed Denial of Service) attacks, which were detected over the Y2K weekend and indeed affected at least one major financial utility, did not actually succeed on a full scale until early February 2000, when defenders had relaxed their prior vigilance.

From the above it is clear that when an incident occurs and how long it takes to fix the systems are very influential on the value losses incurred. What follows is an attempt to develop an economic model of the complex interactions among involved and interested parties in order to be able to determine the impact of various mechanisms for improving, and ideally optimizing, the net value over time to be derived from security measures.

Consideration of the timing of events and time to respond, such as times for patching known vulnerabilities, is generally omitted from the analysis conducted by academic economists, yet such factors have major impact on the net value of security for operational functions. As an example, patching can be a major factor in ensuring that systems are secure. However, the risk of delaying patching will vary with the severity of the vulnerability and likelihood that an exploit will be developed and launched before a patch is installed. The value of specific patches will also be affected by time of day, day of week, the criticality of systems at risk, and so on.

In order to capture the level and variability of the net value of security measures, we use the value-hill concept.[5] The value hill is a means of showing the relationships among value, time and expected response time. Uncertainty or variability in response time may be expressed as the variance of response time. But first, we will examine the motivation and deterrence from the perspective of each category of player that interacts with the other categories of players and with the system.

INVOLVED PARTIES

Who are the involved parties? There are attackers, victims and defenders, and then there are a series of facilitators, intermediaries, detractors, enforcers, and the like. Each category of party has a specific role and set of values, which can be expressed in terms of "utility functions,"[6] and responds to changes in the environment in different ways based on the net value to the party aggregated over time. It is this set of complex interactions that represents the cyber security economic model developed here.

We now examine the various players ... who they are, what their roles are, how they react to specific situations and how their behaviors can be modified in order to optimize the economics.

Attackers

On the attacker side, we have individuals and groups of "black hats," individual criminals or teams of criminals, opportunists who may be operating within an organization (internal threat) or externally, domestic, foreign and international organized crime, terrorists acting independently or under a group leader, and nation states that might purportedly be allies or distinguishable as enemies.

There are also several categories of "hacker."[7] Hackers are, strictly speaking, individuals who supposedly attack systems for the "common good," in order to ferret out vulnerabilities and publicize them so as to encourage vendors and others to come up with patches and other protective mechanisms. Others actually follow through when they find a vulnerability and bring systems down (or otherwise compromise them, such as by defacing websites) as a means of showing off to peers or expressing a political opinion, rather than obtaining personal financial gain. Such individuals likely will try to monetize their skills, either by affiliating with reputable security product and services vendors and performing "ethical hacking," by selling discovered vulnerabilities to the highest bidders, be they government agencies, security vendors, organized crime, terrorists, nation states, and the like, who may use the knowledge for good or evil depending on their orientation. Alternatively they might decide to exploit vulnerabilities directly for their own gain.

Victims

Victims need to be distinguished from defenders, although a single individual or entity could be both a victim and a defender, as in the case when a security-tool vendor is attacked.[8] In general, victims may have no personal responsibility to defend against attacks and they are less likely to have the requisite skills to defend themselves. Certain responsibilities, such as following policy and procedures, updating antivirus and firewall software on their workstations, and the like, are often foisted upon those using the systems by vendors and corporate management in an attempt to avoid or prevent attacks. In the author's opinion, it is unfair and relatively ineffective to have end-users and individual customers be responsible for such activities – they should all be done either "under the covers" or should be done for them by experts. In cases where the victim is an organization, the data compromised can be intellectual property in addition to the personal information of employees, customers, contractors, and the like. When an organization is held responsible, there is an expectation that generally-accepted security practices are in place. This opinion is often unfounded. As an example, the hacker community had been publicizing Sony's apparent poor security for some time before Sony was actually attacked.[9]

Defenders

Defenders are a mixed bag. While companies, government agencies, academic intuitions, and other organizations often have fiduciary responsibility to protect sensitive data, they almost invariably do so according to industry-practice policy and procedures and using tools and services provided by third parties.[10]

These third parties fall into a number of categories. First, there are vendors of security products such as antivirus software, intrusion detection and prevention systems, network and application firewalls. Some of these products are developed and used by military, homeland security, and law enforcement agencies and are subsequently released as commercial versions to the private sector. Many are the creations of individuals and groups performing research in academia, corporate and government-sponsored laboratories, and individuals or small groups who develop products in the proverbial garage. There is a raft of hundreds, if not thousands, of start-ups, self funded, or with angel or venture-capital funding, of which only a handful are really successful.

There are also open-source communities that develop products and make them available at no direct charge, though the software and occasional hardware are usually subject to stringent contractual terms and conditions (Axelrod, 2006). Some of today's most successful security products started out as open source, and many still remain so. Developers who contribute to open source projects are not paid directly for their efforts. Often they are individuals with regular daytime jobs or academics, who believe that making software free and open is for the betterment of mankind. There is money to be made from supporting open-source software, and a number of successful companies have been formed to do just that. Even well established software manufacturers, such as IBM, donate some of their software to open-source communities. The level of altruism varies with open-source participants, as it does with hackers. There have also been a number of high-profile lawsuits about the stealing of open-source programs and incorporating them into commercial software.

With such a variety of players, one can see that trying to determine the incentives governing each segment is a daunting task. Because not only are motivational and deterring factors complex, they change over time and with different relation-ships. The same attacker will treat individuals, corporations, and military, homeland defense, and law enforcement agencies very differently as the "prize" varies, as well as the ability of targeted entities to defend themselves, and their ability and willingness to counter-attack or take legal or other actions.

MOTIVATIONS OF VARIOUS PARTIES

Table 1 shows the author's subjective assessment, based upon experience in the field, of the relative significance of the possible motivations of a variety of attackers. The motivation levels exhibit considerable variation, which explains why researchers frequently comment on the asymmetry of the economics of various types of attack. Clearly, if an attacker anticipates large gains in factors important to him or her, and a relatively small expected downside, then it is highly likely that, given the requisite skills and opportunity to execute, that attacker will do so. On the other hand, if the potential gain is relatively small and the attacker is afraid of the consequences should he or she be caught, then such an attacker might decide not to launch a compromise even when presented with an obvious opportunity.

Table 1. Motivation levels by category of attacker

Category of Attacker	Recognition	Financial Gain	Espionage	Destruction
Opportunistic – insider	Very Low	Substantial	Low	Low
Opportunistic – outsider	Low	High	Low	Low
Hacker – black hat	High	High	Moderate to High	Moderate to High
Hacker – white hat	Moderate	High (Indirect)	Low	Low
Criminal–individual/small group	Moderate	Very High	Very High	Targeted
Organized crime	High	Very High	Very High	Moderate
Terrorist – individual/small group	Very High	High	Moderate	Moderate
Terrorist organization	High	High	Moderate to High	Very High
Nation state	Very Low	Moderate to High	Very High	Moderate to High

Table 2. Motivation levels by category of defender

Category of Defender	Job Security	Financial	Reputation	Preservation	National Security
Internal operation – private sector	High	High	High	High	Low
Security-related software, hardware and services vendors	High	Very high	Very high	Very high	Moderate to High
Outside consultants and contractors	High	Very high	Very high	Very high	Moderate to High
Law enforcement	High	High	Very high	Very high	High
Military	Moderate	Moderate	Very high	High	Highest
Industry groups	High	Moderate	Very high	Very high	Moderate
Private sector	High	High	High	Very high	Moderate
Internal government - Local	Very High	Moderate (current)	High	Very High	Moderate to High
Internal government - Regional	Very High	Moderate (current)	High	Very High	Very high
Internal government - National	Very High	Moderate (current)	Very high	Very High	Highest
Internal government - International	Very High	Moderate (current)	Very high	Very High	Highest

Similarly, the motivations of defenders will vary by type of defender and the factors being affected, as shown qualitatively in Table 2. The degree to which a worker is engaged in the defense of his or her organization is, in the author's experience, highly dependent primarily upon the benefits to be derived personally from such an engagement and secondarily on the benefits accruing to the organization employing the defender.

Table 2 indicates a high degree of motivation level among the various defenders. Some, who have the possibility of receiving substantial financial benefits, such as vendors and consultants, are likely to attract the best researchers and analysts who not only benefit from higher compensation but gain invaluable experience through exposure to many different environments. They not only present tools and services that claim to detect and protect against attacks but also try to demonstrate that the attacks, against which their products defend, are significant and growing.[11]

Internal staff is generally interested in keeping their jobs, getting promoted and/or moving into a more powerful, better-paying position with the same or another entity. For government employees, the job motivation may be, for specific roles, more geared to higher-level goals, such as national security, with the potential of leaving the public sector for a position in the private sector at considerably higher compensation, often having become eligible for a government pension and other benefits (Haystead, 2011).

A major difference between the attitudes of employees in private companies versus law enforcement. in the author's view, is that the former are focused more on continuity of operations whereas the latter are more interested in apprehending perpetrators. This view is supported by reports of law enforcement confiscating equipment, software and data in order to perform forensics analysis, with a resulting detrimental impact on the business. As a result, companies will not inform law enforcement of attacks unless they are forced to by the nature and/or magnitude of the crime or

Table 3. Measures of success factors for various categories of law enforcement

Category of Law Enforcement	Continuance of operations	Preservation of finances	Loss Minimization	Apprehension of Perpetrator(s)	Removal of threats
Internal security	Very high	High	High	Moderate	Moderate
Local law enforcement	Moderate	Moderate	Moderate	Very high	High
Regional law enforcement	Moderate to Low	Low	Low	Very high	Very high
National law enforcement	Moderate/Low	Low	Low	Very high	Very high
International law enforcement	Moderate/Low	Low	Low	Very high	Very high
Military	Low	Low	Low	Very high	Highest

by laws and regulations. In more recent times, law enforcement in the U.S. has become more sensitive to the business needs of companies and has been working with them to a greater degree so as not to be as disruptive. This is done by law enforcement in the hope of being notified by victims more promptly when an incident occurs.

In Table 3, we give examples of differences among what various areas responsible for security and law enforcement believe to be the factors by which their success is measured. Internal corporate security departments, which are often headed by ex-law enforcement personnel, tend to be more protective of the operational stability and financial health of their employers than external law enforcement, although there are groups within various law enforcement agencies that are more sensitive to business needs.[12]

All those impacted by a cyber security breach are influenced by a combination of anticipated personal and organizational gains and losses. Motivators, which are the positive components of such influencing factors, comprise the usual portfolio of money, other asset-enhancing mechanisms, power, reputation, and the like. The author has held for some time that the weightings of motivators differ profoundly between individuals and organizations. For example, a $100,000 personal gain is likely to carry much more personal weight than saving or earning one's employer $10 million. Of course, if the latter leads to the former,

as when someone receives a reward or bonus as a result of the organization's savings or profits, then that individual will be more highly motivated than someone who doesn't see a direct benefit. It is more likely, in the view of the author, that attackers benefit from more direct incentive schemes, as well as more dramatic disincentives.

The money component is measurable, although how it translates into personal value is much more difficult to ascertain. In traditional economics, a $100,000 personal gain is considered to be much more meaningful to someone working for moderate wages than for a multimillionaire. However, it is only when this translation to value is done that comparisons can be made and the likely responses of individuals ascertained.

Other motivators, such as peer admiration, personal reputation, the thrill of the game, and so on, are often much more difficult to measure, if indeed they can be measured at all. And when the complexity of converting such intangible benefits into value terms is considered, the job of determining accurate value measures is well nigh impossible. Nevertheless, using techniques such as those proposed by Douglas Hubbard (Hubbard, 2009), some order-of-magnitude metrics can be derived. The results of a survey about the cost of compliance "with privacy and data protection laws, regulations and policies ..." are published in a recent Ponemon report (Ponemon, 2011). The costs of compliance and noncompliance are presented in direct, indirect and opportunity cost categories, the last of which is defined as "the cost resulting from lost business opportunities as a result of compliance infractions that diminish the organization's reputation and goodwill." These are clearly value-related items.

The author would advise the reader to be wary of some of the experiments that have been done in this area, since the underlying assumptions for decisions are sometimes not well articulated and not actionable in the forms in which they are presented.

For example, on the PBS (Public Broadcasting Company) NOVA documentary "Mind over Money," a group of students were asked to bid on a $20 bill.[13] The apparent conclusion, when the auction ended at a price of $26, was that people deal irrationally when it comes to money. However, if one were to examine the rules of the game more carefully, one would understand more readily why the bids exceeded the intrinsic value of the prize. The rules required that the losing bidder had to pay the winner the amount of the winning bid. Thus there was an incentive not to have to pay a premium to another player. The premium seemingly had a value of $6.

DISINCENTIVES (DETERRENTS)

Just as each category of player is motivated differently, so it is with disincentives or deterrents.[14]

A party will typically subjectively estimate potential losses and the likelihood that they will be incurred. As with gains, as described above, he or she will look differently upon losses which are personal, as opposed to losses that are incurred by the organization for which they work, or losses borne by third parties or society as a whole. We therefore weight these different categories of losses accordingly.

As with motivations, we shall examine the importance of disincentives or deterrents to various categories of attackers and defenders.[15]

Table 4 shows a rough assessment of the relative significance of disincentives affecting a variety of attackers. It shows considerable variation. Clearly, if an attacker anticipates relatively minor losses or slim chance of being subjected to other consequences (such as imprisonment) in factors important to him or her, and a relatively high expected upside, then it is highly likely that, given the requisite skills and opportunity to execute, that attacker will avail himself or herself of the opportunity. On the other hand, if the potential losses are relatively large and the consequences grave when caught, and there is a relatively good chance that the attacker will be apprehended and prosecuted, then such an attacker will tend to shy away from such a crime.

Similarly, the disincentives for defenders, by which we mean factors that might discourage a defender from performing his or her job, will vary by type of defender. The factors that are affected

Table 4. Disincentive levels by type of attacker

Type of Attacker	Recognition	Financial Gain	Espionage	Destruction
Opportunistic – insider	None	High	Low	Low
Opportunistic – outsider	None	High	Low	Low
Hacker – black hat	High	Moderate to High	Low	Low
Hacker – white hat	Moderate	Indirect	Low	Low
Criminal–individual/small group	Low	Very High	Very High	Low
Organized crime	High	Very High	Very High	Low
Terrorist – individual/small group	Very High	High	Moderate	High
Terrorist organization	Very High	High	Moderate	Very High
Nation state	Very Low	Moderate	Very High	High

Table 5. Disincentive levels for engagement by type of defender

Type of Defender	Job-Related Punishment	Personal Injury	Personal Discomfort	External Fines, Penalties, etc.
Internal security	Moderate	Moderate	Moderate	Low
Security vendors	Low	Low	Low	Moderate
Outside consultants	Low	Low	Low	Moderate
Law enforcement	High	High	Very High	Low
Military	High	Very High	Very High	Low
Govt - Local	Moderate	Low	Moderate	Low
Govt - Regional	Moderate	Low	Moderate	Low
Govt - National	Moderate	Moderate	Moderate	Low
Govt - International	Moderate	Moderate	Moderate	Low

are shown qualitatively in Table 5. The degree to which a defender is engaged in actively pursuing an attacker is likely to be affected by the disincentives of such an engagement. For example, those employed in an organization's internal security department may be evaluated based on the degree to which they limit the impact of an attack, and are likely less concerned about going after perpetrators as that could potentially lead to personal risk were the attackers to target internal security individuals. On the other hand, as mentioned above, law enforcement officers are usually oriented towards apprehending perpetrators, and if they are not successful they might be punished by, say, not receiving a promotion, and this would clearly produce personal discomfort.

In Table 6 we take a somewhat different view. Rather than looking at the disincentives or fears that might discourage certain players from engaging in defending victim organizations, we consider how the results of enforcement vary with categories of defenders. For example, the prospect of an organization ceasing business as a result of an attack will be of significant importance to internal staff, senior management and other stakeholders, such as owners or shareholders Yet such a consequence may be relatively unimportant to law enforcement staff who will surely have a different set of views as to the impact and outcome of an investigation.

Every aspect of a cyber security breach is influenced by a combination of anticipated per-

Table 6. Measures of success of various types of enforcement

Type of Enforcement	Continuance of victim's operations	Preservation of finances	Loss Minimization	Apprehension of Perpetrator(s)	Removal of threats
Internal security	Very High	High	High	Low to Moderate	Moderate
Security vendors	Very High	Moderate to High	High	Moderate	Moderate
Outside consultants	Very High	Moderate to High	High	Low	Moderate
Local law enforcement	Moderate	Moderate	Moderate	Very high	High
Regional law enforcement	Moderate/Low	Low	Low	Very high	Very high
National law enforcement	Moderate/Low	Low	Low	Very high	Very high
International law enforcement	Moderate/Low	Low	Low	Very high	Very high
Military	Low	Low	Low	Very high	Highest

sonal and organizational gains and losses. The author has held for some time that the weighting of motivators differs greatly among individuals and organizations. For example, as described above, a $100,000 personal gain is likely to carry much more weight than saving the "company" $10 million or reaping $10 million for a criminal cartel. Of course, if the organizational gain leads to the personal gain, through seeing "part of the action," then the individual will be more highly motivated than if not. It is more likely, in the view of the author, that the attackers will have a more direct incentive scheme, as well as possibly more dramatic disincentives inflicted by their "employers."

ACTIVE AND PASSIVE ATTACKS AND DEFENSES

An attack or a defense can be active, in that somebody, or some system, has to do something actively in order to effect the attack or defensive action. Conversely, passive attacks or defenses do not require specific action by attackers or defenders to trigger them. From an economic perspective, passive attacks and defenses usually involve an initial investment with occasional costs incurred when someone is caught in a trap. On the other hand, active attacks and defenses might require some initial investment, but they might also incur significant variable costs as exploits or tools are invoked.

Attacks: Active and Passive

A passive attack, which might appear to be a contradiction in terms, is defined here as an attack in which a trap is set and the "attacker" waits until someone is caught in it before it is activated, much like a spider building its web and waiting for its prey to get entangled. An example of this would be a malicious website via which visitors are infected with malware upon accessing the website. Phishing, whereby a victim receives an email that may require clicking on a link within the email in order to activate malware downloads, might be considered passive in the sense that it is usually not triggered until the recipient does something, such as clicking on a link. However, phishing might also be considered somewhat active in that the emails have to be generated and sent. This is especially true of "spear phishing," in which specific targets are identified, versus the mass mailings of regular phishing. It should be noted, however, that there are reported email types that do not require any action on the part of the recipient in order to plant malware.

Targeted attacks, such as those experienced by Heartland Payments, RSA, Lockheed Martin, Sony, Bank of America and others are clearly active attacks and involve significant amounts of research, preparation, and operation. Most of the highly publicized attacks are from outside the organization, and relatively few attacks by insiders are disclosed by organizations, if they can avoid such disclosure. This may also be due to limited reporting rather than the actual frequency of incidents.

In terms of costs and benefits, passive attacks tend to be the less expensive than active attacks for attackers to implement, although they might have a much lower yield in terms of percentage of targets victimized. For example, it costs little or no more to send out a few malicious emails versus millions, the upfront costs being in obtaining the lists of email addresses. Even that cost can be avoided if random addresses are generated. Some level of continuing effort is often required as Spam filters quickly learn which emails to block, resulting in a need for the attackers to modify the words and phrases that alert the updated filters. The same is true of worms and viruses, which tend to be passive, but often evolve over time as their creators engage in an effort to outrun the defenders.

Table 7 shows the degree to which a particular category of attack is active or passive. The main aspect important to economic models of attackers

Table 7. The level of active/passive involvement by attack vector

Attack Categories	Active	Passive
Phishing	Somewhat	Mostly
Spear phishing	Fully	-
Viruses, Worms	Somewhat	Mostly
Website scanning	Somewhat	Somewhat
External hacks	Fully	-
Insider hacks	Fully	-

has to do with the level and distribution of costs. Thus, for phishing, there is initial activity and cost in preparing the emails and obtaining the distribution lists, but for the most part the attacker sits back and waits for responses. Once responses come in, then the attacker is again activated to harvest the incoming information and use or sell the data. We differentiate between external attacks, such as website scanning (or "pinging") in which hackers ping huge numbers of websites with the intent of detecting vulnerabilities. and directed attacks, which might be denial-of-service attacks or attempts to gain access to internal networks and systems.

Defenses: Active and Passive

A passive defense is one that essentially sits in wait for someone to fall into a trap, such as a honey pot[16] or intrusion detection system.[17] Such defenses do have active components in their development, preparation and deployment, and then in working on the response when someone gets caught in it. Other methods, such as intrusion prevention systems comprise a detection capability which is augmented with a predetermined response. For example, if certain suspicious messages are detected, they will be blocked.

The degree to which a defense is considered active or passive will vary from one implementation to another. For example, behavioral analysis tools or data-leak prevention tools (such as email monitors) generally have sets of rules "out of the box." The customer of such tools might let them run with the prepackaged patterns or dictionaries, or the customer may be willing and able to introduce specific rules.

Table 8 shows a number of categories of defense tools and the degree to which defenders have to be actively involved or not. The use of antivirus software, for example, requires initial installation and periodic updates. Antivirus software will generally run in the background and require little user intervention. Similarly for intrusion detection systems, which run continuously and report anomalies, but do not require user action unless suspicious activity is detected. On the other hand, intrusion prevention systems will actively block data on the networks or on host computers subject to predetermined rules, requiring oversight and supervision to ensure that valid information is not blocked. When it comes to secure programming and secure architectures, defenders must put in place the policy and procedures to effect them. They don't happen on their own nor can they, as yet, be accomplished by merely installing a set of tools. Secure application coding requires extensive up-front training and continuing monitoring and testing.

PROPOSED ECONOMIC MODEL

The economic model, as proposed here, incorporates consideration and evaluation of motivations and deterrents for all the parties believed to affect,

Table 8. The level of active/passive involvement by defense category

Defense Categories	Active	Passive
Antivirus	Somewhat	Mostly
Intrusion detection	-	Fully
Intrusion prevention	Mostly	Somewhat
Honey pots	Somewhat	Mostly
Access management	Mostly	Somewhat
Behavioral analysis	Somewhat	Mostly
Data leak prevention	Mostly	Somewhat
Secure applications	Fully	-
Secure architecture	Fully	-
Security & privacy awareness & training	Fully	-

or be affected by, some security event or situation. A critical requirement is to be able to express these motivators and detractors using a common measure so that the behavior of the participants can be normalized. The proposed measure is the value increases from positive factors and value reductions from negative influences. As mentioned in (Hubbard, 2009) we are not necessarily looking for a single number. In fact, the model should incorporate ranges and probability distributions in most realistic situations.

Such measures will necessarily be very rough estimates. However, it is important to account first for all known factors affecting all identified players. Prior economic models have tended to consider the effects only on direct attackers and immediate victims. This latter approach is too restrictive and does not account for the influences of all the parties involved and the economic impact of various efforts and outcomes. For example, the involvement of law enforcement or the military might have a major impact on the selection of targets. Thus, if the victim is an individual subjected to identity theft used to access and drain a bank account, then the victim will likely seek recompense from the bank and not utilize law enforcement assistance. On the other hand, the bank involved will often call in law enforcement to find, arrest and prosecute perpetrators.

Asymmetry

A long-time and often-repeated characteristic of the economic behavior of participants in the cyber security space is the asymmetry of the economics gains and losses of the various participants (National Research Council, 2002). At a high level, as shown in Table 9, some groups may be involved in both unauthorized attacks and authorized defense, whereas others are exclusively attackers or defenders. Generally, it is much more difficult and considerably more expensive to defend than to attack in cyberspace, with the attacker looking to exploit one or a few vulnerabilities and the defenders needing to protect against all eventualities. Also, the economic gains accruing to attackers can be orders of magnitude greater than the compensation of defenders.

The economic model presented here suggests that any particular attack might involve one or more parties on the left side of Table 9, and, similarly, the defense might include one or more of the entities on the right side of Table 9.

Thus, if there is an insider attack, the internal security department is usually involved, but it is also possible, though not always the case, that law enforcement will be pulled in, since, in the author's experience, there is a tendency for companies to keep insider incidents out of the public eye. On

Table 9. Attackers and defenders

Attackers	Defenders
Unauthorized insiders (insider threat) – usually individuals	-
Unauthorized outsiders -- individuals and groups	-
-	Insiders (active and passive measures)
-	Authorized external entities (service providers, vendors, etc.)
Criminals or small criminal groups	-
Organized crime	-
Terrorist individuals of groups	-
-	Law enforcement
Military and other government agencies	Military
Nation states (cyber warfare)	Nation states (cyber defense)

the other hand, if there is an attack from outside, victim organizations are more likely to involve law enforcement earlier.

Value Dynamics

The modes of attack and defense are subject to continual change. As attacks become more sophisticated and the lead time from vulnerability detection to exploit creation shortens, the challenges for defenders grow.

As more assets and economic activities are introduced into cyberspace, the need to protect them increases, as does the temptation to attack and exploit them. Commonly, the sequence of events is a follows:

1. New functions and features are introduced into applications, systems and networks
2. Vulnerabilities are discovered ... some are made public, others not
3. Attackers work on developing exploits to take advantage of the vulnerabilities
4. Defenders push to come up with "fixes," which are often in the form of "patches"
5. Vendors, in response, work on developing new or modified security tools to monitor and defend against these known threats
6. Attackers launch their exploits

7. Defenders and vendors urge defenders to implement fixes as quickly as possible to be protected against high-impact, highly-likely attacks
8. Entities, which are slow to implement protection in time, may suffer the attacks, or the nature of attacks might not have been predicted, so that all entities with certain software, system and network attributes will be vulnerable.

The value of security measures will vary over time. If, for example, applying a patch is achieved prior to an attack, then it has the value of all of the costs and other losses that would have been incurred were the attack to have been successful. On the other hand, if the attack occurs before the patch is applied, and the organization suffers significant damage, the value loss will reduce the net value of the subsequent patching effort considerably.

An Illustrative Example

Let us consider a case where a security patch is available and can be installed over the coming weekend or a week later. Because of the prior scheduling of moving certain new program functionality and/or corrective code into production over the near-in weekend, there will be costs of deferring the "production move" to the following week. Those costs can usually be estimated in a relatively straightforward manner. That is to say, if the beneficiaries of these moves can estimate the added value, then the value given up over the week's delay represents the costs of delay, assuming the same operational costs.

On the other hand, the costs of patching of software in advance of an expected attack are considerably more difficult to assess. While the operational cost of patching may be the same for either patching date, the cost of a successful attack on unpatched software is fraught with complexities. For a start, the timing of an attack is not known with any certainty. The challenge here is to try to guess the likelihood that an attack might take place between the two possible patching dates. If it were not to occur, then the rush to patch could have incurred considerable direct and opportunity costs, yet would be of relatively little value, except for some peace of mind, which should not, however, be undervalued. If an attack did occur, but the patch hadn't been installed, then there would be severe negative consequences. While there may be common constituents for either case (i.e., delaying production moves and incurring losses from an attack), there are clearly some areas, such as IT and information security, that would receive the bulk of the blame. One way to assuage this is to have the business units participate in the patching decision process.

From the perspective of attackers, the greatest value is to have in hand a so-called "zero-day exploit," which is an attack against a vulnerability that was not previously known to the defenders and only became known as a result of exploits. If a vulnerability is made public and the vendor is working aggressively to produce and distribute a patch, then the value of an exploit will diminish rapidly once the patch has been developed and sent out to defenders. Frequently, the value of a successful attack is many times greater to the attackers than preventing the success of an attack is to the defenders. If an attack is widespread, then significant damage and fraud might occur before defenders have the opportunity to respond. The incentive for law enforcement and security product and services vendors is also much greater.

Law enforcement, as we have repeated a number of times, is more interested in finding and arresting attackers, but generally does not get involved until an exploit has already achieved considerable success. In highly visible, high-impact cases, the response might be rapid as the net value of the law enforcement effort falls rapidly as significant expenses are incurred and increasing damage is done.

Once the net values over time have been developed for all participants, including attackers, victims, defenders, and law enforcement, they can be put in the form of a value hill which is shown in general form in Figure 1. Iso-value curves indicate a specific constant net value as it varies with the clock time and the expected time to fix a vulnerability. The dashed line shows generally the expected time for the "fix" to be readied, distributed and installed. The concept of the value hill was developed thirty year ago (Axelrod, 1979). In this example, the graph indicates that, for a defender or victim, the value of a defense will increase as the attackers develop exploits, and then diminish as exploits find their way into "the wild."

Where the dashed line intersects with the value hill, we can determine what the net value is at the point of implementation of a fix. This net value will most likely fall off rapidly until there are much-reduced benefits from the fix since successful attacks against the vulnerability will have already taken their toll. In specific cases we are likely to see the expected time to fix diminish over time, but not necessarily meeting the deadlines needed to prevent damage. However, if one goes through the exercise of expressing the dynamic net value of protection and fixes, one can determine the value of accelerating the time to fix.

Figure 1. A "value hill" showing how net value varies over time

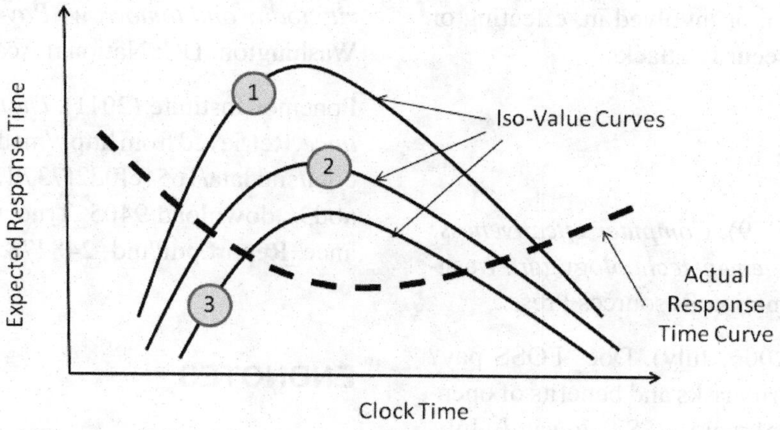

Adapted from C. W. Axelrod, **Computer Effectiveness: Bridging the Management-Technology Gap**, Washington, DC: Information Resources Press, 1979.

The construct of the value hill, which has been discussed here from the perspective of the victim organization, can be extended to attackers and defenders. In this way we can determine the time and effort that maximizes benefits for all defenders.

FUTURE RESEARCH DIRECTIONS

There is clearly a need for empirical evidence in support of the value-based economic model presented here. The suggested approach is to construct surveys for each of the player categories described above and, to the extent possible, have each person complete the specific survey relevant to his or her role. It is recognized that certain groups, particularly criminals and terrorists, will certainly not be approachable. In such cases, the researcher might complete a survey on their behalf, and test the inferred results by running them through the model, observing the results and comparing them to actuality.

The above suggests that it would be worthwhile to develop a computer model of the players, values, and interactions in order to test a range of assumptions. When such a model has been validated, it can then be used to test the impact of a variety of policies and other control mechanisms,

such as pricing, legislation, economic incentives, deterrents, etc.

CONCLUSION

Current cyber security economic models are deficient in their ability to account for the dynamics of value over time, uncertainty related to dynamic value, and the inclusion of the personal values of all those engaged in activities relating to the models. It is evident that there are good reasons for these deficiencies, beginning with the lack of a formal economic model of the motivations and interactions of the various players, and insufficient research addressing the dynamics and fluidity of the factors making up the model. Because of this situation, researchers are not able to determine the effects of various security measures completely or accurately.

This chapter attempts to provide initial formulations of such dynamic models and suggests how such a model might be used to determine the impact of economic, legislative, regulatory and other control mechanisms. We also indicate some potentially fruitful areas for further research that not only would serve to validate the model but also provide a means to observe the impact of various security measures on the population of those committed to, or involved in, effecting or preventing cyber security attacks.

REFERENCES

Axelrod, C. W. (1979). *Computer effectiveness: Bridging the management technology gap*. Washington, DC: Information Resources Press.

Axelrod, C. W. (2006, July). Does FOSS pay? Weighing the security risks and benefits of open-source security software. *ISSA Journal*, July, 6-12. Retrieved from http://www.issa.org/Library/Journals/2006/July/ Axelrod%20-%20Does%20FOSS%20Pay.pdf

Financial Services Roundtable. (2006). *BITS key considerations for securing data in storage and transport: Securing physical media in storage, transport, and for data erasure and destruction*. Retrieved from http://www.bitsinfo.org/downloads/ Publications%20Page/bitsdatatrans.pdf

Haystead, J. (2011). Defining a career path in electronic warfare. *Journal of Electronic Defense*, *34*(8), 26–28.

Hu, Q. (2011). Does deterrence work in reducing information security policy abuse by employees? *Communications of the ACM*, *54*(6), 54–60. doi:10.1145/1953122.1953142

Hubbard, D. W. (2009). *The failure of risk management: Why it's broken and how to fix it*. Hoboken, NJ: Wiley.

Hubbard, D. W. (2010). *How to measure anything: Finding the value of intangibles in business* (2nd ed.). Hoboken, NJ: Wiley.

Lohr, S. (2011, April 15). The business market plays cloud computing catch-up. *The New York Times*.

National Research Council. (2002). *Cybersecurity today and tomorrow: Pay now or pay later*. Washington, DC: National Academy Press.

Ponemon Institute. (2011). *The true cost of compliance*. Retrieved from http://mediazone.brighttalk.com/sitedata/1651cf0d2f737d7adeab84d339dbabd3/ download/9405_True_Cost_of_Compliance_Report.pdf?uid=24847&tid=isc2

ENDNOTES

[1] For a description of SQL Slammer see http://en.wikipedia.org/wiki/SQL_Slammer

[2] The author is personally aware of the networks of several major financial institutions being inoperative, for all intents and purposes, throughout the entire weekend during which SQL Slammer was running rampant.

[3] Unfortunately, the major ISP (Internet Service Provider) in South Korea did not remediate in time and Internet services for the whole country were unavailable the following Monday. See http://www.stratfor.com/memberships/100501/sql_slammer_will_continue_worm_through_south_korean_economy to obtain the article "SQL Slammer Will Continue to Worm Through South Korean Economy," January 27, 2003.

[4] In fact, there were a number of situations where services were taken down due to inadequate remediation. For example, a relatively small African country was knocked out following the date rollover.

[5] The concept of the "value hill" was introduced in (Axelrod, 1979) which was based upon the author's doctoral dissertation.

[6] There are numerous definitions of the term "utility function." One that appears to apply best to the cases considered in this chapter is "A mathematical expression that assigns

a value to all possible choices. In portfolio theory, the utility function expresses the preferences of economic entities with respect to perceived risk and expected return," which is available at http://www.duke.edu/~charvey/Classes/wpg/bfglosu.htm

[7] The original use of the term "hacker" was somewhat benign and referred to those who found vulnerabilities in systems and reported them to manufacturers, vendors and others in order to strengthen the security of those systems. More recently the term has been commonly applied to those who break into systems with evil intent.

[8] Art Coviello, RSA's executive chairman, posted "an open letter" on the RSA website at http://www.rsa.com/node.aspx?id=3872 in regard to the attack.

[9] Regarding Sony's deficiencies, see John C. Dvorak's June 3, 2011 column "Sony Hacker Attack Has Deeper Meaning" available at http://www.pcmag.com/article2/0,2817,2386378,00.asp

[10] The author knows of a major bank that develops some of its own tools and also partners with security product vendors to customize the vendors' technologies to the bank' needs.

[11] There is speculation among reporters and others that some less scrupulous vendors of security tools and services might be tempted to create exploits against particular vulnerabilities in order to generate interest in their products and services and increase sales. There is also believed to be a "market" in vulnerabilities and exploits. In this market, those who discover vulnerabilities and/or develop exploits, which can be shown to be effective, sell the information about such vulnerabilities and/or exploits to interested parties, such as security tools vendors, cyber law enforcement and nation states.

[12] The FBI Infragard website is at http://www.infragard.net and US Secret Service Electronic Crimes Task Force website is at http://www.secretservice.gov/ectf.shtml

[13] The documentary can be viewed at http://video.pbs.org/video/1479100777 The specific segment on the auction of the $20 bill runs from 12:15 minutes to 13:20 minutes within the hour-long film.

[14] The words "disincentive" and "deterrent" are very similar in meaning, but have, in the author's opinion, slightly different nuances. A disincentive implies a form of penalty, financial or otherwise, were a particular action to be taken, and is the opposite of "motivators." On the other hand, a deterrent is something intended o discourage someone from acting, and is the opposite of "incitement." In a sense, a deterrent is more active than a disincentive, which can often be considered passive.

[15] For a thorough analysis of deterrence affecting employees, see (Hu, 2011).

[16] Per Wikipedia: In computer terminology, a honeypot is a trap set to detect, deflect, or in some manner counteract attempts at unauthorized use of information systems. Generally it consists of a computer, data, or a network site that appears to be part of a network, but is actually isolated and monitored, and which seems to contain information or a resource of value to attackers.

[17] Per Wikipedia: An IDS (Intrusion Detection System) is "software and/or hardware designed to detect unwanted attempts at accessing, manipulating, and/or disabling of computer systems, mainly through a network, such as the Internet."

Compilation of References

(2005). *SOSFS 2005:12*. The National Board of Health and Welfare.

3 rd Generation Partnership Project, 3GPP. (2009). *Location service (LCS), service description, stage 1*. 3GPP TS 22.071, Release 9.

3 rd Generation Partnership Project, 3GPP. (2010). *Functional stage 2 description of location service (LCS)*. 3GPP TS 23.271, Release 9.

8052 com. (n.d.). *Introduction to LCD programming tutorial by Craig Steiner Copyright 1997 -2005 by Vault Information Services LLC*. Retrieved from http://8052. com/tutlcd.phtml

Abadi, M., & Fournet, C. (2001). Mobile values, new names, and secure communication. *SIGPLAN Notice*, *36*(3), 104–115. doi:10.1145/373243.360213

Aberer, K., & Despotovic, Z. (2002). Managing trust in a peer-2-peer information system. *Proceedings the Tenth International Conference on Information and Knowledge Management*.

Adida, B. (2008). Helios: Web-based open-audit voting. In the *Proceedings of the 18th Conference on USENIX Security Symposium* (pp. 335–348). Berkeley, CA: USENIX Association.

Agrawal, R., & Srikant, R. (1994). Fast algorithms for mining association rules in large databases. In J. B. Bocca, M. Jarke, & C. Zaniolo, (Eds.), *Proceedings of the 20th International Conference on Very Large Data Bases*, (p. 487). Santiago, Chile.

Agrawal, R., Imielinski, T., & Swami, A. (1993). Mining association rules between sets of items in large databases. In P. Buneman & S. Jajodia (Eds.), *Proceedings of the 1993 ACM SIGMOD International Conference on Management of Data* (SIGMOD '93, Washington, DC, May 26-28), (pp. 207–216). New York, NY: ACM Press.

Åhlfeldt, R.-M. (2008). *Information security in distributed healthcare - Exploring the needs for achieving patient safety and patient privacy*. Doctoral dissertation, Stockholm University, DSV Report series No. 08-003.

Ajam, N., Cuppens, N., & Cuppens, F. (2009). Contextual privacy management in extended role based access control model. *Workshop DPM, DPM-ESORICS, LNCS*, (pp. 121-135). Saint-Malo, France.

Alder, G. S., Noel, T. W., & Ambrose, M. L. (2006). Clarifying the effects of Internet monitoring on job attitudes: The mediating role of employee trust. *Information & Management*, *43*(7), 894–903. doi:10.1016/j.im.2006.08.008

Aljifri, H. A., Pons, A., & Collins, D. (2003). Global e-commerce: A framework for understanding and overcoming the trust barrier. *Information Management & Computer Security*, *11*(3), 130–138. doi:10.1108/09685220310480417

Allan, D., Hahn, T., Szakal, A., Whitmore, J., & Buecker, A. (March 2010). *Security in development: The IBM secure engineering framework*. Retrieved from http://www.redbooks.ibm.com/ redpapers/pdfs/redp4641.pdf

Allcock, W., Chervenak, A., Foster, I., Pearlman, L., Welch, V., & Wilde, M. (2001). *Globus toolkit support for distributed data-intensive science*. In International Conference on Computing in High Energy and Nuclear Physics (CHEP'01). IEEE Press.

AllDataSheet.com. (n.d.). Retrieved from www.alldata-sheet.com/ULN2003/TEXAS/

Allison, D., El Yamany, H., & Capretz, M. (2009). Metamodel for privacy policies within SOA. *Proceedings of the 5th IEEE International Workshop on Software Engineering for Secure Systems in conjunction with the 31st IEEE International Conference of Software Engineering,* Vancouver, Canada, May 19, (pp. 40-46).

Al-Riyami, S. S., & Paterson, K. G. (2003). Certificateless public key cryptography. In Laih, C. S. (Ed.), *ASIACRYPT 2003, LNCS 2894* (pp. 452–473).

Alur, R., & Henzinger, T. (1999). Reactive modules. *Formal Methods in System Design, 15*(1), 7–48. doi:10.1023/A:1008739929481

American Arium Corp. (2009). *Itanium ITP: Intel ICE kit.*

Amin, F., Jahangir, A. H., & Rasifard, H. (2008). Analysis of public-key cryptography for wireless sensor networks security. *Proceedings of World Academy of Science, Engineering and Technology,* Vol. 31.

Anderson, D. P. (2004). BOINC: A System for public-resource computing and storage. In *GRID '04: Proceedings of the Fifth IEEE/ACM International Workshop on Grid Computing* (pp. 4–10). Washington, DC: IEEE Computer Society.

Anderson, D. P., Cobb, J., Korpela, E., Lebofsky, M., & Werthimer, D. (2002). SETI@home: An experiment in public-resource computing. *Communications of the ACM, 45*(11), 56–61. doi:10.1145/581571.581573

Anderson, J. (2002). Why we need a new definition of information security. *Computers & Security, 22*(4), 308–313. doi:10.1016/S0167-4048(03)00407-3

Anderson, J. P. (1972). *Computer security technology planning study.* ESD-TR-73-51, ESD/AFSC, Bedford, MA: Hanscom AFB. (. *NTIS, AD-758,* 206.

Android.com. (n.d.). *Android at Google I/O.* Retrieved from http://www.android.com/

Ansari, N., Sakarindr, P., Haghani, E., Zhang, C., Jain, A. K., & Shi, Y. Q. (2008). Evaluating electronic voting systems equipped with voter-verified paper records. *IEEE Security and Privacy, 6*(3), 30–39. doi:10.1109/MSP.2008.62

Antoniou, A., Korakas, C., Manolopoulos, C., Panagiotaki, A., Sofotassios, D., Spirakis, P. G., & Stamatiou, Y. C. (2007). A trust-centered approach for building e-voting systems. In the *Proceeding of EGO* (pp, 366–377). Springer.

Apple. (n.d.). Retrieved from http://www.apple.com/

Araújo Neto, A., & Vieira, M. (2008). *Towards assessing the security of DBMS configurations.* Intl Conf. Depend. Systems and Networks (DSN 2008), USA.

Araújo Neto, A., & Vieira, M. (2009). *Appraisals based on security best practices for software configurations.* Fourth Latin-American Symposium on Dependable Computing (LADC 2009). João Pessoa, Brasil, Araújo Neto, A., Vieira, M., & Madeira, H. (2009). *An appraisal to assess the security of database configurations.* 2nd Intl Conference on Dependability, DEPEND 2009, Greece.

Archer. (2010). *Compliance management solution.* Retrieved November 3, 2010 from http://www.archer-tech.com

Arkin, B., Stender, S., & McGraw, G. (January 2005). Software penetration testing. *IEEE Security and Privacy,* (pp. 84-87).

Arora, D., Ravi, S., Raghunathan, A., & Jha, N. K. (August 2005). Architectural enhancements for secure embedded processing. *NATO Workshop on Security and Embedded Systems,* Vol. 2, (pp. 18-25).

Athanasopoulos, E., & Antonatos, S. (October 2006). Enhanced CAPTCHAs: Using animation to tell humans and computers apart. *Proceedings of 10th Int. Conf. on Communications and Multimedia Security (CMS 2006), LNCS 4237,* (pp. 97–108).

Atmel corporation. (2000). *AT89S52 data sheet, 8-bit microcontroller with 8k bytes flash.* Atmel Data book, 2000 update.

ATMEL. (2008). *ATMega128 datasheet: 8-bit AVR microcontroller with 128kBytes in-system programable Flash.* Retrieved from http://www.atmel.com/dyn/resources/prod_documents/doc2467.pdf

Aviv, A., C˘erny, P., Clark, S., Cronin, E., Shah, G., Sherr, M., & Blaze, M. (2008). Security evaluation of ES&S voting machines and election management system. *In Proceedings of the Conference on Electronic Voting Technology.* Berkeley, CA: USENIX Association.

Axelrod, C. W. (2006, July). Does FOSS pay? Weighing the security risks and benefits of open-source security software. *ISSA Journal,* July, 6-12. Retrieved from http://www.issa.org/Library/Journals/2006/July/ Axelrod%20 -%20Does%20FOSS%20Pay.pdf

Axelrod, C. W. (1979). *Computer effectiveness: Bridging the management technology gap.* Washington, DC: Information Resources Press.

Bagchi, K., & Udo, G. (2003). An analysis of the growth of computer and internet security breaches. *Communications of the Association for Information Systems, 12,* 684–700.

Baird, H. S., & Bentley, J. L. (January 2005). Implicit CAPTCHAs. *Proceedings of SPIE-IS&T Electronic Imaging, Document Recognition and Retrieval XII, Vol. 5676 of SPIE Proceedings,* (pp. 191–196).

Baker, M., Buyya, R., & Laforenza, D. (2002). Grids and grid technologies for wide-area distributed computing. *Software: Practice and Experience (SPE)* [Wiley Press.]. *Journal, 32*(15), 1437–1466.

Bakker, A., van Steen, M., & Tanenbaum, A. S. (2001). A law-abiding peer-to-peer network for free-software distribution. *IEEE International Symposium on Network Computing and Applications* (pp. 60-67). IEEE Computer Society.

Balepin, I., Maltsev, S., Rowe, J., & Levitt, K. (2002). Using specification-based intrusion detection for automated response. In *Proceedings of 6th International Symposium on Recent Advances in Intrusion Detection,* (pp. 136–154). Springer.

Balzarotti, D., Banks, G., Cova, M., Felmetsger, V., Kemmerer, R., & Robertson, W. ... Vigna, G. (2008). Are your votes really counted? Testing the security of real-world electronic voting systems. In *International Symposium on Software Testing and Analysis* (pp. 237-248). New York, NY: ACM.

Balzarotti, D., Banks, G., Cova, M., Felmetsger, V., Kemmerer, R., & Robertson, W. (2010). An experience in testing the security of real-world electronic voting systems. *IEEE Transactions on Software Engineering, 36*(4), 453–473. doi:10.1109/TSE.2009.53

Baruah, S., Kakoti Mahanta, A., & Sharma, K. C. (2009). A comparative study on client server technology and Web technology in design and implementation of an embedded system used for monitoring and controlling of physical parameters. *Proceedings of 4th International Conference for Internet Technology and Secured Transaction* (ICITST-2009, London, UK, 9-12 November 2009.

Baruah, S., Kakoti Mahanta, A., & Sharma, K. C. (2010). A review of designing and implementing an embedded system using client server and Web technology for monitoring and controlling of physical parameters. *International Journal for Infonomics, 3*(1), 273-282. *ISSN, 1742,* 4712.

Baskerville, R., & Siponen, M. (2002). An information security meta-policy for emergent organizations. *Logistics Information Management, 15*(5/6), 337–346. doi:10.1108/09576050210447019

Beander, B. (1983). *Vax debug: An interactive, symbolic, multilingual debugger.* In ACM SIGSOFT/SIGPLAN Software Engineering Symposium on High-Level Debugging.

Beatty, P., Reay, I., Dick, S., & Miller, J. (2007). P3P adoption on e-commerce web sites. *IEEE Internet Computing, 11*(2), 65–71. doi:10.1109/MIC.2007.45

Bell, D., & La Padula, L. (1973). Secure computer systems: Mathematical foundations. *MITRE Technical Report, 2547,* 1.

Bellovin, S., & Bush, R. (2009). Configuration management and security. *IEEE Journal on Selected Areas in Communications, 27*(3), 268–274. doi:10.1109/JSAC.2009.090403

Bennett, C. (1997). Arguments for the standardization of privacy protection policy: Canadian initiatives and American and international responses. *Government Information Quarterly, 1*(4), 351–362. doi:10.1016/S0740-624X(97)90032-0

Bergadano, F., Crispo, B., & Ruffo, G. (1998). High dictionary compression for proactive password checking. *ACM Transactions on Information and System Security*, *1*, 3–25. doi:10.1145/290163.290164

Bertino, E., Jajodia, S., & Samarati, P. (1995). Database security: Research and practice. *Information Systems Journal*, *20*(7).

Bicakci, K., Yuceel, M., Erdeniz, B., Gurbaslar, H., & Atalay, N. B. (2009). Graphical password as browser extension: Implementation and usability study. *IFIP Advances in Information and Communication Technology*, *300*, 15–29. doi:10.1007/978-3-642-02056-8_2

Biddle, R., Chiasson, S., & van Oorschot, P. C. (2009). *Graphical passwords: Learning from the first generation*. Ottawa, Canada: School of Computer Science, Carleton University.

Bishop, M., & Gates, C. (2008). Defining the insider threat. In *Proceedings of the 2008 Cyber Security and Information Infrastructure Research Workshop*. Oak Ridge, TN.

Bishop, M., Engle, S., Peisert, S., Whalen, S., & Gates, C. (2008). We have met the enemy and he is us. In *Proceedings of the 2008 new Security Paradigms Workshop*. Lake Tahoe, CA.

Bishop, M. (2003). *Computer security: Art and science* (1st ed.). Addison Wesley.

Bishop, M., & Klein, D. V. (1995). Improving system security via proactive password checking. *Computers & Security*, *14*, 233–249. doi:10.1016/0167-4048(95)00003-Q

Bishop, M., & Wagner, D. (2007). Risks of e-voting. *Communications of the ACM*, *50*(11), 120–120. doi:10.1145/1297797.1297827

BitComet. (n.d.). *A free C++ BitTorrent/HTTP/FTP download client*. Retrieved from http://www.bitcomet.com/

BitTorrent. (n.d.). Retrieved from http://www.bittorrent.com

Blakley, G. R. (1979). Safeguarding cryptographic keys. *Proceedings of the National Computer Conference*, (pp. 313–317).

Blakley, G. R. (1980). One-time pads are key safeguarding schemes, not cryptosystems: Fast key safeguarding schemes (threshold schemes) exist. In *Proceedings of the 1980 Symposium on Security and Privacy*, (pp. 108-113). IEEE Press.

Blanchet, B. (2009). Automatic verification of correspondences for security protocols. *Journal of Computer Security*, *17*(4), 363–434.

Blobel, B., & Roger-France, F. (2001). A systematic approach for analysis and design of secure health information systems. *International Journal of Medical Informatics*, *62*, 51–78. doi:10.1016/S1386-5056(01)00147-2

Blonder, G. E. (1996). *Patent n. 5559961*. USA.

Blundo, C., D'Arco, P., Santis, A. D., & Galdi, C. (2004). HYPPOCRATES: A new proactive password checker. *Journal of Systems and Software*, *71*, 163–175. doi:10.1016/S0164-1212(03)00004-9

Boehm, A., & Lowe, D. (2008). *Murach ASP.NET 3.5 web programming with VB 2008*. New Delhi, India: SPD.

Boehm, A., & Murach, J. (2008). *Murach's ASP.NET 3.5 web programming with C#2008*. New Delhi, India: SPD.

Boneh, D., & Franklin, M. (2001). Identity-based encryption from the Weil Pairing. In Kilian, J. (Ed.), *CRYPTO 2001, LNCS 2139* (pp. 213–229). doi:10.1007/3-540-44647-8_13

Bordens, K. S., & Horowitz, I. A. (2001). *Social psychology* (2nd ed.). Lawrence Erlbaum. *Detection of insider threats* (Tech. Rep. No. 2.1). Carnegie Mellon University, CyLab.

Borking, J. (2006). *Privacy rules: A steeple chase for systems architects*. Retrieved November 8, 2010, from www.w3.org/2006/07/privacy-ws/ papers/04-borking-rules/

Borselius, N. (2002). Mobile agent security. *Electronics and Communication Engineering Journal*, *14*(5).

Bort, J. (2000). The best-kept security secrets. *New World (New Orleans, La.)*, *17*(46), 109–114.

Boyd, S. W., & Keromytis, A. D. (2004). *SQLrand: Preventing SQL injection attacks*, (pp. 292-302). Columbia University. Berlin, Germany: Springer.

Bradley, P., & Mangasarian, O. L. (1998). Feature selection via concave minimization and support vector machines. In *Proceedings of the Fifteenth International Conference (ICML)*, (pp. 82-90).

Breiman, L., Friedman, J. H., Olshen, R. A., & Stone, C. J. (1984). *Classification and regression trees*. Belmont, CA: Wadsworth.

Bruckschen, M., Northfleet, C., da Silva, D., Bridi, P., Granada, R., Vieira, R., & Sander, T. (2010). Named entity recognition in the legal domain for ontology population. In *Proceedings of SPLeT-2010*. LREC.

Bryan, D. A., Lowekamp, B. B., & Jennings, C. (2005). SOSIMPLE: A serverless, standards-based, P2P SIP communication system. *First International Workshop on Advanced Architectures and Algorithms for Internet Delivery and Applications (AAA-IDEA'05)* IEEE, Orlando, USA, (pp. 42-49).

Bryan, D. A., Lowekamp, B. B., & Zangrilli, M. (2008). *The design of a versatile, secure P2P SIP communications architecture for the public Internet. IEEE International Symposium on Parallel and Distributed Processing*, IEEE, Miami, USA, (pp. 1-8).

Bryan, D. A., Matthews, P., Shim, E., Willis, D., & Dawkins, S. (2008). *Concepts and terminology for peer to peer SIP*. IETF Internet Draft (draft-ietf-p2psip-concepts-02). Retrieved from http://www.p2psip.org/drafts/draft-ietf-p2psip-concepts-02.html

Bryans, J. W., Littlewood, B., Ryan, P. Y. A., & Strigini, L. (2006). E-voting: Dependability requirements and design for dependability. In the *International Conference on Availability, Reliability and Security (ARES)* (pp. 988-995). Washington, DC: IEEE Computer Society.

Bryl, B., Dalpiaz, F., Ferrario, R., Mattioli, A., & Villafiorita, A. (2009). Evaluating procedural alternatives: A case study in e-voting. *Electronic Government, an International Journal, 6*(2), 213-231

Buchegger, S., & Leboudec, J. Y. (2002). Performance analysis of the CONFIDANT protocol (cooperation of nodes - fairness in dynamic ad-hoc networks). In *Proceedings of MobiHoc 2002*.

Buhr, P. A., Karsten, M., & Shih, J. (1996). *Kdb: A multithreaded debugger for multithreaded applications*. In SIGMETRICS Symposium on Parallel and Distributed Tools.

Butler, R. (2007). A framework of anti-phishing measures aimed at protecting the online consumer's identity. *The Electronic Library, 25*(5), 517–533. doi:10.1108/02640470710829514

California Secretary of State. (2007). *Withdrawal of approval of Diebold Election Systems, Inc, Gems 1.18.24/Accuvote- Tswaccuvote-Os Dre & optical scan voting system and conditional re-approval of use of Diebold Election Systems, Inc., Gems 1.18.24/Accuvote-Tsx/Accuvote-Os Dre & optical scan voting system*. Retrieved April 20, 2008, from https://www.sos.ca.gov/voting-systems/ oversight/ttbr/diebold-102507.pdf

Camtepe, S. A., & Yener, B. (2005). *Key distribution mechanisms for wireless sensor networks: A survey*. Technical Report TR-05-07 Rensselaer Polytechnic Institute, Computer Science Department.

Canadian Council of Better Business Bureaus. (2011). *Canadian BBB*. Retrieved February 11, 2011, from http://www.bbb.org/canada

Canadian Standards Association. (1996). *Model code for the protection of personal information* (Q830-96). Retrieved February 11, 2011, from http://www.csa.ca/cm/ca/en/ privacy-code/publications/view-privacy-code

Cansell, D., Gibson, J. P., & Mèry, D. (2007). Refinement: A constructive approach to formal software design for a secure e-voting interface. *Electronic Notes in Theoretical Computer Science, 183*, 39–55. doi:10.1016/j.entcs.2007.01.060

Cao, F., Bryan, D. A., & Lowekamp, B. B. (2006). Providing secure services in peer-to-peer communications networks with central security servers. *International Conference on Internet and Web Applications and Services (ICIW)*, IEEE, Guadeloupe, French Caribbean, (pp. 105-110).

Cappello, F., Djilali, S., Fedak, G., Herault, T., Magniette, F., Néri, V., & Lodygensky, O. (2004). Computing on large scale distributed systems: XtremWeb architecture, programming models, security, tests and convergence with Grid. *FGCS Future Generation Computer Science, 21,* 417–437. doi:10.1016/j.future.2004.04.011

Cargill, T., & Locanthi, B. (1987). *Cheap hardware support for software debugging and profiling.* In Second International Conference on Architectural Support for Programming Languages and Operating Systems.

Caron, E., & Desprez, F. (2006). Diet: A scalable toolbox to build network enabled servers on the grid. *International Journal of High Performance Computing Applications, 20*(3), 335–352. doi:10.1177/1094342006067472

Cass, A. G., Lerner, B. S., Sutton, S. M., McCall, E. K., Jr., Wise, A., & Osterweil, L. J. (2002). Little-JIL/Juliette: A process definition language and interpreter. In *Proceedings of the 22nd International Conference on Software Engineering,* pp. (754-757). New York, NY: ACM.

Castano, S., Fugini, M. G., Martella, G., & Samarati, P. (1994). *Database security.* ACM Press Books, Addison-Wesley Professional.

Castelluccia, C., & Spognardi, A. (2007). Rok: A robust key pre-distribution protocol for multi-stage wireless sensor networks. In *Proceedings of IEEE SecureComm, International Conference on Security and Privacy in Communication Networks,* Nice, France.

Castellucia, C., & Francillon, A. (2008). *Protéger les réseaux de capteurs sans fil.* Paper presented at the Symposium sur la Sécurité des Technologies de l'Information et des Communications (SSTIC), Rennes, France.

Cattaneo, C., Faruolo, P., Palazzo, V., & Visconti, I. (2010). Proxy smart card systems. *Proceedings of the 4th Workshop in Information Security Theory and Practice* (p. 213-220). Springer.

Catuogno, L., & Galdi, C. (2008). A graphical PIN authentication mechanism with applications to smart cards and low-cost devices. *Information Security Theory and Practices, Smart Devices, Convergence and Next Generation Networks, Second IFIP WG 1.2 International Workshop, WISTP, LNCS 5019,* (pp. 16-35). Seville, Spain: Springer-Verlag.

Catuogno, L., & Galdi, C. (2010). On the security of a two-factor authentication scheme. *Information Security Theory and Practices. Security and Privacy of Pervasive Systems and Smart Devices, 4th IFIP WG 11.2 International Workshop, WISTP 2010, LNCS 6033,* (pp. 245-252). Passau, Germany: Springer-Verlag.

Center for Internet Security. (2010). *CIS benchmarks/scoring tools.* Retrieved August 24, 2010, from http://www.cisecurity.org

Chalmers, J., & Muir, R. (2003). Patient privacy and confidentiality. *British Medical Journal, 326,* 725–726. doi:10.1136/bmj.326.7392.725

Chang, C.-T. (2000). An efficient linearization approach for mixed integer problems. *European Journal of Operational Research, 123,* 652–659. doi:10.1016/S0377-2217(99)00106-X

Chang, C.-T. (2001). On the polynomial mixed 0-1 fractional programming problems. *European Journal of Operational Research, 131*(1), 224–227. doi:10.1016/S0377-2217(00)00097-7

Chebrolu, S., Abraham, A., & Thomas, J. (2005). Feature deduction and ensemble design of intrusion detection systems. *Computers & Security, 4,* 295–307. doi:10.1016/j.cose.2004.09.008

Chellapilla, K., & Simard, P. (2004). Using machine learning to break visual human interaction proofs (hips). In *Advances in Neural Information Processing Systems 17, Neural Information Processing Systems (NIPS),* (pp. 265 – 272).

Chen, H., Kao, C., & Huang, I. (2002). *Analysis of hardware and software approaches to embedded in-circuit emulation of microprocessors.* In 7th Asia Pacific Conference on Computer Systems Architecture.

Chen, Y., Li, Y., Cheng, X.-Q., & Guo, L. (2006). Survey and taxonomy of feature selection algorithms in intrusion detection system. In *Proceedings of Inscrypt 2006, LNCS 4318,* (pp. 153-167).

Chen, Y. H., & Barnes, S. (2007). Initial trust and online buyer behaviour. *Industrial Management & Data Systems, 107*(1), 21–36. doi:10.1108/02635570710719034

Chew, M., & Tygar, J. D. (September 2004). Image recognition CAPTCHAs. In *7ᵗʰ International Information Security Conference, (ISC'04)*, (pp. 268–279).

Chiasson, S., Forget, A., Stobert, E., van Oorschot, P. C., & Biddle, R. (2009). Multiple password interference in text and graphical passwords. *Proceedings of the 16th ACM conference on Computer and Communication Security (CCS)* (pp. 500-511). ACM.

Chiasson, S., van Oorschot, P. C., & Biddle, R. (2007). *Graphical password authentication using cued click points. ESORICS 2007, LNCS 4734* (pp. 359–374). Dresden, Germany: Springer-Verlag.

Chomsky, N. (1957). *Syntactic structures*. London, UK: Mouton.

Chor, B., Goldwasser, S., Micali, S., & Awerbuch, B. (1985). Verifiable secret sharing and achieving simultaneity in the presence of faults. In *Proceedings of 26th IEEE Symposium on Foundations of Computer Science*, Portland, OR, USA, (pp. 151–160).

Christensen, A. S., Møller, A., & Schwartzbach, M. I. (2003). Precise analysis of string expressions. In *Proceedings of the 10ᵗʰ International Static Analysis Symposium, SAS 03, LNCS 2694*, (pp. 1–18). Springer-Verlag.

Cialdini, R., & Goldstein, N. (2004). Social Influence: Compliance and conformity. *Annual Review of Psychology, 55*, 591–621. doi:10.1146/annurev.psych.55.090902.142015

Ciaramella, A., D'Arco, P., Santis, A. D., Galdi, C., & Tagliaferri, R. (2006). Neural network techniques for proactive password checking. *IEEE Transactions on Dependable and Secure Computing, 3*, 327–339. doi:10.1109/TDSC.2006.53

Cobleigh, J. M., Clarke, L. A., & Osterweil, L. J. (2002). FLAVERS: A finite state verification technique for software systems. *IBM Systems Journal, 41*(1), 140-165. ISSN 0018-8670

Cole, E., & Ring, S. (2006). *Insider threat: Protecting the enterprise from sabotage, spying, and theft*. Syngress Press.

Comer, S. (2005). *Internetworking with TCP/IP (Vol. 1-3)*. New Delhi, India: Pearson Education.

Common Criteria. (2009). *Common criteria for information technology security evaluation*. Retrieved November 10, 2009, from http://www.commoncriteriaportal.org/

Compuware Corp. (1999). *Debugging blue screens*. Technical Paper.

Cooley, T. (1888). *A treatise on the law of torts or the wrongs which arise independent of contract* (2nd ed.). Chicago, IL: Callaghan & Co.

Copperman, M. & Thomas, J. (1995). Poor man's watchpoints. *ACM SIGPLAN Notices, 30*(1).

Corelis Corp. (2005). *EMDT/K5 boundary-scan (JTAG) emulator for the AMD K5 processors*.

Cortes, C., & Vapnik, V. (1995). Support-vector networks. *Machine Learning, 20*(3). doi:10.1007/BF00994018

Cranor, L., Langheinrich, M., Marchiori, M., Presler-Marshall, M., & Reagle, J. (2002). *The platform for privacy preferences 1.0 specification*. Retrieved February 11, 2011, from http://www.w3.org/TR/P3P/

Cranor, L. (2002). *Web privacy with* (p. 3P). O'Reilly & Associates.

Cranor, L. F. (1996). Electronic voting: Computerized polls may save money, protect privacy. [New York, NY: ACM.]. *Crossroads, 2*(4), 12–16. doi:10.1145/332159.332163

Cuppens, F., & Cuppens-Boulahia, N. (2007). Modeling contextual security policies. *International Journal of Information Security, 7*(4), 285–305. doi:10.1007/s10207-007-0051-9

Damianou, N., Dulay, N., Lupu, E., & Sloman, M. (2001). The ponder policy specification language. In *Policies for Distributed Systems and Networks, LNCS 1995/2001*, (pp. 18-38). Springer.

Daniel, R. (2005). Monetary incentives, what are they good for? *Journal of Economic Methodology, 12*(2), 265–276. doi:10.1080/13501780500086180

Davis, D., Monrose, F., & Reiter, M. K. (2004). On user choice in graphical password schemes. *Proceedings of the 13th USENIX Security Symposium*, August 9-13, 2004, San Diego, CA, USA, (pp. 151-164).

De Angeli, A., Coventry, L., Johnson, G., & Renaud, K. (2005). Is a picture really worth a thousand words? Exploring the feasibility of graphical authentication systems. *International Journal of Human-Computer Studies, 63*(1-2), 128–152. doi:10.1016/j.ijhcs.2005.04.020

de Lusignan, S., Chan, T., Theadom, A., & Dhoul, N. (2007). The roles of policy and professionalism in the protection of processed clinical data: A literature review. *International Journal of Medical Informatics, 76*, 261–268. doi:10.1016/j.ijmedinf.2005.11.003

Defense Information Systems Agency. (2001). *Database - security tech. implem. guide*, V8, R1.

Delaune, S., Kremer, S., & Ryan, M. (2009). Verifying privacy-type properties of electronic voting protocols. *Journal of Computer Security, 17*(4), 435–487.

DeLuca, A., Denzel, M., & Hussmann, H. (2009). Look into my eyes! Can you guess my password? *Proceedings of the 5th Symposium on Usable Privacy and Security*, (p. 7).

Denger, C., Ciolkowski, M., & Lanubile, F. (2004). Does active guidance improve software inspections? A preliminary empirical study. *IASTED International Conference Software Engineering*. Innsbruck, Austria: ACTA Press.

Denning, D. E. (1986). An intrusion detection model. In *Proceedings of the Seventh IEEE Symposium on Security and Privacy*, (pp. 119–131).

Department of Defense. (1985). *Trusted computer system evaluation criteria*. DoD 5200.28-STDm December 1985, US Department of Defense, December 26, 1985.

Desai, M. S., Richards, T. C., & Desai, K. J. (2003). E-commerce policies and customer privacy. *Information Management & Computer Security, 11*(1), 19–27. doi:10.1108/09685220310463696

Dhamija, R., & Perrig, A. (2000). Dèjà Vu: A user study using images for authentication. *Proceedings of the 9th USENIX Security Symposium* (p. 4). Denver, CO: USENIX.

Dhamija, R., & Tygar, J. D. (May 2005). Phish and hips: Human interactive proofs to detect phishing attacks. In *Second International Workshop on Human Interactive Proofs, (HIP 2005)*, (pp. 127–141). USA.

Dhillon, G. (2007). *Principles of information systems security: Text and cases*. Hoboken, NJ: Wiley Inc.

Dhillon, G., & Backhouse, J. (2000). Information system security management in the new millennium. *Communications of the ACM, 43*(125).

Dhillon, G., & Backhouse, J. (2001). Current direction in IS security research: Towards socio-organizational perspectives. *Information Systems Journal, 11*, 127–153. doi:10.1046/j.1365-2575.2001.00099.x

Dhillon, G., & Torkzadeh, G. (2006). Value-focused assessment of information system security in organizations. *Information Systems Journal, 16*(3), 293–314. doi:10.1111/j.1365-2575.2006.00219.x

di Vimercati, S., & Samarati, P. (1996). Access control in federated systems. In *Proceedings of the 1996 Workshop on New Security Paradigms* (pp. 87–99).

Dicodess. (2006). *Open source model-driven DSS generator*. Retrieved November 11, 2010, from http://dicodess. sourceforge.net

Dietikon, P. L. (2001). *RS232 interface using MAX232, written by Peter Luethi Dietikon*, Switzerland, Revision-1.03.

Dinger, J., & Hartenstein, H. (2006). Defending the Sybil attack in P2P networks: Taxonomy, challenges, and a proposal for self-registration. *Proceedings of the First International Conference on Availability, Reliability and Security* (ARES'06). ISBN: 0-7695-2567-9/06

Douceur, J. R. (2002). The Sybil attack. *Proceedings of the 1st International Workshop of Peer-To-Peer Systems*, 2429. eBay Inc. (2009). *Corporate fact sheet: Q3 2009*. Retrieved from http://ebayinkblog.com/wp-content/uploads/2009/10/FINAL-eBay-Inc-Fact-Sheet-Q309.pdf

Duckham, M., & Kulik, L. (2006). Location privacy and location-aware computing. In Billen, R., Joao, E., & Forrest, D. (Eds.), *Dynamic and mobile GIS: Investigating change in space and time* (pp. 34–51).

Duda, R. O., Hart, P. E., & Stork, D. G. (2001). *Pattern classification*. USA: Wiley-Interscience.

Dunlap, G. W., King, S. T., Cinar, S., Basrai, M., & Chen, P. M. (2002). *Revirt: Enabling intrusion analysis through virtual-machine logging and replay.* In Symposium on Operating Systems Design and Implementation (OSDI).

Dunphy, P., & Yan, J. (2007). Do background images improve draw a secret graphical passwords? *Proceedings of the 14th ACM Conference on Computer and Communications Security*, (p. 47).

Durkan, P., Durkin, M., & Gillen, J. (2003). Exploring efforts to engender online trust. *International Journal of Entrepreneurial Behavior & Research, 9*(3), 93–110. doi:10.1108/13552550310476184

Ebalard, A., & Valadon, G. (2006). *La sécurité dans mobile IPv6.* Paper presented at the Symposium sur la Sécurité des Technologies de l'Information et des Communications (SSTIC), Rennes, France.

Elberzhager, F., Klaus, A., & Jawurek, M. (2009). Software inspections using guided checklists to ensure security goals. *Conference on Availability, Reliability and Security*, (pp. 853-858). Fukuoka.

ElGamal, T. (1985). A public key cryptosystem and a signature scheme based on discrete logarithms. *IEEE Transactions on Information Theory*, 469–472. doi:10.1109/TIT.1985.1057074

Elgoarany, K., & Eltoweissy, M. (2007). Security in mobile IPv6: A survey. *Information Security Technical Report, 12*(1), 32–43. doi:10.1016/j.istr.2007.02.002

Elrakaiby, Y., Cuppens, F., & Cuppens-Boulahia, N. (2010*). From contextual permission to dynamic pre-obligation: An integrated approach*, (pp. 70-78). Paper presented at the ARES Conference.

EMVCo. (2008). *EMV integrated circuit card specification for payment systems.*

Ernst, F., & Armin, F. (1995). *Psychological foundations of incentives* (1st ed.). IEW - Working Papers, Institute for Empirical Research in Economics - IEW.

European Telecommunications Standards Institute, ETSI. (2005). *Open service access (OSA): Parlay X web services: Par 9: Terminal location.* ETSI, ES 202 391-9.

Evans, D., & Larochelle, D. (2002). Improving security using extensible lightweight static analysis. *IEEE Software*, 42–51. doi:10.1109/52.976940

Everitt, K. M., Bragin, T., Fogarty, J., & Kohno, T. (2009). A comprehensive study of frequency, interference, and training of multiple graphical passwords. *Proceedings of the 27th International Conference on Human Factors in Computer Systems* (p. 889-898). Boston, MA: ACM.

Fagan, M. E. (1976). Design and code inspections to reduce errors in program development. *IBM Systems Journal, 38*(2-3), 182–211. doi:10.1147/sj.153.0182

Fan, C., Zhou, S., & Li, F. (2008). Deniable proxy-anonymous signatures. *Proceedings of the 9th International Conference for Young Computer Scientists* (pp. 2131-2136). IEEE Computer Society.

Farmer, W. M., Guttman, J. D., & Swarup, V. (1996). Security for mobile agents: Issues and requirements. *Proceedings of the 19th National Information Systems.*

Feldman, P. (1987). A practical scheme for non-interactive verifiable secret sharing. In *Proceedings of 28th IEEE Symposium on Foundations of Computer Science*, Los Angeles, CA, USA, (pp. 427–437).

Felps, W., Mitchell, T., & Byington, E. (2006). How, when and why bad apples spoil the barrel: Negative group members and dysfunctional groups. *Research in Organizational Behavior, 27*, 181–230. doi:10.1016/S0191-3085(06)27005-9

Fernando, J. I., & Dawson, L. L. (2009). The health information system security threat lifecycle: An informatics theory. *International Journal of Medical Informatics, 78*(12), 815–826. doi:10.1016/j.ijmedinf.2009.08.006

Ferraiolo, D. F., & Kuhn, D. R. (1992). Role based access control. *National Computer Security Conference*, (pp. 554-563).

Fessi, A., Niedermayer, H., Kinkelin, H., & Carle, G. (2007). A cooperative SIP infrastructure for highly reliable telecommunication services. *Proceedings of the 1st International Conference on Principles, Systems and Applications of IP Telecommunications (IPTCOMM'07)*, ACM, New York, USA, (pp. 29-38).

Fettig, A. (2006). *Twisted network programming essentials.* O'Reilly.

Financial Services Roundtable. (2006). *BITS key considerations for securing data in storage and transport: Securing physical media in storage, transport, and for data erasure and destruction.* Retrieved from http://www.bitsinfo.org/downloads/ Publications%20Page/ bitsdatatrans.pdf

Flauzac, O., Krajecki, M., & Steffenel, L. (2010). CONFIIT: A middleware for peer-to-peer computing. *The Journal of Supercomputing, 53*(1), 86–102. doi:10.1007/s11227-009-0349-7

Fleischer, P. (2007). *Google privacy chief calls for international data protection standards.* Retrieved February 8, 2009, from www.bespaci☐c.com/mt/archives/015985. html#015985

Fletcher, N. (2007). Challenges for regulating financial fraud in cyberspace. *Journal of Financial Crime, 14*(2), 190–207. doi:10.1108/13590790710742672

Fok, C. L., Roman, G. C., & Lu, C. (2009). Agilla: A mobile agent middleware for self-adaptive wireless sensor networks. *ACM Transactions on Autonomous and Adaptive Systems, Special Issue on Self-Adaptive and Self-Organising Wireless Networking Systems, 4*(3).

Fonseca, J., & Vieira, M. (2008). Mapping software faults with web security vulnerabilities. *IEEE/IFIP International Conference on Dependable Systems and Networks (DSN 2008),* USA.

Foo, B., Wu, Y., Mao, Y., Bagchi, S., & Spafford, E. (2005). ADEPTS: Adaptive intrusion response using attack graphs in an e-commerce environment. In *Proceedings of 35th IEEE/IFIP International Conference on Dependable Systems and Networks.* Retrieved from http://www.computer.org/portal/web/ csdl/doi/10.1109/DSN.2005.17

Förhécz, A., Kőrösi, G., Millinghoffer, A., & Strausz, G. (2009) Emerald: Legal knowledge engineering using OWL and rules. In G. Governatori (Ed.), *Proceeding of the 2009 Conference on Legal Knowledge and Information Systems: JURIX 2009: The Twenty-Second Annual Conference,* (pp. 53-58). Amsterdam, The Netherlands: IOS Press.

Fortino, G., Aiello, F., Gravina, R., & Guerrieri, A. (2009). MAPS: A mobile agent platform for Java Sun SPOTs. In *Proceedings of the 3rd International Workshop on Agent Technology for Sensor Networks (ATSN-09), jointly held with the 8th International Joint Conference on Autonomous Agents and Multiagent Systems (AAMAS-09).*

Foster, I. T., Kesselman, C., Tsudik, G., & Tuecke, S. (1998). A security architecture for computational grids. *ACM Conference on Computer and Communications Security,* (pp. 83-92).

Foster, I., & Kesselman, C. (1997). Globus: A metacomputing infrastructure toolkit. *The International Journal of Supercomputer Applications, 11*(2), 115–128. doi:10.1177/109434209701100205

Francesconi, E. (2009). An approach to legal rules modelling and automatic learning. In In G. Governatori (Ed.), *Proceeding of the 2009 Conference on Legal Knowledge and Information Systems: JURIX 2009: The Twenty-Second Annual Conference,* (pp. 59-68). Amsterdam, The Netherlands: IOS Press.

Freeman, E. H. (2007). Holistic information security: ISO 27001 and due care. *Information Systems Security*(16), 291-294.

Freenet. (2011). Retrieved February 23, 2011, from http://freenetproject.org/

FSA report. (April 2008). Retrieved February 17, 2009, from http://www.fsa.gov.uk/pubs/other/data_security.pdf

Fuchsbauer, G., & Pointcheval, D. (2008). Anonymous proxy signatures. *Security and Cryptography for Networks, 6th International Conference, LNCS 5229* (p. 201-217). Springer.

Gabillon, A., & Capolsini, P. (2009). Dynamic security rules for geo data. *The Second International Workshop Autonomous Spontaneous Security (SETOP), LNCS,* (pp. 136-152). St. Malo, France.

Gauzente, C. (2004). Web merchants' privacy and security statements: how reassuring are they for consumers? A two sided approach. *Journal of Electronics Commerce Research, 5*(3), 181–198.

Gauzente, C., & Ranchhod, A. (2001). Ethical marketing for competitive advantage on the Internet. *Academy of Marketing Science Review, 1*(10).

Gardner, R., Garera, S., & Rubin, A. (2007). On the difficulty of validating voting machine software with software. In *Proceedings of the USENIX/Accurate Electronic Voting Technology on USENIX/Accurate Electronic Voting Technology Workshop*. Berkeley, CA, USA: USENIX Association.

Gedik, B., & Liu, L. (2008). Protecting location privacy with personalized k-anonymity: Architecture and algorithms. *IEEE Transactions on Mobile Computing, 7*(1), 1–18. doi:10.1109/TMC.2007.1062

Gerber, M., & von Solms, R. (2005). Management of risk in the information age. *Computers & Security, 24*, 16–30. doi:10.1016/j.cose.2004.11.002

Ghiselli, E. E. (1964). *Theory of psychological measurement*. New York, NY: Mc GrawHill.

Ghosh, K. A., & Swaminath, T. M. (2001). Software security and privacy risks in mobile e-commerce. *Communications of the ACM, 44*(2), 51–57. doi:10.1145/359205.359227

Gibson, J. P., Lallet, E., & Raffy, J. L. (2010). Engineering a distributed e-voting system architecture: Meeting critical requirements. In *ISARCS, LNCS* (pp. 89-108). Springer.

Glaseman, S., Turn, R., & Gaines, R. S. (1977). Problem areas in computer security assessment. In *Proceedings of the National Computer Conference* (pp. 13-16).

Goan, T. (1999). A cop on the beat: Collecting and appraising intrusive evidence. *Communications of the ACM, 42*(7), 46–52. doi:10.1145/306549.306569

Goldreich, O., Micali, S., & Wigderson, A. (1987). How to play any mental game or a completeness theorem for protocols with honest majority. *Nineteenth Annual ACM Symposium on Theory of Computing* (pp. 218-229). ACM.

Golle, P., & Wagner, D. (2007). Cryptanalysis of a cognitive authentication scheme (extended abstract). *IEEE Symposium on Security and Privacy*, (pp. 66-70).

Goodhue, D. L., & Straub, D. W. (1991). Security concerns of system users: A study of perceptions of the adequacy of security. *Information & Management, 20*, 13–27. doi:10.1016/0378-7206(91)90024-V

Google. (2010). *Report phishing site*. Retrieved from http://www.google.com/safebrowsing/report_phish/

GPK. (2001). *Gemplus reference manual.*

Grabner-Krauter, S., & Kaluscha, E. (2003). Empirical research in online trust: A review and critical assessment. *International Journal of Human-Computer Studies, 58*(6), 783–812. doi:10.1016/S1071-5819(03)00043-0

Grady, C. L., Mcintosh, A. R., Rajah, M. N., & Craik, F. I. (1998). Neural correlates of the episodic encoding of pictures and words. *Proceedings of the National Academy of Sciences of the United States of America, 95*, 2703–2708. doi:10.1073/pnas.95.5.2703

Grand, J. (2004). Practical secure hardware design for embedded systems. *Proceedings of the 2004 Embedded Systems Conference*, San Francisco, California.

Graunt, N. (2000). Practical approaches to creating a security culture. *International Journal of Medical Informatics, 60*, 151–157. doi:10.1016/S1386-5056(00)00115-5

Gray, G. L., Debreceny, R., & Koreto, R. J. (2000). The electronic frontier. *Journal of Accountancy, 185*(5), 32–38.

GRC-GRID. (2010). *The governance, risk management and compliance global rules information database*. Retrieved November 3, 2010 from http://www.grcroundtable.org/grc-grid.htm

Greene, B., Sternberg, D., & Lepper, M. R. (1976). Overjustification in a token economy. *Journal of Personality and Social Psychology, 34*, 1219–1234. doi:10.1037/0022-3514.34.6.1219

Greenwald, S. (1996). A new security policy for distributed resource management and access control. In *Proceedings of the 1996 Workshop on New Security Paradigms* (pp. 74–86).

GrIDsure Ltd. (2010). *GrIDsure: Strong authentication using one-time passwords*. Retrieved from www.gridsure.com

Grimm, R., Hupf, K., & Volkamer, M. (2010). A formal IT-security model for the correction and abort requirement of electronic voting. In *Electronic Voting* (pp. 89-107).

Group, M. T. (2008, October). *Do you really know what your programmers are doing?* White Paper.

Gupta, A., Jain, A., Raj, A., & Jain, A. (March 2009). Sequenced tagged CAPTCHA: Generation and its analysis. In *International Conference on Advanced Computing, (IACC'09)*, (pp. 1286–1291). India.

Guyon, I., Gunn, S., Nikravesh, M., & Zadeh, L. A. (2006). *Feature extraction: Foundations and applications. Series Studies in Fuzziness and Soft Computing, Physica-Verlag.* Springer.

Guyon, I., Weston, J., Barnhill, S., & Vapnik, V. (2002). Gene selection for cancer classification using support vector machines. *Machine Learning, 46*(1), 389–422. doi:10.1023/A:1012487302797

Hafiz, M. D., Abdullah, A. H., Ithnin, N., & Mammi, H. K. (2008). Towards identifying usability and security features of graphical password in knowledge based authentication technique. *2nd Asian Conference on Modelling and Simulation* (pp. 396-403). Kuala Lumpur, Malaysia: IEEE.

Haley, C. B., Moffett, J. D., Laney, R., & Nuseibeh, B. (2006). *A framework for security requirements engineering.* International Workshop on Software Engineering for Secure Systems. Shanghai, China: ACM.

Halfond, W. G. J., & Orso, A. (2005). *AMNESIA: Analysis and monitoring for neutralizing SQL injection attacks,* (pp. 174-183).

Halfond, W. G., Viegas, J., & Orso, A. (2006). A classification of SQL injection attacks and countermeasures. In *Proceedings of the International Symposium on Secure Software Engineering.*

Hall, M. (1999). *Correlation based feature selection for machine learning.* Unpublished doctoral dissertation, University of Waikato, Department of Computer Science.

Haller, N. (1994). The S/KEY one-time password system. *Symposium on Network and Distributed System Security* (pp. 151-157). Washington, DC: IEEE Computer Society.

Hameed, A., Sleeman, D., & Preece, A. (2002). Detecting mismatches among experts' ontologies acquired through knowledge elicitation. *Knowledge-Based Systems, 15*, 265–273. doi:10.1016/S0950-7051(01)00162-9

Hanacek, P. (2005). Problems of security in ad-hoc sensor network. *Proceedings of MOSIS '05,* MARQ, Ostrava.

Hansson, H., & Jonsson, B. (1994). A logic for reasoning about time and reliability. *Formal Aspects of Computing, 6*(5), 512–535. doi:10.1007/BF01211866

Harada, A., Isarida, T., Mizuno, T., & Nishigaki, M. (2006). A user authentication system using schema of visual memory. *Biologically Inspired Approaches to Advanced Information Technology: Second International Workshop, Bioadit 2006, LNCS 3853,* Osaka, Japan 26-27, (pp. 338-345). Springer.

Harris, S. (2002). *CISSP all-in-one certification exam guide.* New York, NY: McGraw-Hill/Osborne.

Hayashi, E., Dhamija, R., Christin, N., & Perrig, A. (2008). Use your illusion: Secure authentication usable anywhere. *Proceedings of the 4th Symposium on Usable Privacy and Security,* (pp. 35--45).

Haystead, J. (2011). Defining a career path in electronic warfare. *Journal of Electronic Defense, 34*(8), 26–28.

Hedström, K., Dhillon, G., & Karlsson, F. (2010). *Using actor network theory to understand information security management.* Paper presented at the 25th Annual IFIP TC 11.

Hedström, K. (2007). The values of IT in elderly care. *Information Technology & People, 20*(1), 72–84. doi:10.1108/09593840710730563

Heeks, R. (2006). *Implementing and managing egovernment.* London, UK: Sage Publications Ltd.

Heitmeyer, C. L., Archer, M., Leonard, I. E., & McLean, J. (2008). Applying formal methods to a certifiably secure software system. *IEEE Transactions on Software Engineering, 34*(1), 82–98. doi:10.1109/TSE.2007.70772

Henari, T. F., & Mahboob, R. (2008). E-commerce in Bahrain: The non-technical limitations. *Education. Business and Society: Contemporary Middle Eastern Issues, 1*(3), 213–220. doi:10.1108/17537980810909832

Herring, J. R. (2006). *OpenGIS implementation specification for geographic information - Simple feature access - Part 1: Common architecture.* Open Geospatial Consortium Incorporation, OGC 06-103r3.

Hirshleifer, J., & Riley, J. G. (1979). The analytics of uncertainty and information: An expository survey. *Journal of Economic Literature, 17*, 1375–1421.

Hochheiser, H., Feng, J., & Lazar, J. (2008). *Challenges in universally usable privacy and security*. Symposium on Usable Privacy and Security. Pittsburg, PA: ACM.

Höne, K., & Eloff, J. H. P. (2002). *Information security policy - What do international information security standards say?* ISO/IEC 17799 (2005). *International Organization for Standarisation (ISO)*. Retrieved from www.iso.org

Hoppe, T. (2009). *Applying intrusion detection to automotive IT- Early insights and selected short term countermeasures*.

Hoppe, T., Kiltz, S., & Dittmann, J. (2008). Security threats to automotive CAN networks practical examples and selected short-term countermeasures. In *Proceedings of the International Conference on Computer Safety, Reliability and Security* (SAFECOMP), (pp. 235–248).

Hopper, N. J., & Blum, M. (2000). *A secure human-computer authentication scheme*. Carnegie Mellon Technical Report CMU-CS-00-139. Pittsburgh, PA: CMU.

Hopper, N. J., & Blum, M. (2001). *Secure human identification protocols. ASIACRYPT, LNCS 2248* (pp. 52–66). Gold Coast, Australia: Springer-Verlag.

Hopwood, W. S., Sinason, D., & Tucker, R. (2000). Security in a web-based environment. *Managerial Finance, 26*(11), 42–54. doi:10.1108/03074350010766981

Householder, A., Houle, K., & Dougherty, J. (2002). Computer attack trends challenge internet security (Supplement to Computer Magazine). *Computer, 35*(4), 5–7. doi:10.1109/MC.2002.1012422

Housley, R., Polk, W., Ford, W., & Solo, D. (2002). *Internet X509 public key infrastructure: Certificate and certificate revocation list (CRL) profile*. Retrieved from http://www.ietf.org/rfc/rfc3280.txt

Howard, M. (2006, July/August). A process for performing security code reviews. *IEEE Security and Privacy, 4*(4), 74–79. doi:10.1109/MSP.2006.84

Howard, M., & LeBlanc, D. (2002). *Writing secure code* (2nd ed.). Redmond, CA: Microsoft Press.

Howell, N. (2004). *Using Internet information server*. New Delhi, India: PHI.

Hsu, C. W. (2009). Frame misalignment: interpreting the implementation of information systems security certification in an organization. *European Journal of Information Systems, 18*, 140–150. doi:10.1057/ejis.2009.7

Hu, C., & Li, D. (2007). A new type of proxy ring signature scheme with revocable anonymity. *Proceedings of the 8th ACIS International Conference on Software Engineering, Artificial Intelligence, Networking and Parallel/Distributed Computing* (pp. 866-868). IEEE Computer Society.

Hu, C., Liu, P., & Li, D. (2007). A new type of proxy ring signature scheme with revocable anonymity and no info leaked. *Multimedia Content Analysis and Mining, International Workshop, LNCS 4577*, (p. 262-266). Springer.

Hubbard, D. W. (2009). *The failure of risk management: Why it's broken and how to fix it*. Hoboken, NJ: Wiley.

Hubbard, D. W. (2010). *How to measure anything: Finding the value of intangibles in business* (2nd ed.). Hoboken, NJ: Wiley.

Huber, J., Payne, J., & Puto, C. (1982). Adding asymmetrically dominated alternatives: Violations of regularity and the similarity hypothesis. *The Journal of Consumer Research, 9*(1), 90. doi:10.1086/208899

Hu, Q. (2011). Does deterrence work in reducing information security policy abuse by employees? *Communications of the ACM, 54*(6), 54–60. doi:10.1145/1953122.1953142

Hu, Q., & Dinev, T. (2005). Is spyware an internet nuisance or public menace? *Communications of the ACM, 48*(8), 61–66. doi:10.1145/1076211.1076241

Hwang, D., Schaumont, P., Verbauwhede, I., & Yang, S. (2006). Multilevel design validation in a secure embedded system. *IEEE Transactions on Computers, 55*(11), 1380–1390. doi:10.1109/TC.2006.184

HyunGon. K., & ByeongKyun, O. (2008) Secure and low latency handoff scheme for proxy mobile IPv6. In *Mobility '08: Proceedings of the International Conference on Mobile Technology, Applications, and Systems* (pp. 1-9). New York, NY: ACM Press.

IBM. (2004). *The enterprise privacy authorization language (EPAL), EPAL specification*, v1.1. Retrieved November 3, 2010, from http://www.zurich.ibm.com/security/ enterprise-privacy/epal/

IBM. (2005). *Sparcle project*. Retrieved November 3, 2010, from http://domino.research.ibm.com/comm/ research_projects.nsf/pages/sparcle.index.html

IBM. (2006). *REALM project*. Retrieved November 3, 2010, from http://www.zurich.ibm.com/security/ publications/2006/REALM-at-IRIS2006-20060217.pdf

Ingemarsson, I., & Simmons, G. J. (1991). *A protocol to set up shared secret schemes without the assistance of a mutually trusted party. Advances in Cryptology – EURO-CRYPT'90 Proceedings* (pp. 266–282). Springer-Verlag.

International Organization for Standardization (ISO). (1998). *Ergonomics of human-system interaction*. ISO.

ISO/IEC 27002. (2005). *Information technology - Security techniques - Code of Practice for information security management* (2005b).

Iyer, A., & Ngo, H. Q. (2005). Towards a theory of insider threat assessment. In *Proceedings of the 2005 International Conference on Dependable Systems and Networks* (pp. 108–117). Washington, DC: IEEE Computer Society.

Jahnke, M., Thul, C., & Martini, P. (2007). Graph based metrics for intrusion response measures in computer networks. In *Proceedings of the IEEE Conference on Local Computer Networks*, (pp. 1035–1042). doi:10.1109/LCN.2007.45

Jain, A., Jain, A., Raj, A., & Pahwa, T. (2009). Sequenced picture CAPTCHA: Generation and its strength analysis. *International Conference for Internet Technology and Secured Transactions, ICITST 2009*, (pp. 1 – 8).

Jain, A. K., Duin, R. P. W., & Mao, J. (2000). Statistical pattern recognition: A review. *IEEE Transactions on Pattern Analysis and Machine Intelligence In Pattern Analysis and Machine Intelligence, 22*(1), 4–37. doi:10.1109/34.824819

Jansen, W., Gavrila, S., Korolev, V., Heute, T., & Séveillac, C. (June 2004). A unified framework for mobile device security. *Proceedings of the International Conference on Security and Management (SAM'04)*, (pp. 9-14).

JBoss. (2010). *Drools*, v5. Retrieved November 3, 2010 from http://jboss.org/drools/

Jennings, C., Lowekamp, B., Rescorla, E., Baset, S., & Schulzrinne, H. (2010). *Resource location and discovery (RELOAD) base protocol*. IETF Internet Draft (draft-ietf-p2psip-base-09). Retrieved from http://tools.ietf.org/html/draft-ietf-p2psip-reload-00

Jensen, W., Gavrila, S., Korolev, V., Ayers, R., & Swanstrom, R. (2003). *Picture password: A visual login technique for mobile devices*. Gaithersburg, MD: National Institute of Standard and Technologies Interagency Report.

Jermyn, I., Mayer, A., Monrose, F., Reiter, M. K., & Rubin, A. D. (1999). The design and anayisis of graphical passwords. *Proceedings of the 8th USENIX Security Symposium* (pp. 23-26). Washington, DC: USENIX.

Johnson, M. S. (1982). *Some requirements for architectural support of software debugging*. In Symposium on Architectural Support for Programming Languages and Operating Systems.

Jones, D. W. (2003). The evaluation of voting technology (Chap. 1). *Advances in information security* (pp. 3-16). Kluwer Academic.

Josang, A. (1999). An algebra for assessing trust in certification chains. *Proceedings of the Network and Distributed Systems Security (NDSS'99)*, The Internet Society.

Josang, A., Hayward, R., & Pope, S. (2006). Trust network analysis with subjective logic. *Proceedings of the 29th Australasian Computer Science Conference*, Australian Computer Society, Inc., Hobart, Australia, (pp. 85-96).

Josang, A. (2001). A logic for uncertain probabilities. *International Journal of Uncertainty. Fuzziness and Knowledge-Based Systems, 9*(3), 279–311. doi:10.1142/S0218488501000831

Juels, A. Catalano, & D., Jakobsson, M. (2005). Coercion-resistant electronic elections. In *Proceedings of the 2005 ACM Workshop on Privacy in the Electronic Society* (pp. 61-70). New York, NY: ACM.

Jung, C., Elberzhager, F., Bagnato, A., & Raiteri, F. (2010). Practical experience gained from modeling security goals: Using SGITs an industrial project. *International Conference on Availability, Reliability, and Security* (pp. 531-536). Krakow, Poland: IEEE.

Kabay, M. (2002). Using social psychology to implement security policies. *Computer Security Handbook, 35*, 1–35.

Kalsi, H. S. (1999). *Electronic instrumentation*. New Delhi, India: Tata McGraw-Hill Ltd.

Kanneganti, R., & Chodavarapu, P. (2008). *SOA security*. Greenwich, CT: Manning Pub. Co.

Karakaya, F., & Charlton, E. T. (2001). Electronic commerce: Current and future practices. *Managerial Finance*, *27*(7), 42–53. doi:10.1108/03074350110767286

Karau, S. J., & Williams, K. D. (1993). Social loafing: A meta-analytic review and theoretical integration. *Journal of Personality and Social Psychology*, *65*, 681–706. doi:10.1037/0022-3514.65.4.681

Karlof, C., Sastry, N., & Wagner, D. (2004). TinySec: A link layer security architecture for wireless sensor networks. *SenSys'04: Proceeding of 2nd International Conference on Embedded Networked Sensor Systems.*

Kc, G. C., Keromytis, A. D., & Prevelakis, V. (2003). Countering code-injection attacks with instruction-set randomization. In *Proceedings of the ACM Computer and Communications Security (CSS) Conference*, October 2003, (pp. 272-280).

Kenneth, H., Edvall, M. M., & Göran, A. O. (2003). TOMLAB-for large-scale robust optimization. In *Proceedings of the Nordic MATLAB Conference*.

Kenny, S., & Borking, J. (2002). The value of privacy engineering. In *Journal of Information, Law and Technology (JILT), 1*.

Kesh, S., Ramanujan, S., & Nerur, S. (2002). A framework for analyzing e-commerce security. *Information Management & Computer Security*, *10*(4), 149–158. doi:10.1108/09685220210436930

Kessler, P. (1990). *Fast breakpoints: Design and implementation*. In Conference on Programming Language Design and Implementation.

Kheir, N., Cuppens-Boulahia, N., Cuppens, F., & Debar, H. (2010). A service dependency model for cost-sensitive intrusion response. In *Proceedings of the 15th European Symposium on Research in Computer Security, Lecture Notes in Computer Science, 6345*, (pp. 626-642). doi:10.1007/978-3-642-15497-3_38.

Kierkegaard, S. (2005). Privacy in electronic communication- Watch your e-mail: Your boss is snooping. *Computer Law & Security Report*, *21*(3), 226–236. doi:10.1016/j.clsr.2005.04.008

Kilkki, K., & Kalervo, M. (2004, March). *Kk-law for group forming services*. Presented at 15th International Symposium on Services and Local Access.

Kim, Y. S., & Chang, J. H. (2006). Provably secure proxy blind signature scheme. *Eigth IEEE International Symposium on Multimedia* (pp. 998-1003). IEEE Computer Society.

Kinateder, M., Terdic, R., & Rothermel, K. (2005). Strong pseudonymous communication for peer-to-peer reputation systems. *Proceedings of the 2005 ACM Symposium on Applied Computing*, ACM, Santa Fe, New Mexico, (pp. 1570-1576).

King, L. (2008). Ulster Bank loses 10 laptops/ *Computer World*, [Online]. Retrieved February 10, 2009, from http://www.computerworlduk.com/management/security/cybercrime/news/index.cfm?newsid=9165

King, S. T., Dunlap, G. W., & Chen, P. M. (2005). *Debugging operating systems with time-traveling virtual machines*. In Usenix Annual Technical Conference - General Track.

Kluever, K. A., & Zanibbi, R. (July 2009). Balancing usability and security in a video CAPTCHA. In *Proceedings of the 5th Symposium on Usable Privacy and Security 2009*, Mountain View, CA, USA.

Kohno, T., Stubblefield, A., Rubin, A. D., & Wallach, D. S. (2004). Analysis of an electronic voting system. *Symposium on Security and Privacy*, (Vol. 27). IEEE Computer Society.

Koller, D., & Sahami, M. (1996). Toward optimal feature selection. In *Proceedings of International Conference on Machine Learning*.

Koubaa, A., & Alves, M. (2006). Eduardo Tovar: IEEE 802.15.4: A wireless communication technology for large-scale ubiquitous computing applications. *Proceedings of Conference on Mobile and Ubiquitous Systems*, Guimarães, June 29-30.

Kremer, S., & Ryan, D. R. (2005). Analysis of an electronic voting protocol in the applied pi-calculus. *In ESOP '05, LNCS* (pp. 186-200). Edinburgh, UK, April 2005. Springer.

Krumm, J. (2008). A survey of computational location privacy. [London, UK: Springer.]. *International Journal of Personal and Ubiquitous Computing, 13*(6), 391–399. doi:10.1007/s00779-008-0212-5

Kubiatowicz, J., Bindel, D., Chen, Y., Eaton, P., Geels, D., & Gummadi, R. … Zhao, B. (2000). Oceanstore: An architecture for global-scale persistent storage. In *Proceedings of International Conference on Architectural Support for Programming Languages and Operating Systems (ASPLOS)*. ACM Press.

Kumar, M., Garfinkel, T., Boneh, D., & Winograd, T. (2007). *Reducing shoulder-surfing by using gaze-based password entry.* Symposium on Usable Privacy and Security (SOUPS).

Kwiatkowska, M., Norman, G., & Parker, D. (2001). Prism: Probabilistic symbolic model checker. In *Proceedings of PAPM/PROBMIV '01 Tools Session* (pp. 7–12).

Kwon, Y. M., Sundresh, S., Mechitov, K., & Agha, G. (2006). *ActorNet: An actor platform for wireless sensor networks.*

Laboratories, R. S. A. (2009). *PKCS #11: Cryptographic token interface standard.* Retrieved from http://www.rsa.com/rsalabs/ node.asp?id=2133

Lacour, S., Perez, C., & Priol, T. (2004). A network topology description model for grid application deployment. In *Proceedings of the Fifth IEEE/ACM International Workshop on Grid Computing (GRID '04),* (pp. 61–68). Washington, DC: IEEE Computer Society.

Lamport, L. (1981). Password authentication with insecure communication. *Communications of the ACM, 24*(11), 770–772. doi:10.1145/358790.358797

Lamport, L., Shostak, R., & Pease, M. (1982). The Byzantine generals problem. *ACM Transactions on Programming Languages and Systems, 4*(3), 382–401. doi:10.1145/357172.357176

Lange, D., & Oshima, M. (1999). Seven good reasons for mobile agents. *Communications of the ACM, 42.*

Lashkari, A. H., Towhidi, F., Saleh, R., & Farmand, S. (2009). A complete comparison on pure and cued recall-based graphical user authentication algorithms. *Proceedings of the 2nd International Conference on Computer and Electrical Engineering* (pp. 527-532). IEEE.

Latene, B. (1981). The psychology of social impacts. *The American Psychologist, 36,* 343–356. doi:10.1037/0003-066X.36.4.343

Le, L., & Kuo, G.-S. (2007). *Hierarchical and breathing peer-to-peer SIP system. IEEE International Conference on Communications (ICC '07),* IEEE, Glasgow, Scotland, (pp. 1887-1892).

Lee, B., Kim, H., & Kim, K. (2001a). Secure mobile agent using strong non- designated proxy signature. *Information Security and Privacy, 6th Australasian Conference, LNCS 2119,* (p. 474).

Lee, B., Kim, H., & Kim, K. (2001b). Strong proxy signature and its applications. *Symposium on Cryptography and Information Security,* (pp. 603-608).

Lee, W. (1999). A data mining framework for building intrusion detection models. In *IEEE Symposium on Security and Privacy,* (pp. 120–132). Berkeley, California.

Lee, W., Fan, W., Miller, M., Stolfo, S. J., & Zadok, E. (2002). Toward cost-sensitive modeling for intrusion detection and response. *Journal of Computer Security, 10,* 5–22.

Lee, W., & Stolfo, S. (2000). A framework for constructing features and models for intrusion detection systems. *ACM Transactions on Information and System Security, 3,* 227–261. doi:10.1145/382912.382914

Leitheiser, R. L. (2001, January). *Data quality in health care data warehouse environments.* Paper presented at the 34th Hawaii International Conference on System Sciences, Island of Maui, Hawaii.

Leiwo, J., Hanle, C., Homburg, P., & Tanenbaum, A. (2000). Disallowing unauthorized state changes of distributed shared objects. *Information Security for Global Information Infrastructures, IFIP TC11 Fifteenth Annual Working Conference on Information Security, 175,* (pp. 381-390).

Levis, P. (2006). *TinyOS programming*. Retrieved from http://csl.stanford.edu/~pal/pubs/ tinyos-programming.pdf

Lewandowski, S., Van Hook, D. J., O'Leary, G. C., Haines, J. W., & Rossey, L. M. (2002). SARA: Survivable autonomic response architecture. *DARPA Information Survivability Conference and Exposition, 1,* 0077. doi:10.1109/DISCEX.2001.932194

Lewis, D. W. (2003). *Fundamentals of embedded software- Where C and assembly meet*. New Delhi, India: Prentice Hall of India.

Leyton-Brown, K., & Shoham, Y. (2008). *Essentials of game theory: A concise, multidisciplinary introduction*. Morgan & Claypool.

Li, X., & Liu, L. (2003). A reputation-based trust model for peer-to-peer e-commerce communities. *ACM Conference on Electronic Commerce*, (pp. 228-229). New York, NY: ACM Press.

Lidong, Z., & Zygmunt, J. H. (1999). Securing ad hoc networks. *IEEE Network, 13*(6), 24–30. doi:10.1109/65.806983

Linton, M. A. (1990). *The evolution of DBX*. In Usenix Summer Conference.

Lippmann, R. P., Fried, D., Graf, I., Haines, J., Kendall, K., & Mcclung, D. ... Zissman, M. (2000). Evaluating intrusion detection systems: The 1998 DARPA off-line intrusion detection evaluation. In *Proceedings of the on DARPA Information Survivability Conference and Exposition* (DISCEX'00, Hilton Head, South Carolina, Jan. 25-27), (pp. 12–26). Los Alamitos, CA: IEEE Computer Society Press.

Lippmann, R. P., Graf, I., Garfinkel, S. L., Gorton, A. S., Kendall, K. R., & McClung, D. J. ... Zissman, M. A. (1998). The 1998 DARPA/AFRL off-line intrusion detection evaluation. Presented to *the First Intl. Workshop on Recent Advances in Intrusion Detection (RAID-98)*, Lovain-la-Neuve, Belgium, 14–16 September.

Liu, W., Tong, F., Luo, Y., & Zhang, F. (2007). A proxy blind signature scheme based on elliptic curve with proxy revocation. *Proceedings of the 8th ACIS International Conference on Software Engineering, Artificial Intelligence, Networking and Parallel/Distributed Computing* (pp. 99-104). IEEE Computer Society.

Liu, H., & Motoda, H. (2008). *Computational methods of feature selection*. Boca Raton, FL: Chapman & Hall/CRC.

Lohr, S. (2011, April 15). The business market plays cloud computing catch-up. *The New York Times*.

Loukides, M. & Oram, A. (1996). Getting to know GDB. *The Linux Journal, 29*.

Loureiro, S., Molva, R., & Roudier, Y. (2000). Mobile code security. *Proceedings of ISPYAR Code Mobile*, Toulouse, France.

Luethi, M., & Knolmayer, G. F. (2009). *Security in health information systems: An exploratory comparison of U.S. and Swiss hospitals.* Paper presented at the 42nd Hawaii International Conference on System Sciences 5-8 January, Big Island, Hawaii.

Lumenaut. (2006). *Decision tree package*. Retrieved November 24, 2010, from http://www.lumenaut.com/decisiontree.htm

Lunt, T., Tamaru, A., Gilham, F., Jagannathan, R., Neumann, P., Javitz, H., ... Garvey, T. (1992). *A real-time intrusion detection expert system (IDES)*. Final technical report.

Lu, R., Cao, Z., & Dong, X. (2006). Efficient id-based one-time proxy signature and its application in e-cheque. *Cryptology and Network Security, LNCS, 4301,* 153–167. doi:10.1007/11935070_10

Mackenzie, O. J. (Ed.). (2006). *Information science and knowledge management*. Berlin, Germany: Springer-Verlag.

Maenpaa, J., & Camarillo, G. (2010). *Service discovery usage for resource location and discovery (RELOAD)*. IETF Internet Draft (draft-ietf-p2psip-service-discovery-01). Retrieved from https://datatracker.ietf.org/doc/ draft-ietf-p2psip-service-discovery/

Maets, Y., Onno, S., & Heen, O. (2009). Recall-a-story, a story-telling graphical password system. *Proceedings of the 5th Symposium on Usable Privacy and Security* (p. 1). Mountain View, CA: ACM.

Magnusson, P. S., Christensson, M., Eskilson, J., Forsgren, G., Hallberg, G., & Hogberg, J. (2002). Simics: A full system simulation platform. *IEEE Computer Society, 2*(35), 50–58. doi:10.1109/2.982916

Mahoney, M. V., & Chan, P. K. (2003). *An analysis of the 1999 DARPA/Lincoln laboratory evaluation data for network anomaly detection. Technical Report TR CS-2003-02.* Computer Science Department, Florida Institute of Technology.

Mambo, M., Usuda, K., & Okamoto, E. (1996). Proxy signatures for delegating signing operation. *ACM Conference on Computer and Communications Security* (p. 48-57). ACM.

Mambo, M., & Okamoto, E. (1997). Proxy cryptosystem: Delegation of the power to decrypt ciphertexts. *IEICE Transaction Fundamentals. E (Norwalk, Conn.), 80-A*(1), 54–63.

Mandt, T. K. (2006). Certificateless authenticated two-party key agreement protocols. Gjovik University College, 2006.

Mangasarian, O. L. (2007). Exact 1-norm support vector machines via unconstrained convex differentiable minimization (special topic on machine learning and optimization). *Journal of Machine Learning Research, 7*(2), 1517–1530.

Mannila, H., & Toivonen, H. (1996). Discovering generalized episodes using minimal occurrences. In *Proceedings of the 2nd International Conference on Knowledge Discovery in Databases and Data Mining* (Portland, OR, Aug.).

Mannila, H., Toivonen, H., & Verkamo, A. I. (1995). Discovering frequent episodes in sequences. In *Proceedings of the First International Conference on Knowledge Discovery in Databases and Data Mining* (Montreal, Canada, Aug. 20-21).

Martinelli, F. (2002). Symbolic semantics and analysis for crypto-CCS with (almost) generic inference systems. In *Proceedings of the 27th International Symposium on Mathematical Foundations of Computer Science* (pp. 519-531). London, UK: Springer-Verlag.

Martin, R., & Hewstone, M. (2001). Conformity and independence in groups: Majorities and minorities. In Hogg, M. A., & Tindale, S. (Eds.), *Blackwell handbook of social psychology (group processes)* (pp. 209–234). doi:10.1002/9780470998458.ch9

Martin, W. (1995). *The global information society.* Aldershot, UK: Aslib/Gower.

Marwedel, P. (2003). *Embedded system design* (1st ed., pp. 1–8). Kluwer Academic Publishers.

Masoumzadeh, A., James, B., & Joshi, D. (2008). PuRBAC: Purpose-aware role-based access control. In *On the Move to Meaningful Internet Systems (OTM 08)*, (pp. 1104-1121).

Massa, P., & Avesani, P. (2007). Trust-aware recommender systems. *Proceedings of the 2007 ACM Conference on Recommender Systems*, Minneapolis, MN, USA, October 19-20, (pp. 17-24).

Matsumoto, T. (1996). *Human-computer cryptography: An attempt. Computer and Communication Security* (pp. 68–75). New Delhi, India: ACM.

Matsumoto, T., & Imai, H. (1991). *Human identification through insecure channel. EUROCRYPT, LNCS 547* (pp. 409–421). Brighton, UK: Springer-Verlag.

Maxim. (n.d.). *Home page.* Retrieved from www.maxim-ic.com

Mazidi, M. A., & Mazidi, J. G. (2007). *The 8051 microcontroller and embedded systems.* Pearson Education Ltd.

McClure, R. A., & Krüger, I. H. (2005). *SQL DOM: Compile time checking of dynamic SQL statements.* IEEE Explore.

McCrohan, K. F. (2003). Facing the threats to electronic commerce. *Journal of Business and Industrial Marketing, 18*(2), 133–145. doi:10.1108/08858620310463060

McCusker, R. (2006). Transnational organized cyber crime: Distinguishing threat from reality. *Crime, Law, and Social Change, 46*, 257–273. doi:10.1007/s10611-007-9059-3

McDonald, D. L., Atkinson, R. J., & Metz, C. (1995). One time passwords in everything (OPIE): Experiences with building and using stronger authentication. *5th USENIX Security Symposium* (p. 16). Salt Lake City, UT: USENIX.

McFadzean, E., Ezingeard, J.-N., & Birchall, D. (2006). Anchoring information security governance research: Sociological groundings and future directions. *Journal of Information System Security, 2*(3).

McGuire, B. L., & Roser, S. N. (2000). What your business should know about Internet security. *Strategic Finance, 82*(5), 50–54.

McHugh, J. (2000). Testing intrusion detection systems: A critique of the 1998 and 1999 DARPA off-line intrusion detection system evaluation as performed by Lincoln Laboratory. *ACM Transactions on Information and System Security, 3*(4). doi:10.1145/382912.382923

Megliola, M., & Barbieri, L. (2008). *Integrating agent and wireless technologies for location-based services in cultural heritage.* Digital Cultural Heritage - Essential for Tourism, 2nd EVA Conference, 2008, Vienna.

Mellor-Crummey, J. M., & LeBlanc, T. J. (1989). *A software instruction counter.* In Third International Conference on Architectural Support for Programming Languages and Operating Systems.

Menezes, A., van Oorschot, P., & Vanstone, S. (2001). *Handbook of applied cryptography.* Waterloo, Canada: CRC Press.

Mercuri, T. M., & Camp, L. J. (2004). The code of elections. *Communications of the ACM, 47*(10), 52–57. doi:10.1145/1022594.1022623

Merrilees, B., & Frye, M.-L. (2003). E-trust: The in□ uence of perceived interactivity on e-retailing users. *Marketing Intelligence & Planning, 21*(2), 123–128. doi:10.1108/02634500310465461

Metcalfe, B. (1995). Metcalfe's law: A network becomes more valuable as it reaches more users. *InfoWorld, 17*.

Microelectronics, S. T. (2002). *Data book.* Retrieved from http://www.st.com

Microsoft. (n.d.). *Mobile phones: Choose the best phone for you.* Retrieved from http://www.microsoft.com/ windowsmobile/en-my/default.mspx

Miettinen, M., & Korhonen, M. (2008, June). *Information quality in healthcare: Coherence of data compared between organization's electronic patient records.* Paper presented at the 21st IEEE International Symposium on Computer-Based Medical Systems, University of Jyväskylä, Finland.

Mirkovic, J., Prier, G., & Reiher, P. (2002). Attacking DDoS at the source. *Proceedings of 10th IEEE International Conference on Network Protocols*, IEEE, Paris, France, (pp. 312-321).

Misslinger, S. (2005). *Internet worm propagation.* Technical University of Munich. doi:10.1.1.94.7921

Miyazaki, A. D., & Fernandez, A. (2001). Consumer perceptions of privacy and security risks for online shopping. *The Journal of Consumer Affairs, 35*, 27–44. doi:10.1111/j.1745-6606.2001.tb00101.x

Monrose, F., & Reiter, M. (2005). Graphical passwords. In Crantor, L., & Garfinkel, S. (Eds.), *Security and usability: Designing secure systems that people can use* (pp. 157–174). Sebastopol, CA: O'Reilly Media.

Mori, G., & Malik, J. (June 2003). Recognizing objects in adversarial clutter: Breaking a visual CAPTCHA. In *Conference on Computer Vision and Pattern Recognition, (CVPR'03)*, Vol. 1, (pp. 134 – 141).

Morin, B., Me, L., Debar, H., & Ducasse, M. (2009). A logic-based model to support alert correlation in intrusion detection. *Information Fusion, 10*(4), 285–299. doi:10.1016/j.inffus.2009.01.005

Moulton, R., & Coles, R. S. (2003). Applying information security governance. *Computers & Security, 22*(7), 580–584. doi:10.1016/S0167-4048(03)00705-3

Moy, G., Jones, N., Harkless, C., & Potter, R. (2004). Distortion estimation techniques in solving visual captchas. In *IEEE Computer Society Conference on Computer Vision and Pattern Recognition, (CVPR04)*, Vol. 2, (pp. 23–28).

Mozilla. (2010). *Firefox features, anti-malware, anti-phishing.* Retrieved from http://www.mozilla.com/en-US/firefox/features/#anti-phishing

Munawar, W., Alizai, M. H., Landsiedel, O., & Wehrle, K. (2010). Dynamic TinyOS: Modular and transparent incremental code-updates for sensor networks. *Proceedings of ICC*, Cape Town, South Africa.

Nakamura, Y., Tatsubori, M., Imamura, T., & Ono, K. (2005). Model-driven security based on a web services security architecture. *Proceedings of the 2005 IEEE International Conference on Services Computing*, Orlando, Florida, USA, July 11-15, (pp. 7-15).

Nanji, F. (2010). The BP crisis and information security compliance in health care: Parallel disasters? *Journal of Health Care Compliance,* (September-October), 15-23.

National Instruments. (n.d.). *A review of PC -based data logging and recording techniques.* Retrieved from www.ni.com/dataloggers

National Research Council. (2002). *Cybersecurity today and tomorrow: Pay now or pay later.* Washington, DC: National Academy Press.

National Semiconductor Corporation. (2000). *LM35 datasheet, precision centigrade temperature sensors.* Atmel data book, November 2000 update.

National Semiconductor Corporation. (2002). *ADC 0809 data sheet, 8-bit microprocessor compatible A/D converters with 8-channel multiplexer.*

Needham, R. M. (1993). Denial of service. *Proceedings of the 1st ACM conference on Computer and Communication Security.* ACM, Fairfax, USA, (pp. 151-153).

Nelson, T. D. (2001). *E-business.* [Online]. Retrieved February 17, 2009, from http://searchcio.techtarget.com/sDefinition/0,sid182_gci212026,00.html

Network Awareness. (2010). Next-generation intrusion prevention system (NGIPS): Improved security and reduced administrative burden through contextual awareness. In *Sourcefire Cybersecurity.* Retrieved December 1, 2010, from http://www.sourcefire.com/content/ next-generation-intrusion-prevention-system-ngips

Network Working Group. (1999). *S/MIME version 3 message specification.* Retrieved from http://tools.ietf.org/html/rfc2633

Network Working Group. (2008). *The transport layer security (TLS) protocol version 1.2.* Retrieved from http://tools.ietf.org/html/rfc5246

Newman, M. E. J. (2003). The structure and function of complex networks. *SIAM Review, 45,* 167–256. doi:10.1137/S003614450342480

Newman, M. E. J. (2006). Modularity and community structure in networks. *Proceedings of the National Academy of Sciences of the United States of America, 103,* 8577. doi:10.1073/pnas.0601602103

Newman, M. E. J., & Girvan, M. (2004). Finding and evaluating community structure in networks. *Physical Review E: Statistical, Nonlinear, and Soft Matter Physics, 69,* 026113. doi:10.1103/PhysRevE.69.026113

Ng, S. M. S. (2005). *SQL injection protection by variable normalization of SQL statement.* Retrieved from www.securitydocs.com/library/3388

Nguyen, H., Franke, K., & Petrovi'c, S. (2010a). Improving effectiveness of intrusion detection by correlation feature selection, In *Proceedings of the 2010 International Conference on Availability, Reliability and Security (ARES)*, Krakow, Poland, February 2010, (pp. 17-24).

Nguyen, H., Franke, K., & Petrovi'c, S. (2010b). Towards a generic feature-selection measure for intrusion detection. In *20th International Conference on Pattern Recognition,* Istanbul, Turkey, (pp. 1529-1532).

Nokia. (n.d.). *Nokia on the Web.* Retrieved from http://www.nokia.com/

Northcutt, S. (1999). *Network intrusion detection: An analyst's handbook.* Sams.

Northcutt, S., & Novak, J. (2000). *Network intrusion detection: An analysts handbook* (2nd ed.). New Riders Publishing.

O'Rourke, M. (2003). Cyberattacks prompt response to security threat. *Risk Management, 50*(1), 8.

OASIS. (2007). *eContracts specification*, v1.0. Retrieved November 3, 2010, from http://docs.oasis-open.org/ legalxml-econtracts/ legalxml-econtracts-specification-1.0.html

OASIS. (2010). *eXtensible access control markup language* (XACML). Retrieved November 3, 2010, from http://www.oasis-open.org/ committees/tc_home. php?wg_abbrev=xacml

OC1. (2006). *Oblique classifier 1*. Retrieved November 11, 2010, from http://www.cbcb.umd.edu/ ~salzberg/ announce-oc1.html

Odlyzko, A., & Tilly, B. (2009). *A refutation of Metcalfe's law and a better estimate for the value of networks and network interconnections.*

Offensive Computing. (2010). *Community malicious code research and analysis*. Retrieved December 15, 2010, from http://www.offensivecomputing.net

Office of Public Sector Information. (2003). *The privacy and electronic communications (EC Directive) Regulations 2003*. Retrieved February 11, 2011, from http://www.legislation.gov.uk/uksi/ 2003/2426/contents/made

Office of Security Management and Safeguards. (2003). *Further amendment to EO 12958, as amended, classified national security information*. Retrieved February 11, 2011, from http://nodis3.gsfc.nasa.gov/displayEO. cfm?id=EO_13292_

Ogiela, M. R., & Ogiela, U. (2009). Linguistic cryptographic threshold schemes. *International Journal of Future Generation Communication and Networking, 2*(1), 33–40.

Ogiela, M. R., & Ogiela, U. (2009). Secure information splitting using grammar schemes. In Nguyen, N. T., Katarzyniak, R., & Janiak, A. (Eds.), *New challenges in computational collective intelligence: Studies in computational intelligence* (pp. 327–336). Berlin, Germany: Springer-Verlag. doi:10.1007/978-3-642-03958-4_28

Ogiela, M. R., & Ogiela, U. (2009). Security of linguistic threshold schemes in multimedia systems. In Damiani, E., Jeong, J., Howlett, R. J., & Jain, L. C. (Eds.), *New directions in intelligent interactive multimedia systems and services – 2: Studies in computational intelligence* (pp. 13–20). Berlin, Germany: Springer – Verlag. doi:10.1007/978-3-642-02937-0_2

Ogiela, M. R., & Ogiela, U. (2009). Shadow generation protocol in linguistic threshold schemes. In Ślęzak, D., Kim, T.-H., Fang, W.-C., & Arnett, K. P. (Eds.), *Security technology: Communication in computer and information science* (pp. 35–42). Berlin, Germany: Springer-Verlag. doi:10.1007/978-3-642-10847-1_5

Oleshchuk, V. (2007). Trust-based framework for security enhancement of wireless sensor networks. *4th IEEE Workshop on Intelligent Data Acquisition and Advanced Computing Systems: Technology and Applications (IDAACS 2007)*, Dortmund, Germany 6-8 Sept, (pp. 623-627).

Oleshchuk, V., & Zadorozhny, V. (2007). *Trust-aware query processing in data intensive sensor networks. International Conference on Sensor Technologies and Applications (SensorComm)*, Valencia, Spain, 14-20 Oct, (pp. 176-180).

Oostveen, A. M., & den Besselaar, P. V. (2004). Security as belief user's perceptions on the security of e-voting systems. In the *Proceedings of Electronic Voting in Europe* (pp. 73-82).

Openwall. (2010). *John the ripper*. Retrieved from http://www.openwall.com/john/

Organization for Economic Co-operation and Development (OECD). (1980). *Guidelines governing the protection of privacy and transborder flow of personal data*. Geneva, Switzerland: OECD.

Orlov, A. (2008). Project consequence. [PSCA International Ltd.]. *Science and Technology Magazine, 1*, 62–63.

Ornaghi, A., & Valleri, M. (2010). *Man in the middle attacks*. Retrieved from http://www.blackhat.com/presentations/ bh-usa-03/bh-us-03-ornaghi-valleri.pdf

Oscarson, P. (2007). *Actual and perceived information systems security*. Doctoral dissertation, Linköping University, Linköping, Sweden.

Oxid. (2010). *Available at Cain and Abel, password recovery tool for Microsoft operating systems*. Retrieved from http://www.oxid.it/cain.html

P2PSIP. (n.d.). Retrieved from http://www.p2psip.org

Paar, C., & Weimerskirch, A. (2007, January). Embedded security in a pervasive world. *Information Security Technical Report, 12*(3), 155–161. doi:10.1016/j.istr.2007.05.006

Papazoglou, M. P. (2003). Web services and business transactions. *World Wide Web: Internet and Web Information Systems, 6*, 49–91.

Parent, W. (1983). Privacy, morality and the law. *Philosophy & Public Affairs, 12*(4), 269–288.

Park, H. U., & Lee, I. Y. (2001). A digital nominative proxy signature scheme for mobile communication. *Information and Communications Security, Third International Conference, LNCS 2229*, (pp. 451-455). Springer.

Patient Privacy Right Foundation. (2007). *Glossary right to privacy*. Retrieved from http://www.patientprivacyrights.org/site/ pageServer?pagename=glossary_Right_to_privacy

Paul, N., & Tanenbaum, A. S. (2009). Trustworthy voting: From machine to system. [IEEE Computer.]. *Computer, 42*(5), 23–29. doi:10.1109/MC.2009.169

Paxon, V. (1990). *A survey of support for implementing debuggers*.

Pearson, S. (2010). Addressing complexity in a privacy expert system. In E. Hüllermeier, R. Kruse, & F. Hoffmann (Eds.), *Proceedings of IPMU 2010, Part II, CCIS 81*, (pp. 612–621). Berlin, Germany: Springer-Verlag.

Pearson, S., Rao, P., Sander, T., Parry, A., Paull, A., & Patruni, S. … Sharma, P. (2009). Scalable, accountable privacy management for large organizations. In *Proceedings of INSPEC09, 2nd International Workshop on Security and Privacy Distributed Computing, Enterprise Distributed Object Conference Workshops (EDOCW 2009)*, IEEE, (pp. 168-175).

Pearson, S., Sander, T., & Sharma, R. (2010). Privacy management for global organisations. In Garcia-Alfaro, J. (Eds.), *Data Privacy Management and Autonomous Spontaneous Security, LNCS 5939* (pp. 9–17). Berlin, Germany: Springer-Verlag. doi:10.1007/978-3-642-11207-2_2

Pecho, P., Zboril, F., Drahansky, M., & Hanacek, P. (2009). Agent platform for wireless sensor networks with support for cryptographic protocols. *Journal of Universal Computer Science, 6*.

Pedersen, T. (1992). Non-interactive and information-theoretic secure verifiable secret-sharing. In Feigenbaum, J. (Ed.), *CRYPTO 1991, LNCS (Vol. 576*, pp. 129–140). Heidelberg, Germany: Springer.

Peine, H., Jawurek, M., & Mandel, S. (2008). Security goal indicator trees: A model of software features that supports efficient security inspection. *High Assurance Systems Engineering Symposium, HASE* (pp. 9-18). Nanjing, China: IEEE.

Peng, H., Long, F., & Ding, C. (2005). Feature selection based on mutual information: Criteria of max-dependency, max-relevance, and min-redundancy. *IEEE Transactions on Pattern Analysis and Machine Intelligence, 27*(8), 1226–1238. doi:10.1109/TPAMI.2005.159

Pennanen, K., Tiainen, T., & Luomala, H. T. (2007). A qualitative exploration of a consumer's value-based e-trust building process: A framework development. *Qualitative Market Research: An International Journal, 10*(1), 28–47. doi:10.1108/13522750710720387

Pernul, G., & Luef, G. (1992). Bibliography on database security. *SIGMOD Record, 21*(1). doi:10.1145/130868.130884

Perrig, A., & Song, D. (1999). Hash visualization: A new technique to improve real-world security. *Proceedings of the 1999 International Workshop on Cryptographic Techniques and E-Commerce*.

Petri, H. (2003). *Motivation: Theory, research and application* (5th ed.). Wadsworth Publishing.

Ping, Y., Yan, Y., Yafei, H., Yiping, Z., & Shiyong, Z. (2004) Securing ad hoc networks through mobile agent. In *InfoSecu '04; Proceedings of the 3rd International Conference on Information Security*. ACM Press.

Ponemon Institute. (2011). *The true cost of compliance*. Retrieved from http://mediazone.brighttalk.com/sitedata/1651cf0d2f737d7adeab84d339dbabd3/download/9405_True_Cost_of_Compliance_Report.pdf?uid=24847&tid=isc2

Porter, A., & Votta, L. (1. (1998, December). Comparing detection methods for software requirements inspections: A replicated experiment using professional subjects. *Empirical Software Engineering, 3*(4), 355–379. doi:10.1023/A:1009776104355

Postel, J. (1981). *Internet control message protocol.* IETF RFC 792.

Poundstone, W. (1993). *Prisoner's dilemma.* New York, NY: Doubleday.

PRIME. (2008). *Privacy and identity management for Europe.* Retrieved 3 November, 2010, from http://www.prime-project.org.eu

Prince, K. (2008). *A comprehensive study of healthcare data security breaches in the United States from 2000 - 2007.*

Prince, A., & Lowe, D. (2005). *Murach VB.NET 3.5 database programming with ADO.NET.* New Delhi, India: SPD.

Puleo, A. J. (2006). *Mitigating insider threat using human behaviour influence models.* Unpublished Master's thesis, Air Force Institute of Technology, School of Engineering and Management.

PWC. (2008). *Security breaches survey 2008.* PricewaterhouseCoopers on behalf of the UK Department of Business. Retrieved from www.pwc.co.uk.

Qin, Y., & Wu, X. (2008). Cryptanalysis and improvement of two blind proxy signature schemes. *International Conference on Computer Science and Software Engineering* (pp. 762-765). IEEE Computer Society.

Qui, N., Trombetta, A., Bertino, E., & Lobo, J. (2007). *Privacy-aware role based access control,* (pp. 41-50). Paper presented at the 12th ACM symposium on Access control models and technologies, Session Privacy management.

Quinlan, J. R. (1993). *C4.5: Programs for machine learning.* Morgan Kaufmann.

Quisquater, J. J., & Samide, D. (2002). Side channel cryptanalysis. *In Proceedings of the SECI 2002,* (pp. 179-184).

Raaijmakers, J. G., & Shiffrin, R. M. (1992). Models for recall and recognition. *Annual Review of Psychology, 43,* 205–234. doi:10.1146/annurev.ps.43.020192.001225

Rabat, C., Bui, A., & Flauzac, O. (2005). A random walk topology management solution for Grid. In *Proceedings of Innovative Internet Community Systems (I2CS'05), Lecture Notes in Computer Science 3908,* Paris, France. Springer.

Rainer, R. K., Marshall, T. E., Knapp, K. J., & Montgomery, H. G. (2007). Do information security professionals and business managers view information security issues differently? *Information Systems Security, 16*(2), 100–108. doi:10.1080/10658980701260579

Raja, J., & Velmurgan, M. S. (2008). E-payments: Problems and prospects. *Journal of Internet Banking and Commerce, 13*(1), 1–17.

Ramsey, N. (1994). *Correctness of trap-based breakpoint implementations.* In 21st Symposium on Principles of Programming Languages.

Randazzo, M. R., Keeney, M., Kowalski, E., Cappelli, D., & Moore, A. (2005). *Insider threat study: Illicit cyber activity in the banking and finance sector* (Tech. Rep. No. CMU/SEI-2004-TR-021).

Rankl, W., & Effing, W. (2003). *Smart card handbook* (3rd ed.). John Wiley and Sons. doi:10.1002/047085670X

Ratnasingam, P. (2007). A risk-control framework for e-marketplace participation: The findings of seven cases. *Information & Computer Security, 15*(2), 149–166. doi:10.1108/09685220710748029

Ravi, S., Kocher, P., Lee, R., McGraw, G., & Raghunathan, A. (June 2004). Security as a new dimension in embedded system design. In *Proceedings ACM/IEEE Design Automation Conference,* (pp. 753-760).

Ravi, S., Raghunathan, A., & Chakradhar, S. (2004). Tamper resistance mechanisms for secure embedded systems. *In Proceedings of the International Conference of VLSI Design,* (pp. 605-611).

Ravi, S., Raghunathan, A., Kocher, P., & Hattangady, S. (2004). Security in embedded systems: Design challenges. *ACM Transactions on Embedded Computing Systems, 3*(3), 461–491. doi:10.1145/1015047.1015049

Real User Coorp. (1998). *Passfaces.* Retrieved from http://www.realuser.com

Reinhard, K., & Jung, W. (2007). Compliance of POLYAS with the BSI protection profile - Basic requirements for remote electronic voting systems. In *VOTE-ID, LNCS* (pp. 62-75). Springer.

Reinsch, R. (2005). E-commerce: Managing the legal risks. *Managerial Law, 47*(1-2), 168–196. doi:10.1108/03090550510771377

Renaud, K. (2006). *A visuo-biometric authentication mechanism for older users* (pp. 167–182). People and Computers XIX-The Bigger Picture.

Renaud, K. (2009). Guidelines for designing graphical authentication mechanism interfaces. *International Journal of Information and Computer Security, 3*(1), 60–85. doi:10.1504/IJICS.2009.026621

Robbins, J. (1999). Debugging Windows based applications using windbg. *Microsoft Systems Journal, 1999*.

Rodgers, J. L., & Nicewander, W. A. (1988). Thirteen ways to look at the correlation coefficient. *The American Statistician, 42*(1), 59–66. doi:10.2307/2685263

Roesch, M. (1999). Snort - Lightweight intrusion detection for networks. In *Proceedings of the 13th USENIX Conference on System Administration*, (pp. 229-238).

Roth, V., Richter, K., & Freidinger, R. (2004). A PIN-entry method resiliant against shoulder-surfing. *Proceedings of the 11th ACM Conference on Computer and Communications Security* (p. 236-245). Washington, DC: ACM.

Rotter, J. B. (1966). Generalized expectancies for internal versus external control of reinforcement. *Psychological Monographs, 80*(1), 1–28. doi:10.1037/h0092976

Rotter, J. B. (1990). Internal versus external controls of reinforcement. *The American Psychologist, 45*, 489–193. doi:10.1037/0003-066X.45.4.489

Rowe, M., Wilcox, L., & Gadlin, H. (2002, October). Dealing with – or reporting – "unacceptable" behaviour (with additional thoughts about the "bystander effect"). *Computers & Security, 21*(6), 526–531.

Runeson, P., Andersson, C., Thelin, T., Andrews, A., & Berling, T. (2006). What do we know about defect detection methods? *IEEE Software, 23*(3), 82–90. doi:10.1109/MS.2006.89

Rutkowska, J. (2006). *Subverting Vista kernel for fun and profit*. SyScan and Black Hat Presentations.

Sabzevar, A. P., & Stavrou, A. (2008). Universal multi-factor authentication using graphical passwords. *Proceedings of IEEE International Conference on Signal Image Technology and Internet based Systems SITIS* (pp. 625-632). IEEE.

Salehi-Abari, A., Thorpe, J., & Oorschot, P. (2008). On purely automated attacks and click-based graphical passwords. *Proceedings of the 2008 Annual Computer Security Applications Conference*, (pp. 111-120).

Sandhu, R., & Munawer, Q. (1999). The ARBAC99 model for administration of roles. In *Proceedings of the 15th Annual Computer Security Applications Conference*.

Sandhu, R., Bhamidipati, V., & Munawer, Q. (1999). The ARBAC97 model for role-based administration of roles. *ACM Transactions on Information and System Security, 2*(1), 105–135. doi:10.1145/300830.300839

Sandia National Laboratories. (2010). *The information design assurance red team*. Retrieved August 2010 from http://idart.sandia.gov

Sang, X. S. (2009). *Study on some topics of certificate-less public-key cryptography*. Xiamen University, 2009.

Sansone, C., & Harackiewicz, J. M. (2000). *Intrinsic and extrinsic motivation: The search for optimal motivation and performance* (1st ed.). Academic Press.

Sastry, N., & Wagner, D. (2004). Security considerations for IEEE 802.15.4 networks. *Proceedings of the 3rd ACM Workshop on Wireless Security*.

Sastry, N., Kohno, T., & Wagner, D. (2006). Designing voting machines for verification. In *Proceedings of the 15th Conference on USENIX Security Symposium*. Berkeley, CA: USENIX Association.

Sasturkar, A., Yang, P., Stoller, S., & Ramakrishnan, C. (2006). Policy analysis for administrative role based access control. In *Workshop on Computer Security Foundations* (pp. 124–138).

Saunders, M., Lewis, P., & Thornhill, A. (2007). *Research methods for business students* (4th ed.). Harlow, UK: Pearson Education.

Schell, R., & Heckman, M. (1987). Views for multilevel database security. *IEEE Transactions on Software Engineering, SE13*(2).

Schlegel, R., Niccolini, S., Tartarelli, S., & Brunner, M. (2006). *Spam over internet telephony (SPIT). Global Telecommunications Conference (GLOBECOM 06)*, IEEE, San Francisco, USA, (pp. 1-6).

Schmidt, A., Volkamer, M., & Buchmann, J. (2010). An evaluation and certification approach to enable voting service providers. In *Electronic Voting* (pp. 135–148). LNI.

Schneider, G. P. (2004). *Electronic commerce: The second wave*, 5th ed. Wadsworth, UK: Thomson Learning.

Schultz, E. E. (2002, October). A framework for understanding and predicting insider attacks. *Computers & Security, 21*(6), 526–531. doi:10.1016/S0167-4048(02)01009-X

Scott, T., Mannion, R., Davies, H., & Marshall, M. (2003). Implementing culture change in health care: Theory and practice. *International Journal for Quality in Health Care, 15*, 111–118. doi:10.1093/intqhc/mzg021

Seberry, J., & Pieprzyk, J. (1989). *Cryptography: An introduction to computer security*. Englewood Cliffs, NJ: Prentice-Hall.

Seedorf, J. (2006). Security challenges for P2P-SIP. *IEEE Network Special Issue on Securing Voice over IP, 20*, 38-45.

Seedorf, J. (2008). Lawful interception in P2P-based VoIP systems. *Principles. Systems and Applications of IP Telecommunications, 5310*, 217–235.

Sepandar, D. K., Mario, T. S., & Hector, G.-M. (2003). The Eigentrust algorithm for reputation management in P2P networks. *Proceedings of the 12th International Conference on World Wide Web*, ACM, Budapest, Hungary, (pp. 640-651).

Shamir, A. (1984). Identity-based cryptosystems and signature schemes. In *Proceedings of CRYPTO 1984, LNCS 196*, (pp. 47–53). Springer.

Shamir, A. (1979). How to share a secret. *Communications of the ACM, 22*(11), 612–613. doi:10.1145/359168.359176

Shannon, C. E. (1948). A mathematical theory of communication. *The Bell System Technical Journal, 27*, 379–423, 623–656.

Shan, T., & Hua, W. (2006). Service-oriented solution framework for internet banking. *International Journal of Web Services Research, 3*(1), 29–48. doi:10.4018/jwsr.2006010102

Shao, J., Cao, Z., & Lu, R. (2007). Improvement of Yang *et al.*'s threshold proxy signature scheme. *Journal of Systems and Software, 80*(2), 172–177. doi:10.1016/j.jss.2006.02.047

Sharma, S. K., & Gupta, J. N. D. (2002). Securing information infrastructure from information warfare. *Logistic Information Management, 15*(5-6), 414–422. doi:10.1108/09576050210447118

Shepard, R. N. (2006). Recognition memory for words, sentences, and pictures. *Journal of Verbal Learning and Verbal Behavior, 6*, 156–163. doi:10.1016/S0022-5371(67)80067-7

SHIELDS. (n.d.). *DEFECT – Dependability focused inspection tool*. Abgerufen am 11. November 2010 von http://www.shields-project.eu/?q=node/119

SHIELDS. (n.d.). *GOAT modelling tool*. Retrieved from http://www.shields-project.eu/?q=node/32

SHIELDS. (n.d.). *SHIELDS - Detecting known security vulnerabilities from within design and development tools*. Retrieved from http://www.shields-project.eu/

SHIELDS. (n.d.). *Software vulnerability repository services*. Retrieved from https://www.shields-project.eu:8181/SVRS/

Shifrin, T. (2007). *Halifax apologizes after 13,000 customer records stolen from the employee's car*. [Online]. Retrieved February 13, 2009, from http://www.computerworlduk.com/ management/ security/ data control/news/ index. cfm?newsid=2373

Shirali-Shahreza, M., & Shirali-Shahreza, M. H. (January 2008). Online PIX CAPTCHA. *Proceedings of IEEE International Conference on Signal Processing, Communications and Networking (ICSCN2008)*, (pp. 582–585).

Shirali-Shahreza, M., & Shirali-Shahreza, S. (2007). Question-based CAPTCHA. In *ICCIMA '07: Proceedings of the International Conference on Computational Intelligence and Multimedia Applications (ICCIMA 2007)*, (pp. 54 – 58). Washington, DC: IEEE Computer Society.

Shirali-Shahreza, M., & Shirali-Shahreza, S. (April 2008). Advanced collage captcha. In *Proceedings of the 5th International Conference on Information Technology: New Generations (ITNG 2008)*, pages 1234 – 1235, Las Vegas, Nevada, USA.

Shirali-Shahreza, M., & Shirali-Shahreza, S. (December 2007). CAPTCHA for blind people. *Proceedings of 7th IEEE International Symposium on Signal Processing and Information Technology (ISSPIT 2007)*, (pp. 995–998).

Shirali-Shahreza, M., & Shirali-Shahreza, S. (February 2007). Collage CAPTCHA. In *Proceedings of the 20th IEEE International Symposium Signal Processing and Application (ISSPA 2007)*, Sharjah, United Arab Emirates.

Shirali-Shahreza, M., & Shirali-Shahreza, S. (June 2006). Drawing CAPTCHA. *Proceedings of 28th Int. Conf. Information Technology Interfaces (ITI 2006)*, (pp. 475–480).

Shirali-Shahreza, M., & Shirali-Shahreza, S. (May 2008). Motion CAPTCHA. *Proceedings of Conf. on Human System Interaction(HSI 2008)*, (pp. 1042–1044).

Shirali-Shahreza, S., & Shirali-Shahreza, M. (April 2008). A new human interactive proofs system for deaf persons. *Proceedings of 5th International Conference on Information Technology: New Generations (ITNG 2008)*, (pp. 807–810).

Simidchieva, B. I., Marzilli, S. M., Clarke, A. L., & Osterweil, J. L. (2008). Specifying and verifying requirements for election processes. In *Proceedings of the 2008 International Conference on Digital government research* (pp. 63-72). Digital Government Society of North America.

Simmons, G. J. (1992). An introduction to shared secret and/or shared control schemes and their application. In *Contemporary cryptology: The science of information integrity*, (pp. 441–497).

Simmons, G. J. (1993). The subliminal channels of the US digital signature algorithm (DSA). *Proceedings of the Third Symposium on: State and Progress of Research in Cryptography*, Rome (pp. 35–54).

Singh, A., Ngan, T. W., Druschel, P., & Wallach, D. S. (2006). Eclipse attacks on overlay networks Threats and defenses. *Proceedings of 25th IEEE International Conference on Computer Communications (INFOCOM 06)*, IEEE, Barcelona, Spain, (pp. 1-12).

Singh, K., & Schulzrinne, H. (2005). Peer-to-peer internet telephony using SIP. *Proceedings of the International Workshop on Network and Operating Systems Support for Digital Audio and Video*, ACM, Stevenson, Washington, USA, (pp. 63-68).

Singh, K., & Schulzrinne, H. (2005b). *SIPpeer: A session initiation protocol (SIP) based peer-to-peer internet telephony client adapt*. Retrieved from http://ww1.cs.columbia.edu/kns10/ publication/sip-p2p-design.pdf

Siponen, M., & Stucke, C. (January 2006). Effective antispam strategies in companies: An international study. In *39th Annual Hawaii International Conference on System Sciences, (HICSS'06)*, Vol. 6, (pp. 127c – 136c).

Siponen, M. (2006). Information security standards focus on the existence of process, not its content. *Communications of the ACM, 49*(8), 97–100. doi:10.1145/1145287.1145316

SIS. (2003). *SIS handbok 550. Terminologi för informationssäkerhet*. Stockholm, Sweden: SIS Förlag AB.

Skype official website. (n.d.). *Download Skype free now for free calls and internet calls*. Retrieved from http://www.skype.com/intl/en/

SmartCardsBasis. (2011). Retrieved from http://www.smartcardbasics.com/smart-card-types.html

Smith, R. L., Avrunin, G. S., Clarke, L. A., & Osterweil, L. J. (2002). PROPEL: An approach supporting property elucidation. In *Proceedings of the 24th International Conference on Software Engineering* (pp. 11-21). New York, NY: ACM.

Smith, H. J. (1994). *Managing privacy: Information technology and corporate America*. Chapel Hill, NC: University of North Carolina Press.

Snell, J. L. (2003). Expected value and variance. In *Introduction to probability* (pp. 210–230). McGraw-Hill.

Sobrado, L., & Birget, J. C. (2002). Graphical password. *The Rutgers Scholar, An Electronic Bulletin for Undergraduate Research, 4*.

Song, H., Jiang, X., Even, R., & Bryan, D. A. (2010). *P2PSIP overlay diagnostics*. IETF Internet Draft (draft-ietf-p2psip-diagnostics-04). Retrieved from http://tools.ietf.org/html/draft-ietf-p2psip-diagnostics-04

Song, S., Hwang, K., Zhou, R., & Kwok, Y.-K. (2005). Trusted P2P transactions with fuzzy reputation aggregation. *IEEE Internet Computing, 9*, 24–34. doi:10.1109/MIC.2005.136

Spafford, E. H. (1989). The internet worm program: An analysis. *SIGCOMM Computer Communication Review, 19*, 17–57. doi:10.1145/66093.66095

Sparks, R. (2007). SIP: Basics and beyond. *Queue, 5*, 22–33. doi:10.1145/1229899.1229909

Spasov, G., & Kakankov, N. (2004). CGI based applications for distributed systems for monitoring temperature and humidity. In *Proceedings of 5th International Conference on Computer Systems and Technologies-Compsys Tech 2004*, Rousse, Bulgeria, (pp. 1-6). ISBN 954-9641-38-4

Sprott, D., & Wilkes, L. (2004). Understanding service-oriented architecture. *The Architecture Journal, 1*, 10–17.

Spyns, P., & Hogben, G. (2005). Validating an automated evaluation procedure for ontology triples in the privacy domain. In *Frontiers in Artificial Intelligence and Applications: Vol. 134; Proceeding of the 2005 Conference on Legal Knowledge and Information Systems: JURIX 2005: The Eighteenth Annual Conference*, (pp 127-136).

Stakhanova, N., Basu, S., & Wong, J. (2007). A taxonomy of intrusion response systems. *International Journal of Information and Computer Security, 1*(1), 169–184. doi:10.1504/IJICS.2007.012248

Stoica, I., Morris, R., Liben-Nowell, D., Karger, D. R., Kaashoek, M. F., Dabek, F., & Balakrishnan, H. (2003). Chord: A scalable peer-to-peer lookup protocol for internet applications. *IEEE/ACM Transactions on Networking, 11*, 17–32. doi:10.1109/TNET.2002.808407

Stoller, S., Yang, P., Ramakrishnan, C., & Gofman, M. (2007). Efficient policy analysis for administrative role based access control. In *Proceedings of the 14th ACM Conference on Computer and Communications Security* (p. 455).

Strasburg, C., Stakhanova, N., Basu, S., & Wong, J. S. (2009). A framework for cost sensitive assessment of intrusion response selection. In *Proceedings of 33rd Annual IEEE International Computer Software and Applications Conference*, (pp. 355-360).

Straub, D. W., & Welke, R. J. (1998). Coping with systems risk: Security planning models for management decision making. *Management Information Systems Quarterly, 22*(4), 441–469. doi:10.2307/249551

Strooper, P., & Wojcicki, M. A. (2007). Selecting V&V technology combinations: How to pick a winner? *International Conference on Engineering Complex Computer Systems*, (pp. 87-96). Auckland.

Stubblefield, A., & Simon, D. (2004). *Inkblot authentication*. Microsoft Corporation.

Sturton, C., Jha, S., Seshia, A. S., & Wagner, D. (2009). On voting machine design for verification and testability. In *ACM CCS* (pp. 463–476). ACM. doi:10.1145/1653662.1653719

Summers, R. C. (1997). *Secure computing: Threats and safeguards* (pp. 3–11). McGraw-Hill.

Sun, R. A., & Wan Zhong, S. D.-C. (2009, January). Based on embedded database greenhouse temperature and humidity intelligent control system. *WSEAS Transactions on Circuits and Systems 8*(1), 41-52. ISSN: 1109-2734

Sung, A. H., & Mukkamala, S. (2003). Identifying important features for intrusion detection using support vector machines and neural networks. In *Proceedings of the International Symposium on Applications and the Internet (SAINT)*, (pp. 209–217). Los Alamitos, CA: IEEE Press.

Suo, X., Zhu, Y., & Owen, G. S. (2005). Graphical passwords: A survey. *Proceedings of the 21st Annual Computer Security Application Conference (ACSAC)* (pp. 101-202). Tucson, AZ: IEEE.

Sutton, M., Greene, A., & Amini, P. (2007). *Fuzzing: Brute force vulnerability discovery*. Amsterdam, The Netherlands: Addison-Wesley Longman.

Swiderski, F., & Snyder, W. (2004). *Threat modeling*. Washington, DC: Microsoft Press.

Symantec. (2005). *Operational risk management and the financial services sector* [Online]. (Published in 2005). Retrieved February 8, 2009, from http://www.symantec.com/business/library/article.jsp?aid=IN_110705_operational_risk_management

Symantec. (2006). *Symantec Internet security threat report: Trends for January 06–June 06* [Online]. Retrieved March 5, 2009, from http://www.symantec.com/specprog/threatreport/ ent-whitepaper_symantec_Internet_security_ threat_report_x_09_2006.en-us.pdf

Symantec. (2008). *Symantec report on the underground economy* [Online]. Retrieved February 15, 2009, from http://www.symantec.com/business/ theme.jsp?themeid=threatreport

Szor, P. (2005). *The art of computer virus research and defense*. Addison-Wesley and Symantec Press.

Takanen, A., DeMott, J. D., & Miller, C. (2008). *Fuzzing for software security testing and quality assurance*. Artech House Publishers.

Tam, J., Simsa, J., Hyde, S., & Ahn, L. V. (December 2008). Breaking audio CAPTCHAs. In *Advances in Neural Information Processing Systems 21, Proceedings of the Twenty-Second Annual Conference on Neural Information Processing Systems, NIPS*, (pp. 1625–1632). Vancouver, British Columbia, Canada.

Tang, S. (2004). Simple secret sharing and threshold RSA signature schemes. *Journal of Information and Computational Science, 1*, 259–262.

The, S. I. P. Center. (n.d.). *A portal for the commercial development of SIP session initiation protocol*. Retrieved from http://www.sipcenter.com

Thietart, R. A., et al. (2001). *Doing management research: A comprehensive guide* (pp. 58-79). SAGE Publication ltd.

Thomas, D. E., & Moorby, P. R. (1991). *The VERILOG hardware description language*. Norwell, MA: Kluwer Academic Publishers. doi:10.1007/978-1-4615-3992-6

Thomson, K. L., von Solms, R., & Louw, L. (2006). Cultivating an organizational information security culture. *Computer Fraud & Security, 10*, 7–11. doi:10.1016/S1361-3723(06)70430-4

Thorpe, J., & van Oorschot, P. (2007). Human-seeded attacks and exploiting hot-spots in graphical passwords. *Proceedings of 16th USENIX Security Symposium*.

Thorpe, J., & van Oorschot, P. C. (2004). Graphical dictionaries and the memorable space of graphical passwords. *Proceedings of the 13th USENIX Security Symposium, August 9-13, 2004, San Diego, CA, USA*, (pp. 135-150).

Thorpe, J., & van Oorschot, P. C. (2004). Towards secure design choices for implementing graphical passwords. *20th Annual Computer Security Applications Conference (ACSAC 2004), 6-10 December 2004, Tucson, AZ, USA*, (pp. 50-60).

Thunderbird. (2010). *Thunderbird features, anti-malware, anti-phishing*. Retrieved from http://www.mozillamessaging.com/ en-US/thunderbird/features/

Tiresias. (2011). Retrieved from http://www.tiresias.org/research/ guidelines/cards_and_smart_media.htm

Toth, T., & Kruegel, C. (2002). Evaluating the impact of automated intrusion response mechanisms. In *Proceedings of the 18th Annual Computer Security Applications Conference* (ACSAC), 2002

Towhidi, F., & Masrom, M. (2009). A survey on recognition based graphical user authentication algorithms. *International Journal of Computer Science adn Information Security (IJCSIS)*, 119-127.

Tran, E., & Atkinson, M. A. (2002). Security of personal data across national borders. *Information Management & Computer Security, 10*(5), 237–241. doi:10.1108/09685220210446588

Travis, D., Breaux, T. D., & Antón, A. I. (2008). Analyzing regulatory rules for privacy and security requirements. *Transactions on Software Engineering, 34*(1), 5–20. doi:10.1109/TSE.2007.70746

Treasury Board of Canada Secretariat. (2003). *Canadian privacy legislation and policy*. Retrieved February 11, 2011, from http://www.tbs-sct.gc.ca/pgol-pged/ piatp-pfefvp/course2/mod1/mod1-3-eng.asp

Trompeter, C. M., & Eloff, J. (2001). A fremework for implementation of socio-ethical controls in infomration security. *Computers & Security, 20*(5), 384–391. doi:10.1016/S0167-4048(01)00507-7

Udo, G. J. (2001). Privacy and security concerns as major barriers for e-commerce: A survey study. *Information Management & Computer Security, 9*(4), 165–174. doi:10.1108/EUM0000000005808

Undercoffer, J., Pinkston, J., Joshi, A., & Finin, T. (2004). A target-centric ontology for intrusion detection. In *Proceedings of the IJCAI-03 Workshop on Ontologies and Distributed Systems,* (pp. 47-58).

Uner, E. (September 2005). A framework for considering security in embedded systems. *Embedded.com.*

Valadon, G. (2008). *Mobile IPv6: Architectures et protocoles* (PhD Thesis). Paris, France: Université Pierre et Marie Curie.

van Oorschot, P. C., & Wan, T. (2009). TwoStep: An authentication method combining text and graphical passwords. *E-Technologies: Innovation in an Open World, 4th International Conference, MCETECH* (pp. 233-239). Ottawa, Canada: Springer-Verlag.

Van Slyke, C., & Belanger, F. (2003). *E-business technologies.* New York, NY: Wiley.

Vaniea, K., Karat, C., Gross, J. B., Karat, J., & Brodie, C. (2008). Evaluating assistance of natural language policy authoring. In *Proceedings of SOUPS '08: Vol. 337.*

Vapnik, V. (1995). *The nature of statistical learning theory.* Springer.

Varenhorst, C. (2005). *Passdoodles: A lightweight authentication method,* (p. 15). Research Science Institute. Retrieved from http://people.csail.mit.edu/emax/papers/varenhorst.pdf

Vasudevan, A., & Yerraballi, R. (2006). *Cobra: Fine-grained malware analysis using stealth localized-executions.* In IEEE Symposium on Security and Privacy.

Verbauwhede1, I., & Schaumont, P. (July 2007). Design methods for security and trust. *Design, Automation & Test in Europe Conference & Exhibition,* (pp. 1-6).

Vieira, M., & Madeira, H. (2003). *A dependability benchmark for OLTP application environments.* 29th International Conference on Very Large Data Bases, VLDB2003, Berlin, Germany.

Vieira, M., & Madeira, H. (2005). *Towards a security benchmark for database management systems.* Intl Conf. on Dependable Systems and Networks, Yokohama, Japan.

Vieira, R., Agustini, A., Castilho, F., Bruckschen, M., Pizzinato, P., Bridi, P.,... Rao, R. (2010). *Representation and inference of privacy risks using Semantic Web Technologies.* Poster at EKAW 2010 - Knowledge Engineering and Knowledge Management by the Masses.

Villafiorita, A., Weldemariam, K., & Tiella, R. (2009). Development, formal verification, and evaluation of an e-voting system with VVPAT. *IEEE Transaction in Information Forensic Security, 4*(4), 651–661. doi:10.1109/TIFS.2009.2034903

Vitvar, T., Moran, M., Zaremba, M., Haller, A., & Kotinurmi, P. (2007). Semantic SOA to promote integration of heterogeneous B2B services. *Proceedings of the 4th IEEE Conference on Enterprise Computing, E-Commerce and E-Services,* Tokyo, Japan, Jul. 23-26, (pp. 451-456).

Volkamer, M., & Krimmer, R. (2007). Independent audits of remote electronic voting – Developing a common criteria protection profile. In *Proceedings of EDEM'07.*

Volkamer, M. (2009). *Evaluation of electronic voting: Requirements and evaluation procedures to support responsible election authorities: LNBIP.* Berlin, Heidelberg: Springer-Verlag.

von Ahn, L., Maurer, B., McMillen, C., Abraham, D., & Blum, M. (2008, September). Recaptcha: Human-based character recognition via web security measures. *Science Express, 321*(5895), 1465–1468.

von Solms, B. (2000). Information security - The third wave? *Computers & Security, 19,* 615–620. doi:10.1016/S0167-4048(00)07021-8

von Solms, B. (2001). Corporate governance and information security. *Computers & Security, 20*(3), 215–218. doi:10.1016/S0167-4048(01)00305-4

von Solms, B. (2006). Information security - The fourth wave. *Computers & Security, 25,* 165–168. doi:10.1016/j.cose.2006.03.004

von Solms, B., & von Solms, R. (2004). The 10 deadly sins of information security management. *Computers & Security, 23*, 371–376. doi:10.1016/j.cose.2004.05.002

von Solms, B., & von Solms, R. (2005). From information security to....business security? *Computers & Security, 24*, 271–273. doi:10.1016/j.cose.2005.04.004

W3C. (2002). *The platform for privacy preferences, v1.0.* Retrieved November 3, 2010, from http://www.w3.org/TR/P3P/

Wahbe, R. (1992). *Efficient data breakpoints.* In 5th International Conference on Architectural Support for Programming Languages and Operating Systems.

Wahbe, R., Lucco, S., & Graham, S. L. (1993). *Practical data breakpoints: Design and implementation.* In Conference on Programming Language Design and Implementation.

Wang, C. H., Hwang, T., & Tsai, J. J. (1995). *On the Matsumoto and Imai's human identification scheme. EUROCRYPT, LNCS 921* (pp. 382–392). Saint-Malo, France: Springer-Verlag.

Wang, K., Parekh, J., & Stolfo, S. (2006). A content anomaly detector resistant to mimicry attack. In *Recent Adances in Intrusion Detection (RAID)* (pp. 226–248). Anagram. doi:10.1007/11856214_12

Wang, K., & Stolfo, S. (2004). Anomalous payload-based network intrusion detection. In *Recent Adances in Intrusion Detection* (pp. 203–222). RAID. doi:10.1007/978-3-540-30143-1_11

Wang, L., Cao, Z., Li, X., & Qian, H. (2005). Certificateless threshold signature schemes. In Hao, Y. (Eds.), *CIS 2005, Part II, LNAI 3802* (pp. 104–109).

Wang, R. Y., & Strong, D. M. (1996). Beyond accuracy: What data quality means to data consumers. *Journal of Management Information Systems, 12*(4), 5–33.

Waterman, K. K. (2009). *Pre-processing legal text: Policy parsing and isomorphic intermediate representation.* Association for the Advancement of Artificial Intelligence. Retrieved November 8, 2010, from http://dig.csail.mit.edu/2010/Papers/Privacy2010/kkw-preprocessing/waterman.PRIVACY2010. parsing_privacy.pdf

Wei, K., Muthuprasanna, M., & Kothari, S. (2006). Preventing SQL injection attacks in stored procedures. *Proceedings of the 2006 Australian Software Engineering Conference* (ASWEC'06), IEEE, Australia, (pp. 1-7).

Weingart, S. (2000). *Physical security devices for computer subsystems: A survey of attacks and defenses.* Workshop on Cryptographic Hardware and Embedded Systems.

Weinshall, D. (2006). Cognitive authentication schemes safe agains spyware. *IEEE Symposium on Security and Privacy* (pp. 295-300). Berkeley, CA: IEEE Computer Society.

Weldemariam, K. (2010). *Using formal methods for building more reliable and secure e-voting systems.* PhD thesis, University of Trento, via Sommarive 18, Trento, Italy.

Weldemariam, K., & Villafiorita, A. (2008). Modeling and analysis of procedural security in (e)Voting: The Trentino's approach and experiences. In *USENIX/ACCURATE Electronic Voting Workshop (EVT)*. Berkeley, CA: USENIX Association.

Weldemariam, K., Kemmerer, R. A., & Villafiorita, A. (2009). Formal analysis of attacks for an e-voting system. *In International Conference on Risks and Security of Internet and Systems* (pp. 26-34). IEEE.

Weldemariam, K., Kemmerer, R. A., & Villafiorita, A. (2010). Formal specification and analysis of an e-voting system. In the *International Conference on Availability, Reliability and Security (ARES)* (pp. 164-171). IEEE Computer Society.

Weldemariam, K., Villafiorita, A., & Mattioli, A. (2007). Assessing procedural risks and threats in e-voting: challenges and an approach. In *VOTE-ID* (pp. 38–49). Lecture Notes in Computer Science Springer-Verlag. doi:10.1007/978-3-540-77493-8_4

Welling, L., & Thomson, L. (2004). *PHP and MySQL Web development.* Pearson Education.

Weston, J., Mukherjee, S., Chapelle, O., Pontil, M., Poggio, T., & Vapnik, V. (2001). Feature selection for SVMs. *Advances in Neural Information Processing Systems*, 668–674.

Whitman, M. E., & Mattord, H. J. (2003). *Principles of information security.* Boston, MA: Course Technology.

Wiedenbeck, S., Birget, J. C., Brodskiy, A. J. W., & Memon, N. (2005). Authentication using graphical passwords: Effects of tolerance and image choice. *Proceedings of Symposium on Usable Privacy and Security (SOUPS)* (p. 1-12). Pittsburgh, PA: ACM.

Wiedenbeck, S., Waters, J. J.-C., Brodskiy, A., & Memon, N. (2005). PassPoints: Design and longitudinal evaluation of a graphical password system. *International Journal of Human-Computer Studies, 63*(1-2), 102–127. doi:10.1016/j.ijhcs.2005.04.010

Wiedenbeck, S., Waters, J., Sobrado, L., & Birget, J. C. (2006). Design and evaluation of a shoulder-surfing resistant graphical password scheme. [Venice, Italy: ACM.]. *Proceedings of Advanced Visual Interfaces, AVI, 2006,* 177–184.

Wiegers, K. (2002). *Peer reviews in software: A practical guide.* Boston, MA: Addison-Wesley.

Wikipedia. (n.d.). *Liquid crystal display.* Retrieved from http://en.wikipedia.org/wiki/Liquid_crystal_display

Wikipedia. (n.d.). *Temperature measurement.* Retrieved from http://en.wikipedia.org/wiki/temperature-measurement

Wikipedia. (n.d.). *Trojan horse.* Retrieved from http://en.wikipedia.org/wiki/Trojan_Horse

Wilikens, M. (2001). Cofidence and confidentiality: Stimulating e-commerce in Europe. *The Journal of Future Studies. Strategic Thinking and Policies, 3*(2), 135–139. doi:10.1108/14636680110803067

Windows Live Messenger. (n.d.). Retrieved from http://explore.live.com/windows-live-messenger?os=winxp

Wirtz, J., Lwin, M. O., & Williams, J. D. (2007). Causes and consequences of consumer online privacy concern. *International Journal of Service Industry Management, 18*(4), 326–348. doi:10.1108/09564230710778128

Witten, I. H., Frank, E., Trigg, L., Hall, M., Holmes, G., & Cunningham, S. J. (1999). Weka: Practical machine learning tools and techniques with Java implementations. In *Proceedings of the ICONIP/ANZIIS/ANNES'99 Workshop on Emerging Knowledge Engineering and Connectionist-Based Information Systems* (pp. 192–196).

Wojtczuk, R., & Rutkowska, J. (2009). *Attacking SMM memory via Intel CPU cache poisoning.* Invisible Things Lab.

Wolchok, S., Wustrow, E., Halderman, J. A., Prasad, H. K., Kankipati, A., & Sakhamuri, S. K. ... Gonggrijp, R. (2010). Security analysis of India's electronic voting machines. In *Proceedings of the 17th ACM Conference on Computer and Communications Security* (pp. 1-14). ACM.

Worzala, E. M., McCarthy, A. M., Dixon, T., & Marston, A. (2001). E-commerce and retail property in the UK and USA. *Journal of Property Investment & Finance, 20*(2), 142–158. doi:10.1108/14635780210420034

Xi, Q., & Wang, Y. (2009). *P2P reputation model based on trust and recommendation.*

XpertRule. (2006). *Knowledge builder.* Retrieved November 24, 2010 from http://www.xpertrule.com/pages/info_kb.htm

Yahoo. (n.d.). *Messenger - Chat, instant message, SMS, video call, PC calls.* Retrieved from http://messenger.yahoo.com/

Yan, J., & Ahmad, A. S. E. (December 2007). Breaking visual CAPTCHAs with naive pattern recognition algorithms. In *23rd Annual Computer Security Applications Conference, (ACSAC'07),* (pp. 279–291).

Yan, J., & Ahmad, A. S. E. (July 2008). Usability of CAPTCHAs or usability issues in CAPTCHA design. In *Symposium on Usable Privacy and Security, (SOUPS'08),* (pp. 44 – 52).

Yan, J., & Ahmad, A. S. E. (October 2008). A low-cost attack on a Microsoft CAPTCHA. In *15th ACM Conference on Computer and Communications Security, (CCS'08),* (pp. 543 – 554).

Yang, N., Barringer, H., & Zhang, N. (2008). A purpose-based access control model. *The Third International Symposium on Information Assurance and Security,* (pp. 143-148).

Yee, G. (2009). Estimating the privacy protection capability of a Web service provider. *International Journal of Web Services Research, 6*(2), 20–41. doi:10.4018/jwsr.2009092202

Yee, G., & Korba, L. (2005). Semi-automated derivation and use of personal privacy policies in e-business. *International Journal of E-Business Research*, *1*(1), 54–69. doi:10.4018/jebr.2005010104

Yu, E. (1993). *Modeling organizations for information systems requirements engineering*. Paper presented at The IEEE International Symposium on Requirements Engineering.

Yu, D., & Frincke, D. (2007). Improving the quality of alerts and predicting intruder's next goal with hidden colored Petri-Net. *Computer Networks: The International Journal of Computer and Telecommunications Networking*, *51*(3), 632–654. doi:doi:10.1016/j.comnet.2006.05.008

Yumin, Y. (2006). A threshold proxy signature scheme with nonrepudiation and anonymity. [Springer.]. *Computer and Information Sciences, LNCS*, *4263*, 1002–1010.

Zaki, M. J. (2000). Scalable algorithms for association mining. *IEEE Transactions on Knowledge and Data Engineering*, *12*(3), 372–390. doi:10.1109/69.846291

Zanero, S., Carettoni, L., & Zanchetta, M. (2005). *Automatic detection of Web application security flaws*. Black Hat Briefings.

Zheng, X., & Oleshchuk, V. (2009). Improvement of chord overlay for P2PSIP-based communication systems. *International Journal of Computer Networks & Communications*, *1*, 133–142.

Zheng, Y., Hardjono, T., & Seberry, J. (1994). Reusing shares in secret sharing schemes. *The Computer Journal*, *37*, 199–205. doi:10.1093/comjnl/37.3.199

Zhou, X. (2008). Anonymous proxy authorization signature scheme with forward security. *International Conference on Computer Science and Software Engineering* (pp. 872-875). IEEE Computer Society.

Zhu, Q. Z., & Dong, X. L. (2006). *Efficient and secure certificateless key agreement protocol*, 2008.

Zou, C. C., Gong, W., & Towsley, D. (2002). Code red worm propagation modeling and analysis. In *Proceedings of the 9th ACM Conference on Computer and Communications Security*, (pp. 138–147). doi: 10.1145/586110.586130

About the Contributors

Manish Gupta received his PhD in Management Science and Systems and an MBA in Information Systems and Finance from State University of New York, Buffalo, NY, USA in 2011 and 2003, respectively. He received his undergraduate degree in Mechanical Engineering from Institute of Engineering and Technology, Lucknow, India in 1998. He has more than twelve years of experience in information systems, security policies, and technologies. He currently works in a Northeast US bank in information security division. He has published 4 books in the area of information security, ethics, and assurance. He has authored or co-authored more than 50 research articles in leading journals, conference proceedings, and books, including *DSS, ACM Transactions, IEEE,* and *JOEUC*. His papers have received best paper awards. He serves in editorial boards of several international journals and has served in program committees of several international conferences. He holds several professional designations including CISSP, CISA, CISM, CRISC, ISSPCS, CIW Security Analyst, and PMP. He is a member of Sigma Xi, Beta Gamma Sigma, ISACA, and ISC2. He received prestigious 2008 ISC^2 information security scholarship (awarded on to only 7 researchers around the world) from ISC^2 and also received PhD Student Achievement Award from SUNY Buffalo.

John Walp has more than 17 years of Information Technology experience, more than half of which has been focused on information security challenges. He currently serves as Administrative Vice President and Corporate Information Security Officer for M&T Bank, a $70 billion financial institution headquartered in Buffalo, NY. Previously, he held the role of Vice President, Network Security Solutions Manager for M&T. His responsibilities include forming and executing the overall strategy for Information Security and Privacy at M&T Bank. This includes groups that focus on external and internal network security, which are made up of key security systems such as firewalls, intrusion detection/prevention systems, and security information management platforms. In addition, his organization supports the functions of access management, and compliance and risk management. Mr. Walp was selected as the 2009 North East Information Security Executive of the Year, an honor given by the Executive Alliance. The ISE Northeast Awards recognize information security executives and their teams who demonstrate outstanding leadership in risk management, data asset protection, regulatory compliance, privacy, and network security across the region including the states of Connecticut, Maine, Massachusetts, New Hampshire, New Jersey, New York, Rhode Island, and Vermont. John is a Certified Information Systems Security Professional (CISSP) as well as a Certified Information Security Manager (CISM). He is a graduate of the FBI Citizens Academy and serves as Executive Vice President of the FBI's Buffalo InfraGard Membership Alliance. Mr. Walp also serves on the advisory board of the Center of Excellence in Information Systems Assurance Research and Education (CEISARE) at the University of Buffalo. He is a member of the High-Tech Crime Consortium and the U.S. Secret Services Electronic Crimes Task Force. A Veteran of the United State Air Force, he served his country for 22 years, which included both active and reserve service. In 2004, Mr. Walp was recalled to active duty and deployed to the Kingdom of Kuwait in support of Operation Iraqi Freedom and Operation Enduring Freedom. He was selected as part of an elite logistics cadre to aid in establishing the Central Command's Deployment and Distribution Operations Center. He holds a Bachelor of Science in Computer Information Systems from State University of New York College at Buffalo. He and his wife Laurie have four children and make their home in Amherst, NY.

Raj Sharman is an Associate Professor in the Management Science and Systems Department of the State University of New York at Buffalo. His expertise is in Information Assurance, Disaster Preparedness and Response Management, Patient Safety and Health Care Systems, Business Value of Information Technology investments, Technology Valuation and Performance, and Imaging Systems. He has published in national and international journals and is the recipient of several grants from university and external agencies, including the National Science Foundation.

* * *

Nabil Ajam received his Engineering in Mobile Networks (2003) and his Master of Science degree in Networks (2005) from the higher School of Communication (SupCom), Tunisia. From September 2003 to March 2006, he was an Intelligent Network (IN) Engineer for mobile networks at Tunisia Telecom. Then, he received the Ph. D. degree in Computer Science from Telecom Bretagne, Institut Telecom, France in 2010. His research work focuses on service creation in mobile networks and how to protect user privacy within. From September 2009 to August 2010, he was an Assistant Professor at Institut Polytechnique de Bordeaux (Enseirb -Matmeca). And since September 2010, he has been an Assistant Professor at Rennes University (IUT Lannion).

David S. Allison is currently pursuing his PhD in Software Engineering at the University of Western Ontario, where he has previously completed his Master of Engineering Science and Bachelor of Engineering Science degrees, both specializing in Software Engineering. Mr. Allison was awarded an NSERC CGS D scholarship to help fund his PhD research. His Master's thesis focused on privacy for service-oriented architecture and Web services and was funded in part by an OGS scholarship. During his undergraduate studies, he partook in a sixteen month internship at IBM, where he worked as a database performance analyst.

Kasra Amirtahmasebi earned his M.Sc. degree in Networks and Distributed Systems in 2010 from Chalmers University of Technology in Sweden. His research interests center around network and security, especially vehicular networks. He has done his Master's thesis in cooperation with Volvo Company on the subject of Vehicular Networks – Security, Vulnerabilities, and Countermeasures by in depth analysis of various possible attack scenarios and their countermeasures on both inter and intra-vehicle networks. He is currently working for Huawie technologies (A leading telecom solutions provider) as a Core Network Engineer.

C. Warren Axelrod, Ph.D., is a Senior Consultant with Delta Risk, a consultancy specializing in cyber security, risk management, and business resiliency, and Research Director for Financial Services for the U.S. Cyber Consequences Unit. Previously, he was the Business Information Security Officer and Chief Privacy Officer for US Trust, the Private Wealth Management division of Bank of America. He was a founding member of the Financial Services Information Sharing and Analysis Center (FS/ISAC) and represented financial services cyber security interests in the National Information Center in Washington, DC during the Y2K date rollover weekend. He testified before Congress in 2001 on the subject of cyber security. He recently led the Software Assurance Initiative for the Financial Services Technology Consortium (FSTC). Dr. Axelrod won the 2009 Michael Cangemi Best Book/Best Article Award for his article "Accounting for Value and Uncertainty in Security Metrics," published in the *ISACA Journal*, Volume 6, 2008. He was honored with the prestigious Information Security Executive (ISE) Luminary Leadership Award in 2007. He received a Computerworld Premier 100 IT Leaders Award in 2003. Dr. Axelrod has written three books, two of which are on computer management, and numerous articles on information technology and information security topics. His third book is Outsourcing Information Security (Artech House, 2004), and he was coordinating editor of Enterprise Information Security and Privacy (Artech House, 2009). He participated in the updating of the report Security Guidance for Critical Areas of Focus in Cloud Computing, and contributed major sections to the whitepaper Domain 10: Guidance for Application Security, both for the Cloud Security Alliance. He recently published two articles in *CrossTalk Magazine*; one is "Investing in Software Resiliency," which appeared in the September/October 2009 issue, and the other is "The Need for Functional Security Testing," which is in the March/April 2011 issue. He holds a Ph.D. in managerial economics from Cornell University, as well as an honors M.A. in Economics and Statistics and a first-class honors B.Sc. in Electrical Engineering, both from the University of Glasgow. He is certified as a Certified Information Systems Security Professional (CISSP) and Certified Information Security Manager (CISM).

Alessandra Bagnato is a research scientist and project manager within the Corporate Research Division of TXT e-solutions. She holds an MSc in Computer Science from the University of Genoa, Italy. She has worked in numerous EU projects related to software/service development and security, and she was also the dissemination and exploitation manager of the EU project SHIELDS. Her research interests include secure software development as well as security and privacy issues, model driven engineering, model driven modernisation of complex systems, and model-based methods and tools for embedded systems development.

Siddhartha Baruah is an Associate Professor and HOD of MCA Department at Jorhat Engineering College. He received MCA from Jorhat Engineering College, Jorhat, ASSAM in 1990 and PhD in Technology, Computer Science from the Department of Computer Science, Gauhati University. Dr. Baruah has more than 20 years of teaching experience in MCA and BE computer science students. He has published 3 papers in international referred journals and 7 papers in proceedings of national and international conferences, and out of these, the following two were presented outside India: (1) WORLD-COMP `08 in the International Conference on Embedded Systems and Applications held from 14th to 17th July 2008 at Las Vegas, USA, and (2) ICITST-2009, International Conference for Internet Technology and Secured Transaction, London, UK, 9-12 November 2009. He is actively involved in designing and modifying curriculum of MCA and BE (Comp. Sc.) Course time to time. He introduced Embedded

System Course in MCA and set up Embedded System Design Laboratory at MCA Department. Serving as Member Board of Studies, Computer Science Dibrugarh University also member of expert committee for Department of Computer Application, Nort Eastern Hill University, Shillong, Assam, India. His areas of interest include: computer networking, operating systems, Web technology, and embedded systems.

Miriam A. M. Capretz is currently an Associate Professor and Associate Dean (Acting), Research and Graduate at the Faculty of Engineering at the University of Western Ontario, Canada. Before joining the University of Western Ontario, she was an Assistant Professor in the Software Engineering Laboratory at the University of Aizu, Japan. Dr. Capretz received her BSc and MESc degrees from UNICAMP, Brazil and her PhD from the University of Durham, UK. She has been involved with organization of several workshops and symposia as well as has been serving on program committee in several international conferences. She was a Program Co-Chair of the IEEE Workshop Web2Touch – living experience through web (W2T) in 2008 and 2009 and was the Program Chair of the IEEE Symposium on Human and Socio-Cultural Service Oriented Computing 2009. She has been working in the software engineering area for more than 25 years. Her current research interests include service oriented architecture, ontology and semantic integration, business process management, software security, and grid computing.

Giuseppe Cattaneo was born in Bari in 1960. He took a Laurea degree cum laude in Scienze dell'Informazione from University of Salerno in 1983. In 1984 he has been Technical Consultant at the Dept. of Computer Science. Since 1986 he is Research Associate at Dept. of Computer Science at University of Salerno. In 1987, with a post-graduate fellowship he went at LITP at University of Paris. His current research interests are algorithm engineering.

Luigi Catuogno got his Laurea in 1999 and his PhD in Computer Science in 2004, from the Università degli Studi di Salerno (Italy). From July to September 2002, he has been a visiting researcher at the Computer Science Department, New York University, New York, (USA). He has been post-doctoral fellow at Horst Görtz Institute for IT-Security, University of Bochum (DE) in 2009. His research interests focus on operating system security.

Frédéric Cuppens is a full Professor at the Telecom Bretagne LUSSI department. He holds an engineering degree in Computer Science, a PhD, and an HDR. He has been working for more 20 years on various topics of computer security including definition of formal models of security policies, access control to network and information systems, intrusion detection, reaction and counter-measures, and formal techniques to refine security policies and prove security properties. He has published more than 150 technical papers in refereed journals and conference proceedings. He served on several conference program committees and was the Programme Committee Chair of ESORICS 2000, IFIP SEC 2004, of SARSSI 2006 and general chair of ESORICS 2009.

Nora Cuppens-Boulahia is a teacher/researcher at the TELECOM Bretagne LUSSI department. She holds an Engineering degree in Computer Science, a PhD from SupAero, and an HDR from University Rennes 1. Her research interest includes formalization of security properties and policies, cryptographic protocol analysis, formal validation of security properties and thread and reaction risk assessment. She has published more than 50 technical papers in refereed journals and conference proceedings. She has been member of several international program committees in information security system domain and the Programme Committee Chair of Setop 2008, Setop2009, SAR-SSI 2008, and the co-general chair of ESORICS 2009. She is the French representative of IFIP TC11 "Information Security," and she is he co-responsible of the information system security axis of SEE.

Martin Drahansky obtained the Master degree in Informatics and Computer Science at FEECS Brno University of Technology (BUT), Brno (Czech Republic) and in electrotechnics at FernUniversity in Hagen (Germany) - both in 2001. He finished the dissertation at the Faculty of Information Technology, BUT in 2005 and the habilitation at FIT BUT in 2009. His field of study is biometrics, further artificial intelligence, sensorics, security, and cryptography. Now he works as Associate Professor at FIT BUT.

Frank Elberzhager is a researcher in the Department of Information Systems Quality Assurance at the Fraunhofer Institute for Experimental Software Engineering (IESE) in Kaiserslautern, Germany. He received his diploma (Master) in Computer Science from the University of Kaiserslautern, Germany. His research interests include software quality assurance in general, static quality assurance techniques such as software inspections or reviews in particular, and the combination of static and dynamic quality assurance techniques. He is the author of more than 20 publications, including one that received a best-paper award.

Pompeo Faruolo was born in Salerno in 1975. He got his Laurea (M.Sc. equivalent) cum laude in Computer Science in 2001 and his PhD in Computer Science in 2005 from the University of Salerno. Currently, He holds an Assegno di Ricerca (postdoctoral fellowship) at the University of Salerno. His research includes algorithm engineering, distributed systems, and network security.

Olivier Flauzac is a Professor at the Université de Reims Champagne-Ardenne, France since 2006, and was Associate Professor at the same university from 2000 to 2006. He obtained a Ph.D. in Computer Science in 2000 at the Université Technique de Compiègne, France. His research interests include distributed systems, algorithmic, and fault tolerance.

Katrin Franke is Professor of Information Security at NISlab, Department of Computer Science and Media Technology, Gjøvik University College, Gjøvik, Norway. She received a Diploma in Electrical Engineering from the Technical University Dresden, Germany in 1994 and her Ph.D. in Artificial Intelligence from the Groningen University, The Netherlands in 2005. Her research interests include computational forensics, biometrics, document and handwriting analysis, computer vision, and computational intelligence. She has published several scientific journal articles, peer-reviewed conference papers, and edited books.

Clemente Galdi got his Laurea (*cum laude*) and PhD in Computer Science from the Università degli Studi di Salerno in 1997 and 2002, respectively. In May 2000 and from May to September 2001 he has been a visiting researcher at Telcordia Technologies and DIMACS, New Jersey, USA. He has been post-doctoral fellow at Computer Technology Institute (Greece) and Department of Computer Engineering and Informatics of the University of Patras (Greece) (2001-2004) and with Università di

Salerno (2004-2006). Since April 2006, he is Assistant Professor at the Università di Napoli 'Federico II'. His research focuses on cryptography, data security, and algorithm theory.

Petr Hanacek obtained the Master degree in Computer Engineering at FEECS Brno University of Technology (BUT), Brno (Czech Republic) in 1988. He finished the dissertation at FEECS BUT in 1997 and the habilitation at FIT BUT in 2003. His fields of study are: parallel and distributed algorithms, computer security, wireless and mobile networks, and applied cryptography. Now he works as Associate Professor at FIT BUT.

Karin Hedström is Senior Lecturer of Informatics at Örebro University, Örebro, Sweden. She holds a PhD in Information Systems from Linköping University, Sweden. Her research interests concern the ethics of information- and communication technologies (ICT), with a focus on how different interests and values influence the design of ICTs. She is interested in the social and ethical effects of developing and using ICTs. She is especially interested in the development and use of IT in healthcare. She has published several journal- and conference articles on the issue of values of IT in health care. She is a member of the research group MELAB.

Jan Horacek was born in April 1985. Jan is a PhD student at Faculty of Information Technology at Brno University of Technology since 2009. Jan's main area of interest is autonomous agents in wireless sensor networks. Jan is also focusing on porting our agent platform to secured nodes to provide proper interpretation of agent code. Jan started professional orientation at high school in Jihlava that was focused on electronic devices and computers, followed with study at Faculty of Information technology where Jan studied Bachelor and Master degree. Jan's master thesis was also focused on agents in wireless sensor networks and continues with this work in actual study.

Ashish Jain has completed his graduation (Bachelor's in Engineering) from Netaji Subhas Institute of Technology, New Delhi, India. His branch in engineering was Information Technology. The course of study included the core subjects of Computers and Electronics with more emphasis on computer subjects. He is particularly interested in the field of computer graphics, so he chose image processing as his research domain. It has been a long journey since he started out, and now he has numerous international IEEE publications. Presently he is working with a software company, looking forward to gain quality work experience and apply for post-graduation in the field of computer graphics some years down the line.

Seyed Reza Jalalinia earned his M.Sc. degree in Networks and Distributed Systems in 2010 from Chalmers University of Technology in Sweden. His research interests are vehicular networks, network, security, internet technology, and wireless networks. He did his Master thesis in cooperation with Volvo Company on the subject of Vehicular Networks – Security, Vulnerabilities, and Countermeasures by in depth analysis of various possible attack scenarios and their countermeasures on both Inter and Intra-vehicle networks. He is currently working for MTN Company (A global communications partner and world-class cellular network) as a Disaster Recovery Manager.

Christian Jung works as a Security Engineer in the Department Information Systems Quality Assurance at the Fraunhofer Institute for Experimental Software Engineering (IESE) in Kaiserslautern.

He graduated with a diploma in "Technical Computer Science" from the University of Technology in Kaiserslautern (November 2008). During his university studies, Christian Jung focused on security in distributed systems and as member of the security team at the Distributed Computer Systems Lab (disco) at the University of Technology in Kaiserslautern he conducted research in securing wireless networks. At Fraunhofer IESE his research areas include software- and system-security as well as quality improvements in the software development process.

Fredrik Karlsson is an Associate Professor of Informatics at Örebro University. He received his PhD in Information Systems Development from Linköping University. His research about information security, tailoring of systems development methods, and computer aided method engineering (CAME) tools has appeared in a number of IS journals and conferences. He is currently heading the Methodology Exploration Lab at Örebro University and is Deputy Head of the Örebro University School of Business.

Ella Kolkowska is a Lecturer at Örebro University School of Business in Sweden. Her research is about social and organizational aspects in information security, value conflicts, as well as compliance with information security policies. She has published several conference articles on the issue of values and value conflicts in relation to information security. She is a member of the research group MELAB.

Zhongwen Li received MS and Ph.D. degree from College of Computer Science and Engineering of UESTC in 1998 and 2001, respectively. In 2001, she had worked as a Postdoctoral research fellow in College of Communication Technology of UESTC. From 2003 to 2010, she had been worked in the Department of Computer Science of Xiamen University. During the period, she worked as the New Century Excellent Talents of Xiamen University, New Century Excellent Talents in Fujian Province, and deputy director of the Department of Computer Science. Now, she is the vice dean of the College of Information Science and Technology of Chengdu University.

Chen Liang is a graduate student of Xiamen University, and he focuses on the research about P2P network security.

Anjana Kakoty Mahanta is Professor and HOD of Computer Science, Department at Gauhati University, Guwahati, Assam, India. He has published 10 papers in referred International & National journals and more than 12 papers in International & National Conference. His fields of research include embedded systems, data mining and algorithms, and automated reasoning.

Janardan Misra received his Bachelor's degree in Computer Science and Engineering from the University of Lucknow, India in 1999 and Master of Technology in Computer Science from Indian Statistical Institute, Kolkata, India in 2001. Further he received his Master of Science degree in Computer Science from National University of Singapore in 2005. During his professional and academic career he has been associated with Honeywell Technology Solutions Research Lab, India, James Cook University, Singapore, Dayananda Sagar Institutions, and Texas Instruments India Pvt, Ltd. His research interests include enterprise security, social network analysis, formal methods, and complex adaptive systems.

Afonso Araújo Neto has MSc. in Computer Science from the Universidade Federal do Rio Grande do Sul, Brazil, in the field of cryptography and holds a Ph.D. student position at the Department of Informatics Engineering of the University of Coimbra, Portugal, where he is finishing his PhD research in the area of security benchmarking of transactional systems. He is also an Information Technology Analyst working at *Centro de Processamento de Dados of Universidade Federal do Rio Grande do Sul*. Afonso has a fair amount of research experience and industry experience in the domains of security and databases.

Hai Thanh Nguyen is Doctoral researcher of Information Security at NISlab, Department of Computer Science and Media Technology, Gjøvik University College, Gjøvik, Norway. He received his diploma and Master degree in Applied Mathematics and Computer Science from Moscow State University named after M. V. Lomonosov in 2007. His research interests include intrusion detection, cryptography, and computational intelligence.

Florent Nolot obtained his PhD degree in Computer Sciences in 2002. He is an Associate Professor at the University of Reims Champagne-Ardenne, France, since 2003 where he is in charge of a Master in Systems Administration and Network Security. Florent Nolot has been involved in undergraduate and graduate courses in Computer Sciences for 10 years. He created a Cisco Networking Academy in June 2007 in his university, and he is certified Cisco CCDA, Cisco CCNP and IPV6Forum Gold Trainer. Florent Nolot is doing his research on ad-hoc networks and developing new security solutions for the network according to the Grid of security approach.

Marek R. Ogiela, DSc, Ph.D., works at the AGH University of Science and Technology in Krakow. In 1992, he graduated from the Mathematics and Physics Department at the Jagiellonian University. In 1996, for his honours doctoral thesis on syntactic methods of analysis and image recognition, he was awarded the title of Doctor of Control Engineering and Robotics at the Faculty of Electrical, Automatic Control, Computer Science and Electronic Engineering of the AGH University of Science and Technology. In 2001 he was awarded the title of Doctor Habilitated in Computer Science for his research on medical image automatic analysis and understanding. In 2005 he received a Professor title in Technical Sciences. Member of numerous world scientific associations as well as of the Forecast Committee "Poland 2000 Plus" of the Polish Academy of Science and member of Interdisciplinary Scientific Committee of the Polish Academy of Arts and Sciences (Bio cybernetics and Biomedical Engineering Section). He is author of more than 200 scientific international publications on pattern recognition and image understanding, artificial intelligence, IT systems, and biocybernetics. He is also author of recognised monographs in the field of cryptography and IT techniques and author of an innovative approach to cognitive medical image analysis. For his achievements in these fields, he was awarded many prestigious scientific honors, including Prof. Takliński's award (twice) and the first winner of Prof. Engel's award.

Urszula Ogiela is an Economist and Computer Scientist. She received Master of Science degree and Master of Business Administration in Information Management from AGH University of Science and Technology in Krakow in 2002. Currently, she works at the AGH University of Science and Technology, leading her research on linguistic aspect of information data sharing, as well as grammar extensions for secret splitting threshold protocols.

Vladimir Oleshchuk is Professor of Computer Science at University of Agder, Norway. He received his MSc in Applied Mathematics (1981) and PhD in Computer Science (1988) from Kiev Taras Shevchenko University, Ukraine. From 1981 to 1985 he was a Software Development Engineer at Glushkov Institute of Cybernetics, Kiev, Ukraine. From 1987 to 1991 he was Assistant Professor and then Associate Professor at Kiev Taras Shevchenko University. He has been working at University of Agder since 1992. His current research interests include formal methods and information security and privacy with special focus on applications in telecommunication area.

Trailokya Oraon is both Freelancer and an Adjunct Faculty at Jorhat Engineering College, Jorhat, Assam, India. He also worked as a security consultant for Fourth Dimension, a software and web designing firm. He attended numerous conferences and embedded system application workshops for last 7 years. He has taken interest on security of embedded systems 3 years back. Since then he is trying to detect subtle, but crucial errors in working embedded systems that make the entire system malfunction. He currently pursuing his research on security on data acquisition system and accuracy of delivering data to/from computer systems from/to embedded devices applied in green-house environment and in other similar environments.

Tushar Pahwa has completed his graduation (Bachelors in Engineering) from Netaji Subhas Institute of Technology, New Delhi, India. His branch in engineering was Information Technology. His interest has always been towards research side as he likes to innovate and put new ideas into practice He is particularly interested in the field of security and privacy in computer vision. He has numerous international IEEE publications. He is passionate to work in research oriented projects and dreams of doing his Master's Degree in Computer Science from a reputed college of United States of America.

Siani Pearson is a senior researcher in the Cloud and Security Research Lab (HP Labs Bristol, UK), HP's major European long term applied research centre. She has an MA in Mathematics and Philosophy from Oxford and a PhD in Artificial Intelligence from Edinburgh. She was a Fellow at the Computer Lab in Cambridge University, and for the last 17 years has worked at HP Labs in a variety of research and development programs including collaborations with HP business units and EU PRIME (Privacy and Identity Management for Europe) project. Siani's research focus is on privacy enhancing technologies. She is currently a technical lead on regulatory compliance projects with HP Privacy Office and HP Enterprise Services, and on the collaborative TSB-funded EnCoRe (Ensuring Consent and Revocation) project.

Slobodan Petrović is Professor of Information Security at NISlab, Department of Computer Science and Media Technology, Gjøvik University College, Gjøvik, Norway. He received his Ph.D. degree in 1994 from the University of Belgrade, Serbia. His research interests include cryptology, intrusion detection, and digital forensics. He is the author of more than 40 papers published in renowned international journals and conferences.

Cyril Rabat is an Associate Professor at the Université de Reims Champagne-Ardenne, France since 2009. He obtained a Ph.D. in Computer Science in 2008 at the same university. His research interests include distributed systems and simulation of ad-hoc networks.

Mohammad Mahfuzur Rahman received his first BSc. degree in the field of Physics from National University Bangladesh, Dhaka in 1994, second B.A. degree in the field of Business Administration from Independent University Bangladesh, Dhaka in 2002, and third B.A. degree in the field of Business Administration from University of East London, United Kingdom in 2009. His research topic was "*Information Security and Threats: A Study on E-Commerce*", supervised by Dr. Karim Mohammed Rezaul. He is a member of Applied Research Centre for Business and Information Technology (ARCBIT, UK). His research interests include stock markets, economics, finance, business information systems, information security, and e-commerce.

Fabio Raiteri is a software developer in the Corporate Research Division of Txt e-solutions in Milan Italy. He received his Master in Computer Science from the University of Milan Bicocca, Italy. His research interests include secure software development and content management systems.

Aditya Raj is a graduate (Bachelors in Engineering) from Netaji Subhas Institute of Technology, New Delhi, India. His branch in engineering was Information Technology. His interest areas in research include computer vision, image processing, security and privacy, artificial intelligence, computer graphics and operating systems with numerous IEEE publications. He is particularly interested in working in projects on next-generation cutting-edge technologies. He is looking forward to pursue his post-graduation from United States of America.

Karim Mohammed Rezaul was awarded a PhD degree in Computing and Communications Technology from North East Wales Institute (NEWI) of Higher Education, University of Wales, UK in October 2007. He received his BSc. degree in the field of Naval Architecture and Marine Engineering from Bangladesh University of Engineering and Technology (BUET), Dhaka in 1998 and MSc. degree in Marine Technology from Norwegian University of Science and Technology (NTNU), Trondheim, Norway in 2001. His PhD research topic was "*Estimating Long-range dependent self-similar Network traffic: performance evaluation and control,*" supervised by Professor Vic Grout. He is a member of the Institute of Electrical and Electronics Engineers (IEEE), Association for Computing Machinery (ACM), Centre for Applied Internet Research (CAIR, UK), and a fellow of Institution of Engineers Bangladesh (IEB, Bangladesh). In February 2002, Dr. Karim was appointed as visiting Lecturer in the department of Computing, Communications Technology and Mathematics at London Metropolitan University, and continued until June 2005. He is currently working as the Director of Studies and Senior Lecturer at St. Peter's College of London. He is the founder and director of Applied Research Centre for Business and Information Technology (ARCBIT). He is an author of a numerous scientific and business articles in scholarly & refereed publications which include book, book chapters, journals and International conference papers. He is an editor of several international journals and member of the technical program committee (TPC) of multiple International conferences. He is an Academic advisor / Programme director of various international colleges in UK. His research interests include e-business, network traffic engineering, long-range dependence phenomena (which appear in network traffic, stock markets, oil price, cardiology, economics, finance, hydrology, climate, weather, etc.), time series analysis, quantitative development, business information systems & design, information security, designing algorithm & data structures, statistical computing, internet technology & grid computing, quality of service (QoS) control, and traffic modelling & simulation.

Tomas Sander is a Research Scientist at Hewlett-Packard Labs in Princeton, New Jersey. He is a member of the Cloud and Security Research Lab at HP which conducts research in trust, security, and privacy technologies as well as cloud computing. Before joining HP, he worked for STAR Lab, the research lab of InterTrust Technologies in Santa Clara, California on a broad range of topics relevant to advanced digital rights management (DRM). Tomas Sander received a Doctoral degree in Mathematics from the University of Dortmund, Germany in 1996. From September 1996 to September 1999, he was a postdoctoral researcher at the International Computer Science Institute in Berkeley, California. He founded the ACM DRM Workshop in 2001. His research interests include privacy, computer security, cryptography and digital rights management. In the last few years he has been researching and developing technology that assists implementing good privacy practices in large organizations. In addition he is interested in creating new consumer technology that leverages insights from psychology to positively impact human well-being.

Kanak Ch Sarma, *is Professor in* Instrumentation at Gauhati University, Guwahati. He received Ph.D from Gauhati University in 1990 and MSc. from Gauhati University in 1974. He has published 25 papers in refereed international & national level journals and more than 25 papers in international & national conference proceedings. His fields of research include embedded system, electronic & opto-electronic instrumentation, thin films, and semiconductor nanomaterials.

Luiz Angelo Steffenel is an Associate Professor at the Université de Reims Champagne-Ardenne, France since 2007. He obtained a Ph.D. in Computer Science in 2005 at the Institut National Polytechnique de Grenoble, France, and a MSc. in Communication Systems in 2002 from the École Polytechnique Fédérale de Lausanne, Switzerland. Luiz Angelo Steffenel is certified Cisco CCDA and CCNP BSCI/ISCW Instructor. His research interests include parallel and distributed systems, grid computing, performance modeling, fault tolerance, and pervasive computing. Luiz Angelo Steffenel is also the scientific responsible for the Reims site inside the French countrywide ALLADIN/Grid'5000 project.

Chris Strasburg is a Cyber Security Analyst at The Ames Laboratory, US Department of Energy as well as a Ph.D. candidate in the Computer Science Department at Iowa State University. He received his MS degree in Information Assurance from Iowa State University, and has over ten years of experience in information management, with more than five in cyber security management and implementation. Chris' research interests include security, machine learning, & knowledge representation. He was invited to join the Upsilon Pi Epsilon and Golden Key honors societies. He has published several papers in peer reviewed conferences and is a member of IEEE Computer Society, ACM, and the Society for Industrial and Applied Mathematics (SIAM).

Amit Vasudevan is a Research Systems Scientist for CyLab at Carnegie Mellon University. He earned his Ph.D. degree in Computer Science and Engineering from UT Arlington. He received his Master's and Bachelor's degree in Computer Science and Engineering from UT Arlington and Bangalore University (India), respectively. Amit's primary research interests lie in the areas of computer systems and security. His current research focuses on hypervisor-based trusted code execution, execution logging and binary-code re-engineering and analysis. He is also interested in mobile device virtualization and OS Kernel Architectures.

Marco Vieira is an Assistant Professor at the University of Coimbra, Portugal. Marco Vieira is an expert on dependability benchmarking and is co-author of the first dependability benchmark proposal known – the DBench-OLTP. His research interests also include experimental dependability evaluation, fault injection, security benchmarking, software development processes, and software quality assurance, subjects in which he has authored or co-authored tens of papers in refereed conferences and journals. He has participated in many research projects, both at the national and European level. Marco Vieira has served on program committees of the major conferences of the dependability area and acted as referee for many international conferences and journals in the dependability and databases areas.

Adoflo Villafiorita received the MS degree from the University of Genoa, Italy, in 1993, and the PhD degree from the University of Ancona, in 1997, both in Computer Science. He is a senior researcher and the head of ICT4G research Unit in the Center of Information Technology at the Fondazione Bruno Kessler, Italy. His current interests include ICT4D, software and system engineering, security, formal methods, and safety analysis. He has participated and led several industrial projects related to the development of safety critical applications in the railway, aerospace, and e-Government sector. Adolfo Villafiorita is a member of IEEE and ACM.

Ivan Visconti is Assistant Professor at the Applicazioni of the University of Salerno, supported by ECRYPT, ECRYPT II, AEOLUS, and FRONTS. He got his Laurea degree cum laude in Computer Science in 1998 and the PhD in Computer Science in 2003 from Università di Salerno. Then he has been a Post-Doctoral fellow at the University of Salerno and in Paris, at the Departement d'Informatique of the cole Normale Suprieure, in the Crypto Team. He has been visiting Professor at the Center for Information and Computation Security, of UCLA (University of California, Los Angeles).

Komminist Weldemariam received the BS degree in Computer Science from Addis Abeba University, Ethiopia, in 2003, the MS degree in Computer Science and Engineering from Indian Institute of Technology, Bombay, India, in 2006, and PhD degree in Computer Science from the University of Trento, Italy, in 2010. He is currently a researcher at the Fondazinoe Bruno Kessler, Italy. He has been visiting scholar at the Computer Security Group of the University of California in Santa Barbara. His research interests include software engineering, security, electronic voting systems, and ICT4G. He is a member of the IEEE.

Johnny Wong is a Professor & Associate Chair of the Computer Science Department at Iowa State University. His research interests include software systems & networking, security & multimedia systems. Most of his research projects are funded by government agencies and industries. He is the President/CEO of a startup company EndoMetric, with products for Medical Informatics. He has served as a member of program committee of various international conferences on intelligent systems and computer networking. He was the program co-Chair of the COMPSAC 2006 and General co-Chair of the COMPSAC 2008 conference. He has published over 100 papers in peer reviewed journals and conferences. He is a member of IEEE Computer Society and ACM.

Zhibin Xu is a graduate student of Xiamen University. His mentor is Zhongwen Li, who is the chapter's lead author. During the graduate studies, he focuses on the research about P2P and network security.

Hany F. EL Yamany is an Assistant Professor in the Department of Computer Science Faculty of Computers and Informatics at Suez Canal University, Ismailia, Egypt. He received his PhD in Software Engineering at the University of Western Ontario, Canada. He has completed his Master's Degree in Computer Science from Ain Shams University, in Cairo, Egypt. Previously, he obtained his BSc in Computational Science from Suez Canal University, in Ismailia, Egypt. Dr. Hany EL Yamany has more than 5 years of industry experience, working in the field of Database Applications. His research interests include software engineering, service-oriented architecture, Web Services, intelligent information security, and intelligent systems.

Frantisek Zboril, Jr. is an Assistant Professor at Brno University of Technology. He has been active in the area of agent systems and modelling of intelligent systems for more than ten years. His main interest includes implementation of (multi)agent principles into discrete modeling techniques and development of distributed systems that may host the intelligent agents. Recently his research is aimed to implementation of intelligent mobile codes to heterogeneous distributed computation systems, wireless sensor networks, RFID systems etc. and security issues relating with such mobile codes. He has been published his research results at many respected international conferences and scientific journals.

Xianghan Zheng is PhD student of Computer Science at University of Agder, Norway. He received his BSc in Computer Science (2005) from Wuhan University of Technology, China and MSc in Distributed System from University of Agder (2007). From 2005 to 2007, he was a Research Assistant at Agder Mobility Lab (AML) and Ericsson Germany. His current research interests include networking and communication security with special focus on P2PSIP communication systems.

Index